BARRON'S

THE TRUSTED NAME IN TEST PREP

T0007896

Digital PSAT/NMSQT®
Study Guide
Premium
2024

Brian W. Stewart, M.Ed.
Founder and President
BWS Education Consulting, Inc.

Dedication

Dedicated to Caitlin, Andrew, and Eloise—without your love and support, this book would not have been possible. I would like to especially thank my mom, my dad, Andy, Pam, Hannah, Mitchell, Michal, Julia, and Lydia for their invaluable help with this undertaking. I am grateful to all the support from my publisher, especially Jennifer Goodenough and Angela Tartaro.

Thanks so much to all of my students over the years—I have learned far more from you than you have learned from me.

Published by Kaplan North America, LLC, d/b/a Barron's Educational Series
1515 W. Cypress Creek Road
Fort Lauderdale, FL 33309
www.barronseduc.com

ISBN: 978-1-5062-8754-6

10 9 8 7 6 5 4 3 2 1

Kaplan North America, LLC, d/b/a Barron's Educational Series print books are available at special quantity discounts to use for sales promotions, employee premiums, or educational purposes. For more information or to purchase books, please call the Simon & Schuster special sales department at 866-506-1949.

Table of Contents

4   Advanced Writing Drills 205

MATH

5   Math Review 237

PRACTICE TESTS

APPENDIX

About the Author

Brian W. Stewart is the founder and president of BWS Education Consulting, Inc., a boutique tutoring and test preparation company based in Columbus, Ohio. Brian is a nationally recognized test preparation expert, having over 30,000 hours of direct instructional experience with a wide variety of learners from all over the world. He has earned perfect scores on many standardized tests, helped hundreds of students reach their college admissions goals, and presented on best tutoring practices at national conferences.

Brian has used his experience and expertise to write several best-selling books with Barron's, including *Barron's ACT* and *Barron's SAT*. He is a former high school teacher and graduate of Princeton University (A.B.) and The Ohio State University (M.Ed.).

Brian resides in Columbus with his wife, two children, and an assortment of pets.

To learn more about Brian's online tutoring and group presentations, please visit www.bwseducationconsulting.com.

How to Use This Book

This book is designed to allow for highly targeted preparation for the new Digital SAT. Based on your previous PSAT test scores or the PSAT diagnostic test in this book, review the strategies and content knowledge that are most relevant to your needs. There are hundreds of drills that range in difficulty from easy to challenging so that you can achieve the very best results for your personal situation. In writing this new edition for the digital PSAT, I used information available from released practice questions and the test specifications from the College Board. I was able to create a variety of brand new questions that will help you be ready for test day. What you find in the text is aligned with the information about the digital PSAT available in the fall of 2022. You should check the latest information from the College Board for the latest updates.

Diagnostic Test

First, take the diagnostic test to gain an understanding of your strengths and weaknesses. It is a complete test with answer explanations and a question-type analysis guide, so you know what types of concepts need the most attention.

Review and Practice

The Reading, Writing, and Math sections each have:
- Proven test-taking strategies that allow you to customize your approach
- Extensive review of key concepts, particularly grammar and math knowledge
- Practice questions fully aligned with PSAT content
- Advanced practice drills for those students seeking National Merit recognition

Practice Tests

The final section of the book offers the opportunity to take two full-length practice tests that include all question types found on the actual PSAT for the Reading, Writing, and Math sections. Comprehensive answer explanations are provided for each question.

Online Practice

In addition to the diagnostic test and two practice tests within this book, there is also one full-length online practice exam. You may take this exam in practice (untimed) mode or in timed mode. All questions include answer explanations. Further, there is a vocabulary resource available in the online practice if you need to improve your performance on word-in-context questions.

For Students

Every strategy and explanation is based on what I have found works best for students on the actual PSAT. No matter your personal goals and background knowledge, you will find practice drills and test-taking strategies that are geared toward your situation.

Best of luck,
Brian W. Stewart

For Teachers

While many students will like working through this book independently, others will maximize their learning when they have a great teacher or tutor as their guide. Help your students work smarter instead of simply working harder by utilizing the concept reviews and drills most appropriate for your students' needs. Also, you can coach your students on which test-taking strategies will be the best fit based on their past performance. I am hopeful that the skills that students develop from using this book will help them not just with the PSAT, but also with their academic coursework and future careers. If you have any suggestions for future editions, please reach out via the publisher.

Sincerely,
Brian W. Stewart

Introduction to the Digital PSAT/NMSQT

The New Digital PSAT/NMSQT

The PSAT is a preliminary SAT exam that is used both for assessing student academic progress and for determining eligibility for the National Merit Scholarship competition. Over 4,000,000 high school students take the PSAT or PSAT 10 each year. It is such a popular test because the PSAT helps students gauge their college readiness as well as prepare for the SAT exam. There are different PSAT exams, including PSAT 8/9, PSAT 10, and PSAT/NMSQT, which are typically based on a student's grade level.

What Does the PSAT Test Do?

The PSAT tests the skills and general knowledge you will need to be successful in college and beyond.

Reading Comprehension Skills
- Determining what you can infer from a reading passage
- Finding what evidence in a passage supports a claim
- Establishing the meaning of words in context
- Analyzing graphs as they relate to a reading passage

Writing and Language Skills
- Knowledge of English grammar fundamentals (punctuation, subject-verb agreement, verb tense, etc.)
- Understanding how best to organize writing to help the flow of ideas
- Awareness of proper English language use (idioms, words in context, essay tone, etc.)

Math Problem-Solving Skills
- Solving questions with an emphasis on Algebra 1 and Algebra 2 (just a handful of questions may relate to geometry and precalculus)
- Analyzing and problem-solving using charts and graphs
- Understanding and solving real-world applications

Starting in the fall of 2023, the PSAT is scheduled to shift to a digital format. The new digital PSAT will have two Evidence-Based Reading and Writing modules (sections) and two Math modules. The test will be **adaptive**—the second modules of both the Reading/Writing and the Math will change in difficulty based on how students do on the first modules of each type. Students who perform better on the first modules will have more challenging questions in the second modules, while students who do not perform as well will have easier questions in the second modules. Here is a summary of the format of the new digital PSAT:

Digital PSAT Format

PSAT Module	Format
Reading and Writing One	32 Minutes, 27 Questions, Standard Difficulty
Reading and Writing Two	32 Minutes, 27 Questions, Adaptive Difficulty (easier or harder questions depending on how you did on the first Reading/Writing section)
Break—10 Minutes	
Math One	35 Minutes, 22 Questions, Standard Difficulty
Math Two	35 Minutes, 22 Questions, Adaptive Difficulty (easier or harder questions depending on how you did on the first Math section)

If you have previously taken or prepared for the paper-based version of the PSAT, here are some of the key differences between the older and newer digital versions of the PSAT:

Test Length

Old PSAT	Digital PSAT
■ About three hours long, including breaks and administration ■ 60 minutes for Reading ■ 35 minutes Writing and Language ■ 25 minutes for Non-Calculator Math ■ 45 minutes for Calculator Math	■ A little over two hours long; assesses the same skills as the longer PSAT by having an *adaptive* format ■ Less time needed for test administration because students can download the testing app ahead of time

Test Format

Old PSAT	Digital PSAT
■ One test form for all students on a particular test day ■ Paper test booklets with scantron sheets for answers ■ Can go back to questions within a section before time is called ■ Students should bring their own watches and calculators—they are not provided. ■ Can write on the test booklet ■ Experimental questions (ones that don't count towards your score), if given, are in a section after the test.	■ Different test questions for different students ■ Taken on a laptop that students provide or that the test center makes available ■ Can still go back and review questions. Questions can be flagged. ■ Countdown clock and calculator built into the program, although students can still bring a watch and calculator if they would like. ■ Can write on provided scrap paper ■ A few experimental questions are incorporated into each test section.

Reading and Writing & Language

Old PSAT	Digital PSAT
■ Reading passages are 500–750 words long and have 9–10 questions each. ■ Reading genres include fiction, social science, historical documents, and natural science. ■ Writing and Language passages are about 450 words long and have 11 questions each.	■ Reading and Writing passages are no longer than 150 words. Each passage has just one question accompanying it. ■ Will have a greater variety of reading genres represented. Along with the existing PSAT reading genres, there will be humanities, drama, and poetry excerpts.

Math

Old PSAT	Digital PSAT
■ Non-Calculator and Calculator sections ■ Formula sheet provided at the beginning of the test section ■ Students need to bring their own calculators.	■ Calculator permitted throughout the test ■ Formula sheet and digital calculator available in the program ■ Word problems are typically more concise than they were before.

Why Is the College Board Making This Change to the PSAT?

- **Adaptive tests have a long track record of success.** The GRE and GMAT, both of which are used for graduate school admissions, are computer-based adaptive assessments. These tests are shorter than they would otherwise be since they adjust the difficulty of the questions based on student performance.
- **Students have become more comfortable with computer-based assessments.** With so many students learning remotely over the past couple of years, digital learning has become far more common.
- **The test should be easier to administer.** Testing administrators will not have to secure test booklets, and schools will not have to take nearly as much time out of the day to offer the PSAT.
- **Test security should be improved.** Since students will have different test questions, it is far more difficult to cheat. Also, it will be far less likely that a test security breach will lead to score cancellations.

What Should I Take to the Test?

Be certain to bring the following on test day:
- Pens or pencils you can use on the scrap paper.
- Your own laptop or tablet if you have one. (If you don't, you will be given one by the test administrator). If you want to use your own laptop or tablet for the PSAT, be sure to download the testing app ahead of time and make sure your device is fully charged.
- A permitted calculator (see *https://www.collegeboard.org/psat-nmsqt/approved-calculators* for a complete list). Although there is a calculator embedded in the testing program, you may prefer to use your own.
- A watch to monitor your pacing if you would prefer to not rely on the timer embedded in the testing program. (Be sure it doesn't make noise and cannot connect to the internet.)
- A photo ID. (If you are taking the exam at your own school, you will likely not need one.)
- An e-mail address, so colleges can contact you and you can access your scores online.
- A snack or drink for your break. Be sure you do not place these on your desk.
- Do NOT bring a cell phone. You don't want to risk it going off accidentally. Also, you won't be able to check it during a break.

What Should I Do in the Days Leading Up to the PSAT?

If the PSAT were a test for which you could cram, it would make sense to stay up late studying the night before. Since it is more of a critical thinking test, you need to be as relaxed and as well rested as possible to do your best. Here are some things you should do before the PSAT.

- Download the PSAT testing app ahead of time and familiarize yourself with the program. Don't let the day of the PSAT be the first time you use the computer-based format.
- Go to bed at a reasonable hour starting a week before the test. If you wait until the night before the test to get a good night's sleep, you may not be rested enough on test day. After all, calming down and relaxing the night before a major assessment can be extremely difficult.
- Know the test directions—you do not want to waste time reading the directions on each section. At a minimum, know that you SHOULD INCLUDE AN ANSWER for every question since there is no guessing penalty.
- Become comfortable with timing. Do at least some practice with timing so you will not work too quickly or too slowly on test day.
- Know your strategic approach ahead of time—this way you can devote your full attention to solving problems instead of experimenting with strategies during the test.

What Is a National Merit Scholarship and How Do I Qualify?

The National Merit Scholarship is a prestigious award administered by the National Merit Scholarship Corporation that recognizes students based on their academic merit, using PSAT scores as the principal eligibility factor. The scores are used to compute the selection index. Your section scores from the Reading, Writing and Language, and Math sections are each doubled to give you a selection index between 48 and 228. (So even though the Reading and the Writing and Language sections comprise half of the PSAT, they make up two-thirds of your selection index calculation.) Depending on which state you live in, a selection index between 212 and 223 may qualify you for some type of National Merit recognition.

National Merit Scholarships range from single-payment $2,500 scholarships to college-sponsored scholarships that provide a full ride for tuition and room/board, plus a stipend for all four years of school. Out of the roughly 1.6 million high school juniors who take the PSAT/NMSQT, about 50,000 receive some sort of National Merit recognition, such as being named a Commended Scholar or a Semi-Finalist. Only about 7,500 students nationwide receive a National Merit Scholarship. In order to be a National Merit Scholar, you must typically perform in the top 0.5 percent of students. To learn more about the National Merit program, go to *www.nationalmerit.org*.

In addition to the National Merit Scholarship program, PSAT scores are now used to determine eligibility for other academic recognition programs. If you are African American, Hispanic American or Latino, or Indigenous, and/or live in a rural area, you may be eligible to apply for academic recognition by the College Board. You can go to *www.psat.org/recognition* and the appendix of this book for the latest information on these programs.

What Are the Requirements to Participate in the National Merit Scholarship Program?

- Take the PSAT/NMSQT no later than the third year of high school—typically this is the junior year for students who take the full four years to graduate.
- Be a high school student in the United States or its territories, or be a U.S. citizen or resident attending high school abroad.
- Be on track for high school graduation and college admission the fall after high school graduation.

What If I Miss the PSAT/NMSQT Because of an Emergency?

You or a school official should write to the National Merit Scholarship Corporation as soon as possible (at the latest, April 1 after the PSAT) to request information about alternate entry into the scholarship program. The mailing address is:

National Merit Scholarship Corporation
1560 Sherman Avenue, Suite 200
Evanston, IL 60201-4897
Go to *www.nationalmerit.org* for more details.

What About PSAT Accommodations and Extended Time?

If you are a student who has special learning needs and you have an IEP or 504 plan with your school, you may be eligible for accommodations on the PSAT. Some of the different types of accommodations offered include 50 percent or 100 percent extended time and extra breaks. Some students may qualify to take the PSAT in a paper-based format instead of a digital format. Applying for accommodations on the PSAT is easiest and fastest if you do so through your school. Keep in mind that you should allow at least seven weeks for the College Board to review your request. You can find more information about PSAT testing with accommodations at *https://accommodations.collegeboard.org/*.

What If English Is Not My Native Language?

The College Board offers testing options to students who have English language support in school and are considered to be *English learners* by the state or federal government. Students with English learner support may be able to use 50 percent extra time, an approved bilingual dictionary, and translated test directions. Unlike special needs accommodations, extended time for English learners is available only on the test date for which you register. Speak to your school counselor, ESL teacher, or administrator for help on PSAT English learner testing support.

What Is the PSAT 10? How Will This Book Help Me Prepare for It?

The PSAT 10 is the same test as the PSAT/NMSQT. Thus, if you would like to prepare for the PSAT 10, this book is exactly what you need. Although the tests themselves are identical, there are three important differences between the PSAT 10 and the PSAT/NMSQT.

- The PSAT 10 is offered in the spring, while the PSAT/NMSQT is offered in the fall.
- The PSAT 10 is for tenth-grade students, while the PSAT/NMSQT is for eleventh-grade students (although many first-years and sophomores take the PSAT/NMSQT).
- The PSAT 10 will not enter students in the National Merit Scholarship competition, while juniors who take the PSAT/NMSQT can enter this competition. Students who take either exam will be considered for other scholarship programs through the Student Search Service.

If your school does not offer the PSAT 10 and you would like to try the PSAT as a tenth grader, talk to your guidance counselor about taking the PSAT/NMSQT in the fall of your tenth-grade year.

How Can I Manage My Test Anxiety?

With only one shot to perform well on the PSAT for National Merit consideration, taking the PSAT can be a very stressful process. Being nervous is completely normal. Here are a few things to keep in mind if you find anxiety interfering with your ability to perform your best.

- When it comes to college admissions, how you perform on the actual SAT and/or ACT will be much more important than your PSAT performance. You will have many opportunities to take the SAT and/or ACT.
- Colleges will receive your scores only if you opt-in to the informational services.
- Mentally rehearse ahead of time to think about how you can best respond to the pressure of the PSAT. Are you someone who tends to rush through tests? Are you someone who tends to get stuck on questions? Knowing your tendencies will help you recognize if your thought process is off track, enabling you to make adjustments to your test-taking strategies for test day.

Realize that if the PSAT doesn't go well even after quite a bit of preparation, you will have built skills that will help you on both the SAT and ACT since those two tests have questions very similar to much of what you will find on the PSAT.

How Can I Use This Book to Prepare?

This book allows you to focus on your areas of weakness. It also helps you customize your strategies and mindset depending on your situation. Not only can you spend your time practicing math, for example, but you can also spend your time practicing the types of math questions that are most challenging for you, be they algebra or data analysis. The practice exercises are designed to give you comprehensive coverage of all the types of questions and concepts you will face. If you work through everything in this book, it is unlikely that you will encounter surprises on test day.

If you are unsure what areas of the test are most difficult for you, start by taking the full-length PSAT diagnostic test. Evaluate your performance to see what types of passages and questions give you the most difficulty. Then review the strategies and materials from the different chapters to sharpen your skills. When you are done with the chapters, do more practice with the two full-length PSAT practice tests at the end of the book and the additional one online. To really push yourself, try the advanced practice drills and online resources for extra-challenging questions.

If you wish to do even more long-term preparation, you should read a wide variety of well-written texts. At a minimum, install an e-reading app on your phone and use it to spend a few minutes each day reading, no matter where you are. If you want to go all out, seek the types of reading that you find most difficult. Read more material from those genres so that your weaknesses turn into strengths. Reading books will help improve your reading comprehension skills, your ability to pick up the meaning of vocabulary in context, and your feel for English grammar.

TIP

Remember that the strategy that works for one student may not work for another student. This book is designed to help you customize your strategy and practice.

What If I Have a Limited Amount of Time to Prepare?

Here are some suggested plans depending on how long you have to prepare.

- If you have one day, read through the strategies in the chapters for each test section: Reading, Writing and Language, and Math. Look through the full-length diagnostic test to become familiar with the directions, time requirements, and structure of the PSAT. Try a few practice questions.

- If you have one week, take the full-length diagnostic test under timed conditions to determine your strengths and weaknesses. Then review the strategies in the chapters for each of the test sections. Target your areas of weakness based on the diagnostic test by working through selected review drills. The drills are broken down by categories, so it will be easy to pick out where you should focus.

- If you have one month, systematically work through everything in this book. The strategies, content review, drills, and practice tests will give you the best possible preparation to achieve a top score on the PSAT/NMSQT.

If you are a sophomore or freshman, you may want to take the PSAT when it is offered at your school even though it will not count toward National Merit consideration. The pressure of this actual test will prepare you for when it is most important for you to do well on the PSAT—in October of your junior year. The better prepared you are, the less nervous you will feel on test day.

Let's get to work!

> Be sure to check out the appendix in this book—"After the PSAT"—once your scores come back to help you understand how to use your PSAT results to help plan future testing.

Diagnostic Test

Diagnostic Test

A full-length PSAT diagnostic test is on the pages that follow. Allow a little over two hours of uninterrupted time to complete the entire test. Find a spot to take the test where you will not be distracted. You can take a ten-minute break after the two Reading and Writing modules and before the Math modules.

Note: On the following pages, there is an answer sheet you can use to write down your letter choices and math answers. Feel free to use the sheet to record your answers or simply circle and write down your answers in the test as you go.

Completing this diagnostic test will help you determine your PSAT strengths and weaknesses. Think about the following after you take the test.

- How are you with timing?
- Do you find certain types of reading questions to be challenging?
- Do particular reading texts and genres give you more difficulty than others?
- Do you need to review English grammar concepts?
- Do some types of writing questions give you more trouble than others?
- Do you need to review or learn some math concepts?
- What kinds of math questions are toughest for you?

After completing the test, review your answers with the "Diagnostic Test Analysis Guide" to determine what types of questions and concepts you most need to study.

Good luck!

ANSWER SHEET
Diagnostic Test

Reading and Writing Module 1

1. _____	8. _____	15. _____	22. _____
2. _____	9. _____	16. _____	23. _____
3. _____	10. _____	17. _____	24. _____
4. _____	11. _____	18. _____	25. _____
5. _____	12. _____	19. _____	26. _____
6. _____	13. _____	20. _____	27. _____
7. _____	14. _____	21. _____	

Reading and Writing Module 2

1. _____	8. _____	15. _____	22. _____
2. _____	9. _____	16. _____	23. _____
3. _____	10. _____	17. _____	24. _____
4. _____	11. _____	18. _____	25. _____
5. _____	12. _____	19. _____	26. _____
6. _____	13. _____	20. _____	27. _____
7. _____	14. _____	21. _____	

ANSWER SHEET
Diagnostic Test

Math Module 1

1. _____   7. _____   13. _____   19. _____

2. _____   8. _____   14. _____   20. _____

3. _____   9. _____   15. _____   21. _____

4. _____   10. _____   16. _____   22. _____

5. _____   11. _____   17. _____

6. _____   12. _____   18. _____

Math Module 2

1. _____   7. _____   13. _____   19. _____

2. _____   8. _____   14. _____   20. _____

3. _____   9. _____   15. _____   21. _____

4. _____   10. _____   16. _____   22. _____

5. _____   11. _____   17. _____

6. _____   12. _____   18. _____

Diagnostic Test

SECTION 1: READING AND WRITING MODULE 1

32 MINUTES, 27 QUESTIONS

> **DIRECTIONS:** You will be tested on a variety of important reading and writing skills. Each question has one or more passages, possibly including a graph or table. Carefully read each passage and question and choose the best answer to the question based on the passage(s).
>
> Every question in this section is multiple-choice with four possible answers. Each question has only one best answer.

1. This cycle was broken by the unification of five Iroquois tribes in The Confederacy of Peace and Power. The confederacy was born from a Huron woman who had a dream that her son would be a prophet. She named him Deganawidah, or "the prophet." He preached to his people, but his words fell on deaf ears. Consequently, he left the Huron and traveled through the Iroquois spreading his message of peace. Within the Iroquois he collected many followers, including Hiawatha.

   As used in the text, what does the word *collected* most nearly mean?

   (A) Placated
   (B) Composed
   (C) Catalogued
   (D) Gathered

2. To begin to understand the possibilities of time, we first need a brief introduction of spacetime. We're all familiar with our three-dimensional world, but we need to consider a fourth dimension as well—time. Time passes. Therefore, you can sit still in a chair not traveling in three dimensions, but traveling in spacetime. We think of time as passing forward.

   As used in the text, what does the word *passing* most nearly mean?

   (A) Living
   (B) Moving
   (C) Throwing
   (D) Succeeding

3. In science class, the two friends frantically mixed their chemical solutions together. They had failed to meet over the weekend and their assignment was nowhere close to being finished. When they received a failing grade, the teacher remarked that the _____ to their problem would come from adequate preparation.

Which choice completes the text with the most logical and precise word or phrase?

(A) resolution
(B) mixture
(C) choice
(D) origin

4. Electricity in the kitchen, of course, ushered in a new age of powered cooking appliances, but perhaps none is more curious, clever, and common than the microwave oven. The epitome of speed cooking, the microwave uses a wholly different approach to heating food than any of its predecessors—however, its remarkable swiftness comes at the expense of precision, particularly when dealing with physically dense foodstuffs. In consequence, the microwave is a fantastic device for thawing stored vegetables, but should hardly be relied upon to properly prepare, say, a Thanksgiving turkey, or perhaps a mammoth steak.

Which choice best states the function of the underlined sentence in the text as a whole?

(A) To consider objections to a widespread viewpoint
(B) To discuss the scientific underpinnings of a theory
(C) To clarify the optimal uses for an appliance
(D) To suggest avenues for further research

5. By painting the idle vacationers from behind, and obscuring any visible faces in the impressionist-landscape style, Boudin's patrons could purchase premade a work articulating the mood, activity, colors and locale of their holiday without the monetary and temporal obstacles of a traditional, commissioned painting. For comparison, Renoir's painting of models from the rear—far from making the work more commercially viable—was executed as a stylistic affront to classical notions of portraiture. Suffice to say that Boudin's mercantile techniques were, at least among the impressionists, rather unique.

The selection serves to demonstrate that the primary aspect of Boudin's work that made it distinct from those of his contemporaries was its

(A) economic viability.
(B) impressionist style.
(C) focus on natural landscapes.
(D) affront to common sensibilities.

6. **Text 1**

Since coming to a head in 2004, the high fructose corn syrup crisis and its role in the emergent obesity epidemic has faced unwavering denial from the food industry; yet the efforts to defend the additive on scientific grounds have been dubious at best. We are all familiar with the pitiful syllogism: corn syrup comes from corn, and corn is natural; corn syrup, therefore, is natural. However true this may be, it provides no proof whatsoever as to corn syrup's safety for human consumption.

Text 2

Despite ongoing proof that genetically modified crops not only are perfectly safe for consumption but also have in fact saved an estimated 600 million people from starvation over the past two decades, fears and skepticism toward them persist simply because they are popularly perceived as *unnatural*, and thus, somehow, unhealthy.

It can most reasonably be inferred that the two authors would disagree with those who declared a food to be healthy simply because it is

(A) engineered.
(B) genetically modified.
(C) natural.
(D) metabolized.

7. **Text 1**

We teach in schools that a presidential candidate must receive an absolute majority of the electoral college votes to win the presidential election, but we don't teach the mechanics of how a candidate actually receives these votes. A party's electors are chosen in a variety of ways, but they're typically reputable members of the party. When citizens cast a vote during the presidential election, they are actually voting for a particular party's electors to cast their votes for the presidential candidate to whom they have pledged.

Text 2

More than 200 years of complacency have left us with something resembling less a federal government than a yard sale of antiquated institutions, with none more dusty than the electoral college. Consider that it's theoretically possible to receive just eleven votes, have your opponent receive 200 million, and still win the election under the electoral college.

The relationship between the passages can best be described as which of the following statements?

(A) Text 1 and Text 2 both cite political authority figures to make their cases.
(B) Text 1 focuses more on voting technicalities while Text 2 focuses on historical context.
(C) Text 1 presents more of a pious view of the founding of the United States than does Text 2.
(D) Text 1 focuses more on political dishonesty while Text 2 focuses on economic repercussions.

8. Social media in the workplace has gotten a bad rap; in many ways, it deserves it. But the role it can play—when embraced appropriately—in networking, collaboration, and retention proves that it isn't as simple as that. Like any new and rapidly changing technology, it will take time and adaptability for its advantages and pitfalls to be clear. The smart company will find it necessary to consider the implications social media presents for its future—is it really something that can just be ignored or banned altogether?

Which of the following statements best expresses the main idea of the text?

(A) Social media has already proven to be one of the most valuable workplace tools.

(B) Social media should not be disregarded as a potentially valuable tool in the workplace.

(C) The risks of social media are far too great to allow it in the workplace.

(D) Employees should be able to decide for themselves how to best use social media while working.

9. Though humans have likely marveled at the spectacle of Halley's Comet for thousands of years (the Talmudic astronomers of the first century describe a star that appears once every seventy years to wreak havoc on nautical navigation), it was little more than 300 years ago that Edmond Halley—a friend of Sir Isaac Newton's—used Newton's newly conceived laws of gravity to explain the motion and predict the periodicity of comets. Using these equations in tandem with historical records, Halley surmised that the comets observed in 1531 by German humanist Petrus Apianus, in 1607 by Johannes Kepler, and by himself and Newton in 1683 were one and the same. Moreover, he predicted its return for 1758.

The scientist Halley's relationship to the ideas of Newton most resembles the relationship between

(A) a musician who uses music theory to enable creative compositions.

(B) a politician who uses philosophical maxims to predict societal outcomes.

(C) a mathematician who uses scientific data to justify algebraic theories.

(D) an engineer who uses the laws of physics to build long-lasting constructions.

10.

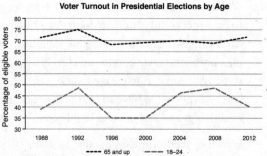

Source: 2012 U.S. Census Bureau: *http://www.census.gov/prod/2014pubs/p20-573.pdf*.

According to the information in the graph, during what year were the voter turnout rates of Americans ages 65 and older and Americans ages 18−24 closest to one another?

(A) 1992

(B) 2000

(C) 2004

(D) 2008

11. In the early 1990s, a scientist found an extremely large virus that infected an amoeba. The scientist noted that the size and composition of the virus's capsid outer coating was very similar to the protein structure of the nuclear membrane of a eukaryote, which is an organism with a clear nucleus. The scientist hypothesized that the modern cell nucleus may itself have originated from a similar viral infection.

Which finding, if true, would most support the scientist's hypothesis?

(A) Confirmation that the same virus has successfully reproduced in a new environment

(B) Experimental confirmation that the inner components of a virus are similar to those of a cell nucleus

(C) Observation of the destruction of a large virus by specially-designed antiviral medication

(D) A scientific literature review that found other scientists investigating amoeba biology in recent decades

12. "Holy Sonnet 10" is an early 1600s poem by John Donne. In the poem, the speaker suggests that death is more of a random process than one of clear destiny: _____

Which quotation from "Holy Sonnet 10" most effectively illustrates the claim?

(A) "Death, be not proud, though some have called thee / Mighty and dreadful, for thou are not so;"

(B) "For those whom thou think'st [Death] dost overthrow / Die not, poor Death, nor yet canst thou kill me."

(C) "And soonest our best men with [Death] do go, / Rest of their bones, and soul's delivery."

(D) "[Death] art slave to fate, chance, kings, and desperate men, / And dost with poison, war, and sickness dwell,"

13. *The text is adapted from the 1949 Geneva Conventions, which protects the human rights of those captured in war.*

Until recent times war was ordinarily preceded by a regular diplomatic ceremonial. Before there was any resort to arms, there was a declaration of war by one of the opposing parties, followed by the inauguration of a state of war by both belligerents with all the legal consequences which that entailed, both in relation to nationals and in relation to enemy nationals and enemy property. Consequently, in those days, in theory, where war had not been declared, or the state of war had not been recognized by one of the parties for one reason or another, the applicability of the Convention might be contested. The danger arising in such cases is _____.

Which choice most logically completes the text?

(A) unexpected

(B) inconclusive

(C) historical

(D) obvious

14. *The following text is from Kate Chopin's 1899 novel* The Awakening.

"Ask Mrs. Pontellier what she would like to hear me play," she requested of Robert. She sat perfectly still before the piano, not touching the keys, while Robert carried her message to Edna at the window. A general air of surprise and genuine satisfaction fell upon everyone as they saw the pianist enter. There was a settling down, and a prevailing air of expectancy everywhere. Edna was a trifle embarrassed at being thus signaled out for the imperious little woman's favor. She would not dare to choose and begged that Mademoiselle Reisz would please herself in her selections.

Upon being asked to select songs for Mademoiselle Reisz to play, Edna could best be described as

(A) eager.
(B) indecisive.
(C) sheepish.
(D) thrilled.

15. In retrospect, I should _____ my bat a reprieve from the endless punishment; we should allow ourselves to rest, likewise.

Which choice completes the text so that it conforms to the conventions of Standard English?

(A) of given
(B) of give
(C) have given
(D) have give

16. There are a variety of vital skills necessary for one to be a successful candidate for a job. At the top of the list are strong critical thinking skills and complex problem-solving, followed closely by problem sensitivity and deductive reasoning. _____ can be expected to have strengths in analyzing, evaluating, and interpreting highly complex data.

Which choice completes the text so that it conforms to the conventions of Standard English?

(A) You
(B) I
(C) One
(D) She

17. Today we can produce even very large sheets of glass of nearly uniform thickness using the *float glass* process invented by Sir Alastair Pilkington in the mid-1950s. As the name implies, this technique _____

Which choice completes the text so that it conforms to the conventions of Standard English?

(A) involve floated molten glass on a bath of molten tin.
(B) involve floating molted glass with a bath of molted tin.
(C) involves floated molted glass on a bath of molted tin.
(D) involves floating molten glass on a bath of molten tin.

18. Boiled down to its essence, the problem _____ to learn other languages I must speak other languages, but I rarely have the opportunity to do so.

Which choice completes the text so that it conforms to the conventions of Standard English?

(A) is this:
(B) is, this
(C) is this
(D) is this,

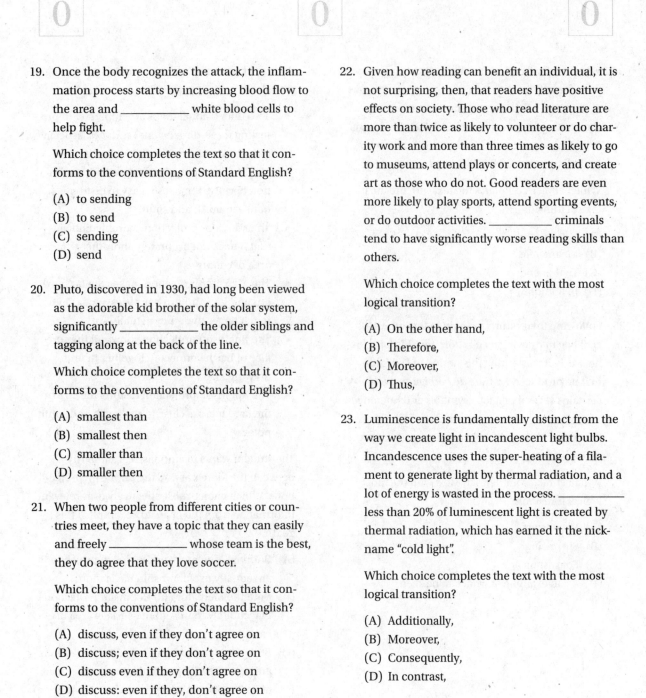

19. Once the body recognizes the attack, the inflammation process starts by increasing blood flow to the area and _____ white blood cells to help fight.

    Which choice completes the text so that it conforms to the conventions of Standard English?

    (A) to sending
    (B) to send
    (C) sending
    (D) send

20. Pluto, discovered in 1930, had long been viewed as the adorable kid brother of the solar system, significantly _____ the older siblings and tagging along at the back of the line.

    Which choice completes the text so that it conforms to the conventions of Standard English?

    (A) smallest than
    (B) smallest then
    (C) smaller than
    (D) smaller then

21. When two people from different cities or countries meet, they have a topic that they can easily and freely _____ whose team is the best, they do agree that they love soccer.

    Which choice completes the text so that it conforms to the conventions of Standard English?

    (A) discuss, even if they don't agree on
    (B) discuss; even if they don't agree on
    (C) discuss even if they don't agree on
    (D) discuss: even if they, don't agree on

22. Given how reading can benefit an individual, it is not surprising, then, that readers have positive effects on society. Those who read literature are more than twice as likely to volunteer or do charity work and more than three times as likely to go to museums, attend plays or concerts, and create art as those who do not. Good readers are even more likely to play sports, attend sporting events, or do outdoor activities. _____ criminals tend to have significantly worse reading skills than others.

    Which choice completes the text with the most logical transition?

    (A) On the other hand,
    (B) Therefore,
    (C) Moreover,
    (D) Thus,

23. Luminescence is fundamentally distinct from the way we create light in incandescent light bulbs. Incandescence uses the super-heating of a filament to generate light by thermal radiation, and a lot of energy is wasted in the process. _____ less than 20% of luminescent light is created by thermal radiation, which has earned it the nickname "cold light".

    Which choice completes the text with the most logical transition?

    (A) Additionally,
    (B) Moreover,
    (C) Consequently,
    (D) In contrast,

24. When sweating or swimming, sunscreen products can be easily washed away. _____ a new application will not set the timer to zero: only time out of the sun will do that. What this means is that frequent applications (at least every two hours) and breaks from the sun are important.

Which choice completes the text with the most logical transition?

(A) Subsequently,
(B) Meanwhile,
(C) To that end,
(D) In addition,

25. Following their return to Spain in the late 1940s, Dali began drawing inspiration from his faith for his work. It was during this period of Dali's life that he produced *La Gare de Perpignan*, which contains several religious symbols and references. _____ there is the shadow of Christ on the cross bearing his thorny crown near the center of the painting.

Which choice completes the text with the most logical transition?

(A) In contrast,
(B) Surprisingly,
(C) For instance,
(D) As an example of what can be seen,

26. A student takes the following notes for her geography class:

- Two dimensional maps are imperfect in projecting three-dimensional surfaces, especially planetary surfaces like that of Earth.
- The Mercator projection is good for navigation because it makes it easy to distinguish between north and south.
- The Mercator projection is problematic in that it does not accurately show the surface area of countries.
- The Mercator projection makes the far northern and far southern countries appear to be much larger than they actually are.
- The Robinson projection shows all the surface of Earth connected together in one drawing.
- The Robinson projection distorts the size of the land masses close to the north and south poles.

The student wants to emphasize a similarity between the Mercator and the Robinson projections. Which choice most effectively uses relevant information from the notes to accomplish this goal?

(A) Both the Mercator and Robinson projections are equally useful for ship navigation.
(B) Both the Mercator and Robinson projections inaccurately represent the surface area of each part of Earth.
(C) Both the Mercator and Robinson projections are accurate in representing the surface area of Earth towards upper latitudes near the poles.
(D) Neither the Mercator nor the Robinson projection can be drawn on a two-dimensional surface.

27. While researching a topic, a student has taken the following notes:

- Before the Incas and Aztecs, Teotihuacan flourished in what is today known as Mexico.
- Teotihuacan was a large city built in the Valley of Mexico and was at peak importance between 500 and 550 AD.
- Teotihuacan is responsible for some of the most intact ruins and some of the most impressive pyramids in North America, including the Pyramid of the Sun and the Pyramid of the Moon.
- The city was the most important cultural center of Mesoamerica in its time and produced much of the art, music, and other culturally important concepts of the time.
- Teotihuacan eventually crumbled for reasons unknown; many archeologists suspect an uprising of the peasant class contributed to the demise of the once-great city.

The student wants to emphasize elements of Teotihuacan that are most likely still physically visible by people today. Which choice most effectively uses relevant information from the notes to accomplish this goal?

(A) Much of the culture in modern-day Latin American traces its influence to the concepts of the Inca.

(B) The large city of Teotihuacan was constructed over 1,500 years ago in the Valley of Mexico.

(C) Students today can still view the well-preserved Pyramid of the Sun and Pyramid of the Moon.

(D) Just as the civilization in Teotihuacan eventually deteriorated, our modern-day society is under the threat of class conflict.

SECTION 1: READING AND WRITING MODULE 2

32 MINUTES, 27 QUESTIONS

DIRECTIONS: You will be tested on a variety of important reading and writing skills. Each question has one or more passages, possibly including a graph or table. Carefully read each passage and question and choose the best answer to the question based on the passage(s).

Every question in this section is multiple-choice with four possible answers. Each question has only one best answer.

1. Juan was surprised by what he heard but
_____ the information as lies. He knew many of his peers were jealous of his success, but he doubted they would stoop so low.

Which choice completes the text with the most logical and precise word?

(A) reduced
(B) forgot
(C) conceded
(D) dismissed

2. When the speaker was done, the crowd rose and clapped vigorously. Yet, at the question and answer session, attentive spectators _____ several points—particularly that the speech's moral lesson came off as condescending and was generally unfounded.

Which choice completes the text with the most logical and precise word or phrase?

(A) increased salary
(B) elevated
(C) put forward
(D) nourished

3. At the turn of the nineteenth century, a prominent physicist stated that physics as a field of study was finished due to the belief that everything about the physical world had already been discovered. Newtonian Mechanics had held sway for over two hundred years and our understanding of the atom had not advanced much beyond the concepts of the ancient Greeks. The view of a static universe was the accepted construct and humanity's ignorance was a kind of simple bliss and arrogance.

As used in the text, what does the word *construct* most nearly mean?

(A) Building
(B) Observation
(C) Theory
(D) Astronomy

4. Whatever your preference, the method by which a product finds its way to you, the consumer, is logistics. <u>Originally a term that described the flow of materiel for the military in the conflicts around the globe</u>, it has now found its way into every element of consumerism. Major retailers have emerged that specialize in on-line shopping; others have outlet stores and websites where the buyer can choose a channel for procurement.

Which choice best states the function of the underlined phrase in the text as a whole?

(A) To define current usage of a phrase

(B) To address a likely reader objection

(C) To use primary source evidence

(D) To explain the root of a concept

5. Disinterested in a bleak future of more debt and less freedom, and wary of aligning themselves within partisanship, today's youth are doubtful of a government that promises few of the assurances it once pledged. Naturally, this trend is disquieting for a nation that depends on its voters and an interest in representation, both of which are in a state of deterioration. <u>Yet, some may applaud the veer from partisanship—a phenomenon that has left more undone than accomplished.</u> Still, if democracy is to survive, something must be done to align the cynical millennials with a system that desperately needs their interference.

What is the purpose of the underlined sentence in the text?

(A) To state the thesis of the text

(B) To give details about the pitfalls of partisanship

(C) To acknowledge a contrasting viewpoint

(D) To cite an expert point of view

6. The intrinsic difficulty of predicting a comet's greatness makes the consistency of Halley's visibility even more remarkable. Most great comets will pass near Earth only once every several thousand years, whereas Halley's does so on a cycle of about seventy-five years—making it the only great comet with the potential to appear twice in a human lifetime. With an eccentricity of 0.967, the orbit of Halley's Comet is extremely elliptical; at one end of its major axis Halley's is roughly the same distance from the sun as Pluto, whereas at the other it passes between the orbits of Mercury and Venus. The highly elliptic character of Halley's orbit means that, apart from having one of the highest velocities of any body in our solar system, it passes near Earth both during its approach and its return from the sun.

Which choice best states the main purpose of the text?

(A) Discuss the physical definition of elliptical eccentricity

(B) Provide scientific justification for the rarity of Halley's predictable visibility

(C) Give historical evidence of human observation of Halley's velocity

(D) Differentiate Halley's from other celestial bodies, such as planets and meteors

7. **Text 1**

One promising alternative fuel source is ethanol. This alternative fuel is made by fermenting crops such as wheat, corn, and sugarcane. One glucose molecule is broken down to form two ethanol molecules and two carbon dioxide molecules. Because it is made from organic matter, it is renewable—a big pro compared to oil. Another benefit is that it's domestically made, so we don't have to rely on other countries for it.

Text 2

Despite decades of apocalyptic forecasting of peak oil, petroleum output is as healthy as ever. In fact, petroleum companies are leaving the industry not because oil reserves are dwindling, but rather because oil production is so massive that demand is falling considerably.

The author of Text 1 would most likely state that the author of Text 2 needs to make what important clarification to the underlined statement in the text?

(A) To what extent this applies to just domestic petroleum production
(B) Whether the petroleum produced is organic and renewable
(C) If the petroleum production will generate greenhouse gases
(D) If the petroleum mentioned here will be more or less expensive than ethanol

8. **Text 1**

There is and must remain a standard by which good writing is measured and acknowledged. Take a moment to consider the alternative, and you'll surely come to agree with me. Without a standard, anything and everything could be considered *literature*. More so, it would change from person to person and place to place based solely on the rudimentary preference of varied individuals.

Text 2

Many will adore language that others detest, and some will gasp appreciatively at a metaphor that makes the masses vomit. And so I say, to each their own. What is thoughtful, good, and stirring is without impartiality, contingent not only on the reader but also on the reader's mood, location, and even on what the reader has recently read. Therefore, write what you will and read what you wish, and if you like it, then declare with authority that it is indeed exceptional.

Which option best expresses the overall relationship between the texts?

(A) Text 1 argues for the existence of literary objectivity, whereas Text 2 argues for the opposite.
(B) Text 1 asserts the primacy of reading literature, whereas Text 2 asserts that writing is the only gateway to understanding.
(C) Text 1 contends that good literature makes readers uncomfortable, whereas Text 2 contends that good literature is what is most popular.
(D) Text 1 focuses on the *great books*, whereas Text 2 focuses on excellence in poetic expression.

9. *The following text is from Nathaniel Hawthorne's 1852 novel* The Blithedale Romance.

I recognized no severe culture in Zenobia; her mind was full of weeds. It startled me, sometimes, in my state of moral as well as bodily faint-heartedness, to observe the hardihood of her philosophy. She made no scruple of oversetting all human institutions and scattering them as with a breeze from her fan. A female reformer, in her attacks upon society, has an instinctive sense of where the life lies, and is inclined to aim directly at that spot. Especially the relation between the sexes is naturally among the earliest to attract her notice. Zenobia was truly a magnificent woman.

Based on the text, what aspect of society is Zenobia most eager to reform?

(A) Xenophobic universities

(B) Widespread economic corruption

(C) Antiquated gender roles

(D) Environmental negligence

10. *The following text is from Irina Petrov's 1917 work* More than Many Sparrows.

Already that winter, [Kolya] had fed [the fire in the fireplace] half the books in his great grandfather's library. It had eaten up all the Napoleonic settees and tables that once adorned his ancestral home. He'd even offered it his mother's beloved mando-lin, letting the strings on which she'd plucked his somber lullabies catch fire, snap, and turn to ash. He watched it happen, and felt nothing. Nothing, that is, but warm. It was winter, and sentimental-ity was not in season—nor had it been for many months. Besides, no one still living in the house knew how to play it.

What is a main idea of the text?

(A) The narrator's ancestral library must be pre-served at all costs.

(B) Offerings to the gods may ward off misfortune.

(C) The narrator longs for the companionship of his deceased mother.

(D) The need for comfort overcomes familial nostalgia.

11.

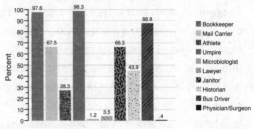

Likelihood a Job Will Be Done by a Machine

Source: npr.org

Using the information in the graph, which state-ment is true?

(A) GPS and automation will lead to bus drivers being obsolete.

(B) Careers with a high likelihood of a machine performing the job have poor employment outlooks.

(C) Historians are less likely to have their job per-formed by a machine than janitors are.

(D) More people are employed as umpires than any other profession.

12. I used to revel at my anxiety after turning in an assignment in my first years of my creative writing degree. One moment, I was quite sure that my work was genius. And another, I was the most dim-witted simpleton to ever put pen to paper. I had absolutely no idea whether my fiction would come back with an *A* or an *F* stamped on it—no clue how the professor might decide between the two. Often, I'd pull decent grades, but moan aloud when the instructor picked out my very favorite sentence—the one that was going to mark me the next Vonnegut or Kerouac—and crossed it out in red ink. Rethink this she'd scribble underneath. It took me two years and the onset of carpal tunnel to realize that there is no real way to know what's good, and that what's good is entirely subjective.

Which of the following, if true, would present the greatest challenge to the argument of the text?

(A) Some people adore Shakespeare, while others do not care for his work.

(B) Well-trained literary minds are able to use more sophisticated language to give their views on the quality of different texts.

(C) American book readership has steadily declined in the past three decades.

(D) The writer's academic evaluators graded in a hurried, haphazard way.

13. Encryption, as evident from the preceding information, has advanced throughout the centuries from rudimentary to labyrinthine: today's encryption systems are even more complicated than they were in 1970. And, frankly, that's with good reason; from nuclear launch codes to social security numbers to human intelligence gathered on enemy attack plans, information has never been more dangerous. To some nefarious sorts, that means it's never been more *valuable,* which means it's never been more *vulnerable.*

The text most strongly implies that

(A) the modern era stands far behind the ancient era in the technological sophistication of its encryption.

(B) the primary focus of organized criminal activity is the decryption of secret communications.

(C) the greater the importance of the information, the more likely criminals will seek to obtain it.

(D) it is difficult to determine the reasons that people decide to become criminals.

14. Though today the familiar names of French Impressionism—Degas, Pissarro, Cézanne, Renoir, and Monet—are nearly synonymous with what we may inscrutably refer to as *great art*, in its own time the impressionist movement was often identified with artistic dissidence, the avant-garde, and painterly provocateurs. In its development, the impressionist style boldly challenged the entrenched principles of French painting, and ultimately transformed art for most of the Western world.

It can reasonably be inferred that the narrator's general attitude towards impressionism can best be characterized as

(A) warm appreciation.
(B) awestruck reverence.
(C) dispassionate objectivity.
(D) mild contempt.

15. The issues of both convenience and synchronous exposure in color photography were eventually solved by two professional, classical musicians—Leopold Mannes and Leopold Godowsky, Jr.—working recreationally for the Eastman Kodak Company. Together they designed a film that consisted of three separate emulsion layers mounted on a single flexible base, each of which captured and individually filtered the lens image. Their design was marketed by Kodak under the name *Kodachrome* and was the first system to make the use of color film widely available to lay photographers. With respect to their photographic research, Mannes and Godowsky can best be described as _____

Which choice most logically completes the text?

(A) serendipitous tinkerers.
(B) scholarly thinkers.
(C) scientific masterminds.
(D) musical prodigies.

16. _____ the Parthenon is one of the most popular tourist attractions in the world, enticing millions of people each year and warranting an ongoing restoration project currently in its third decade.

Which choice completes the text so that it conforms to the conventions of Standard English?

(A) In the contemporary world in which we reside,
(B) In the world of today,
(C) Contemptuously,
(D) Today,

17. Apart from the drum, there is perhaps no instrument more widespread among the world's ancient cultures than the curious noisemaker known severally as the *bullroarer*, _____ *tundun*, or *whizzing-stick*.

Which choice completes the text so that it conforms to the conventions of Standard English?

(A) rhombus',
(B) *rhombus*,
(C) rhombus,
(D) rhombus

18. Pitch modulation can be achieved by altering the speed of rotation, or the length of the cord. The capacity for pitch modulation has _____ to the idea that bullroarers could be used to communicate coded messages, with certain meanings attached to certain pitches.

Which choice completes the text so that it conforms to the conventions of Standard English?

(A) lent credence
(B) lended credibility
(C) loaned credibility
(D) lending credence

19. We know with surprising certainty not only the composition of the bodies in our solar system _____ that of many interstellar bodies, and even some intergalactic ones as well.

Which choice completes the text so that it conforms to the conventions of Standard English?

(A) from also
(B) but also
(C) also
(D) and

20. The tough competition and demanding prerequisites for the job market need not be deterrents. Leading journalism _____ students leave undergraduate programs with all the tools necessary for success.

Which choice completes the text so that it conforms to the conventions of Standard English?

(A) department's are reassuring that their
(B) departments' are insuring that they're
(C) departments are assuring there
(D) departments are ensuring that their

21. A newly formed photon carries with it a sort of chemical *signature* called an emission spectrum, which is _____ to the element from which it was emitted.

Which choice completes the text so that it conforms to the conventions of Standard English?

(A) one of the only of its kind
(B) partial
(C) uniquely
(D) specific

22. Marjorie, an immensely popular young woman, is plagued by Bernice, her dull cousin who fails to entertain _____ Marjorie's many social environments.

Which choice completes the text so that it conforms to the conventions of Standard English?

(A) or be entertained by
(B) and entertainment
(C) with the entertaining of
(D) of the entertaining for

23. Nearly all tortoiseshell and calico cats are female. This is because the gene that dictates whether the cat's fur is orange or black is located on the X chromosome. Since male cats have XY chromosomes, they will usually only have one allele coding for either orange fur or black fur. Males would be calico or tortoiseshell if they had two X chromosomes along with a Y, _____ this is very rare.

Which choice completes the text with the most logical transition?

(A) so
(B) if
(C) but
(D) moreover

24. The Depression arrived at a moment in time in which Sweden was particularly ripe for comprehensive reform; in hopes of stabilizing a rapidly declining economy, the Swedish people elected the Social Democratic Party to power in 1932. _____ contemporary socialist parties in Europe, Sweden's Social Democrats—rather than calling for the full socialization of private industry—made combating unemployment through bipartisan, interventionist legislation their main priority.

Which choice completes the text with the most logical transition?

(A) Also
(B) Unlike
(C) Consequently
(D) Therefore

25. For ten months while I was in high school, I lived with a host family in Germany. I attended tenth grade in a German upper school, traveled through northern Europe and, truth be told, learned a bit of German. _____ a German student traveling to the U.S., staying with a host family, and attending school for the same amount of time seems to learn significantly more English.

Which choice completes the text with the most logical transition?

(A) Therefore,
(B) However,
(C) Additionally,
(D) As a result,

26. While researching a topic, a student has taken the following notes:

- Humans are susceptible to infection by a variety of parasitic worms. These infections can be anywhere from a mild annoyance to life-threatening.
- Dracunculiasis, also known as guinea worm disease, starts when the host drinks water contaminated with the parasite.
- Incubation of the guinea worm can be a year and ends with a blister forming on the body. The blister becomes very painful as the parasite emerges. Hosts often put their body into water to ease the pain, which unfortunately stimulates the guinea worm to release larvae contaminating that water and perpetuating the cycle.
- To remove the guinea worm from the body, the worm is slowly wound around a stick or bit of gauze or fabric until the worm exits the body.

The student wants to emphasize the possible range of severity that could result from a parasitic worm infection. Which choice most effectively uses relevant information from the notes to accomplish this goal?

(A) Guinea worms are quite dangerous and should only be removed by a highly trained medical professional.
(B) The infection resulting from a parasitic worm can range from being mildly annoying to life-threatening.
(C) If you ingest contaminated water, you are more likely to contract a guinea worm infection.
(D) The self-perpetuating cycle of guinea worm disease has required very targeted programs and education to make guinea worm disease eradicated in many parts of the world.

27. While researching a topic, a student has taken the following notes:

   - Land conservation and land preservation are two different concepts.
   - Preservation focuses on keeping the land as it is as a sort of natural museum, unable to be used in any significant way by humanity. It preserves the nature as it is.
   - Conservation focuses on keeping lands usable for anyone who might want to experience the outdoors. It allows people to use the land for recreation and ensures that cities and other human growth do not destroy natural areas.
   - Teddy Roosevelt was one of the first proponents of conservationism in the United States. He started the National Parks System to ensure that generations of Americans could still see the wonders of the land.

   The student wants to show a contrast between land preservation and land conservation. Which choice most effectively uses relevant information from the notes to accomplish this goal?

   (A) Teddy Roosevelt was a major personality who inspired long-term investments in both land conservation and land preservation.

   (B) Land conservation entails ensuring humans can use the land recreationally, while land preservation ignores this goal.

   (C) While land preservation will cause existing human habitation to be removed, land conservation encourages urban development.

   (D) Museumgoers are more likely to enjoy experiencing land in a similar way—therefore, the investment in national parks is worthwhile.

SECTION 2: MATH MODULE 1

35 MINUTES, 22 QUESTIONS

- All expressions and variables use real numbers.
- All figures are drawn to scale.
- Every figure lies in a plane.
- The domain of given functions is the set of all real numbers for which the corresponding value of the function is real.

For multiple-choice questions, solve the problem and pick the correct answer from the provided choices. Each multiple-choice question has only one correct answer.

For student-produced response questions, solve each problem and enter your answer following these guidelines:

- If you find more than one correct answer, enter just one answer.
- You can enter up to five characters for a positive answer and up to six characters (this includes the negative sign) for a negative answer.
- If your answer is a fraction that does not fit in the given space, enter the decimal equivalent instead.
- If your answer is a decimal that does not fit in the given space, enter it by stopping at or rounding up at the fourth digit.
- If your answer is a mixed number (like $4\frac{1}{2}$), enter it as an improper fraction (9/2) or its decimal equivalent (4.5).
- Do not enter symbols like a comma, dollar sign, or percent sign.

Examples

Answer	Acceptable Entries	Unacceptable Entries That Will Receive Zero Credit
4.5	4.5 4.50 9/2	41/2 4 1/2
$\frac{8}{9}$	8/9 .8888 .8889 0.888 0.889	0.8 .88 0.88 0.89
$-\frac{1}{9}$	−1/9 −.1111 −0.111	−.11 −0.11

1. If $x^2 > y^2$ which statement must be correct?

   (A) $x > y$

   (B) $x < y$

   (C) $x \neq y$

   (D) $x^3 > y^3$

2. What is the product of xy given the system of equations below?

   $$4 + y = 32x$$
   $$y = 2x + 2$$

   (A) $\frac{6}{25}$

   (B) $\frac{12}{25}$

   (C) 12

   (D) 15

3. Eloise is told by her doctor that she should try to average 9 hours of sleep a night, since that is what a typical teenager needs for optimal mental and physical health. If Eloise has been awake for 126 hours in a given week, how many additional hours of sleep should she have had in order to follow her doctor's advice?

4. What are the values of a in this equation?

   $$3a^2 - 27a - 108 = 0$$

   (A) $-9, -3$

   (B) $6, -4$

   (C) $9, 6$

   (D) $12, -3$

5. What is the difference between $7a^2 + 3ab - 8b$ and $-2a^2 + ab - 2b$?

   (A) $5a^2 + 4ab - 10b$

   (B) $9a^2 + 4ab - 8b$

   (C) $9a^2 + 2ab - 6b$

   (D) $7a + 3ab - 10$

6. If $2x + 3 = 4$, what is the value of $6x + 9$?

7. If a circle has a diameter of 8 centimeters, what is its circumference rounded to the nearest whole centimeter?

8. Allison is purchasing a new car that costs $25,000. She is trading in a used car that is worth $5,000, according to the dealer. The amount she pays for the new car is the new car price minus the amount she receives as a credit for the used car trade-in. If she has to pay 7% sales tax on the entire purchase, what expression would give the total amount she pays?

   (A) $0.07(25,000 - 5,000)$

   (B) $0.07(25,000) + 5,000$

   (C) $1.07(25,000 - 5,000)$

   (D) $1.7(25,000 + 5,000)$

9. Which of the following operations could we perform on both sides of the inequality $-2x > 4$ in order to make it necessary to change the direction of the inequality sign while keeping x on the left hand side of the inequality?

   (A) Add 4

   (B) Subtract 7

   (C) Multiply by 12

   (D) Divide by -2

10. The variables x and y have a linear relationship; the table below contains several corresponding x-y values for the line:

x	y
-1	-6
1	2
5	18
7	26

What is the equation of the line made up of x-y values?

(A) $y = 4x - 2$
(B) $y = 2x$
(C) $y = -2x + 4$
(D) $y = -4x + 2$

11. Maria currently has \$10,000 in her retirement fund. She wants to see how much money she will have in her fund for several different years in the future, assuming that her portfolio has a steady annual growth rate of 10%. What function $f(n)$ would model the amount she should have in her portfolio in n years?

(A) $f(n) = 10,000^n$
(B) $f(n) = 10,000 \times 0.1^n$
(C) $f(n) = 10,000 \times 1.1^n$
(D) $f(n) = 10,000 \times 1.11^n$

12. A cylinder has a height of 4 feet and a diameter of 2 feet. What is the cylinder's volume in cubic feet?

(A) 3π
(B) 4π
(C) 8π
(D) 16

13. A convenience store has a *change bowl* on its counter in which there can be 5-cent nickels and/or 1-cent pennies. The store manager insists that whenever there is a dollar (100 cents) or more in the bowl, some change must be removed. What expression gives the range of P pennies and N nickels that could be in the change bowl at any given time without the cashier needing to remove any coins?

(A) $100P - N > 5$
(B) $6(P + N) < 100$
(C) $0.01P + 0.05N < 100$
(D) $P + 5N < 100$

14. The data are collected from a survey of 500 randomly selected people in the United States. The researcher asked participants their ages and the type of social media they use the most frequently: video sharing, photo sharing, text sharing, or none. The goal of the researcher was to determine the general characteristics of social media use by different age groups throughout the United States.

Type of Social Media Use by Numbers of People in Different Age Groups					
Age Group	Video Sharing	Photo Sharing	Text Sharing	No Social Media	Total
12–18	40	32	20	2	94
19–30	31	51	43	6	131
31–45	20	20	40	24	104
46–60	9	8	36	35	88
61–up	2	3	29	49	83

If one were to create a graph with age groupings (from younger to older) as the variable along the x-axis and percentage of group members who use video sharing (from smaller to larger) along the y-axis, what would be the relationship portrayed by the data?

(A) Positive correlation
(B) Negative correlation
(C) Equivalence
(D) Exponentially inverse

15. The variables m and n have a directly proportional relationship, given by the equation $m = kn$ where k is a constant of proportionality. When $m = 10$, $n = 2$. What will be the value of n if m is 38?

16. A parallelogram has one interior angle that measures 50 degrees. What is the measure of the largest interior angle of the parallelogram?

(A) 130 degrees
(B) 150 degrees
(C) 250 degrees
(D) 310 degrees

17. A new business uses a crowdfunding website to raise money for its expansion. The graph below plots the number of new investment pledges per week, collecting the data once at the end of each week after the crowdfunding has begun (For example, *Week 1* gives the total number of pledges at the very end of week 1).

Number of New Investment Pledges Per Week

Week Number

A marketing professional defines the point at which something goes *viral* as the point at which the item shifts from linear to exponential growth. During what week does the value of the new investment pledges become viral?

(A) 2
(B) 3
(C) 6
(D) 10

18. A dry cleaner has a computer program to determine the price it will charge an individual customer to clean a bag full of shirts (S) and pairs of pants (P). The total cost in dollars (C) is given by the following expression:

$$C = 10S + 6P + 5$$

What does the constant 5 most likely represent in the above expression?

(A) A set fee the cleaner assesses to do any amount of cleaning
(B) The cost to clean a shirt
(C) The cost to clean a pair of pants
(D) The total minimum cost to clean either one shirt or pair of pants

19. How many more kilograms (to the nearest hundredth) will a 2 cubic meter balloon that is filled with air weigh than an identical balloon that is filled with helium, given that helium has a density of $0.179 \frac{kg}{m^3}$ and air has a density of $1.2 \frac{kg}{m^3}$?

(A) 0.21
(B) 1.02
(C) 1.38
(D) 2.04

20. A pretzel stand has fixed costs for the facility and cooking supplies of $500. The cost for the labor and supplies to cook one pretzel after the pretzel stand has been set up is $2 per pretzel. What is the graph of the cost function $c(x)$ given x pretzels?

(A)

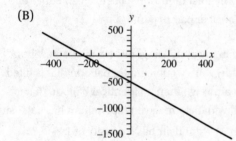

(B)

(C)

(D)

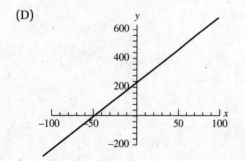

21. In the equation $y = 2x^n$, in which x is an integer greater than 1, what is a possible value of n that will ensure that the expression has exponential growth?

   (A) 0
   (B) 1
   (C) 4
   (D) Not sufficient information

22. The function $f(x) = (x - 3)(x + 2)((x - 1)^2)$ will intersect the x axis how many times?

SECTION 2: MATH MODULE 2

35 MINUTES, 22 QUESTIONS

1. What are the values of y that satisfy these conditions?

$$x = y^2 - 3y + 1$$
$$2x = 10$$

(A) −4 and 2
(B) −1 and 4
(C) 3 and 4
(D) 6 and 10

2. When Andrew does his homework, he always takes 10 minutes to set up his desk and get totally ready to begin. Once he starts working, he is able to complete one homework problem every 5 minutes. Assuming that Andrew studies for over 10 minutes time, which of the following represents the total number of homework problems, p, Andrew is able to complete in m minutes?

(A) $p = 5m + 10$
(B) $p = 5m - 1$
(C) $p = \frac{1}{5}(m - 10)$
(D) $p = \frac{1}{10}(m - 5)$

3. How many solutions does the equation below have?

$$3x - 4y = 73$$

(A) None
(B) Exactly 1
(C) Exactly 2
(D) Infinite

4. $\left(2x^2 + 4xy + 2y^2\right) \times \dfrac{1}{2x + 2y} =$

(A) $y + x$
(B) $\dfrac{2x + 4y + 2}{x + y}$
(C) $2x + 4xy + 2y$
(D) 2

5. A professor will cancel his sociology class if the number of students in attendance is less than or equal to 10. Which of the following expressions would give the range of students S necessary for the professor to have class, given that S is a whole integer?

(A) $S < 10$
(B) $S > 10$
(C) $S \le 10$
(D) $S \ge 10$

6. What is a possible value for x in the expression below?

$$-6 < \frac{8}{3}x < -\frac{1}{4}$$

(A) 8
(B) 1
(C) −2
(D) −5

7. A politician proposes a new federal tax bracket system for single tax payers with the following tax rates for the given ranges of income:

Taxable Income Range	Tax Rate
$0 up to $9,000	15%
Greater than $9,000 up to $50,000	20%
Greater than $50,000	30%

If Julian has only $8,000 in taxable income, what is the total amount of federal tax he would pay under the proposed system?

(A) $400
(B) $800
(C) $1,200
(D) $1,600

8. If the line given by the equation $y = 4x + 7$ is reflected about the x axis, what will be the graph of the resulting function?

(A)

(C)

(B)
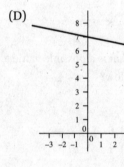

(D)

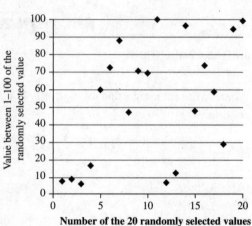

Number of the 20 randomly selected values

9. What is the solution(s) for x in this equation?

$$\frac{12}{\sqrt[3]{x}} = 4$$

(A) −3 and 81

(B) −27 and 27

(C) 9 only

(D) 27 only

10. How many solution(s) does this system of equations have?

$$m + 2n = 1$$
$$6n + 3m = 9$$

(A) None

(B) 1

(C) 2

(D) 3

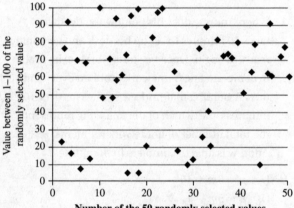

Number of the 50 randomly selected values

11. Suppose that the random selection process of numbers between 1 and 100 were conducted for a group of 100 values and a group of 1,000 values. After the selection process is completed, the range of each group is determined. What would most likely be closest to the difference between each group's range of values?

(A) 0

(B) 20

(C) 50

(D) 100

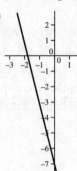

12. Which of these equations when combined into a set of equations with $4x = 2y - 6$ will result in no solutions to the set?

    (A) $y = x - 4$
    (B) $y = 2x + 10$
    (C) $y = 4x - 1$
    (D) $y = \frac{1}{4}x - 6$

13. The amount of money (A) in a bank account after a principal amount (P) is on deposit for t years at an annual interest rate r compounded n times per year is given by this equation:

    $$A = P\left(1 + \frac{r}{n}\right)^{nt}.$$

    Suppose that a banker would like to determine how changes in these variables would cause the bank to pay *less* interest to its clients. Which of the variables P, r, n, and t, if minimized, would cause less interest paid to clients?

    (A) P only
    (B) r and t only
    (C) n and t only
    (D) P, r, n, and t

14. In a certain right triangle, the sine of angle A is $\frac{5}{13}$ and the cosine of angle A is $\frac{12}{13}$. What is the ratio of the smallest side of the triangle to the median side of the triangle?

15. If $x > 0$ and $x^2 + 10x = 11$, what is the value of $x + 5$?

16. If a set of 20 different numbers has its smallest and largest values removed, how will that affect the standard deviation of the set?

    (A) It will increase.
    (B) It will decrease.
    (C) It will remain the same.
    (D) Not sufficient information.

17. Jay is purchasing gifts for his four friends' high school graduation. He has a budget of at most $150. He is purchasing a restaurant gift card of $25 for one friend, a tool set that costs $40 for another friend, and a $35 college sweatshirt for a third friend. For his fourth friend, he wants to see how many $0.25 quarters ($Q$) he can give for him to use for laundry money. What expression gives the range of quarters he can purchase given his budgetary restrictions?

    (A) $1 \le Q \le 300$
    (B) $1 \le Q \le 200$
    (C) $10 \le Q \le 120$
    (D) $40 \le Q \le 60$

18. What will happen to the graph of the function $f(x) = 4x^2 - 18$ if it is transformed into this function? $g(x) = 4(x - 2)^2 - 15$?

(A) It will shift down 2 units and shift to the left 3 units.

(B) It will shift up 3 units and shift to the right 2 units.

(C) It will shift up 2 units and shift to the left 3 units.

(D) It will shift down 3 units and shift to the right 2 units.

19. What is the surface area in square units of a right rectangular prism with edges of 2, 3, and 4 units?

20. Which of the following could be a value of x in this equation?

$$8x^2 = -16x - 2$$

I. $-1 - \dfrac{\sqrt{3}}{2}$

II. $\dfrac{1}{2}(-2 - \sqrt{6})$

III. $\dfrac{1}{2}(\sqrt{3} - 2)$

(A) I only

(B) II only

(C) I and III only

(D) II and III only

21. A botanist plants a small ivy plant and evaluates its growth function. She finds that at 2 months after planting, the plant is 5 inches tall; at 4 months after planting, the plant is 8 inches tall. Additionally, she has noticed that the plant has grown at a constant rate since its initial planting. Given this information, what was the plant's height in inches at the time it was planted?

22. An interior designer is selling wood flooring to be used by his client for a new room. The client has already purchased a set length of trim, which goes between the edge of the wood flooring and the wall. The trim is straight, and cannot be curved, yet it can be joined to make right angle corners. The client does not wish to purchase any more trim and would like to use all of his trim in building the new room. If the interior designer wants to maximize the amount of wood flooring that the client purchases, while satisfying the client's requirements, what should be the relationship between the length (L) and width (W) of the room's dimensions?

(A) $L = W$

(B) $L = 2W$

(C) $W = L^2$

(D) $L = W^3$

ANSWER KEY
Diagnostic Test

Reading and Writing Module 1

1.	D	8.	B	15.	C	22.	A
2.	B	9.	B	16.	C	23.	D
3.	A	10.	D	17.	D	24.	D
4.	C	11.	B	18.	A	25.	C
5.	A	12.	D	19.	C	26.	B
6.	C	13.	D	20.	C	27.	C
7.	B	14.	C	21.	B		

Reading and Writing Module 2

1.	D	8.	A	15.	A	22.	A
2.	C	9.	C	16.	D	23.	C
3.	C	10.	D	17.	B	24.	B
4.	D	11.	C	18.	A	25.	B
5.	C	12.	D	19.	B	26.	B
6.	B	13.	C	20.	D	27.	B
7.	A	14.	A	21.	D		

Math Module 1

1.	C	7.	25	13.	D	19.	D
2.	B	8.	C	14.	B	20.	C
3.	21	9.	D	15.	7.6	21.	C
4.	D	10.	A	16.	A	22.	3
5.	C	11.	C	17.	C		
6.	12	12.	B	18.	A		

Math Module 2

1.	B	7.	C	13.	D	18.	B
2.	C	8.	A	14.	$\frac{5}{12}$ or 0.4166 or 0.4167	19.	52
3.	D	9.	D			20.	C
4.	A	10.	A	15.	6	21.	2
5.	B	11.	A	16.	B	22.	A
6.	C	12.	B	17.	B		

Diagnostic Test Analysis Guide

Use this guide to determine which skills you should focus on when you review the chapters. As you go through the test, circle the questions you missed. This will let you easily identify the areas in which you need to improve. The test questions that correspond to different skills are organized below.

Reading and Writing Module 1

Reading: Words in Context	1, 2, 3
Reading: Text Structure and Purpose	4, 5
Reading: Cross-Text Connections	6, 7
Reading: Central Ideas and Details	8, 9
Reading: Command of Evidence	10, 11, 12
Reading: Inferences	13, 14
Writing: Standard English Conventions	15, 16, 17, 18, 19, 20, 21
Writing: Expression of Ideas	22, 23, 24, 25, 26, 27

Reading and Writing Module 2

Reading: Words in Context	1, 2, 3
Reading: Text Structure and Purpose	4, 5, 6
Reading: Cross-Text Connections	7, 8
Reading: Central Ideas and Details	9, 10
Reading: Command of Evidence	11, 12
Reading: Inferences	13, 14, 15
Writing: Standard English Conventions	16, 17, 18, 19, 20, 21, 22
Writing: Expression of Ideas	23, 24, 25, 26, 27

Math Module 1

Algebra	2, 3, 5, 6, 9, 10, 13, 18
Problem-Solving and Data Analysis	8, 11, 14, 17
Advanced Math	1, 4, 15, 19, 20, 21, 22
Geometry and Trigonometry	7, 12, 16

Math Module 2

Algebra	2, 3, 5, 6, 10, 12, 17
Problem-Solving and Data Analysis	7, 11, 13, 16, 21
Advanced Math	1, 4, 8, 9, 15, 18, 20
Geometry and Trigonometry	14, 19, 22

Digital PSAT Scoring Chart

This will give you an approximation of the score you would earn on the Digital PSAT[1]. Tally the number of correct answers from the Reading & Writing section (out of 54) and the Math section (out of 44). Take the total for each of these and find the corresponding section score in the tables below.

Number of correct reading and writing questions (out of 54)	Reading and writing test score (out of 760)
0	160
1	170
2	180
3	190
4	200
5	210
6	220
7	230
8	240
9	250
10	260
11	270
12	290
13	300
14	310
15	320
16	340
17	350
18	360
19	370
20	390
21	400
22	420
23	430
24	450
25	460
26	470

[1] Keep in mind that some of the questions on an actual SAT test will be research questions that will not count towards your actual score. For the sake of simplicity, we are including possible research questions in your calculation.

Number of correct reading and writing questions (out of 54)	Reading and writing test score (out of 760)
27	480
28	490
29	500
30	510
31	520
32	530
33	540
34	550
35	560
36	570
37	580
38	590
39	600
40	610
41	620
42	630
43	640
44	650
45	660
46	670
47	680
48	690
49	700
50	710
51	720
52	730
53	750
54	760

Number of Correct Math Questions (Out of 44)	Math Section Score (Out of 760)
0	160
1	180
2	190
3	200
4	210
5	240
6	260
7	280
8	300
9	310
10	320
11	340
12	350
13	360
14	370
15	390
16	400
17	410
18	420
19	440
20	450
21	460
22	470
23	480
24	490
25	500
26	510
27	520
28	530
29	540
30	550
31	560
32	570
33	580

Number of Correct Math Questions (Out of 44)	Math Section Score (Out of 760)
34	590
35	610
36	620
37	640
38	650
39	660
40	680
41	710
42	730
43	750
44	760

Add the Reading and Writing score and the Math section score to find your total PSAT test score:

_____ Reading and Writing score +

_____ Math section score =

_____ **Total PSAT test score (between 320 and 1520)**

Approximate your testing percentiles (1st–99th) using this chart:

Total Score	Section Score	Total Percentile	Reading and Writing Percentile	Math Percentile
1520	760	99+	99+	99
1420	710	98	98	96
1320	660	94	94	91
1220	610	86	86	84
1120	560	74	73	75
1020	510	59	57	61
920	460	41	40	42
820	410	25	24	27
720	360	11	11	15
620	310	3	3	5
520	260	1	1	1
420	210	1	1	1
320	160	1	1	1

Scoring data based on information at Collegeboard.org

Diagnostic Self-Assessment

Check any areas you feel you need to work on.

Reading

- ☐ Reading timing
- ☐ Overthinking Reading questions
- ☐ Not sure how to think through Reading questions
- ☐ Careless errors on Reading questions
- ☐ Other issues?

Writing

- ☐ Writing timing
- ☐ Writing grammar review
- ☐ Overthinking Writing questions
- ☐ Not sure how to think through Writing questions
- ☐ Careless errors on Writing questions
- ☐ Other issues?

Math

- ☐ Math timing
- ☐ Math formula and concept review
- ☐ Overthinking Math questions
- ☐ Not sure how to think through Math questions
- ☐ Careless errors on Math questions
- ☐ Other issues?

General

- ☐ Test anxiety and testing mindset issues?

Answer Explanations

Reading and Writing Module 1

1. **(D)** On the vocabulary questions, the wisest strategy is to insert each of the options into the text to determine the best choice in context. "Within the Iroquois, he *gathered* many followers" is the most sensible possibility, as seen in choice (D), since he is creating a group of people who follow him.

2. **(B)** *Passing* in this context means "going" or "progressing" because the sentence is expressing the nature of time. The best answer is *moving*, since it comes closest to meaning "going" or "progressing." It is not (A), *living*, because time is not a living thing, and is not described in this way—even metaphorically—in the surrounding sentences. It is not (C), because the type of movement that time undergoes is not a physical throw, but an abstract process. It is not (D), because although *succeeding* can mean "following," *passing* is describing an ongoing process, not a series of separate events.

3. **(A)** You can put your own synonym in here pretty easily. An "answer" or *resolution* to a problem is the intended meaning, so (A) works best. (B) refers to the first usage of *solution*, a mixture of liquids. (C) denotes an "option." (D) inaccurately signifies that the teacher is referencing the cause—a lack of preparation—rather than the solution, adequate preparation.

4. **(C)** The text describes how the microwave presents an innovation in cooking technology, with the final sentence showing the uses that are most suitable for the microwave: thawing food and not cooking large cuts of meat. This understanding most closely aligns with choice (C). It is not (A), because it does not consider objections. It is not (B), because it does not go into detail about science. And it is not (D), because it does not suggest further avenues for research.

5. **(A)** Boudin's works were economically viable, i.e., they could be sold to consumers successfully, because he painted the vacationers and locations in a way that enabled them to capture the essence of their destinations without having to pay the added expense of a customized painting. Choices (B) and (C) would be widely applicable to most all impressionist art, and choice (D) would apply to certain artists other than Boudin.

6. **(C)** Both authors debunk the connection between natural and healthy, so (C) is correct. Only Text 2 explicitly considers (B), and implicitly considers (A), since *engineered* would be similar to genetic modification. Finally, since *metabolism* is the name for how our bodies function, (D) is an imprecise choice.

7. **(B)** Text 1 delves into the mechanics of how the electoral college works, while Text 2 puts the electoral college in the historical context of the past 200 years—all of this lines up with choice (B). It is not (A), because neither text cites political authority figures. It is not (C), because Text 1 does not address the founding of the United States. And it is not (D), because Text 2 does not address the economy.

8. **(B)** The text argues that the advantages of social media need to be considered in the workplace, so (B) is the correct choice. The author provides evidence of (A) to support the thesis, but it is not the thesis itself. (C) represents a general argument that the text questions. (D) is not discussed.

9. **(B)** Newton's theories gave Halley a general structure he could use to make better predictions about the behavior of comets. Out of the options, this is most similar to a politician who uses philosophical maxims to predict societal outcomes, since the philosophical maxims would give the theoretical structure that the politician would use to predict what would come next. It is not choice (A), because the musician is not making predictions. It is not (C), because the mathematician is using the data to create theories, whereas Halley was using the theory to make experimental predictions as to what the data would be. And it is not (D), because the engineer is not focused on making predictions about data but using established laws of physics for construction.

10. **(D)** The lines are closest to one another in 2008, so (D) is correct. The other choices provide years where the deviation between voters is greater than it is in 2008.

11. **(B)** *Experimental confirmation that the inner components of a virus are similar to those of a cell nucleus* would give further evidence that the modern cell nucleus originated from a viral infection. Choices (A), (C), and (D) would not relate to origin of the cell nucleus.

12. **(D)** By stating that death is a "slave to fate, chance," the poet suggests that death is more of a random process than one of clear destiny, in which the future would be more pre-determined. While the other options all mention death, they do not mention its randomness.

13. **(D)** The "cases" the text refers to in the final sentence are those in which due to confusion as to whether a war actually began, the applicability of the Geneva Convention would be "contested." Certain parties in the war may not consider respecting the human rights of those that they capture. This would therefore result in an *obvious* danger. The other options do not highlight the clear danger to combatants that such confusion would cause.

14. **(C)** The text states: "Edna was a trifle embarrassed at being thus signaled out for the imperious little woman's favor. She would not dare to choose, and begged that Mademoiselle Reisz would please herself in her selections." Edna's embarrassment indicates that she was *sheepish,* which is a word describing embarrassment. Edna certainly was not *eager* or *thrilled*, but was rather quite reluctant instead. Edna was not *indecisive*, as she never intended to make a decision in the first place.

15. **(C)** In colloquial English, people use choice (A), but it ultimately is not correct usage. *Should have given* is the correct conjugation here. Remember that *should of, could of,* and *would of* are never correct verb usages. *Should have, could have,* and *would have* are the proper usages.

16. **(C)** Earlier in the text, the author uses "one." To be consistent with this pronoun use, use *one* in this instance as well. The other options would not match this pronoun usage.

17. **(D)** *Technique* is the singular subject, so the verb should be *involves*. (D) also uses the correct forms of *floating* and *molten* to describe the class—*molted* does not work as a word in this context—*molted* means for an animal to have shed its exterior coat. *Molten* means "liquified," which would be appropriate to describe hot glass. Choices (A) and (B) have plural verbs, and choice (C) uses *molted* instead of *molten*.

18. **(A)** "Boiled down to its essence, the problem is this" is an *independent clause,* meaning that it could be a full sentence on its own. It needs sufficient punctuation to separate it from what comes after. A colon would be best in this case because it acts as a lead-in to the second clause. Choice (A) is the correct answer. Choices (B) and (C) lack punctuation at the end of the independent clause. Choice (D) would be a comma splice.

19. **(C)** It is important to maintain parallelism within a clause. Notice how "increasing" is used first. It is necessary to maintain the gerund (-ing) form for the second action. *Sending* is the only option that appropriately maintains parallelism.

20. **(C)** *Than* is used for comparisons, while *then* is used as a sequencing term. Eliminate choices (B) and (D), as this is a comparison. When making comparisons, it is far better to use an -*er* word, like *smaller*, rather than an -*est* word, like *smallest*. Choice (C) is the correct answer.

21. **(B)** Recall that a semicolon is the best way to connect two independent clauses (two clauses that could otherwise be full, complete sentences). Choice (B) uses a semicolon effectively. Choice (A) is a comma splice. Choice (C) is a run-on sentence. Choice (D) is flawed in that it introduces an unnecessary comma.

22. **(A)** The best option here is a contrasting transition. Essentially, *good readers are active,* but *bad readers tend to end up as criminals.* A vast generalization, but that's the structure of the sentence. *On the other hand* is the only contrasting transition. *Therefore* and *thus* are cause-and-effect transitions. *Moreover* means "also."

23. **(D)** Choice (D) is the only option that demonstrates a contrast between the relatively wasteful process of incandescence and the far more efficient process of luminescence.

24. **(D)** This sentence provides an additional explanation that helps the reader understand how sunscreen is not a perfect solution in and of itself—responsible behavior, like taking breaks from the sun, is essential to sun safety. It is not Choice (A) because this is not a subsequent, or next, event. It is not Choice (B) because the previous and current sentences do not contrast with one another. And it is not Choice (C) because the current sentence is not simply elaborating on the previous sentence but providing a new point.

25. **(C)** *For instance* provides a connection between the general statement made about the artwork in the previous sentence, followed by a specific example in the current sentence. Choices (A) and (B) do not provide this sort of transition, and choice (D) is too wordy.

26. **(B)** Both of these projections inaccurately display the area of all surfaces of Earth, skewing the size based on where on Earth the section is found. The Mercator projection "does not accurately show the surface area of countries" and the Robinson projection "distorts the size of the land masses close to the North and South poles." It is not (A), because the Mercator is likely more useful for ship navigation. It is not (C), because the projections are not accurate in displaying relative land area in latitudes close to the poles. It is not (D), because both projections can indeed be drawn on a two-dimensional surface.

27. **(C)** The student wants to emphasize what can be likely seen by people who want to see elements of Teotihuacan today. Since the Pyramid of the Sun and the Pyramid of the Moon are both well-preserved, they would be excellent elements of this past civilization that people today could visibly see. It is not Choice (A) because this relates to the Inca, not to Teotihuacan. It is not (B) because this does not tell us what can physically be seen today. It is not (D) because this makes a general parallel between ancient and modern civilization.

Reading and Writing Module 2

1. **(D)** Here, *dismissed* means "discredited." (A) refers to a lower price. There is no suggestion that he has *forgotten* the information, as in (B). (C) means that he would "allow" this information to go forward, which is illogical.

2. **(C)** This line is referring to viewers who brought up, or presented, points that weakened the speaker's credibility. Therefore, the meaning is that they *put forward* several points. (A) is the type of *raise* one might get at a job. (B) is the definition for *raise* when it refers to lifting something up. (D) indicates bringing up and caring for someone, as a mother might raise a child. Make sure to read the sentence with the choices replacing the underlined portion if you are struggling between two answer choices.

3. **(C)** On vocabulary problems, if there is any uncertainty, it is best to plug the options into the text in place of the word. *Theory*, in this case, makes far more sense than *building*, *observation*, or *astronomy*. *Construct* isn't often used as a noun rather than verb, but when it is, its meaning is generally *an idea or theory*.

4. **(D)** The phrase is used to describe what the concept of *logistics* initially meant: it was a war term used to describe the delivery of ammunition. It is thus *to explain the root of a concept*, as in Choice (D). Choice (A) is flawed in that the phrase defines *past*, not current, usage of a phrase. There is no likely reader objection, as in Choice (B). To what would the reader possibly object? There is no primary source evidence provided, as in Choice (C).

5. **(C)** This sentence serves as the author's acknowledgment of a possible objection that would find a move away from partisanship a positive trend in American politics, so (C) is accurate. These lines show an opposing view, ruling out (A), and do not go into details as in (B). Finally, choice (D) is incorrect because the lines do not include a citation.

6. **(B)** The author uses this text to give scientific reasons, such as Halley's unusually elliptical orbit, as to why Halley's Comet is a uniquely observable comet. The other options do not give you the *primary* purpose of the text, just minor things that are mentioned.

7. **(A)** The underlined selection states that "petroleum output is as healthy as ever." Now, consider how the first author might respond. Choices (B), (C), and (D) are not variable: petroleum is not renewable, always generates greenhouse gases, and is less expensive than ethanol. (A) works because the first author would want to consider how much oil is available domestically since it impacts our self-sufficiency.

8. **(A)** The first text argues that literature is a term reserved for writing that is artistically superior and timeless, pursuing beauty, purpose, and meaning. The second text, on the other hand, postulates that standards of evaluation are illusory and biased. Therefore, (A) is the only option that captures the overall relationship between the two texts.

9. **(C)** Zenobia is most interested in the "relation between the sexes" when it comes to social reform, so she is most interested in reforming antiquated gender roles. There is no evidence that her primary reform objective is to change universities that are hostile towards foreigners (choice A), problems with economic fairness (choice B), or destruction of the environment (choice D).

10. **(D)** When answering questions like these, the challenge is recognizing the big picture idea of the text. You need to be able to fully understand the text and put the main idea of the text in your own words. In this text, the main idea is that Kolya is putting family heirlooms into a fire in order to keep warm in the bitter cold. Instead of prioritizing the sentimental value of these items, he is more interested in being comfortable in the harsh environment. Therefore, choice (D) makes the most sense since Kolya's need for comfort overcomes his familial nostalgia (sentimental longing). The incorrect choices will often trap you by presenting ideas that may represent small portions of the text, but do not accurately represent the text as a whole. Choice (A) states that the library must be preserved at all costs, which is inaccurate given that so many of the library books are being burned. Choice (B) incorrectly suggests that the narrator is making some sort of sacrifice to the gods; instead, he is simply trying to stay warm. Choice (C) suggests that the narrator would like to be reunited with his deceased mother; while this may be true, there is no textual evidence to draw this conclusion, and this statement does not accurately represent the main idea of the text.

11. **(C)** Only use the evidence given. You cannot make conclusions about any employment outlooks, as in (A) and (B). Nor can you make assumptions about the number of people currently employed in these professions, as in (D). However, you can use the graph to show that janitorial jobs are more likely to be completed by machinery than historian jobs, making (C) correct.

12. **(D)** The author of Text 2 believes that the quality of writing is "entirely subjective," and bases this argument on inconsistent grading. So, choice (D) would rule out the evidence and undermine the author's argument. (A) would support the argument of the text. (B) and (C) don't affect the argument either way.

13. **(C)** The surrounding context is helpful in figuring out this question. The text in which this excerpt is found states that encryption has become extremely complex, so choice (A) is incorrect. There is nothing in the text or these lines that refers to the primary focus of criminal activity, as in choice (B), or to the motivations that cause people to become criminals, as in choice (D).

14. **(A)** The narrator has an attitude of warm appreciation as evidenced especially by the second sentence of the text, in which the narrator describes impressionist art as "boldly" challenging the older principles of art, "transforming" it into something new. Choice (B) is too positive, choice (C) too neutral, and choice (D) too negative.

15. **(A)** The text describes Mannes and Godowsky as more casual tinkerers (as opposed to dedicated researchers) "working recreationally, "who had backgrounds in music rather than professional science. Thus, their discovery can best be described as *serendipitous*, i.e., a fortunate finding by chance. The other options are all associated with focus in particular fields of study, which was not the case for Mannes and Godowsky with respect to their photographic research.

16. **(D)** This choice concisely expresses the intended idea. Choices (A) and (B) are too wordy. Choice (C) likely wants to say something along the lines of *contemporary*, but the word given actually means "with contempt."

17. **(B)** This is the only option consistent with the use of Italics throughout the sentence to denote a different name for this instrument.

18. **(A)** This is the only option that uses the correct present perfect tense. Choice (B) is past. Choice (C), *loaned*, is always incorrect. Choice (D) is in the progressive tense.

19. **(B)** The proper phrase is *not only . . . but also. . . .* The other options can work as transitions but not in this context given the earlier part of the sentence.

20. **(D)** This choice correctly does not have an apostrophe after *departments* because this word is functioning as the subject, not as a possessive adjective. Choices (A) and (B) incorrectly have apostrophes after *departments*. Choice (D) is correct also because *ensuring* means to "make sure," which fits the context. *Assure* means to "reassure," and *insure* has to do with financial transactions.

21. **(D)** *Specific* in this case means "unique," stating that the particular chemical signature given off by each element is unique to it. Choice (A) is too wordy. Choice (B) is incorrect because *partial to* means "to prefer" something. Choice (C) uses an adverb instead of an adjective.

22. **(A)** The writer uses an interesting turn of phrase to state that Bernice does not listen to (entertain) or find amusing (be entertained by) Marjorie's social activities. Choice (B) does not work because a transitional word would be needed after *entertainment*. Choices (C) and (D) result in nonsensical meanings.

23. **(C)** This is the only option that provides a needed contrast between what could potentially cause males to be calico or tortoiseshell and the fact that such a possibility is quite rare.

24. **(B)** "Unlike" is the only option to show the necessary contrast between the view of the contemporary socialist parties that seek out full socialization of private industry and the more moderate Social Democrats who sought compromise.

25. **(B)** For transition questions, diagnose the relationship between this sentence and the preceding one. The author is arguing that, *even though* she learned some German, she didn't learn as much of the native language as a German student would learn of English in the United States. That *even though* is important, as it denotes a contrast between the two sentences. *However* is the only contrasting choice.

26. **(B)** Since the student wants to show the possible range of severity that could result from a parasitic worm infection, Choice (B) is the most effective option. It outlines how an infected person could feel anything from mild annoyance to having potentially life-threatening consequences. The other options relate to infection, but do not discuss the possible range of severity.

27. **(B)** The notes state that land preservation does not factor in the potential use of the land by humans, while land conservation does factor in such use—this makes Choice (B) the most logical option. Choices (A) and (D) do not draw a contrast, and Choice (C) is inconsistent with the definitions of the ideas presented in the notes.

Math Module 1

1. **(C)** x and y could both either be negative or positive to make this true. Therefore, the only thing we can safely assume is that x and y are different. You can try this with sample values that make this expression true:

x	y	$x^2 > y^2$
-5	4	$25 > 16$
6	-1	$36 > 1$
3	0	$9 > 0$

2. **(B)** Solve for x and y by using substitution:

$$4 + y = 32x \text{ and } y = 2x + 2 \rightarrow$$

$$4 + (2x + 2) = 32x \rightarrow 6 = 30x \rightarrow x = \frac{1}{5} \rightarrow$$

Substitute $\frac{1}{5}$ in for x to solve for y: $y = 2 \times \frac{1}{5} + 2 = \frac{12}{5}$

Then, multiply x and y to solve for their product: $\frac{1}{5} \times \frac{12}{5} = \frac{12}{25}$

3. **(21)** In a typical week, Eloise should get $9 \times 7 = 63$ hours of sleep. We can see how much sleep she has gotten by subtracting the total hours she has been awake from the total hours in a week: $24 \times 7 - 126 = 42$. Then, we can calculate the additional hours of sleep she should get by subtracting how many hours she *actually* got (42) <u>from</u> the amount of sleep she *should have* gotten (63):

$63 - 42 = 21$ additional hours she should get.

4. **(D)** You could work backwards from the choices if you are so inclined. Algebraically, divide the expression by 3 to simplify:

$$3a^2 - 27a - 108 = 0 \rightarrow a^2 - 9a - 36 = 0 \rightarrow$$

Factor it: $(a - 12)(a + 3) = 0$

If $a = 12$, $(a - 12)$ is 0, making the entire expression equal to 0. Similarly, if $a = -3$, $(a + 3)$ is 0, making the entire expression equal to 0.

Therefore, the solutions are $12, -3$.

5. **(C)** The *difference* between two terms is the result when you subtract one term from another. Let us subtract one term from another—this is easiest to do if you place one term over the other so you can easily match up common terms and carefully apply the negative sign:

$$(7a^2 + 3ab - 8b)$$
$$\underline{- (-2a^2 + ab - 2b)}$$
$$9a^2 + 2ab - 6b$$

6. **(12)** Triple the given equation $2x + 3 = 4$ to give you the equation $6x + 9 = 12$:

$$2x + 3 = 4 \rightarrow 3 \bullet 2x + 3 \bullet 3 = 3 \bullet 4 \rightarrow 6x + 9 = 12$$

Alternatively, if you do not recognize this pattern, solve for x and plug the value into to $6x + 9 = 12$ to see the value of the expression.

7. **(25)** Use the circumference formula, $2\pi r$, to solve for the circumference. Since the diameter is 8 centimeters, the radius will be half of this: 4 centimeters. Plug 4 into the circumference formula to solve for the circumference:

$$2\pi(4) = 8\pi = \approx 25.12$$

Round it to the nearest whole centimeter to get 25.

8. **(C)** The total price on which the sales tax will be applied is $25,000 − $5,000 , since the new car is $25,000 and Allison receives $5,000 on the trade-in. To calculate the total after the sales tax is applied, take 100% of (25,000 − 5,000) and add 7% to it. Move the decimal point to the left two spots for each percentage: 100% becomes 1.00 and 7% becomes 0.07. So, multiply (25,000 − 5,000) by 1.07 to get the correct answer: 1.07(25,000 − 5,000).

9. **(D)** Multiplying or dividing an inequality by a negative number will change the direction of the inequality sign. The other operations mentioned will not do so. Here is how it would work with dividing the expression by −2:

$$-2x > 4 \rightarrow \frac{-2x}{-2} < \frac{4}{-2} \rightarrow x < -2$$

If you try some sample values that would work for x, such as −3 or −5, you will see that the inequality is true.

10. **(A)** Take the slope of the line using relatively simple points from the table, like (1, 2) and (5, 18):

$$\text{Slope} = \frac{Rise}{Run} = \frac{y_2 - y_1}{x_x - x_1} = \frac{18 - 2}{5 - 1} = \frac{16}{4} = 4$$

The only choice with a slope of 4 is (A).

11. **(C)** For each year she has the portfolio, it increases 10%. Therefore, the amount after one year of growth over the original amount at the beginning of that year will be 1.1 times the original amount. This process will repeat for each year she has the portfolio growing at this rate, making $f(n) = 10{,}000 \times 1.1^n$

You can also see this using concrete numbers. If she starts with $10,000, after 1 year, she will have 10% interest added to the original amount:

$$10\% \text{ of } 10{,}000 = 0.1 \times 10{,}000 = 1{,}000$$

Then, you can add 1,000 to the original 10,000 to have $11,000 after the first year. Then, to see how much money she will have after two years, find 10% of this new total:

$$10\% \text{ of } 11{,}000 = 0.1 \times 11{,}000 = 1{,}100$$

Then, add this to the original 11,000 to find how much she will have in her account at the end of year 2:

$$11{,}000 + 1{,}100 = 12{,}100$$

The only option that fits these concrete numbers is choice (B).

12. **(B)** Use the provided formula for the volume of a cylinder:

$$V = \pi r^2 h$$

The height is 4 feet and the radius is half the diameter: 1 foot. Plug these values into the equation to solve for the cylinder's volume:

$$V = \pi r^2 h \rightarrow \pi(1^2)4 = 4\pi \text{ cubic feet}$$

13. **(D)** Each penny is 1 cent and each nickel is 5 cents. So, the total number of cents given by the total coins in the change bowl will be $P + 5N$. This needs to be less than 1 dollar total, i.e., 100 cents. This gives us the inequality $P + 5N < 100$ as our solution.

14. **(B)** As the age groups gradually increase in value (from 12 through 61+), the number of group members using video sharing steadily decreases (from 40 to 2). A negative correlation is defined as the relationship between two variables such that when one variable increases, the other variable decreases. So the relationship between age groups and percentage of group members using video sharing can best be described as a negative correlation.

    A positive correlation is when the variables increase with one another. Equivalence simply means the variables are equal. An exponentially inverse relationship means that as one variable increases, the other decreases at an exponential rate. The decrease in video sharing is relatively steady, so the terms cannot be described as having an exponentially inverse relationship.

15. **(7.6)** Plug in the given values for m and n to determine what the value of the constant k is:

$$m = kn$$
$$10 = k \times 2$$
$$5 = k$$

Now, plug 38 in for m and 5 for k to get the value of n:

$$38 = 5n$$
$$7.6 = n$$

16. **(A)** A parallelogram has two sets of equivalent interior angle measures. Also, it is a quadrilateral that has a total interior angle measure of 360 degrees. Since one of the interior angles is 50 degrees, one of the other angles will also be 50 degrees. The other two angles will then add up to a total measure of $360 - 2(50) = 260$ degrees. Solve for the larger angle by dividing 260 by 2:

$$\frac{260}{2} = 130.$$

17. **(C)** The slope of the function is steady and linear until around week 6, at which point it starts curving upwards exponentially. An exponential function is one that goes up at a rapidly increasing rate or goes down at a rapidly decreasing rate, as opposed to a steady, linear rate.

18. **(A)** No matter how many shirts or pants are cleaned, the cleaner has a $5 fee. The only logical explanation out of the given choices is that this is some kind of set fee. The cost to clean a shirt is 10, since it multiplies the shirt variable. The cost to clean a pair of pants is 6, since it multiplies the pants variable. And the total minimum cost to clean either one shirt or one pair of pants is 11, since it would be:

$$C = 10S + 6P + 5 \rightarrow C = 10 \times 0 + 6 \times 1 + 5 = 11$$

19. **(D)** The weight of the balloon itself is irrelevant since the balloon is identical in both situations. $1.2 - 0.179 = 1.021$ is the difference in density between the two balloons. Since you have a 2 cubic meter balloon, simply multiply 1.021 by 2 to give approximately 2.04.

20. **(C)** The fixed costs for the pretzel stand are $500, and the variable costs are $2. So, the cost function $c(x)$ given x pretzels is $c(x) = 2x + 500$. The graph of this function will therefore have a y-intercept of 500, and a slope of 2:

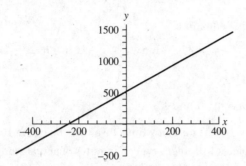

21. **(C)** A value of 4 for n will ensure that the expression has exponential growth since any power of 2 or greater will ensure exponential growth in the function. Anything raised to the 0 power simply equals 1. Anything raised to an exponent of 1 is simply itself. So choices (A) and (B) result in lines, not exponential functions.

22. **(3)** There are 3 values of the function where it will intersect the x axis, which we can see by looking at the graph of the equation below:

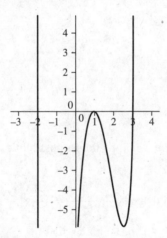

The values of 3, -2, and 1 are all zeros of the function.

You can perhaps more easily determine the zeros of the function if you recognize that the function is already factored:

$$f(x) = (x - 3)(x + 2)((x - 1)^2)$$

All you need to do is look at the values of x that would make the entire expression equal to zero. If $(x - 3) = 0$, or $(x + 2) = 0$, or $(x - 1) = 0$, the entire expression is equal to zero. Also, since $(x - 1)$ is squared, the $(x - 1)$ term repeats, so we will have only three zeros even though this will end up being a quartic equation (to the fourth power).

Math Module 2

1. **(B)** It is easiest to do substitution for x into the first equation.

$$2x = 10 \rightarrow x = 5$$

Substitute 5 into the first equation:

$$5 = y^2 - 3y + 1 \rightarrow y^2 - 3y - 4 = 0 \rightarrow$$

Factor it: $(y + 1)(y - 4) = 0$

Therefore, the solutions are -1 and 4.

2. **(C)** Whenever Andrew begins his study time, he always takes the 10 minutes of time to get set up. Then, he completes 1 problem every 5 minutes of actual study. So, the number of minutes he takes to do p problems is $10 + 5p$. If we set up the equation for this, it is $m = 10 + 5p$. Then, if we solve for p, we will get the correct answer:

$$m = 10 + 5p \rightarrow m - 10 = 5p \rightarrow \frac{(m - 10)}{5} = p \rightarrow p = \frac{1}{5}(m - 10)$$

3. **(D)** Since this is one equation with two variables, it will have infinite solutions. If we knew another line with which this equation intersected, the two equations would have a solution. To see how this equation has more than two solutions, try some sample values for x and y into the equation:

$$3x - 4y = 73$$

If x is 1, y is -17.5

If x is 2, y is -16.75

If x is 3, y is -16.

You can keep on going and you will find endless possibilities for x and y.

4. **(A)**

$$\left(2x^2 + 4xy + 2y^2\right) \times \frac{1}{2x + 2y} = \frac{2x^2 + 4xy + 2y^2}{2x + 2y} \rightarrow$$

$$\frac{x^2 + 2xy + y^2}{x + y} = \frac{(x + y)(x + y)}{(x + y)} = x + y = y + x$$

5. **(B)** The professor will cancel if there are 10 or fewer students in the class. So, there must be more than 10 students. Therefore, the answer is $S > 10$.

6. **(C)** What is a possible value for x in the expression below?

Take the original expression: $-6 < \frac{8}{3}x < -\frac{1}{4}$

Multiply everything by $\frac{3}{8}$ in order to get x by itself:

$$-\frac{9}{4} < x < -\frac{3}{32}$$

Make it easier by converting each fraction to a decimal so it is easier to determine what numbers would fall within this range. The fractions would convert to the following range expressed as decimals:

$$-2.25 < x < -0.09375$$

-2 is the only choice within this range.

7. **(C)** Since the amount of money he earns is only $8,000, it falls within the first tax bracket of 15%. Multiply 0.15 by $8,000 to find the total amount of tax on his income:

$$0.15 \times 8,000 = 1,200$$

8. **(A)** Take both the slope and the y-intercept and multiply them by -1 to get the reflection of the line. For $y = 4x + 7$ this will be the equation $y = -4x - 7$

   The general rule for a reflection of a function $f(x)$ across the x axis is that the reflection is $-f(x)$.

9. **(D)** Solve for x as follows:

$$\frac{12}{\sqrt[3]{x}} = 4 \rightarrow 12 = 4\sqrt[3]{x} \rightarrow 3 = \sqrt[3]{x} \rightarrow \text{Cube both sides} \rightarrow 27 = x$$

10. **(A)** $m + 2n = 1$ and $6n + 3m = 9$ are parallel lines that will not intersect, since they have the same slopes and different y intercepts. Since they do not intersect at all, they will have no common solutions.

11. **(A)** The range is the difference between the maximum and minimum values in the set. With such large data sets, it is highly likely that both sets would have a wide range of large and small values, with both almost certainly having a value close to or at 1 and a value close to or at 100. So the range for both sets would be about 100. The difference between the ranges is calculated by subtracting one range from the other: $100 - 100 = 0$.

12. **(B)** We can begin by determining the slope of the line in the given equation by putting it in slope-intercept form $(y = mx + b)$:

$$4x = 2y - 6 \rightarrow 2y = 4x + 6 \rightarrow y = 2x + 3$$

   The line portrayed in choice (B), $y = 2x + 10$, is the only option that has the same slope of the line in the problem. This means that the two lines will never intersect and will have no common solutions since they are parallel to one another. Be mindful that this will only be true as long as the y-intercepts of the lines are different; if the y-intercepts are the same, then the lines will overlap.

13. **(D)** Minimizing all of the variables will decrease the amount of money in the account after a given period of time. While you could plug in a variety of sample values and test the impact of changing each variable on the overall amount of money in the account, this is easier to simply think through using common sense. If you start off with less money, have a lower interest rate, and have less frequent compounding of interest, there will be less money in the account.

14. **($\frac{5}{12}$ or 0.4166 or 0.4167)** The triangle as described looks like this:

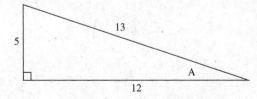

   Given this sine and cosine, the triangle will be a multiple of the special right triangle, 5-12-13. The smallest side is 5 and the median side is 12, so the ratio of the smallest side of the triangle to the median side of the triangle is $\frac{5}{12}$.

   Another way to think about it is that this is asking for what the tangent of angle A would be, which is the opposite side over the adjacent, giving you $\frac{5}{12}$.

15. **(6)** Look for a way to seamlessly make the original expression a variation on $x + 5$. Add 25 to both sides of the equation: $x^2 + 10x = 11$, and the result can be expressed as $(x + 5)^2 = 36$. Therefore, $x + 5 = 6$.

Alternatively, you could determine the value of x using the quadratic formula, $\dfrac{-b \pm \sqrt{b^2 - 4ac}}{2a}$, but this will be more labor-intensive than noticing the short-cut.

16. **(B)** The smaller the range of values in a data set, the lower the standard deviation will be. If the smallest and largest values are removed, this will decrease the range of values, therefore decreasing the standard deviation.

To be more precise, you can calculate standard deviation using this formula:

$$\text{Standard Deviation} = \sqrt{\text{Average of the squared distances of the data points from their mean}}$$

For example, the standard deviation of the set $\{1, 5, 6, 7, 10\}$ is approximately 3.3, while the standard deviation of the same set with the highest and lowest values removed $\{5, 6, 7\}$ would be 1. So, using this example, you can see that removing the smallest and largest values from the set will decrease the standard deviation of the set.

17. **(B)** After purchasing gifts for his other friends, Jay has \$50 left. \$50 has 200 quarters, so the range of what Jay can give his friend is between 1 and 200 quarters inclusive, which is expressed as $1 \leq Q \leq 200$.

18. **(B)** When you add a positive number to the y value of a function, the function shifts up; when you subtract a number from its x value, the function shifts to the right. This function has 3 added to its y value and 2 subtracted from its x value, so it will shift up 3 units and shift to the right 2 units.

19. **(52)** Each of the six faces of a right rectangular prism (a box) is a rectangle—you can calculate the area of a rectangle by multiplying its length by its width. So, for a right rectangular prism with edges of x, y, and z units, the surface area can be calculated as follows:

$$2xy + 2xz + 2yz$$

Plug in 2 for x, 3 for y, and 4 for z to calculate the total surface area:

$$2(2)(3) + 2(2)(4) + 2(3)(4) = 12 + 16 + 24 = 52 \; \textit{square units}$$

20. **(C)** Which of the following could be a value of x in this equation?

$$8x^2 = -16x - 2$$
$$8x^2 + 16x = -2$$
$$x^2 + 2x = -\frac{1}{4}$$

Complete the square:

$$(x + 1)^2 = \frac{3}{4} \rightarrow x^2 + 2x + 1 = \frac{3}{4} \rightarrow x^2 + 2x + \frac{1}{4} = 0$$

Use the quadratic equation to find the answers:

$$\frac{-b \pm \sqrt{b^2 - 4ac}}{2a} \rightarrow \frac{-2 \pm \sqrt{2^2 - 4 \cdot 1 \cdot \frac{1}{4}}}{2 \cdot 1} = \frac{-2 \pm \sqrt{3}}{2 \cdot 1} = -1 \pm \frac{\sqrt{3}}{2}$$

Then, simplify the two $\pm$ solutions to see what they equal:

$$-1 + \frac{\sqrt{3}}{2} = \frac{-2}{2} + \frac{\sqrt{3}}{2} = \frac{1}{2}(\sqrt{3} - 2)$$

And $-1 - \frac{\sqrt{3}}{2}$.

21. **(2)** The plant increases 3 inches in height every 2 months. Simply backtrack 2 months from the time when it is 5 inches tall in order to see how tall it was when it was planted. $5 - 3 = 2$ inches.

22. **(A)** In order to maximize the area of floor while minimizing the floor perimeter, a square floor would be the best choice. A square will always have at least as much and typically more area for a particular perimeter than a rectangle will of the same perimeter. Therefore, the length and width should be equivalent.

To see this, try using concrete numbers. If we have a square and a rectangle, each with a perimeter of 20 units, the length of each side for the square must be 5, and the lengths of the sides of the rectangle could be a wide range of possibilities, such as 2, 8, 2, 8. The area of the square with a side of 5 is $5^2 = 25$. The area of the rectangle is $2 \times 8 = 16$, which is much less than the area of the square. You can try this with other sample values for the rectangle's sides, but you will consistently find that having the sides equivalent will lead to the greatest possible area.

Reading

1

Reading

Reading For The Digital PSAT

The new Digital PSAT Reading and Writing section combines both reading comprehension questions with grammar and editing questions to give you your total *Reading and Writing* score. How is this different from the old PSAT Reading format?

Old PSAT Reading	New Digital PSAT Reading
■ Reading passages are 500–750 words long and have 10–11 questions each.	■ Reading and Writing passages no longer than 150 words. Each passage has just one question accompanying it.
■ Reading genres include fiction, social science, historical documents, and natural science.	■ Will have a greater variety of reading genres represented. With the current SAT reading genres, there will be humanities, drama, and poetry excerpts.

The new Digital PSAT Reading and Writing section is structured as follows:

Reading and Writing Module One	32 Minutes, 27 Questions, Standard Difficulty
Reading and Writing Module Two	32 Minutes, 27 Questions, Adaptive Difficulty (easier or harder questions depending on how you did on the first Reading/Writing section)

- Out of the 54 total questions in the two modules, a little over half of them will likely be reading questions.
- Each reading question will have a small passage that accompanies it, ranging between 25 and 150 words. Some of the passages will also have a graph of some sort.
- 50 of the questions will count towards your score and four of the questions are *pre-test* questions that will not count but are used by the College Board to test future questions. *Do not worry about determining which questions are pre-test; just do your best on every question you encounter.*

This chapter contains:
- **14 Key strategies for success on PSAT Reading questions**
- **Question-specific strategies and practice** for the six types of PSAT Reading questions you will encounter:
  - **Information and Ideas**
    - *Central Ideas and Details*
    - *Command of Evidence*
    - *Inferences*
  - **Craft and Structure**
    - *Words in Context*
    - *Text Structure and Purpose*
    - *Cross-Text Connections*

Reading Strategies

1. Take your time.

A major shift in the digital SAT is to make it an easier test to complete within the time constraints. Most test-takers will find that the PSAT Reading section is quite manageable to complete. Take approximately **70 seconds for each question** on the Reading and Writing section. To manage your time, utilize the countdown clock that is embedded in the testing program.

You will likely do your best if you use the full amount of time to read the passages well, and think through the questions carefully. There is no prize for finishing the section early. In fact, if you find yourself finishing the Reading and Writing section with time to spare, you may want to try reading the more challenging passages a couple of times before attempting the questions. If you do have difficulty finishing the PSAT Reading, you can pick your battles by focusing on just those passages and questions that come to you most easily, and guessing on the questions you do not have time to attempt, since there is no guessing penalty.

2. Consider reading the questions before reading the passages.

Since each reading text has just one question that accompanies it, you may find it easier to focus on what you need to look for if you read the question before reading the text. This could be especially helpful on questions that ask you to focus on something more specific in the text: words in context, text structure and purpose, and command of evidence. On questions that involve determining the meaning of the passages in a more general way—central ideas and details, inferences, and cross-text connections—you may want to go ahead and read the passage before doing the questions.

3. Focus on the overall meaning of the text(s) as you read.

You should be able to restate the *gist* of what you have read—don't worry about memorizing details from the text. This is especially important for questions that ask about the general meaning or the primary function of the text. Sometimes there will be a brief note at the beginning of the text that will tell you the name of the author, the book, and the date—these pieces of information will help you preview the text, so be sure to read them. To help you stay focused as you ascertain the overall gist, use the provided scrap paper to take notes and briefly summarize the text in your own words.

4. Read Actively, Not Passively.

Simply moving your eyes over the page is not enough to be sure that you understand what you are reading. What makes active reading and passive reading different?

Active Reading	Passive Reading
Paraphrase—You put the ideas of the text into your own words. You can state the main idea of what you read.	**No paraphrasing**—You get lost in the details and are unable to summarize what is happening.
Ask questions—You ask yourself questions about the text, such as, "Who is this character?" "What is going to happen next?" "What is the point of the text?"	**Don't ask questions**—Although you may be reading, you are not interacting with the text.
Focus on the task at hand—You think about the text, and if your mind wanders, you quickly refocus.	**Your mind is elsewhere**—You may look like you're reading but don't refocus when you become bored or distracted.

If you have trouble reading actively, what can you do to improve?

FIND SOMETHING ABOUT THE TEXT THAT CAN INTEREST YOU: Reading actively is easy when the text is something you would read for pleasure. If the text is not on a topic you find particularly interesting, try to think of some connection you can make to the text from your schoolwork or life experiences. Suppose you had a text about human anatomy. Even if you haven't specifically studied the subject in school, you might be able to understand the concepts based on experiences you had going to the doctor or studying the biology of different animals.

MAKE SURE YOU ARE WELL RESTED: It is more difficult to focus on reading when you are fatigued. Try your best to get about 8–9 hours of sleep on the nights leading up to the PSAT.

RECOGNIZE WHICH PASSAGE TYPES ARE MORE CHALLENGING FOR YOU AND ALLOW MORE TIME ON THEM: Often, students find that older texts require more time to fully comprehend. Fiction texts may have flashbacks and metaphors that require a closer reading; historical texts may be over 200 years old, making some of the language antiquated. Experiment with reading the different text types so that you have a sense of which ones you can complete in less than 70 seconds and which may need more time.

5. Do not hesitate to skip and come back to questions.

You can flag questions in the testing program, making it easy to revisit the questions that you skipped. If you find yourself stuck on a question, come back to it so that you can allow your subconscious mind to process the possibilities. Once you come back to the question with fresh eyes, you will often surprise yourself at how well you can think through it at that point. Also, if you know that the reading questions are more difficult for you than the grammar questions in the same testing module, you could do the grammar questions first and save the reading questions for later. Recognize that you are in control of the order that you do things within the testing module, so do things in the order that best suits you.

6. Fully understand every part of the question.

A careless mistake in reading a question will likely lead to a wrong answer. Instead of quickly reading through the question, and then having to reread it, read it one time well. This will ensure that you not miss wording critical to understanding what the question is asking, such as *not, primary, infer, suggest*, etc.

7. Do not look at the answer choices until you have an idea of what you are looking for.

On factual recall tests, checking out the answers before you have formulated an answer can help you narrow it down. With the critical thinking questions on the PSAT, in contrast, you will often find yourself misled by persuasive but ultimately incorrect answers. Take control of the questions and don't let them control you. Try your best to come up with an idea of the answer before actually looking at the answer choices.

8. Go back to the passage as often as needed.

Most tests we take are closed-book—the PSAT Reading section is open-book. If you had an open-book test in school, you would surely use your textbook and notes to help you answer the questions. With the PSAT questions giving you key words and underlined selections, it makes sense to use the passage whenever necessary.

9. The answers will be 100 percent correct or totally wrong.

A single word can contaminate an answer, making it completely wrong. When you narrow the choices down to two options, don't just look for the *best* answer—look for the *flawless* answer. Try to quickly debate with yourself the correctness or incorrectness of each answer, knowing that there is one that is definitely correct, and three that are definitely incorrect. The College Board has put a great deal of effort into creating the questions you will see on the PSAT, so you can safely assume they will be of the very highest quality.

10. Focus on meaning, not matching.

On ordinary school tests, we are often used to matching the choices with facts we recall from the assigned reading or the in-class lecture. On the PSAT, the fact that an answer has wording that matches parts of the passage text is no guarantee that it is correct. There is nothing wrong with picking an answer because it *does* have wording that is in the passage; just don't pick an answer *only because* it has matching wording. Be certain the overall meaning of an answer gives the correct idea.

11. Don't try to guess how you did.

Since the digital SAT is adaptive, the later sections will change in difficulty depending on your performance on earlier sections. It will do no good to try to evaluate how difficult the later section questions are—you will waste time and energy that could be spent on figuring out the problems in front of you. Do your best to stay in the moment and not think back about how you performed on earlier sections. Moreover, be mindful that four of the Reading and Writing questions you encounter will be experimental and not scored—if a question seems a bit odd to you, do your best and don't dwell on it.

12. Practice with the testing application ahead of time.

You will be able to download the software that you will use on the actual digital SAT—go to collegeboard.org for the latest details on how to do so. You can practice with this program on your own computer or on one at a library or school. Familiarize yourself with the software interface—the timer, the question-flagging feature, and the adaptive question style. The program will allow you to mark off answers you have eliminated and zoom in on the passages if you want to focus on part of the text. Since the passages are fewer than 150 words, you should have no difficulty seeing the entirety of the passage on the screen while you work through the question.

13. Give every question your best effort.

With fewer questions on the digital SAT, each question has a larger impact on your score. Given the adaptive nature of the digital SAT, the questions you will be given on the later modules are designed to be of a difficulty appropriate for you. Be sure to give every question your very best effort—do not allow yourself to become frustrated and quickly guess.

14. When in doubt about your strategy, give the PSAT the benefit of the doubt.

On poorly written tests, tricks and gimmicks can help you succeed—such shortcuts *will not* help you perform well on the new PSAT. The digital PSAT is an extraordinarily well-constructed assessment, given the amount of time and resources the College Board has devoted to its overhaul. As a result, do not waste your time and energy while taking the PSAT looking for flaws in the test. Instead, give the PSAT reading section the benefit of the doubt and focus on how *you* can improve your reading comprehension and critical thinking skills.

Central Ideas and Details

These questions will ask you to interpret the overall meaning of the text. For example, they may ask you something like this:

Which choice best states the main idea of the text?

How should you handle these specific types of questions?

- **Carefully read and thoroughly paraphrase the text before examining the answer choices.** While this is good advice on almost all PSAT reading questions, it is particularly important on central ideas questions. The meaning will likely be based on the text as a whole rather than one small part of it, so understand the entirety of what is given.
- **Be careful of latching on to answers just because they mention specific parts from the text.** If you don't fully grasp the general meaning of the text, it will be easy to become trapped by answers that are partially right in citing specific language in the selection.

Practice Exercises

1. *The following text is from Anatole France's 1912 French novel* The Gods Will Have Blood.

"As an appetizer for your capon, I've made some vegetable soup with a slice of bacon and a big beef bone. There's nothing gives soup a flavor better than a marrow bone."

"A praiseworthy maxim, (Gamelin)," replied old Brotteaux. "And you will do wisely, if tomorrow, and the next day, and all the rest of the week, you put this precious bone back into the pot, so that it will continue to flavor it. The wise woman of Panzoust used to do that: she made a soup of green cabbages with a rind of bacon and an old *savorados*. That is what they call the tasty and succulent medullary bone in her country, which is also my country."

"This lady you speak of, monsieur," . . . Gamelin put in, "wasn't she a little on the careful side, making the same bone last so long?"

Based on the text, Citizen Brotteaux and Citizeness Gamelin have what respective attitudes towards the reuse of food?

(A) Both agree that no effort should be spared to make food as delicious as possible to give refuge from the political difficulties of the time.

(B) There is no need for conservation, given the abundant supply of poultry; use every part of the poultry—let nothing go to waste.

(C) Both agree that given the scarcity of food, every effort should be made to conserve and reuse food.

(D) Be wise by craftily reusing food as much as possible; don't take conservation of food to an extreme.

2. *The text is from Booker T. Washington's 1901 autobiography.*

My mother, I suppose, attracted the attention of a purchaser who was afterward my owner and hers. Her addition to the slave family attracted about as much attention as the purchase of a new horse or cow. Of my father I know even less than of my mother. I do not even know his name. I have heard reports to the effect that he was a white man who lived on one of the near-by plantations. Whoever he was, I never heard of his taking the least interest in me or providing in any way for my rearing. But I do not find especial fault with him.

The source of information Washington primarily draws upon for the information in the text is most likely

(A) a publication.

(B) hearsay.

(C) statistical analysis.

(D) a scholarly article.

3. Finding a job directly out of college is, for many, a catch-22. Employers want experience, and graduates are hard pressed to gain the experience needed to, well, gain experience. As a remedy, universities are encouraging internships, opportunities to enter the workforce temporarily and train in a position of interest. The idea is that both sides will come out the better – the intern strengthening his or her resume and building a strong social network, the employer expanding its workforce and investing in a prospective employee. But now, more students are questioning exactly who is getting their money's worth when many internships are unpaid. Rather than doubting the value of experience, they wonder at its fairness and practicality. Internships, when paid, are not only more valuable, but also more meaningful.

Which choice best states the main argument of the text?

(A) Ambitious college students should embrace any work opportunity that becomes available.

(B) Employers should do away with the obsolete practice of college internships.

(C) In order to create a mutually beneficial opportunity, internships should be compensated.

(D) So that employers do not have to waste time training inexperienced new hires, they should focus on only hiring applicants with experience.

4. *The following is Carl Sandburg's 1916 poem "Fog."*

The fog comes
on little cat feet.

It sits looking
over harbor and city
on silent haunches
and then moves on.

What is the most suitable description of fog as presented in the poem?

(A) Gentle and fleeting

(B) Invasive and dominating

(C) Quiet and subversive

(D) Animalistic and destructive

5. *This selection is adapted from Lincoln's 1863 Gettysburg Address.*

   Now we are engaged in a great civil war, testing whether that nation, or any nation so conceived and so dedicated, can long endure. We are met on a great battle-field of that war. We have come to dedicate a portion of that field, as a final resting place for those who here gave their lives that that nation might live. It is altogether fitting and proper that we should do this.

   Which choice best states the main idea of the text?

   (A) Defeating the enemy is essential to creating the type of nation the United States should become.
   (B) While the civil war rages on, we must have hope that there will be a peaceful resolution.
   (C) It is important for policy makers to understand the importance of constructing a burial ground.
   (D) Dedicating a cemetery for those who died in a vital national battle is the right thing to do.

6. *The following text is from Ralph Waldo Emerson's 1862 lecture "American Civilization."*

   The power of Emancipation is this, that it alters the atomic social constitution of the Southern people. Now their interest is in keeping out white labor; then, when they must pay wages, their interest will be to let it in, to get the best labor, and, if they fear their blacks, to invite Irish, German, and American laborers. Thus, whilst Slavery makes and keeps disunion, Emancipation removes the whole objection to union. Emancipation at one stroke elevates the poor white of the South, and identifies his interest with that of the Northern laborer. [...]

   What option best summarizes the text?

   (A) Emancipation will lead to the political dominance of European immigrants.
   (B) Emancipation will ensure an equitable redistribution of income across the races.
   (C) An end to slavery will cause the Southern constitution to be amended.
   (D) An end to slavery will realign Southern economic interests in favor of union.

Answer Explanations

1. **(D)** Brotteaux's attitude is seen when he advocates reusing a cooking bone; Gamelin's attitude is seen in the final paragraph of the text in which she questions the sensibility of reusing a bone so much. Neither would support choice (A) or (B), and only Brotteaux would support (C).

2. **(B)** Washington has acquired the little knowledge he has of his family through informal conversations and speculation. This is most evident when Washington states that he has "heard reports" about his family. This type of conjecture and secondary-witness testimonial is best represented as *hearsay*. There were no *publications* of his family; he mentions nothing written at all. Similarly, there were no *statistics*. Washington did not learn of his family through *scholarship* or academia; there was nothing to be studied.

3. **(C)** The passage initially presents the dilemma that both employers and potential employees face—workers will be better prepared with experience, but they can only get experience if they become workers. The author argues that a way to solve this dilemma is for internships to be paid so that they are both valuable and meaningful. This argument aligns with choice (C). Neither (A) nor (B) is presented in the passage, whereas (D) inaccurately summarizes the general argument given.

4. **(A)** The fog comes in very gently "on little cat feet." Then it sticks around for a bit before it "moves on," showing that it is impermanent or *fleeting*. It does not have the negative and violent elements suggested in (B) with *invasive and dominating*, in (C) with *subversive*, or in (D) with *destructive*. While the fog could be described as *quiet* and also having some animal qualities, the entirety of the answer must be correct to work.

5. **(D)** Lincoln sets the stage by stating that there is a great civil war going on. He then states that he is dedicating a portion of the battlefield as a "final resting place" for deceased soldiers, and that this is a "fitting and proper" thing to do. This aligns with choice (D). It is not (A) or (B), because there is not a primary focus on defeating an enemy and on ending the war, but on taking a pause to dedicate this cemetery. It is not (C), because the burial ground has already been made—it is just being ceremonially dedicated at this point.

6. **(D)** To paraphrase the text, emancipation will change Southern culture in ways that will unify the nation. Thus, (D) best captures this idea. Emerson only mentions immigrants to argue that emancipation opens up labor options. Choice (B) is a distorted exaggeration. (A) Southern constitution, as in (C), was never mentioned.

Command of Evidence

These questions will ask you to analyze textual and quantitative evidence to determine what is justified based on the given information. For example, they may ask you things like this:

Which quotation from Hamlet *most effectively illustrates this idea?*

Which choice most effectively uses information from the graph to complete the example?

Which finding from the experiments, if true, would most strongly support the scientist's theory?

How should you handle these specific types of questions?

- **Realize that you do not need to understand everything, just enough to answer the question.** It will likely be easiest to read the question first to focus on what context clues you should pay close attention to.
- **Recognize that you do not need any background knowledge.** Do not let yourself be intimidated by unfamiliar graphs or concepts—everything you need to figure out evidence-based problems will be right there in the material.
- **Give yourself plenty of time to understand the graphs, poems, text, or other information.** On graph questions be sure to carefully examine the labels and axes so you can evaluate the data. With challenging texts, like poems, allow yourself time to read through the text a couple of times if need be.

Practice Exercises

1. Intentional cultivation of non-native invasive plants is generally far more beneficial than accidental introduction.

   Which of the following, if true, would most undermine the statement made above?

   (A) A historical investigation into the origins of invasive plants that demonstrates that the majority were introduced by accident
   (B) A global statistical analysis that demonstrates the net harmful effect from purposefully introduced invasive plant species
   (C) A genetic analysis that establishes that invasive plant species share several fundamental characteristics in their DNA
   (D) Discovery of three instances of invasive plant introduction that had a beneficial impact on the surrounding environments

2. "A Jelly-Fish" is an early 1900s poem by Marianne Moore. In the poem, the speaker metaphorically alludes to giving up on trying to find meaning: _____

   Which quotation from "A Jelly-Fish" most effectively illustrates the claim?

   (A) "Visible, invisible, / A fluctuating charm, / An amber-colored amethyst / Inhabits it;"
   (B) "your arm / Approaches, and / It opens and / It closes"
   (C) "You have meant / To catch it, / And it shrivels; / You abandon / Your intent—"
   (D) "It opens, and it / Closes and you / Reach for it— / The blue / Surrounding it / Grows cloudy,"

3. Many accounts from people immersed in a language that is not their own have, throughout several centuries, pointed to profanity as by far the most difficult aspect of a novel language to master. There is, in our profanity, a high cultural learning curve that demands intimate knowledge and sensitivity to the subtleties of social interactions.

   The selection could most effectively be used by which of the following persons to accomplish their stated goal?

   (A) A film censor who wishes to eliminate controversial vocabulary from an upcoming movie
   (B) A world language teacher who wanted to pacify students eager to immediately learn translated *swear words*
   (C) A businessperson who wants to communicate the benefits of their products to potential clients in other countries
   (D) A translator of cookbooks who wants to convert customary measurements to metric ones

4. Primarily, Boudin painted beach scenes on the shores of Brittany and Normandy. Alongside Monet, he was among the first of the impressionists to embrace painting *en plein air*, and he was also one of very few artists to show canvases in all eight of the Paris Impressionist exhibitions. But despite his proximity to the avant-garde, Boudin's work remained, for the most part, conspicuously marketable throughout his career.

   The information in the selection gives the strongest evidence that which of the following labels applied towards Boudin would be most <u>unjustified</u>?

   (A) Savvy businessman
   (B) Starving artist
   (C) Skillful impressionist
   (D) Independent thinker

5. In a presidential system, the executive and legislative branches of government are completely independent of one another, such as in the United States of America. The president, elected directly by the people, is a national figure that is at once the head of government and state, but is separate and distinct from Congress, the lawmaking body. On the other hand, a parliamentary system is a fusion of executive and legislative powers with the executive, most often called *prime minister*, being a member of Parliament. In the latter arrangement, members of Parliament, the legislative assembly, are elected by the people, but then choose amongst themselves the most fit to be executive. Most often, a monarch, like in Great Britain, is given the responsibility of heading the state and being the icon of national ceremony.

   Suppose a country with a parliamentary system and a country with a presidential system were choosing representatives to a global sports competition like the Olympics. Based on the text, which respective governmental officials from the parliamentary and the presidential system would be the most desirable and fitting representatives?

   (A) Prime minister, congressperson
   (B) Judge, military general
   (C) King, president
   (D) Queen, senator

6.

Principal USDA Food Guides, 1940s–1980s

U.S. Food Guide Time Period	Number of Food Groups	Protein-Rich Foods	Breads	Fruits and Vegetables	Other
1940s Basic Seven Foundation Diet	7	Milk and milk products: 2 or more cups Meat, poultry, fish, eggs, dried beans, peas, nuts: 1–2	Bread, flour, and cereals: Every Day	Leafy green/yellow: 1 or more Potatoes, other fruit/veg: 2 or more Citrus, tomato, cabbage, salad greens: 1 or more	Butter, fortified margarine: some daily
1956–70s Basic Four Foundation Diet	4	Milk group: 2 or more cups Meat group: 2 or more (2–3 oz. serving)	Bread, cereal: 4 or more (1 oz. dry, 1 slice, ½–¾ cup cooked)	Vegetable-fruit group: 4 or more (including dark green/yellow vegetables frequently and citrus daily, ½ cup or average-size piece)	None
1979 Hassle-Free Foundation Diet	5	Milk-cheese group: 2 (1 cup, 1 ½ oz. cheese) Meat, poultry, fish, and beans group: 2 (2–3 oz. serving)	Bread-cereal group: 4 (1 oz. dry, 1 slice, ½–¾ cup cooked)	Vegetable-fruit group: 4 (including vitamin C source daily and dark green/yellow vegetable frequently, ½ cup or typical portion)	Fats, sweets, alcohol: Use dependent on calorie needs
1984 Food Guide Pyramid Total Diet	6	Milk, yogurt, cheese: 2–3 (1 cup, 1 ½ oz. cheese) Meat, poultry, fish, eggs, dry beans, nuts: 2–3 (5–7 oz. total/day)	Breads, cereals, rice, pasta: 6-11 servings –Whole grain –Enriched (1 slice, ½ cup cooked)	Vegetable: 3–5 –Dark green/deep yellow –Starchy/legumes –other (1 cup raw, ½ cup cooked) Fruit: 2–4 –Citrus –Other (½ cup or average)	Fats, oils, sweets: Total fat not to exceed 30% of calories Sweets vary according to calorie needs

Source: USDA.Gov

According to the table, the recommendations regarding sweets have historically been

(A) explicit.

(B) ambiguous.

(C) lenient.

(D) static.

7.

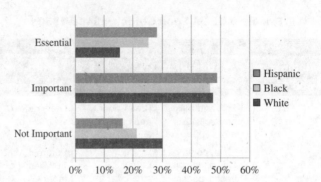

Forbes: How Important Is it That Americans Learn a Second Language?

Most Americans agree on the importance of language education—approximately _____ of white, Black and Hispanic Americans believe that learning another language is important or essential.

Which choice most effectively uses data from the chart to complete the example?

(A) 20 percent

(B) 50 percent

(C) 70 percent

(D) 100 percent

8.

STAY-AT-HOME PARENTS, IN MILLIONS

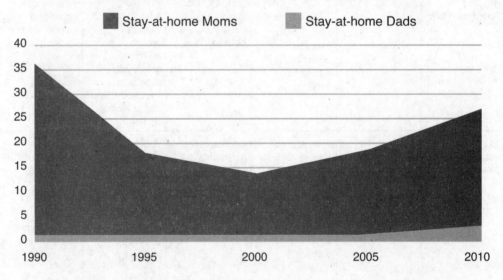

An often-overlooked change in a workforce evermore reliant on technology is the increasing number of employees who find themselves staying at home during the workday.

_____

Which choice most effectively uses data from the chart to complete the example?

(A) From 1990 to 2000, the number of stay-at-home moms declined, whereas the number of stay-at-home dads remained steady.

(B) From 1995 to 2005, the number of stay-at-home moms increased slightly, whereas the number of stay-at-home dads remained steady.

(C) From 1990 to 2010, the number of stay-at-home moms somewhat declined, whereas the number of stay-at-home dads slightly increased.

(D) From 2000 to 2010, the number of stay-at-home moms and stay-at-home dads both increased.

Answer Explanations

1. **(B)** The author argues in these lines that intentional cultivation of non-native plants is usually a good thing. A global analysis demonstrating that non-native plants are typically harmful when introduced would therefore undermine, i.e. weaken, this argument. It is not (A), because knowing that most invasive plants were introduced by accident would not give information about their relative benefit. It is not (C), because this too would not give any facts about how harmful the plants were to their surroundings. And it is not (D), because this would be too small a sample size to make such a sweeping claim.

2. **(C)** In the last part of choice (C) it states *You abandon / Your intent*, which metaphorically illustrates that the speaker is giving up on trying to find meaning. The other options focus on the physical description of and the narrator's interaction with the jelly-fish.

3. **(B)** The text states that profanity is the most difficult aspect of a new language to learn, so if a world language teacher wanted to discourage students from learning *translated swear words*, the teacher could explain the inherent difficulty in doing so. It is not (A), because this has nothing to do with different languages. It is not (C) or (D), because the passage focuses on profanity, not on descriptive business prose or the language of measurement.

4. **(B)** The narrator asserts that Boudin's works were "conspicuously marketable," which means that consumers were willing to purchase them. Hence, it wouldn't make sense to refer to him as a *starving artist* since he was able to make money off his paintings. The other options would properly characterize Boudin in the eyes of the narrator.

5. **(C)** From the context, we know that presidential systems expect the president to be both government leader and national figure. In contrast, a parliamentary system has a government executive that is separate from the national icon, most commonly a monarch. So, (C) is the correct choice.

6. **(B)** Analyze the table for this question. Never is there a definite, clear recommendation for how many servings of sweets one should or should not eat. This is an example of something *ambiguous*, which is another word for *unclear*. *Explicit* is the opposite of the desired choice. *Lenient* means "permissive," while *static* means "constant." Neither of those choices is correct, either.

7. **(C)** Analyze the accompanying graph for this question. The best way to determine the percentage of those who feel it is essential or important is to determine the percentage of people who do *not* feel that it is important, and then subtract this percentage from 100. Analyzing the graph, 30 percent of white people do not feel that it is important, whereas the percentages of Blacks and Hispanics who do not feel it is important are roughly 20 percent and 15 percent, respectively. Theoretically, the mathematics could become a little complicated because there are more whites than Blacks or Hispanics, but the percentage of people who do feel that is important must be somewhere between 70 percent and 85 percent; only choice (C) falls in this range.

8. **(D)** The correct answer is (D) because in 2000, both the number of stay-at-home moms and the number of stay-at-home dads were lower than they were in 2010; this data supports the claim in the previous sentence that there is an "increasing number of employees who find themselves staying at home during the workday." Choices (A), (B), and (C) make accurate statements based on the data in the graph, but they would not support the claim made in the previous sentence.

Inferences

These questions will ask you to read between the lines as you demonstrate deeper understanding of a text—what the author is implying or what the reader can infer. For example, they may ask you something like this:

Which choice most logically completes the text?

How should you handle these specific types of questions?

- **Do not be overly literal.** Look for what the author may be saying indirectly—what is being suggested or implied? Especially watch out for overly literal interpretations when you read genres like fiction, poetry, and drama.
- **Create a possible insertion of your own before evaluating the options.** Inference questions often involve asking you to consider what would most logically complete the text. Although it is tempting to immediately plug each of the choices into the text, you will likely perform better on these types of questions if you create a possible insertion in your own words first. Doing so will make you less susceptible to persuasive yet incorrect answer choices.

Practice Exercises

1. Students should not study math until high school; and at that point, they should be thrown into rigorous algebra, geometry, and calculus courses and be expected to excel. _____ That's because it is. Yet, it is precisely what we do for foreign language study in most school systems.

    Which choice most logically completes the text?

    (A) Sounds absurd, doesn't it?
    (B) Math is an essential part of a high school education.
    (C) Foreign language study deserves more attention.
    (D) Why would we want to study these subjects?

2. It might be easy to chalk up the younger generation as careless and unconcerned and altogether misdirected, but that's the easy way out, and it is flawed. Students are largely civic-minded; they volunteer, worry about public policies, and even congregate to debate solutions to everything from environmental issues to human rights to health care. Significant events like the war in Iraq in 2003 or Barack Obama's running for president in 2008 or gay marriage rights may generate an influx in youth participation, but overall, young voters are disengaged from American democracy and looking at other ways of tackling society's problems. It is not that they are merely apathetic, but instead that they have lost faith in electoral politics and are highly suspicious of party labels.

    The author most strongly suggests that younger Americans are most likely to take what approach to solving societal problems?

    (A) Active participation in the political process
    (B) General apathy and lack of activity
    (C) Attacking problems outside of a governmental paradigm
    (D) Focusing on their own individual interests above all

3. When General Fulgencio Batista assumed power in Cuba by canceling elections and enacting a *disciplined democracy*, Castro planned a popular uprising. His assault failed, and after a year-long imprisonment, Castro fled to Mexico to regroup. _____: of the 82 men who sailed back to Cuba on the *Granma*, Castro was one of the 18 to survive and flee to the Sierra Maestra Mountains.

   Which choice most logically completes the text?

   (A) He decided to remain there indefinitely
   (B) He was unable to recruit more followers
   (C) He gave up on his quest to overthrow Batista
   (D) His return was similarly unsuccessful

4. As a compassionate and passionate educator, I know the competition your child faces. I am interested in breaking down the barriers that intimidate students and providing the path that will get them better college offers, better careers, and most significantly, a better quality of life. To do this, I adopt a perspective of peak preparation at all costs.

   The text most strongly implies that the author places a premium on

   (A) physical exertion.
   (B) intellectual contemplation.
   (C) rigorous expectations.
   (D) logical reasoning.

5. Employees say working from home means fewer dollars spent on gas and daycare. Employers brag that they can reduce real estate, diminish employee turnover, and end the practice of employees' disregarding their attendance obligations. _____

   Which choice most logically completes the text?

   (A) Employees find working from home to be an unneeded chore.
   (B) All in all, working from home may be a win-win.
   (C) Gas prices may impact the willingness of employers to pay for employee commutes.
   (D) To summarize, the culture of an office is difficult to replicate at home.

6. *The following text is from Harriet Beecher Stowe's 1852 novel* Uncle Tom's Cabin.

And suiting the action to the word, the door flew open, and the light of the candle which Tom had hastily lighted, fell on the face of Eliza. "I'm running away, Uncle Tom and Aunt Chloe—carrying off my child. Master [Shelby] sold him."

"Sold him?" echoed both, holding up their hands in dismay.

"Yes, sold him!" said Eliza firmly. "I crept into the closet by mistress's door to-night, and I heard master tell missus that he had sold my Harry and you, Uncle Tom, both to a trader, and that the man was to take possession to-day."

Slowly, as the meaning of this speech came over Tom, he collapsed on his old chair, and sunk his head on his knees.

The passage most strongly implies that Tom's reaction to hearing of Mr. Shelby's plans for him is one of

(A) unanticipated peacefulness.
(B) delighted relief.
(C) surprised despondency.
(D) playful mockery.

Answer Explanations

1. **(A)** The narrator outlines a rather absurd idea—namely that students should not study math until high school and should be immediately thrown into rigorous courses. Then, the narrator goes on to state that this is the approach that is used with foreign language study. The most logical option to connect these ideas is the rhetorical question in choice (A). (B) does not connect to the following part of the text. (C) does not connect to the previous part of the text. (D) is off-topic since the issue is not with whether these subjects are worth studying but with the approach that the educational system takes in studying them.

2. **(C)** Given the overall argument in the text, it is safe to assume that the author believes the younger generation is concerned with solving social issues but prefers to do so outside of political spheres. They are looking at "other ways of tackling society's problems." The text argues against (A). Choices (B) and (D) are refuted in the first sentence of the text.

3. **(D)** The paragraph starts by stating that Castro's initial assault failed. It continues after the underlined portion to state that most of the people who fled perished and Castro had to retreat to the mountains. The most logical connection is to state that his return was similarly unsuccessful. It is not (A), because he is not staying in Mexico indefinitely since he goes back to Cuba. It is not (B), because there is no indication that he recruited more followers. It is not (C), because we do not see that he gave up on his quest to overthrow Batista, only that he regrouped and retreated.

4. **(C)** The text conveys the author's priority to prepare students for the challenges ahead "at all costs." So, we can assume that the author places an emphasis on (C), rigorous expectations. There is no evidence that the author values physical exertion as in (A). Choice (B) more closely resembles what the author of Passage 1 might stress. Finally, (D) usually refers to a process by which one supports and gives logical evidence for an argument or position.

5. **(B)** The first sentence states the benefits that employees receive from at-home work, and the second sentence states the benefits that employers receive. Choice (B) summarizes this by stating that both employers and employees can win from this arrangement. Choices (A) and (C) only focus on one group instead of both, and (D) is overly negative based on the context.

6. **(C)** The final paragraph indicates that upon hearing the news, Tom is shocked and dejected once the full meaning of what happened became clear. Despondency refers to hopelessness and joylessness. His reaction is neither peaceful, relieved, nor playful so (A), (B), and (D) are incorrect.

Words in Context

These questions will ask you determine which words are the best fit for a given context and what the definitions of words are based on context clues. For example, they may ask you things like this:

Which choice completes the text with the most logical and precise word or phrase?

As used in the text, what does the word compromise *most nearly mean?*

How should you handle these specific types of questions?

- **Create a synonym of your own when asked to complete the text with a word or phrase.** Having a synonym before reviewing the answer choices is like having a shopping list before going to the store—you will be more decisive and accurate in picking what you actually need.
- **Just because you do not know a word's meaning does not mean it is wrong.** One of the most frequent mistakes students make on word-in-context questions is going with a word that *sort of works* simply because they know the meaning of the word. If you narrow the question down to two words, one of which you know and doesn't quite fit, and the other of which you do not know, *go with the word you do not know since it has the* <u>potential</u> to be 100-percent correct.
- **Work on picking up on context clues with word definitions.** While memorizing vocab will still help you prepare for these types of questions, you should especially sharpen your skills in picking up on the meanings of words based on context. Even if you know the definitions of words, you will need to determine which definition is most applicable in the particular situation. Build on this skill by making a habit of trying to pick up on definitions as you read.

Practice Exercises

1. The author's rebuttal to such concerns is _____. First, he uses tongue-in-cheek humor to brush off such concerns, by assuring his parents that he will not end up homeless. Second, and more effectively, he uses facts to the contrary.

   Which choice completes the text with the most logical and precise word?

   (A) complex
   (B) understated
   (C) lacking
   (D) twofold

2. The skills developed through studying philosophy train us to clear up confusions. Sometimes, when two people are discussing a significant life issue, they talk past one another and use the same terms in different ways. Learning to analyze concepts helps us to step back and clarify what we mean by the terms we use, to realize the assumptions we are making in holding certain views, and to make important distinctions.

   As used in the text, what does the phrase *talk past* most nearly mean?

   (A) Speak about the same topic but with different understandings of the topic
   (B) Enter into verbal altercations with one another
   (C) Clearly define the topics about what one another is speaking
   (D) Carefully analyze the shortcomings of the other person's argument

3. Outward expansion of cities was necessary as we continued to deplete the resources near our urban centers. Modern transportation _____ that need, as the necessities for life could be brought in over long distances.

Which choice completes the text with the most logical and precise word?

(A) encouraged
(B) designated
(C) created
(D) nullified

4. Why does one listen to music? Or dance? Or look to the stars? Amusement, surely. Communication and complex stimulation, absolutely. But mostly, I write in the name of indomitable creativity. I am of the distinct opinion that creativity is the most _____ ingredient of erudition, expression, and future success, and being so, must be encouraged inside the classroom.

Which choice completes the text with the most logical and precise word?

(A) effusive
(B) essential
(C) attainable
(D) discouraging

5. President Franklin Delano Roosevelt signed into effect the first minimum wage law in 1933. The Supreme Court overturned this first minimum wage law as unconstitutional, arguing that Congress lacked the legislative _____ for such a far-reaching mandate.

Which choice completes the text with the most logical and precise word or phrase?

(A) authority
(B) ideology
(C) consensus
(D) disparity

6. The bad rap of traditional dietary fats is unjustified. While fats may be high in calories, the human body is excellent at transforming fats into long-lasting energy. This isn't to say that all fats are good; the highly processed fats that in the last fifty years have become ubiquitous are bad for the body because the body cannot easily process them. However, modern studies have demonstrated that unrefined fat—e.g., that in milk, butter, eggs, and meat—poses no danger to a healthy person. Instead, in contrast to the 1950s AMA recommendations, people should monitor their intake of sugars and highly processed foods to maintain healthy lifestyles.

As used in the text, what does the word *poses* most nearly mean?

(A) Postures
(B) Positions
(C) Presents
(D) Displays

7. An Enigma operator was given a message to encrypt. As he typed in each letter, a lamp randomly selected a letter different from the first. The letter substituted by the lamp was recorded as the encrypted message. Each key press moved a rotor so that the subsequent key would use a different electrical pathway, which led to the substitution of a whole new letter. The entire initial, unencrypted message would be typed in, and Enigma would produce the encrypted message.

    As used in the text, what does the word *initial* most nearly mean?

    (A) Original
    (B) Personalized
    (C) Literary
    (D) Decoded

8. The governmental structure of the League was rather uncomplicated. The women of each tribe would select men to represent the tribe at the council. Each village and tribe operated independently outside of the council and the council came together to discuss issues important to the entire league. The Iroquois did not vote individually but as tribes. Debates would rage for long periods of time because the Iroquois never had majority rule; they would come to a consensus. All decisions made were made unanimously. The league had no power to enforce decisions; if a tribe did not agree, it could simply ignore the decision. Thus, consensus was crucial.

    As used in the text, what does the word *rage* most nearly mean?

    (A) Embitter
    (B) Go on
    (C) Cause ire
    (D) Dispute

9. The electoral college served its purpose in years past when smaller states were concerned that larger states would _____ their authority.

    Which choice completes the text with the most logical and precise word or phrase?

    (A) usurp
    (B) invade
    (C) touch
    (D) decline

Answer Explanations

1. **(D)** The sentence goes on to state two things about what describes the rebuttal, making *two-fold* the most logical word. The response has just two aspects, making *complex* too extreme. It is not *understated*, because the author is very direct and vocal with his arguments. It is not *lacking*, because the text speaks of the author's rebuttal in positive terms.

2. **(A)** The sentence clears this up with the later context that states that the people "use the same terms in different ways." So, this would go with (A) because the people would speak about the same topic but have different understandings of it. It is not (B), because while there is confusion, there is no mention of hostility. It is not (C), because the people are not clearly defining the topics. It is not (D), because the people are entrenched in their own points of view, unable to carefully analyze the other person's argument.

3. **(D)** The second sentence states that necessities could be brought into cities over long distances, making the outward expansion of cities no longer necessary, thereby *nullifying* this need. It is not (A) or (C), because these would suggest that modern transportation made this need for outward expansion rather than getting rid of it. It is not (B), because to *designate* is to "name" something, which would not make sense in this context.

4. **(B)** The narrator speaks of creativity in extremely positive terms, making it most logical to call it the *essential* ingredient for success. It is not (A), because the narrator does not suggest that creativity is essentially expressive. It is not (C), because the narrator does not suggest that it is easy to be creative. It is not (D), because this is overly negative.

5. **(A)** Since the Supreme Court overturned this law, the Court would have argued that Congress lacked the *authority* to do so—in other words, Congress would not have had the legitimate power to pass this law. While Congress may have had an *ideology* or *consensus*, these would not necessarily give Congress the rightful power to pass the law. *Disparity* means "difference," which is illogical in this context.

6. **(C)** Substitute the choices into the sentence to determine which option is most appropriate in context. The sentence "Modern studies have demonstrated that unrefined fat . . . *presents* no danger to a healthy person" is the most sensible substitution, because the fats do not cause a danger in the author's estimation.

7. **(A)** The sentence in which we find "initial" states that "The entire initial, unencrypted message would be typed in, and Enigma would produce the encrypted message." It is most reasonable to conclude that an unencrypted message would be the original message that would need to be put into coded form. Thus, choice (A) makes the most sense. It is not choice (B), because the message would not necessarily be personalized. It is not choice (C), because it is unlikely that military communication would take on literary qualities. It is not choice (D), because the message would not likely have been decoded since it had not yet been put into coded form.

8. **(B)** The paragraph states that debates would rage for "long periods of time" until consensus was reached—this is a process that has the potential to be quite inefficient, making choice (B) the best option. It is not choice (A) or choice (D), because with all the debates there would surely be communication and transparency (openness). It is not choice (C), because there is no tyrannical dictatorial structure in this governmental arrangement.

9. **(A)** *Usurp* means to "seize power," usually inappropriately. This would be the best word to convey the fears that the smaller states had. The larger states are not going to literally *invade*, *touch*, or *decline* authority over smaller states.

Text Structure and Purpose

These questions will ask you determine the primary purpose and function of both entire texts and smaller selections within texts. For example, they may ask you things like this:

Which choice best states the main purpose of the text?

Which choice best states the function of the underlined sentence in the text as a whole?

How should you handle these specific types of questions?

- **Distinguish between *purpose* and *summary*.** Students often answer structure/purpose questions by summarizing the text instead of finding the purpose of the text. A summary tells you what the text is about, whereas the purpose tells you why the text was written—these are two very different tasks.
- **Use the surrounding context to pick up on the function of underlined selections.** To understand the purpose of an underlined sentence, you will likely need to fully grasp the entirety of the text. Do not limit yourself to just the underlined sentence when you need to determine the sentence's function and purpose.
- **If the question asks about the purpose of the entire text, be sure you keep the big picture in mind.** It might be tempting to pick an answer that gives you the purpose of some small part of the text instead of the entirety of the text. Be aware of this temptation when doing these types of questions.

Practice Exercises

1. Think traditions. Think stories, dances, jokes, and old fairy tales. But don't stop there. Think about ways of living and expressing oneself–maybe through language, or cooking, or laughing, or rituals. The Center for Folklore Studies at Ohio State University defines it this way: <u>"Folklore may be seen as the products of human work and thought that have developed within a limited community and that are communicated directly from generation to generation, usually orally, with the author or creator unknown."</u>

   Which choice best states the function of the underlined sentence in the text as a whole?

   (A) To explain a method whereby a topic will be researched
   (B) To analyze a specific work of folklore artistry
   (C) To cite an authoritative source in order to clarify an idea
   (D) To highlight the shortcomings of folklore as a communication approach

2. *The following text is from Kate Chopin's 1899 novel* The Awakening.

The very first chords which Mademoiselle Reisz struck upon the piano sent a keen tremor down [Edna's] spinal column. It was not the first time she had heard an artist at the piano. Perhaps it was the first time she was ready, perhaps the first time her being was tempered to take an impress of the abiding truth.

[Edna] waited for the material pictures which she thought would gather and blaze before her imagination. She waited in vain. She saw no pictures of solitude, of hope, of longing, or of despair. But the very passions themselves were aroused within her soul, swaying it, lashing it, as the waves daily beat upon her splendid body. She trembled, she was choking, and the tears blinded her.

The text primarily serves to illustrate that Edna was

(A) viscerally upset by the themes of the songs.
(B) surprised at her newfound reaction to the music.
(C) weary at the lengthy delay in her entertainment.
(D) distraught at her inability to visualize as she listened.

3. It is important to acknowledge that research has identified several serious health risks associated with the chronic overconsumption of sugar, and perhaps of fructose in particular. These risks, however, are by no means limited to foodstuffs containing high fructose corn syrup. Depending on the formula, corn syrup contains between 42 percent and 55 percent fructose by volume. For comparison, cane sugar, honey, and agave nectar—three popular sweeteners touted as *natural,* and therefore, more healthful—contain 50 percent, 52 percent, and 85 percent fructose, respectively. Thus, whereas it is true that fructose should be consumed only in moderation, the singling out of products that contain high fructose corn syrup is not merely insufficient action to curb the fructose-associated obesity epidemic in our country, it's also patently misleading to consumers.

Which choice best states the function of the underlined sentence in the text as a whole?

(A) Demonstrate that corn syrup is especially harmful to consumers
(B) Show that corn syrup is undeservingly singled-out for criticism
(C) Argue that fructose is but one reason that corn syrup is maligned
(D) Illustrate that many foodstuffs contain great quantities of sugar

4. Research shows that animal companionship supports mental and physical health, increasing life expectancy despite the lack of tyrannous flora or fauna. Pets are associated with lower blood pressure, lower triglyceride and cholesterol levels, and a reduced risk of heart disease. Pet owners are known to be more active, less anxious, and more socially adept. Similarly, pets can improve relationship bonds and unite families around a shared responsibility.

Which choice best states the main purpose of the text?

(A) Discuss the latest advances in medical science
(B) Present a method to improve heart health
(C) Critique those who dislike animal owners
(D) Describe the benefits of pet ownership

5. Consider the work that you most enjoy doing. How do you figure out what to do when complications arise? Relationships with family members, friends, and others enrich our lives. What makes those relationships go well? Many forms of recreation contribute to living a good life. But is there any ultimate meaning or purpose to these temporary activities, or even to life itself? Studying philosophy equips us with the skills needed to understand these and many other important questions.

Which choice best states the main purpose of the text?

(A) Ask questions critical to picking an ideal career
(B) Persuade the reader of the need to study a particular subject
(C) Encourage readers to seek out more recreational activities
(D) Suggest the ultimate answer to life's major questions

6. *The following text is from* Meditations on First Philosophy, *by René Descartes, 1641, in which he muses about the nature of knowledge.*

Several years have now elapsed since . . . I was convinced of the necessity of undertaking once in my life to rid myself of all the opinions I had adopted, and of commencing anew the work of building from the foundation, if I desired to establish a firm and abiding superstructure in the sciences. But as this enterprise appeared to me to be one of great magnitude, I waited until I had attained an age so mature as to leave me no hope that at any stage of life more advanced I should be better able to execute my design. On this account, I have delayed so long that I should henceforth consider I was doing wrong were I still to consume in deliberation any of the time that now remains for action.

Which choice best states the function of the underlined sentence in the text as a whole?

(A) He believes that the foundations for knowledge are error ridden.
(B) The intellectual project he is tackling is so important.
(C) His mental and physical health have begun to decline.
(D) He has chosen this point in time to write this work.

Answer Explanations

1. **(C)** Prior to the underlined sentence, the narrator states that the idea of folklore can be defined in this way, and the narrator defines folklore by citing the Center for Folklore Studies—an authoritative source. So, (C) is the most logical option. It is not (A), because there is no mention of the methodology that will be used to study folklore. It is not (B), because the description of folklore is very general, not of a specific work. It is not (D), because the selection is a definition, not a mentioning of shortcomings.

2. **(B)** The text demonstrates that Edna expected to have mental images of various emotions in response to the emotion. Instead, though, it states that she could *feel* those emotions instead of simply picturing them, which is a far stronger response than Edna anticipated. She was, thus, *surprised at her newfound reaction to the music*. Choice (A) is flawed because Edna does not indicate that this is an unpleasant happening. Choice (C) is flawed because there is nothing to express fatigue. Choice (D) is flawed because she *can* in fact visualize as she listens, so she certainly would not be distraught.

3. **(B)** The text states that the health risks are misdirected at corn syrup; realistically, they are associated with fructose, which is prevalent in "cane sugar, honey, and agave nectar" as well. So, (B) is correct. Corn syrup has comparable or even lesser amounts of fructose than the author's other examples, so (A) is not supported. (C) misunderstands the argument—fructose, not corn syrup, is problematic. (D), although true, does not address the fact that the high amounts of fructose in other foodstuffs contradict the case against corn syrup.

4. **(D)** The text presents numerous reasons that pet ownership can be beneficial: it can increase life expectancy, help heart health, and improve social skills. So, choice (D) best captures this overall presentation. It is not (A), because while the text does make references to research, it does not focus on the latest research developments throughout. It is not (B), because the reference to heart health is only in the second sentence. It is not (C), because the text has a positive tone, suggesting the benefits for those who choose to own pets instead of criticizing those who do not do so.

5. **(B)** The last sentence of the text is key in summarizing the main purpose—the author encourages the reader to study philosophy in order to develop the skills needed to understand the important questions of life. This most logically aligns with (B), because the text serves to persuade the reader to study the subject of philosophy. It is not (A), because the focus is not on career choices. It is not (C), because the narrator is encouraging the reader to develop philosophical thinking skills instead of embark on a particular course of recreation. It is not (D), because the narrator emphasizes the importance of asking questions without giving an idea as to what the ultimate answer to those questions will be.

6. **(D)** The underlined portion refers to the fact that Descartes has waited until an optimal age to try to break down his false principles, making (D) accurate. (A) and (B) are alluded to earlier in the text, and (C) is not supported by the text.

Cross-Text Connections

These questions will ask you determine the primary purpose and function of both entire texts and smaller selections within texts. For example, they may ask you something like this:

Based on the texts, how would the author of Text 2 most likely describe the view of the historians presented in Text 1?

How should you handle these specific types of questions?

- **Paraphrase the thesis of each text.** With non-fiction texts in particular, each text will most likely have some sort of argument it is making. Determine each author's position on the topic and you will be in excellent shape with the question.
- **Recognize the complexity of the text relationship.** It is unlikely that the relationship between the two texts will be completely in opposition to each other. Instead, the texts will likely have some overlapping thoughts and some opposing thoughts. Try not to oversimplify the relationship between the texts.

Practice Exercises

1. **Text 1**

   If both Chicago and Indianapolis expanded their radii by fewer than 100 miles, they would spill into one another. All the farmland between the two would be gone. It's a rather scary enigma: we expand our cities because our population is growing, yet we decrease our ability to sustain ourselves by doing so.

   Text 2

   If done correctly, vertical expansion would greatly decrease our need for cars. A *large city* would actually be made up of many *mini-communities*. Each community would be a self-serving network of high rises. Food would likely still need to be imported, but the people in each community would be able to walk to the grocery store. Residents would walk to work. Each community would have workers specialized in the various essential professions.

   Which of the following best describes the relationship between the texts?

   (A) Text 1 demonstrates how the approach advocated in Text 2 is impractical.
   (B) Text 2 provides a possible solution to the problem described in Text 1.
   (C) Text 1 argues that existing technology can overcome the obstacles in Text 2.
   (D) Text 2 is focused on urban developments while Text 1 is not.

2. **Text 1**

Students should be permitted to leave school during lunch periods. Having the opportunity to get off school grounds and recharge will build student morale and empower students to be more focused when they return from their meal. Additionally, giving students the chance to leave school for lunch will likely encourage more physical activity, as many students will walk home or to a nearby restaurant.

Text 2

Many people are rightly concerned that some students cannot be trusted to act appropriately with the freedom to leave school during lunch. Rather than letting a few bad apples spoil the barrel, schools should prohibit troublemakers from leaving the school grounds, while allowing responsible students the freedom to make their own choices.

The two texts differ in arguments in that

(A) Text 2 uses metaphorical language, whereas Text 1 does not.

(B) Text 1 argues for students to be free to leave during lunch periods, whereas Text 2 disagrees.

(C) Text 2 does not consider the likely objections of others, whereas Text 1 does.

(D) Text 1 cites evidence from scholarly publications, whereas Text 2 does not.

3. **Text 1**

Some non-native plants are introduced to new territories accidentally via interregional soil and food trade. Accidental introduction of non-native organisms can often have negative and unforeseen consequences. For example, the Asian chestnut blight fungus was unexpectedly brought to the United States through the trade of plants; this fungus nearly wiped out the entire American chestnut population, harming many animals that depended on chestnuts for food.

Text 2

For the past fifty years, it has been the conventional credence of ecologists and biologists alike that invasive, non-native plant species are, without exception, detrimental to the host ecosystem. However, recent studies at Penn State University indicate that the eradication of invasive plants—specifically fruit-bearing shrubs—can do more harm than good for the native animal populations.

Based on the texts, how would the author of Text 2 describe the overall view presented in Text 1?

(A) Unusual

(B) Typical

(C) Unfounded

(D) Correct

4. **Text 1**

If the eruption of smartphones has been the vanguard of anything, it is the near soci-etal takeover of social media. Within the workplace, most supervisors quickly block sites like Facebook, Twitter, and Instagram from company computers, and for good reason. Productivity is likely to decrease if three hours of an eight-hour workday are spent *liking* and *tweeting* and *pinning*. Then there is company bad-mouthing to consider. In the digital age, nothing one says or does or records online is private—nothing.

Text 2

The unique ability of social media to market company services and extend company reputa-tion is indispensable. Many startup businesses find that they simply cannot compete without a social media page to deliver their mission and broaden their contacts. It can simply be the best tool available for advertising, marketing, expansion, and customer feedback. Likewise, it provides an unrivaled medium for market research.

It can be reasonably concluded that the authors of both Text 1 and Text 2 would most likely agree with which of the following statements?

(A) While it can be inefficient for employees to use social media during the workday, it can be quite helpful for business to utilize it.

(B) Social media provides an unnecessary distraction to both businesses and to their employees and should be removed from the workplace.

(C) Employers often overstep their bounds by interfering with the social media use of their employees.

(D) Privacy is the foremost concern for internet users, and strict measures should be taken to safeguard personal information.

5. **Text 1**

According to the American Academy of Sleep Medicine, teenagers (13–18 years old) should aim for 8–10 hours of sleep during each 24-hour period. According to a national survey, how-ever, 73 percent of students reported not getting enough sleep during school nights.

Text 2

The early start time for high school is a major problem for students. When I was of high school age, I found it exceedingly difficult to fall asleep before midnight, despite my best efforts to go to bed around 10 PM. When the alarm clock woke me up at 6 AM, I was exhausted and certainly not in the best frame of mind to learn.

What would the authors of the texts most likely consider to be a reasonable solution to teen-age sleep deprivation?

(A) Mandate that high school students get at least 12 hours of sleep every evening

(B) Find an alternative waking notification method to the relatively shrill noise of an alarm clock

(C) Shift the start time of high school to later in the day so students can get more sleep

(D) Educate teens on the importance of being alert during the school day so that they can maximize learning

6. *Text 1 is from Sojourner Truth's 1815 speech at the Women's Convention in Akron, Ohio. Text 2 is from Carrie Chapman Catt's 1917 Address to the Congress on Women's Suffrage.*

Text 1

That man over there says that women need to be helped into carriages and lifted over ditches, and to have the best place everywhere. Nobody ever helps me into carriages, or over mud-puddles, or gives me any best place! And ain't I a woman? Look at me! Look at my arm! I could have ploughed and planted, and gathered into barns, and no man could head me! And ain't I a woman?

Text 2

Your party platforms have pledged women suffrage. Then why not be honest, frank friends of our cause, adopt it in reality as your own, make it a party program, and *fight with us*? . . . We shall all be better friends, we shall have a happier nation, we women will be free to support loyally the party of our choice, and we shall be far prouder of our history.

Both texts use which of the following argumentative techniques?

(A) Rhetorical questions
(B) Individual attacks
(C) Personal anecdotes
(D) Historical references

Answer Explanations

1. **(B)** The problem outlined in Text 1 is that as cities grow, the land available for the cities decreases. Text 2 proposes a solution of vertical expansion to overcome this, making (B) the most logical option. It is not (A) or (C), because Text 1 does not address the specifics of the solution discussed in Text 2. It is not (D), because both texts consider urban developments, i.e., cities.

2. **(A)** Text 2 uses the phrase "letting a few bad apples spoil the barrel," which is metaphorical, not literal, language. Text 1 does not use any metaphorical language and is very matter-of-fact. It is not (B), because Text 2 also believes that students should have the freedom to leave school during lunch periods. It is not (C), because Text 2 begins by considering the objections of others. It is not (D), because neither text cites scholarly evidence.

3. **(B)** Text 1 describes invasive plants as generally negative in their influence on the environment, which would align with the "conventional credence" that non-native species are detrimental. *Conventional* is close to *typical* in meaning, making choice (B) correct. It is not (A), because Text 2 would consider this text *usual* rather than *unusual*. To call it *unfounded* would be overly negative—Text 2 would most likely acknowledge that there are justifications to this viewpoint, although recent research has shown exceptions. It is not (D), because Text 2 argues that the general view in Text 1 is not completely correct.

4. **(A)** Text 1 argues that due to time wasting and privacy considerations, employers are correct in blocking social media use by employees at work. Text 2 argues that there are tremendous benefits to businesses that can use social media. So, choice (A) would be the best fit. It is not (B), because Text 2 argues that businesses should be able to use social media. It is not (C), because neither text argues that a social media ban in the workplace is an invasion of boundaries. It is not (D), because whereas Text 1 acknowledges concerns about privacy, Text 2 does not give evidence in support of this position.

5. **(C)** Text 1 states that 73 percent of students are not getting enough sleep during school nights, and Text 2 gives a personal anecdote about the difficulty of getting to sleep as a high school student. Putting these arguments together, both authors would likely consider shifting the start time of high school to later in the day to be a good solution. It is not (A), because this would be too extreme a solution. It is not (B), because the issue is not about the annoyance from an alarm clock but about the lack of sleep. It is not (D), because a lack of education does not seem to be at the heart of the issue.

6. **(A)** Both passages use rhetorical questions, i.e., questions given for dramatic effect in which the answer is already known. Text 1 asks "ain't I a woman?" and Text 2 asks "why not be honest, frank friends of our cause?" Neither uses individual attacks. Text 1 uses personal anecdotes, whereas Text 2 does not. Text 2 puts the situation in a historical context, whereas Text 1 focuses on the present.

Troubleshooting

Here are some further pointers for common issues.

"I can't stay focused when I read."

- Be certain you get a good night's sleep before the PSAT. You will start the PSAT with the Reading section. So if you are tired and groggy, it will go poorly. Staying focused is extremely difficult when you are exhausted. Don't stay up late the night before the test doing last-minute cramming; it is not worth it.
- Don't try to remember too much when you read. You only need to remember the general meaning of the text—you should go back when you need to find details. This is not a school-based test for which you need to memorize many details.
- Try doing the questions in an order you choose. The simple act of choosing what texts to try first empowers you to take more ownership of what you read, instead of feeling that you're stuck reading a boring text out of necessity. Build momentum by starting with the texts that come easiest to you.

"I finish too early."

- Consider what would be the best use of your extra time—surely it is not to just sit there and stare off into space for several minutes at the end of the test. Perhaps you can spend more time reading the texts, formulating your own answers to questions, or carefully dissecting the answer choices. Experiment with some practice texts to see where the extra time will be most helpful for you.
- Have a watch when you take the test so you can be mindful of how quickly you are working. Try to maintain about a 70 second per question pace. You can also use the timer that is embedded into the testing program if you would rather not wear a watch.

"I go too slowly."

- Diagnose what is taking you the most time. Typically, students spend too much time either reading the texts or evaluating each answer choice. If you are spending too much time reading the text remind yourself that this is an open-book test and that you only need to paraphrase the general idea. If you are spending too much time breaking down the choices, shift your energy to reading the questions more carefully and formulating your own answer; that way, you will be much more decisive when you go to the answer choices.
- Let go of perfectionist tendencies. You will not have time to double-check every answer, and you may not have time to do every question. The PSAT is heavily curved, and you can likely still achieve National Merit recognition even if you miss some questions.

"I get it down to two choices, and I can't decide."

- Even though this isn't the Math section know that there will be one answer that is definitely correct. If you are not seeing it, make sure you understand the context and make sure you have a firm grasp of what the question is asking. Do not allow yourself to become frantic and panicked because you feel you have come across a "trick" question.
- Look for "contamination" in the choices. Even one incorrect word can ruin an entire answer choice. Instead of looking for the "best" answer, look for the "flawless" answer—this mind-set will help you more rigorously analyze the answer choices without being seduced by the incorrect options.

TIP

Do not underestimate how important it is to be well-rested for test day.

TIP

Practice under timed conditions so that proper pacing becomes second nature.

Further Preparation

What else can I do beyond this book to prepare for the PSAT Reading Test?

TIP

Don't forget to try reading passages in the next chapter, "Advanced Reading Drills," for more challenging practice.

- Practice with Barron's books for the SAT: *Barron's SAT* has plenty of practice tests you can try.
- Use the online vocabulary resource that accompanies this book if you have trouble with the words-in-context questions. See the card at the front of this book for online access.
- Use the free reading practice tests and resources provided by the College Board on *KhanAcademy.org*.
- Focus on your most difficult passage types—and turn them into strengths. To challenge yourself even further, you may want to try reading passages for the GRE, GMAT, and MCAT; the passages you find on graduate school admissions tests will surely be more challenging than what you will face on test day.
- Read, read, read. At a minimum, read high-quality books for pleasure, such as ones that have won the Pulitzer Prize or Booker Prize. At a maximum, seek out articles and books that you find most challenging, and read those in your spare time. The more widely you read, the greater the likelihood that you will have some baseline familiarity with the topics you encounter on the PSAT.

2

Advanced Reading Drills

To earn National Merit recognition, you will need to score at an elite level on the PSAT. The following 12 drills will help you develop the skills you need to be successful by giving you texts that are longer and more difficult than you will actually face on test day. You can practice all of these or focus on the passages that give you the most difficulty:

- Fiction: *Almayer's Folly*
- Fiction: "The Fall of the House of Usher"
- Fiction: "Adventure"
- Great Global Conversation: Jefferson
- Great Global Conversation: Frederick Douglass
- Great Global Conversation: Emerson and Arnold
- Social Science: Russian Depopulation
- Social Science: The Emu War
- Science: Caffeine
- Science: Fungi
- Science: Methanogenesis
- Science: Wound Healing

To practice these passages under timed conditions, take about 12 minutes per drill. Answer explanations for each drill are at the end of the chapter.

Fiction

Fiction: *Almayer's Folly*

Almayer's Folly is Joseph Conrad's first novel, published in 1895. Almayer, a poor businessman, dreams of acquiring wealth.

"Kaspar! Makan!"

The well-known shrill voice startled Almayer from his dream of splendid future into the unpleasant realities of the present hour. An unpleasant voice too. He had heard it for many

Line years, and with every year he liked it less. No matter; there would be an end to all this soon.

(5) He shuffled uneasily, but took no further notice of the call. Leaning with both his elbows on the balustrade of the verandah, he went on looking fixedly at the great river that flowed—indifferent and hurried—before his eyes. He liked to look at it about the time of sunset; perhaps because at that time the sinking sun would spread a glowing gold tinge on the waters of the Pantai, and Almayer's thoughts were often busy with gold; gold he had

(10) failed to secure; gold the others had secured—dishonestly, of course—or gold he meant to secure yet, through his own honest exertions, for himself and Nina. He absorbed himself in his dream of wealth and power away from this coast where he had dwelt for so many years, forgetting the bitterness of toil and strife in the vision of a great and splendid reward. They would live in Europe, he and his daughter. They would be rich and respected. Nobody

(15) would think of her mixed blood in the presence of her great beauty and of his immense wealth. Witnessing her triumphs he would grow young again, he would forget the twenty-five years of heart-breaking struggle on this coast where he felt like a prisoner. All this was nearly within his reach. Let only Dain return! And return soon he must—in his own interest, for his own share. He was now more than a week late! Perhaps he would return to-night.

(20) Such were Almayer's thoughts as, standing on the verandah of his new but already decaying house—that last failure of his life—he looked on the broad river. There was no tinge of gold on it this evening, for it had been swollen by the rains, and rolled an angry and muddy flood under his inattentive eyes, carrying small driftwood and big dead logs, and whole uprooted trees with branches and foliage, amongst which the water swirled and roared angrily.

(25) One of those drifting trees grounded on the shelving shore, just by the house, and Almayer, neglecting his dream, watched it with languid interest. The tree swung slowly round, amid the hiss and foam of the water, and soon getting free of the obstruction began to move down stream again, rolling slowly over, raising upwards a long, denuded branch, like a hand lifted in mute appeal to heaven against the river's brutal and unnecessary vio-

(30) lence. Almayer's interest in the fate of that tree increased rapidly. He leaned over to see if it would clear the low point below. It did; then he drew back, thinking that now its course was free down to the sea, and he envied the lot of that inanimate thing now growing small and indistinct in the deepening darkness. As he lost sight of it altogether he began to wonder how far out to sea it would drift. Would the current carry it north or south? South, probably,

(35) till it drifted in sight of Celebes, as far as Macassar, perhaps!

Macassar! Almayer's quickened fancy distanced the tree on its imaginary voyage, but his memory lagging behind some twenty years or more in point of time saw a young and slim Almayer, clad all in white and modest-looking, landing from the Dutch mail-boat on the dusty jetty of Macassar, coming to woo fortune in the godowns of old Hudig. It was an

(40) important epoch in his life, the beginning of a new existence for him. His father, a subor-dinate official employed in the Botanical Gardens of Buitenzorg, was no doubt delighted to place his son in such a firm. The young man himself too was nothing loth to leave the

poisonous shores of Java, and the meagre comforts of the parental bungalow, where the
father grumbled all day at the stupidity of native gardeners, and the mother from the depths
(45) of her long easy-chair bewailed the lost glories of Amsterdam, where she had been brought
up, and of her position as the daughter of a cigar dealer there.

Almayer had left his home with a light heart and a lighter pocket, speaking English well,
and strong in arithmetic; ready to conquer the world, never doubting that he would.

1. How do the opening lines of the essay, lines 1–4 ("Kaspar . . . this soon"), serve to illustrate
    the overall internal conflict throughout the passage?

    (A) Almayer's dreams of wealth are interrupted by mundane reality.
    (B) Almayer's lack of cultural proficiency prevents him from achieving internal peace.
    (C) Almayer's relatively low personal assertiveness keeps him from having fulfilling
        relationships.
    (D) Almayer's struggles with hallucinations haunt his quest for rational thought.

2. How does Almayer contrast himself with those who have been more financially successful?

    (A) He argues that he is more intelligent.
    (B) He acknowledges that they are more motivated.
    (C) He asserts that he is more virtuous.
    (D) He grants that they are more clever.

3. Which option gives the best evidence for the answer to the previous question?

    (A) Lines 5–7 ("He shuffled . . . his eyes")
    (B) Lines 9–11 ("Almayer's . . . Nina")
    (C) Lines 14–17 ("They would . . . prisoner")
    (D) Lines 19–21 ("He was . . . river")

4. As used in line 19, "share" most closely means

    (A) part.
    (B) communication.
    (C) gift.
    (D) disclosure.

5. Almayer's attitude as expressed in lines 31–33 ("It did . . . darkness") compares in what way to
    his attitude when he first set out on his journey?

    (A) More optimistic
    (B) Less troubled
    (C) More hopeless
    (D) Less honest

6. Which option gives the best evidence for the answer to the previous question?

   (A) Lines 16–17 ("Witnessing . . . prisoner")
   (B) Lines 25–26 ("One of . . . interest")
   (C) Lines 44–46 ("the mother . . . there")
   (D) Lines 47–48 ("Almayer . . . would")

7. It is most reasonable to infer that Dain is someone who Almayer believes

   (A) is a skilled seafarer.
   (B) will help him become rich.
   (C) is a close relative.
   (D) will take him and his daughter to Europe.

8. As used in line 32, "free" most closely means

   (A) willful.
   (B) unhindered.
   (C) empowered.
   (D) inexpensive.

9. What personality characteristic does the author most strongly suggest that Almayer has taken from his parents?

   (A) A disappointment that he is continually unable to find adequate nourishment
   (B) A cosmopolitan open-mindedness to new cultures and experiences
   (C) A fear of venturing too far from one's native land
   (D) A disregard for what he believes his station in life should be and what it actually is

Fiction: "The Fall of the House of Usher"

Below is the opening excerpt from Edgar Allan Poe's 1839 short story, "The Fall of the House of Usher," in which an unnamed narrator approaches the home of his childhood friend Roderick Usher after not having seen him for many years.

During the whole of a dull, dark, and soundless day in the autumn of the year, when the clouds hung oppressively low in the heavens, I had been passing alone, on horseback, through a singularly dreary tract of country, and at length found myself, as the shades of the evening drew on, within view of the melancholy House of Usher. I know not how it was—

Line
(5) but, with the first glimpse of the building, a sense of insufferable gloom pervaded my spirit. I say insufferable; for the feeling was unrelieved by any of that half-pleasurable, because poetic, sentiment, with which the mind usually receives even the sternest natural images of the desolate or terrible. I looked upon the scene before me—upon the mere house, and the simple landscape features of the domain—upon the bleak walls—upon the vacant eye-like

(10) windows—upon a few rank sedges—and upon a few white trunks of decayed trees—with an utter depression of soul which I can compare to no earthly sensation more properly than to the after-dream of the reveller upon opium—the bitter lapse into every-day life—the hideous dropping off of the veil. There was an iciness, a sinking, a sickening of the heart—an unredeemed dreariness of thought which no goading of the imagination could torture into

(15) aught of the sublime. What was it—I paused to think—what was it that so unnerved me in the contemplation of the House of Usher? It was a mystery all insoluble; nor could I grapple with the shadowy fancies that crowded upon me as I pondered. I was forced to fall back upon the unsatisfactory conclusion, that while, beyond doubt, there *are* combinations of very simple natural objects which have the power of thus affecting us, still the analysis of

(20) this power lies among considerations beyond our depth. It was possible, I reflected, that a mere different arrangement of the particulars of the scene, of the details of the picture, would be sufficient to modify, or perhaps to annihilate its capacity for sorrowful impression; and, acting upon this idea, I reined my horse to the precipitous brink of a black and lurid tarn that lay in unruffled lustre by the dwelling, and gazed down—but with a shudder even

(25) more thrilling than before—upon the remodelled and inverted images of the gray sedge, and the ghastly tree-stems, and the vacant and eye-like windows.

Nevertheless, in this mansion of gloom I now proposed to myself a sojourn of some weeks. Its proprietor, Roderick Usher, had been one of my boon companions in boyhood; but many years had elapsed since our last meeting. A letter, however, had lately reached me

(30) in a distant part of the country—a letter from him—which, in its wildly importunate nature, had admitted of no other than a personal reply. The MS. gave evidence of nervous agitation. The writer spoke of acute bodily illness—of a mental disorder which oppressed him—and of an earnest desire to see me, as his best and indeed his only personal friend, with a view of attempting, by the cheerfulness of my society, some alleviation of his malady. It was the

(35) manner in which all this, and much more, was said—it was the apparent *heart* that went with his request—which allowed me no room for hesitation; and I accordingly obeyed forthwith what I still considered a very singular summons.

Although, as boys, we had been even intimate associates, yet I really knew little of my friend. His reserve had been always excessive and habitual. I was aware, however, that his

(40) very ancient family had been noted, time out of mind, for a peculiar sensibility of temperament, displaying itself, through long ages, in many works of exalted art, and manifested, of late, in repeated deeds of munificent yet unobtrusive charity, as well as in a passionate

devotion to the intricacies, perhaps even more than to the orthodox and easily recognizable beauties, of musical science. I had learned, too, the very remarkable fact, that the stem of
(45)   the Usher race, all time-honored as it was, had put forth, at no period, any enduring branch; in other words, that the entire family lay in the direct line of descent, and had always, with very trifling and very temporary variation, so lain.

1. Which option best describes what happens in the passage?

    (A) A traveler contemplates the best solution to a problem.
    (B) A man attempts to reconnect with his childhood best friend.
    (C) A character recounts his impressions and analysis of a situation.
    (D) A narrator tells the story of a famous and idiosyncratic family.

2. The tone of the first paragraph is one of

    (A) destruction.
    (B) sorrow.
    (C) foreboding.
    (D) mindfulness.

3. What best captures the narrator's sentiments about his capacity to understand the mystery of the House of Usher?

    (A) He feels intellectually capable.
    (B) He feels professionally untrained.
    (C) He feels largely optimistic.
    (D) He feels generally inadequate.

4. Which option gives the best evidence for the answer to the previous question?

    (A) Lines 6–8 ("I say . . . terrible")
    (B) Lines 13–15 ("There was . . . sublime")
    (C) Lines 16–17 ("It was . . . pondered")
    (D) Lines 23–25 ("I reined . . . before")

5. As used in line 34, "society" most closely means

    (A) civilization.
    (B) culture.
    (C) association.
    (D) order.

6. It can most reasonably be inferred from the passage that the narrator responds as he did to the letter out of a sense of

    (A) obligation.
    (B) sorrow.
    (C) longing.
    (D) terror.

7. Which option gives the best evidence for the answer to the previous question?

    (A) Lines 4–5 ("I know . . . spirit")

    (B) Lines 13–16 ("There was . . . Usher")

    (C) Lines 34–37 ("It was . . . summons")

    (D) Lines 39–41 ("I was . . . exalted art")

8. As used in line 39, "reserve" most closely means

    (A) greed.

    (B) openhandedness.

    (C) preparedness.

    (D) detachment.

9. Lines 44–47 ("I had . . . so lain") suggest that at any point in its history, the Usher family would have had how many heirs at a given time?

    (A) None

    (B) One

    (C) Two or more

    (D) The family had no heirs.

Fiction: "Adventure"

The passage below is adapted from "Adventure," in Sherwood Anderson's 1919 short-story collection Winesburg, Ohio.

Alice Hindman, a woman of twenty-seven when George Willard was a mere boy, had lived in Winesburg all her life. She clerked in Winney's Dry Goods Store and lived with her mother, who had married a second husband.

Line
(5) At twenty-seven Alice was tall and somewhat slight. Her head was large and overshadowed her body. Her shoulders were a little stooped and her hair and eyes brown. She was very quiet but beneath a placid exterior a continual ferment went on.

When she was a girl of sixteen and before she began to work in the store, Alice had an affair with a young man. The young man, named Ned Currie, was older than Alice. He, like George Willard, was employed on the *Winesburg Eagle* and for a long time he went to see
(10) Alice almost every evening. Together the two walked under the trees through the streets of the town and talked of what they would do with their lives. Alice was then a very pretty girl and Ned Currie took her into his arms and kissed her. He became excited and said things he did not intend to say and Alice, betrayed by her desire to have something beautiful come into her rather narrow life, also grew excited. She also talked. The outer crust of her life, all
(15) of her natural diffidence and reserve, was torn away and she gave herself over to the emotions of love. When, late in the fall of her sixteenth year, Ned Currie went away to Cleveland where he hoped to get a place on a city newspaper and rise in the world, she wanted to go with him. With a trembling voice she told him what was in her mind. "I will work and you can work," she said. "I do not want to harness you to a needless expense that will prevent
(20) your making progress. Don't marry me now. We will get along without that and we can be together. Even though we live in the same house no one will say anything. In the city we will be unknown and people will pay no attention to us."

Ned Currie was puzzled by the determination and abandon of his sweetheart and was also deeply touched. He had wanted the girl to become his mistress but changed his mind.
(25) He wanted to protect and care for her. "You don't know what you're talking about," he said sharply; "you may be sure I'll let you do no such thing. As soon as I get a good job I'll come back. For the present you'll have to stay here. It's the only thing we can do."

On the evening before he left Winesburg to take up his new life in the city, Ned Currie went to call on Alice. They walked about through the streets for an hour and then got a rig
(30) from Wesley Moyer's livery and went for a drive in the country. The moon came up and they found themselves unable to talk. In his sadness the young man forgot the resolutions he had made regarding his conduct with the girl.

They got out of the buggy at a place where a long meadow ran down to the bank of Wine Creek and there in the dim light became lovers. When at midnight they returned to town
(35) they were both glad. It did not seem to them that anything that could happen in the future could blot out the wonder and beauty of the thing that had happened. "Now we will have to stick to each other, whatever happens we will have to do that," Ned Currie said as he left the girl at her father's door.

The young newspaper man did not succeed in getting a place on a Cleveland paper and
(40) went west to Chicago. For a time he was lonely and wrote to Alice almost every day. Then he was caught up by the life of the city; he began to make friends and found new interests in life. In Chicago he boarded at a house where there were several women. One of them

attracted his attention and he forgot Alice in Winesburg. At the end of a year he had stopped writing letters, and only once in a long time, when he was lonely or when he went into one

(45) of the city parks and saw the moon shining on the grass as it had shone that night on the meadow by Wine Creek, did he think of her at all.

1. The major thematic focus of the passage is on what characteristic of love?

   (A) Its impermanence
   (B) Its beauty
   (C) Its wholesomeness
   (D) Its potential for abuse

2. It is reasonable to infer that George Willard was approximately what age at the time that Alice initiated her affair with Ned Currie?

   (A) Unborn
   (B) Seven
   (C) Sixteen
   (D) Twenty-three

3. As an adult, the attitude that Alice has toward her past is best described as

   (A) fond.
   (B) forgetful.
   (C) unsettled.
   (D) sedate.

4. Which option gives the best evidence for the answer to the previous question?

   (A) Lines 4–5 ("At twenty-seven . . . brown")
   (B) Lines 5–6 ("She was . . . went on")
   (C) Lines 39–40 ("The young . . . every day")
   (D) Lines 43–46 ("At the end . . . her at all")

5. As used in line 24, "touched" most closely means

   (A) assaulted.
   (B) dashed.
   (C) matched.
   (D) moved.

6. Compared to Ned, Alice is much more

   (A) willing to make sacrifices for the benefit of their relationship.
   (B) determined to advance her professional status.
   (C) motivated by physical attractiveness.
   (D) interested in moving away from their provincial small-town life.

7. Which option gives the best evidence for the answer to the previous question?

   (A) Lines 7–8 ("When she . . . man")
   (B) Lines 14–16 ("She also . . . love")
   (C) Lines 23–24 ("Ned . . . touched")
   (D) Lines 28–29 ("On the . . . Alice")

8. As used in line 31, "resolutions" most closely means

   (A) promises.
   (B) purposes.
   (C) solutions.
   (D) entreaties.

9. The surrounding context around Ned's statement in lines 36–37, "Now we . . . do that," suggests that this quote was

   (A) an outright deception.
   (B) somewhat disingenuous.
   (C) given under duress.
   (D) motivated by true love.

Great Global Conversation

Great Global Conversation: Jefferson

Below are two letters sent by Thomas Jefferson of the United States of America, the first to Benjamin Franklin in 1777 and the second to George Washington in 1781.

Passage 1

Honorable Sir,

I forbear to write you news, as the time of Mr. Shore's departure being uncertain, it might be old before you receive it, and he can, in person, possess you of all we have. With respect to the State of Virginia in particular, the people seem to have laid aside the monarchical,
(5)   and taken up the republican government, with as much ease as would have attended their throwing off an old and putting on a new suit of clothes. Not a single throe has attended this important transformation. A half dozen aristocratical gentlemen, agonizing under the loss of pre-eminence, have sometimes ventured their sarcasms on our political metamorphosis. They have been thought fitter objects of pity than of punishment. We are at present in
(10)   the complete and quiet exercise of well organized government, save only that our courts of justice do not open till the fall. I think nothing can bring the security of our continent and its cause into danger, if we can support the credit of our paper. To do that, I apprehend one of two steps must be taken. Either to procure free trade by alliance with some naval power able to protect it; or, if we find there is no prospect of that, to shut our ports totally to all the
(15)   world, and turn our colonies into manufactories. The former would be most eligible, because most conformable to the habits and wishes of our people. Were the British Court to return to their senses in time to seize the little advantage which still remains within their reach from this quarter, I judge that, on acknowledging our absolute independence and sovereignty, a commercial treaty beneficial to them, and perhaps even a league of mutual offence and
(20)   defence, might, not seeing the expense or consequences of such a measure, be approved by our people, if nothing in the mean time, done on your part, should prevent it. But they will continue to grasp at their desperate sovereignty, till every benefit short of that is for ever out of their reach. I wish my domestic situation had rendered it possible for me to join you in the very honorable charge confided to you. Residence in a polite Court, society of literati of the
(25)   first order, a just cause and an approving God, will add length to a life for which all men pray, and none more than

Your most obedient
and humble servant,
Th: Jefferson.

Passage 2

(30)   Sir,

I have just received intelligence, which, though from a private hand, I believe is to be relied on, that a fleet of the enemy's ships have entered Cape Fear river, that eight of them had got over the bar, and many others were lying off; and that it was supposed to be a reinforcement to Lord Cornwallis, under the command of General Prevost. This account,
(35)   which had come through another channel, is confirmed by a letter from General Parsons at Halifax, to the gentleman who forwards it to me. I thought it of sufficient importance to be

communicated to your Excellency by the stationed expresses. The fatal want of arms puts it out of our power to bring a greater force into the field, than will barely suffice to restrain the adventures of the pitiful body of men they have at Portsmouth. Should any more be added *(40)* to them, this country will be perfectly open to them, by land as well as water.

I have the honor to be, with all possible respect,
Your Excellency's most obedient
and most humble servant,
Th: Jefferson.

1. In Passage 1, Jefferson describes the Virginia governmental transition as

    (A) peaceful and orderly.
    (B) challenging and violent.
    (C) vengeful and political.
    (D) easy and trivial.

2. In Passage 1, Jefferson suggests that the American people would be open to which of the following with the British?

    (A) Political dependence
    (B) Economic reconciliation
    (C) Religious integration
    (D) Intellectual exchange

3. Which option gives the best evidence for the answer to the previous question?

    (A) Lines 9–12 ("We are . . . our paper")
    (B) Lines 13–15 ("Either to . . . manufactories")
    (C) Lines 19–21 ("a commercial . . . prevent it")
    (D) Lines 23–26 ("I wish . . . more than")

4. As used in line 12, "apprehend" most closely means

    (A) believe.
    (B) capture.
    (C) cease.
    (D) invent.

5. Jefferson uses lines 15–16 ("The former . . . people") to imply most directly that

    (A) Americans would prefer to continue to be able to purchase manufactured goods from abroad.
    (B) Americans are eager to achieve economic independence by creating domestic factories.
    (C) Americans are unwilling to engage in an entangling alliance with another country that would require the United States to enter foreign conflicts.
    (D) Americans are weary of the revolutionary conflict and would like to see its swift end.

6. The implied meaning of Jefferson's message in Passage 2 is that at the time of the letter, the American defense against the invading British force was

   (A) incapable of resistance.
   (B) likely to collapse if there were British reinforcements.
   (C) likely to defeat the insignificant force at Portsmouth.
   (D) capable of meeting and defeating the British on an open battlefield.

7. As used in line 37, "want" most closely means

   (A) desire.
   (B) abundance.
   (C) lack.
   (D) danger.

8. Both Passage 1 and Passage 2 have a tone of

   (A) obedience and inferiority.
   (B) aggression and anxiety.
   (C) practicality and avarice.
   (D) formality and deference.

9. Which of Jefferson's statements from Passage 1 demonstrated the greatest foresight given the issues mentioned in Passage 2?

   (A) Lines 7–9 ("A half dozen . . . metamorphosis")
   (B) Lines 9–11 ("We are . . . the fall")
   (C) Lines 13–14 ("Either to . . . protect it")
   (D) Lines 23–24 ("I wish . . . to you")

10. The respective general themes of Passage 1 and Passage 2 are

   (A) militaristic and economic.
   (B) personal and reflective.
   (C) strategic and tactical.
   (D) pedestrian and urgent.

Great Global Conversation: Frederick Douglass

Below is the beginning of the autobiography Narrative of the Life of Frederick Douglass, *which was published in 1845 and became significant to the abolitionist movement.*

I was born in Tuckahoe, near Hillsborough, and about twelve miles from Easton, in Talbot County, Maryland. I have no accurate knowledge of my age, never having seen any authentic record containing it. By far the larger part of the slaves know as little of their ages as horses know of theirs, and it is the wish of most masters within my knowledge to keep *(5)* their slaves thus ignorant. I do not remember to have ever met a slave who could tell of his birthday. They seldom come nearer to it than planting-time, harvest-time, cherry-time, spring-time, or fall-time. A want of information concerning my own was a source of unhappiness to me even during childhood. The white children could tell their ages. I could not tell why I ought to be deprived of the same privilege. I was not allowed to make any inquiries *(10)* of my master concerning it. He deemed all such inquiries on the part of a slave improper and impertinent, and evidence of a restless spirit. The nearest estimate I can give makes me now between twenty-seven and twenty-eight years of age. I come to this, from hearing my master say, some time during 1835, I was about seventeen years old.

My mother was named Harriet Bailey. She was the daughter of Isaac and Betsey Bailey, *(15)* both colored, and quite dark. My mother was of a darker complexion than either my grandmother or grandfather.

My father was a white man. He was admitted to be such by all I ever heard speak of my parentage. The opinion was also whispered that my master was my father; but of the correctness of this opinion, I know nothing; the means of knowing was withheld from me. My *(20)* mother and I were separated when I was but an infant—before I knew her as my mother. It is a common custom, in the part of Maryland from which I ran away, to part children from their mothers at a very early age. Frequently, before the child has reached its twelfth month, its mother is taken from it, and hired out on some farm a considerable distance off, and the child is placed under the care of an old woman, too old for field labor. For what this separa- *(25)* tion is done, I do not know, unless it be to hinder the development of the child's affection toward its mother, and to blunt and destroy the natural affection of the mother for the child. This is the inevitable result.

I never saw my mother, to know her as such, more than four or five times in my life; and each of these times was very short in duration, and at night. She was hired by a Mr. Stewart, *(30)* who lived about twelve miles from my home. She made her journeys to see me in the night, travelling the whole distance on foot, after the performance of her day's work. She was a field hand, and a whipping is the penalty of not being in the field at sunrise, unless a slave has special permission from his or her master to the contrary—a permission which they seldom get, and one that gives to him that gives it the proud name of being a kind master. I *(35)* do not recollect of ever seeing my mother by the light of day. She was with me in the night. She would lie down with me, and get me to sleep, but long before I waked she was gone. Very little communication ever took place between us. Death soon ended what little we could have while she lived, and with it her hardships and suffering. She died when I was about seven years old, on one of my master's farms, near Lee's Mill. I was not allowed to be *(40)* present during her illness, at her death, or burial.

She was gone long before I knew any thing about it. Never having enjoyed, to any considerable extent, her soothing presence, her tender and watchful care, I received the tidings of her death with much the same emotions I should have probably felt at the death of a stranger.

1. The general point Douglass conveys in the first paragraph (lines 1–13) about knowing one's age is that

   (A) slaves managed to celebrate birthdays through careful estimations of their actual ages.
   (B) slaves were not granted basic personal identifying characteristics taken for granted by others.
   (C) there were some kind masters who overcame societal prejudice to see slaves as people, not property.
   (D) slaves did not know the fundamentals of arithmetic, having been denied math education by their masters.

2. As used in line 7, "want" most closely means

   (A) desire.
   (B) obstacle.
   (C) lack.
   (D) command.

3. Douglass expresses that his primary vehicle for learning about his origins was

   (A) his mother's private conversations.
   (B) the anecdotes of others.
   (C) documentary evidence.
   (D) spiritual revelation.

4. Which option gives the best evidence for the answer to the previous question?

   (A) Lines 10–11 ("He deemed . . . spirit")
   (B) Lines 17–18 ("My father . . . my father")
   (C) Lines 32–34 ("unless . . . master")
   (D) Lines 35–36 ("She was . . . gone")

5. It can reasonably be inferred from lines 24–26 that Frederick Douglass

   (A) was disappointed in his mother's lack of affection toward him.
   (B) was conditioned to feel little emotion toward his mother.
   (C) understands the true reason for the separation from his mother.
   (D) feels that the lack of his mother in his life hindered his intellectual development.

6. Douglass suggests that he met his father at what point in time?

   (A) As an infant
   (B) As a young child
   (C) As an adult
   (D) At no point

7. Douglass implies that his mother visited him only during the night because

   (A) she would face a harsh reprisal if she visited during the day.
   (B) she had other economic priorities besides child rearing.
   (C) she lived at an insurmountable distance from her son.
   (D) she had an unusual biological clock that made daytime activity a challenge.

8. Which option gives the best evidence for the answer to the previous question?

   (A) Lines 28–30 ("I never . . . home")
   (B) Lines 31–34 ("She was . . . master")
   (C) Lines 35–36 ("She was . . . gone")
   (D) Lines 37–38 ("Very little . . . suffering")

9. As used in line 42, "tidings" most closely means

   (A) news.
   (B) offerings.
   (C) remnants.
   (D) causes.

Great Global Conversation: Emerson and Arnold

The first passage is adapted from Ralph Waldo Emerson's essay "Nature," a foundational text of transcendentalism. Matthew Arnold, inspired by Emerson, wrote Literature and Science, *which is adapted for the second passage.*

Passage 1

Our age is retrospective. It builds the sepulchres of the fathers. It writes biographies, histories, and criticism. The foregoing generations beheld God and nature face to face; we, through their eyes. Why should not we also enjoy an original relation to the universe? Why should not we have a poetry and philosophy of insight and not of tradition, and a religion
(5)   by revelation to us, and not the history of theirs? Embosomed for a season in nature, whose floods of life stream around and through us, and invite us by the powers they supply, to action proportioned to nature, why should we grope among the dry bones of the past, or put the living generation into masquerade out of its faded wardrobe? The sun shines to-day also. There are new lands, new men, new thoughts. Let us demand our own works and laws
(10)   and worship.

Undoubtedly we have no questions to ask which are unanswerable. We must trust the perfection of the creation so far, as to believe that whatever curiosity the order of things has awakened in our minds, the order of things can satisfy. Every man's condition is a solution in hieroglyphic to those inquiries he would put. He acts it as life, before he apprehends it
(15)   as truth. In like manner, nature is already, in its forms and tendencies, describing its own design. Let us interrogate the great apparition, that shines so peacefully around us. Let us inquire, to what end is nature?

All science has one aim, namely, to find a theory of nature. We have theories of races and of functions, but scarcely yet a remote approach to an idea of creation. We are now so far
(20)   from the road to truth, that religious teachers dispute and hate each other, and speculative men are esteemed unsound and frivolous. But to a sound judgment, the most abstract truth is the most practical. Whenever a true theory appears, it will be its own evidence.

Passage 2

Practical people talk with a smile of Plato and of his absolute ideas; and it is impossible to deny that Plato's ideas do often seem unpractical and impracticable, and especially when
(25)   one views them in connexion with the life of a great work-a-day world like the United States. The necessary staple of the life of such a world Plato regards with disdain; handicraft and trade and the working professions he regards with disdain; but what becomes of the life of an industrial modern community if you take handicraft and trade and the working professions out of it? The base mechanic arts and handicrafts, says Plato, bring about a natural
(30)   weakness in the principle of excellence in a man, so that he cannot govern the ignoble growths in him, but nurses them, and cannot understand fostering any other. Those who exercise such arts and trades, as they have their bodies, he says, marred by their vulgar businesses, so they have their souls, too, bowed and broken by them.

Nor do the working professions fare any better than trade at the hands of Plato. He draws
(35)   for us an inimitable picture of the working lawyer, and of his life of bondage; he shows how this bondage from his youth up has stunted and warped him, and made him small and crooked of soul, encompassing him with difficulties which he is not man enough to rely on justice and truth as means to encounter, but has recourse, for help out of them, to falsehood and wrong. And so, says Plato, this poor creature is bent and broken, and grows up from boy

(40) to man without a particle of soundness in him, although exceedingly smart and clever in his own esteem.

One cannot refuse to admire the artist who draws these pictures. But we say to ourselves that his ideas show the influence of a primitive and obsolete order of things, when the warrior caste and the priestly caste were alone in honour, and the humble work of the world *(45)* was done by slaves. We have now changed all that; the modern majority consists in work, as Emerson declares; and in work, we may add, principally of such plain and dusty kind as the work of cultivators of the ground, handicraftsmen, men of trade and business, men of the working professions.

1. The fundamental question raised by the first paragraph of Passage 1 is

   (A) why is it that scientific inquiry is dismissed in favor of political dogma?
   (B) why are philosophers considered superior to more practical professionals?
   (C) why shouldn't archaeology take precedence over historical research?
   (D) why can't modern society directly have transcendental experiences?

2. As used in line 3, "original" most closely means

   (A) special.
   (B) creative.
   (C) inventive.
   (D) formal.

3. According to Passage 1, Emerson has what attitude toward the human capacity for understanding?

   (A) Optimism
   (B) Skepticism
   (C) Abstraction
   (D) Historicism

4. Which option gives the best evidence for the answer to the previous question?

   (A) Lines 3–5 ("Why should . . . theirs")
   (B) Lines 11–13 ("Undoubtedly . . . satisfy")
   (C) Lines 16–17 ("Let us . . . nature")
   (D) Line 18 ("All science . . . nature")

5. According to Passage 2, Matthew Arnold has what overall feelings about Plato's ideas?

   (A) That they are interesting yet overly practical
   (B) That they are comprehensive yet indecipherable
   (C) That they are admirable yet outdated
   (D) That they are melancholy yet applicable

6. Which option gives the best evidence for the answer to the previous question?

    (A) Lines 31–33 ("Those who . . . by them")

    (B) Lines 39–41 ("And so . . . his own esteem")

    (C) Lines 42–45 ("But we say . . . by slaves")

    (D) Lines 46–48 ("and in work . . . professions")

7. As used in line 40, "soundness" most closely means

    (A) safety.

    (B) strength.

    (C) intelligence.

    (D) eloquence.

8. In Passage 2, Arnold's description of Plato's philosophy toward work can be summarized as

    (A) true strength is evident only in those who put the needs of others before themselves.

    (B) those who cannot make themselves useful to society are little more than parasites.

    (C) the demands of one's profession will limit the loftiness of one's being.

    (D) true nobility of soul is more likely to be found among those who work by hand than in those who use machines.

9. According to Passage 1 and Passage 2, Emerson and Plato, respectively, place great value on what in their pursuits of wisdom?

    (A) Religious revelation and scientific inquiry

    (B) Practical observation and abstract ideas

    (C) Legal theory and mathematical reasoning

    (D) Professional experience and industrial engineering

10. Which statement from Passage 1 is it reasonable to infer that Plato would have found most offensive?

    (A) Line 3 ("Why should . . universe")

    (B) Line 9 ("There are . . . thoughts")

    (C) Line 16 ("Let us . . . around us")

    (D) Lines 20–21 ("speculative . . . frivolous")

Social Science

Social Science: Russian Depopulation

Russia, the geographically largest country in the world, is facing the biggest long-term problem any country can: depopulation. This problem is difficult to solve, however, as no one factor caused it. Rather, the roots of the issue lie in low life expectancy, low birth rates, and the gradual disintegration of the traditional Russian family.

Line
(5)   The beginning of the demographic problem is in Russia's low life expectancy. The life expectancy at birth for Russian males is only 64.7 years, and while the life expectancy for women is much longer, having the male half of the population die so early, before many men in the United States even retire, causes great concern.[1] This low male life expectancy has been attributed to both an increase in alcoholism and to the breakup of the Soviet

(10)   Union, which have led to high labor turnover and increased crime rates.[2] Compared to many less developed countries in the world, a life expectancy of 64.7 is fairly high. These less developed countries, however, are not experiencing the drastic drop in population with which Russia is currently struggling. This is due to the high birth rates that counteract the low life expectancy. Russia, unfortunately, has no such advantage.

(15)   Low birth rates are the most critical factor in the Russian population crisis. The average fertility rate for Russian women is at 1.61 children per women; this results in a population growth rate of –0.04 each year. Russian women have practically ceased having children altogether, putting extreme pressure on the population.

These demographic numbers show a society that desires family and children very
(20)   little. Generally, in richer countries, the birth rate drops as the quality of life increases. Yet in Russia, the high quality of life that would justify the present low rates does not exist. The low birth rates must then point to some societal lack of value of family and children. Interestingly, this contention is not supported by a survey conducted in 2007 that found that sixty-seven percent of Russian people thought that the love of the parents was the most
(25)   important aspect in raising any child, and around sixty percent of all age groups found family, home, and comfort to be "very important" in their lives.[3]

Despite Russian people espousing these values of family life, reality says something different. Studies of the artwork of children who draw family life, as well as the children's game of "house" show that the average Russian father is often absent in daily life.[4] Thus,
(30)   while Russians see parental love and care as being vital to the wellbeing of their children, in general, men in Russia do not act to give this love and care to their children. As rational humans, it can be concluded that the women of Russia, wanting their children to have good lives, are less likely to have kids since they know that it is very possible that their children will have absentee fathers. This may be a conscious or unconscious decision but it seems
(35)   to have been imprinted upon the people of Russia, giving the entire society an attitude whereby they value children but they don't have any themselves. With each generation that passes, this mindset grows, the men drift further, and the birth rate drops. This low birth rate is the main factor in the population decline in Russia.

[1]All demographic information sourced from the CIA World Factbook. https://www.cia.gov/library/publications/the-world-factbook/

[2]Julie DaVanzo and Clifford Grammich, *Dire Demographics: Population Trends in the Russian Federation* (Santa Monica: Rand, 2001), 40.

[3]E.I. Pakhomova, "Is It Reasonable to Speak of a Crisis of the Family?" *Russian Social Science Review* 48, no. 5(2007): 70, 79.

[4]Pakhomova, 70, 79.

All of these problems—the low life expectancy, low birth rate, and dissolution of the
(40) traditional family—are contributing to population declines in Russia. Vladimir Putin, in
his 2006 State of the Nation Address, showed that he fails to see the underlying causes of
the problem: the lack of family support and the deep societal lack of desire for children. He
focused on the economic problems instead, encouraging social programs to help pay for
children.[5] He understands there is a problem but doesn't know how to fix it, which lies in
(45) the mindset, not necessarily the pocketbooks, of the Russian people. Without a change in
mindset, the population of Russia is destined to grow ever smaller.

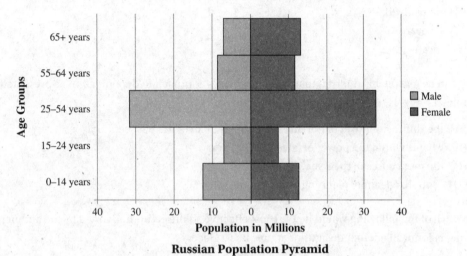

Russian Population Pyramid
Information Source: CIA World Factbook

1. It is most reasonable to infer that the author considers the problem of Russian depopulation
   to be

   (A) complex yet manageable.
   (B) dire yet common.
   (C) serious and multifaceted.
   (D) unfortunate and nebulous.

2. Which option gives the best evidence for the answer to the previous question?

   (A) Lines 1–3 ("Russia . . . caused it")
   (B) Lines 11–14 ("These . . . advantage")
   (C) Lines 19–21 ("These . . . exist")
   (D) Lines 36–38 ("With . . . Russia")

3. The author's primary purpose in lines 10–14 is to demonstrate how

   (A) statistical precision is difficult to come by in demographic research.
   (B) Russia's demographic problems are not unique.
   (C) Russia's economic development is worse than that of developing countries.
   (D) data taken in isolation could lead to a mistaken conclusion.

[5]Vladimir Putin, "State of the Nation Address 2006," *Population and Development Review* 32, no. 2 (2006), 386.

4. As used in line 11, "fairly" most closely means

   (A) justly.
   (B) relatively.
   (C) equally.
   (D) exclusively.

5. As used in line 34, "absentee" most closely means

   (A) dead.
   (B) uninvolved.
   (C) far away.
   (D) incarcerated.

6. It can be reasonably inferred that Vladimir Putin's approach to depopulation as presented in lines 42–44 ("He focused . . . children") focuses on

   (A) the shifting mindset in the Russian population over the past century.
   (B) what is within the power of government to do.
   (C) the root causes of the issue.
   (D) centralized family planning.

7. Which of the following would be the most effective solution (unmentioned by the author) to the major problem that the author argues Russia faces?

   (A) More precise statistical study of demographic trends
   (B) Changing the Russian attitude toward fatherhood
   (C) Allowing increased immigration to Russia
   (D) Convincing Russians of the value of childhood

8. If Russia were able to follow the advice of the author, how would a reformed population distribution chart compare to the figure provided in the passage?

   (A) It would have a greater percentage of youth.
   (B) It would have a greater percentage of elderly.
   (C) It would have a greater percentage of people in their 40s and 50s.
   (D) It would have relatively more males than females.

9. Based on the figure provided and the passage, how does the distribution of ages within the 65+ group of women most likely compare to the distribution of ages within the 65+ group of men?

   (A) More divergent
   (B) Less divergent
   (C) Nearly identical
   (D) Differing values for the youngest ages

10. Which option gives the best evidence for the answer to the previous question?

   (A) Lines 5–8 ("The beginning . . . concern")
   (B) Lines 8–11 ("This low . . . high")
   (C) Lines 15–18 ("Low birth . . . population")
   (D) Lines 22–26 ("The low . . . their lives")

Social Science: The Emu War

The best-laid plans often have unexpected consequences. Popular among chaos theorists, the butterfly effect refers to the interdependence of all events, and how even seemingly trivial changes in any of these can cause disproportional differences
Line in the non-linear space-time continuum. Chances are that following World War I,
(5) when British veterans were encouraged by the government to farm wheat in Western Australia, they had no idea they would be setting into motion another deadly conflict: The Great Emu War of 1932.

The end of World War I had many positive effects on the world: the end of world violence, the beginning of talks of worldwide peace organizations and treaties. However, there were
(10) also negative impacts. The end of the war also meant the end of many war-related jobs. Additionally, thousands of soldiers were returning home to economies already unable to provide enough employment opportunities to citizens. While different countries had different solutions to the problem, in Australia the government encouraged British veterans to take up farming. Subsidies were guaranteed but either failed to be provided, or weren't
(15) enough. As a result, by October 1932, wheat prices fell dangerously low.

Justifiably outraged, the farmers and government entered a time of rising tensions. Matters were made appreciably worse when over 20,000 emus entered the scene. Emus follow predictable migration patterns and when the farmers settled the land, the emus were residing in the coastal regions. In October, they started their migration toward the warmer,
(20) inland areas of Australia. Due to the extensive farming that had taken place, the land had been cleared—allowing easier migration—and there was a plentiful water supply from irrigation systems. In essence, the emus had found a perfect habitat. They destroyed much of the underpriced crop the farmers had painstakingly grown. This was the final straw for the farmers and they demanded the government provide them military aid.

(25) The government assigned the emu mission to Major G.P.W. Meredith along with two soldiers to assist him. Beginning in November, Major Meredith, the two soldiers, two Lewis guns, and 10,000 rounds of ammunition arrived to "take care of" the emu problem. Similar to a typical war involving humans on both sides, there were several "engagements" in this "war." A variety of borderline comical events took place from the soldiers underestimating
(30) the emus' military prowess (they broke into several guerilla like groups), to the Lewis guns jamming, to Major Meredith deciding to mount the guns on a military vehicle. In the end, the war was an overall failure and Major Meredith and his men returned home with only a fraction of the emu pelts they were supposed to have acquired.

The retreat of Major Meredith allowed the emus to return to the farmlands and once
(35) again ravage the crops. The farmers again called on the government for aid, and the Minister of Defense approved another military engagement with the emus. Despite his previous failure, Major Meredith was sent back to the field. Drawing on his previous experience, he was reportedly much more successful this time around.

Following the "war," word travelled and eventually reached Great Britain. Several news-
(40) papers had comical responses to the so-called "Great Emu War." While it undoubtedly had comedic threads, the emus did have a devastating effect on an already tenuous situation. A bounty system was reinstated to avoid government involvement and potential future embarrassment should they lose another "war" to these large, flightless birds. Despite this, the farmers called again for government aid in 1934, 1943, and 1948. However, the bounty
(45) system ended up being much more effective as locals were more well equipped and knowledgeable about hunting the emus than was the military.

Significant Events in Emu War

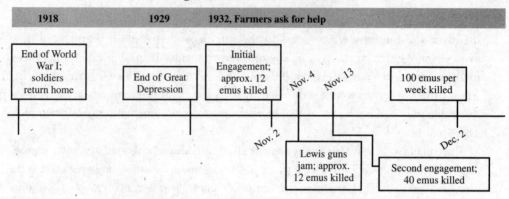

1. The author uses the introductory paragraph (lines 1–7) to

    (A) demonstrate how a military decision led to environmental catastrophe.
    (B) anticipate objections that the reader will have to the main argument.
    (C) provide a personal anecdote to draw the reader's attention.
    (D) place the topic of the passage in a greater context.

2. The author suggests that the military's initial mindset on their capacity to remove the emus was one of

    (A) overconfidence.
    (B) bravery.
    (C) humility.
    (D) fanaticism.

3. Which option gives the best evidence for the answer to the previous question?

    (A) Lines 4–7 ("Chances . . . 1932")
    (B) Lines 22–24 ("They . . . military aid")
    (C) Lines 29–30 ("A variety . . . groups")
    (D) Lines 34–36 ("The retreat . . . emus")

4. As used in line 14, the phrase "take up" most closely means

    (A) seize.
    (B) engage in.
    (C) study for.
    (D) invent.

5. Out of the following choices, which does the narrator suggest was of the greatest importance for people to fight the emus effectively?

    (A) Military training from elite academies
    (B) First-hand experience with the emus
    (C) A scholarly understanding of emu anatomy
    (D) A sophisticated relationship with the media

6. Which option gives the best evidence for the answer to the previous question?

    (A) Lines 23–24 ("This was . . . aid")
    (B) Lines 39–40 ("Following . . . War")
    (C) Lines 42–43 ("A bounty . . . birds")
    (D) Lines 44–46 ("However . . . military")

7. What is the author's primary purpose in using quotation marks in the sentence in lines 27–29 ("Similar . . . 'war' ")?

    (A) To quote primary source information
    (B) To highlight the global importance of this event
    (C) To underscore the irony of these labels
    (D) To dispute the veracity of certain claims

8. As used in line 41, "tenuous" most closely means

    (A) precarious.
    (B) fatalistic.
    (C) biological.
    (D) cosmopolitan.

9. The figure is most useful in elaborating on which of the following selections from the passage?

    (A) Lines 25–26 ("The government . . . him")
    (B) Lines 26–27 ("Beginning . . . problem")
    (C) Lines 27–29 ("Similar . . . 'war' ")
    (D) Lines 29–31 ("A variety . . . vehicle")

10. Based on the figure, the military's effectiveness in fighting the emus can best be described as

    (A) gradually increasing over time.
    (B) steadily decreasing over time.
    (C) relatively constant over time.
    (D) generally inconsistent.

Science

Science: Caffeine

Passage 1

All told, there exist just over sixty species of plant known to produce caffeine, among the mostly widely cultivated of which are coffee from the berries of the *Coffea arabica* plant, tea from the leaves of *Camellia sinesis,* and chocolate from the seeds of the *Theobroma cacao* tree. Caffeine, curiously enough, is in its structure quite closely related to adenine and gua-
(5) nine, the two purine nitrogenous bases that comprise about half of our DNA. Moreover, it is precisely this structural similarity between caffeine and nucleic acids that gives coffee, tea, and chocolate their uniquely stimulating properties. While amphetamine, ephedrine, nicotine, cocaine, and the vast majority of other common psychoactive stimulants work to modulate the dopaminergic circuits of the central nervous system, the stimulation we feel
(10) from ingesting caffeine arises from a completely distinct neural pathway.

Within every metabolically active cell of the human body, a molecule called adeno-sine triphosphate acts as a major reservoir of transferrable chemical energy. That is, in the thermodynamically favorable liberation of phosphate groups from adenosine, free energy is released that can be harnessed to drive forward a variety of the thermodynamically unfa-
(15) vorable chemical reactions required to sustain life. For our purposes, the main implications of this system are fairly intuitive: cells with significant energy reserves will be those with a large amount of adenosine triphosphate at their disposal, while those that have exhausted their reserves will contain merely adenosine, and inorganic phosphate.

Throughout our evolution, the neurons that make up our brain and spinal cord have
(20) adapted to detect the presence of adenosine, and to react to it by increasing the secre-tion of melatonin from the pineal gland, which in turn mediates feelings of "drowsiness" or somnolence. The purpose, one might reason, is simply to promote sleep; a state that is minimally taxing to the metabolism of the central nervous system, and will allow its cells an opportunity to replenish their energy stores.

(25) Adenosine itself is made up merely of an adenine nitrogenous base attached via a beta-glycosidic bond to a pentose sugar. Thus, it is simply the approximate structural correspondence between caffeine and adenosine that enables caffeine to interact with and antagonize adenosine-sensing receptors without chemically activating them. The end result is a general blunting of the brain's ability to perceive how much energy it has
(30) expended; though the effect, it should be mentioned, is self-limited. As the concentration of adenosine increases to critical levels, adenosine displaces caffeine from its inhibitory position on the receptor in a phenomenon known colloquially to some consumers of coffee and cola beverages as "the crash."

Passage 2

Caffeine, admittedly, seldom kills. A toxic dose to an adult is roughly equivalent to the
(35) amount contained in somewhere between eighty and one-hundred mid-sized cups of cof-fee. This is not to say, however, that caffeine is completely innocuous. By some estimates, more than 90% of the American adult population uses caffeine on a daily basis, and it is far and away the most widely consumed psychostimulant worldwide. It is somewhat shock-ing, therefore, that its distribution remains wholly unregulated by the Food and Drug
(40) Administration.

While the recreational use of caffeine is infrequently fatal, abuse of caffeinated supplements, medications, and beverages can precipitate a wide range of detrimental effects on the body, particularly among individuals with underlying vulnerabilities. For instance, in those already at risk for osteoporosis—such as post-menopausal women, and those suf-
(45) fering from hyperparathyroidism—caffeine has been shown to significantly accelerate the rate of bone loss, chiefly by increasing basal metabolic rate. Similarly, multiple studies have demonstrated a positive correlation between the agitating, stimulant-effects of caffeine use on the limbic system and acute exacerbations of panic disorder and anxiety disorders. Caffeine increases blood pressure. It promotes electrical dysrhythmias of the
(50) heart. It is anything but harmless, and yet contrary to popular belief, the most commonly heard health complaint concerning caffeine is something of a fallacy. That is to say, while chemical dependence, tolerance, and withdrawal from the stimulant are familiar entities to those who consume large quantities, genuine pathological addiction to caffeine has not been documented in humans, and as such is omitted from both the DSM-5, and the ICD-10
(55) as well.

1. The respective purposes of Passage 1 and Passage 2 are best described as

(A) analytical and narrative.
(B) persuasive and descriptive.
(C) expository and argumentative.
(D) medical and economic.

2. Which of these gives the correct sequence of processes as described in the paragraphs in lines 11–24?

(A) Adenosine triphosphate is formed in the pineal gland from the reaction between natural melatonin and artificial adenosine.
(B) Adenosine and adenosine triphosphate stimulate the production of melatonin in the pineal gland.
(C) Adenosine and melatonin from the pineal gland cause energy to be released in the creation of adenosine triphosphate.
(D) Melatonin is released from the pineal gland as a result of detection of adenosine, which comes from the breakdown of adenosine triphosphate.

3. As used in line 13, the phrase "thermodynamically favorable" most closely refers to a reaction in which

(A) the reactants are exclusively biological.
(B) a subject consciously chooses to undergo the process because of its positive effects.
(C) the reactants have more energy than the products.
(D) the products have more energy than the reactants.

4. The process whereby caffeine works, according to Passage 1, is best paraphrased as

(A) caffeine tricks the body into thinking it has not used as much energy as it in fact has.
(B) caffeine causes the release of adenosine, stimulating the central nervous system.
(C) caffeine strongly hinders the body's ability to produce adenosine, resulting in greater alertness.
(D) caffeine helps the body generate more adenosine triphosphate storage, creating greater stores of energy.

5. Which option gives the best evidence for the answer to the previous question?

    (A) Lines 11–15 ("Within . . . life")

    (B) Lines 22–24 ("The purpose . . . stores")

    (C) Lines 26–30 ("Thus . . . self-limited")

    (D) Lines 30–33 ("As the . . . 'the crash' ")

6. As used in line 36, "innocuous" most closely means

    (A) harmless.

    (B) stimulating.

    (C) legal.

    (D) popular.

7. Which of the following does the author of Passage 2 suggest is a way that caffeine does NOT present a danger to humans?

    (A) Through exacerbation of panic disorders

    (B) Through pathological addiction

    (C) Through increasing blood pressure

    (D) By accelerating bone loss among at-risk populations

8. Which option gives the best evidence for the answer to the previous question?

    (A) Lines 43–46 ("For instance . . . rate")

    (B) Lines 46–49 ("Similarly . . . disorders")

    (C) Lines 49–50 ("Caffeine . . . heart")

    (D) Lines 51–55 ("That is . . . well")

9. When taken together, these two passages present a solid overview of caffeinated stimulation's

    (A) origins and history.

    (B) benefits and pitfalls.

    (C) causes and effects.

    (D) evolution and devolution.

Science: Fungi

With good reason, biologists have frequently described fungi as the "forgotten kingdom." Despite demonstrating a diversity and evolutionary resilience to rival plants and animals alike, for many of us, our day-to-day familiarity with fungi reaches little further than to a handful of domesticated mushrooms, and perhaps the *Penicillium* molds that imbue blue
Line
(5)   cheese with their distinctive color and smell. In reality, fungi are all around us, and contribute biochemically to a remarkable variety of both natural and artificial processes: from the vital decomposition of organic matter commonly described as "rotting" to the yeast-mediated fermentation of polysaccharides into ethanol and gaseous carbon dioxide which allows a baker's bread to rise. Even so, perhaps due to their obscure, soil-dwelling lifestyles,
(10) the manifold functions that fungi execute in our lives are more often than not inconspicuous, and all too easily overlooked.

The health sciences especially are rife with novel applications for mycology (that is, the branch of biology emphasizing fungi). Famously, the first commercially available antibiotics capable of curing streptococcal and staphylococcal infections were discovered quite by
(15) accident when Scottish scientist Alexander Fleming noticed how the growth of a staphylococcus culture had been drastically inhibited following its contamination with a *Penicillium chrysogenum* mold. Notably, the unique mechanism by which this inhibitory effect is accomplished has since led to the development of not one but three distinct classes of antimicrobial medications—penicillins, cephalosporins, and beta-lactamase inhibitors—and
(20) accelerated a set of fascinating genetic mutations which confer antibiotic resistance among strains of bacteria.

In penicillins and cephalosporins, the so-called "beta-lactam ring" is known to be the principle structure responsible for their antimicrobial properties. This ring binds avidly to specialized cross-linking proteins found within the peptidoglycan layer of bacterial cell
(25) walls, subsequently blocking a bacterium's attempts at reproduction, as well as the replication of its intracellular organelles. As it is not found naturally within the cells of animals, plants, or fungi, peptidoglycan polymers are highly peculiar to bacteria, and antimicrobial agents targeting peptidoglycan possess a very low potential for toxic cross-reactivity with other types of cells.
(30) Even into the 21st century, beta-lactam compounds still comprise more than half of all antibiotics prescribed worldwide, and it is widely believed that their pervasive usage has helped to promote the novel synthesis of beta-lactamases among a wide array of common pathogenic bacterial species. To clarify, beta-lactamases are a class of enzymes capable of hydrolyzing the beta-lactam ring, and are often secreted in the presence of antibiotics.
(35) While these enzymes are nigh ubiquitous among bacteria today, prior to the commercial availability of penicillin, their endogenous synthesis was limited to a fairly small number of gram-negative organisms. The startling rapidity with which bacteria have developed resistance against beta-lactams may have far reaching implications for the health of human populations in the future.
(40) Although penicillin is perhaps the most memorable example, it is hardly the only contribution fungi have made to improving human health. In recent years, a number of medicinally significant fungal isolates have emerged to treat not just infection, but metabolic, immunologic, and neoplastic diseases as well. Of particular note, 3-hydroxy-3-methylglutaryl-CoA reductase inhibitors—more commonly called "statins"—are considered the
(45) first-line pharmacological therapy for hypercholesterolemia, and are the only cholesterol-lowering class of medications that have been proven in peer-reviewed longitudinal studies

to lower an individual's risk of major cardiovascular disease. Mechanistically, rather than blocking the absorption of dietary cholesterol or enhancing its excretion, statins work to reduce the *de novo* biosynthesis of cholesterol molecules in the body by inhibiting the rate-

(50) limiting enzyme in its anabolic pathway.

It would not be overstating the matter to say that statins have transformed the treatment of both acquired and congenital cholesterol-related diseases. But what's more, the first generation of statins was discovered, oddly enough, by Japanese scientist Akira Endo during his research into the antimicrobial properties of the mold *Penicillium citrinum*. Not unlike

(55) Alexander Fleming one-half century earlier, Endo serendipitously discovered yet another compound from this curious genus of fungi destined to do no less than revolutionize the medical maintenance of human health. One must wonder, therefore, what more we stand to learn from fungi, and what still-greater mysteries they may yet be concealing in the soil.

1. As described in the passage, the gradual process of changes in bacterial resistance to antibiotics is most similar to which of the following situations?

   (A) An artificial intelligence program analyzes multiple instances of computer viruses, increasing its antiviral effectiveness as it gathers more applicable data.
   (B) A television show is extremely popular in its first season but becomes less popular as its novelty wears off.
   (C) A school initiates antiplagiarism software that is highly useful in stopping cheating at the outset but becomes less useful as more students catch on.
   (D) A car's tires become worn thin after thousands of miles of wear and tear.

2. The author primarily uses the introductory paragraph, lines 1–11, to

   (A) demonstrate the applications of fungi in cooking.
   (B) refute widespread misinformation about fungi.
   (C) establish the relevance of the essay's topic.
   (D) point out the easy visibility of fungal influence.

3. As used in line 10, "execute" most closely means

   (A) destroy.
   (B) camouflage.
   (C) entice.
   (D) perform.

4. The author suggests that some of the most important fungi-related medical innovations came about primarily as a result of

   (A) luck.
   (B) evolution.
   (C) economic investment.
   (D) genetic engineering.

5. Which option gives the best evidence for the answer to the previous question?

   (A) Lines 17–21 ("Notably . . . bacteria")
   (B) Lines 30–33 ("Even into . . . species")
   (C) Lines 43–47 ("Of particular . . . disease")
   (D) Lines 54–57 ("Not unlike . . . health")

6. As used in line 27, "peculiar" most closely means

   (A) strange.
   (B) unique.
   (C) diseased.
   (D) helpful.

7. The author implies that a property of antibiotics that makes them particularly helpful to diseased animals is that they

   (A) are not widely recognized and can therefore be inconspicuous.
   (B) cause the diseased tissue to mutate into healthy tissue.
   (C) help the organism develop long-term immunity against infection.
   (D) attack the bacteria without attacking the host organism.

8. Which option gives the best evidence for the answer to the previous question?

   (A) Lines 9–11 ("Even so . . . overlooked")
   (B) Lines 17–21 ("Notably . . . bacteria")
   (C) Lines 26–29 ("As it is . . . cells")
   (D) Lines 37–39 ("The startling . . . future")

9. The author most likely uses the final sentence of the passage (lines 57–58, "One must . . . soil") to suggest

   (A) that geological exploration deserves funding.
   (B) that further study of fungi is warranted.
   (C) skepticism about the prospects for scientific research.
   (D) a more balanced approach to the analysis of fungi.

Science: Methanogenesis

Methanosphaera stadtmanae, the first single-celled (archaeal) commensal (i.e., two organisms have a relationship wherein one benefits, and the other has no harm nor benefit) organism to have its genome sequenced, is an anaerobic, non-moving, sphere-shaped organism that inhabits the human gastrointestinal tract. Of all methanogenic (methane-
(5) producing) Archaea, *Methanosphaera stadtmanae* has been found to have the most restrictive energy metabolism as it can generate methane only by reduction of methanol with H_2 and is dependent on acetate as a carbon source. These unique energy conservation traits are what make *Methanosphaera stadtmanae* beneficial to its human host and not an opportunistic pathogen.

(10) *Methanosphaera stadtmanae*'s genome lacks 37 protein-coding sequences present in the genomes of all other methanogens. Among these are the protein coding sequences for synthesis of molybdopterin, which is required for the enzyme catalyzing the first step of methanogenesis from CO_2 and H_2, as well as for the synthesis of the CO dehydrogenase/acetyl-coenzyme A synthase complex. This explains why *Methanosphaera stadtmanae* can-
(15) not reduce CO_2 to methane nor oxidize methanol to CO_2. While this is the typical path of methanogenesis for many archaeal methanogens, it is not the path for *Methanosphaera stadtmanae*.

Methanogenic Archaea are naturally occurring components of the human gut microbiota. The two original methanogenic species belonging to the order Methanobacteriales,
(20) *Methanobrevibacter smithii* and *Methanosphaera stadtmanae,* were identified over 30 years ago by the detection of methane in the breath, and eventually isolated from fecal samples. *Methanosphaera stadtmanae*, one of the major archaeal inhabitants of the gut, is able to thrive in the human digestive system because methanol is a product of pectin degradation in the intestine by *Bacterioides* species and other anaerobic bacteria. *Methanosphaera*
(25) *stadtmanae* reduces methanol produced by the anaerobic bacteria with H_2 present to produce methane. Production of methane in this manner is beneficial to the human host because of energy conservation. Methanogens, like *Methanosphaera stadtmanae*, also play an important role in digestion by improving efficiency of polysaccharide fermentation by helping to prevent accumulation of acids, reaction end products, and gaseous hydrogen. It
(30) is thought that *Methanosphaera stadtmanae*'s energy conserving methanogenesis process is one of the ways it helps in maintaining homeostasis (biological equilibrium) within the human gut microbiota.

Homeostasis of the human gut microbiota is a delicate balance, and if disrupted can cause serious issues for humans. One of these issues is the growing number of cases of IBD
(35) (Inflammatory Bowel Disease). IBD is a term used in the medical field to describe conditions of the gastrointestinal tract that have chronic or recurring immune responses and inflammation. *Methanosphaera stadtmanae*'s commensal role with the human can be disrupted when other bacteria in the highly immunologically active intestinal tract stop performing their normal processes. While the details of all of the processes that bacteria per-
(40) form are not completely known, it is understood that *Methanosphaera stadtmanae* reacts to the adverse effects by inducing the release of proinflammatory cytokine TNF in peripheral blood cells. By releasing this, *Methanosphaera stadtmanae* produces a four-times stronger response than any other methanogen of the gut microbiota. This response causes increased inflammation in the gastrointestinal tract, and can only stop when balance within the gut
(45) microbiota is restored.

One method physicians have found to help restore the homeostasis of the gut microbiota is the administration of archaebiotics. Archaebiotics colonize in the gastrointestinal tract to help restore balance by eliminating and controlling bacteria or archaea that disrupted the balance in the first place. Archaebiotics also help by keeping commensal methanogens, like

(50) *Methanosphaera stadtmanae,* so that they can continue to perform their necessary role of methanogenesis. It is imperative to maintain methanogenesis so that proper digestion and energy conservation can happen for the human.

Understanding the role *Methanosphaera stadtmanae* plays in the human gastrointestinal tract has been extremely important in the advancement of understanding IBD, as well as

(55) the development of treatments. Identification of additional archaeal and bacterial species will continue to help develop the field so that scientists and physicians can better understand how different organisms work with each other or against each other.

Pathway	Complete/Incomplete/ Absent	Intermediates
Glycolysis (Embden-Meyerhof)	Incomplete	Missing glucose and D-glucose 6-phosphate
Entner-Doudoroff (Semi-phosphorylative Form)	Both Absent	Missing all intermediates
Pentose Phosphate	Incomplete	Missing all intermediates except D-ribulose-5-phosphate and D-ribose-5-phosphate
Pyruvate Oxidation	Complete	All intermediates present
Citrate Cycle (Glyoxylate Cycle)	Both Incomplete	Missing citrate and isocitrate as intermediates. Pyruvate feeds into the Citrate Cycle via oxaloacetate. Glyoxylate Cycle only contains oxaloacetate and malate.
Reductive Citrate Cycle	Incomplete	Missing all intermediates except oxaloacetate and malate
Calvin Cycle	Incomplete	Missing Erythrose-4P, Sedoheptulose 1,7P, Sedoheptulose 7P, and Ribulose 1,5P
Methanogenesis	Complete	All intermediates present (can only use methanol and H_2 to produce methane)
Reductive Acetyl-CoA	Incomplete	Missing all intermediates except 5,10-Methylene-THF and THF (come in from a different pathway)

Figure 1. The above chart lists the known mechanisms that bacterial and archaeal organisms use for energy purposes. The chart lists if *M. stadtmanae* has the necessary intermediates present in the human digestive system to have a functional energy pathway given a particular mechanism.

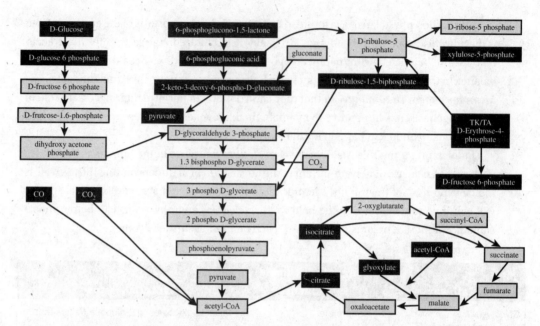

Figure 2. The intermediates in the black boxes are ones that *M. stadtmanae* cannot use or does not have. The intermediates in the gray boxes are ones that *M. stadtmanae* does use or has.

1. It is most reasonable to infer that the author of the passage believes that scientific understanding of how archaeal and bacterial species interact with the human digestive system is

   (A) largely settled.
   (B) making progress.
   (C) generally mystified.
   (D) static.

2. According to the third paragraph (lines 18–32), the presence of methanogenic species in the human digestive system was first detected from

   (A) observation of a product of a chemical reaction.
   (B) isolation from human bowel movements.
   (C) the decoding of the DNA of methanogens.
   (D) the discovery of its essential role in human homeostasis.

3. As used in line 25, "reduces" most closely means

   (A) subtracts.
   (B) diminishes.
   (C) transforms.
   (D) persecutes.

4. What is the primary purpose of lines 40–42 ("it is . . . cells")?

   (A) To address an objection
   (B) To provide speculation
   (C) To explain a process
   (D) To cite an authority

5. As used in line 41, "inducing" most closely means

    (A) causing.
    (B) suggesting.
    (C) releasing.
    (D) persuading.

6. According to the passage as a whole, the overall role of *Methanosphaera stadtmanae* with respect to human health is

    (A) uniformly positive.
    (B) primarily beneficial.
    (C) somewhat harmful.
    (D) mostly parasitic.

7. The processing or lack thereof of which chemical intermediate shown in Figure 2 does the author argue is particularly distinctive for *Methanosphaera stadtmanae* relative to other methanogens?

    (A) H_2
    (B) Oxaloacetate
    (C) CO_2
    (D) Succinate

8. Which option gives the best evidence for the answer to the previous question?

    (A) Lines 10–11 ("*Methanosphaera* . . . methanogens")
    (B) Lines 14–17 ("This explains . . . *stadtmanae*")
    (C) Lines 22–24 ("*Methanosphaera* . . . bacteria")
    (D) Lines 27–29 ("Methanogens . . . hydrogen")

9. How does the information in Figures 1 and 2 help make the author's case that *Methanosphaera stadtmanae* is helpful to humans, relative to many other similar bacteria and archaeal organisms?

    (A) The figures show that pentose phosphate does not have the needed intermediates to carry out the development of methanol.
    (B) The figures demonstrate that *M. stadtmanae* is genetically similar to the more common *Methanobrevibacter smithii*.
    (C) The figures detail the chemical process whereby inflammatory bowel disease can be avoided.
    (D) The figures show that *M. stadtmanae* lacks the necessary intermediates for most of the common energy pathways.

10. Which option gives the best evidence for the answer to the previous question?

    (A) Lines 4–9 ("Of all . . . pathogen")
    (B) Lines 19–21 ("The two . . . samples")
    (C) Lines 33–39 ("Homeostasis . . . processes")
    (D) Lines 46–51 ("One method . . . methanogenesis")

Science: Wound Healing

An Occupational Therapist Describes the Process of Wound Healing

Even when a laceration as small as a paper cut happens to a person, complex reactions begin within the body almost instantaneously. Were these processes to be disrupted for any number of reasons, even the most insignificant of scrapes could prove fatal for the victim.

Line
(5) Thus, it is of the utmost importance to know the typical progression for how a wound heals so that the afflicted can seek medical attention should the wound prove aggravated.

Immediately after the initial laceration transpires, the body responds and initiates action. Known as the "inflammatory phase" of wound healing, this is when the body first begins to repair the damage it encountered. In order to prevent excessive blood loss, the first step is vasoconstriction in which the blood vessels near the affected area are constricted. Nearly

(10) concurrently, phagocytosis begins as white blood cells are sent to the wound. Phagocytes are cells that consume the debris in the wound, which aids in the cleansing of damaged tissue as well as foreign matter.

Phagocytosis is completed quite quickly—a mere 30 minutes for culmination and inception of the next stage. Following the cleaning, mast cells arrive and release histamine which

(15) causes vasodilation; this opening of the blood vessels vastly increases the flow of fluid into the affected area and results in the inflammation for which this stage is named. This inflammation decreases the available capacity of the area and leads to increased amounts of pain and discoloration in and around the wound site. From vasoconstriction to dilation, the inflammatory phase may last between two days and two weeks (depending on the severity

(20) of the wound).

Following this somewhat preparatory stage, the proliferative phase marks the beginning of the actual healing process. Within this second stage, there are four mini steps that are crucial for the wound to close properly. Granulation is the first of these four steps. It is indicated by the body beginning to lay down different connective tissues like collagen; these

(25) tissues help fill the empty space or hole created by the affliction. The body, however, is not only constructed of connective tissue. Angiogenesis, the second of the four steps, is when the body embarks on the arduous process of growing new blood vessels. Intertwining networks of vessels are laid down, oft called capillary beds. These growing, weaving vessels give a new wound its distinctive pink coloration. The third stage, wound contraction, is the first

(30) stage in which the raw edges of the wound begin to adjoin to each other. The wound does not experience complete closure until the final stage of the four stages of proliferation—epithelization. Epithelial cells—or skin cells—move over the granulated tissue from the first step. The four stages of the proliferative phase can last anywhere from 3–21 days. The timeline is, once again, dependent on how poignant the wound is.

(35) It is critical to be protective of a newly healed wound at the beginning of the third stage: maturation. The new skin is quite fragile and can easily reopen if too much stress is placed on it. The maturation stage can last up to two years as the scar forms and hardens. In some cases the scar will disappear with time, but in others it's a permanent addendum to a person's body. Even once the scar has fully matured, scar tissue is only 80% as strong as skin,

(40) meaning it is prone to re-injury.

Several factors can influence the quality and timeliness of wound healing, many of which—circulation, chemical stress, temperature of the wound bed, amount of moisture in and around the wound, and age—are outside the control of the individual. The individual

can control other factors, like nutrition, medication, and infection. Maintaining a well-
(45) balanced diet, consulting a doctor about medications, and keeping the wound site clean
can all have a positive effect on wound closure and healing.

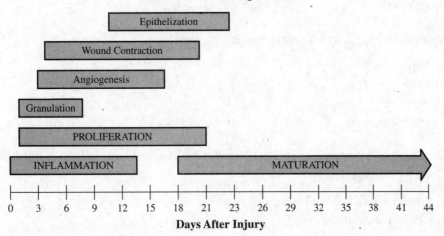

The Wound Healing Process

Days After Injury

1. What is the overall structure of the passage?

    (A) Chronological
    (B) Pro and con
    (C) Spatial
    (D) Persuasive

2. What is the primary purpose of the passage?

    (A) To highlight medical abnormalities
    (B) To argue in favor of a theory
    (C) To detail helpful information
    (D) To confront conventional wisdom

3. Which option gives the best evidence for the answer to the previous question?

    (A) Lines 1–2 ("Even . . . instantaneously")
    (B) Lines 4–5 ("Thus . . . aggravated")
    (C) Lines 41–43 ("many . . . individual")
    (D) Lines 44–46 ("Maintaining . . . healing")

4. What is the primary function of the sentence in lines 10–12 ("Phagocytes . . . matter")?

    (A) To clarify a specialized term
    (B) To explain the derivation of a word
    (C) To highlight an irony
    (D) To offer a solution to a health care predicament

5. As used in line 30, "raw" most closely means

   (A) unprocessed.
   (B) primal.
   (C) uncooked.
   (D) inflamed.

6. As used in line 35, "critical" most closely means

   (A) important.
   (B) harsh.
   (C) negative.
   (D) analytical.

7. The passage and the figure, respectively, portray the steps of wound healing in which of the following different ways?

   (A) Concurrent and chronological
   (B) Gradual and sudden
   (C) Sequential and simultaneous
   (D) Internal and external

8. If the author wished to extend the x-axis of the figure to portray the point at which a wound would nearly certainly be healed without extending the graph unnecessarily, which of the following would serve as the most logical final value for days?

   (A) 10
   (B) 100
   (C) 1,000
   (D) 10,000

9. Which option gives the best evidence for the answer to the previous question?

   (A) Lines 13–15 ("Phagocytosis . . . vasodilation")
   (B) Lines 21–23 ("Following . . . steps")
   (C) Lines 32–34 ("Epithelial . . . wound is")
   (D) Lines 36–37 ("The new . . . hardens")

Answer Explanations

Fiction: *Almayer's Folly*

1. **(A)** The passage begins with an "unpleasant voice" interrupting Almayer's dreams of a "splendid future." This pattern is characteristic of the passage as a whole. Almayer imagines a life of wealth but is constantly reminded of his dull, wretched reality, making choice (A) correct. Choices (B) and (C) are not evidenced by the passage; actually, Almayer demonstrates both cultural proficiency and assertiveness. Choice (D) wrongfully assumes that Almayer wishes to be grounded in the rational when actually he prefers his wishful fantasies.

2. **(C)** Almayer justifies his failure to secure gold by asserting that those successful few have secured it dishonestly. He, instead, hopes to gain wealth and power "through his own honest exertions." Therefore, his contrast is one of virtue and morality. Choice (A) is not evidenced, although he might, too, believe this. Choices (B) and (D) are not only without evidence but also contrary to Almayer's character.

3. **(B)** Lines 8–11 tell us that Almayer contrasts himself to the dishonest procurers of gold, providing evidence for the previous question. Choice (A) provides detail of Almayer's response to the call but does not talk about financial circumstances. Choice (C) creates images of Almayer's fantasy of wealth and power but does not address his opinion toward those more financially successful. Choice (D) reports Almayer's thoughts about Dain and his belated return but, again, doesn't address the previous question.

4. **(A)** Here, Almayer reassures himself that his fantasies are within reach if only Dain returns. Likewise, Dain must return for "his own share." Since Dain is obviously connected to Almayer's desire for wealth, we can substitute "share" with "part of the money," making choice (A) the correct option. It is nonsensical to think that Dain must return for his own "communication" or "disclosure." Although choice (C) may be tempting, we cannot assume that Almayer is gifting something to Dain but, instead, that Dain has a stake in the gold per previous agreement.

5. **(C)** Throughout the passage, we can see that Almayer still wishes for wealth but is constantly in despair because of his grim, impoverished circumstances. In comparison to the hopeful Almayer who "left his home with a light heart . . . ready to conquer the world," we can infer that he is now more hopeless than earlier in life when he never doubted his success. Now, he hopes for wealth but certainly has doubts and dark thoughts, making choices (A) and (B) incorrect. We have no evidence for choice (D), particularly because Almayer still considers himself to be very honest.

6. **(D)** Lines 47–48 reference the beginning of Almayer's journey when he embarked optimistically and "ready to conquer the world." This is in stark contrast to his current internal turmoil that reveals his feelings of hopelessness and disempowerment. Choice (A) actually refers to how he imagines he will feel when he obtains wealth. Choice (B) might be tempting because it is close to the lines referenced in the above question and deals with Almayer's interest in the tree; however, it reveals nothing about his attitude earlier in life. Choice (C) does, in fact, deal with Almayer's early life but with the attitude of his mother rather than of himself.

7. **(B)** To approach this question, ask yourself what we know about Dain. We know that Almayer impatiently awaits Dain's return because his arrival is somehow tied to a prosperous future—a future "nearly within his reach." Therefore, we can reasonably conclude that Dain is somehow aiding Almayer in his financial goals. Although choices (A), (C), and (D) could all be true, they are not evidenced and so could equally be false.

8. **(B)** Here, the powerless and formerly stuck tree is now "free" to drift into the sea. So we could substitute *unimpeded* or *no longer restrained*, which makes choice (B) correct. Choice (A) conveys the idea that the tree has a feeling or an attitude of its own. Choice (C) is tempting but again evokes the idea that the tree has gained power rather than merely escaped to freedom. Choice (D) refers to free as a financial concept, as in *without cost*, which does not fit here.

9. **(D)** Look for evidence about what Almayer's parents believed. His father, a "subordinate," is delighted at his son's prospects for a better future. His mother is nostalgic for Amsterdam and her former "position." Thus, both parents are concerned with social mobility. Since this pattern coincides with Almayer's own refusal to accept a low social position, choice (D) is the correct choice. Choices (A) and (C) are not evidenced in the passage. Choice (B) can be ruled out by Almayer's father's intolerant reaction to the natives.

Fiction: "The Fall of the House of Usher"

1. **(C)** This is a big-picture question. First, the narrator tells us about a time when he approached a particularly gloomy-looking house, explains the events that led to his arrival, and then delivers a general sense of his relationship to the home's occupant. Choice (C) is the only option that fits this pattern, an impression of the house and then an analysis of how the narrator came to be there. The narrator does not suggest that he is solving a problem as in choice (A). Although he may attempt to reconnect with an old friend, the events of the passage take place before that. Choice (D) serves as a detail of the passage but not an overall description.

2. **(C)** Words like "dull," "dark," "dreary," "gloom," and "desolate" provide evidence to support choice (C). Although the narrator is certainly aware, as in choice (D), of how the home is in a destructive state, as mentioned in choice (A), and that he feels both despair and melancholy, found in choice (B), none of these describes the tone, or the general attitude, of the paragraph. Since "foreboding" means a feeling that something bad will happen, it is the correct answer.

3. **(D)** Throughout the passage, the narrator is generally aware of the gloomy, ominous feeling the house gives off, but he cannot explain it. Even after trying to change his attitude and his view of the house, he cannot express why or how it has such power over him. So choice (D) is correct. Choices (A) and (C) describe feelings opposite of uncertainty. Since it doesn't have to do with professional training, you can rule out choice (B) as well.

4. **(C)** Lines 16–17 explicitly state the narrator's feeling that "[i]t was a mystery" and thus back up the answer for the previous question. Choices (A), (B), and (D) depict scenes in which the narrator feels unnerved but cannot shake his apprehension. As such, they evidence how the house makes the narrator feel but not how he understands his ability to assess that reaction.

5. **(C)** A good approach to this question is to replace "society" with a simple synonym like *company*, which is closest to choice (C). The other choices all refer to the alternate meaning of society that refers to an aggregate of people living together under a system of order.

6. **(A)** From the passage, we know the narrator and his friend haven't seen each other for a long time. However, they were friends "in boyhood" and Roderick is ill, hoping to feel better in the presence of "his only personal friend." Thus, we can infer the narrator feels obligated, as in choice (A), to submit to the request. His feelings of "sorrow" and "terror" are brought on by the house, not by his friend's letter. Choice (C) is too extreme since it implies that the narrator held a strong desire or yearning to visit his old friend.

7. **(C)** Here, the narrator states that "it was the apparent *heart*" of the letter, despite the odd request, that made him say yes. This provides sufficient evidence that the narrator feels a certain responsibility to his friend and yields the answer for the previous question. Choices (A) and (B) merely discuss his uneasiness upon approaching the house. Choice (D) highlights the narrator's limited knowledge concerning Roderick's family history.

8. **(D)** Use context clues. Despite their intimacy, the narrator doesn't know much about his friend. So "reserve" must mean something like shyness or reticence, making choice (D) the correct answer. Choice (B) is an antonym. On the other hand, neither greed nor preparedness means that Roderick is detached or unwilling to share much about himself.

9. **(B)** This is tough reading, but don't be intimidated; break it down. The family is peculiar, or odd; has a great interest in art, charity, and musical science; but is not enduring. In fact, the line of descent is direct and has always been so. Thus, there is only one descendant. We know that the family has a long history and that Roderick is the current heir, ruling out choices (A) and (D). The word "direct" implies that the inheritance has always been passed down from one to the next without any extra heirs, eliminating choice (C).

Fiction: "Adventure"

1. **(A)** The question asks for the thematic focus, which can be summarized as two lovers whose circumstances bring them together and then gradually apart. Thus, love is fleeting, transient, or temporary, making choice (A) the correct answer. Although love may be beautiful or wholesome more generally speaking, this passage focuses on its impermanence. Choice (D) is misleading because the two characters do not wish to abuse love but, instead, drift apart despite their good intentions.

2. **(A)** We know from line 1 that George is only a boy when Alice is twenty-seven. Since her affair with Ned began when she was sixteen, eleven years have passed. If George is a small boy now, we can reasonably assume that eleven years ago, he was unborn. Choices (C) and (D) would make him much older than he is. Although choice (B) might be tempting, that would make George eighteen at the time of this passage, not a boy.

3. **(C)** The imagery in lines 4–6 reveals a lot about Alice as an adult. She is "stooped" and "quiet," despite the "ferment" brewing under her surface. Synonyms of *ferment* include tumult, turmoil, and disquiet, so "unsettled" is the correct answer. Although she may be fond of Ned, their unresolved love affair has taken its toll on her—she still lives with her mother and there is no evidence to suggest she has since moved on to another lover. Choice (B) is characteristic of Ned, not Alice. The word "sedate," which means calm and peaceful, describes Alice's exterior but remains in contrast to her restless interior.

4. **(B)** As stated above, the description of the adult Alice occurs in the first two paragraphs, eliminating choices (C) and (D), which describe instances of Alice's teenage years. When deciding between choices (A) and (B), you should focus on the words "beneath a placid exterior a continual ferment went on." Even if you don't know what "ferment" means, you can assume that it is in contrast to her placid, quiet exterior. Choice (A), in contrast, deals more with her physical appearance and not her attitude.

5. **(D)** Here, Ned is "puzzled" but "touched." He had desired Alice only physically, but here "changed his mind" and became more emotionally attached to her. So, if you substitute a word or words for "touched," you might use *stirred emotionally* or "moved" as in choice (D). Choice (A) refers to touching someone physically in a violent manner. Choice (B) can be used as a verb meaning to hurry or as a feeling of disappointment as in *dashed hopes*; neither fits here. Choice (C) is irrelevant since it might mean to correspond or resemble another, or to be equal to something in quality or strength.

6. **(A)** The evidence for this question is scattered throughout the essay. Alice is both willing to move to a new city and to live unmarried with Ned. For her, their being together is most important. Ned is "puzzled," or confused, by her devotion. Despite his intention to "protect and care" for Alice, he is unwilling to take her with him, becomes interested in other women, and very nearly forgets her altogether. Choices (B), (C), and (D) better describe Ned than Alice.

7. **(C)** Lines 23–24 reveal much about both Alice's and Ned's feelings. He is confused but pleased by Alice's devotion. A good approach to this question is to eliminate the other answer choices. Choice (A) gives us only facts about Alice, not anything about their attitudes toward the affair itself. Choice (B) gives us information about Alice's infatuation but nothing about Ned's feelings. Choice (D), like choice (A), reports facts but reveals little about the couple's inward emotions. Choose choice (C) because it's the only choice that provides evidence of how both lovers feel toward one another.

8. **(A)** Ned, sad about leaving his home and his sweetheart, forgets his "resolutions" concerning Alice. Before this, he has refused to live with her unmarried and, instead, resolves to return to care for her in more traditionally appropriate ways. Instead, he forgets that plan. The couple, ignited by emotions, become lovers and make further promises that are likewise disregarded. Thus, choice (A) is the correct option. It is not appropriate to say he forgot his "purposes" or "solutions." Choice (D) means requests rather than pledges.

9. **(B)** Lines 36–38 consist of Ned's promise to always be with Alice. Since he later glosses over this commitment to Alice, it is appropriate to infer that he was disingenuous, misleading, or insincere. Choice (A) is an extreme that is ultimately unfair to Ned, who attempts, somewhat halfheartedly, to keep the love alive through his letters. Choice (C) indicates that he committed himself to Alice under great pressure or force, which is untrue. Choice (D) is another extreme that lacks evidence; later, he casually neglects Alice for present, temporary amusements.

Great Global Conversation: Jefferson

1. **(A)** Jefferson explains the transition from monarchy to republic as one as natural and easy as "throwing off an old and putting on a new suit of clothes." Hence, choice (A) is correct. Choices (B) and (C) describe situations contradictory to the one Jefferson presents. Choice (D) is incorrect because of the word "trivial," which means "insignificant" or "inconsequential."

2. **(B)** Jefferson prefers the first of his two proposals, "Free trade by alliance with some naval power." He argues that if the British Court were willing, an alliance "might . . . be approved by our people." Hence, Jefferson suggests that the people would see the benefits of economic trade with the British, as in choice (B). Choices (A) and (D) don't express the idea of free trade. Choice (C) does not work because the passage does not focus on the desire of the American people as a whole for religious integration with the British.

3. **(C)** Lines 18–21 supply Jefferson's direct proposal that a free trade alliance with Britain will benefit both countries and be generally supported by the American people. Choice (A) discusses Virginia's smooth transition into a republic. Choice (B) is Jefferson's proposal but fails to address how the American people might react. Choice (D) expresses Jefferson's desire to be serving with Benjamin Franklin, for whom he obviously has great respect.

4. **(A)** Read the sentence before looking at the answer choices. You might substitute "apprehend" with *anticipate* or *think* since Jefferson is proposing his ideas. Thus, choice (A) is correct. Choices (B) and (C) refer to the other meaning of "apprehend," as in arresting someone for an offense or crime. Choice (D) implies creation rather than opinion.

5. **(A)** Check the sentence before this one. Jefferson says free trade with an alliance is preferable because it aligns with the American people's "habits and wishes." Here, he implies that Americans would like to have access to imports from abroad rather than making everything themselves. This coincides with choice (A) but contradicts choices (B) and (C). Choice (D) brings up the American Revolution. Although it seems plausible that Americans do not desire further conflict, that is not the subject of these lines.

6. **(B)** The meaning of his second letter concerns "a fleet of the enemy's ships" that will easily have access to America's shores "[s]hould any more be added to them." Hence, Jefferson worries that American defenses will fail if more British ships arrive, as in choice (B). Choice (C) says the opposite. Choice (D) is wrongly concerned with the "open battlefield." Although choice (A) is tempting, it is too extreme. Certainly, Jefferson believes American defenses can resist. However, he also believes that they will be quickly overcome if the situation gets any worse.

7. **(C)** Here, the "want of arms" inhibits America from bringing the amount of forces necessary to defeat the British fleet. So Jefferson means that there is a continual need or demand for limited military power. It is the "lack" of arms that prevents appropriate defense operations. If America had an abundance of military powers, as in choice (B), this would not be an issue. Since this is dealing with the availability of military forces, "danger" is not an appropriate choice. Choice (A) is appealing because Jefferson does desire more forces. However, read the sentence with "desire" in place before you choose it. It is not the desire for arms itself that prevents adequate defense but, instead, that the desire cannot be fulfilled.

8. **(D)** The tone, or overall feel/attitude, of the passages can be described as serious, official, and respectful. Choice (D) best describes these feelings since "formality" refers to a stateliness and "deference" implies a respectfulness. Jefferson offers ideas of his own, rather than submitting himself as subservient like in choice (A). Although Jefferson may be anxious because of the severity of his letters, he is far from aggressive. Practical could readily describe Jefferson's tone, but avarice, or greed, does not.

9. **(C)** First, think about what the question is asking. "Foresight" means that Jefferson was able to predict what might happen. So we are looking in the first passage for a prediction that comes true or could come true according to the second passage. Choice (C) is the only choice in which Jefferson anticipates America's vulnerability at its coasts, which is the topic of the second passage.

10. **(C)** Notice the word "respective" in the question, meaning that these answers have to go in order: the first word has to describe the first passage and the second should apply to Passage 2. In the first passage, Jefferson proposes ideas about how to move forward economically. In the second, he plans for military engagement. Choice (A) has these switched, so eliminate it. Jefferson never shows evidence of being overly concerned with his personal issues, as in choice (B). The first passage is far from "pedestrian," or dull and unconcerned.

Great Global Conversation: Frederick Douglass

1. **(B)** Notice the question asks for a general point, or main idea, from the first paragraph. In these lines, Douglass discusses his broad autobiographical information, his birthplace and age, emphasizing the obscurity about his age. The rest of the paragraph expresses that this ignorance is commonplace among slaves. Choice (A) wrongly assumes celebration, which is not mentioned here. Choice (C) is not evidenced; "kind" masters are referenced as those who give their slaves permission to visit another plantation—an allowance that is far from overcoming prejudice. Math education, although conceivable as a detail, is not the main point of the first paragraph, eliminating choice (D).

2. **(C)** In lines 7–9, Douglass validates his distress at not having access to his own basic personal information. If you replace "want" with *absence*, you can see that choice (C) is appropriate. Although choice (A) might be tempting, read the sentence with *obstacle* substituted for "want." You'll quickly see that the desire for information is not what produced unhappiness but that the need was denied. It isn't appropriate to say the "obstacle" or "command" of information produced unhappiness.

3. **(B)** What the author does know about himself comes from others' conversations or stories, making choice (B) correct. We know Douglass didn't speak much with his mother, and she died while he was very young. Choice (C) is incorrect because this evidence was purposefully denied him. Choice (D) is not discussed in the passage.

4. **(B)** To approach this question, look for lines in which Douglass receives information about his past through others, as in choice (B). Choice (A) evidences the master's tendency to refuse to answer questions concerning a slave's past. Choice (C) explains why it was especially tough for Douglass's mother to visit him. Choice (D) gives the only example of Douglass's history that he seems to remember for himself.

5. **(B)** In these lines, Douglass describes the effects of taking mothers from their children under institutionalized slavery. He concludes that this tendency impeded the child's affection and curtailed the mother's nurturing. Hence, choice (B) is correct. Although Douglass may have wished for a better relationship with his mother, he seems quite fond of, rather than disappointed by, her commitment to seeing him whenever possible. Choice (C) is appealing, but Douglass says himself that he can't be sure why. He doesn't discuss his intellectual development, eliminating choice (D).

6. **(D)** Douglass is unsure of who his father is, so choice (D) is correct. Although Douglass admits that a rumor spread that his master was his father, the rumor was never confirmed. So Douglass does not suggest that he actually met his father. Since this information is completely withheld from him, we cannot assume choice (A), (B), or (C).

7. **(A)** Douglass's mother sneaks out at night, walks 12 miles to visit him, and then has to make the journey again before morning so she can work in the fields all day. Her priorities are not economic as in choice (B). Although 12 miles is quite a bit to walk, her presence proves that it is not insurmountable, making choice (C) incorrect. Choice (D) is never mentioned.

8. **(B)** Beginning in line 31, we learn about the circumstances under which Douglass's mother visits him, risking "a whipping" if not back "in the field at sunrise." Hence, these lines provide direct evidence for the previous question. Choices (A), (C), and (D) tell us briefly about Douglass's relationship with his mother but not why she was forced to visit only at night.

9. **(A)** Here, Douglass describes his numbness at the news of his mother's death. "Tidings" means news or information, making choice (A) correct. Although choices (B) and (C) don't describe this same idea of hearing about her death, choice (D) might tempt you. Just remember that it's inaccurate to say Douglass would receive the "causes" of her death.

Great Global Conversation: Emerson and Arnold

1. **(D)** In the first passage, Emerson is concerned with why the current age is retrospective, or always looking back into the past. He advocates, instead, for "a poetry and philosophy of insight" rather than relying on traditional discourses. Similarly, he says we should "demand our own works" and interrogate what is natural. Hence, he raises the question of why we rely on what others have said instead of having our own experiences and creating our own theories, making choice (D) correct. He is not concerned with feuds or inconsistencies between separate fields as in choices (A), (B), and (C).

2. **(A)** Here, Emerson argues that past generations "beheld God and nature face to face" while the current generation experiences them only through the words and records of those who have come before. So "original" means "unique" or "special," making choice (A) correct. We can rule out choices (B) and (C) because they mean the same thing, both suggesting that the new ways be somehow groundbreaking. Choice (D) is wrong because Emerson does not suggest that the relationship be ceremonial in any way.

3. **(A)** Emerson believes in "the perfection of the creation so far," arguing that man can "satisfy" all "curiosity." So Emerson's attitude is optimistic that as long as we pose questions, we can intelligently and coherently discover answers. Choice (B) is the opposite. Although Emerson's argument is abstract, or existing through ideas and theoretical concepts, this doesn't describe his attitude toward human understanding. Similarly, historicism is the theory that culture is determined by history. This is what Emerson desires to change. Again, it is not accurate in describing his attitude toward human understanding.

4. **(B)** These lines summarize Emerson's belief that all questions can be answered and all curiosities can be satisfied, and thus provide evidence that he is optimistic that the current generation can come to their own understanding of the human experience. Choice (A) is merely where Emerson's question is posed. Choice (C) suggests that the current generation must look for its own answers but does not explicitly reveal his attitude toward the possibility of accomplishing this task. Choice (D) simply states what Emerson believes is the objective of science.

5. **(C)** Of Plato, Arnold says that "[o]ne cannot refuse to admire the artist," yet his notions are "primitive," making choice (C) correct. Plato, who held disdain for the man who worked rather than spent all his time thinking and speculating, is viewed as neither practical nor applicable, ruling out choices (A) and (D). Since Arnold summarizes Plato's beliefs, it is not accurate to call them "indecipherable" as in choice (B).

6. **(C)** Here, Plato's ideas are called "primitive," based on a time when society was categorized into warriors, priests, and slaves. Further, his ideas are "admirable" because the first sentence of the selection states that one "cannot refuse to admire the artist who draws these pictures." Choices (A) and (B) both explain Plato's argument. Choice (D) does not focus on what Arnold thinks of Plato's ideas.

7. **(B)** This word is used in Plato's description of the "working lawyer" who is bonded, "bent and broken . . . without a particle of soundness in him." A good approach to this question is to substitute a word like *health*. The example paints the picture of a man "smart and clever" who has not been able to meet his potential because of the strains of life, ruling out choice (C). It is inaccurate to say somebody doesn't have "safety" in them. The word "eloquence" means being articulate or expressive. Plato does not think the lawyer cannot be persuasive but, instead, that the lawyer doesn't have the time or strength to devote to his own refinement.

8. **(C)** Simply put, Plato is scornful of all working professions. So look for an answer that says something to the effect of labor detracting from one's self-worth. That is choice (C). Choices (A) and (D) favor those who work or service others and so contradict Plato's belief. Choice (B) is too extreme since Plato seems to pity the "bent and broken" victims of the labor force.

9. **(B)** To approach this question, think of what we know Emerson and Plato value. In the first passage, Emerson values independent thinking, observing, and asking questions. Emerson is briefly mentioned in the second passage as advocating for working professionals since they are "the modern majority." Plato, on the other hand, believes any kind of organized work or profession detracts from one's strength and intellectual potential. Hence, choice (B) is correct. Plato never advocates for mathematical reasoning or industrial engineering, eliminating choices (C) and (D). Although choice (A) is tempting, recall that religious revelation is only one detail of Emerson's argument and that Plato is not focused on the sciences but on the pursuit of knowledge apart from the burden of a job.

10. **(D)** Know what you are looking for by paraphrasing this question. We want to find what Emerson said that would explicitly offend Plato. Choice (D) is correct because here Emerson voices a common belief that "speculative men," or men like Plato who spend their time thinking, are "unsound and frivolous." Choices (A), (B), and (C) consist of Emerson's argument that the current generation should seek its own knowledge, an idea with which Plato would most likely agree.

Social Science: Russian Depopulation

1. **(C)** The author presents several contributing factors to the population problem and ends on a less than hopeful note that the population will continue to decline if great changes are not made. Thus, choice (C) makes the most sense here. Choice (A) might tempt you, but "manageable" implies that the problem could be taken care of without difficulty, which is not the author's opinion. Since Russia seems to be an aberration rather than the norm, we can rule out choice (B). "Nebulous" means "unclear," but the author seems to believe he knows the factors behind the decline in population, which eliminates choice (D).

2. **(A)** In the very first paragraph, the author states that Russia faces "the biggest long-term problem" and lists the many factors influencing the problem. This provides direct evidence for the previous question, making choice (A) correct. Choice (B) supports the idea that Russia is an anomaly. Choices (C) and (D) discuss the author's opinions regarding Russian family values. Only choice (A) gives evidence of the author's overall attitude toward the issue.

3. **(D)** This is a purpose question. Ask yourself what the author is doing in these lines. These lines compare Russia to less-developed countries, illustrating how life expectancy alone cannot explain Russia's decline in population. Instead, Russia is combatting a more complex problem where life expectancy and birth rates are simultaneously low. These lines show how we need more than one number to evaluate Russia's situation effectively, making choice (D) correct. We are given precise data, so choice (A) doesn't work. These lines actually contradict choice (B). Be careful with choice (C); we are examining demographics, not economics.

4. **(B)** "Fairly" can be substituted with *comparably* here. So choice (B) is the correct choice. The idea is that the expectancy can be considered high in relation to less-developed countries. Choice (A) wrongly assumes we are using morals as judgment measures. Choice (C) inaccurately equates the expectancy rates. Choice (D) would mean that we are looking at a sole figure rather than comparing multiple figures.

5. **(B)** This line refers to fathers who are often absent, or "uninvolved," in the raising of their children. We cannot assume the fathers are in jail, deceased, or geographically distant.

6. **(B)** The author sees Putin's solution as limited because it "fails to see the underlying causes" and instead focuses on "economic programs." Choices (A) and (C) contradict this view. Choice (D) assumes too much; although the article references social programs, it does not include details.

7. **(C)** We are looking for two things here. First, we want a solution that would increase Russia's population. Second, we want something that was not considered in the passage. Hence, choice (C) is correct. Choices (B) and (D) were both mentioned by the author. Choice (A) wouldn't actually change the population at all.

8. **(A)** This question has two parts. First, decide what the author offered as advice. The author argues that the mindset of Russians has to change. She identifies the causes as lack of family support and lack of desire for children. So, if those two things changed to increase the population, Russians would have more children. Hence, the new figure would show an increase in the youth population. Choice (A) accurately describes that change. Choice (B) wrongly implies that the author suggests a solution that extends life expectancy. Choices (C) and (D), by emphasizing other subsections of the population, both fail to account for the rise in births that the author ultimately advocates for.

9. **(A)** The question asks for the difference in Russia's male and female elderly populations. We know from the passage that women live much longer than men in Russia. Hence, their ages will diverge more. Choice (D) is nonsensical, claiming different values for the same numbers. Choices (B) and (C) don't account for the tendency for elderly women to live longer than elderly men.

10. **(A)** Look for the lines that indicate the gap in life expectancy between males and females in Russia. Since that occurs around lines 5–8, choice (A) is correct. Choice (B) explains some causes of the low male life expectancy. Choice (C) transitions into birth rates. Choice (D) examines the inconsistencies between demographic data and supposed family values.

Social Science: The Emu War

1. **(D)** The question is asking what the first paragraph *does*. That paragraph discusses the butterfly effect generally before closing in on a particular instance between British veterans and emus in Western Australia. So choice (D) is correct. This paragraph is concerned with introducing the topic in a creative way, not in demonstrating a decision (which comes much later in the passage) or countering objections. Choice (C) is incorrect because the first paragraph does not utilize a personal story.

2. **(A)** We know that the military initially thought they could easily handle the emus, but they failed miserably, making choice (A) correct. The author does not suggest that it requires extraordinary bravery to face flightless birds, ruling out choice (B). Choice (C) is actually the lesson learned from the military's overconfidence: because it was particularly presumptuous, the military learned a lesson in modesty. Choice (D) means excessively enthusiastic or extreme, which is not accurate here.

3. **(C)** These lines specifically state that the troops underestimated the emus and failed to accomplish their mission. Hence, they give direct support for the previous question. Choice (A) introduces the event but doesn't reveal the military mindset toward the emus. Choice (B) explains the damage inflicted by the emus. Choice (D) affirms the major's failure but, again, doesn't give evidence of his initial attitude.

4. **(B)** Here, the veterans are encouraged to participate in farming. Choice (B) sounds most like that. Choice (A) inaccurately implies that the veterans should *grab* farming. Choice (C) is wrong because no evidence is given that the veterans had to study farming first; instead, they are involved in actual farming. Of course, the veterans were not inventing or creating farming for the first time, making choice (D) incorrect.

5. **(B)** It might be helpful to paraphrase this question. *What changed between the ineffective and the effective raids on the emus?* The passage attributes Major Meredith's minimal success his second time around to "his previous experience." Later, the locals succeed because they are "well equipped and knowledgeable." So choice (B) is the correct answer. No evidence indicates that the major or the locals receive further training, academic or military. Choice (D) inappropriately implies that the media were somehow responsible for the more successful onslaughts.

6. **(D)** These lines state that the bounty system—a measure that prevented government involvement—worked well because the locals were better able to hunt the emus. Thus, we can infer that their first-hand experience gave them an advantage. Choice (A) states only that government aid was requested. Choice (B) references the media's involvement but, of course, does not connect the media with the successful fight against the emu population. Choice (C) includes the lines where the bounty system is explained, but fails to explain why it was successful. So choice (D) is the only answer that gives evidence as to what attributed to the effective attacks on the emus.

7. **(C)** Why might the author choose to use quotation marks here? You might be thinking for dramatic effect. The usage of "war" in this context is comical because a military force is being called in to fight birds, and the birds are ironically winning. So these terms usually mean something very different in warfare. Hence, choice (C) is correct. The author is not citing quotations or research. This event is actually quite trivial in the global context of war. Choice (D) is tempting but implies that the author is disputing facts, whereas he/she is actually calling attention to the absurdity of equating a fowl hunt to true warfare.

8. **(A)** To approach this question, use context clues and substitute your own synonym. The successful resistance of the emus, though humorous, was actually harmful to the veterans' already dangerously uncertain situation. Choice (A) sounds most like *uncertain* or *unpredictable*. Choice (B) is too extreme because it implies a submission to fate, but the veterans/farmers are not merely resigned to fail. Choice (C) just means that the situation is related to living organisms. Choice (D) means cultivated in the sense of being well traveled.

9. **(C)** This question focuses on what the figure can help explain. So first ask what the figure does. It gives a general timeline of the war very similar to the ones constructed to outline the battles of extended warfare. Then ask which of these choices discusses the varied events of the so-called war. Choice (C) specifically mentions the engagements of the war, and so it is correct. Choice (A) just tells who was assigned to the task. Choice (B) describes what the forces took for the first engagement. Choice (D) again describes one event but doesn't reference several like (C) does.

10. **(A)** From the figure, we can see that the forces were generally ineffective at first, improved with time, and then became particularly efficient by December. Choice (A) accurately accounts for this gradual increase in efficiency. Choices (B) and (C) do not reflect this improvement, and choice (D) inaccurately implies that we cannot find a general pattern.

Science: Caffeine

1. **(C)** Passage 1 examines how caffeine works in the body by inhibiting the body's ability to sense how much adenosine is in the body. It is neutral and informative. Passage 2 seems to serve as a warning to the reader that although caffeine isn't typically deadly, it does have many negative health consequences. Passage 2 is primarily persuasive. Therefore, choice (C) is correct. Choice (A) is wrong because, although Passage 1 is analytical, Passage 2 is not narrative, or telling a story. Choice (B) is wrong because it flips the two passages. Choice (D) is incorrect because, although Passage 1 is somewhat medical, Passage 2 doesn't focus on economics.

2. **(D)** The first of these two paragraphs says that in a thermodynamically favorable reaction, adenosine triphosphate releases its phosphates and free energy, leaving just adenosine and inorganic phosphate. The next paragraph talks about how we have neurons that have evolved to detect the presence of adenosine and then to direct the pineal gland to secrete melatonin. This sequence is described by answer choice (D). Choice (A) is wrong because the pineal gland secretes melatonin, rather than forms adenosine triphosphate. Choice (B) is wrong because the detection of just adenosine triggers the melatonin response; the presence of adenosine triphosphate does not have this effect. Choice (C) doesn't work because the energy is released when adenosine triphosphate decomposes to adenosine and inorganic phosphate.

3. **(C)** This paragraph describes the process by which adenosine triphosphate undergoes a thermodynamically favorable process to form adenosine and inorganic phosphate and to release free energy. If energy is released in the reaction, it means that energy was being stored in the reactants, so the reactants have more energy than the products, choice (C). Choices (A) and (B) are incorrect because this term refers to an energy differential. Choice (D) is backward.

4. **(A)** In paragraph 3, the author talks about how the body knows to sleep when a large amount of adenosine is sensed by receptors in the neurons. In the last paragraph, the author says that caffeine (because it has a very similar structure to adenine) can interact with these receptors, tricking the body into thinking less adenosine is present than really is. This corresponds to choice (A), because energy consumption in the body corresponds to conversion of adenosine triphosphate into adenosine. Choices (B), (C), and (D) aren't supported anywhere in the passage.

5. **(C)** The correct answer is choice (C) because this is the part of the passage that discusses how caffeine works. These lines talk about caffeine interacting with adenosine receptors that are intended to sense how much energy the body has expended. Choice (A) is wrong because it introduces the concept of adenosine triphosphate as a source of energy. Choice (B) merely suggests a purpose for sleep. Choice (D) is wrong because it talks about a time when caffeine doesn't work—when the body has simply expended too much energy and the body's adenosine levels have become too high.

6. **(A)** This line is used to contrast the beginning of the paragraph, which states that caffeine isn't typically deadly. The "however" in this line tips us off to the fact that the author wants to make a contrast. What he's saying is that although caffeine isn't deadly, it's also not _____. It makes sense to say that although caffeine isn't deadly, it's also not "harmless," which is choice (A). Choices (B), (C), and (D) are incorrect because caffeine is all of these things.

7. **(B)** The author states in the final paragraph that pathological addiction to caffeine has never been documented in humans, so the correct answer is choice (B). The rest of the answer choices are mentioned as detriments of caffeine.

8. **(D)** Choice (D) is correct because these lines state that pathological addiction to caffeine has never been documented. The other choices all mention negative effects of caffeine: bone loss, anxiety, and heart dysrhythmias.

9. **(C)** Passage 1 primarily examines how caffeine stimulation works in the body. Passage 2 argues that although caffeine isn't deadly, it can have many negative side effects in certain groups of people. Therefore, the correct answer is choice (C). Choice (A) is wrong because, although Passage 1 does touch on the origins of caffeine, it doesn't discuss the history. Choice (B) is wrong because Passage 1 talks about how caffeine works rather than its benefits. Choice (D) is incorrect because neither passage discusses the evolution of caffeine stimulation.

Science: Fungi

1. **(C)** First summarize what happened with antibiotics and antibiotic resistance: certain classes of antibiotics were wildly effective in eradicating bacteria, but some were resistant. As these classes of antibiotics were used more rampantly, much larger numbers of the bacteria became resistant. Thus, the situation described is one in which initial efficiency decreases as something becomes better at beating the system. This matches choice (C): the software is initially effective. However, as more students learn to beat the system, the software loses its effectiveness. Choice (A) isn't the same, because its efficiency increases over time. Choices (B) and (D) are tempting, but nothing is learning to beat the system in either case.

2. **(C)** This paragraph gives a general introduction to fungi, emphasizing that many people don't realize how prevalent they are in our lives. The essay then goes on to discuss several examples of the applications of fungi. Therefore, the answer is choice (C): the author relates fungi to our lives. Choice (A) is wrong because the author mentions fungi only as food here, but the essay doesn't focus on it. Choice (B) doesn't work because the author simply says that many people don't realize how important fungi are—not that they're wrong about fungi. Choice (D) is incorrect because the author says that the importance of fungi is easily overlooked rather than easily visible.

3. **(D)** This line says that fungi execute many functions in our lives. In other words, they *perform* many functions, which is choice (D). Choice (A) is another definition of "execute." However, the fungi aren't destroying functions, they're carrying out functions. They're also not hiding functions, as in choice (B), or enticing functions, as in choice (C).

4. **(A)** The author talks about Alexander Fleming somewhat accidentally discovering the antibiotic properties of penicillin (lines 13–17) and Akiro Endo discovering the benefits of statins while attempting to study *Penicillium citrinum*'s antimicrobial properties. What these major discoveries have in common is that they were somewhat accidental. Thus, the answer is choice (A). These discoveries weren't a product of evolution or genetic engineering as in choice (B) or (D). Although they may have required economic investment, as in choice (C), the author doesn't mention this.

5. **(D)** The correct answer is choice (D) because these lines state that both Alexander Fleming and Akira Endo made their discoveries serendipitously, meaning with a bit of chance or luck. Choice (A) talks about how Fleming's discovery contributed to science, but none of the answer choices from the previous question apply. Choice (B) talks about how widespread use of antibiotics contributed to antibiotic resistance—not exactly a medical innovation. Choice (C) simply defines statins.

6. **(B)** Consider the context. These lines state that peptidoglycan polymers are highly peculiar to bacteria and that the antimicrobial agents that target peptidoglycan don't harm other cells. In other words, only bacteria are affected by these agents because only bacteria have peptidoglycan polymers. Therefore, the polymers are *unique* to bacteria, choice (B). Choice (A) is another common use of the word "peculiar." In this case, though, it is somewhat opposite of what the author means since peptidoglycans are common to bacteria. Choice (C) is wrong because these polymers are normal, not diseased. Choice (D) is wrong because, although peptidoglycans certainly are helpful, this doesn't fit the contrast in the latter part of the sentence.

7. **(D)** The answer can be found in the third paragraph, where the author details the mechanism by which antibiotics work. He says that antibiotics target peptidoglycan polymers, which are present only in bacteria. Therefore, antibiotics harm the bacteria without harming the host's cells, choice (D). Choice (A) is incorrect as evidenced by the fact that many bacteria have developed antibiotic resistance. Neither choice (B) nor choice (C) is supported anywhere in the passage.

8. **(C)** The correct answer is choice (C). These lines state that antibiotics work by targeting something present strictly in bacteria. Choice (A) doesn't discuss antibiotics. Choice (B) merely mentions that a fungus led to the development of three classes of antibiotics. Choice (D) references antibiotic resistance but not what makes antibiotics effective.

9. **(B)** This sentence beckons the reader to ask what is left to be discovered if some of our biggest findings in medicine have been the accidental results of studying fungi. The author is hinting that it's almost certain that fungi have more benefits to provide but that we must look for them. Thus, choice (B) is correct. Choice (A) is wrong because the author mentions neither geology nor funding. Choice (C) is wrong because the author thinks there's much research left to be done, and choice (D) is wrong because nowhere in the passage does the author criticize mycology.

Science: Methanogenesis

1. **(B)** The answer to this question can be found in the last paragraph. The author states that understanding *Methanosphaera stadtmanae* has been immensely helpful in understanding and treating IBD. He also acknowledges that further understanding of archaeal and bacterial species will lead to a better understanding of how all of these things interact. Therefore, progress is being made on the subject, choice (B). It isn't choice (A), "largely settled," because he admits that it can be better understood. It isn't choice (C) because he talks about how scientists have come to better understand the relationships. It isn't choice (D) because scientists are still working to understand how archaeal and bacterial species interact with the human anatomy.

2. **(A)** According to lines 18–21, methanogenic bacteria were first identified in the gut microbiota after methane was detected in the breath. Methanogens are defined throughout the passage as species that produce methane, so this presence of methane in the breath eventually led to the identification of methanogenic species in the human digestive system. Thus, the answer is choice (A). Choice (B) is incorrect because it says that the methanogens were eventually identified in fecal samples, but this wasn't how they were originally discovered. Choices (C) and (D) are details of the passage mentioned in other paragraphs but not in the third paragraph and not about how methanogens were discovered.

3. **(C)** In these lines, the author is referring to methanol being reduced to methane. Since these are two different chemical compounds, you can infer that methanol is being converted or *transformed* into methane, choice (C). The other choices are all different meanings of the word that don't apply here, as methanol cannot be subtracted, diminished, or persecuted into methane.

4. **(C)** Consider the context. Prior to these lines, the author stated that *Methanosphaera stadtmanae* is somehow connected to the occurrence of IBD. These lines serve to explain to the reader the role that *M. stadtmanae* plays in this process—it triggers the proinflammatory cytokines. Thus, he is explaining a process, choice (C). The answer isn't choice (A) because the author hasn't introduced any objections that he's trying to disprove. The answer isn't choice (B) because he's talking about a partially known scientific fact rather than a speculation. Choice (D) is incorrect because the author doesn't attribute this fact to anyone.

5. **(A)** This line says that *Methanosphaera stadtmanae* induces the release of proinflammatory cytokine TNF. This seems to be a cause-and-effect relationship: *M. stadtmanae* senses something and makes something else happen. Another way to describe this might be that *M. stadtmanae* triggers the release, or *causes* the release, choice (A). Choices (B) and (D) are too personified—it's more automated than something that is suggested or persuaded. Choice (C) doesn't work because the organisms can't release a release.

6. **(B)** The author states that *Methanosphaera stadtmanae* is helpful to humans because it conserves energy and aids in digestion (lines 46–52). He also says that it likely contributes to IBD in some individuals. Therefore, *M. stadtmanae* plays an important and helpful role in the body. However, if homeostasis is not maintained, it can also have negative effects in the body. Therefore, it is primarily beneficial, choice (B). It isn't uniformly positive, choice (A), because of its role in IBD. It isn't somewhat harmful, as in choice (D), because the author explicitly states in the first paragraph that *M. stadtmanae* is beneficial to humans. It's necessary for energy conservation and digestion.

7. **(C)** In the second paragraph, the author explains how *Methanosphaera stadtmanae* is different from other methanogens. These other methanogens can reduce CO_2 to methane, but *M. stadtmanae* lacks the enzyme to initiate this pathway. Thus, *M. stadtmanae* can reduce methanol only to methane. Therefore, the inability to process CO_2 sets the species apart from other methanogens. Choice (A) is incorrect because all of the methanogens the author references use H_2 in reduction. Choices (B) and (D) aren't mentioned in the passage.

8. **(B)** Choice (B) is the correct answer because these lines explicitly state that the inability of *Methanosphaera stadtmanae* to reduce carbon dioxide to methane is what sets it apart from other methanogens. Lines 10–11 and 22–24 also give examples of differences among *M. stadtmanae* and other methanogens, but these lines don't mention any of the answers to the previous question. Choice (D) provides a similarity between *M. stadtmanae* and the other methanogens.

9. **(D)** First, consider why the author says that *Methanosphaera stadtmanae* is beneficial to the host. In the first paragraph, he talks about how this species has a particularly restrictive energy metabolism, stating that "these unique energy conservation traits are what make *Methanosphaera stadtmanae* beneficial to its human host and not an opportunistic pathogen." Thus, we're looking for an answer choice from the figures that shows that this species conserves energy. Notice that for most of the pathways, Figure 1 implies that at least some sort of intermediate is missing. In Figure 2, many of the boxes are black, meaning intermediates are missing. Thus, the answer is choice (D). Choices (A) and (B) aren't mentioned in the passage, and choice (C) isn't supported by the figures.

10. **(A)** The correct answer is choice (A). These lines suggest that this species is helpful to humans rather than harmful because it has a very restrictive metabolism, meaning it's limited in its pathways. This is what's being shown by the two figures. Choice (B) is about the history of the discovery of methanogens in the gut. Choice (C) is a negative side effect of what can happen if the balance of methanogens isn't maintained, so it's about how they can be harmful to humans, rather than helpful. Choice (D) is about how homeostasis of the gut microbiota may be restored when it's disturbed. However, choice (D) is unrelated to the figures, as well as to how *M. stadtmanae* is beneficial to humans.

Science: Wound Healing

1. **(A)** The passage starts with what happens immediately after a laceration occurs and continues through the stages of wound healing; thus, it is chronological as in choice (A). Choices (B) and (D) are incorrect because the passage is merely informative and does not consider pros and cons or attempt to be persuasive. Choice (C) is incorrect because these steps all occur in the same space.

2. **(C)** The main purpose of the passage is to inform the reader of what happens after a person sustains a wound so that he or she may know to seek medical attention if a wound isn't properly healing. This makes choice (C) the correct answer. Choice (A) is wrong because the author details the normal healing process rather than any abnormalities. Choices (B) and (D) are incorrect because the author is simply stating the current understanding of wound healing rather than arguing anything.

3. **(B)** Lines 4–5 give the author's purpose: to detail the typical wound progression so that a reader may know what to expect and when to be concerned. So choice (B) is correct. Furthermore, either the beginning or the end of the first paragraph is often where the author will clearly state their thesis, so it is unsurprising to find the answer in these lines. Choice (A) only introduces the reader to the topic of wound healing without stating why it is important that a reader understands the subject. Choice (C) lists aspects of wound healing that a reader can't control. Choice (D) gives the reader some advice. However, both choices (C) and (D) miss the big picture by merely providing details.

4. **(A)** Consider the context here. The previous sentence introduces the term *phagocytosis*. Because this is a scientific term that not all readers will know, the author then clarifies what phagocytes do in the process of phagocytosis. Therefore, the author is clarifying a specialized term, making choice (A) correct. Choice (B) is incorrect because the author doesn't tell where the word comes from. Choices (C) and (D) are incorrect because the sentence does neither of these things.

5. **(D)** In this case, "raw" is referring to the edges of the wound. The author means raw as in damaged or inflamed, as is expected after the inflammatory stage, choice (D). Choice (A) is incorrect because, although it is a definition of the word "raw," it refers to materials rather than a wound. Choice (B) doesn't work because the skin isn't primitive. Choice (C) is a common definition of raw, but it refers more to uncooked food rather than to a wound.

6. **(A)** The author is emphasizing here that it is important to protect a wound in this stage, choice (A). Neither choice (B) nor choice (C) works because each has a negative connotation. The author is just emphasizing something, not passing judgment. Choice (D) is wrong because one wouldn't say that protecting something is analytical.

7. **(C)** The passage lists the steps in terms of one occurring, then the body moving on to the next. Therefore, the passage lists the steps in a sequential or chronological order. However, the figure shows great overlap among the steps; for instance, angiogenesis and wound contraction occur almost entirely at the same time. Therefore, the figure shows them as being concurrent or simultaneous. Thus, the correct answer is choice (C) as it classifies the passage's description as sequential and the figure's description as simultaneous. Choice (A) has the passage and the figure backward. Choice (B) is incorrect because both show that the processes are gradual. Choice (D) is wrong because the figure simply shows a time depiction of when the steps occur but states nothing of where they occur.

8. **(C)** Line 37 states that the last step of healing, the maturation stage, may last up to two years. The inflammatory phase lasts between 2 and 14 days, and the proliferative phase lasts between 3 and 21 days. Therefore, the whole healing phase may last 14 + 21 + 365 + 365 = 765 days. Thus, the closest answer is 1,000. In 1,000 days, the wound will almost certainly be healed, choice (C).

9. **(D)** Lines 36–37 give the timeline for the longest-lasting stage—up to two years. Therefore, we know that even the worst wounds should be healed in just over two years, making 1,000 days a reasonable estimate. Choices (A) and (C) give the timeline for much faster steps, but they don't give a reasonable estimate of the whole timeline. Choice (B) doesn't discuss time.

Writing

3

Writing

Frequently Asked Questions

How Is the Writing Component Structured?

- Part of the Reading and Writing section (2 modules of 27 questions each, 32 minutes each)
- The first Reading and Writing module will be of standard difficulty, and the second module will be more or less difficult depending on your performance on the first module.
- Approximately 25 of the 54 total Reading and Writing questions are Writing ones.
- Out of these 25 questions, about 14 relate to Standard English conventions and about 11 relate to the expression of ideas.

What Are the Most Important Things I Can Do to Be Successful?

1. **CAREFULLY REVIEW THIS CHAPTER.** It comprehensively covers the major grammar and editing concepts you will need to know for the PSAT.
2. **WORK THROUGH THE READING AND WRITING TESTS IN THIS BOOK.** They are carefully designed to align with what you will face on test day and are based on careful analysis of the released materials from the College Board.
3. **READ WIDELY.** The more familiar you are with what good writing should look like, the easier it will be for you to spot the best options in this section.
4. **PRACTICE WITH OTHER MATERIALS IF NEEDED.** The PSAT Reading and Writing section is virtually identical to the SAT Reading and Writing section. So, if you run out of practice materials in this book, check out *Barron's SAT* or any of the other Barron's books for the SAT. You can find further practice at *KhanAcademy.org*, the official College Board practice website. Also, since the PSAT Writing questions closely mirror the content covered by the ACT English section, you can improve your PSAT Writing and Language performance by practicing ACT English passages.

Writing Strategies

1. Use the Full Amount of Time.

The PSAT Writing questions are typically easy to finish for most students. You can take approximately 70 seconds to complete each Writing question. You are much more likely to make careless errors if you rush through the questions. Instead, do the questions one time well so that you do not miss the subtle issues that many questions test. Even though with many tests it makes sense to finish early so that you have time to check your work, it is advisable with the PSAT Writing questions to pace yourself to finish right on time. You are more likely to avoid careless errors if you catch them the first time, rather than if you go through the test quickly and then quickly scan over your answers to check.

2. Mouth It Out as You Read.

"Hear" the passage in your head and test out the sound of the different options. You don't have to know the exact rules for misplaced modifiers and proper sentence construction to recognize that this sounds wrong: "Excited was I the brand new science fiction movie to see." When you are doing the PSAT Reading and Writing test, you must answer the questions correctly—you do not need to write out a justification for each answer. This chapter comprehensively covers the grammar rules you will need to know—study them, and you will be much more confident and decisive. Coupled with this knowledge, you will put yourself in the best position to succeed if you filter the questions not just through your eyes but through your ears as well.

3. Make Sure That Everything Makes Sense Given the Context.

To determine if a sentence provides an effective introduction, you must understand the paragraph as a whole. To see if a verb has the correct tense, you must see how the verbs in nearby sentences are used. Some questions will require that you look only at the sentence that the underlined portion is in, whereas other questions will require a couple of paragraphs of context. When you have any doubt about how much of the surrounding context to consider, err on the side of reading *too much* rather than *too little*. Since the Reading and Writing section is relatively easy to finish, you should take the necessary time to be certain everything is consistent and logical.

4. Understand That There Will Not Be Grammar Gimmicks—Just Grammar Rules.

The PSAT will only test you on topics where there are clearly defined grammar rules. Topics on which there is disagreement on proper English usage (using the Oxford comma, using "but" or "because" to start a sentence, and whether it is OK to use the first person "I" or second person "you" in formal papers) will not be tested. In addition, you do not need to worry about if there will be two right answers—the PSAT is an extremely well-crafted test, and it is a virtual certainty that it will be free of errors. So, instead of wasting your time trying to determine the "tricks" of the test, boost your grammar knowledge and go in with confidence.

5. Guess Intelligently, Not Just Randomly.

Remember—there is no penalty for guessing on the PSAT. Thus, be certain that you answer every single test question. If two or three of the answers are extremely similar, it is highly unlikely that one of those will be the correct choice. For example, if a question has these choices—(A) but, (B) however, (C) nevertheless, and (D) consequently—the answer is most likely choice (D) because the other choices are all synonymous. Come back to questions if you do not feel confident. Doing this will allow you to reexamine the question with fresh eyes after you've given your mind a chance to subconsciously process what the question was asking.

Transitions Questions

Questions about the best connections between different parts of the passage *are among the most frequent question types on the PSAT*. These questions require you to consider what wording would make the flow of the passage most logical and meaningful. Be sure you know the "big three" transitional words—"but," "also," and "because"—and some of their common synonyms.

BUT: however, on the other hand, in contrast to, yet, still, nevertheless, conversely, in spite of, despite, unlike, besides, although, instead, rather, otherwise, regardless, notwithstanding

ALSO: additionally, moreover, further, as well, besides, likewise, what is more, furthermore, in addition, similarly

BECAUSE: consequently, so, therefore, as a result, thus, hence, in order to, if . . . then, since, so that, due to, whenever

Tactic: Treat the Transitional Wording as a Blank, and Then Consider What Type of Transition Is Needed Given What Comes Around It.

What comes around the transitional wording could be in contrast to one another, be in support of one another, or have some other relationship. Look at as much of the text as needed—sometimes just a couple of sentences, sometimes the entire paragraph—to determine what wording is needed.

> **Example**

Those not accustomed to the effects of caffeine may experience jitteriness upon initial consumption. Despite this, many students try caffeine for the first time the morning of the PSAT in an effort to be alert. _____ they should rely on a good night's sleep and natural adrenaline to maximize performance.

7. Which choice completes the text with the most logical transition?
   (A) As a result,
   (B) Instead,
   (C) Consequently,
   (D) Moreover,

The sentence that precedes the question states that students try caffeine in order to improve their test performance. The sentence that follows states that students should rely on more natural solutions to improve performance. Choice (B) is the only option that shows the needed contrast between these two ideas. "As a result" and "consequently" both show cause and effect, and "moreover" is synonymous with "also."

Transitional Wording Drill

Write appropriate transitional words in the underlined portions. Use the "word bank" of transitions—each word will be used only once.

Word Bank

while	and	in fact
but	since	perhaps

_____ it is unusual that I enjoy waiting in line for hours on the opening night of a big movie, _____ I am not alone. _____, dozens of other moviegoers wait along with me, _____ we enjoy passing the time speculating on the movie's potential plot twists. _____ it could be expected that tempers would be short as people stood patiently in line, the truth is that people are extremely polite. _____ we are all full of hopeful anticipation, everyone is in a fairly good mood.

Answer

<u>Perhaps</u> it is unusual that I enjoy waiting in line for hours on the opening night of a big movie, <u>but</u> I am not alone. <u>In fact</u>, dozens of other moviegoers wait along with me, <u>and</u> we enjoy passing the time speculating on the movie's potential plot twists. <u>While</u> it could be expected that tempers would be short as people stood patiently in line, the truth is that people are extremely polite. <u>Since</u> we are all full of hopeful anticipation, everyone is in a fairly good mood.

Transitions Skill-Building

❶ <u>When I was young, I could not put down books.</u> I read all the Harry Potter books several times over and was a big fan of other fantasy and science fiction texts. Once I entered middle school, I lost much of the joy of reading. ❷ <u>Since I loved</u> reading for fun, I had to read certain books for summer reading. Not only did I have to read them, I had to take careful notes on the texts ❸ <u>from</u> when school started again, there would inevitably be a major reading test. I suppose it is like going to see a

1. Which choice provides the best introduction to the paragraph?
   (A) NO CHANGE
   (B) Books have always fascinated me.
   (C) Some of the best books are ones you would not expect.
   (D) Some of my happiest memories come from my childhood travel.

2. (A) NO CHANGE
   (B) As a result of
   (C) In addition to
   (D) Instead of

3. (A) NO CHANGE
   (B) until
   (C) because
   (D) by

4 movie—if you had to take notes for a quiz while watching the film, you would probably just stay out in the lobby!

[1] Fortunately, my new English teacher helped reawaken my love of reading. [2] Not surprisingly, when you can read a book that actually interests you, you tend to do much better when it comes to recall. [3] **5** In contrast, I don't even mind taking a few notes or highlighting key phrases if it helps me understand a well-written story's plot. **6** Rather than forcing us to read certain books, she gave us considerable leeway in choosing which books most interested us.

My newfound attitude toward reading comes at just the right time. I am about to take some much more challenging AP courses, and **7** you surely cannot believe what happened, there will be some material in the classes that will be rather dry. If I still had my middle-school mentality toward reading, I would likely surf the web for book summaries instead of actually reading the texts.

4. Which choice best concludes the sentence with a logical explanation?
   (A) NO CHANGE
   (B) Who has the money to see a movie in a crowded theater when you can enjoy it much more comfortably at home?
   (C) Both movies and books have plot lines, character development, and metaphorical imagery.
   (D) Nobody enjoys a movie when it is interrupted by delinquents who talk and text through its entirety.

5. (A) NO CHANGE
   (B) In fact,
   (C) Without equivocation,
   (D) Unfortunately,

6. What is the most logical placement of the underlined sentence in this paragraph?
   (A) Where it is now
   (B) Before sentence 1
   (C) Before sentence 2
   (D) Before sentence 3

7. Which choice provides the best transition at this point in the sentence?
   (A) NO CHANGE
   (B) the classes will take place in my school
   (C) despite my misgivings about the teachers
   (D) let's face it

❽ On the other hand, I am able to find interesting articles and blogs to divert my attention from studying.

8. Which option would provide the best conclusion to the paragraph?
   (A) NO CHANGE
   (B) Instead, I am able to buckle down when I need to read an antiquated historical document or a chapter about balancing chemical equations.
   (C) Middle school was a tough time for me in general—it was difficult for me to figure out to which group I really belonged.
   (D) After all, online videos are far more interesting than the boring films our teachers force upon us in school.

Answer Explanations

1. **(A)** The paragraph shows a shift in the narrator's attitude toward reading—as a young child, she enjoyed reading, and as she progressed in school, she lost her joy in reading. Choice (A) best introduces this paragraph because it is the only option that previews this transition in attitude. Choices (B) and (D) are simply positive, and choice (C) is too loosely related to what follows.

2. **(D)** The previous sentence establishes that the narrator has lost joy in reading. The current sentence serves to explain how this shift in attitude came about—namely, rather than reading recreationally, the narrator was required to read certain texts. Choice (D) is the only option that shows this contrast. Choices (A) and (B) both show cause and effect, and choice (C) indicates a list.

3. **(C)** A cause-and-effect transition is needed here because the narrator is stating that she has to take notes so that she could be prepared for the test upon her return from vacation—choice (C) is the only option that provides a cause-and-effect transition.

4. **(A)** The paragraph as a whole states that the narrator became progressively less interested in reading as it became something she was required to do, instead of something she chose to do. Choice (A) makes sense in this context because it provides an analogy that shows how being forced to watch a movie for school makes the experience much less enjoyable. Choices (B), (C), and (D) are somewhat connected to the sentence but are not relevant to the paragraph.

5. **(B)** The sentence that comes before this makes the general point that it is easier to read books that are interesting to you. The remainder of the current sentence states that the narrator is fine with taking notes and highlighting words if doing so will help her better understand a story she finds interesting. Choice (B) is the best option because it provides a transition indicating a clarification. None of the other options indicates a clarification is taking place—choices (A) and (D) show contrast, and choice (C) shows certainty.

6. **(C)** This sentence should be placed before sentence 2 because it provides a logical transition after sentence 1, which states that the English teacher helped the narrator become interested once again in reading. Without having this sentence moved to this place,

the paragraph would not have a clear elaboration on how the teacher accomplished this shift in the narrator's attitude. All of the other options would prevent this clear elaboration from taking place.

7. **(D)** "Let's face it" uses concise language that matches the relatively informal tone of the essay. Choice (A) is too wordy and extreme, choice (B) is illogical and irrelevant, and choice (C) changes the emphasis from the reading requirements to the teachers themselves.

8. **(B)** This paragraph states that the narrator now has a mindset that enables her to read material that is academic and dry. Choice (B) concludes this paragraph well because it concretely illustrates how being able to read less entertaining texts can be helpful. Choice (A) confuses the intended meaning, and choices (C) and (D) are too disconnected from the topic of the paragraph.

Notes Analysis Questions

A new type of question on the Digital PSAT is the notes analysis question. You will be asked to consider the notes that a student has taken on a topic and determine the best way to use the information in the notes to present or emphasize a particular idea. On questions like these, be sure to really focus on what the question asks so that you can zero in on the most relevant evidence.

❯ Example

While researching a topic, a student has taken the following notes:

- A solar eclipse occurs when the moon passes between the Earth and sun, thereby blocking the sun's light.
- Some solar eclipses are partial, in which some of the sunlight is obscured by the moon.
- On rare occasions, there can be a total solar eclipse in which the moon fully blocks the sun's circular disk.
- Astronomy enthusiasts sometimes travel to the site of a solar eclipse to observe it, since at any given spot on the Earth, it may take about four centuries for an eclipse to occur.
- Ancient societies understandably were unsettled by solar eclipses, since they often feared some unusual supernatural force was at work.

The student wants to draw a contrast between partial and total solar eclipses. Which choice most effectively uses relevant information from the notes to accomplish this goal?

(A) Even though it might take nearly 400 years for a total solar eclipse, it is exciting to see one if possible.

(B) Since ancient societies felt that eclipses were the result of supernatural forces, they did not see any difference between total and partial eclipses.

(C) A total eclipse occurs when the moon is between the Earth and Sun, whereas a partial eclipse occurs when the Earth is between the moon and sun.

(D) While a partial eclipse some of the sun's light, a total eclipse will fully block the sun's circular disk.

Explanation

The question asks you to draw a contrast between a partial and total solar eclipse. Choice **D** effectively accomplishes this task by incorporating the information about the partial eclipse only blocking out some of the sun's light, while a total eclipse blocks out the sun's circular disk. It is not Choice A because it does not highlight a difference between the two types of eclipse. It is not Choice B because it ignores the possibility of a difference between the eclipse types. It is not C because both eclipse types occur when the moon is between the Earth and Sun.

Notes Analysis Practice

1. While researching a topic, a student has taken the following notes:

   - People hold their writing utensil in many ways.
   - A functional grasp is one that produces legible writing and does not cause pain or inefficiency for the writer.
   - An inefficient grasp can cause illegible writing, pain, very slow writing, and excessive fatigue when writing.
   - Three common functional writing utensil grasps are dynamic tripod, quadrupod, and modified tripod.
   - Many people write using a grasp that falls outside of the common functional grasps. As long as the unique grasp is functional for the individual and not inefficient, there is no cause for concern.

   The student wants to emphasize the potential negative consequences if someone does not hold a pen properly. Which choice most effectively uses relevant information from the notes to accomplish this goal?

   (A) An inefficient grasp is less preferable than a functional one.
   (B) Individuals can decide as to what type of grasp best suits them.
   (C) Without a proper grasp of the writing utensil, pain, fatigue, and slow writing may result.
   (D) Increased legibility might be an undesirable outcome of not holding a pen properly.

2. While researching a topic, a student has taken the following notes:

   - The French Legion of Honor is an award for great personal and professional merit.
   - This award is given to both military and non-military recipients.
   - Following similar categories to ranks of chivalry, the Legion of Honor was established by Napoleon Bonaparte in 1802.
   - The American Congressional Medal of Honor is the highest military decoration in the United States.
   - The Medal of Honor was established during the U.S. Civil War to recognize those who distinguished themselves with acts of bravery.

The student wants to describe a difference between the general types of recipients of the Medal of Honor and Legion of Honor. Which choice most effectively uses relevant information from the notes to accomplish this goal?

(A) Though the Medal of Honor is given to members of the military, the Legion of Honor is given only to citizens who are not in the armed forces.

(B) While both military and non-military persons can receive the Legion of Honor, the Medal of Honor is given to military recipients.

(C) The French Legion of Honor was established at an earlier historical date than the U.S. Medal of Honor.

(D) The U.S. Medal of Honor deemphasizes recognition of accomplishment, while the French Legion of Honor seeks to reestablish a medieval feudal order.

3. While researching a topic, a student has taken the following notes:

- The creator of "Star Wars" is George Lucas.
- George Lucas made episodes 4–6 and waited to make episodes 1–3 until further technological advancement.
- Lucas Films produced the movies which were later bought by Disney in 2012.
- Upon Disney taking over the "Star Wars" franchise, Dave Filoni and Jon Favreau became the new creative directors.
- As of 2022, there have been 9 core films, multiple spinoffs, and tv shows.

The student wants to highlight the change in the management of the Star Wars franchise at a particular point in time. Which choice most effectively uses relevant information from the notes to accomplish this goal?

(A) The number of Star Wars films created—at least nine as of 2022—is quite impressive.

(B) Dave Filoni, Jon Favreau, and George Lucas are among the persons who have managed the famous Star Wars franchise.

(C) While initially created by George Lucas, Disney took over the Star Wars franchise in 2012.

(D) George Lucas, famously known as the creator of Star Wars, held off on making new Star Wars films until technology could advance.

4. While researching a topic, a student has taken the following notes:

- Many people experience eye floaters.
- Eye floaters often appear as clear squiggles or small spots that float across the field of vision.
- Eye floaters appear as they do because they are shadows cast on the retina from small stuck-together pieces of vitreous in the eye.
- Most of the time, eye floaters are not a cause for concern, but they can have serious causes, such as retinal detachment.
- If there is a sudden change in eye floaters, an eye care professional should be alerted.

The student wants to emphasize floater symptoms that should not prompt concern. Which choice most effectively uses relevant information from the notes to accomplish this goal?

(A) If the retina becomes detached, be sure to seek out a doctor.

(B) When the spots from floaters rapidly increase, try to remain calm.

(C) Stuck-together pieces of vitreous in the eye can cause one's vision to be impeded.

(D) Consistently small squiggles in the field of vision are likely nothing to worry about.

5. While researching a topic, a student has taken the following notes:

- Digestion means the breakdown of food.
- There are two kinds of digestion: chemical and mechanical.
- Chemical digestion is the breakdown of food through enzymes and hormones.
- Mechanical digestion is simply breaking down the food into smaller pieces.
- In the mouth, chewing (a mechanical digestive process) is the main type of digestion that occurs, but small amounts of salivary amylase are released to chemically degrade starches.

The student wants to point out a similarity between chemical and mechanical digestion. Which choice most effectively uses relevant information from the notes to accomplish this goal?

(A) Chemical and mechanical digestion equally contribute to the digestion that takes place in the mouth.

(B) While mechanical digestion is more prevalent in the mouth, chemical digestion is more prevalent in the intestines.

(C) Both mechanical and chemical digestion involve breaking down food.

(D) Saliva is used as a key component of both mechanical and chemical digestion.

Answer Explanations

1. **(C)** This option is the only choice that accomplishes the goal of showing what negative consequences will result from not holding a pen correctly. Choices A and B do not focus on negative consequences, and Choice D is a positive outcome.

2. **(B)** This option accurately points out that there is a general difference between the possible recipients of the two honors since civilians are only eligible for the Legion of Honor. The other options do not accurately reflect the information in the notes.

3. **(C)** This question asks the student to highlight a small portion of the information presented, namely about how the management of the franchise changed at a point in time. Choice C is the only option that connects to the change in management.

4. **(D)** This choice is the only option that emphasizes specific symptoms of floaters—like small squiggles—that should not make patients worry. Choices A and B focus on more severe symptoms, and Choice C focuses on the causes of floaters.

5. **(C)** This option points out a similarity between chemical and mechanical digestion—they both break down food. Choice A is not supported by the given information. Choice B points out a difference. Choice D is inaccurate since saliva is involved in chemical, not mechanical digestion.

Sentence Structure

Sentence Fragments and Run-On Questions

A **sentence** *expresses a complete thought with both a subject and predicate (i.e., a subject and a verb)*. A subject will be a noun—a person, place, or thing. The predicate will have a verb—a word that expresses an *action*, such as "is," "were," "ate," "choose," or "eat." Here are some examples of complete sentences:

What is this?
He won the match.
There is great trouble brewing in the town.

A **sentence fragment** *expresses an incomplete thought. It typically has just a subject or a predicate.* Here are some examples of sentence fragments:

From my place.
Homework for tomorrow's big test.
Your neighbor's house, which is next to the spooky mansion on the hill.

A **run-on sentence** *consists of two or more complete sentences that are not joined together with appropriate punctuation or transitions*. Here are some examples of run-on sentences.

Finish your meal it is really good for you to do so.
I was excited to see the new show I stayed up really late to see it.
The moon will be full tonight, let's stay up and enjoy its beauty.

Tactic: Evaluate Whether a Sentence Is Complete by Determining If It Has a Subject and a Verb—Don't Make Assumptions Based Simply on the Length of the Sentence.

A sentence can be complete while being quite short. For example, "I am" is a complete sentence. A selection can be a fragment even though it is rather long. For example, "For the benefit of the United States of America, today, tomorrow, and in the years to come" is a fragment. Consider each sentence on a case-by-case basis to make a determination.

❯ Example

We will need to get to the bottom of this news _____ he is a winner in the hotly contested election.

8. Which choice completes the text so that in conforms to the conventions of Standard English?
   (A) story. Whether
   (B) story. If
   (C) story. Whether or not
   (D) story as to whether

Choices (A), (B), and (C) all have a sentence fragment after the period. Choice (D) is the only option that joins the wording together in a way that provides one complete sentence.

Sentence Structure Drill

Determine if the sentence is complete, a run-on, or a fragment.

1. To whom this letter may concern.
2. She wept.
3. I am looking forward to the movie I plan on standing in line for a couple of hours.

4. Whenever they leave the doors unlocked of their brand new automobile.

5. My best friend, whom I have known since childhood, will be visiting from out of town this upcoming weekend.

Answers

1. Fragment
2. Complete
3. Run-on
4. Fragment
5. Complete

Modifier Placement Questions

Consider these two improper sentences:

The fish loved its new aquarium, swimming quickly.

While reading the brand new book, many people were annoying.

These two sentences have confusing meaning. The first sentence literally expressed that the aquarium is swimming quickly. In the second sentence, it is unclear who is reading the new book. These sentences can be fixed by making sure the modifying words, like adjectives, and the words they modify, like nouns, are clearly stated and in a proper sequence. Here are proper versions of the two sentences:

The fish, swimming quickly, loved its new aquarium.

While I was reading the brand new book, many people annoyed me.

When it comes to modifier clarity and placement, remember this tip:

Tactic: Make Sure That the *Literal* Meaning and the *Intended* Meaning Are the Same.

> **Example**

My teacher asked me a question, but _____ a prompt response.

22. Which choice completes the text so that in conforms to the conventions of Standard English?
    (A) too tired was I for giving
    (B) giving was too tired for me
    (C) I was giving too tired
    (D) I was too tired to give

To clearly express what is doing the action, "I" should follow the "but." Choices (A) and (B) have convoluted word order. Choice (C) has the correct placement of "I," but jumbles the wording later in the selection. Choice (D) has clarity of wording and a logical sequence throughout.

Modifier Placement Drill

Make corrections, if needed, to give the sentences proper modifier placement and word order. There are multiple ways to fix these sentences.

1. While reading the book, forgot to leave a bookmark I did.

2. My car was unavailable for the road trip, which was in the repair shop.

3. The player's last game was rather abysmal, not practice very well leading up to it.

4. Route 1 was a beautiful stretch of freeway on our way to vacation, a six-lane superhighway.

5. Read all the way to the end of the book, and confusion will be replaced with clarity.

Answers with Possible Corrections

1. While reading the book, **I forgot to leave a bookmark.**

2. My car**, which was in the repair shop,** was unavailable for the road trip.

3. The player's last game was rather abysmal **since he did** not practice very well leading up to it.

4. Route 1, **a six-lane superhighway,** was a beautiful stretch of freeway on our way to vacation.

5. Fine as is. The sentence implies that the reader is being directly addressed.

Verb Use Questions

The PSAT requires you to be comfortable with the essentials of verb conjugation. Most students become familiar with the terminology for proper verb conjugation when they take a foreign language in high school—here is an overview of the key verb conjugation information that you may already know intuitively.

Table 3.1 contains a summary of some of the basic conjugation patterns of verbs.

Table 3.1 Basic Verb Conjugations

Past	Present	Future
He ate They were She ran We walked	He eats They are She runs We walk	He will eat They will She will run We will walk
Past Perfect	**Present Perfect**	**Future Perfect**
I had eaten They had been She had run We had walked	I have eaten They have been She has run We have walked	I will have eaten They will have been She will have run They will have walked

Although many verbs follow a simple pattern, quite a few verbs have irregular conjugations, particularly for the past and past perfect forms. These irregular verbs are often called "strong" verbs since they form a past tense without the aid of the "ed" ending as with "weak" verbs. Table 3.2 shows a sampling of some irregular verbs you might encounter.

Table 3.2 Irregular Verb Conjugations

Present Tense (*I am.*)	Past Tense (*I was.*)	Past Participle (What comes after "have" in the Present Perfect— *"I have been."*)
Become	Became	Become
Begin	Began	Begun
Bring	Brought	Brought
Choose	Chose	Chosen
Do	Did	Done
Draw	Drew	Drawn
Drink	Drank	Drunk
Drive	Drove	Driven

Present Tense (*I am.*)	Past Tense (*I was.*)	Past Participle (What comes after "have" in the Present Perfect— "*I have been.*")
Fly	Flew	Flown
Get	Got	Gotten
Go	Went	Gone
Grow	Grew	Grown
Have	Had	Had
Hear	Heard	Heard
Know	Knew	Known
Lay (i.e., place)	Laid	Laid
Lead	Led	Led
Lie (i.e., recline)	Lay	Lain
Light	Lit	Lit
Ride	Rode	Ridden
Ring	Rang	Rung
Rise	Rose	Risen
Run	Ran	Run
See	Saw	Seen
Shine	Shone	Shone
Show	Showed	Shown
Sing	Sang	Sung
Sink	Sank	Sunk
Swim	Swam	Swum
Swing	Swung	Swung
Take	Took	Taken
Wake	Woke	Woken
Wear	Wore	Worn

Tactic: Look at the Context Surrounding the Verb to See What Verb Tense, Mood, or Voice Is Appropriate.

> ### Example

Three years ago on our trip to India, we visited Humayan's Tomb and _____ the Siddhivinayak Temple.

24. Which choice completes the text so that in conforms to the conventions of Standard English?
    (A) see
    (B) saw
    (C) seeing
    (D) shall see

The sentence refers to events that took place three years ago, making the entire sentence in the past tense. Choice (B) is the only option in the past tense. Choice (A) is in the present tense, choice (C) uses the gerund form of the verb, and choice (D) uses the future tense.

Verb Use Drill

Make corrections, if needed, to give the sentences proper verb use. There are multiple ways to fix these sentences.

1. A decade ago, I decide to focus more intently on my studies.
2. The customer service message needs to be answered by you.
3. If you was able to find a job, you would not have the financial worries you currently did.
4. In 1992, Caitlin won the prize, but only after she practice for many months.
5. My teacher demands that I am quiet during the test.

Answers with Possible Corrections

1. A decade ago I **decided** to focus more intently on my studies. *Put it in the past tense since it was a decade ago.*
2. **You need to answer** the customer service message. *Avoid the passive voice—use the active voice instead.*
3. If you **were** able to find a job, you would not have the financial worries you currently **do**. *Use the subjunctive mood to express something contrary to fact, and use the present tense since the sentence says "currently."*
4. In 1992, Caitlin won the prize, but only after she **had practiced** for many months. *Use the past perfect tense to indicate that the practice was ongoing for a period in the past.*
5. My teacher demands that I **be** quiet during the test. *Since this is a demand, use "be" rather than "is."*

Pronoun Number Questions

Matching pronouns with the nouns they represent is easy when the words are close to each other. For example,

Jennifer ate her entire lunch.

It becomes more challenging to match pronouns when the pronouns and the nouns are more separated. For example,

The man who left the calculator on top of the board games cabinet needs to pick up his property.

Tactic: Match Singular Pronouns with Singular Nouns and Plural Pronouns with Plural Nouns.

Even though the pronouns and nouns may be separated from one another, be sure they are numerically consistent. These types of questions take a bit more focus because simply "mouthing them out" won't necessarily alert you to a grammatical problem; the separation between the pronouns and nouns makes the sentences sound pretty good as they are.

❯ Example

When two scientists work together, _____ become smarter than would be possible if working independently.

3. Which choice completes the text so that in conforms to the conventions of Standard English?
   (A) he
   (B) you
   (C) they
   (D) it

In the first part of the sentence, "two scientists" are mentioned as working together—this is a plural subject. So, it would be logical to have the plural pronoun "they" match up with this. The other pronouns are singular, and so would not work.

Pronoun Number Drill

Make corrections, if needed, to give the sentences proper pronoun number. There are multiple ways to fix these sentences.

1. No matter your feelings on the vote, be sure that you are true to oneself.
2. Whenever I see someone struggling with math, I can't help but wonder if they missed some of the fundamentals earlier in school.
3. A sperm whale will probably have scars from deep-sea battles with giant squids all over their skin.
4. Members of the orchestra have to submit practice records before you are allowed to attend rehearsal.
5. Skilled surgeons are likely quite proud of their training.

Answers with Possible Corrections

1. No matter your feelings on the vote, be sure that you are true to **yourself**. *Keep it consistent with "your" throughout.*
2. Whenever I see someone struggling with math, I can't help but wonder if **he or she** missed some of the fundamentals earlier in school. *This is referring to a singular person given the use of "someone."*
3. A sperm whale will probably have scars from deep-sea battles with giant squids all over **its** skin. *This refers to "a" sperm whale, so use the singular.*
4. Members of the orchestra have to submit practice records before **they** are allowed to attend rehearsal. *"They" will be consistent with "members of the orchestra."*
5. No change is needed to this sentence because "surgeons" is plural and "their" is also plural.

Sentence Structure Skill-Building

❶ The increased use of smartphones and Internet technology profoundly interaction with our friends and family. Class reunions and opening holiday

1. (A) NO CHANGE
   (B) The increased use of smartphones and Internet technology have profoundly influenced how we interact with our friends and family.
   (C) The increased using of smartphones and Internet technology had profoundly affected how we will interact with our friends and family.
   (D) The increased use of smartphones and Internet technology has profoundly affected how we interact with our friends and family.

greeting cards ❷ <u>was once</u> highly anticipated events that would offer updates on the goings-on of distant acquaintances. Now, a quick scan of a social media feed gives a real-time update. On the other hand, look at any group of people out for dinner or just hanging out, and you will inevitably find many of the group members buried in their phones, ❸ <u>immersed in their own stimulation instead of meaningful interactions to be had with the people right in front of them.</u> Is it possible to have both the blessings of instantaneous communication and the minimization of the effects of distraction and ❹ <u>dehumanization</u>?

It is possible to do so if we put ourselves on an "information diet." Instead of having your phone set to notify you every time there is a message or a new post, give ❺ <u>oneself</u> a reasonable schedule for updates. If you are working on a major project with other people, ❻ <u>and</u> you should probably check your phone more frequently. If you are on vacation, take advantage of "away" messages and ❼ <u>as your gatekeeper let the computer serve,</u> informing people that you will be available to respond upon your return. If you can take control of technology rather than letting it control you, you ❽ <u>will be</u> empowered to have the benefits of new technology while minimizing its pitfalls.

2. (A) NO CHANGE
   (B) has been the
   (C) were once
   (D) is now

3. (A) NO CHANGE
   (B) immersed in stimulation of their own instead of with the people right in front of them having meaningful interactions.
   (C) immersed in their own stimulation instead of having meaningful interactions with the people right in front of them.
   (D) immersed with the people right in front of them with meaningful interactions instead in their own stimulation.

4. (A) NO CHANGE
   (B) dehumanizing
   (C) to dehumanize
   (D) for the dehumanizing

5. (A) NO CHANGE
   (B) yourself
   (C) themselves
   (D) us

6. (A) NO CHANGE
   (B) but
   (C) because
   (D) DELETE the underlined portion.

7. (A) NO CHANGE
   (B) the computer you should let as your gatekeeper serve,
   (C) let the computer serve as your gatekeeper,
   (D) the computer should be served by you as the gatekeeper,

8. (A) NO CHANGE
   (B) shall
   (C) had been
   (D) have

Answer Explanations

1. **(D)** Choice (D) uses parallel structure and proper tense to make a clear, flowing sentence. Choice (A) is a sentence fragment. Choice (B) uses the plural "have" instead of "has" to match up with the singular "use." Choice (C) improperly uses "using" instead of "use."

2. **(C)** Choice (C) uses a plural and past tense verb, "were," which is consistent with the fact that this refers to a past state of affairs, and that there is a compound subject of "reunions" and "cards." All of the other choices use singular verb forms.

3. **(C)** Choice (C) puts the words in the most logical and flowing order and clarifies the meaning of the sentence. Choice (A) does not have a parallel structure, choice (B) has jumbled word order with the phrase "instead of with the people right in front of them having," and choice (D) changes the intended meaning.

4. **(A)** Choice (A) is the only option to use wording that parallels the "communication" and "distraction" that come before in the sentence. Choices (B), (C), and (D) all convey the same idea, but they do not do so in a way consistent with the rest of the sentence.

5. **(B)** The author is directly addressing the reader using the informal second person in this sentence, earlier stating "your phone" and "notify you." To be consistent with this wording, "yourself" is correct. The other options are inconsistent with the use of "you" elsewhere in the sentence.

6. **(D)** The "If" at the beginning of the sentence already serves to create an implied transition. Because of this, no transitional word is needed at this point.

7. **(C)** Choice (C) maintains the parallel structure established earlier in the sentence in which the narrator directly addresses the reader, stating that he or she should "take advantage." The other options all lack this parallel structure.

8. **(A)** Choice (A) is the only option that properly uses the future tense. Choice (B) could work if it said "shall be," and choices (C) and (D) both would be used to refer to past actions.

Conventions of Usage

Pronoun Clarity Questions

Pronouns can improve the flow of one's writing. Consider this sentence:

Bill went to Bill's house before Bill decided what Bill was going to have for Bill's dinner.

It would be far preferable to rewrite the sentence like this:

Bill went to his house before deciding what he was going to have for dinner.

The second version is far less choppy because it doesn't continually reintroduce the subject. If what a pronoun refers to is unclear, clarification is needed. For example:

Mark and Jason could not wait to see his new car.

There are two men mentioned—Mark and Jason—but we do not know whose car they cannot wait to see since the "his" could refer to either Mark or Jason. The sentence could be fixed by saying "Mark and Jason could not wait to see Mark's new car." If a PSAT question clarifies a vague pronoun with a noun, *do not worry about whether the replacement is true*—focus only on if the substitution is grammatically correct.

Tactic: Pronouns Are Fine to Use, as Long as What They Stand for Is 100 Percent Clear.

If what the pronoun stands for is not 100 percent clear, choose an option that provides a clarification.

> **Example**

When I go to Susan and Marsha's hometown, I love to visit with _____ family.

14. Which choice completes the text so that in conforms to the conventions of Standard English?
(A) her
(B) this
(C) Susan's
(D) they're

Susan and Marsha both live in the same town, but the narrator has not made clear which of the two families she wishes to visit. Choice (C) is the only option that clarifies which family the narrator will see. Choice (A) could refer to either Susan or Marsha. Choice (B) is also vague. Choice (D) means "they are" and is not a possessive pronoun.

Pronoun Clarity Drill

Make corrections, if needed, to clarify vague pronouns. There are multiple ways to fix these sentences.

1. At the business, they do a nice job of making customers happy.
2. Whenever Kristen decides to take on a project, she always manages to do an excellent job.
3. Eloise laughed with her mother as she told the funny story.
4. Soon after the school contracted with the company, they were disappointed.
5. My brother enjoyed reading the book by the famous author that opened his mind to the new possibilities of space travel.

Answers with Possible Corrections

When a pronoun is vague, there are many possible ways it can be clarified. On the PSAT, as long as the substitution for a vague pronoun is grammatically appropriate, it is a valid choice.

1. At the business, **the sales associates** do a nice job of making customers happy.
2. Fine as is.
3. Eloise laughed with her mother as **Eloise** told the funny story.
4. Soon after the school contracted with the company, **the school officials** were disappointed.
5. My brother enjoyed reading the book by the famous author—**it opened my brother's** mind to the new possibilities of space travel.

Possession Questions

The PSAT will assess your understanding of possessive pronouns. Table 3.3 summarizes what you need to know.

Table 3.3 Possessive Pronouns

Pronoun	Meaning	Example
There vs. Their vs. They're	*there:* place *their:* possession *they're:* "they are"	They're excited to implement their new ideas when they travel over there.
Its vs. It's	*its:* possession *it's:* "it is" (*its'* is always incorrect)	It's a great day to take the car to be washed and vacuum all of its carpeting.
Your vs. You're	*your:* possession *you're:* "you are"	Your best friend tells you when you're not acting like yourself.
Whose vs. Who's	*whose:* possession *who's:* "who is"	Who's about to decide whose project wins the grand prize?

Tactic: Pronouns That Show Possession Do Not Have Apostrophes, Unlike Most Nouns.

Pronouns that use apostrophes are the contraction forms, like "they're" and "you're." Pronouns are different from most other words in that they show possession without apostrophes.

⟩ Example

When you try to turn on your computer, be sure that _____ plugged into the wall outlet.

18. Which choice completes the text so that in conforms to the conventions of Standard English?
    - (A) it's
    - (B) its
    - (C) its'
    - (D) it is going to be

In the above sentence, the required meaning of the underlined portion is "it is," making choice (A) correct. Choice (B) is used to show possession, choice (C) is never correct, and choice (D) is too wordy.

Possession Drill

Make corrections, if needed, to clarify possession. There are multiple ways to fix these sentences.

1. The chair was nonfunctional—its' legs no longer worked.
2. You're patience is appreciated as you wait for the next customer service representative.
3. I am confident that they're going to be on time.
4. Whose calculator needs new batteries?
5. While it's a nice day, please be sure to wash your car—it's windows are filthy.

Answers with Possible Corrections

1. The chair was nonfunctional—**its** legs no longer worked.
2. **Your** patience is appreciated as you wait for the next customer service representative.
3. Fine as is.
4. Fine as is.
5. While it's a nice day, please be sure to wash your car—**its** windows are filthy.

Subject-Verb Agreement Questions

Subject-verb agreement would be easy to determine if all sentences had the subject and verb close to one another. For example,

Birds fly in the air.

When the subject and verb are separated from each other, creating agreement can be more challenging. For example,

The movie about the terrifying monsters and evil ghosts were most frightening.

The subject "movie" and the verb "were" do not match numerically. Here is the corrected version:

The movie about the terrifying monsters and evil ghosts was most frightening.

When you encounter subject-verb agreement questions remember this next tactic.

Tactic: Cut Out the Words Between the Subject and Verb to See If the Subject and Verb Are Both Singular or Both Plural.

> **Example**

___

The general who led legions of soldiers
_____ triumphant in the battle.

25. Which choice completes the text so that in conforms to the conventions of Standard English?
    (A) were
    (B) are
    (C) was
    (D) have been

The subject in the sentence is "general," which is singular. Choice (C) is the only option that has a singular verb. Choices (A), (B), and (D) are all plural, and thus incorrect. It would be easy to be confused about the subject and think that it was the plural "legions" or "soldiers."

Number Agreement Drill

Make corrections, if needed, to a lack of number agreement. There are multiple ways to fix these sentences.

1. The company of actors do a wonderful production.
2. My teacher or his teaching assistant is in charge of grading the assignment.
3. Gender roles over the past century has evolved significantly.
4. My favorite summer diversion, reading and swimming, are quite enjoyable.
5. Each person on the train were glad to arrive at the destination.

Answers with Possible Corrections

1. The company of actors **does** a wonderful production.
2. Fine as is.
3. Gender roles over the past century **have** evolved significantly.
4. My favorite summer **diversions**, reading and swimming, are quite enjoyable.
5. Each person on the train **was** glad to arrive at the destination.

Punctuation

Proper use of punctuation is a major area that is tested on the PSAT. Tables 3.5 through 3.9 show the rules for proper usage of commas, semicolons, colons, dashes, and apostrophes. These tables also include examples showing the correct usage of punctuation marks.

Commas

Table 3.5 Comma Rules and Examples

General Rule	Proper Use
Separate a phrase (dependent clause) from a complete sentence (independent clause).	When you open your birthday present, remember to whom you should send thank you notes.
Join two complete sentences when there is a transitional word, like the "FANBOYS": *for, and, nor, but, or, yet,* and *so.*	I am eager to receive my PSAT test scores online, but they will not come out for several weeks.
Separate extra information from the rest of the sentence.	The Hubble Telescope, which orbits our planet, has provided fantastic pictures of deep space.
Separate items in a list with commas.[1]	I will order a pizza topped with cheese, pepperoni, mushrooms, and green peppers.
Don't use commas to separate parts of a sentence if everything in the sentence is needed to make it clear and logical. (In this case, clarifying that the boat is sinking).	The boat that is sinking needs Coast Guard personnel to come rescue its passengers.
Just because a sentence is long doesn't mean that it needs a comma. Look more at the structure of the sentence than at its length.	The Great Barrier Reef off the coast of Australia offers some of the best snorkeling and scuba diving anywhere in the world.
A clarifying parenthetical phrase needs to be separated with commas. If the name is sufficient to know who the person is, commas are needed to separate the description. If the description is too vague to precisely narrow down the item, then no commas should separate descriptive phrases.	Eddie George, winner of the 1995 Heisman Trophy, had a successful professional football career after college.

[1]The PSAT has traditionally preferred the serial or "Oxford" comma (i.e., having a comma between the second-to-last and last items in a list), but since there is not a universally accepted rule about whether the serial comma should be used, it is extremely unlikely that the PSAT would include a test question about it.

Comma Drill

Make changes, if needed, to the comma usage.

1. Joe Montana winner of multiple Super Bowls, is undoubtedly one of the best to ever play football.
2. You are doing pretty well but you could be doing even better.
3. No I did not call the doctor.
4. *Gone With the Wind,* a nearly four-hour-long movie is so long that it has an intermission.
5. The horse currently winning the race will probably finish first.

Answers

1. Joe Montana, winner of multiple Super Bowls, is undoubtedly one of the best to ever play football.
2. You are doing pretty well, but you could be doing even better.
3. No, I did not call the doctor.
4. *Gone With the Wind*, a nearly four-hour-long movie, is so long that it has an intermission.
5. Fine as is.

Semicolons

Table 3.6 Semicolon Rules and Examples

General Rule	Proper Use
You can use a semicolon to separate two complete, related sentences.	My friend did most of the driving on our trip; she has much better stamina than I do.
Use a semicolon to separate items in a list when each item has a comma or commas within it.	On my European trip during college, I went to Paris, France; London, England; and Rome, Italy.
Put a semicolon before a conjunctive adverb (e.g., however, consequently, and nevertheless) when it joins two independent clauses.	Be sure to wear a raincoat today; otherwise, you will be soaked.

Semicolon Drill

Make changes, if needed, to the semicolon usage.

1. Please clean up after yourself I don't want to find any messes.
2. My dad was convinced she was lying, however, I was not so sure.
3. Although my husband's snoring is quite annoying, I try my best to ignore it.
4. Cyberbullying is a major problem, consequently, we need to do something to stop it.
5. On our "foundation of the nation" vacation we traveled to Boston, Massachusetts, Philadelphia, Pennsylvania, and Washington, D.C.

Answers

1. Please clean up after yourself; I don't want to find any messes.
2. My dad was convinced she was lying; however, I was not so sure.
3. Fine as is.
4. Cyberbullying is a major problem; consequently, we need to do something to stop it.
5. On our "foundation of the nation" vacation we traveled to Boston, Massachusetts; Philadelphia, Pennsylvania; and Washington, D.C.

Colons

Table 3.7 Colon Rules and Examples

General Rule	Proper Use
Use a colon after a complete sentence to set off a list.	Whenever I go on a trip, I am certain to take the following items: my passport, a cell phone, and my wallet.
Use a colon after a complete sentence to set off a clarification. (A colon can work if it can be replaced by the word "namely.")	I was surprised at how my boyfriend proposed to me: he did so at the spot of our very first date.

Colon Drill

Make changes, if needed, to the colon usage.

1. Be sure to do the following in the interview, make eye contact, listen carefully, and answer from the heart.
2. I whiffed something burning from downstairs it was the stove.
3. Lead paint should be avoided it can cause lower intelligence and delayed growth.
4. The player had a major announcement: he was retiring for good.
5. Both of the job candidates have major flaws, one candidate is inexperienced and the other is unprofessional.

Answers

1. Be sure to do the following in the interview: make eye contact, listen carefully, and answer from the heart.
2. I whiffed something burning from downstairs: it was the stove.
3. Lead paint should be avoided: it can cause lower intelligence and delayed growth.
4. Fine as is.
5. Both of the job candidates have major flaws: one candidate is inexperienced and the other is unprofessional.

Dashes

Table 3.8 Dash Rules and Examples

General Rule	Proper Use
While other punctuation can often work (in this case, a colon or semicolon could work instead of the dash), the dash can provide variety in your writing when you need to indicate an interruption or change of thought.	Shut the door behind you—it is freezing outside.
A dash can be used to interrupt a sentence and provide a change of voice.	She won the prize—this came as no surprise to me—and shared her prize money with all her friends.
Dashes can set off a parenthetical phrase. If you start with a dash on one end of the phrase, you need to use a dash on the other end of it for consistency.	Summer vacation—considered by many educators to be outdated—is probably my favorite time of year.

Dash Drill

Make changes, if needed, to the dash usage.

1. Hold on a second please wait for me to finish.
2. Sam took just three things with him to class a laptop, reading glasses, and a ballpoint pen.
3. New York City—home of the Statue of Liberty and the Empire State Building, is a major tourist attraction.
4. My brand new phone charger does not work nearly as well as my old one did.
5. My stomach was full I couldn't eat another bite.

Answers

1. Hold on a second—please wait for me to finish.
2. Sam took just three things with him to class—a laptop, reading glasses, and a ballpoint pen.
3. New York City—home of the Statue of Liberty and the Empire State Building—is a major tourist attraction.
4. Fine as is.
5. My stomach was full—I couldn't eat another bite.

Apostrophes

Table 3.9 Apostrophe Rules and Examples

General Rule	Proper Use
Use an apostrophe before the "s" to indicate that a singular entity possesses something.	The cat's claws needed to be trimmed.
Use an apostrophe after the "s" to indicate that a plural entity possesses something.	The class officers' retreat was extremely productive.
Use an apostrophe before the "s" to indicate possession after an already-plural noun.	Children's theater is often far more interesting than adults'.

Apostrophe Drill

Make changes, if needed, to the apostrophe usage.

1. One dog's leash is sometimes just as expensive as two dog's leashes.
2. Womens restrooms frequently have longer lines than mens.
3. Your car's windows are so dirty I can write my name on them with my finger.
4. My one friends house is quite a bit more spacious than his.
5. Whale's skin is extremely thick in order to protect the animals from cold water.

Answers

1. One dog's leash is sometimes just as expensive as two **dogs'** leashes.
2. **Women's** restrooms frequently have longer lines than **men's**.
3. Fine as is.
4. My one **friend's** house is quite a bit more spacious than his.
5. **Whales'** skin is extremely thick in order to protect the animals from cold water.

Frequent Types of Punctuation Questions

End-of-Sentence Questions

It is unlikely that you will find an end-of-sentence punctuation question that asks you to identify the basic usage of a period or a question mark, since these concepts are typically mastered in elementary school.

Tactic: End-of-Sentence Punctuation Questions Will Probably Be About Unusual Situations.

> **Example**

My friend was wondering if it would be OK for me _____?

6. Which choice completes the text so that in conforms to the conventions of Standard English?

(A) to take him home?

(B) taking him home?

(C) to take him home.

(D) take him home!

Although the friend is asking a question, it is given indirectly. As a result, no question mark is needed, making choice (C) the correct choice. Choices (A) and (B) both improperly make this into a direct question, and choice (D) incorrectly makes this into an exclamation.

Items-in-a-Series Questions

As with end-of-sentence punctuation questions, items-in-a-series questions are unlikely to test basic concepts, such as knowing that a list of three or more items requires each item to be separated by punctuation of some kind. Be on the lookout for unusual situations with items in a series of questions, paying close attention to this next tactic.

Tactic: Make Sure the Punctuation Separates One Complete Item from Another.

❯ Example

When traveling in the Western United States, be sure to visit _____ _____.

19. Which choice completes the text so that in conforms to the conventions of Standard English?

(A) Yosemite National Park, Yellowstone National Park, and San Francisco.

(B) Yosemite National Park Yellowstone National Park, and San Francisco.

(C) Yosemite, National Park, Yellowstone National Park, and San Francisco.

(D) Yosemite National Park Yellowstone National Park and San Francisco.

Choice (A) is the only option that correctly separates each destination from one another. Choices (B) and (D) jumble the destination names together, and choice (C) breaks up "Yosemite National Park" unnecessarily.

Parenthetical-Phrase Questions

A parenthetical phrase provides extra, clarifying information that can be removed and the sentence will still be complete. For example,

My good friend Jen—a champion horseback rider—is one of the most talented people I have ever met.

Commas, dashes, and parentheses can all set off parenthetical phrases. Be sure of one thing:

Tactic: Start a Parenthetical Phrase in the Same Way That You End It.

If the parenthetical phrase begins with a comma, end it with a comma; if it starts with a dash, end it with a dash. Do not mix and match punctuation types in these cases.

> **Example**

The widely respected _____ _____ able to develop a solution to the seemingly intractable problem.

8. Which choice completes the text so that in conforms to the conventions of Standard English?

(A) engineer, winner of numerous industry awards—was

(B) engineer—winner of numerous industry awards—was

(C) engineer, winner of numerous industry awards was

(D) engineer winner of numerous industry awards was

The phrase "winner of numerous industry awards" is not essential to making this sentence complete, although it does provide helpful clarifying information. The only option that sets this phrase out of the way using consistent punctuation is choice (B). Choice (A) mixes a comma with a dash, and choices (C) and (D) do not set the parenthetical phrase aside.

Unnecessary-Punctuation Questions

Some students tend to over-punctuate, feeling that PSAT answer choices with more elaborate punctuation are more sophisticated. Other students tend to under-punctuate, picking options that read like a stream of consciousness.

Tactic: Find a Balance Between Too Much and Too Little Punctuation. Use Exactly What Is Needed, No More and No Less.

> **Example**

In the _____ _____ sure to enjoy time with your family and high school friends.

22. Which choice completes the text so that in conforms to the conventions of Standard English?

(A) summer months before, you start college, be

(B) summer months, before you start college be

(C) summer months before you start college, be

(D) summer months before you start college be

The introductory phrase of the sentence, "In the summer months before you start college," needs to be kept unified because it gives a precise description of the time period under discussion. Choices (A) and (B) interrupt this phrase. Choice (D) has no punctuation to separate the introductory clause from the complete sentence that follows. Choice (C) is the only option that correctly places a comma just after the introductory phrase.

Punctuation Skill-Building

The extent of one's extracurricular ❶ participation is a vital factor in college admissions decisions. There are innumerable ways to become involved in your school and ❷ community, running for class office, starting a new club, and volunteering as a tutor or mentor. Extracurricular participation should not be ❸ burdensome you should find activities that you find enjoyable and pursue them with passion. ❹ Despite what many people think, selective colleges are looking for a well-rounded class, not necessarily well-rounded students. What do we mean ❺ by this! An elite college would rather have a community of specialists than a group of generalists. ❻ So in choosing your extracurricular activity; go for in-depth involvement in one or two areas instead of superficial involvement in many areas.

1. (A) NO CHANGE
   (B) participation, is a vital factor in college admissions decisions.
   (C) participation is a vital factor, in college admissions decisions.
   (D) participation, is a vital factor in college, admissions decisions.

2. (A) NO CHANGE
   (B) community running, for class office starting
   (C) community running for class office; starting
   (D) community: running for class office, starting

3. (A) NO CHANGE
   (B) burdensome, you should
   (C) burdensome—you should
   (D) burdensome; you, should

4. (A) NO CHANGE
   (B) Despite what many people—think selective
   (C) Despite what many people think selective
   (D) Despite—what many people think—selective

5. (A) NO CHANGE
   (B) by this? An
   (C) by this. An
   (D) by this; an

6. (A) NO CHANGE
   (B) So, in choosing your extracurricular activity, go
   (C) So, in choosing your extracurricular activity; go
   (D) So, in choosing your extracurricular activity: go

Answers

1. **(A)** Even though this is a longer phrase, no commas are required. Choices (B) and (D) would separate the subject from the verb, and choice (C) interrupts the phrase "factor in college admissions."

2. **(D)** A colon is appropriate here as it sets off a list of three different ways that one can become involved. Choices (A) and (B) do not provide a sufficient pause, and choice (C) does not work because a semicolon must have a complete sentence both before and after.

3. **(C)** The dash provides an appropriately heavy pause to break up the two independent clauses. Choice (A) provides no break, choice (B) makes this a run-on sentence, and choice (D) has a comma inappropriately placed after "you."

4. **(A)** Choice (A) has a comma after the introductory dependent clause. Choice (B) places the pause too soon, choice (C) has no breaks at all, and choice (D) has too many breaks.

5. **(B)** This is the only option that correctly treats this as a question. Given the first part of the sentence, "What do we mean . . . ," it is clear that this should take the form of a question.

6. **(B)** This option correctly places commas around the parenthetical phrase. Choices (A), (C), and (D) are all incorrect because there must be a complete sentence before both a semicolon and a colon—"So, in choosing your extracurricular activity" is instead a fragment.

Skill-Building Exercises

Punctuation Exercise

Recovering History

The title of Erna ❶ Brodber's third novel, *Louisiana,* has a triple meaning: it refers to a state in the United States, a place of the same name in Jamaica, and the name taken by Ella ❷ Townsend the novel's protagonist. Ultimately, the word's fluidity emphasizes the connection between African Americans and African Caribbeans, as well as between the living and dead. The eponymous ❸ protagonist: a Colombian anthropology student ventures to St. Mary, Louisiana, to study Black folk life and, instead, finds herself taken over by the spirit of Mammy. Mammy, formally civil rights activist Sue Ann Grant King and more generally called Anna, is Ella's research target. A matriarch of

1. (A) NO CHANGE
   (B) Brodber's third novel *Louisiana*, has
   (C) Brodbers' third novel, *Louisiana* has
   (D) Brodber's third novel,
        Louisiana—has

2. (A) NO CHANGE
   (B) Townsend; the novel's protagonist.
   (C) Townsend, the novel's protagonist.
   (D) Townsend: the novels protagonist.

3. (A) NO CHANGE
   (B) protagonist, a Colombian anthropology student, ventures
   (C) protagonist, a Colombian anthropology student ventures
   (D) protagonist a Colombian anthropology student ventures

obscure but certain significance, Mammy gradually reveals her own history (as well as Ella's) via a psychic, spiritual ❹ connection that changes the young academic's trajectory in unexpected ways.

Ella Townsend earned a fellowship in 1936 to collect and record the history of Blacks of Southwest Louisiana using one of the university's first tape recorders but never returned. The text opens with a confusing transcript of multiple voices that are all but nonsense to the ❺ reader, Ella, later called Louisiana, endeavors for most of the novel to make sense of the data collected on the tape recorder, confronting her own preconceptions of voodoo and acknowledging her supernatural connection with two dead women, Anna (Mammy) and Louise. ❻ Ella embraces this spiritual connection only after listening through the tape recorder's reel and witnessing her own out-of-body experiences. Although she has no recollection of her interactions on the tape, she hears her voice speaking unintelligibly, a phenomenon that she must either investigate or accept as proof of her insanity.

After Mammy's funeral, Ella begins to understand the recorded transcript as a tri-party ❼ dialogue an interaction among her, Anna, and Anna's long-dead friend, Louise. Louisiana then gets her name by combining those of her spiritual sisters. When Caribbean sailors visit Ella and sing folk songs to her, Ella's past is revealed to her in a trance-like vision and formally initiates her into the art

4. (A) NO CHANGE
   (B) connection, that changes the young academic's trajectory in unexpected ways.
   (C) connection that changes, the young academic's trajectory, in unexpected ways.
   (D) connection that changes the young academics' trajectory, in unexpected ways.

5. (A) NO CHANGE
   (B) reader; Ella later called Louisiana, endeavors
   (C) reader: Ella—later called Louisiana, endeavors
   (D) reader; Ella, later called Louisiana, endeavors

6. (A) NO CHANGE
   (B) Ella embraces this spiritual connection, only after listening through, the tape recorder's reel and witnessing her own out-of-body experiences.
   (C) Ella embraces this spiritual connection only after listening through the tape recorder's reel; and witnessing her own out-of-body experiences.
   (D) Ella embraces this spiritual connection only after listening, through the tape recorder's reel and witnessing her own out-of-body experiences.

7. (A) NO CHANGE
   (B) dialogue—an interaction among her, Anna, and
   (C) dialogue, an interaction among her Anna and
   (D) dialogue; an interaction among her, Anna and

of prophecy. **8** <u>From then on: her journey is one of guiding</u> other diaspora in reliving their pasts and speaking with Louise and Anna to recover a communal history of resistance.

9 <u>Louisianas supernatural powers however, are</u> not universally commended. She faces isolation from academia, her parents, and the larger Western social sphere. When she finally completes her project and sketches out Mammy's family history, Louisiana nears death. The reader accompanies Louisiana on her revelation and expansion of the original transcription, engaging with oral folk traditions to rewrite history. Brodber's novel testifies to African **10** <u>survivals; folk traditions that</u> have made it through the Middle Passage.

8. (A) NO CHANGE
   (B) From then on, her journey is one of guiding
   (C) From then on; her journey is one of guiding
   (D) From then on her journey, is one of guiding

9. (A) NO CHANGE
   (B) Louisianas' supernatural powers, however are
   (C) Louisiana's supernatural powers, however are
   (D) Louisiana's supernatural powers, however, are

10. (A) NO CHANGE
    (B) survivals; folk traditions, that
    (C) survivals: folk traditions that
    (D) survivals: folk traditions, that

Answer Explanations

1. **(A)** "Erna Brodber" is a singular person. To show that she possesses the novel, the apostrophe must be placed like this: *Brodber's*. The name of the novel can also be set off/separated from the rest of the sentence by commas because the description that precedes it—Brodber's third novel—is sufficient to narrow down the information to exactly which novel it is. The answer is not choice (B) because there is not a comma after "novel." It is not choice (C) because of improper apostrophe and comma use. It is not choice (D) because the punctuation that starts and ends a parenthetical description must be consistent. Parenthetical information cannot start with a comma and end with a dash.

2. **(C)** This choice properly places a comma before the clarifying description; it also correctly uses the apostrophe and *s* after "novel" to indicate singular possession. Choice (A) is incorrect because there is no break before the clarifying phrase. The answer is not choice (B) because a semicolon must have a complete sentence both before and after it. Choice (D) is wrong because this option does not properly show possession.

3. **(B)** This is the only option that properly sets off the appositive phrase with commas. Choice (C) does so only at the beginning of the phrase. Choice (D) has no commas. Choice (A) does not correctly use the colon since a colon must have a complete sentence before it.

4. **(A)** There is no need to insert commas into this phrase since the phrase is describing an essential characteristic of the spiritual connection. All of the other options insert unnecessary punctuation.

5. **(D)** This choice separates the two independent clauses with a semicolon. Moreover, it surrounds the parenthetical phrase with commas. Choice (A) is wrong because this option results in a run-on sentence. Choice (B) is incorrect because there is not a comma at the beginning of the parenthetical phrase. The answer is not choice (C) because there is inconsistent punctuation around the parenthetical phrase.

6. **(A)** No additional punctuation is needed in this complete and logical sentence. Choices (B) and (D) insert unnecessary commas, which interrupt the sentence. Choice (C) does not have a complete sentence after the semicolon.

7. **(B)** A dash can provide the heavy pause needed to come before a clarification like this. The answer is not choice (A) because there is no pause between "dialogue" and the clarification that follows. It is not choice (C) because this option lacks needed commas to differentiate the items in the list. The answer is not choice (D) because there is not a complete sentence after the semicolon.

8. **(B)** This choice provides a break between the introductory phrase and the complete sentence that follows. The answer is not choice (A) because there is not a complete sentence before the colon. Choice (C) is incorrect because there is not a complete sentence before the semicolon. Choice (D) is wrong because the comma provides an interruption too late in the sentence.

9. **(D)** This is the only option that places needed commas around the word "however." In addition, this option properly uses the apostrophe to indicate singular ownership.

10. **(C)** This option provides a clear break before the clarification. The answer is not choice (A) or (B) because there is not a complete sentence after the semicolon. It is not choice (D) because there is an unnecessary comma after "traditions."

Transitions Skill-Building

The Benefits of Earthquakes

An earthquake results from tectonic plate activity, which starts from forces within the Earth that eventually break blocks of rock in the outer layers of the Earth. The rocks then move along a fault, or crack, ❶ and most of the energy that is released travels away from the fault in different types of seismic waves.

❷ Because earthquakes are often called natural disasters, in and of themselves, they

1. (A) NO CHANGE
   (B) but
   (C) since
   (D) while

2. (A) NO CHANGE
   (B) For
   (C) Although
   (D) Therefore

are part of the forces of nature that actually help to sustain life on Earth. ❸ On the other hand, the carbon cycle is made possible by plate tectonics, which, together with the water cycle, keep nutrients, water, and land available for life. This process also regulates the global temperature. Tectonic activity builds mountains and forms lakes and waterfalls as well, providing an environment in which plant and animal life can flourish. ❹ In addition to their contributions to Earth's habitability, earthquakes also help scientists to make discoveries. By using seismographs around the Earth to measure seismic waves, geophysicists can determine the structure of Earth's interior.

Despite these benefits, it is still common to think of the damage that earthquakes cause. ❺ Unfortunately, most earthquakes have not been disastrous. There are as many as a million earthquakes per year, ❻ because most occur below the oceans sometimes as deep as about 435 miles below the Earth's surface. There was also more tectonic plate activity earlier in Earth's history, which released trapped nutrients, methane, and hydrogen that provided sufficient energy for some life-forms. Providing for a greater diversity and amount of life ❼ although prepared an environment that could support advanced life. Today, the amount of earthquakes is not so great as to prevent humans from living in cities.

❽ Furthermore, some earthquakes are destructive. Such destruction, however, could be avoided. About ninety-five percent of earthquakes happen in the Pacific Belt and the Mediterranean Belt. Even though it is known where earthquakes are likely to happen with a strong degree of confidence, there are still

3. (A) NO CHANGE
   (B) For example,
   (C) As a result,
   (D) Nevertheless,

4. (A) NO CHANGE
   (B) Of
   (C) In consideration with
   (D) As a result of

5. (A) NO CHANGE
   (B) Also,
   (C) And,
   (D) However,

6. (A) NO CHANGE
   (B) but
   (C) with
   (D) moreover

7. (A) NO CHANGE
   (B) shall
   (C) in turn
   (D) as

8. (A) NO CHANGE
   (B) To illustrate,
   (C) Subsequently,
   (D) Nevertheless,

large cities in these areas that people have chosen to develop. Building cities ❾ <u>to</u> soft ground in earthquake-prone areas leads to more damage and a greater loss of life. Structures can be built that are able to withstand even the most intense earthquakes, but this has often not been done. While tectonic plate activity provides a number of benefits, moving to locations ❿ <u>when</u> earthquakes occur without the proper structures sometimes results in disasters.

9. (A) NO CHANGE
   (B) on
   (C) through
   (D) with

10. (A) NO CHANGE
    (B) which
    (C) where
    (D) that

Answer Explanations

1. **(A)** "And" correctly expresses that the author is simply continuing the line of thought from the first part of the sentence into the second part of the sentence.

2. **(C)** "Although" gives a contrast between the ideas that earthquakes are both natural disasters and life-sustaining events.

3. **(B)** "For example" connects the previous statement that earthquakes are life sustaining and the example of the carbon cycle that follows.

4. **(A)** "In addition to" connects the previous sentence, which focuses on some of the ways in which earthquakes make Earth more habitable, to the current sentence, which makes the additional statement that earthquakes help scientific research.

5. **(D)** The previous sentence acknowledges that there is a widespread belief that earthquakes are associated with damage. The current sentence states that this is not as widespread as is commonly thought, so the contrast that "however" provides is appropriate.

6. **(B)** "But" provides a contrast between the statement that there are so many earthquakes and the statement that many earthquakes happen deep within the planet.

7. **(C)** "In turn" is the only option that uses proper wording to express the cause-and-effect relationship within the sentence.

8. **(D)** The previous paragraph asserts that earthquakes are not all that harmful, while the current paragraph starts with the assertion that some earthquakes are destructive. Therefore, a contrasting word like "nevertheless" is appropriate.

9. **(B)** Although "building" can be paired with any of these options, in this context, "building on" is logical since one would build a city *on* the ground.

10. **(C)** Since the sentence is referring to physical locations, "where" is appropriate.

Expression of Ideas Practice Questions Set 1

1. While reading a social studies text about economics and inflation, a student takes the following notes:

- Inflation involves an increase in the money supply.
- Inflation is associated with increasing prices for goods and services.
- Those who have fixed prices for their long-term debt payments may find inflation beneficial.
  - Fixed debt payments will become relatively less expensive over time with inflation.
- Those who are on fixed incomes may find inflation detrimental.
  - Fixed income recipients may find their purchasing power decrease in an inflationary environment.

The student is doing a presentation in which she needs to create an example of a person who would most likely be harmed by inflation. Based on the notes, which of these examples would best accomplish the student's goal?

(A) A homeowner with fixed monthly mortgage payments

(B) A retiree on a pension with a set income every month

(C) A car owner who has $500 monthly payments until the car is fully paid off in five years

(D) A gardener who grows most of his food at home, thereby avoiding purchasing food at stores

2. Still, modernism isn't let off easy in Fitzgerald's well-liked short story. _____ Marjorie is preferred socially, she is flagrantly rude and always needing to be entertained.

Which choice completes the text with the most logical transition?

(A) When

(B) While

(C) Because

(D) Since

3. Journalism includes the gathering and distribution of news through a variety of mediums,

_____.

Which choice most specifically elaborates on the first part of this sentence?

(A) building upon the long-standing professional excellence with which journalism is associated.

(B) growing its reach to include urban, suburban, and rural population centers.

(C) which have recently expanded to incorporate smartphones, tablets, and blogs.

(D) demonstrating that seeking the average public opinion is most objective.

4. Athenians collected their most lavish possessions inside the Parthenon among a host of statues, sculptures, precious metals, and treasures taken in the conquest of the Persians. _____ the project and all it stood for were short-lived: just seven years after the Parthenon was constructed, war broke out with Sparta.

Which choice completes the text with the most logical transition?

(A) Yet,

(B) Additionally,

(C) In conclusion,

(D) As a result,

5. Some bat species have altered their mating and living habits to help protect themselves, and it is through observation of these adaptations that researchers _____, so preservationists can make the necessary interventions.

Which choice is most logically inserted in the underlined portion of the sentence?

(A) have decided how the species are thriving

(B) are learning which species are in the most danger

(C) are finding the preferred cultural associations of bats

(D) may locate major bat predators

6. Perhaps nowhere are timeless marital troubles better illustrated than in the second narrative of the suite, "The Clerk's Tale." _____ we find the greatest power imbalance of any of Chaucer's unhappy couples.

Which choice completes the text with the most logical transition?

(A) In the story of "The Clerk's Tale,"

(B) In this medieval narrative found in The Canterbury Tales,

(C) Here

(D) Therefore

7. I have found my work as a professional architect to be _____ Architects are rarely afforded a regular workweek. Instead, we spend hours upon hours preparing and re-preparing scale drawings, looking into environmental and safety regulations, and meeting with clients.

If the author wishes to express both the positive and negative nature of architecture, which of the following choices best accomplishes her goal?

(A) undoubtedly rewarding and mercilessly demanding.

(B) fearsomely boring and drearily trivial.

(C) moderately enjoyable and somewhat interesting.

(D) terribly impersonal and pleasantly dispassionate.

Answer Explanations

1. **(B)** The student wants to create an example of someone who is likely to be harmed by inflation. Based on the notes, someone who has fixed income payments would likely find inflation detrimental because their purchasing power would decrease over time. A retiree with a set income each month would fall under this description. It is not (A) or (C), because these represent fixed debt payments that would become relatively less expensive over time. It is not (D), because this person would not be significantly impacted by changes in the money supply since they do not need as much money to grow their own food as they would if they purchased the food at a store.

2. **(B)** *While* is the only option that provides a contrast within the sentence between how Marjorie is preferred socially and her rudeness.

3. **(C)** The first part of the sentence states that journalism gathers and distributes news in a wide variety of ways, and choice (C) gives specific examples of the technology that does this. Choices (A), (B), and (D) are irrelevant to the first part of the sentence.

4. **(A)** This is the only option that expresses the needed contrast between the previous sentence and the current one since there is a contrast between the glorious construction of the Parthenon and the fact that the glory was very short-lived. The other options do not express the needed contrast.

5. **(B)** Consider what immediately follows the insertion point—"so preservationists can make the necessary interventions." Preservationists would naturally be most interested in helping those species in need of intervention because the species were in danger of becoming extinct. So the statement *are learning which species are in the most danger* most logically connects to this. Choice (A) is the opposite of what is needed. Choice (C) is irrelevant. Even though choice (D) relates a bit to the information that follows, it does not give as strong a connection as choice (B) does. Preservationists would more likely find information about which bat species most need help more useful than information about bat predator locations.

6. **(C)** There is no need to repeat the name of the story, as choice (A) does, since it is mentioned immediately before this sentence. Choice (B) is not correct because it is wordy and adds no substance to the sentence. Choice (D) is incorrect because the current sentence is simply expanding on the previous one, not showing cause and effect.

7. **(A)** Stating that architecture is both *rewarding* and *demanding* clearly indicates the positive and negative aspects of this field. Choice (B) has two negative adjectives, choice (C) has two positive adjectives, and choice (D) has two neutral adjectives.

Expression of Ideas Practice Questions Set 2

1. Humorism held medical discovery back for centuries at a time when the pure sciences _____ it established a systemic insularity in the field that cut medicine off from discoveries in biology, chemistry, and physics, and generated a remarkably long-lived illusion of comprehensiveness that categorically rejected revision and innovation.

   The writer would like to emphasize how humorism prevented medical discovery from advancing. Which choice best accomplishes this goal?

   (A) were conducting medical research;
   (B) were shifting from the foreground to the background;
   (C) considered questions of knowledge and learning;
   (D) were preparing for a renaissance;

2. I recited this _____ to my first college roommate.

   Which choice completes the text most effectively?

   (A) childhood memory from the early part of my life
   (B) childhood memory
   (C) memory from my time period as a child
   (D) childhood memory and recollection

3. Newly licensed occupational therapists have a minimum of a four-year undergraduate degree and a two-year master's degree. Many occupational therapists also have a doctorate. Occupational therapy assistants have a two-year associate degree and work under the supervision of an occupational therapist. Occupational therapists and occupational therapy assistants work in a wide variety of settings like hospitals, skilled nursing facilities, schools, home health, outpatient clinics, sports medicine, and private practice alongside all types of health care practitioners.

   The writer is considering deleting the underlined sentence. Should the sentence be kept or deleted?

   (A) Kept, because it gives the first mention of the educational qualifications to become an occupational therapist
   (B) Kept, because it gives further elaboration on the educational possibilities for occupational therapists
   (C) Deleted, because it repeats information stated elsewhere in the passage
   (D) Deleted, because it contradicts information found later in the paragraph

4. The findings at Fermi Lab are at once unsettling, in that they will soon necessitate a considerable reform to our understanding of particle physics, _____ titillating in that they may well lead to a more sophisticated and penetrating understanding not only of particle asymmetry but also of the nature and origin of the universe itself.

   Which choice completes the text with the most logical transition?

   (A) but
   (B) and
   (C) moreover
   (D) for

5. Though Frick survived the assassination attempt, and ultimately won the conflict when it entered the courts, his relationship with Carnegie was _____, and his reputation as *America's most hated man* was solidified for years to come.

Which choice would best complete the text to express that Frick's relationship with Carnegie was beyond repair?

(A) irrevocably blemished
(B) rather tarnished
(C) mostly stained
(D) firmly tainted

6. _____ One of the most highly regarded surrealist artists, Salvador Dali, often drew on symbols that he saw in his dreams and incorporated them into his paintings. Dali's formal art education began in 1921 at the School of Fine Arts in Madrid, where he studied for several years. However, Dali was expelled shortly before graduating because he claimed that none of the teachers was competent enough to examine him. In this same year he painted *Basket of Bread*, which features four slices of buttered bread in a basket with one set off from the others and missing a bite. The painting uses a dematerializing lighting technique that shows just how far Dali's skill had already developed when he was only 22.

Given that all are true, which choice completes the text with the best introduction to the paragraph?

(A) The use of discrete symbolism is essential to the surrealist movement.
(B) Art has been appreciated by millions of museum goers the world over.
(C) Salvador Dali was born in Spain in the city of Figueres.
(D) It is rare to find artistic works that have truly stood the test of time.

7. Their proposal held that objects that were in orbit around the sun (but not around another planet) _____ could be considered planets. Unfortunately, Pluto didn't meet these stipulations.

Which of these options best completes the text by elaborating on the topic of the sentence with the most specific detail?

(A) were quite large and had a resulting large amount of gravitation,
(B) were constituted of a great deal of mass and matter, and possessed sufficient gravitational pull to have a significant impact on their surroundings,
(C) had enough mass to become nearly round due to pressure, and had enough gravity to clear their orbit of any other bodies,
(D) had a tremendously large amount of mass, while enough gravity to be quite noticeable,

Answers Explanations

1. **(D)** A *renaissance* is a "rebirth." So, choice (D) properly emphasizes the fact that the theory of humors held back society, especially given the advances in science alluded to immediately after this. Choice (A) does not logically lead into the context that follows. Choices (B) and (C) are vague.

2. **(B)** All four choices communicate the exact same sentiment, but choices (A), (C), and (D) are excessively wordy versions of choice (B), which is concise without sacrificing content.

3. **(B)** The previous sentence discusses some of the educational degree possibilities for occupational therapists, and the underlined sentence continues that focus. It is not redundant, giving us information that is helpful to understanding the full range of educational options for occupational therapists, making it best to leave it as is.

4. **(B)** When using the phrase *at once . . .* one needs to use *and* to transition to the second item in the list. Why? Because these two things exist *at once*, so *and* is an appropriate way to join them to one another.

5. **(A)** If something is *irrevocable*, it cannot be reversed or changed; *blemished* indicates a major flaw. This is the most thoroughly and permanently negative option. The other options are not as negative or permanent, using words like *rather*, *mostly*, and *tainted*.

6. **(A)** This sentence begins the paragraph with a general introduction to the subject that is specifically elaborated upon in the next sentence. Choices (B) and (D) are too broad, and choice (C) is too specific.

7. **(C)** The important part of this question is *specificity:* a choice is needed that provides the most relevant, logical, and *specific* information. Eliminate choices (A) and (D) for being far too general: they lack *specific* substance. Choice (B) manages to be lengthy and yet shallow at the same time. *A great deal of mass and matter* is the best example of this wordiness. Moreover, it still doesn't provide the specificity of choice (C), which wastes no words while still providing ample detail.

Standard English Conventions Practice Questions Set 1

1. The United States is the only country in the world to use an electoral college system to elect its chief executive. Each state has a certain number of electors based on _____ of senators and congresspersons.

   Which choice completes the text so that it conforms to the conventions of Standard English?

   (A) there number
   (B) their numbers
   (C) its number
   (D) our number

2. The areas of _____ of ways people use their time—that an occupational therapist considers when working with clients include activities of daily living, instrumental activities of daily living, rest and sleep, education, work, play, leisure, and social participation.

   Which choice completes the text so that it conforms to the conventions of Standard English?

   (A) occupations—or categories
   (B) occupations: categories
   (C) occupations; or categories
   (D) occupations, or categories

3. It is much like how humans would rather hear about someone's trip to a foreign country _____ at photographs of the country on the internet.

   Which choice completes the text so that it conforms to the conventions of Standard English?

   (A) then to look merely
   (B) then to merely look
   (C) than too look merely
   (D) than merely look

4. Following physicist Carl D. Anderson's 1932 gamma ray _____ anticipated the discovery of negatively baryon-charged antimatter throughout the universe in quantities that would precisely counterbalance the positive baryon charge of matter.

   Which choice completes the text so that it conforms to the conventions of Standard English?

   (A) experiment which demonstrated the existence of antimatter, scientists
   (B) experiment, which demonstrated the existence of antimatter, scientists
   (C) experiment; which demonstrated the existence of antimatter, scientists
   (D) experiment which demonstrated the existence of antimatter scientists

5. Faulkner first introduces Sarty at his father's trial where he is accused of burning a local farm. It is through Sarty's inner toil _____ the reader becomes distinctly aware of Abner's guilt.

   Which choice completes the text so that it conforms to the conventions of Standard English?

   (A) which
   (B) from
   (C) for
   (D) that

6. When struck by a wave of electromagnetic radiation, every element _____ an *excited state*, in which the electrons surrounding the nucleus *jump* to higher energy levels.

   Which choice completes the text so that it conforms to the conventions of Standard English?

   (A) enter
   (B) entering
   (C) enters
   (D) entries

7. Marjorie, a quintessentially modern girl, represents the destruction of conventional norms and former ideas of femininity. Young and beautiful, she is interested only in having a good time and being good company to the many suitors _____ flock to her.

   Which choice completes the text so that it conforms to the conventions of Standard English?

   (A) whom
   (B) who
   (C) whose
   (D) who's

Answer Explanations

1. **(C)** "Its" refers to each singular state taken on its own, not as part of a group, while the other options do not the number agreement established in the context.

2. **(A)** A dash is needed to set off the parenthetical phrase in the same way the parenthetical phrase is ended, namely with another dash. (B) and (C) are incorrect because a complete sentence must come before a semicolon or a colon. (D) would start the parenthetical phrase with a comma, while it ends with a dash—this would be fine if it also ended with a dash.

3. **(D)** *Than* is used when comparing, and *to* is used when joined to a verb, like in this case *to look.*

4. **(B)** The sentence can still function as a complete sentence without the phrase "which demonstrated the existence of antimatter," so it is appropriate to use commas to set it aside. Choice (A) does not have a necessary pause before the phrase, choice (C) does not have the necessary completed sentence before the semicolon, and choice (D) has no pauses whatsoever.

5. **(D)** *That* works because it begins an essential phrase in the sentence that cannot be set aside with commas, as would be the case with *which.* The answer is neither choice (B) nor (C) because it is incorrect to say *through . . . from* or *through . . . for* in a sentence like this.

6. **(C)** The subject of this sentence, "element," is singular. Even though the author is referring to many different elements, she is doing so one element at a time. So the singular verb *enters* is needed. Choice (A) is plural, choice (B) is progressive, and choice (D) is a noun.

7. **(B)** *Who* is correct since it stands for a subject that is human. Choice (A) is used in reference to objects. Choice (C) shows possession. Choice (D) means "who is."

Standard English Conventions Practice Questions Set 2

1. She instructs Bernice in social protocol in a _____ sentences, causing the reader to question the frivolous hedonism that dominates the early twentieth century.

   Which choice completes the text so that it conforms to the conventions of Standard English?

   (A) few short
   (B) short few
   (C) few, short
   (D) short, few

2. Although the digital age has understandably discouraged popularity in some traditional forms of _____ is the digital platform more than making up for the moderate declines in traditional news sources but also research shows that Americans are spending more time consuming news than they have since the early 1990s.

   Which choice completes the text so that it conforms to the conventions of Standard English?

   (A) news media the field itself is optimistic, not only
   (B) news media, the field itself is optimistic, not only
   (C) news media, the field itself is optimistic: not only
   (D) news media the field itself; is optimistic not only

3. The building's miraculous design comes not from its magnitude, but from the curvatures between its platform and columns that offer an illusion of symmetry that exceeds its true dimensions, and in the elaborate engravings within its marble surfaces _____ centuries of calamity.

   Which choice completes the text so that it conforms to the conventions of Standard English?

   (A) that having to outlast
   (B) which has to outlast
   (C) that have outlasted
   (D) which had outlasted

4. While Neanderthals appear to have maintained a stable population during the Ice Age, _____ leaving only the strongest and most intelligent to survive and carry on the species.

   Which choice completes the text so that it conforms to the conventions of Standard English?

   (A) a drastic genetic bottleneck was experienced by our African ancestors,
   (B) a drastic genetic bottleneck by our African ancestors was experienced,
   (C) our African ancestors drastically experienced a bottleneck that was genetic,
   (D) our African ancestors experienced a drastic genetic bottleneck,

5. Griselda consents to each demand precisely as she promised on their wedding day, and one begins to imagine that the Marquis is not so much testing his wife's devotion _____ exploring the extent to which his power reaches.

Which choice completes the text so that it conforms to the conventions of Standard English?

(A) so they are

(B) when they were

(C) so he was

(D) as he is

6. A teacher's workday starts and ends with the training and shaping of the next generation; and for many, there's no better way to invest their own training _____ in the opening of young minds.

Which choice completes the text so that it conforms to the conventions of Standard English?

(A) compared

(B) than

(C) then

(D) related

7. Although in life the two considered themselves plenary _____ begin to realize that the worlds envisioned by Strindberg and Ibsen were perhaps not so different as they believed.

Which choice completes the text so that it conforms to the conventions of Standard English?

(A) opposites as drama continues to evolve into the postmodern era, we may

(B) opposites as drama continues, to evolve into the postmodern era we may.

(C) opposites, as drama continues to evolve into the postmodern era, we may

(D) opposites as drama continues to evolve into the postmodern era we may

Answer Explanations

1. **(A)** When adjectives have to be ordered a certain way to provide a logical meaning, there should be no commas separating them. In this case, it only makes sense to use *few short sentences*, not *short few sentences*, making choice (A) the only viable option. Choices (B) and (D) change the meaning, and choice (C) has an unnecessary comma.

2. **(C)** This choice places a comma after the introductory dependent clause ending in *media* and puts a colon before a clarification of how the field is optimistic. Choice (A) lacks a necessary comma after *media* and leads to a run-on sentence. Choice B leads to a run-on. Choice (D) puts a semicolon between a subject and a verb, which should not be separated.

3. **(C)** The fact that these engravings have lasted for a long time is an essential part of their description, so *that* is needed instead of *which*. Choice (C) also uses the proper tense. Choice (A) uses the incorrect verb tense. Choices (B) and (D) use *which*, which works for nonessential characteristics of described objects.

4. **(D)** This choice concisely expresses the idea using logical word order. Choices (A) and (B) use passive voice. Choice (C) jumbles the word order such that the meaning is confused.

5. **(D)** This phrase completes the idiomatic expression *is not so much . . . as he is*. The other options do not connect appropriately to this earlier phrasing.

6. **(B)** *Than* completes the comparative phrase *better . . . than*. Choice (A) can work for comparisons but not in this context. Choice (C) is for time, and choice (D) does not lead to a comparison.

7. **(C)** The commas set aside the phrase *as drama continues to evolve into the postmodern era* that leads into the rest of the sentence. Choice (A) lacks a needed comma. Choice (B) breaks up the phrase *continues to evolve*. Choice (D) gives no break whatsoever.

Troubleshooting

Here are some further pointers for common issues.

"I never learned grammar rules."
- Review the concepts presented throughout this chapter—the rules are presented in an extremely concise, easy-to-grasp way.
- Realize that you don't need to know the precise grammatical terminology for a concept being tested. As long as you have a good sense of what is correct, you do not need to give an elaborate justification for your answer—simply get it right.
- Actually read the editing marks and comments teachers make on your papers. Instead of just looking at your grade, look at what grammar mistakes you made and be sure you understand *why* they were mistakes. That way, you will gradually remedy gaps in your grammar knowledge.

"I finish too quickly."
- Try reading the text before you look at the questions. Having a sense of the broad flow of the text can be useful to you in answering many of the big-picture questions. This will be a more effective use of your time than doing nothing for several minutes at the end of the Reading and Writing section.
- Pace yourself to take the full amount of time per question. If you do not check your time as you go, you will likely rush to the end. Try to take the full 70 seconds per question.

"I finish too slowly."
- Do not spend time overanalyzing your choice after you have made it. If you have read enough context and fully understand the requirements of the question, you have done all you can do; it is time to pick an answer choice and move on.
- Practice with timing so that on test day you do not fall prey to "paralysis by analysis." Any tendencies you have to go too slowly will only be exacerbated by the stresses of the actual PSAT.
- Try to spend no more than 90 seconds on a difficult question. If you have spent this much time and are not getting anywhere, you should cut your losses and take a guess. After all, there is no guessing penalty on the PSAT. You will not need to answer every question correctly to achieve National Merit recognition.

Further Preparation

What else can I do beyond the drills and practice tests in this book to prepare for the PSAT Writing?

- Practice with the other Barron's books for the SAT: *Barron's SAT* has plenty of practice tests you can try.
- Use the free practice tests and resources provided by the College Board on *KhanAcademy.org*.
- Practice with ACT English tests—the grammar concepts and editing skills tested on the ACT are virtually identical to those tested on the PSAT Writing questions.
- Edit your friends' papers, and have them edit yours. The more practice you have with editing, the better you will do.
- Read a variety of high-quality texts so that you develop a great feel for excellent writing.

Advanced Writing Drills

The following eight drills represent the most challenging types of writing concepts you may encounter on the PSAT. They are longer and more difficult than what you will face on the actual writing questions, helping push you to do your best. Completing these will help you prepare to score at the elite level required for National Merit recognition. The body of passages comprehensively covers the most difficult concepts you might find. Here are the titles of the passages should you wish to mark them off as you complete them:

- *Abeng*
- Beauty and Peril
- Carbon
- Court Reporter
- Hatfields and McCoys
- Hornsby
- President
- Risk

To practice these passages under timed conditions, take about 9 minutes per drill. Answer explanations for each drill are at the end of the chapter.

Advanced Writing Drills

Abeng

[1] In contemporary critical work examining female subjectivities in ❶ <u>womens'</u> fiction, there is a tendency to privilege the overt insurgent over more ❷ <u>direct instances of insubordination.</u> [2] For most, it seems that the better story lies with psychically fragmented protagonists deviating from the world in which they live. [3] Michelle Cliff's 1984 *Abeng* tells the story of Clare Savage, a light-skinned Jamaican girl whose mixed racial heritage—in a world of strict oppositional binaries—incapacitates her chances for wholeness. [4] While Clare's complex subjectivity under the constraints of colonialist White supremacy certainly ❸ <u>calls for</u> examination as well as acclaim, other female characters' counter hegemonic personalities and actions, often less conspicuous, go predominantly ❹ <u>unseen and unnoticed.</u> [5] Thus, there is a presumption that these female characters are less courageous, less risky, less intellectual, less *something.* ❺

The novel, in some ways, magnifies the difference between insurgent and pacifist women in its juxtaposition of Nanny and Sekesu—the former a legendary leader of the Windward Maroons, and ❻ <u>the later</u> her sister who remained a slave. Accordingly, the islanders descend from either one or the other—rebel or conformist—implying a congenital difference in the people of Jamaica. A closer reading of several of the characters, however, suggests an identity more complex than mere compliance with White

1. (A) NO CHANGE
   (B) women's
   (C) womans'
   (D) womens

2. Which of the following provides the most logical ending to this sentence?
   (A) NO CHANGE
   (B) conspicuous happenings of belligerence.
   (C) indirect depictions of inconsistency.
   (D) subtle representations of resistance.

3. (A) NO CHANGE
   (B) call for
   (C) calls of
   (D) call of

4. (A) NO CHANGE
   (B) without anyone actually seeing them.
   (C) mostly without being viewed.
   (D) unnoticed.

5. The author wishes to place the following sentence into the previous paragraph.

   "In Caribbean women's fiction specifically, this commonality likely coincides with the tradition's inclination to be inherently subversive."

   Where would it most logically be placed?

   (A) Before sentence 1
   (B) Before sentence 2
   (C) Before sentence 3
   (D) Before sentence 4

6. (A) NO CHANGE
   (B) the opposition
   (C) the latter
   (D) the other one

patriarchal ideologies, a subjectivity amid the mire of institutionalized oppression that resists and survives in more nuanced ways. **❼** Rather than relying on colonialist binaries, the female characters in *Abeng* demarcate a complex gradation of resistance from varying marginal spaces that ultimately works to dismantle the conceptual order of Western metaphysics. By interrogating the subjectivities of characters like Kitty, Mad Hannah, and Miss Winifred, readers can begin to understand various degrees of female resistance. **❽** Moreover, they will understand the roots of the motivations that empowered them to stand up for themselves.

Cliff's novel is within the tradition of Jamaica Kincaid's *Annie John* **❾** (1985) Merle Hodge's *Crick Crack Monkey* (1981), Oonya Kempadoo's *Buxton Spice* (1999), and Edwidge Danticat's *Clare of the Sea Light* (2013), in which young Caribbean girls' gender awakenings coincide with their political awakenings while they struggle to construct a Black female self without coherent mother-daughter relationships and without a clear sense of history. Clare typifies the **❿** double consciousness, her White external self attempts to reconcile internal feelings of Blackness. In essence, the quest for Black female subjectivity coexists with the struggle against patriarchy, concurring with the feminist perspective that loving Blackness is itself political resistance. **⓫** Hence, actions taken by women like Kitty, Mad Hannah, and Miss Winifred that may seem inconsequential actually serve socially and politically to challenge notions of patriarchal discourse by creating spaces of agency that refute, undermine, or opt out of systemic oppression.

7. Which of the following would provide the most effective and logical introduction to this sentence?
   (A) NO CHANGE
   (B) Instead of acting in a relativist fashion,
   (C) In contrast with some documentary evidence,
   (D) As opposed to seeing things along a spectrum,

8. The author is considering deleting the underlined sentence. Should it be kept or removed?
   (A) Kept, because it provides a needed clarification
   (B) Kept, because it justifies the author's line of thinking
   (C) Removed, because it is unrelated to the previous sentence
   (D) Removed, because it repeats an idea already expressed

9. (A) NO CHANGE
   (B) (1985), Merle Hodge's *Crick Crack Monkey* (1981) Oonya
   (C) (1985) Merle Hodge's, *Crick Crack Monkey* (1981) Oonya
   (D) (1985), Merle Hodge's *Crick Crack Monkey* (1981), Oonya

10. (A) NO CHANGE
    (B) double consciousness: her White external self attempts to reconcile internal feelings of Blackness.
    (C) double consciousness her White external self, attempts to reconcile internal feelings of Blackness.
    (D) double consciousness—her White external self—attempts to reconcile internal feelings of Blackness.

11. (A) NO CHANGE
    (B) Additionally,
    (C) Moreover,
    (D) However,

Beauty and Peril

One would be hard-pressed to find more gorgeous scenery ❶ than that in California and the Pacific Northwest. From the Santa Monica Mountains to the Malibu lagoons, from the gorgeous Cascades and Mount Rainier to Puget Sound, the entirety of the coast from California to Washington is breathtaking. Tucked beneath that striking veneer, sinister and lurking, however, ❷ is secrets of a magnitude of which we are suspicious but uncertain. The reality, though, is as follows: ❸ a conspiracy is afoot.

For one, the region is threatened by the San Andreas fault line. Popularized by countless Hollywood films in the previous decades, San Andreas is perhaps the most recognizable (though, unfortunately, perhaps not even the most potentially destructive) of Pacific geological hazards. ❹ Extending for 810 miles in length through the bulk of California, the San Andreas fault line had its largest recorded earthquake in 1906, the infamous San Francisco earthquake with a magnitude of 7.8 on the Richter scale. The death count was 3,000, ❺ and that must be accompanied by the disclaimer that the population was significantly less than it is today.

❻ In addition to the previously mentioned things, there is also the Juan de Fuca tectonic plate. This plate comprises part of the Cascadia subduction zone. Cascadia stretches all the way from Northern California to Canada's

1. (A) NO CHANGE
   (B) than
   (C) then those in
   (D) then

2. (A) NO CHANGE
   (B) was
   (C) are
   (D) has

3. Which of the following would provide wording that focuses on the overall message of the essay?
   (A) NO CHANGE
   (B) people need to get their priorities straight.
   (C) leadership depends on deeds, not words.
   (D) something cataclysmic is coming this way.

4. (A) NO CHANGE
   (B) Extending through
   (C) Extending for 810 miles through
   (D) Passing by

5. (A) NO CHANGE
   (B) moreover
   (C) but
   (D) also

6. Which of the following provides the best combination of the underlined sentences?
   (A) Additionally to the Juan de Fuca plate is the following, a plate that comprises part of the Cascadia subduction zone.
   (B) What is more, the Juan de Fuca tectonic plate is comprised with the Cascadia subduction zone.
   (C) Furthermore, the Juan de Fuca tectonic plate is the major component which partially comprises the zone, known as the "Cascadia subduction" zone.
   (D) Then there is the Juan de Fuca tectonic plate, which comprises part of the Cascadia subduction zone.

British Columbia, and this is the place where seismologists predict is the most likely spot for the "Big One." ❼ For centuries North Americas continental shelf has ground against Juan de Fuca, and the shelf has been compressed upward all the while—every moment, every day, every century, a little bit more all the time. Predictions are that this sort of unrelenting stress ❽ is approaching its breaking point of both literal and figurative nature. When that finally occurs (and advanced computer models put the likelihood of that catastrophe at greater than one in three in the next fifty years), it's difficult to affix an accurate estimation of the impending damages. Tens of thousands of deaths, hundreds of thousands of casualties, and billions of dollars in damaged property are not outside the scope of possibility. ❾ Moreover, as both San Andreas and Juan de Fuca are coastal, subsequent tidal waves would accompany the earthquakes. And, at this point in our ❿ wild goose chase, perhaps it is best not to venture any further down our path of apocalyptic prediction.

⓫ Despite all of these frightening possibilities, by no means am I advocating avoiding the Pacific coastal states. We must refuse to allow fear to dictate the courses of our lives—refuse to be deterred in our pursuit of happiness by the fragile futility of, "*Well, what if . . . ?*"

7. (A) NO CHANGE
   (B) For centuries, North Americas'
       continental
   (C) For centuries, North America's
       continental
   (D) For centuries North Americas'
       continental

8. (A) NO CHANGE
   (B) is approaching their
   (C) are approaching its
   (D) are approaching their

9. (A) NO CHANGE
   (B) Moreover as both San Andreas, and
       Juan de Fuca are coastal subsequent
   (C) Moreover as both San Andreas and
       Juan de Fuca are coastal subsequent
   (D) Moreover—as both San Andreas and
       Juan de Fuca are coastal subsequent

10. Which of the following would be most
    consistent with the tone and meaning of
    the passage?
    (A) NO CHANGE
    (B) conjecture
    (C) guesstimate
    (D) wisdom

11. Which of these options provides the
    most effective introduction to this sentence and paragraph as a whole?
    (A) NO CHANGE
    (B) Given the imminent catastrophe,
    (C) With the utter pointlessness of rampant speculation,
    (D) Granted that this is all hypothetical,

Percent of Human Body

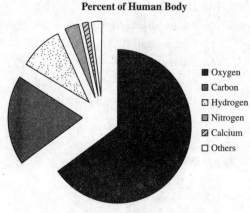

- ■ Oxygen
- ▦ Carbon
- ☐ Hydrogen
- ▨ Nitrogen
- ▧ Calcium
- ☐ Others

Source: OpenStax College

Carbon

You can burn me for energy or find me in plastics. When I am soft, pliable, and dark, I am used to write with. When I am diamond shaped and clear, I go on your left hand. I might be in your stocking or your gas tank, and I always show up to the family barbecues. I make up **❶** 2% of the human body, forming the basis of your very DNA. I am life when mixed with oxygen but death without enough of it. **❷** It takes a lot to melt me, my nature is quite unreactive. With an atomic number of 6 and a weight of 12.011, I am the fourth most common element in the entire universe. I'm all about the bonds, attaching to up to four atoms at one time. **❸** Chemists, casually refer to me as the basis of all plant and animal life, so you could say I have some big footprints to fill. **❹**

If you guessed iron, you're wrong. If you guessed nitrogen, you are equally incorrect. **❺** Sulfur, lacking in many of the characteristics of other atomic elements, is not suitable for this purpose. Carbon is the name; living organisms are the game.

1. Which of the following is supported by the information in the accompanying graph?
   - (A) NO CHANGE
   - (B) 10%
   - (C) 19%
   - (D) 65%

2. (A) NO CHANGE
   - (B) It takes a lot to melt me my nature is quite unreactive.
   - (C) It takes a lot to melt me: while my nature is quite unreactive.
   - (D) It takes a lot to melt me; my nature is quite unreactive.

3. (A) NO CHANGE
   - (B) Chemists casually refer to me, as the basis of all plant and animal life,
   - (C) Chemists casually refer to me as the basis of all plant and animal life,
   - (D) Chemists casually refer to me as the basis of all plant and animal life

4. Which option, if inserted here, would provide the most logical conclusion to the paragraph and the most effective transition to the next?
   - (A) What am I?
   - (B) Where am I?
   - (C) What are these?
   - (D) Who is this?

5. Which of the following is most consistent with the tone and style of the passage as a whole?
   - (A) NO CHANGE
   - (B) Nope, sulfur isn't cutting it either.
   - (C) If you considered picking sulfur, that too would be a deleterious inclination.
   - (D) Sulfur ain't right, too.

And it just so happens that I form more compounds than any other element, making me a building block of life on Earth. You might **6** have heard of my most common isotope, carbon-12, because it occurs naturally and makes up 99% of the carbon on your planet. If you happen to be more versed in the wonders of the chemical world, you might recognize me as the basis of graphene, a material stronger than steel but more flexible than rubber.

[1] My versatility is both gift and curse. [2] When I can find two oxygen atoms, I make carbon dioxide, which is found in Earth's atmosphere and used in photosynthesis. [3] Carbon footprint refers to the amount of greenhouse gas emissions generated by a particular country, organization, etc., and damages to Earth's ozone layer. [4] Hence, carbon dioxide—essential to life—can be detrimental in excess quantities. [5] **7** Accordingly, when I join with only one oxygen atom, I form a toxic gas known as carbon monoxide and **8** are responsible for fatal poisonings. **9**

For millions of years, I operated **10** between a balanced cycle. Plant life extracts me from the atmosphere in large quantities for food and energy, and I return to the atmosphere through respiration, **11** decomposing, and combustion. But humans disrupted my cycle by burning fossil fuels at rapid rates and destroying forests and plant life. Since I'm so critical to life, you may want to be more careful in the future.

6. (A) NO CHANGE
   (B) of heard of
   (C) have heard have
   (D) of heard have

7. (A) NO CHANGE
   (B) Furthermore,
   (C) Nevertheless,
   (D) Consequently,

8. (A) NO CHANGE
   (B) is
   (C) were
   (D) am

9. The author would like to insert the following sentence into the preceding paragraph.

   "However, too much of a good thing can be bad, really bad."

   Where would it most logically be placed?

   (A) After sentence 1
   (B) After sentence 2
   (C) After sentence 3
   (D) After sentence 4

10. (A) NO CHANGE
    (B) among
    (C) within
    (D) for

11. (A) NO CHANGE
    (B) decompose,
    (C) decomposed,
    (D) decomposition,

Court Reporter

In the court of law, a judge is the public official who presides over the hearing and is ultimately responsible for the administration of justice. An attorney or a lawyer advises and represents individuals, businesses, or agencies in legal disputes. Defense attorneys and prosecutors are the specific names given to lawyers ❶ whom represent the accused or whom represent local, state, or federal agencies as they accuse others of crimes, respectively. The jury consists of a body of people appointed to listen, consider evidence, and give a verdict on a ❷ specific trial—essentially, jurors represent a panel of judges. Responsible for maintaining order in the court is an officer, much like a police officer. And a court clerk maintains records of the court proceedings. Other than interested parties like the defendant and the witnesses, this list ❸ composes those occupants found in a normal legal proceeding. ❹ *Or will they?*

❺ Court reporting an often-overlooked occupation of legal services—is essential to trials, depositions, committee meetings, and basically any legal proceeding you can think of. A court reporter provides a verbatim record of court proceedings using recording equipment, stenographs, and stenomasks. ❻ For this reason, a court reporter transcribes any spoken dialogue, recorded speech, gestures, actions, etc. that occur in a legal environment where exact record of occurrences is mandatory. Hence, the oversight does not reflect the significance of the occupation itself. Court reporters are very important to the judicial system.

1. (A) NO CHANGE
   (B) who represent the accused or who
   (C) whom represent the accused or who
   (D) who represent the accused or whom

2. (A) NO CHANGE
   (B) specific trial, essentially jurors represent a panel of judges.
   (C) specific trial: essentially jurors represent, a panel of judges.
   (D) specific trial; essentially jurors, represent a panel of judges.

3. (A) NO CHANGE
   (B) compromises
   (C) comprises
   (D) comprising

4. Which of the following would provide the most logical and effective conclusion to this paragraph and transition to the next paragraph?
   (A) NO CHANGE
   (B) *Or does it?*
   (C) *Or can you?*
   (D) *Or did it?*

5. (A) NO CHANGE
   (B) Court reporting—an often-overlooked occupation of legal services, is essential to trials, depositions, committee
   (C) Court reporting, an often-overlooked occupation of legal services is essential to trials, depositions committee
   (D) Court reporting, an often-overlooked occupation of legal services, is essential to trials, depositions, committee

6. (A) NO CHANGE
   (B) In other words,
   (C) In contrast,
   (D) Because of this

Stenographs are machines like keyboards that use key combinations rather than single characters **❼** for effective communication. A court reporter using a stenomask, on the other hand, actually speaks into a covered microphone recording dialogue and reporting actions that a computer then transcribes. Recording equipment might consist of anything from a traditional tape recorder to more advanced digital audio recording with voice recognition technology. Whatever a court reporter chooses to use, **❽** they are charged with generating exact records of what was said inside the courtroom and then providing accurate copies to courts, counsels, and other involved parties.

As you might guess, the occupational skills valued in a court reporter encompass clerical, listening, and writing skills; selective hearing; attention to detail; and knowledge of legal codes, jargon, and court procedures. That being said, it might surprise **❾** you to learn that most entry-level positions require only an associate's degree or certificate program, and completion of licensing exams. **❿** You are on your way to a six-figure salary and a front-row seat at local, state, or federal court proceedings in as little as two years. In addition, **⓫** a given court reporter's salary is more likely to be within a consistent range than the salaries of other major legal fields, making it a job you can count on to give you a solid paycheck.

Average Salaries for Legal Occupations, 2014

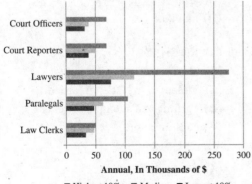

Source: Onetonline.org

7. Which of the following provides the most logical and effective ending to this sentence?
   (A) NO CHANGE
   (B) for technological advantage.
   (C) for speedy typing.
   (D) to discourage sickness.

8. (A) NO CHANGE
   (B) you are
   (C) one are
   (D) he or she is

9. (A) NO CHANGE
   (B) him or her
   (C) one
   (D) them

10. Which of the following is both the most logical introduction to the sentence and supported by the information in the accompanying graph?
    (A) NO CHANGE
    (B) You will earn more than the typical American worker
    (C) You will pay off your student loans in no time
    (D) You could be on your way to a $60,000 salary

11. Which of the following properly uses information from the graph to build upon the author's argument in this paragraph?
    (A) NO CHANGE
    (B) court reporters earn an average salary that exceeds the median legal professional salary,
    (C) court reporters are more likely to be hired for entry-level positions,
    (D) a given court reporter's compensation is likely to be as much as the salaries of the attorneys who appear before them,

Hatfields and McCoys

Like many of history's most legendary battles, the lawless family feud between the Hatfields and McCoys ❶ boiling down to the differences between two men. William Anderson Hatfield, known widely as "Devil Anse," was a mountain dweller and successful timber merchant. Randolph McCoy, or "Ole Ran'l," ❷ owned some land, and livestock in the same region; the borderlands dividing Kentucky and West Virginia. The clash between the two families brands the American memory—in the Midwest, the vendetta rivals that of the Capulets and Montagues but with a uniquely "hillbilly" twist.

Legend has it that the feud began somewhere near 1865 with the murder of Randolph's brother, Asa, who was accused of treason for fighting for the Union during the Civil War. ❸ As a result, the Hatfield family ran the Logan Wildcats, the local militia group responsible for Asa's murder. Years of deep dislike, bitter resentment, and minor confrontations passed before Randolph McCoy accused Floyd Hatfield of stealing a hog in 1878. Devil Anse's influence over the courts resulted in a quick clearing of Floyd's name but not before a McCoy relative testified on the Hatfield's behalf. ❹ The disloyalty sealed the witness's fate—he was violently killed by other McCoys. It wasn't until the 1880s, though, that things spiraled out of control. Johnse Hatfield, son of Devil Anse, began dating Randolph's daughter, Roseanna. They devoted themselves to each other despite their ❺ family's disapproval. However, Johnse later left a pregnant Roseanna and married her cousin Nancy, stirring intra- and inter-familial conflicts. Things were unstable to say the least in August 1882, when three of Randolph's sons confronted two Hatfield brothers. ❻ The face-off turned to violence with quickness and rapidity, and Ellison Hatfield was stabbed and shot. To ❼ venge the family name, a group of Hatfields found the three

1. (A) NO CHANGE
   (B) boils
   (C) boil
   (D) OMIT the underlined portion.

2. (A) NO CHANGE
   (B) owned some land, and livestock in the same region, the borderlands dividing Kentucky and West Virginia.
   (C) owned some land and livestock in the same region, the borderlands dividing Kentucky and West Virginia.
   (D) owned some land and livestock in the same region the borderlands dividing Kentucky and West Virginia.

3. (A) NO CHANGE
   (B) Nonetheless, the
   (C) Contradictorily, the
   (D) The

4. Which of the following would provide the most logical and effective introduction to this sentence?
   (A) NO CHANGE
   (B) He managed to keep his word
   (C) The judge and jury were unimpressed
   (D) The historical record did him no favors

5. (A) NO CHANGE
   (B) families
   (C) familys
   (D) families'

6. (A) NO CHANGE
   (B) The face-off turned violent,
   (C) Violent to the face-off turned,
   (D) Turning to a situation of violent confrontation,

7. (A) NO CHANGE
   (B) revenging
   (C) vengeance
   (D) avenge

sons, bound them, and fired more than 50 bullets into them. Again, the prominent family **8** eluded arrest.

[1] The media caught on, and the Hatfield/McCoy clash reached commercial popularity. [2] Suddenly newspapers produced article after article, painting the Hatfield family as particularly vicious and violent. [3] By 1887, the Hatfields spent most of their time dodging increasingly large bounties. [4] To put an end to the family rivalry, the Hatfields sought to end the McCoys once and for all. [5] In 1888, they ambushed the McCoy household, killing **9** Old Ran'l's son and daughter, and brutally beating his wife. [6] Nine were arrested in connection to the atrocious crime. **10**

Eventually, the case made its way to the U.S. Supreme Court where eight of the nine received life in prison. **11** The ninth, a mentally handicapped Ellison Mounts, was hanged in February 1890. Today, both families hold celebrity status in the American consciousness.

8. (A) NO CHANGE
(B) alluded
(C) illuded
(D) illuminated

9. The author is considering changing this phrase to "Mr. McCoy's." Is this change necessary?
(A) Yes, because it provides a needed clarification.
(B) Yes, because it uses more formal language.
(C) No, because this logically refers to Mr. Hatfield.
(D) No, because this nickname was already established in the essay.

10. The author would like to insert the following sentence into the previous paragraph:

"With the journalistic sensationalism, the feud was revived."

Where would it most logically be placed?

(A) Before sentence 1
(B) Before sentence 3
(C) Before sentence 5
(D) After sentence 6

11. Should the underlined sentence be kept or deleted?
(A) Kept, because it provides a relevant clarification
(B) Kept, because it gives a needed justification
(C) Removed, because it is off topic
(D) Removed, because it shifts the analysis too quickly

Hornsby

I struggle with the phenomenon of fame. ❶ <u>Perhaps, as Andy Warhol once quipped, we are all destined to occupy the spotlight for fifteen minutes.</u> But what, I ask, of those whose notoriety is longer sustained? How can a Hollywood family of dullards and never-do-wells mesmerize the whole of a nation with a smash-hit reality TV series, while someone of actual import and accomplishment—say, a heroic police officer or selfless organ donor— ❷ <u>passes</u> the entirety of their life in the thankless shadows? I don't wish to waste your time disputing the nature or purpose of celebrity, but pardon my tangential musing as I approach ❸ <u>my true question, where is the love, for Bruce Hornsby?</u>

❹ <u>Powerfully,</u> I now must tell you who Bruce Hornsby is, which further illustrates the criminality of his anonymity. A man so talented should require no introduction whatsoever. Alas, Hornsby is a singer, songwriter, and—in my esteemed opinion—as fine a piano player as Billy Joel (a man who requires no introduction, ❺ <u>my point about the arbitrary nature of fame having been thus solidified</u>). When Bruce plays the piano, the sound is so wonderfully rich that your brain can't help but be puzzled at the thought of human hands moving so deftly over the keys.

1. The author is considering deleting the underlined sentence. Should this sentence be kept or removed?
   (A) Kept, because it provides a relevant elaboration
   (B) Kept, because it introduces the main person to be analyzed
   (C) Deleted, because it is inconsistent with the essay's tone
   (D) Deleted, because it distracts from the essay's principal argument

2. (A) NO CHANGE
   (B) pass
   (C) passing
   (D) past

3. (A) NO CHANGE
   (B) my true, question; where is the love for Bruce Hornsby?
   (C) my true question—where is the love for Bruce Hornsby.
   (D) my true question: where is the love for Bruce Hornsby?

4. Which word provides the most logical transition at this point in the essay?
   (A) NO CHANGE
   (B) Imaginatively,
   (C) Inevitably,
   (D) Obliquely,

5. (A) NO CHANGE
   (B) giving the solidity of a case to my point about the arbitrary nature of fame.
   (C) further solidifying my point about fame's arbitrary nature
   (D) making my point about the solidifying of the arbitration of fame

And when he sings, there is a molasses-sweet timbre that communicates volumes about the human condition. **6**

Even more puzzling about Hornsby's lack of name recognition is that he has had a moderate amount of success throughout his career. Hornsby has won three Grammy awards (most notably in 1987 for best new artist), and his album *The Way It Is* attained multiplatinum status by selling more than two million units. His songs continue to receive radio airplay on **7** variety various stations, and he has toured and collaborated with such dynamos as The Grateful Dead; Don Henley; Bob Dylan; Stevie Nicks; Bonnie Raitt; and Crosby, Stills and Nash **8** (all of whom have succeeded him greatly in notoriety and recognition). Moreover, Bruce Hornsby's music has transcended genre; it is a little-known fact that hip-hop legend Tupac Shakur's megahit "Changes" was actually an adaptation of Hornsby's "The Way It Is."

6. The author wishes to insert an aside to underscore his self-deprecating self-awareness that readers likely will not share his views about Hornsby. Which of the following would best be inserted at this point to accomplish the author's goal?
   (A) There are those who can appreciate Hornsby, and there are those who not only cannot appreciate his work, but have no artistic sensibility whatsoever.
   (B) Forgive my hyperbole, but so profound is my love for his music that I cannot help but get carried away with my adulation.
   (C) As someone with extensive musical training, I can assure you that if you miss out on Hornsby, you are truly missing out.
   (D) To listen to him play is like watching Michelangelo painting the Sistine Chapel—it is to see a master at work.

7. (A) NO CHANGE
   (B) various variety
   (C) variety, various
   (D) various, variety

8. The author is considering deleting the underlined portion of the sentence. Should this portion be removed?
   (A) Yes, because it does not focus on the essay's primary topic.
   (B) Yes, because it unfairly disparages the protagonist of the passage.
   (C) No, because it underscores the author's thoughts about Hornsby's lack of recognition.
   (D) No, because it provides specific details in support of the following sentence.

9 Perhaps, like van Gogh's or F. Scott Fitzgerald's, Bruce Hornsby's legacy will grow with time. Perhaps society just isn't quite ready to award him his deserved credentials. **10** Consequently, I fear the opposite: now more than ever, we are a Justin Bieber and Eminem crowd. Bruce's time is past, and his just desserts will forever elude him as we continue to turn our attention to increasingly **11** lessening worthy recipients.

9. (A) NO CHANGE
   (B) Perhaps like van Gogh or F. Scott Fitzgerald Bruce Hornsby's legacy
   (C) Perhaps, like van Gogh or F. Scott Fitzgerald Bruce Hornsby's, legacy
   (D) Perhaps, like van Gogh or F. Scott Fitzgerald Bruce Hornsby's legacy

10. (A) NO CHANGE
    (B) But,
    (C) Therefore,
    (D) Accordingly,

11. (A) NO CHANGE
    (B) less worthy
    (C) fewer worthy
    (D) fewer worth of the

President

{1}

The first three articles of a 1789 document—formally known as the United States Constitution—delineate the separation of powers ❶ in the core of American democracy. Divided into three branches, the federal government assigns law making to the legislative, law enforcing to the executive, and law interpreting to the judicial system. ❷ The separation of powers doctrine largely originated with the ideas of the French political philosopher, Baron de Montesquieu. The President of the United States is the nucleus of the Executive Branch, serving as both Head of State and Commander in Chief, and is the most prominent figure of American government. ❸ Thus, if one's career goals involve establishing oneself as one of the most important and well-known people in the world, then running for the national presidency makes a great deal of sense.

{2}

[1] The requirements are pretty straightforward: one must be a natural-born citizen who ❹ is at least the age of 35 years and for at least the duration of 14 years resided in the United States. [2] What it actually takes, however, is labyrinthine. [3] At the forefront of a successful campaign for presidency ❺ lie charisma. [4] One's public image must be maintained with a skeleton-free closet and consistent political views—nothing sabotages a presidential campaign like scandal or irregularity. [5] Even then, a likely candidate should endeavor to appeal to average Americans, appearing in churches and small businesses often and visiting frequently with

1. (A) NO CHANGE
   (B) with
   (C) at
   (D) on

2. The author is considering deleting the underlined sentence. Should it be removed?
   (A) Yes, because it interrupts the flow of the paragraph.
   (B) Yes, because it is unrelated to the facts of the paragraph.
   (C) No, because it defines a key term in the passage.
   (D) No, because it provides a relevant historical anecdote.

3. (A) NO CHANGE
   (B) Thus, if ones career goals involve establishing oneself
   (C) Thus if your career goals involve establishing yourself
   (D) Thus, if your career goals involve establishing oneself

4. (A) NO CHANGE
   (B) is at least 35 years old and has resided in the United States for 14 years or more.
   (C) is 35 and has lived in the U.S. for a long time.
   (D) meets the requirements as laid out in the Constitution.

5. (A) NO CHANGE
   (B) lay
   (C) lays
   (D) lies

veterans, blue-collar workers, and farmers.
[6] Personal military experience never hurt
anyone either. **❻**

{3}

❼ Past presidents' age ranges from 44 (John
F. Kennedy) to 76 (Ronald Reagan) but average at about 55 years old. U.S. presidents tend
to be married with children and hold advanced
degrees in law or business from elite universities.
Most candidates possess resumes boasting of
years in public service and political positions; the
fast track to presidential candidacy comprises
elected posts like mayor, governor, and senator. **❽** Still allure, a spotless background, and
years in diplomatic service are a dime a dozen in
presidential races. One needs money, and plenty
of it, to run for the presidency.

{4}

Even after an exploratory committee predicts
success and a potential candidate registers
with the Federal Election Commission, one
has to win support in a caucus, triumph in
a primary, **❾** following an earning nationally in a convention, and raise millions of
dollars in funds before the general election. **❿** Surprisingly, the *Washington Post*
reported that both presidential candidates in
2012, Barack Obama and Mitt Romney, raised
over $1 billion each to run their campaigns.
Thinking of the White House as a future residence? Work on that billion-dollar smile. **⓫**

**Desirable Characteristics in the
Next U.S. President, 2016**

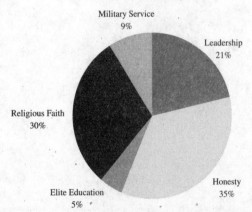

Military Service
9%

Leadership
21%

Religious Faith
30%

Honesty
35%

Elite Education
5%

Survey of 1,000 randomly selected likely voters

6. The author would like to insert the
following sentence into the previous
paragraph:

"But mastering the charm, attractiveness,
and likability to please the cameras—
arguably one of the more mystifying
qualifications of presidency—by itself
falls short of an election."

Where would it most logically be inserted?

(A) After sentence 1
(B) After sentence 2
(C) After sentence 3
(D) After sentence 5

7. (A) NO CHANGE
(B) Past president's ages range
(C) Past president's age range
(D) Past presidents' ages range

8. (A) NO CHANGE
(B) Still, allure, a spotless background, and
(C) Still, allure a spotless background and
(D) Still, allure a spotless background, and

9. NO CHANGE
(A) earn a following in a national
convention,
(B) follow an earning nationally in a
convention,
(C) follow a national earning in a
convention

10. (A) NO CHANGE
(B) As a result,
(C) For instance,
(D) However,

11. The author would like to use the data
from the accompanying chart to create a
relevant sentence to insert in the essay.
To which paragraph should such a sen-
tence be added?
(A) Paragraph 1
(B) Paragraph 2
(C) Paragraph 3
(D) Paragraph 4

Risk

I remember the class well. ❶ We seniors understood academic principles and knew the roles that we would play when we moved into management jobs after graduation ❷ since we felt well-prepared for the profession we were about to enter. Most programs had a capstone course that pulled all of our coursework together, and this was no different. Our guide for this course was an experienced executive and not the normal academic ❸ who walked these halls. "What is the basic job of a general manager?" he asked. Hands shot up. "Maximize shareholder equity!" "Maximize profit." "Develop a strategic vision!" "Increase market share." To these responses and others, he said a simple "no." Finally, he told us what we would be doing as managers ❹ for the field. "Your job is to take risk. When analysis will not provide an answer, you have to make a decision and move the ball forward. ❺ Your decision-making performance will determine your worth to the enterprise."

1. (A) NO CHANGE
   (B) Us
   (C) That
   (D) This

2. The author is considering deleting the underlined portion. Should this selection be removed?
   (A) Yes, because it digresses from the main idea of the sentence.
   (B) Yes, because it repeats ideas already implied in the sentence.
   (C) No, because it provides relevant details in support of a claim.
   (D) No, because it provides a needed contrast.

3. (A) NO CHANGE
   (B) whom walked
   (C) who walking
   (D) whom walking

4. (A) NO CHANGE
   (B) fielding.
   (C) out in the field.
   (D) with a field.

5. Which of the following provides the most logical and relevant conclusion to the paragraph?
   (A) NO CHANGE
   (B) Significant wealth will inevitably follow.
   (C) Be sure you incorporate thorough analysis before you decide on your course of action.
   (D) Remember these words of advice when you go back to school.

Taking risk involves the understanding that various outcomes can arise when you make a choice. ❻ <u>Some outcomes may spell disaster for your company, others may create exceptional financial returns for the shareholders.</u> But hiding behind every one of these possible futures is the uncertainty of which one or some hybrid of several will actually occur. An ❼ <u>affective</u> manager has the confidence to face these outcomes and the inherent unknowns.

[1] Let's take a simple example. [2] How much inventory of a certain item should you hold so that you can provide exceptional customer service and not run out of product? [3] What affects the success of a chosen number of items to put on the shelf? [4] The other is the lead time that it takes to replenish the inventory when it begins to run low. [5] The tricky part is that both the demand for the product and the lead time to replenish are typically not known with certainty. [6] ❽ <u>Books are going the way of the record player—technology has made mobile electronics far more preferable.</u> [7] The publisher may tell you that the standard lead time is 8 weeks, but this can change due to other business it may be running in the printing factory. [8] And if you are at Amazon.com, there are millions of these decisions that are made, and ❾ <u>the success of the business will be driven by how well you manage these variations.</u>

6. (A) NO CHANGE
   (B) Some outcomes, may spell disaster for your company: others may create exceptional financial returns for the shareholders.
   (C) Some outcomes—may spell disaster for your company—others may create exceptional financial returns for the shareholders.
   (D) Some outcomes may spell disaster for your company; others may create exceptional financial returns for the shareholders.

7. (A) NO CHANGE
   (B) affecting
   (C) effective
   (D) effecting

8. Which of the following would provide the most specific example in support of the claim made in the previous sentence?
   (A) NO CHANGE
   (B) If Oprah selects a given book for her monthly review, copies will run off of the shelves and backorders will occur.
   (C) The definition of "lead time" varies a great deal depending on the business professor to whom you speak.
   (D) Publishers try to increase demand for profitable books, using methods like online advertising and public relations firms.

9. (A) NO CHANGE
   (B) the success of the business, will be driven by how well you manage these variations.
   (C) the success, of the business will be driven, by how well you manage these variations.
   (D) the success of the business will be driven by how well, you manage these variations.

[9] If you don't have the item, the customer will simply click on a competitor's website and make the purchase. [10] If you put too much on the shelf, the investment cost of this **10** <u>moving slowly inventory</u> can consume the working capital of the business. **11**

10. (A) NO CHANGE
    (B) slow inventory with respect to moving
    (C) slowly moving inventory
    (D) inventory, which is slowly moving at times,

11. The author wishes to place the following sentence into the previous paragraph:

    "One factor is the demand that you expect over a given time period, such as a month or quarter."

    Where would it most logically be placed?

    (A) Before sentence 2
    (B) Before sentence 4
    (C) Before sentence 9
    (D) Before sentence 10

Answer Explanations

Abeng

1. **(B)** A choice is needed that encompasses *fiction of women*. A possessive is required, and possession is demonstrated using *s*. Choice (D) can be eliminated, as it has no apostrophe. Choice (C) can be eliminated, as it reads as *fiction of womans*. Choice (A) can be eliminated as it reads as *fiction of womens*. Choice (B) is the only logical option.

2. **(D)** This question is largely about the vocabulary. A choice is needed that contrasts with "overt insurgent," which essentially means clear instance of rebellion. Choice (D), particularly with its usage of "subtle . . . resistance," forms a perfect contrast since *subtle* is an antonym for *overt*. Choices (A) and (B) are flawed in that they mean the same thing as "overt insurgent." Choice (C) is not logical in context. Instead, it is irrelevant to the topic.

3. **(A)** The subject is "subjectivity," which requires the singular verb form "calls." Eliminate choices (B) and (D) accordingly. One "calls for" rather than "calls of." Eliminate choice (C).

4. **(D)** All four choices represent the exact same sentiment. To be concise and avoid wordiness, choice (D) is the best option.

5. **(C)** The proposed insertion mentions "Caribbean women's fiction." Sentence 3 references a story in Jamaica, which would be an example of "Caribbean women's fiction." The new sentence should therefore be inserted before sentence 3. In that position, the new sentence can act as an introductory sentence to the discussion of *Abeng*.

6. **(C)** A common verbal pattern involves the usage of *former* and *latter* in conjunction. This sentence is a perfect example of that pattern, and "the latter" is the correct answer. Choice (A), "the later," is used as an adjective or adverb, not as a noun. Choices (B) and (D) break with the pattern completely.

7. **(A)** Immediately before this sentence, the author writes about resisting oppression in more "nuanced" ways. The author then states that the characters act along a more "complex gradation of resistance." In other words, the characters act in such a way that their behavior should be considered to be along a spectrum. Therefore, choice (A) is the most logical, because "relying on colonialist binaries" is a simplified way of interpreting their actions, as a "binary" provides only two extreme options. Choices (B) and (D) are incorrect because they express the opposite of what is intended. Choice (C) is incorrect because the author is suggesting how the interpretation of literature should be done—there is no question about the quality of the documentary sources themselves.

8. **(D)** In the sentence immediately before the underlined portion, the author states that "by interrogating the subjectivities of characters like Kitty, Mad Hannah, and Miss Winifred, readers can begin to understand various degrees of female resistance." Subjectivity refers to one's personal point of view, which gives insight into the person's motivations. The female resistance refers to actions one would take to stand up for oneself. Therefore, this sentence provides a subtle repetition of the idea expressed in the previous sentence. Choices (A) and (B) are incorrect because they would leave in an unneeded sentence. The answer is not choice (C) because the underlined sentence is, in fact, related to the previous sentence.

9. **(D)** Notice the pattern here: there is an author, a title, a year, and then a comma. Eliminate choices (A) and (C) for neglecting the comma after "(1985)." Eliminate choice (B) since it does not include a comma after "(1981)."

10. **(B)** This sentence first mentions "double consciousness" and then proceeds to define that phrase. There must be adequate punctuation to separate the term from the definition. With choice (A), a comma isn't a strong enough pause. A colon or dash would be ideal, and a semicolon could arguably work. However, a comma is not appropriate since it leaves a comma splice. Choice (C) neglects punctuation altogether. Choice (D)'s initial dash is acceptable, but the second dash is unnecessary. This isn't a parenthetical phrase and should not be treated as such. After eliminating those three choices, analyze choice (B). Notice that it is properly punctuated, with the colon serving as a lead-in between the term and the definition.

11. **(A)** When working with transitions, analyze both the current sentence and the previous sentence to determine how they interrelate. In this case, there is a *cause-and-effect* relationship. "Hence" may not have been familiar to you, but it is a close approximation for *as a result, therefore,* or *accordingly.* Since "hence" can be used to transition between a cause and its effect, it is the best option. Notice that choices (B) and (C) mean the same thing. So they can be eliminated for that reason. The word "however," in choice (D) is a *contrasting* transition, but the sentences do not contrast.

Beauty and Peril

1. **(A)** Maintain a logical comparison in this sentence. "Then" is not used for comparisons, so eliminate choices (C) and (D). Keep in mind that this is comparing the *scenery* of California to the *scenery* of other places, as opposed to comparing *California* itself to other places. Choice (B) attempts to compare apples to oranges, so it must be eliminated. Choice (A) is the only option that logically compares one place's scenery to another place's scenery.

2. **(C)** The subject comes after the verb, which can be confusing. Nonetheless, the subject is "secrets," a plural noun that requires a plural verb for agreement. Choices (A), (B), and (D) are all *singular* verbs and therefore must be eliminated. "Are" is the only acceptable option.

3. **(D)** This is a question that perhaps requires reading a little bit further into the passage to diagnose the theme, which is the possibility of "cataclysmic" natural disasters on the Pacific Coast. The passage has nothing to do with a "conspiracy," with people who "need to get their priorities straight," or with the concept of "leadership." Choice (D), with its speculation on the possibility of impending, devastating natural disasters, is the only logical solution.

4. **(C)** Eliminate choice (D) immediately, as "passing by" California is incorrect; the San Andreas fault goes *through* California. From there, find the choice that has the perfect balance between concision and content. In choice (A), it is unnecessary to say "810 miles *in length.*" *Length* is already implied. Choice (B) eliminates too much, as "810 miles" is still relevant and provides new, productive information. Choice (C), then, is the perfect balance.

5. **(C)** This question illustrates the principle of coordination and subordination. Essentially, to paraphrase this sentence: *the death toll then was only 3,000,* **but** *keep in mind that the death toll from a similar earthquake would probably be much higher today.* Choice (C) is the only option that expresses that disclaimer effectively. Choices (A), (B), and (D) really all communicate the same message of *additionally,* which is not logical in this sentence; the clauses do not build on each other. Also keep in mind that there can be only one correct answer, so any choices that are essentially identical must be eliminated.

6. **(D)** Choices (A), (B), and (C) all have some major flaw, and sometimes they have multiple flaws. There are grammatical issues with choice (A), too, but its largest flaw is that it treats Juan de Fuca and Cascadia as two separate things, whereas the former is actually part of the latter. In choice (B), the proper phrase is *comprised of*, not "comprised with." Choice (C) uses "which" where it should use "that"; it also places an unnecessary comma after "zone." Choice (D) is without flaw, and its use of "which" rather than *that* is perfect.

7. **(C)** The idea that should be expressed as a possessive is *the continental shelf of North America*. Choice (A), by omitting an apostrophe, fails to illustrate possession. Choices (B) and (D) read as if the continent were *North Americas*, as opposed to the correct *North America*.

8. **(A)** It can be argued that the item "approaching its breaking point" is either "stress" or *the plate*. Nonetheless, both are singular nouns that require singular verbs for concordance. Eliminate choices (C) and (D) for using plural verbs. Next, the possessive pronoun form of one thing is "its." "Their" is used for multiple items, as in choice (B). Choice (A) is therefore the correct answer.

9. **(A)** The principal matter that separates the correct answer from all three incorrect choices is the issue of comma placement between "coastal" and "subsequent." The independent, main clause of the sentence is "subsequent tidal waves would accompany the earthquakes." The clause "as both San Andreas and Juan de Fuca are coastal," is separate and *dependent*. (It depends on the second clause to constitute a full sentence.) Since the two are separate clauses, the comma must be placed between them for separation.

10. **(B)** "Conjecture" most clearly means speculation, theory, or hypothesis. Since the author is speculating about the future throughout the passage, choice (B) is the correct answer. A "wild goose chase" is a hectic, often-futile undertaking. This doesn't fit in context. "Wisdom" doesn't fit in context since the author actually *knows* nothing of the future but is merely speculating. "Guesstimate" is a *portmanteau* (combination of two words) that is too casual for the purposes of this passage.

11. **(A)** Choice (B) can be quickly eliminated since the author has made clear that the catastrophe is not "imminent" but, rather, *probable given a long enough period of time*. The paragraph goes on to address fear and to warn that we must not allow it to dictate our lives. Choices (C) and (D) address the futility of speculation, which does capture part of the paragraph's theme. However, they ultimately fail to make any mention of "fear." Choice (A) is the only option that addresses the concept that fear based on speculation is unproductive.

Carbon

1. **(C)** Analyze the graph for this question. It's impossible to say *exactly* how much carbon is in the human body as there are no numbers provided. However, the carbon slice makes up just under one-fourth or one-fifth of the pie. The only answer that is even close to the 20% to 25% of the actual slice is 19%.

2. **(D)** The underlined section contains two *independent clauses:* they could be full sentences by themselves. Accordingly, we need to separate the two clauses. Choice (D) uses a semicolon to do this. Choice (A) is a comma splice. Choice (B) is a run-on sentence. Choice (C) would be acceptable if we had used a colon and maintained the two initial clauses. However, the use of "while" changes the second clause from independent to dependent, which doesn't function.

3. **(C)** There are two independent clauses here, with "so" used as a conjunction to unite them. Choice (A), by placing a comma after "chemists," breaks the first independent clause. Choice (B) incorrectly treats the phrase as an appositive. Choice (D) is a run-on sentence. Choice (C) is correct; it adds no unnecessary commas while still managing to insert the required one after "life."

4. **(A)** Analyze the first sentence of the next paragraph, "If you guessed iron, you're wrong." Iron is not a place, so eliminate choice (B). It is not plural, so eliminate choice (C). It is not a person, so eliminate choice (D). It is a singular thing, which makes choice (A) the correct answer.

5. **(B)** First, recognize tone: it is very casual, almost like an informal conversation. Choices (A) and (C) are far too formal. Choice (D) is incorrect, as one would say "sulfur ain't right, *either*" as opposed to "sulfur ain't right, *too.*" Choice (B) is both informal and without enormous grammatical flaws.

6. **(A)** Eliminate choices (B) and (D) since the verb tense is "have heard." "Might of" is never a correct construction. Choice (C)'s error is in having an extra "have." One hears *of* something as opposed to hears *have* something.

7. **(B)** Analyze the relationship between this sentence and the previous sentence to diagnose the relationship between the two. In this case, each sentence independently builds on the statement in the first sentence of the paragraph that says that carbon can be a "curse." "Furthermore" is the best way to list an additional aspect to an argument. "Accordingly" and "consequently" express cause and effect, which is not what we want. "Nevertheless" is contrasting, which is equally incorrect.

8. **(D)** The subject is difficult to isolate, but it is "I." One would say, "I am," not *I are/is/were*.

9. **(B)** This sentence is most logically placed after sentence 2. A good thing, life-giving photosynthesis, is mentioned at the end of sentence 2. Then sentence 3 transitions to a contrasting bad thing—namely, the carbon footprint. Any of the other placements would make this logical transition unclear.

10. **(C)** When paraphrased, the clause becomes "I operated *inside* a balanced cycle," or "I operated *as part of* a balanced cycle." Choice (A), "between," requires operating *between two things*. Choice (B), "among," requires operating *among three or more things*. However, carbon is part of only *one thing*: as the cycle. Choice (D) implies a causal relationship that is not logical.

11. **(D)** Pay attention to context in order to maintain parallelism. The other words in the list are "respiration" and "combustion"—both nouns that end in -*tion*. "Decomposition" is one of two noun options, but it is the -*tion* ending that maintains parallelism better than the gerund "decomposing." Choices (B) and (C) are not nouns. Rather, they are verbs that do not maintain parallelism in the list.

Court Reporter

1. **(B)** When deciding on *who* versus *whom,* remember to rewrite the sentence using *he* or *him*. In this case, one would say *he represents* rather than *him represents.* Recall that he = who and him = whom, so one must use *who* here. Choices (A), (C), and (D) all have at least one instance of misusing *whom,* so choice (B) is the only possible answer.

2. **(A)** The clause up to the word "trial" is independent, as is the clause after "trial." Accordingly, sufficient punctuation is needed to separate the two. Eliminate choice (B) because it is a comma splice. In the second clause, "jurors represent a panel of judges," we want no punctuation separating the subject and predicate. Choices (C) and (D) both add unnecessary commas.

3. **(C)** This question is more a matter of vocabulary than anything else. After eliminating choice (D)—a gerund that leaves a fragment in its wake—one must simply select the most apt vocabulary. *To comprise* means "to consist of," so this is the most logical option. *To compromise* is to come to an agreement, which isn't logical. *To compose* is to create, which is equally illogical.

4. **(B)** First, maintain verb parallelism. The rest of the passage is in present tense, so eliminate choice (D) for being past tense. Our proposed question refers to the previous sentence that refers to a list that "comprises those occupants found in a normal legal proceeding." The most logical follow-up is "Or does it?" This phrase means *does this list really comprise the occupants in the legal proceeding*? Choices (A) and (C) use pronouns that aren't logical in context.

5. **(D)** The phrase "an often-overlooked occupation of legal services" is a parenthetical phrase. If you remove it from the sentence, the clause still functions perfectly well. The rule for parenthetical phrases is that they can be separated from the main clause using either two commas or two dashes. Choices (A) and (C) bungle the parenthetical phrase completely. Choice (B) is close, but it uses one dash and one comma, whereas one needs to use two of the same punctuation marks.

6. **(B)** Notice that choices (A) and (D) convey *the exact same meaning*. As there can be only one correct answer, eliminate those two (the relationship is not causal). Choice (C) declares a contrast, but this sentence does not contrast with the previous one. What actually happens is that the second sentence restates the first sentence in a more explanatory fashion. "In other words" is the correct answer.

7. **(C)** Consider what the sentence is implying: by using key combinations, it would be much quicker to type than if one had to punch each letter key individually. Choice (C) is most logical and effective. Choices (A) and (B) are logical, but they aren't terribly descriptive and thus not very effective. Choice (D) is completely irrelevant.

8. **(D)** The pronoun in the underlined portion must refer back to the singular "court reporter," which only choice (D) successfully does. Choice (A) uses the plural "they." Choice (B) changes this from third person to second person. Choice (C) uses an incorrect verb.

9. **(A)** Notice the context of this paragraph: it is written in second person, consistently referring to *you*. Maintain that parallelism by staying in second person instead of switching to third person as the other choices do.

10. **(D)** Analyze the graph for this question, particularly the data about court reporter salaries. Notice that the top 10% make roughly $60,000 dollars per year, thus making choice (D) the most logical and specific option. Choice (A) is incorrect, as this is a five-figure salary. Choice (B) is true but is not directly supported by the information in the graph since there are no statistics about the average American worker's salary, just statistics about those in legal professions. In this context, choice (C) and "student loans" are wholly irrelevant.

11. **(A)** Analyze the graph for this question. Choice (B) is simply not supported by the data. Choice (C) is equally unsupported as there are no data on entry-level hiring. Choice (D) is entirely false; attorneys earn much more. After eliminating the three illogical choices, all that remains is the correct answer. Analyze choice (A) just to make certain, and it is true.

Hatfields and McCoys

1. **(B)** The subject here is "feud," which is a singular noun that requires a singular verb. Eliminate choice (C) accordingly. Choice (A) would result in a sentence fragment. Delete choice (D) for producing a fragment. "Boils" is the correct answer.

2. **(C)** The first issue is not to include an unnecessary comma between "land and livestock." No comma is required in a list of just two items. Eliminate choices (A) and (B) for that reason. Choice (D) neglects necessary punctuation after "region," rendering it a run-on sentence.

3. **(D)** Choose the correct transitional word by analyzing the relationship between the current sentence and the previous sentence. There is no cause-and-effect relationship, so eliminate choice (A). There is no contrasting relationship, so eliminate choices (B) and (C). Ultimately, a transition wasn't necessary at all, and sometimes that is perfectly fine. Choice (D) is the correct answer.

4. **(A)** The concept here is that the McCoy witness's betrayal of his own family led to his death. The betrayal thus *sealed his fate*, and he was subsequently murdered by his family members. Choices (B), (C), and (D) provide no relevant, logical connection to the man being killed.

5. **(D)** In essence, we must select a possessive form of *disapproval of families*. Since there are plural *families*, eliminate choice (A). Choices (B) and (C) neglect the necessary apostrophe that demonstrates possession.

6. **(B)** This choice uses concise wording that is in a logical order. Choice (A) is too wordy. Choice (C) uses awkward word order along with an unneeded "to." Choice (D) is also too wordy.

7. **(D)** We must work with the "to" already provided at the beginning of the sentence. This demonstrates that we need an infinitive verb. "Venge" is an archaic verb that was abandoned centuries ago. "Vengeance" is a noun, not a verb. "Revenging" would not work with the preceding "to" to create an infinitive.

8. **(A)** To "illude" means to create an illusion, so this is not logical in context. To "allude" is to refer to something, which is equally illogical. To "illuminate" is to shine light upon, which still does not make sense. To "elude," however, means to escape or avoid, which is perfect in this sentence.

9. **(D)** In the first paragraph, Randolph McCoy is referred to as "Old Ran'l." Continuing to refer to him as "Old Ran'l" avoids the ambiguity that would be caused by referring to him as "Mr. McCoy." In effect, everyone in the passage is either a Hatfield or a McCoy. So writing *Mr. McCoy* leaves the reader uncertain as to which McCoy is intended. Eliminate choice (A), as this actually is *less* a clarification than a cause of confusion. Eliminate choice (B), as "old Ran'l" has already been established as acceptable and therefore formalities have already been abandoned. Choice (C)'s statement is simply incorrect.

10. **(B)** Sentence 2 refers to the publishing of inflammatory articles by newspapers, which matches the "journalistic sensationalism" mentioned in the proposed insertion. The insertion, then, must come either *before* or *after* sentence 2 in order to maintain coherence. As *before sentence 2* is not an option, "before sentence 3" (or *after sentence 2*) is the most logical selection.

11. **(A)** If the underlined sentence were deleted, most readers would wonder what was exceptional about the ninth person that permitted him to avoid life in prison. Thankfully, our underlined sentence answers this question for us: *the ninth wasn't so lucky; in fact, he was probably the least lucky of all.* Thus, the sentence must be kept as it "provides a relevant clarification" that removes confusion that might arise otherwise.

Hornsby

1. **(A)** If the author were to delete the sentence, it would then be unclear *why* he struggles with the phenomenon of fame. It "provides a relevant elaboration," as in choice (A). Choice (B) is incorrect as Bruce Hornsby, not Andy Warhol, is "the main person to be analyzed."

2. **(A)** The subject here is "someone of actual import," and *someone* is a singular noun that requires a singular verb. Eliminate choice (B) for being a plural verb, and eliminate choice (D) for not being a verb at all. Choice (C), *a gerund*, does not provide a complete sentence. "Passes," however, is a singular verb.

3. **(D)** Choice (A) places an unnecessary comma after "love." Choice (B) places an unnecessary comma after "true." Choice (C) neglects to end with a question mark. Choice (D) is correct; the colon acts as a nice lead-in to the question.

4. **(C)** "Obliquely" means *indirectly,* and there is nothing indirect about the statement, just as there is nothing *imaginative* or *powerful* about it, as described by choices (A) and (B). "Inevitably" means *unavoidably.* The author's point is that he *unavoidably* has to tell you who Hornsby is, and the fact that this is necessary is unfortunate.

5. **(C)** This question is difficult in that the choices are all fairly similar. Choice (A) transitions to passive voice, which is best to avoid if possible. In choice (B), saying both "case" and "point" is wordy and unnecessary. ("Case in point" is a common phrase, but using "case" and "point" separately in this instance does not use the common idiom.) In choice (D), "arbitration" is a process through which two parties resolve differences and is not connected with the adjective *arbitrary.*

6. **(B)** Choice (A) is not "self-deprecating" but, rather, deprecates *others.* Choice (C) is not self-deprecating in any way; rather, it reads almost as more of a boast. Again, choice (D) features nothing of self-deprecation. Choice (B), however, fits the question. Its use of "forgive my hyperbole" is an acknowledgment that the author is aware that he is *going overboard* in his praise, so to speak.

7. **(B)** This sentence reads awkwardly at first, particularly with the use of both "various" and "variety." But if you look closer, you will see that a "variety station" is a genre of radio channel and the "various" refers to the prevalence of those stations. Eliminate choices (A) and (C) for not recognizing "variety stations." Just as one wouldn't say, "There are two, cars," one can't say, "various, variety stations." The quantifier must not be separate from what it is describing. Eliminate choice (D) because of that unnecessary comma.

8. **(C)** Without the underlined portion, many high school readers would not recognize the fame of the musicians mentioned; thus, it provides an important distinction that again "underscores the author's thoughts about Hornsby's lack of recognition." In effect, *why are Hornsby's peers so much more famous than he is*?

9. **(A)** "Like van Gogh's or F. Scott Fitzgerald's" is an *appositive*. If you remove this portion, the sentence still functions perfectly acceptably. A correctly used appositive must be set off from the surrounding sentence with two commas or two dashes. Choice (B) forgets the punctuation completely. Choice (C) incorrectly diagnoses what the appositive actually is by misplacing the second comma. Choice (D) neglects the second comma. In addition, choice (A) is the only option that makes a logical comparison, using the possessive "Gogh's" and "Fitzgerald's" to make these implicitly comparable to "Hornsby's legacy."

10. **(B)** The relationship between this sentence and the previous one is *contrasting*. When paraphrased, the sentences are *Maybe Hornsby will be famous later. However, I doubt it.* "But" is the only option that executes the contrast. Choices (A), (C), and (D) all are *cause-and-effect* transitions.

11. **(B)** To quantify adjectives, it is appropriate to use "less." For example, one would never say *he is fewer fast*. Rather, one would say *he is less fast*. Eliminate choices (C) and (D) accordingly. "Lessening" cannot be used as a determiner, which is what this sentence requires.

President

1. **(C)** Certain expressions are used frequently in the English language, and it is important to use the common preposition when using these expressions. The phrase "at the core" is an example of one of those expressions. Using "at" is far preferable to the other choices if only because that is the way this expression is typically written.

2. **(A)** The problem with this sentence is that it needed to be placed earlier if it was going to be used at all. The passage has drifted away from discussion of the separation of powers. To return to the topic would be flighty at this point, breaking with the flow of the passage. Choice (A) is the correct answer.

3. **(A)** Choice (B) is flawed because it omits an apostrophe on "one's." Choice (C) forgets a necessary comma after "thus." Choice (D) changes from second person to third person during the course of the sentence. Choice (A) is without blemish, and it is the correct answer.

4. **(B)** Choice (A) is very wordy. For instance, "for the duration of 14 years" can be much more effective if it is shortened to "for 14 years." Choice (C) reads as if the president must be exactly 35. Choice (D) is terribly general, providing us with no relevant, specific information. Choice (B) is the best combination of concision and specificity.

5. **(D)** "Charisma," a singular noun, is the subject. It requires a singular verb to maintain concordance. Eliminate choices (A) and (B) accordingly. At this point, the decision is about "lies" versus "lays," which are two commonly confused verbs. To *lay* is the act of physically taking something and placing it elsewhere. To *lie* is the act of an object remaining at rest. "Lies" is far more appropriate in this context.

6. **(C)** Sentence 3 mentions "charisma." The proposed insertion practically gives us the complete definition of charisma by using the words "charm, attractiveness, and likability." The insertion, then, is best placed after sentence 3, which is choice (C).

7. **(D)** The first part of the question regards proper use of the possessive for *the ages of presidents*. As there are multiple presidents, the apostrophe must go *after* the *s*. Eliminate choices (B) and (C) accordingly. Now, as there were multiple presidents, there were multiple ages. Choice (A) reads as if the presidents all had one age—the same age. Choice (D), then, is the correct answer.

8. **(B)** "Still" is separate from the main clause. (In effect, if we remove "still," the clause is still perfect.) So we must place a comma after "still" to denote that required separation. Eliminate choice (A) accordingly. From there is a list of three things: "allure, a spotless background, and years in diplomatic service." Eliminate choices (C) and (D) for neglecting the comma after "allure."

9. **(B)** Take note of parallelism in this sentence: "one has *to win*" (to win is an infinitive verb) and "triumph" (*one has to* is implied, which makes this an infinitive verb). Therefore, eliminate choice (A) since "following" is not an infinitive verb. We can eliminate choice (D) for omitting the listing comma after "convention." From there, we can analyze the context to see what is most *logical*. To "earn a following" means to gain supporters, while to "follow an earning" is nonsensical. Choice (B) is the best answer.

10. **(C)** For transitions, analyze both the current sentence and the previous sentence to determine how they interrelate. The second sentence here gives a supporting example to bolster the claim made in the first sentence. "For instance" is the best option to illustrate an example. The second sentence isn't surprising but, rather, is to be expected based on sentence 1. Eliminate choice (A) for that reason. Choice (B) implies a cause-and-effect relationship that is not apparent, while choice (D) implies a contrast that is equally absent.

11. **(B)** Analyze the chart for this question. Notice that the chart refers to personal characteristics that voters have stated would be important to them in a presidential candidate. Paragraph 2 refers to personal characteristics, which makes that paragraph the most suitable place to insert a relevant sentence based on the data in our chart. Paragraph 1 is introductory, and there isn't any mention of personal characteristics there. Paragraph 4 refers to financial matters. Paragraph 3 is close, but it refers to more *concrete* qualifications, like education, seniority, and political credentials. Choice (B) is the correct answer.

Risk

1. **(A)** For one, notice that "we" is used throughout the sentence. That's indicative of the need to remain in first person plural, so eliminate choices (C) and (D). Now ask, *Is it better to say "we understood" or "us understood"?* "We," of course, is the proper pronoun. Choice (A) is correct.

2. **(B)** When deciding to delete a portion, ask yourself, *Is this information relevant?* Then ask, *Does it repeat information or feature information that can be readily inferred?* Since the passage already states that the narrator knew the roles he or she would fulfill upon graduation, "we felt well-prepared for the profession we were about to enter" is a restatement of what is already known. Choice (B) is the correct answer. This portion must be deleted because it does not provide meaningful, new information.

3. **(A)** When deciding between *who* and *whom*, remember to rewrite the clause using *he* or *him*. We would say *he walked* rather than *him walked*, so we must use *who*. Eliminate choices (B) and (D) accordingly. "Who walking" would leave a fragment—and a rough one at that—so choice (A), "who walked," is the correct answer.

4. **(C)** There are certain phrases that the test writers assume are widely known. "Out in the field" is one of those. The meaning isn't that one is *literally* in a body of grass but, rather, that one is in a professional environment—i.e., the *field of business management* in this case. Choices (A), (B), and (D) simply do not suit the required purpose as choice (C) does.

5. **(A)** Choice (D) can be immediately deleted as the professor is referring to *after* leaving school rather than returning to it. Choice (B) is somewhat relevant but is not a logical, effective conclusion to the argument. Choice (C) is relevant, but it *isn't effective;* it lacks the attention-getting quality of choice (A), which essentially says, *You've taken all these courses to be a better manager. But the true value comes down to one simple question: can you take calculated risk?* Choice (A), then, is by far the best answer.

6. **(D)** There are two independent clauses, with the first ending at "company" and the second beginning at "others." Choice (A) is a comma splice. Choice (B) is flawed in multiple ways, but the first mistake is with the inclusion of an unnecessary comma after "outcomes." Choice (C) incorrectly attempts to employ a parenthetical phrase. Choice (D), however, correctly links the two independent clauses with a semicolon.

7. **(C)** "Affective" is a psychological term relating to moods and feelings, and it isn't logical here. Eliminate "affecting" for the same reason. "Effecting" is a word that isn't traditionally an adjective and isn't particularly logical in this case. This leaves only "effective," which is the correct answer.

8. **(B)** The question requires "the most specific example," with *specific* being the operative word. Choices (A) and (D) aren't relevant to the concept of trying to determine lead time. Choice (C) regards attempts to *define* lead time rather than calculate it for an actual business. Choice (B) provides a very *specific* example of how lead time can fluctuate in a *specific* industry after a *specific* event occurs.

9. **(A)** This is an example of an independent clause. The subject is "the success of the business," and the predicate is "will be driven by how well you manage these variations." There is no reason to insert any punctuation to separate the subject and predicate, so eliminate choices (B), (C), and (D) accordingly.

10. **(C)** Choices (B) and (D) lack concision; eliminate them because they are wordy. The adverb "slowly" functions much more effectively when placed before "moving" as opposed to after. Choice (C), then, is the correct answer.

11. **(B)** Notice how sentence 4 says "the other" but is ambiguous in context. *What is the other?* The proposed insertion clarifies this, beginning with "one factor." "The other," then, refers to *the other factor,* which is much more logical when the insertion is placed before sentence 4.

Math

5

Math Review

What Is Tested on the Math Section?

The following is the typical breakdown of all the Math Test questions from both modules combined:

- Algebra (primarily linear equations and systems): approximately 14 questions
- Problem-Solving and Data Analysis (primarily demonstrating literacy with data and real-world applications): approximately 8 questions
- Advanced Math (primarily more complicated equations): approximately 13 questions
- Geometry and Trigonometry: approximately 5 questions

If you have studied Algebra 1, Geometry, and Algebra 2, then you most likely will have covered the concepts tested on the PSAT Math sections.

How Should I Use This Chapter?

Examine the following list. If there is anything you need to review or practice, check it out. After you complete the review, try the "Math Essentials Review Quiz" to be sure that you don't have any gaps in your knowledge.

Algebra

Problem-Solving and Data Analysis

Advanced Math

Geometry and Trigonometry

Algebra

Order of Operations

Remember the proper sequence of mathematical operations by using the acronym **PEMDAS:** *Please Excuse My Dear Aunt Sally.*

Parentheses ( ) or other grouping symbols, like $\sqrt{\ }$ or { }

Exponents x^y

Multiplication $x \times y$

Division $x \div y$

Addition $x + y$

Subtraction $x - y$

> **Example**

$$(-2)(4 + 3)^2 = ?$$

✓ **Solution**

Simplify what is in the parentheses first, square it, and then multiply it by -2.

$$(-2)(4 + 3)^2 =$$
$$(-2)(7)^2 =$$
$$(-2)49 = -98$$

FOIL

Remember how to multiply simple polynomials by "FOILing" the expression. This corresponds to the order in which you multiply parts of the factored expression:

First, **O**uter, **I**nner, **L**ast

In the expression $(a + b)(x + y)$, you can simplify by multiplying parts in the FOIL sequence and then simplifying like terms by combining them together:

First $= ax$ Outer $= ay$ Inner $= bx$ Last $= by$

Add them all together: $ax + ay + bx + by$

Here are examples of FOIL in action:

$$(4 + x)(2 - x) = 4 \cdot 2 - 4x + 2x - x^2 = 8 - 2x - x^2$$
$$(x + 2y)(x - 3y) = x \cdot x - 3xy + 2xy - 6y^2 = x^2 - xy - 6y^2$$

Order of Operations Drill

1. $(x + 4) + (x - 2) = ?$
2. $3(m + n) - n = ?$
3. $x^2 + 2x^2 = ?$
4. $\dfrac{2x + 3x}{x} = ?$
5. $\dfrac{3 \times (5n)^2}{n} = ?$

6. $(2 + x)(5 + x) = ?$

7. $(3x - 4)(2x + 5) = ?$

8. $5n(2n + 1)^2 = ?$

9. Solve for x: $2x + 5 = 7$

10. Solve for x: $\dfrac{-5}{x} = 10$

Solutions

1. The parentheses can be ignored since there is nothing on the outside of the parentheses:

$$(x + 4) + (x - 2) =$$
$$x + 4 + x - 2 = 2x + 2$$

2. Distribute the 3 and multiply it by each term within the parentheses. Then combine like terms to simplify:

$$3(m + n) - n =$$
$$3m + 3n - n = 3m + 2n$$

3. Add the like terms together:

$$x^2 + 2x^2 =$$
$$1x^2 + 2x^2 = 3x^2$$

4. Combine the parts on the top, and then divide both the top and bottom by x:

$$\frac{2x + 3x}{x} =$$
$$\frac{5x}{x} =$$
$$\frac{5\cancel{x}}{\cancel{x}} = 5$$

5. First simplify what is in the parentheses by squaring it, and then multiply and divide:

$$\frac{3 \times (5n)^2}{n} =$$
$$\frac{3 \times (25\,n^2)}{n} =$$
$$\frac{75\,n^2}{n} = 75n$$

6. FOIL the expression:

$$(2 + x)(5 + x) =$$
$$10 + 2x + 5x + x^2 =$$
$$10 + 7x + x^2 \rightarrow x^2 + 7x + 10$$

7. FOIL the expression:

$$(3x - 4)(2x + 5) =$$
$$6x^2 + 15x - 8x - 20 = 6x^2 + 7x - 20$$

8. First FOIL what is in the parentheses, and then distribute the $5n$ through the expression:

$$5n(2n + 1)^2 =$$
$$5n((2n + 1)(2n + 1)) =$$
$$5n(4n^2 + 4n + 1) = 20\,n^3 + 20\,n^2 + 5n$$

9. $2x + 5 = 7$

$\qquad 2x = 7 - 5$

$\qquad 2x = 2$

$\qquad x = 1$

10. $\dfrac{-5}{x} = 10$

$\qquad -5 = 10x$

$\qquad -\dfrac{5}{10} = x$

$\qquad -\dfrac{1}{2} = x$

Substitution and Elimination to Solve a System of Equations

Substitution

A common way to solve a system of equations with two variables is through *substitution* of one variable in terms of the other.

> **Example**

Solve for x and y in the equations below.

$$2x = y$$
$$y - 3x = -5$$

✓ Solution

Substitute $2x$ for y in the second equation:

$$(2x) - 3x = -5$$
$$-x = -5$$
$$x = 5$$

Plug 5 in for x into the first equation to solve for y:

$$2x = y$$
$$2(5) = 10$$
$$y = 10$$

Elimination

When two equations are similar to one another, *elimination* of terms and variables may be the easiest way to solve for the variables. Multiply both sides of one of the equations by a number that allows you to add or subtract one equation easily from another, making it easy to eliminate one of the variables.

Two equations have infinitely many solutions if the equations are identical. For example, $x + y = 2$ and $2x + 2y = 4$ together have infinitely many solutions since the equations are simply multiples of one another. Some equations, like $x + y = 2$ and $2x + 2y = 10$, have no solutions. They do not intersect at all because their graphs are parallel to each other.

> **Example**

Solve for both x and y in the system of equations below:

$$3x + 2y = 7$$
$$2x - y = 0$$

✓ **Solution**

Multiply the second equation by 2:

$$3x + 2y = 7$$
$$4x - 2y = 0$$

Then add the second equation to the first equation to eliminate the y-variables:

$$3x + 2y = 7$$
$$\underline{+4x - 2y = 0}$$
$$7x + 0 = 7$$

Divide both sides by 7 to get the answer: $x = 1$.

Then solve for y by plugging 1 in for x in the first equation:

$$3x + 2y = 7$$
$$3 \times 1 + 2y = 7$$
$$2y = 4$$
$$y = 2$$

The PSAT will generally have systems of equations with one or two variables. Be mindful that there should typically be as many *equations* as there are *variables* in order to solve a given system. For example, in order to solve for two variables, you should have two equations; to solve for three variables, you should have three equations.

Distance, Rate, and Time

When considering the relationship among distance, speed/rate, and time, use the following formula:

$$\text{Distance} = \text{Rate} \times \text{Time}$$

For example, if you were biking 80 miles at 10 miles per hour, it would take you 8 hours to do so. See how that situation fits into the equation:

$$80 \text{ miles} = 10 \frac{\text{miles}}{\text{hour}} \times 8 \text{ hours}$$

Variations on the distance, speed/rate, and time formula can also be used to solve for whichever variable is needed:

$$\text{Rate} = \frac{\text{Distance}}{\text{Time}} \text{ and Time} = \frac{\text{Distance}}{\text{Rate}}$$

> **Example**

If Fred has to drive 200 miles in 5 hours, at what average speed should he drive?

✓ Solution

Insert the given information into the formula and solve for rate (speed):

$$\text{Distance} = \text{Rate} \times \text{Time}$$
$$200 \text{ miles} = \text{Rate} \times 5 \text{ hours}$$
$$\frac{200}{5} = 40 \text{ miles per hour}$$

With distance, rate, and time questions, be sure to check that the units in the solution (mph, miles, hours, etc.) match the units required by the question.

Substitution and Elimination to Solve a System of Equations Drill

In questions 1–5, solve for x and y in these systems of equations:

1. $3x = 2y$
   $x = y + 1$

2. $y = x - 1$
   $7x = -3y + 2$

3. $x + 4y = 2$
   $-x + y = 8$

4. $x - \frac{1}{2}y = 3$
   $2x + y = 10$

5. $4x + 2y = 1$
   $8x + 4y = 2$

6. If Nischal is traveling at 40 miles per hour for 3 hours, how far will he have traveled?

7. What is the rate in feet per second a hockey puck travels if it goes 30 feet in 10 seconds?

Solutions

1. Use substitution to solve this system of equations:

$$3x = 2y$$
$$x = y + 1$$

Plug in $y + 1$ for x into the first equation:

$$3(y + 1) = 2y$$
$$3y + 3 = 2y$$
$$y + 3 = 0$$
$$y = -3$$

Then substitute -3 in for y into the second equation:

$$x = y + 1$$
$$x = -3 + 1$$
$$x = -2$$

So the solution is $x = -2$ and $y = -3$.

2. Use substitution to solve this system of equations:

$$y = x - 1$$
$$7x = -3y + 2$$

Plug in $x - 1$ for y into the second equation:

$$7x = -3(x - 1) + 2$$
$$7x = -3x + 3 + 2$$
$$7x = -3x + 5$$
$$10x = 5$$
$$x = \frac{1}{2}$$

Now, plug this value of x into the first equation:

$$y = x - 1$$
$$y = \frac{1}{2} - 1$$
$$y = -\frac{1}{2}$$

So the solution is $x = \frac{1}{2}$ and $y = -\frac{1}{2}$.

3. Use elimination to solve this system of equations:

$$\begin{array}{r} x + 4y = 2 \\ -x + y = 8 \\ \hline 0 + 5y = 10 \end{array}$$

Then, solve for y:

$$5y = 10$$
$$y = \frac{10}{5}$$
$$y = 2$$

Then, plug 2 back in for y and solve for x:

$$x + 4y = 2$$
$$x + 4(2) = 2$$
$$x + 8 = 2$$
$$x = -6$$

So the solution set is $x = -6$ and $y = 2$.

4. Solve using elimination by doubling the first equation and adding it to the second:

$$2\left(x - \frac{1}{2}y = 3\right) \rightarrow 2x - y = 6$$

$$\begin{array}{r} 2x - y = 6 \\ 2x + y = 10 \\ \hline 4x + 0 = 16 \end{array}$$

Then solve for x and plug it into either original equation to solve for y:

$$4x = 16$$
$$x = 4$$

$$2x + y = 10$$
$$2(4) + y = 10$$
$$8 + y = 10$$
$$y = 2$$

So the solution is $x = 4$ and $y = 2$.

5. Multiply the first equation by 2 to notice a pattern:

$$4x + 2y = 1$$
$$8x + 4y = 2$$

As you may recognize, this is identical to the second equation: $8x + 4y = 2$.

Since the two equations are identical and would therefore overlap if graphed in the *x-y* coordinate plane, there would be *infinitely* many solutions.

6. Multiply the rate by the time to find the total distance:

$$40 \times 3 = 120$$

So Nischal has traveled a total of 120 miles.

7. Divide the distance by the time to find the rate:

$$30 \div 10 = 3$$

So the puck is traveling 3 feet/second.

Fractions

The *numerator* is the number on top of a fraction, while the *denominator* is the number on the bottom of the fraction. For example, in the fraction $\frac{1}{2}$, "1" is the numerator and "2" is the denominator. To simplify fractions, put them in their *lowest terms*. Do so by canceling out the same number as a factor of both the numerator and the denominator. For example:

$$\frac{6}{10} = \frac{3 \cdot 2}{5 \cdot 2} = \frac{3 \cdot 2}{5 \cdot 2} = \frac{3}{5}$$

The number 2 can be taken out of both the numerator and denominator, leaving just $\frac{3}{5}$. We know that the fraction is now in lowest terms because no factors are shared by 3 and 5 besides 1.

Adding and Subtracting Fractions

To add two fractions, follow these two simple steps.

STEP 1   Find the least common denominator of each fraction (i.e., the lowest common multiple of the denominators) so that the fractions have the same number on the bottom.

Consider the problem $\frac{3}{7} + \frac{5}{14}$. The least common multiple of the denominators is 14, so $\frac{3}{7}$ can be rewritten like this:

$$\frac{3}{7} \times \frac{2}{2} = \frac{6}{14}$$

Now both fractions have 14 as the denominator. The addition problem looks like this:

$$\frac{6}{14} + \frac{5}{14} =$$

Let's do our second step to solve the problem.

STEP 2   Once you have the same denominator for the fractions, add their numerators.

With $\frac{6}{14} + \frac{5}{14}$, just add the 6 and 5 together:

$$\frac{6}{14} + \frac{5}{14} = \frac{6 + 5}{14} = \frac{11}{14}$$

To subtract a fraction from another, find the least common denominator and subtract the numerators. For example:

$$\frac{8}{9} - \frac{1}{6} =$$

$$\frac{2}{2}\left(\frac{8}{9}\right) - \frac{3}{3}\left(\frac{1}{6}\right) = \frac{16}{18} - \frac{3}{18}$$

The least common denominator is 18. Now subtract one numerator from the other:

$$\frac{16 - 3}{18} = \frac{13}{18}$$

Multiplying and Dividing Fractions

Multiply fractions using this rule:

$$\frac{a}{b} \cdot \frac{c}{d} = \frac{ac}{bd} \quad \text{(Neither } b \text{ nor } d \text{ can equal zero, or it will be undefined.)}$$

Visualize fraction multiplication with actual numbers:

$$\frac{3}{4} \cdot \frac{2}{5} = \frac{3 \cdot 2}{4 \cdot 5} = \frac{6}{20} \rightarrow \text{reduce the fraction} \rightarrow \frac{3}{10}$$

Divide fractions using the following rule:

$$\frac{a}{b} \div \frac{c}{d} = \frac{a}{b} \cdot \frac{d}{c} \quad (b, c, \text{ and } d \text{ cannot equal zero, or it will be undefined.})$$

Visualize fraction division with actual numbers:

$$\frac{2}{5} \div \frac{3}{4} = \frac{2}{5} \cdot \frac{4}{3} = \frac{8}{15}$$

Fractions Drill

1. Reduce $\frac{12}{18}$ to its lowest terms.

2. Reduce $\frac{2}{7}$ to its lowest terms.

3. $\frac{1}{4} + \frac{3}{4} = ?$

4. $\frac{2}{3} + \frac{1}{9} = ?$

5. $\frac{7}{8} - \frac{1}{2} = ?$

6. $\frac{15}{16} - \frac{3}{4} = ?$

7. $\frac{2}{9} \times \frac{4}{5} = ?$

8. $\frac{2}{3} \times \frac{3}{8} = ?$

9. $\frac{4}{3} \div \frac{1}{3} = ?$

10. $\frac{5}{8} \div \frac{2}{3} = ?$

Solutions

1. $\frac{12}{18} =$

   $\frac{2 \cdot 6}{3 \cdot 6} =$

   $\frac{2 \cdot 6}{3 \cdot 6} = \frac{2}{3}$

2. $\frac{2}{7}$ cannot be reduced further.

3. $\frac{1}{4} + \frac{3}{4} =$

   $\frac{1 + 3}{4} =$

   $\frac{4}{4} = 1$

4. $\frac{2}{3} + \frac{1}{9} =$

   $\frac{6}{9} + \frac{1}{9} = \frac{7}{9}$

5. $\frac{7}{8} - \frac{1}{2} =$

$\frac{7}{8} - \frac{4}{8} = \frac{3}{8}$

6. $\frac{15}{16} - \frac{3}{4} =$

$\frac{15}{16} - \frac{12}{16} =$

$\frac{15 - 12}{16} = \frac{3}{16}$

7. $\frac{2}{9} \times \frac{4}{5} =$

$\frac{2 \times 4}{9 \times 5} = \frac{8}{45}$

8. $\frac{2}{3} \times \frac{3}{8} =$

$\frac{2}{3} \times \frac{3}{8} =$

$\frac{2}{8} = \frac{1}{4}$

9. $\frac{4}{3} \div \frac{1}{3} =$

$\frac{4}{3} \times \frac{3}{1} =$

$\frac{4}{3} \times \frac{3}{1} =$

$\frac{4}{1} = 4$

10. $\frac{5}{8} \div \frac{2}{3} =$

$\frac{5}{8} \times \frac{3}{2} =$

$\frac{5 \times 3}{8 \times 2} = \frac{15}{16}$

Inequalities

An inequality is an expression that indicates that something is less than or greater than something else. The open end of the ">" goes toward the larger number. For example:

$$4 < 8 \text{ and } 7 > 2$$

When an inequality has a line underneath the "greater than" sign or the "less than" sign, it indicates that the terms on either side can also equal one another. For example:

$$x \leq 5 \text{ means that } x \text{ is less than or equal to } 5$$

When working with inequalities, solve them just as you would typical equations EXCEPT in two situations:

1. When you multiply or divide both sides of the inequality by a *negative* number, change the direction of the inequality sign.

❯ Example

Solve for x: $-5x > 2$

✓ Solution

Divide both sides by –5 and turn the > around to <.

$$-5x > 2$$

$$\frac{-5x}{-5} < \frac{2}{-5}$$

$$\frac{-5x}{-5} < \frac{2}{-5}$$

$$x < -\frac{2}{5}$$

2. If you take the reciprocal with an inequality, and the variables have the same sign (positive or negative), you must change the direction of the inequality sign. If the variables have opposite signs, do not change the direction of the inequality sign.

› Example

Simplify this expression, in which x and y are both positive: $\frac{1}{x} > \frac{1}{y}$

✓ Solution

Cross multiply, and then flip the sign to put the variables in the numerator:

$$\frac{1}{x} > \frac{1}{y}$$
$$x < y$$

When graphing inequalities on a number line, a hollow circle indicates $<$ or $>$ and a solid circle indicates $\leq$ or $\geq$. Figure 1 shows the graph of two different inequalities.

$n > 2$ is graphed as:

$n \leq 5$ is graphed as:

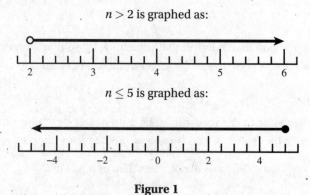

Figure 1

Inequalities Drill

1. Solve for x: $4x + 2 \leq 6$
2. How would you graph the inequality $x > 2$ on a number line?
3. Solve for x: $-3x \geq 9$

Solutions

1. $4x + 2 \leq 6$

    $4x \leq 4$

    $x \leq 1$

2. Since the inequality includes a $>$ sign with no "equal" underneath, make the circle where it intersects 2 *hollow*:

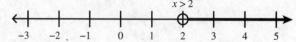

3. When you multiply or divide an inequality by a negative number, the direction of the inequality sign changes:

$$-3x \geq 9 \rightarrow x \leq -3$$

Absolute Value

Absolute value is the distance that a number is from zero along the number line. It doesn't matter if you are considering -3 or $+3$. Since both are the same distance from zero on the number line, both have an absolute value of 3.

If you want the absolute value of 9, express it like this: $|9|$.

When computing the value of an absolute value expression, simply determine the value of what is inside the two bars and then make that number positive, no matter if it was originally positive or negative. Here are some examples:

$$|25| = 25$$
$$|-12| = 12$$
$$|-3 + 8| = 5$$
$$|-2 \times 9| = 18$$

When solving absolute value equations, set them up as equal to both a positive and a negative value. If, for example, you are going to solve $|x + 2| = 4$, you should write it as two different equations since what occurs inside the absolute value signs can have either a positive or a negative value and can make the expression true.

$$|x + 2| = 4$$

$$\begin{array}{ccc} x + 2 = 4 & & x + 2 = -4 \\ x = 2 & \text{and} & x = -6 \end{array}$$

So x could be either 2 or -6.

Absolute Value Drill

1. What is the value of $|8|$?
2. What is the value of $|-25 + 4|$?
3. What are the possible solutions for x: $|x + 5| = 7$?
4. How many solutions are there for x in this equation? $|x - 5| = -2$

Solutions

1. 8

2. $|-25 + 4| \rightarrow |-21| \rightarrow 21$

3. Turn $|x + 5| = 7$ into two equations and solve:

$$\begin{array}{ccc} x + 5 = 7 & & x + 5 = -7 \\ x = 2 & \text{and} & x = -12 \end{array}$$

So the solutions for x are 2 and -12.

4. Since an absolute value must give a value that is greater than or equal to zero, there are *no* solutions to this equation.

Linear Relationships

Slope-Intercept Form

Determine the graph of a line by putting it in *slope-intercept form*:

$$y = mx + b$$

m = slope of the line, the "rise" over the "run," calculated with $\dfrac{(y_2 - y_1)}{(x_2 - x_1)}$

b = y-intercept of the line, i.e., where the line intersects the y-axis

> **Example**

Graph the following equation:

$$y = 3x + 2$$

> **✓ Solution**

Based on the slope-intercept formula, the line has a slope of 3 and a y-intercept of 2.

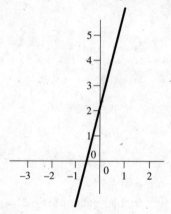

Parallel and Perpendicular Lines

Lines that are *parallel* to one another have *identical slopes*—they will never cross one another. (Parallel lines should have different y-intercepts, or they will simply be overlapping lines.) Figure 2 is a graph of two parallel lines in the x-y coordinate plane, $y = 3x$ and $y = 3x + 2$:

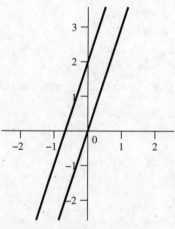

Figure 2

Perpendicular lines intersect at a 90° angle and have slopes that are *negative reciprocals* of one another. For example, if one line has a slope of 4, a line perpendicular to it has a slope of $-\frac{1}{4}$. Figure 3 is an example of two perpendicular lines and their graph, $y = -\frac{1}{5}x - 1$ and $y = 5x - 3$:

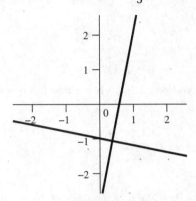

Figure 3

Slope Formula, Positive and Negative Correlations

To find the slope between two points, (x_1, y_1) and (x_2, y_2), plug the coordinates of the points into this formula:

$$\text{Slope} = \frac{\text{Change in } y}{\text{Change in } x} = \frac{(y_2 - y_1)}{(x_2 - x_1)}$$

(It is not important which point you consider the first or second set of coordinates, so long as your calculation is consistent.)

> **Example**

If a line includes the points (6, 4) and (2, 9), what is the slope of the line?

✓ **Solution**

You can determine the slope as follows:

$$\frac{(y_2 - y_1)}{(x_2 - x_1)} = \frac{(9 - 4)}{(2 - 6)} = -\frac{5}{4}$$

You can examine the slope of a line to see whether the variables have a positive or a negative correlation. If the x-values and y-values increase together or decrease together, the variables have a *positive correlation*. The line has a *positive slope*. If the x-values increase while the y-values decrease, or vice versa, the variables have a *negative correlation*. The line has a *negative slope*.

Linear Relationships Drill

1. What is the y-intercept of the line given by $y = -4x + 13$?

2. What is the slope of a line with points $(1, -2)$ and $(-4, 6)$?

3. What is the slope of the line given by $-8x + 2y = 10$?

4. If (3, 5) is a point on a line that goes through the origin, what is the slope of this line?

5. If a line has a slope of $-\frac{2}{3}$, what is the slope of a line perpendicular to it?

6. If two lines have the same slope but different y-intercepts, how often will the lines intersect?

7. In the equation $y = 5x$, are x and y positively or negatively correlated?

Solutions

1. The line is in slope-intercept form, $y = mx + b$, so the y-intercept corresponds to the b: 13.

2. Use the slope formula, $\dfrac{(y_2 - y_1)}{(x_2 - x_1)}$, to solve for the slope of the line with these points:

$$\frac{(y_2 - y_1)}{(x_2 - x_1)}$$

$$\frac{(6 - -2)}{(-4 - 1)} = \frac{8}{-5} = -\frac{8}{5}$$

3. Rearrange the parts of the equation so that it is in slope-intercept form:

$$-8x + 2y = 10$$
$$2y = 8x + 10$$
$$y = 4x + 5$$

The slope is 4.

4. The origin has the coordinates $(0, 0)$. So take the slope of the two points using the slope formula:

$$\frac{(y_2 - y_1)}{(x_2 - x_1)}$$

$$\frac{(5 - 0)}{(3 - 0)} = \frac{5}{3}$$

5. Take the negative reciprocal of $-\dfrac{2}{3}$ to find the slope of a perpendicular line. Multiply $-\dfrac{2}{3}$ by -1 and flip the fraction.

$$-\frac{2}{3} \times -1 = \frac{2}{3}$$

$$\frac{3}{2}$$

6. Lines with the same slope but different y-intercepts are parallel to each other. Therefore, they never intersect. For example, the lines $y = 2x$ and $y = 2x + 2$ have identical slopes but different y-intercepts, making them parallel:

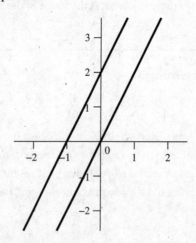

7. The variables are *positively* correlated with one another because the line of this equation has a positive slope. As x increases, y also increases.

Problem-Solving and Data Analysis

Interpreting Functions

Linear, Quadratic, and Exponential Models

A linear *relationship* between two variables is represented by a graph with a *constant slope*. For example, the equation $y = x$ represents a linear relationship between x and y, as you can see in the graph in Figure 4.

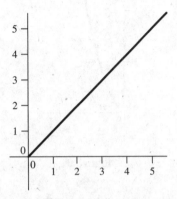

Figure 4

TIP

If you have a question that says some quantity is increasing at a "constant" rate, realize that this is code for a linear relationship.

A *quadratic relationship* between two variables, x and y, is generally represented by an equation of the form $y = kx^2$ or $y = ax^2 + bx + c$, in which k, a, b, and c are constants. It is called a quadratic relationship because "quad" means *square*. Figure 5 shows a portion of the graph of $y = x^2$, in which x and y have a quadratic relationship.

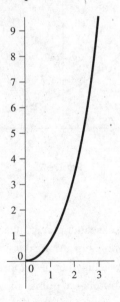

Figure 5

TIP

Generally the most rapid growth or decay is found with an exponential function, and the least rapid growth or decay is found with a linear function.

An *exponential relationship* between two variables, x and y, is generally expressed in the form $y = cb^x$ or $y = ab^x + c$, in which a, b, and c are constants. Figure 6 shows a portion of the graph of $y = 3^x - 1$, which is an exponential function. (Notice that the exponential relationship puts the x in the exponent part of the equation.)

Figure 6

Keep in mind that functions can have negative linear, quadratic, and exponential relationships. In other words, these functions can express decay rather than growth. For example, the function $y = 20 \times 0.5^x$ shows decay because as x increases to infinity, the y-value decreases. The graph of the function is shown in Figure 7.

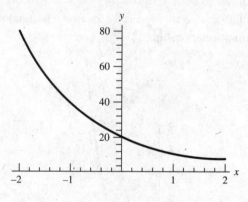

Figure 7

Scatter Plots

The PSAT will test your understanding of scatter plot graphs. Scatter plots provide a graph of different points that together show a relationship among data. To see the relationship among the data, draw a "line of best fit" that shows a line that best approximates the data points. A line of best fit typically has roughly the same number of points above it and beneath it, unless there are significantly outlying points. Figure 8 is an example of a scatter plot with a line of best fit.

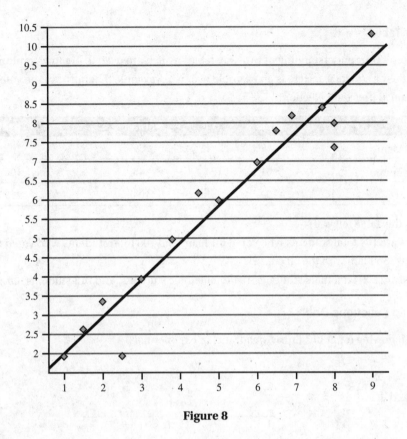

Figure 8

Histograms

Another type of graph on the PSAT is the histogram—it shows the frequency of different values in a data set. For example, consider the histogram in Figure 9.

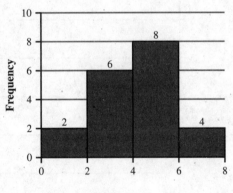

Figure 9

What does this histogram portray?

- 2 values in the set between 0 and 2
- 6 values between 2 and 4
- 8 values between 4 and 6
- 4 values between 6 and 8

Two-Way Tables

The PSAT tests your understanding of two-way tables, which are used to organize multiple variables and their frequencies. Here is an example of a two-way table that portrays the votes in a student council president election:

	Male	Female	Total
Voted for Liam	48	59	107
Voted for Emma	61	45	106
Total	109	104	213

What does this table tell you?

- There are 107 total students who voted for Liam and 106 total students who voted for Emma. So Liam won the election.
- There are 109 total male students, 104 total female students, and 213 students altogether.

Interpreting Functions Drill

1. Are the following functions linear, quadratic, or exponential?
   a. $y = 2x^2 - 5$
   b. $y = 4x + 2$
   c. $y = 6^x + 5$

2.

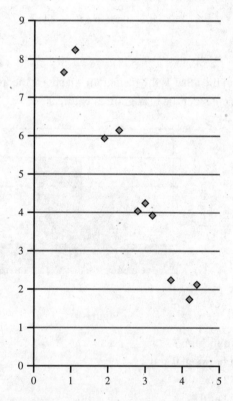

Consider the scatter plot above. When rounded to the nearest whole number, what is the slope of the line of best fit for this scatter plot?

3.

	Seniors Graduating with Honors	Seniors Graduating without Honors	Total
Lincoln High School	50	240	290
Jefferson High School	80	170	250
Total	130	410	540

Consider the table above.

a. How many seniors are graduating from Jefferson High School without honors?

b. How many seniors are at both schools?

c. How many seniors are at just Lincoln High School?

Solutions

1. a. $y = 2x^2 - 5$ is a quadratic function since the x is raised to the second power.

b. $y = 4x + 2$ is a linear function since it has a constant slope of 4.

c. $y = 6^x + 5$ is an exponential function since the 6 is raised to the x power.

2. To estimate the slope, sketch a best-fit line:

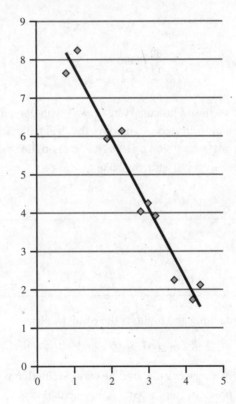

The line roughly has points at (1, 8) and (3, 4). So the slope would approximately be:

$$\frac{(y_2 - y_1)}{(x_2 - x_1)}$$

$$\frac{8 - 4}{1 - 3} =$$

$$\frac{4}{-2} = -2$$

3. a. 170

   b. 540. Include seniors from both schools, both those who are graduating with honors and those who are graduating without honors.

   c. 290. Include only seniors from Lincoln, both those who are graduating with honors and those who are graduating without honors.

Percentages

The general formula for percentages is:

$$\frac{\text{Part}}{\text{Whole}} \times 100 = \text{Percent}$$

❯ Example

You took a test with 80 questions, and you answered 60 of them correctly. What percentage of the questions did you answer correctly?

✓ Solution

$$\frac{\text{Part}}{\text{Whole}} \times 100 = \text{Percent}$$
$$\frac{60}{80} \times 100 =$$
$$0.75 \times 100 = 75\%$$

On the calculator-permitted section, a practical way to work with percentages is to convert them to decimals. First, remove the percent sign. Then, move the decimal point 2 spots to the left. Finally, multiply the last decimal expression by 100. Note that on the non-calculator section, you may want to convert the percentages to a fraction, like $\frac{1}{2} = 50\%$.

❯ Example

What is 45 percent of 300?

✓ Solution

Convert the percentage to a decimal and multiply the result by 300:

$$45\% \text{ of } 300 = 0.45 \times 300 = 135$$

When doing multistep percentage calculations, be very careful that you are considering the increases or decreases from previous steps in your later calculations.

❯ Example

A book regularly costs $20, but it is on sale for 10% off. A customer also has a coupon for 30% off the price of the book in addition to any sale discounts. What will be the price of the book the customer pays using only the sale? What will then be the price also using the coupon? Ignore any sales tax.

✓ Solution

First determine the sale price of the book by subtracting the 10% discount from the original price:

$$\$20 - (0.1 \times \$20) = \$20 - \$2 = \$18$$

Then subtract 30% of the new price from the new price to find the fully discounted price:

$$\$18 - (0.3 \times \$18) = \$18 - \$5.40 = \$12.60$$

Alternatively, you could calculate 90% of the original amount and then calculate 70% of that new amount. This method takes away the need to do subtraction:

$$\$20 \times 0.9 = \$18 \rightarrow \$18 \times 0.7 = \$12.60$$

Another useful approach to percentage calculations is to use 100 as a sample starting value.

❯ Example

If Michal's blood pressure increased by 20% from 6 P.M. to 7 P.M. and then decreased by 10% from 7 P.M. to 8 P.M., what was the overall percentage change in her blood pressure from 6 P.M. to 8 P.M.?

✓ Solution

Although you can calculate this percentage change using variables, it is far easier if you use 100 as the original number. If you assume Michal's initial blood pressure at 6 P.M. is 100, then a 20% increase will result in a new blood pressure of 120 at 7 P.M. Why? Because 20% of 100 is 20, and you add it to 100, giving 120. Then to calculate the change from 7 P.M. to 8 P.M., simply take 10% of 120, which is $120 \times 0.10 = 12$, and subtract it from 120: $120 - 12 = 108$. So 108 represents an 8% increase over 100. The overall percentage change in her blood pressure is 8%.

Sometimes you can save time on percentage problems by substituting fractions for the percentage. Certain percentages are easily converted to fractions, like $25\% \rightarrow \frac{1}{4}$ or $50\% \rightarrow \frac{1}{2}$.

❯ Example

If a shirt that costs $60 is on sale for 50% off, what is the discounted price of the shirt?

✓ Solution

To solve this without the use of a calculator, use the fraction $\frac{1}{2}$ instead of 50% to easily find the discounted price:

$$\$60 \times \frac{1}{2} = \$30$$

$30 taken away from $60 gives you a discounted price of $30.

Percentages Drill

1. What is 25% of 200?

2. What is 110% of 50?

3. If there are 50 questions on a test and you answered 36 questions correctly, what is your percent score on the test?

4. If a book regularly costs $20 but you have a coupon for 15% off the book, what would you pay altogether for the book after 7% sales tax is added?

5. Lydia has $1,000 in her savings account on January 1 of this year. If she earns 2% interest, compounded annually, how much money will she have on January 1 two years from now (assuming she makes no additional deposits or withdrawals)?

Solutions

1. $0.25 \times 200 = 50$

2. $1.10 \times 50 = 55$

3. $\frac{36}{50} \times 100 = 72\%$

4. First determine the discounted price for the book:

$$\$20 - (0.15 \times \$20) = \$17$$

Then, add the 7% sales tax to the price to get the total price paid:

$$\$17 + (0.07 \times \$17) = \$18.19$$

Alternatively, combine the addition and subtraction steps to save time in your calculations:

$$\$20 \times (0.85) = \$17$$

$$\$17 \times (1.07) = \$18.19$$

5. A 2% increase on an original amount of x is calculated like this:

$$x + 0.02x = 1.02x$$

To compound the 2% interest on the original sum of $1,000 over two years, multiply the original amount by 1.02 *twice* to get the total amount of money:

$$1.02 \times 1.02 \times \$1,000 = \$1,040.40$$

Ratios, Proportions, and Direct and Inverse Variation

Ratios and Proportions

Recognize when numbers and expressions involve the application of ratios and proportions. This will most frequently occur with word problems.

❯ Example

A cookie recipe calls for 6 cups of sugar and 4 cups of milk. Brendan has 18 cups of sugar. If Brendan wants to use all of that sugar, how many cups of milk will he need?

✓ Solution

Set up a ratio that has the same units in the numerator and the same units in the denominator:

$$\frac{4 \text{ cups milk}}{6 \text{ cups sugar}} = \frac{x \text{ cups milk}}{18 \text{ cups sugar}}$$

$$\frac{2}{3} = \frac{x}{18}$$

Cross multiply:

$$2 \times 18 = 3x$$

Divide both sides by 3:

$$\frac{2 \times 18}{3} = x$$

$$\frac{36}{3} = 12 = x$$

Brendan will need 12 cups of milk.

Direct and Inverse Variation

The variables a and b vary *directly* with one another (also called "directly proportional") if as a increases, then b increases, and if as a decreases, then b also decreases. The general form for an equation in which a and b are directly proportional is:

$$b = ka \quad (k = \text{constant})$$

As a real-world example, the greater the quantity of a certain food, the more calories there are in that food. You could say the food quantity and caloric quantity are directly proportional.

The variables a and b vary *indirectly* with one another (also called "inversely proportional") if as a increases, then b decreases, and if as a decreases, then b increases. The general form for an equation in which a and b are inversely related is:

$$b = \frac{k}{a} \quad (k = \text{constant})$$

As a real-world example, the more people who split a pizza, the smaller the size is of each person's piece of pizza. The number of people and the size of each piece are inversely related.

❯ Example

Consider the variable n in this equation:

$$n = \frac{x}{y}$$

To which variable is n directly proportional, and to which variable is n inversely proportional?

✓ Solution

Since n and x are both on top in the equation, if x becomes greater, so does n. (You can consider n to be a fraction with n as the numerator and 1 as the denominator.) The variable y is in the denominator, so as y increases, n decreases. As a result, n is directly proportional to x and is inversely proportional to y.

Ratios, Proportions, and Direct and Inverse Variation Drill

1. If 3 teaspoons are in 1 tablespoon, how many teaspoons are in 4 tablespoons?

2. If the U.S. dollar exchanges for 71 Indian rupees, how many dollars will be needed to purchase a toy that costs 426 rupees?

3. A town requires that in every new development, there are 2 acres of park for every 3 acres that are zoned for residential and/or commercial purposes. How many acres of park would be required in a new development that is 50 acres total?

4. When a car is traveling 40 kilometers per hour, how fast will it be going in meters per second (to the nearest tenth)? Note: There are 1,000 meters in a kilometer.

5. The physics equation that describes the relationship among pressure (p), force (F), and surface area (A) is $p = \dfrac{F}{A}$. Based on this equation, pressure is directly proportional and is inversely related to which variables?

6. Variables a and b are related by the equation $b = ka$, in which k is the constant of proportionality. If b is 5 when a is 10, what is the value of k?

Solutions

1. Set up a proportion to solve the problem:

$$\frac{3 \text{ teaspoons}}{1 \text{ tablespoon}} = \frac{x \text{ teaspoons}}{4 \text{ tablespoons}}$$

Cross multiply:

$$3 \times 4 = 12 \text{ teaspoons}$$

2. Solve using a proportion:

$$\frac{1 \text{ dollar}}{71 \text{ rupees}} = \frac{x \text{ dollars}}{426 \text{ rupees}}$$

Cross multiply:

$$426 = 71x$$

$$\frac{426}{71} = 6 \text{ dollars}$$

3. For a given development, there will be 2 park acres for every 5 total acres since 2 park acres + 3 non-park acres = 5 total acres. Solve this question using a proportion:

$$\frac{2 \text{ park acres}}{5 \text{ total acres}} = \frac{x \text{ park acres}}{50 \text{ total acres}}$$

Cross multiply:

$$50 \times 2 = 5x$$

$$\frac{100}{5} = 20 \text{ park acres}$$

4. There are 1,000 meters in 1 kilometer and 3,600 seconds in an hour (60 minutes $\times$ 60 seconds = 3,600). Solve by converting the units:

$$40\frac{\text{kilometers}}{\text{hour}} \times 1,000\frac{\text{meters}}{\text{kilometer}} \times \frac{\text{hour}}{3,600 \text{ seconds}} \rightarrow$$

$$40\frac{\cancel{\text{kilometers}}}{\cancel{\text{hour}}} \times 1,000\frac{\text{meters}}{\cancel{\text{kilometer}}} \times \frac{\cancel{\text{hour}}}{3,600 \text{ seconds}} = \frac{40 \times 1,000}{3,600} = 11.1\frac{\text{meters}}{\text{second}}$$

5. In this equation, $p = \dfrac{F}{A}$, p and F are both in the numerator. So pressure (p) and force (F) are directly proportional to one another—as p increases, F also increases. Surface area (A) is in the denominator while p is in the numerator. So A and p are inversely related to one another—as A increases, p decreases.

6. Plug the values for a and b into the equation to solve for k:

$$b = ka$$

$$5 = k(10)$$

$$\frac{5}{10} = k$$

$$\frac{1}{2} = k$$

Mean, Median, and Mode

Table 5.1 gives the definitions of mean, median, and mode.

Table 5.1 Mean, Median, and Mode

Definition	
Mean	$\dfrac{\text{Sum of Items}}{\text{Number of Items}} = \text{Mean}$ What you usually think of when you calculate the average.
Median	The middle term of a set of numbers when those numbers are lined up from smallest to largest. When the number of terms is even and the two terms in the middle are not the same, take the mean of the two middle terms to find the median.
Mode	The most frequent term in a set of numbers. In a set of numbers, if each number appears only once, there is no mode. However, if two or more numbers are tied for appearing the most times, that set has multiple modes.

> **Example**

Compute the mean, median, and mode for the following set of numbers:

$$\{1, 4, 4, 5, 8, 13, 22\}$$

✓ **Solution**

The mean:

$$\frac{1 + 4 + 4 + 5 + 8 + 13 + 22}{7} = \frac{57}{7} \approx 8.14$$

The mean is 8.14.

The median:

The numbers are already in order from smallest to largest. There are 7 numbers in the set. The median is 5 since it is in the middle of the set.

The mode:

The most frequent term is 4, so it is the mode.

A common application of the mean is when you calculate the missing term in a set when you already know the mean. Here is an example.

> **Example**

Sam has taken three exams, each worth a maximum of 50 points, over the course of her semester. She scored 40, 35, and 27 on her three exams. What must she score on a fourth exam, also out of 50 points, in order to average 35 points on her four exams?

✓ **Solution**

Set up the problem using the formula for finding the mean:

$$\frac{\text{Sum of Items}}{\text{Number of Items}} = \text{Mean}$$

Plug in the terms that you know:

$$\frac{40 + 35 + 27 + x}{4} = 35$$

Cross multiply by 4:

$$(4)\frac{40 + 35 + 27 + x}{4} = 35(4)$$

$$40 + 35 + 27 + x = 140$$

Solve for x:

$$40 + 35 + 27 + x = 140$$
$$102 + x = 140$$
$$x = 38$$

Sam would need to score a 38 on her fourth exam.

Mean, Median, and Mode Drill

1. Consider this set of numbers: {1, 3, 4, 5, 5, 7, 10}.
   a. What is the mean of this set?
   b. What is the median of this set?
   c. What is the mode of this set?

2. If the set of numbers {4, 6, 7, 7, 9} had the number 10 added to it, what would change?
   I. The set's mean
   II. The set's mode
   III. The set's median

3. A restaurant wants the average calories for each item in a meal to be 300. If a meal is to consist of a serving of pasta (500 calories), a salad (200 calories), and a side dish, what must the calories in the side dish be to meet the restaurant's requirement?

Solutions

1. a. The formula for the mean is $\frac{\text{Sum of Items}}{\text{Number of Items}} = \text{Mean}$. Add the numbers in the set together, and divide by how many numbers there are in the set:

$$\frac{1 + 3 + 4 + 5 + 5 + 7 + 10}{7} = \frac{35}{7} = 5$$

   b. The numbers are already organized in order from least to greatest, so find the fourth value of the set since it is in the middle:

$$(1, 3, 4, \mathbf{5}, 5, 7, 10)$$

The median is therefore 5.

   c. The mode is the most frequent member of the set. Since 5 appears twice while the other numbers appear only once, 5 is the mode of the set.

2. The current set is {4, 6, 7, 7, 9}, and the new set is {4, 6, 7, 7, 9, 10}.

The mean of the set would change. The original mean is $\dfrac{4+6+7+7+9}{5} = \dfrac{33}{5} = 6.6$, while the new mean would be $\dfrac{4+6+7+7+9+10}{6} = \dfrac{43}{6} \approx 7.2$. You could also estimate that the mean would change because if you add only a number that is greater than the mean to a set, it will make the mean larger as a result.

The mode of the set would NOT change because 7 is still the most frequent number in each set.

The median of the set would NOT change. In the original set, 7 is the middle number. In the new set, 7 is the value we get when we take the average of the two middle values of the new set (since there is an even number of members of the set): $\dfrac{7+7}{2} = 7$. If the two middle values in a set that has an even number of elements are the same, then the median will simply be one of these middle values.

3. Set up an equation for the mean, where x represents the calories in the side dish:

$$\frac{500 + 200 + x}{3} = 300$$

$$\frac{700 + x}{3} = 300$$

Cross multiply:

$$700 + x = 3 \times 300$$
$$700 + x = 900$$
$$x = 200$$

There must be 200 calories in the side dish.

Probability and Statistics

Probability Basics

Probability is the *likelihood that a given event will happen*, expressed as a fraction, decimal, or percentage. If there is no chance an event will occur, it has a probability of 0. If there is a 100 percent chance something will happen, it has a probability of 1.

To calculate probability, take the number of cases of a success and divide it by the total number of possible outcomes:

$$\text{Probability} = \frac{\text{Number of Successes}}{\text{Number of Possible Outcomes}}$$

> **Example**

If Janice has 3 red marbles out of the 200 total marbles in her collection, what is the probability that she will randomly pick a red marble?

✓ **Solution**

The number of successes is 3, and the number of possible outcomes is 200:

$$\frac{\text{Number of red marbles}}{\text{Number of total marbles}} = \frac{3}{200} = 0.015 = 1.5\%$$

Independent/Dependent Counting Problems

Counting problems are either independent or dependent.

Independent Counting Problems (Drawing With Replacement)

Independent counting problems involve drawing an object and then replacing it before drawing again. In these types of problems, each choice is computed *independently*. In other words, what you pick the first time has *no impact* on what you pick the second time, which has no impact on what you pick the third time, and so on. Such problems include flipping a coin several times because the flip of one coin has no impact on the later coin flips.

> ### Example

Hazel is choosing a 3-letter combination for her safe. Whether or not the letters are repeated does not matter. How many unique combinations can Hazel make?

✓ Solution

What Hazel picks for one letter does not impact what she picks for another letter. Since there are 26 letters in the alphabet, calculate the total number of possible combinations as follows:

$$26 \times 26 \times 26 = 17,576 \text{ possible combinations}$$

Dependent Counting Problems (Drawing Without Replacement)

Dependent counting problems involve drawing an object and not replacing it before drawing again. In these types of problems, each choice *depends* on what was previously chosen. In other words, what you pick the first time *has an impact* on what you pick the second time, which has an impact on what you pick the third time, and so on. Such problems include drawing names out of a hat because you do not want to pick the same name more than once.

✓ Example

John is choosing a 3-letter combination for his locker. The letters *cannot* be repeated. How many unique combinations can John make?

✓ Solution

What John picks for the first letter does impact what he picks for the second, which impacts what he picks for the third. So he will have one fewer possible letters for each subsequent choice. He can compute the total number of unique 3-letter combinations with no repeating letters as follows:

$$26 \times 25 \times 24 = 15,600 \text{ possible combinations}$$

Range and Standard Deviation

The PSAT will emphasize analyzing data sets. So be comfortable with the important concepts of range and standard deviation.

Range

Range is defined as the difference between the smallest and the largest values in a set of data.

Standard Deviation

Standard deviation measures how spread out or how varied the data points are in a set. It can be calculated using the following equation:

Standard deviation = $\sqrt{\text{Average of the squared distances of the data points from their mean}}$

Rather than having you conduct elaborate calculations to find the standard deviation of a set of data, you will need to have a feel for what the standard deviation represents. If the standard deviation is small, the data points have little variation. If the standard deviation is large, the data points have great variation.

> **Example**

Compare the ranges and standard deviations of Set A and Set B.

   Set A: {1, 3, 4, 6, 8}
   Set B: {1, 8, 50, 200, 380}

✓ **Solution**

The range and standard deviation of Set B are greater than the range and standard deviation of Set A. Why? The values in Set A range from only 1 to 8 and do not vary much from the average of Set A (4.4). The values in Set B range from 1 to 380 and vary quite a bit from the average of Set B (127.8). The sets are simple enough that you can likely determine the general trends with standard deviation and range without doing detailed calculations.

The most common graph involving standard deviation is the *normal distribution*—the typical distribution of a large sampling of values in a bell curve shape. Figure 10 shows a normal distribution. About 68% of the values are within 1 standard deviation of the mean. About 95% of the values are within 2 standard deviations of the mean. About 99.7% of the values are within 3 standard deviations of the mean.

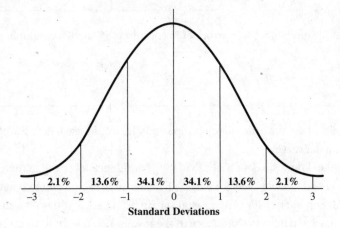

Figure 10

Confidence Interval and Margin of Error

When collecting a sample of data from a population, you need to be sure that the results give a true snapshot of the population as a whole. Two important terms are associated with the quality of data sampling: confidence interval and margin of error.

> Use common sense when thinking about data. To get an accurate snapshot of public opinion, you want to ask as MANY RANDOM people your questions as you can!

Confidence Interval

The confidence interval is a range of values defined so that there is a predetermined probability that the value of an unknown parameter under investigation will fall within the range. The higher the confidence level is, the more likely the parameter will fall within that interval.

> Example

Suppose a stockbroker has research indicating a 95% confidence interval that a company's stock will have a return between −7.8% and +9.5% during the next year. What does this mean?

✓ Solution

In this case, the unknown parameter is the average stock return for the year. This means that if all economic conditions remain the same, there is a 95% chance that the stock will have an average return in this interval of −7.8% to +9.5%.

Margin of Error

The margin of error is the maximum expected difference between the actual (unknown) parameter and the estimate for that parameter obtained through a sample. The smaller the margin of error is, the more accurate the survey results are.

> Example

Suppose that a survey has a margin of error of plus or minus 5% at 96% confidence. What does this mean?

✓ Solution

This means that 96% of the time the survey is repeated, the results are within 5% of the amount reported in the original survey.

You do not need to know the details of calculating confidence level and margin of error for the PSAT. Instead, you need to have a feel for what will make survey results more reliable. The confidence level and margin of error for survey results are interrelated. If you want a smaller margin of error, you may have to have less confidence in the results. If you want to be more confident in your results, you should allow for a larger margin of error. In order to maximize confidence in the results and minimize the margin of error, make sure that the sample is *as large and as random* as possible.

Probability and Statistics Drill

1. If a particular pet store has five dogs, four cats, and 12 guinea pigs available for purchase (and no other pets for sale), what is the probability that a randomly purchased pet will be a cat?

2.

	Write Using Cursive	Write Using Print	Total
Teachers	12	4	16
Students	40	280	320
Total	52	284	336

Consider the table above that portrays the teachers and students at a particular high school and their preferred writing styles.

a. What is the probability that a randomly selected teacher prefers to write using print?

b. What is the probability that a randomly selected person at the school prefers to write using cursive?

3. At the school cafeteria, there are three main courses and four desserts from which to choose. What is the total number of possible meals that a student can choose, assuming he or she wants both a main course and a dessert?

4. In Kim's closet, she has eight different dresses. She is packing for a three-day trip; she wants to wear a different dress on each day of the trip. What is the total number of combinations of dresses Kim could pack?

5. Consider the set of numbers {3, 4, 7, 11}. What positive number could be added to the set to double the set's range?

6. If someone added the number 20 to the set of numbers {1, 2, 4, 5, 12}, would that increase or decrease the standard deviation of the set?

7. Which of these approaches would give the best indication of how a particular town is planning on voting on an issue in an election?

a. Interviewing 100 political activists in the town as to their predictions

b. Taking a phone survey of 500 randomly selected likely voters

c. Having 500 pedestrians in the main city park complete a survey

Solutions

1. Total the number of pets:

$$5 + 4 + 12 = 21$$

Then divide the number of cats (4) by the number of total pets (21) to get the probability that a randomly purchased pet will be a cat:

$$\frac{4}{21}$$

2. a. There are 16 total teachers, and 4 of them prefer to write using print. So divide 4 by 16 to get the probability:

$$\frac{4}{16} = \frac{1}{4}$$

This is the same as 0.25 if you want to express the answer as a decimal.

b. There are 336 total people in the school, and 52 of them prefer to write using cursive. So divide 52 by 336. Your answer can be expressed as a reduced fraction or as a decimal:

$$\frac{52}{336} = \frac{13}{84} \text{ or } 0.155$$

3. Multiply the number of main courses by the number of desserts to find the total number of possible meals:

$$3 \times 4 = 12$$

4. After Kim wears one dress, she does not want to wear it again. Therefore, the number of dress options each day decreases by 1. Calculate the total number of combinations as follows:

$$8 \times 7 \times 6 = 336 \text{ total possible combinations}$$

5. The range of the set $\{3, 4, 7, 11\}$ is currently $11 - 3 = 8$.
   Double the current range to find the new range:

$$8 \times 2 = 16$$

Since the smallest number in the set is 3, add 16 to 3 to find the number that would need to be added to make the range of the set 16:

$$3 + 16 = 19$$

So the new set would be $\{3, 4, 7, 11, 19\}$ with 19 as the added number. It would have a range of 16, twice the original range of 8.

6. If 20 was added to this set, the new set would be $\{1, 2, 4, 5, 12, 20\}$. The average deviation from the mean would increase since the spread of the numbers would increase. Therefore, the standard deviation would increase.

7. Interviewing the political activists and the park pedestrians would not be ideal since the sample set would not be randomized. Performing a phone survey of the randomly selected voters would ensure that the sample was randomized, giving much better results.

Advanced Math

Factoring

When simplifying an equation, take out any common factors.

> **Example**

Factor $nx + ny$.

> ✓ **Solution**

$nx + ny$ can be expressed as $n(x + y)$ by factoring out the n.

> **Example**

Factor $\dfrac{2x^3 + 6x}{3x}$.

> ✓ **Solution**

$\dfrac{2x^3 + 6x}{3x}$ can be expressed as $\dfrac{2x(x^2 + 3)}{3x}$ since you can factor $2x$ out of the numerator. Then you can cancel out an x from the numerator and denominator:

$$\frac{2x(x^2 + 3)}{3x} = \frac{2x(x^2 + 3)}{3x} = \frac{2}{3}(x^2 + 3)$$

You also should know how to factor equations like $x^2 - x - 12 = 0$. Try to express it as two binomials that are multiplied by each other. The factored form looks like:

$$(x + \text{something})(x - \text{something}) = 0$$

In the case of $x^2 - x - 12 = 0$, you can rewrite it as $(x + 3)(x - 4) = 0$. -12 is equal to 3×-4, and $-x$ is equal to $-4x + 3x$, making it possible to visualize how the expression can be factored. If you use FOIL to multiply the left-hand side (i.e., multiply the **F**irst terms together, then the **O**uter terms, then the **I**nner terms, and finally the **L**ast terms), you will get the original equation:

$$(x + 3)(x - 4) = 0$$
$$x^2 - 4x + 3x - 12 = 0$$
$$x^2 - x - 12 = 0$$

Common Factoring Patterns

Memorize these patterns so you can recognize them on the PSAT Math Test and save time.

- Multiplying Binomials

$$(a + b)(a + b) = a^2 + 2ab + b^2$$

Example:

$$(x + 3)(x + 3) = x^2 + 6x + 9$$

$$(a + b)(a - b) = a^2 - b^2$$

Example:

$$(m + 2)(m - 2) = m^2 - 4$$

$$(a - b)(a - b) = a^2 - 2ab + b^2$$

Example:

$$(3 - y)(3 - y) = 9 - 6y + y^2$$

- Sum of Cubes

$$(a + b)(a^2 - ab + b^2) = a^3 + b^3$$

Example:

$$(2 + x)(4 - 2x + x^2) = 2^3 + x^3 = 8 + x^3$$

- Difference of Cubes

$$(a - b)(a^2 + ab + b^2) = a^3 - b^3$$

Example:

$$(y - 4)(y^2 + 4y + 16) = y^3 - 4^3 = y^3 - 64$$

Factoring Drill

1. Factor this expression: $4x + 8y$

2. Simplify this expression: $\dfrac{3x - 6y}{3}$

3. Simplify this expression: $\dfrac{12x^4}{3x^2}$

4. Factor this expression: $25x^2 - 9y^2$

5. Factor this expression: $27 - 8x^3$

Solutions

1. $4x + 8y \rightarrow 4(x + 2y)$

2. $\dfrac{3x - 6y}{3} =$

   $\dfrac{3(x - 2y)}{3} =$

   $\dfrac{3(x - 2y)}{3} = x - 2y$

3. $$\frac{12x^4}{3x^2} =$$

$$\frac{3 \cdot 4 \cdot x^2 \cdot x^2}{3x^2} =$$

$$\frac{3 \cdot 4 \cdot x^2 \cdot x^2}{3x^2} = 4x^2$$

4. $25x^2 - 9y^2 = (5x - 3y)(5x + 3y)$

5. This is a difference of cubes, where $a^3 - b^3 = (a - b)(a^2 + ab + b^2)$. In this case, a is equal to 3, and b is equal to $2x$. So the solution is:

$$27 - 8x^3 =$$

$$3^3 - ((2x)^3) =$$

$$(3 - 2x)(3^2 + 3(2x) + (2x)^2) = (3 - 2x)(9 + 6x + 4x^2)$$

Advanced Equation Concepts

Quadratic Formula

A second-degree equation containing the variable x, the constants a, b, and c, and written in the form $ax^2 + bx + c = 0$ can be solved using the quadratic formula:

$$x = \frac{-b \pm \sqrt{b^2 - 4ac}}{2a}$$

> **Example**

What are the values of x in the equation $2x^2 - 2x - 12 = 0$?

✓ **Solution**

The values of the constants are $a = 2$, $b = -2$, and $c = -12$. Solve for x by plugging a, b, and c into the quadratic formula:

$$x = \frac{-b \pm \sqrt{b^2 - 4ac}}{2a}$$

$$x = \frac{-(-2) \pm \sqrt{(-2)^2 - 4(2)(-12)}}{2(2)}$$

$$x = \frac{2 \pm \sqrt{4 + 96}}{4}$$

$$x = \frac{2 \pm \sqrt{100}}{4}$$

$$x = \frac{2 \pm 10}{4}$$

$$x = \frac{1}{2} \pm \frac{5}{2}$$

$$x = 3 \text{ or } -2$$

Completing the Square

Another way to solve quadratic equations is by completing the square—turning each side of the equation into parts that can be squared. Here is how you can solve for x using this method. Consider the following equation:

$$x^2 - 6x - 16 = 0$$

Start by adding 16 to both sides so the x-terms are all on the left.

$$x^2 - 6x = 16$$

Then take half of -6, which is -3, square it, and add it to both sides of the equation.

$$x^2 - 6x + 9 = 16 + 9$$

You can now rewrite the left-hand side in simplified, squared form:

$$(x - 3)^2 = 25$$

Take the square root of both sides:

$$x - 3 = \pm 5$$

Solve for x:

$$x - 3 = -5 \qquad \text{and} \qquad x - 3 = 5$$
$$x = -2 \qquad\qquad\qquad x = 8$$

Therefore, $x = 8$ and $x = -2$

Undefined Functions

A function can be undefined when *it is divided by zero*. The value at which a function is undefined indicates that the function has *no solution* for that value. This makes sense because it would be impossible to divide something into *zero* parts.

> **Example**

When is this function undefined?

$$f(x) = \frac{x^2 + 5}{x - 7}$$

✓ **Solution**

Find the value of x that would make this function have zero in the denominator. The denominator is $x - 7$, so set this equal to zero and solve for x:

$$x - 7 = 0$$
$$x = 7$$

So the function is undefined when $x = 7$.

Extraneous Solutions

Sometimes you should test solutions to see if they work in the original expression.

> **Example**

What is (are) the solution(s) for x in this equation?

$$x = \sqrt{24 - 2x}$$

✓ **Solution**

The logical first step to solve this equation is to square both sides:

$$x^2 = 24 - 2x$$

This can then be arranged and factored:

$$x^2 + 2x - 24 = 0$$
$$(x - 4)(x + 6) = 0$$
$$x - 4 = 0 \quad x + 6 = 0$$
$$x = 4 \qquad x = -6$$

So 4 and -6 both appear to be solutions. However, only 4 works in the original expression since the square root of a real number cannot be negative. Therefore, just 4 is the answer. Check for extraneous solutions when you start multiplying and dividing expressions containing square root symbols.

Advanced Equation Concepts Drill

1. Solve for x: $2x^2 - 5x + 1 = 0$

2. For what value of x is the following function undefined?

$$y = \frac{14x - 5}{2x + 3}$$

3. If x is going to have only imaginary solutions, what are the possible values of c in this equation? (If needed, see "Imaginary Numbers" on page 285.)

$$x^2 + 2x + c = 0$$

4. What is the solution (or solutions) to this equation?

$$x = \sqrt{12 - x}$$

5. Solve for x by completing the square: $x^2 - 8x - 20 = 0$.

Solutions

1. Use the quadratic equation to solve:

$$x = \frac{-b \pm \sqrt{b^2 - 4ac}}{2a}$$
$$x = \frac{-(-5) \pm \sqrt{(-5)^2 - 4(2)(1)}}{2 \cdot 2}$$
$$x = \frac{5 \pm \sqrt{25 - 8}}{4}$$
$$x = \frac{5 \pm \sqrt{17}}{4}$$

2. In order for the function $y = \frac{14x - 5}{2x + 3}$ to be undefined, the denominator, $2x + 3$, should equal zero. Set up an equation to solve:

$$2x + 3 = 0 \rightarrow 2x = -3 \rightarrow x = -\frac{3}{2}$$

3. Consider the quadratic equation: $x = \dfrac{-b \pm \sqrt{b^2 - 4ac}}{2a}$. If x is going to have only imaginary solutions, the *discriminant* $(b^2 - 4ac)$ in the quadratic formula must be *negative*. Why? If the discriminant was negative, you would be taking the square root of a negative number, which will result in imaginary solutions. For the equation $x^2 + 2x + c = 0$, the value of a is 1, the value of b is 2, and c is a variable. Set up an inequality to solve:

$$b^2 - 4ac < 0$$
$$2^2 - 4 \cdot 1 \cdot c < 0$$
$$4 - 4c < 0$$
$$4 < 4c$$
$$1 < c$$

As long as c is greater than 1, there will be an imaginary solution to the equation.

4. Start by squaring both sides of the equation:

$$x = \sqrt{12 - x}$$
$$x^2 = 12 - x$$
$$x^2 + x - 12 = 0$$

Then factor the equation:

$$x^2 + x - 12 = 0$$
$$(x + 4)(x - 3) = 0$$

It looks like -4 and 3 will work as solutions. However, you need to check for extraneous solutions by plugging these possible solutions back into the original equation.

Plug in 3 for x:

$$x = \sqrt{12 - x}$$
$$3 = \sqrt{12 - 3}$$
$$3 = \sqrt{9}$$
$$3 = 3$$

So 3 works.

Now plug in -4 for x:

$$-4 = \sqrt{12 - (-4)}$$
$$-4 = \sqrt{12 - (-4)}$$
$$-4 = \sqrt{16}$$
$$-4 \neq 4$$

So -4 is extraneous, and the only solution is 3.

5. Start by adding 20 to each side of the equation:

$$x^2 - 8x - 20 = 0$$
$$x^2 - 8x = 20$$

Now take half of -8, which is -4, square it, and add it to both sides:

$$x^2 - 8x + 16 = 20 + 16$$
$$x^2 - 8x + 16 = 36$$
$$(x - 4)^2 = 6^2$$
$$\sqrt{(x - 4)^2} = \sqrt{6^2}$$
$$x - 4 = \pm 6$$

The two solutions for x can be found as follows:

$$x - 4 = 6 \quad \text{and} \quad x - 4 = -6$$
$$x = 10 \qquad\qquad x = -2$$

So x can be either 10 or -2.

Synthetic Division

Synthetic division is the way students typically learn how to divide polynomials. Here is a brief review of how $2x^2 - 5x + 7$ would be divided by $x + 1$ using synthetic division.

Set up the synthetic division by taking the coefficients of the terms of the polynomial $(2, -5, 7)$ and placing the numerical term of the divisor $x + 1$ (multiplied by -1) to the left of them as follows:

$$-1 \,\big|\, 2 \quad -5 \quad 7$$

Then, bring down each of the coefficients, multiplying the columns one by one by the -1. Create sums to determine the divided polynomial and remainder:

$$
\begin{array}{r|rrr}
-1 & 2 & -5 & 7 \\
   &   & -2 & 7 \\
\hline
   & 2 & -7 & 14
\end{array}
$$

So the answer is $2x - 7$ with a remainder of $\dfrac{14}{x+1}$.

Important fact: $x + 1$ is NOT a factor of $2x^2 - 5x + 7$ since the remainder is not zero.

Synthetic Division Drill

1. Is $(x - 2)$ a factor of $x^2 + 3x - 10$?

2. What is the remainder when $5x^2 - 3x + 2$ is divided by $x - 2$?

Solutions

1. To determine if $(x - 2)$ is a factor of $x^2 + 3x - 10$, divide $x^2 + 3x - 10$ by $(x - 2)$ to see if there is a remainder. If the remainder is zero, then $(x - 2)$ is a factor. Use synthetic division to divide:

$$
\begin{array}{r|rrr}
2 & 1 & 3 & -10 \\
  &   & 2 & 10 \\
\hline
  & 1 & 5 & 0
\end{array}
$$

The remainder is zero, so $(x - 2)$ is a factor.

2. Use synthetic division to divide:

$$
\begin{array}{r|rrr}
2 & 5 & -3 & 2 \\
  &   & 10 & 14 \\
\hline
  & 5 & 7 & 16
\end{array}
$$

The remainder is 16 divided by $x - 2$:

$$\frac{16}{x - 2}$$

Function Notation and Manipulation

In school, you are probably comfortable with equations written in one of the following two ways:

A function written like this:

$$y = 4x - 2$$

is the same as a function written like this:

$$f(x) = 4x - 2$$

If you are told that $x = 3$, you can just plug 3 in for x into each equation:

$$y = 4(3) - 2$$
$$f(3) = 4 \cdot 3 - 2$$

The PSAT will also assess your understanding of *composite functions*, which involve functions that depend on one another. For example, consider these two functions:

$$f(x) = x + 5$$
$$g(x) = 3x - 1$$

If you are asked to solve $f(g(2))$, you need to work from the *inside out*. Start with the $g(x)$ function, plugging in 2 for x:

$$g(x) = 3x - 1$$
$$g(2) = 3 \cdot 2 - 1$$
$$g(2) = 5$$

Then, plug 5 into $f(x)$:

$$f(x) = x + 5$$
$$f(5) = 5 + 5$$
$$f(5) = 10$$

So $f(g(2)) = 10$.

Function Notation and Manipulation Drill

1. If $f(x) = -3x + 5$, what is the value of $f(4)$?

2. If $f(x) = 3x$ and $g(x) = x - 4$, what is the value of $f(g(5))$?

3. What is the value of $f(x + 2) = 5x - 6$ when $x = 4$?

Solutions

1. Plug in 4 for x:

$$f(x) = -3x + 5$$
$$f(4) = -3(4) + 5$$
$$f(4) = -12 + 5$$
$$f(4) = -7$$

2. Start by calculating the value of $g(5)$:

$$g(x) = x - 4$$
$$g(5) = 5 - 4$$
$$g(5) = 1$$

Now, plug 1 into $f(x)$:

$$f(x) = 3x$$
$$f(1) = 3(1)$$
$$f(1) = 3$$

3. Plug in 4 for x on the left-hand side to determine what value should be plugged in for x on the right-hand side:

$$f(x + 2) = 5x - 6$$
$$f(4 + 2) = 5(4 + 2) - 6$$
$$f(6) = 5(6) - 6$$
$$f(6) = 24$$

Exponents

Table 5.2 shows the most important exponent rules along with some concrete examples. It also includes ways to remember these rules.

Table 5.2 Exponent Rules

Exponent Rule	Concrete Example	Way to Remember
$x^a x^b = x^{(a+b)}$	$x^3 x^4 = x^{(3+4)} = x^7$	Remember the acronym **MADSPM**. **M**ultiply exponents, **A**dd them. **D**ivide exponents, **S**ubtract them. **P**arentheses with exponents, **M**ultiply them.
$\dfrac{x^a}{x^b} = x^{a-b}$	$\dfrac{x^7}{x^2} = x^{7-2} = x^5$	
$(x^a)^b = x^{ab}$	$(x^3)^5 = x^{15}$	
$x^{-a} = \dfrac{1}{x^a}$	$x^{-5} = \dfrac{1}{x^5}$	If you are "bad" (negative), you are sent down below!
$x^{\frac{a}{b}} = \sqrt[b]{x^a}$	$x^{\frac{2}{7}} = \sqrt[7]{x^2}$	The root of a tree is on the bottom. Similarly, the root is on the bottom and on the left-hand side!

Exponential Growth and Decay

One of the most common ways that the PSAT will assess your understanding of exponents is by asking you to calculate the future value of a quantity after interest is applied to it. Here is a formula you can use to determine *exponential growth*:

$$(\text{Future Value}) = (\text{Present Value})(1 + (\text{Interest Rate as a Decimal}))^{\text{Number of Periods}}$$

The number of periods indicates the number of times the interest is compounded.

> **Example**

If Sara starts a savings account with $500 and the money in the account earns 3% interest compounded once a year, how much money will she have in the account after two years?

✓ **Solution**

The present value of the money is $500. The interest rate, expressed as a decimal, is 0.03. The number of periods for which the money is compounded is 2 since there are two years. By plugging this all into the formula, you get the following:

$$(\text{Future Value}) = (500)\left(1 + (0.03)\right)^2$$
$$500 \times 1.03^2 = \$530.45$$

If a function decreases exponentially over time, slightly modify the formula by subtracting the interest rate to determine *exponential decay*:

$$(\text{Future Value}) = (\text{Present Value})\left(1 - (\text{Interest Rate as a Decimal})\right)^{\text{Number of Periods}}$$

> **Example**

Suppose the cost of a television is currently $600, but the price of the television will decrease by 5% each year. What will be price of the television exactly three years from now?

✓ **Solution**

The present value of the price is $600. The interest rate, expressed as a decimal, is 0.05. The number of periods for which the price is compounded is 3 since there are three years. By plugging this all into the formula, you get the following:

$$(\text{Future Value}) = (600)\left(1 - (0.05)\right)^3$$
$$600 \times 0.95^3 \approx \$514.43$$

Exponents Drill

1. Simplify: $3x^2 + 7x^2$

2. Simplify: $4(x^3)^2$

3. Simplify: $\dfrac{5x^3 + 10x}{5x}$

4. Simplify without the negative exponent: $2x^{-4}$

5. Simplify without the exponent form: $x^{\left(-\frac{2}{5}\right)}$

6. Simplify this expression: $\dfrac{x^{\left(\frac{3}{4}\right)}}{x^{-\left(\frac{1}{4}\right)}}$

7. Simplify this expression: $\left(\sqrt[3]{x^2}\right)\left(\sqrt[6]{x^8}\right)$

8. If Neha is 50 inches tall and she grows 5% in height each year, what is her height after two years have passed?

Solutions

1. $3x^2 + 7x^2 = 10x^2$

2. $4(x^3)^2 = 4x^{(3 \times 2)} = 4x^6$

3. $\dfrac{5x^3 + 10x}{5x} =$

   $\dfrac{5x(x^2 + 2)}{5x} =$

   $\dfrac{5x(x^2 + 2)}{5x} = x^2 + 2$

4. $2x^{-4} = \dfrac{2}{x^4}$

5. $x^{\left(-\frac{2}{5}\right)} = \dfrac{1}{x^{\left(\frac{2}{5}\right)}} = \dfrac{1}{\sqrt[5]{x^2}}$

6. $\dfrac{x^{\left(\frac{3}{4}\right)}}{x^{-\left(\frac{1}{4}\right)}} =$

   $x^{\left(\frac{3}{4}\right)} x^{\left(\frac{1}{4}\right)} =$

   $x^{\left(\frac{3}{4} + \frac{1}{4}\right)} = x^1 = x$

7. $\left(\sqrt[3]{x^2}\right)\left(\sqrt[6]{x^8}\right) =$

   $\left(x^{\frac{2}{3}}\right)\left(x^{\frac{8}{6}}\right) =$

   $\left(x^{\frac{2}{3}}\right)\left(x^{\frac{4}{3}}\right) =$

   $x^{\left(\frac{2}{3} + \frac{4}{3}\right)} = x^{\left(\frac{6}{3}\right)} = x^2$

8. You can use this equation to solve:

$$\text{(Future Value)} = \text{(Present Value)}(1 + \text{(Interest Rate as a Decimal)})^{\text{Number of Periods}}$$

The present value is 50 inches, the interest rate expressed as a decimal is 0.05, and the number of periods is 2 since you need the height after two years. By plugging this all into the formula, you get the following:

$$\text{(Future Value)} = (50)(1 + 0.05)^2 = 55.125 \text{ inches}$$

Zeros and Parabolas

Roots or Zeros

The root or zero of a function is the value for which the function has a value of zero. A function can have more than one root/zero. To find the root(s) of a function, either examine the equation of the function or look at the function's graph.

> **Example**

What are the zeros of $y = x^2 - 10x + 21$?

✓ **Solution**

The equation is graphed below:

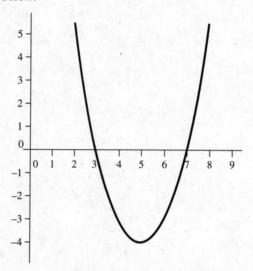

The function has roots/zeros at 3 and 7 since that is where the function intersects the *x*-axis. Since the function intersects the *x*-axis twice, the function has 2 solutions.

You can also determine the roots/zeros of the function by factoring it and setting the function equal to zero. Then solve for *x*. Let's do that with the above function:

$$y = x^2 - 10x + 21$$
$$0 = (x - 3)(x - 7)$$
$$(x - 3) = 0 \text{ and } (x - 7) = 0$$
$$x = 3 \text{ and } 7$$

The values of *x* that give a *y*-value of 0 are 3 and 7. Depending on the situation, use the graph or a simplified equation to determine roots/zeros.

Alternatively, you can use the quadratic formula to determine the roots:

$$y = x^2 - 10x + 21$$
$$x = \frac{-b \pm \sqrt{b^2 - 4ac}}{2a}$$
$$x = \frac{-(-10) \pm \sqrt{(-10)^2 - 4(1)(21)}}{2(1)}$$
$$x = \frac{10 \pm \sqrt{100 - 84}}{2}$$
$$x = \frac{10 \pm \sqrt{16}}{2}$$
$$x = \frac{10 \pm 4}{2}$$
$$x = 5 \pm 2$$
$$x = 3 \text{ or } 7$$

Parabolas

Sometimes you will need to look at the equation of a U-shaped curve, known as a parabola, and determine certain properties of it.

- The vertex form of a parabola is $y = a(x - h)^2 + k$.
- The vertex has the coordinates (h, k). If the parabola is facing up, the vertex is the bottom point of the U-shape. If the parabola is facing down, the vertex is the top point of the U-shape.
- The x-coordinate of the vertex provides the *axis of symmetry* for the parabola.

A parabola with the equation $y = (x - 1)^2 + 2$ has a vertex of $(1, 2)$. The equation for the axis of symmetry for the parabola is $x = 1$. The parabola is graphed in Figure 11:

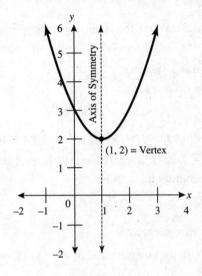

Figure 11

When a parabola is written in the form $y = ax^2 + bx + c$, you can determine the x-coordinate of the parabola's vertex using this formula:

$$x = -\frac{b}{2a}$$

❭ Example

Given a parabola with the equation $y = 5x^2 - 4x + 7$, what is the x-coordinate of the parabola's vertex?

✓ Solution

Use the formula $x = -\frac{b}{2a}$, and plug in the correct values: $a = 5$ and $b = -4$. Therefore:

$$x = -\frac{b}{2a}$$
$$x = -\frac{(-4)}{2 \cdot 5}$$
$$x = \frac{4}{10}$$
$$x = 0.4$$

Zeros and Parabolas Drill

1. What are the zeros of the function $y = (x - 9)(x + 1)$?

2. Where does the function $y = (x + 4)(x - 7)$ intersect the x-axis?

3. What are the zeros of the parabola $y = x^2 + x - 12$?

4. What is the x-coordinate of the vertex of a parabola with the equation $y = (x + 2)(x - 4)$?

5. A parabola with the equation $y + 4 = 3(x - 5)^2$ has what coordinates for its vertex?

6. What are the x- and y-coordinates for the vertex of a parabola with the equation $y = 3x^2 - 6x + 5$?

Solutions

1. Consider where y will equal zero. If $x - 9 = 0$ or $x + 1 = 0$, the function will equal zero. Therefore, x can equal 9 or -1.

2. The function intersects the x-axis where the value of y is zero. Find the zeros of $y = (x + 4)(x - 7)$ to solve. If $(x + 4) = 0$ or $(x - 7) = 0$, y will be zero. So x could be -4 or 7.

3. Factor the equation to determine the zeros:

$$y = x^2 + x - 12$$
$$y = (x + 4)(x - 3)$$

So the zeros are at -4 and 3 since those two values of x make y equal zero.

4. The parabola $y = (x + 2)(x - 4)$ has zeros at -2 and 4. To easily determine the x-coordinate of the vertex, find the midpoint between -2 and 4:

$$\frac{-2 + 4}{2} = \frac{2}{2} = 1$$

So the x-coordinate of the vertex is simply 1.

Alternatively, you could FOIL the equation and find $-\frac{b}{2a}$ in the new expression:

$$y = (x + 2)(x - 4)$$
$$y = x^2 - 4x + 2x - 8$$
$$y = x^2 - 2x - 8$$

For this equation, $a = 1$ and $b = -2$. So:

$$-\frac{b}{2a} \rightarrow -\frac{-2}{2(1)} = \frac{2}{2} = 1$$

Therefore, this approach also results in 1 as the x-coordinate of the vertex.

5. Put the parabola with the equation $y + 4 = 3(x - 5)^2$ into vertex form, $y = a(x - h)^2 + k$. Easily do so by subtracting 4 from both sides:

$$y + 4 = 3(x - 5)^2$$
$$y = 3(x - 5)^2 - 4$$

In parabolas of the form $y = a(x - h)^2 + k$, (h, k) is the vertex. Therefore, in the equation $y = 3(x - 5)^2 - 4$, the vertex is $(5, -4)$.

6. For parabolas in the form $y = ax^2 + bx + c$, the x-coordinate of the vertex is found using this formula: $x = -\frac{b}{2a}$. For the equation $y = 3x^2 - 6x + 5$, find the x-coordinate of the vertex:

$$x = -\frac{(-6)}{2(3)} = \frac{6}{6} = 1$$

Then, solve for the y-coordinate of the vertex by plugging 1 into the equation for the parabola:

$$y = 3x^2 - 6x + 5$$
$$y = 3(1)^2 - 6(1) + 5$$
$$y = 3 - 6 + 5$$
$$y = 2$$

The coordinates of the vertex are $(1, 2)$.

Imaginary Numbers

A complex number includes the square root of a negative number and is expressed using i, which is $\sqrt{-1}$. Some examples of imaginary numbers include:

$$\sqrt{-64} = 8i$$

$$\sqrt{-4} = 2i$$

$$7i + 4i = 11i$$

$$i \times i = -1$$

$$\frac{7i^3}{3i} = \frac{7}{3}i^2 = -\frac{7}{3}$$

$$3i^4 = 3 \times (i \times i) \times (i \times i)$$

$$= 3 \times (-1) \times (-1)$$

$$= 3$$

> Imaginary numbers have a recurring pattern when they are in exponential form:
>
> $i^1 = i$
> $i^2 = -1$
> $i^3 = -i$
> $i^4 = 1$
> $i^5 = i$
> $i^6 = -1$
>
> **and so on**

Imaginary Numbers Drill

1. $3i + 8i = ?$

2. $(4i) \times (3i) = ?$

3. $\dfrac{-12i^2}{4i^4} = ?$

4. The *conjugate* of $a + bi$ is $a - bi$. Using the concept of conjugate, simplify the following expression so there are no imaginary numbers in the denominator: $\dfrac{12}{x + i}$.

Solutions

1. $3i + 8i = 11i$

2. $(4i) \times (3i) = 12i^2$
$$= 12(-1)$$
$$= -12$$

3. $\dfrac{-12i^2}{4i^4} = \dfrac{-12}{4} \times \dfrac{i^2}{i^4}$
$$= -3 \times i^{-2}$$
$$= \dfrac{-3}{i^2}$$
$$= \dfrac{-3}{-1}$$
$$= 3$$

4. To simplify this expression, multiply both the numerator and the denominator by the *conjugate* of the denominator, $x - i$. This will cause the imaginary numbers in the denominator to be canceled:

$$\frac{12}{x + i} \times \frac{x - i}{x - i} = \frac{12(x - i)}{x^2 - ix + ix - i^2}$$
$$= \frac{12x - 12i}{x^2 - i^2}$$
$$= \frac{12x - 12i}{x^2 + 1}$$

Geometry and Trigonometry

Trigonometry

The three sides in a right triangle (a triangle with a 90° angle) each have special names that are based on the angles.

- **Hypotenuse:** This side is always the longest and is across from the 90° angle.
- **Opposite:** This side depends on the location of the angle you are using. It is always *directly opposite* the angle.
- **Adjacent:** This side also changes depending on the location of the angle you are using. It is always *adjacent* (next) to the angle you are using.

People often confuse the adjacent with the hypotenuse. Just remember that the hypotenuse is always the longest side in a right triangle. All three sides in a right triangle are shown in Figure 12.

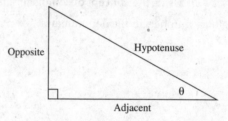

Figure 12

Use the acronym **SOH-CAH-TOA** to remember the key trigonometric ratios, as shown in Table 5.3.

Table 5.3 A Mnemonic to Remember Trigonometric Ratios

SOH	CAH	TOA
$\sin \theta = \dfrac{\text{Opposite}}{\text{Hypotenuse}}$	$\cos \theta = \dfrac{\text{Adjacent}}{\text{Hypotenuse}}$	$\tan \theta = \dfrac{\text{Opposite}}{\text{Adjacent}}$

Let's take a look at an example to see what the different trigonometric values are in the same right triangle.

> **Example**

A right triangle has side lengths of 3, 4, and 5. The angle θ is opposite from the side with length 3. What are the different trigonometric values for angle θ?

☑ **Solution**

Draw the triangle to determine the different trigonometric values.

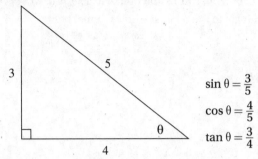

$$\sin \theta = \frac{3}{5}$$

$$\cos \theta = \frac{4}{5}$$

$$\tan \theta = \frac{3}{4}$$

To solve for an unknown angle in a right triangle, use an *inverse* of one of the trigonometry functions. In the triangle above, use an inverse function to solve for θ:

$$\sin \theta = \frac{3}{5}$$

$$\sin^{-1} (\sin \theta) = \sin^{-1} \left(\frac{3}{5} \right)$$

$$\theta \approx 36.87°$$

This could have been calculated using an inverse of the tangent or the cosine functions as well.

You can save time in your calculations if you recognize common special right triangles and Pythagorean triples:

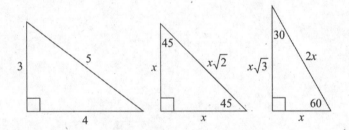

Some other common triples are **5-12-13** and **7-24-25**—you can plug these in to the Pythagorean theorem, and they will work as sides in a right triangle:

$$5^2 + 12^2 = 13^2 \text{ and } 7^2 + 24^2 = 25^2$$

Trigonometry Drill

1.

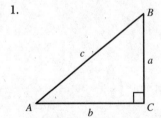

In this right triangle, what are the values of the following?

a. sin*A*

b. cos*B*

c. tan*A*

2. What is the length of the hypotenuse of a right triangle with two legs that each have a length of 4?

3. If $\sin X = \frac{1}{2}$ and angle X is between 0° and 90°, what is the degree measure of angle X?

4. If a right triangle has a hypotenuse of 13 and one of its legs is 5, what is the measure of the smallest angle in the triangle to the nearest whole degree?

Solutions

1.

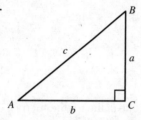

(a) $\sin A = \dfrac{\text{side opposite of angle A}}{\text{hypotenuse of the triangle}} = \dfrac{a}{c}$

(b) $\cos B = \dfrac{\text{side adjacent to angle B}}{\text{hypotenuse of the triangle}} = \dfrac{a}{c}$

(c) $\tan A = \dfrac{\text{side opposite of angle A}}{\text{side adjacent to angle A}} = \dfrac{a}{b}$

2. Use the Pythagorean theorem to solve, plugging in 4 for both a and b since the length of each leg is 4:

$$a^2 + b^2 = c^2$$
$$4^2 + 4^2 = c^2$$
$$16 + 16 = 32$$
$$c^2 = 32$$
$$c = \sqrt{32}$$
$$c = \sqrt{2 \times 16}$$
$$c = 4\sqrt{2}$$

Alternatively, you could recognize this is a multiple of a special right triangle: x, x, $\sqrt{2}\,x$. You could then just multiply 4 by $\sqrt{2}$ and get the same result.

3.

$$\sin X = \frac{1}{2}$$
$$\sin^{-1}(\sin X) = \sin^{-1}\left(\frac{1}{2}\right)$$
$$X = \sin^{-1}\left(\frac{1}{2}\right)$$

With the calculator set in degree mode (not radian mode), find that $\sin^{-1}\left(\frac{1}{2}\right) = 30°$.

4. If a right triangle has a hypotenuse of 13 and one of its legs as 5, the length of the other leg will be 12. You can find this by either realizing this is a 5-12-13 special right triangle or by calculating the unknown side by using the Pythagorean theorem:

$$a^2 + b^2 = c^2$$

$$5^2 + x^2 = 13^2$$
$$25 + x^2 = 169$$
$$x^2 = 169 - 25$$
$$x^2 = 144$$
$$\sqrt{x^2} = \sqrt{144}$$
$$x = 12$$

The triangle will look like this:

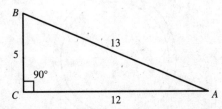

The smallest angle will be the one across from the side of length 5, angle A. So find the measure of angle A using trigonometry:

$$\sin A = \frac{5}{13}$$
$$\sin^{-1}(\sin A) = \sin^{-1}\left(\frac{5}{13}\right)$$
$$A \approx 22.62°$$

The answer is 23° since the question asks for the nearest whole degree. You could have calculated the value of this angle using tangent or cosine as well.

Circles

Circumference and Area

You should know some important circle definitions.

- The *radius* goes from the center of the circle to the circle itself, as shown in Figure 13.

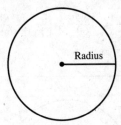

Figure 13

■ The *diameter* goes from one point on a circle, through the center, to another point on the circle, as shown in Figure 14.

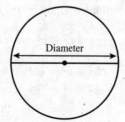

Figure 14

■ A circle has 360°, as shown in Figure 15.

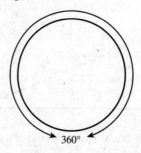

Figure 15

The *area* of a circle is computed with the following formula, where r is the radius:

$$\text{Area} = \pi r^2$$

For example, the area of a circle that has a radius of 6 is $\pi 6^2 = 36\pi$.

The *circumference* of a circle is computed with the following formula, where r is the radius:

$$\text{Circumference} = 2\pi r$$

For example, the circumference of a circle that has a radius of 6 is $2\pi 6 = 12\pi$.

A common application of circle concepts on the PSAT is calculating the length of an arc or the area of a sector. The formula for *arc length* is the following:

$$\frac{\text{Part}}{\text{Whole}} = \frac{\text{Angle}}{360°} = \frac{\text{Length of Arc}}{\text{Circumference}}$$

❯ **Example**

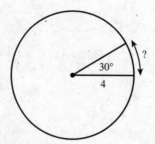

If a circle has a radius of 4 with an arc of 30° as shown above, what is the length of the arc?

✓ Solution

Use the part-whole ratio to solve this problem:

$$\frac{\text{Part}}{\text{Whole}} = \frac{30°}{360°} = \frac{1}{12} = \frac{\text{Length of Arc}}{\text{Circumference}} = \frac{x}{2\pi4} = \frac{x}{8\pi}$$

Set up a proportion to solve for the arc length:

$$\frac{1}{12} = \frac{x}{8\pi}$$
$$8\pi = 12x$$
$$\frac{8\pi}{12} = x$$
$$\frac{2}{3}\pi = x$$

The formula for *sector area* is the following:

$$\frac{\text{Part}}{\text{Whole}} = \frac{\text{Angle}}{360°} = \frac{\text{Area of Sector}}{\text{Area of Circle}}$$

❯ Example

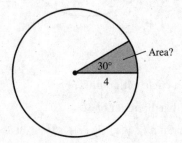

If a circle has a radius of 4 with a sector of 30° as shown above, what is the area of the sector?

✓ Solution

Use the part-whole ratio to solve this problem:

$$\frac{\text{Part}}{\text{Whole}} = \frac{30°}{360°} = \frac{1}{12} = \frac{\text{Area of Sector}}{\text{Area of Circle}} = \frac{x}{\pi4^2} = \frac{x}{16\pi}$$

Set up a proportion to solve for the sector area:

$$\frac{1}{12} = \frac{x}{16\pi} \rightarrow \frac{16\pi}{12} = x \rightarrow \frac{4}{3}\pi = x$$

Circle Formula

The following formula provides the graph of a circle in the *xy*-plane:

$$(x - h)^2 + (y - k)^2 = r^2$$
$$h = x\text{-coordinate of center}$$
$$k = y\text{-coordinate of center}$$
$$r = \text{radius}$$

> **Example**

What are the center and radius of the following equation? What is its graph?

$$(x - 3)^2 + (y - 2)^2 = 9$$

✓ **Solution**

$(x - 3)^2 + (y - 2)^2 = 9$ has a center at (3, 2) and a radius of 3. Its graph is shown:

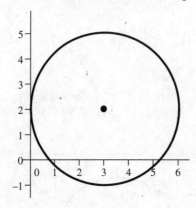

Circles Drill

1. What is the circumference of a circle with radius 5?

2. What is the area of a circle with a diameter of 6?

3. Consider a circle with the equation $(x - 1)^2 + (y + 4)^2 = 36$.

   a. What are the coordinates of the center of the circle?
   b. What is the radius of the circle?

4.

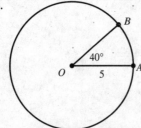

Consider a circle with a radius of 5 as shown above. Arc $\widehat{AB}$ in this circle has a measure of 40°.

a. What is the length of arc $\widehat{AB}$?
b. What is the area of the sector formed by arc $\widehat{AB}$?

Solutions

1. Use the formula for circumference, $2\pi r$, and plug in 5 for the radius:

$$C = 2\pi r$$
$$C = 2\pi 5$$
$$C = 10\pi$$

2. Use the area formula for a circle, πr^2, and plug in half the diameter, 3, for the radius:

$$A = \pi r^2$$
$$A = \pi(3)^2$$
$$A = 9\pi$$

3. a. From the formula for a circle, $(x - h)^2 + (y - k)^2 = r^2$, the center of the circle is point (h, k). So in the circle with the equation $(x - 1)^2 + (y + 4)^2 = 36$, the center is $(1, -4)$.

   b. The radius of a circle of the form $(x - h)^2 + (y - k)^2 = r^2$ is r. So in the circle with the equation $(x - 1)^2 + (y + 4)^2 = 36$, take the square root of 36 to find the radius:

$$\sqrt{36} = 6$$

4. a. $\dfrac{\text{Part}}{\text{Whole}} = \dfrac{40°}{360°} = \dfrac{1}{9} = \dfrac{\text{Length of Arc}}{\text{Circumference}} = \dfrac{x}{2\pi 5} = \dfrac{x}{10\pi}$

   Set up a proportion to solve for the arc length:

$$\frac{1}{9} = \frac{x}{10\pi}$$
$$10\pi = 9x$$
$$\frac{10\pi}{9} = x$$

   If you simplify without the π, the solution is approximately 3.49.

   b. $\dfrac{\text{Part}}{\text{Whole}} = \dfrac{40°}{360°} = \dfrac{1}{9} = \dfrac{\text{Area of Sector}}{\text{Area of Circle}} = \dfrac{x}{\pi 5^2} = \dfrac{x}{25\pi}$

   Set up a proportion to solve for the sector area:

$$\frac{1}{9} = \frac{x}{25\pi}$$
$$25\pi = 9x$$
$$\frac{25\pi}{9} = x$$

   If you simplify without the π, the solution is approximately 8.73.

PSAT Reference Formulas

The PSAT will provide you with the following facts and formulas. Memorizing these facts will save you time and help you think about what formula may be needed for a particular problem. However, if you do forget a formula, you can always click open the option to see it.

Radius of a circle = r
Area of a circle = πr^2
Circumference of a circle = $2\pi r$

Area of a rectangle = length $\times$ width = lw

Area of a triangle = $\frac{1}{2} \times$ base $\times$ height = $\frac{1}{2}bh$

Pythagorean theorem: $a^2 + b^2 = c^2$

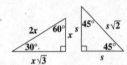

Special right triangles: 30-60-90 and 45-45-90

Volume of a box = length $\times$ width $\times$ height = lwh

Volume of a cylinder = $\pi r^2 h$

Volume of a sphere = $\frac{4}{3}\pi r^3$

Volume of a cone = $\frac{1}{3}\pi r^2 h$

Volume of a pyramid = length $\times$ width $\times$ height = $\frac{1}{3}lwh$

Key Facts:

- A circle has 360 degrees.
- There are 2π radians in a circle.
- There are 180 degrees in a triangle.

Math Essentials Review Quiz

Even though the PSAT provides you with some formulas, it doesn't provide all the ones you will need. Complete this quiz to determine which concepts you may still need to memorize.

1. To find the perimeter P of a rectangle with length L and width W, what is the correct formula?

    (A) $P = L \times W$ OR   (B) $P = 2L + 2W$

2. Which of these statements is true?

    (A) An isosceles triangle is always equilateral.   OR   (B) An equilateral triangle is always isosceles.

3.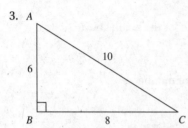

    What is the value of the sine of angle C in the triangle above?

    (A) $\frac{3}{5}$ OR   (B) $\frac{4}{5}$

4. What is the y-intercept and slope of the line with the equation $y = 4x + 3$?

    (A) y-intercept: 4 and slope: 3   OR   (B) y-intercept: 3 and slope: 4

5. What is an expression to calculate the slope between the points (A, B) and (C, D)?

    (A) $\frac{B - D}{A - C}$ OR   (B) $\frac{A - C}{B - D}$

6. A line that is parallel to the line $y = 5x - 3$ would have what slope?

    (A) 5   OR   (B) -3

7. What is the slope of a line perpendicular to the line with the equation $y = -\frac{1}{5}x - 7$?

    (A) -5 OR   (B) 5

8. What is another way of writing $(a + b)(a - b)$?

    (A) $a^2 - b^2$ OR   (B) $a^2 + b^2$

9. What does $(4x - 3)^2$ equal?

    (A) $16x^2 - 24x + 9$ OR   (B) $16x^2 + 9$

10. Which of these expresses an equivalent relationship?

    (A) $|-3| = -|3|$ OR   (B) $|3| = |-3|$

11. Which of these expresses that x is 40% of y?

    (A) $x = 0.4y$ OR   (B) $y = 0.4x$

12.

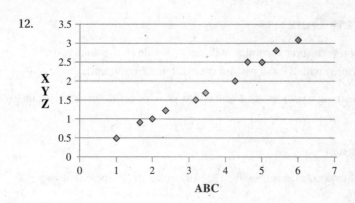

What is the best approximation of the slope of a best-fit line for the graph above?

(A) $\frac{1}{2}$ OR   (B) 2

13. How should you calculate the arithmetic mean of this set of numbers?

$$\{2, 3, 5, 7, 11\}$$

(A) Simply choose the middle value, 5   OR   (B) $\frac{2 + 3 + 5 + 7 + 11}{5}$

14. Which is larger for this set of numbers, the mode or the range?

$$\{1, 1, 4, 5, 12, 71\}$$

(A) Mode   OR   (B) Range

15. What is the probability that a two-sided coin will turn up heads when flipped?

(A) 0.5   OR   (B) 2

16. Which of these expressions states that x is less than or equal to 3?

(A) $x < 3$ OR   (B) $x \le 3$

17. If $f(x) = 2x$ and $g(x) = x + 3$, what is the value of $f(g(2))$?

(A) 10   OR   (B) 13

18. Which of these is the correct quadratic formula for equations in the form $ax^2 + bx + c = 0$?

(A) $x = \dfrac{-b \pm \sqrt{b^2 - 4ac}}{2a}$ OR   (B) $x = \dfrac{b \pm \sqrt{b^2 + 4ac}}{a}$

19. Which of these systems of equations has infinitely many solutions?

(A) $y = 2x$ OR   (B) $y = 2x + 1$
    $y = x + 5$ $3y = 6x + 3$

20. The function $f(x) = \dfrac{x^2 + 5}{x - 3}$ is undefined when x equals what number?

(A) $x = 3$ OR   (B) $x = \sqrt{5}$

21. $\frac{2}{3} + \frac{1}{4} = ?$

    (A) $\frac{11}{12}$ OR   (B) $\frac{3}{7}$

22. $\frac{x+3}{3} = ?$

    (A) x OR   (B) $\frac{x}{3} + 1$

23. $x^3 x^4 = ?$

    (A) x^7 OR   (B) x^{12}

24. $(x^2)^5 = ?$

    (A) x^7 OR   (B) x^{10}

25. If $x > 0$, $\frac{\sqrt[3]{x^2}}{\sqrt[6]{x}} = ?$

    (A) $\sqrt[3]{x}$ OR   (B) $\sqrt{x}$

26. What is 40% of 80?

    (A) 32   OR   (B) 48

27. If someone travels 200 miles in 4 hours, what is the person's speed in miles per hour?

    (A) 40 mph   OR   (B) 50 mph

28. What are the zeros of the function $y = (x+2)(x-4)$?

    (A) -2 and 4 OR   (B) 2 and -4

29. What is the vertex of a parabola with the equation $y = 2(x-4)^2 - 5$?

    (A) $(4, -5)$ OR   (B) $(2, 4)$

30. What is the x-coordinate of the vertex of a parabola with the equation $y = 2x^2 + 3x - 6$?

    (A) $\frac{1}{3}$ OR   (B) $-\frac{3}{4}$

Answer Explanations

Solutions	Concept Review
1. **(B)** $P = 2L + 2W$ Perimeter is the sum of the lengths of the sides in the figure. As you can see in the figure below, the rectangle has two sides of width W and two sides of length L. The sum of all these sides is $L + L + W + W = 2L + 2W$. 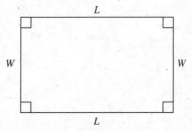	**Rectangle Area = Length × Width** and **Rectangle Perimeter =** **(2 × Length) + (2 × Width)**
2. **(B)** An equilateral triangle is always isosceles. An isosceles triangle needs to have only *two* sides and angles equivalent. In contrast, an equilateral triangle must have *all three sides and angles equivalent*. (An isosceles triangle can also have three angles and sides equivalent, but it is not a necessary condition to be isosceles.) So if a triangle is equilateral, it will definitely be isosceles as well. (This is similar to stating that a square is always a rectangle.)	**Isosceles Triangle:** At least 2 equal sides; at least 2 equal angles. **Equilateral Triangle:** 3 equal sides; 3 equal angles (all 60°).
3. **(A)** $\frac{3}{5}$ Here is a drawing of the sides of the triangle relative to angle C: 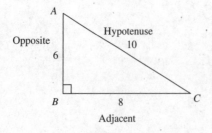	$\sin \theta = \dfrac{\text{Opposite}}{\text{Hypotenuse}}$ $\cos \theta = \dfrac{\text{Adjacent}}{\text{Hypotenuse}}$ $\tan \theta = \dfrac{\text{Opposite}}{\text{Adjacent}}$ **Pythagorean Theorem:** $$a^2 + b^2 = c^2$$

Calculate the sine of angle *C* by taking the length of the opposite side (length 6) and dividing it by the length of the hypotenuse (length 10):

$$\frac{6}{10} = \frac{3}{5}$$

Special Right Triangles and Pythagorean Triples:

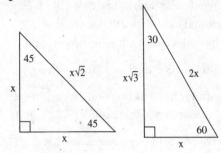

3-4-5   5-12-13   7-24-25

---

4. **(B)** *y*-intercept: 3 and slope: 4

The equation is in slope-intercept form. So the slope of the line is 4 and its *y*-intercept is 3. Here is a drawing of the line:

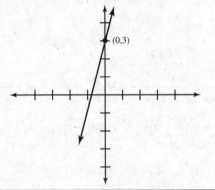

Slope-Intercept Form of a Line:

$y = mx + b$

$m =$ slope $b = y$-intercept

---

5. **(A)** $\frac{B - D}{A - C}$

Slope is the rise over the run. For the given two points, take the difference between the *y*-coordinates and divide it by the difference between the *x*-coordinates. Be careful to maintain the same order. If you subtract the *y*-coordinate of point 1 from the *y*-coordinate of point 2, you must subtract the *x*-coordinate of point 1 from the *x*-coordinate of point 2.

For a line with the points (x_1, y_1) and (x_2, y_2):

Slope $= \dfrac{y_2 - y_1}{x_2 - x_1}$

---

6. **(A)** 5

Parallel lines never intersect since they run parallel to one another. They therefore have identical slopes. Since this line is in slope-intercept form, we can tell that the slope is 5. So any line parallel to it will also have a slope of 5.

Parallel Lines: Slopes are the same.

7. (B) 5

Perpendicular lines intersect at a 90-degree angle and have slopes that are negative reciprocals of each other. The slope of the line in the equation is $-\frac{1}{5}$. To find the negative reciprocal, first find the reciprocal and then multiply that result by –1. To find the reciprocal of $-\frac{1}{5}$, determine what number you would multiply $-\frac{1}{5}$ by to get 1.

$-\frac{1}{5} \times (-5) = 1$

So the reciprocal is -5. To get the negative reciprocal, multiply this by -1, giving $(-1)(-5) = 5$. Thus, the slope of the line perpendicular to the given line is 5.

A shortcut to finding the slope of a line perpendicular to another is simply to invert the fraction and flip the sign.

Perpendicular Lines: Slopes are *negative reciprocals of each other* (e.g., 3 and $-\frac{1}{3}$).

---

8. (A) $a^2 - b^2$

If you don't remember this pattern, you can use FOIL (first, outer, inner, last) with this expression:

$(a + b)(a - b) \rightarrow$

$a^2 - ab + ab - b^2 \rightarrow$

$a^2 - b^2$

9. (A) $16x^2 - 24x + 9$

FOIL the expression:

$(4x - 3)^2 \rightarrow$

$(4x - 3)(4x - 3) \rightarrow$

$16x^2 - 12x - 12x + 9 \rightarrow$

$16x^2 - 24x + 9$

Common Factoring Patterns:

$(a + b)(a + b) = a^2 + 2ab + b^2$
Example:

$(x + 4)(x + 4) = x^2 + 8x + 16$

$(a + b)(a - b) = a^2 - b^2$
Example:

$(m + 2)(m - 2) = m^2 - 4$

$(a - b)(a - b) = a^2 - 2ab + b^2$
Example:

$(5 - y)(5 - y) = 25 - 10y + y^2$

Sum of Cubes
$(a + b)(a^2 - ab + b^2) = a^3 + b^3$
Example:

$(2 + x)(4 - 2x + x^2) = 8 + x^3$

Difference of Cubes
$(a - b)(a^2 + ab + b^2) = a^3 - b^3$
Example:

$(y - 4)(y^2 + 4y + 16) = y^3 - 4^3 = y^3 - 64$

10. **(B)** $\left|3\right| = \left|-3\right|$

Treat the absolute value sign like parentheses with the order of operations. Just like parentheses come first in the order of operations, you should calculate the absolute value expressions first before dealing with the negatives outside the absolute values. In choice (A), the left-hand side equals 3 since –3 is 3 units away from 0. However, on the right-hand side, the negative sign on the outside of the absolute value makes the expression negative:

$$-\left|3\right| = -3$$

Absolute Value: Distance along the number line from zero.

Examples: $\left|8\right| = 8$ and $\left|-8\right| = 8$

Remark: Taking the absolute value of something should always give a nonnegative result since absolute value represents a distance.

---

11. **(A)** $x = 0.4y$

To find the percent, turn 40% into a fraction by dividing 40 by 100:

$$\frac{40}{100} = 0.4$$

Write an equation to show that x equals 40% of y:

$$x = 0.4y$$

General Percent Formula:

$$\frac{\text{Part}}{\text{Whole}} \times 100 = \text{Percent}$$

---

12. **(A)** $\frac{1}{2}$

Estimate the coordinates of a couple of points in the graph. Then calculate the slope. We can use (0, 0) and (6, 3). Plug these into the slope formula to solve:

$$\frac{y_2 - y_1}{x_2 - x_1} = \frac{3 - 0}{6 - 0} = \frac{3}{6} = \frac{1}{2}$$

Best-Fit Lines: Look for a general trend in the data (if it exists), and draw a line to model the trend.

---

13. **(B)** $\frac{2 + 3 + 5 + 7 + 11}{5}$

The mean is the simple average. Add the individual values ($2 + 3 + 5 + 7 + 11$), and divide by the total number of values (5).

$$\text{Mean} = \frac{\text{Sum of Items}}{\text{Number of Items}}$$

Median: The middle term of a set of numbers when lined up small to large. Note that when the number of terms is even and the two terms in the middle are not equal, take the mean of the two middle terms to find the median.

Mode: The most frequent term in a set of numbers. Note that if in a set of numbers each number appears only once, there is no mode. If a set of numbers has 2 or more numbers tied for appearing the most times, the set has multiple modes.

14. **(B)** Range

The mode is 1 for this set of numbers since 1 appears more frequently than any other number.

The range is $71 - 1 = 70$ since that is the difference between the smallest and largest terms in the set.

Therefore, the range is greater than the mode.

Range: The difference between the smallest and largest values in a set of data.

---

15. **(A)** 0.5

When the coin is flipped, it can land on either heads or tails. So there is a 1 out of 2 chance it will land on heads. In other words, 1 outcome results in success (heads) out of 2 possible outcomes (heads or tails). So the probability is $\frac{1}{2} = 0.5$.

Probability: The likelihood that a given event will happen, expressed as a fraction or decimal between 0 and 1 inclusive. Note that a probability of 0 means an event has no chance of occurring. A probability of 0.5 means there is a 50% chance it will occur. A probability of 1 means the event is certain to occur.

In general, we can find the probability by taking the number of successes divided by the number of possible outcomes.

---

16. **(B)** $x \leq 3$

The line underneath the $>$ or $<$ sign signifies equivalence.

$<$ means less than.

$>$ means greater than.

$\leq$ means less than or equal to.

$\geq$ means greater than or equal to.

---

17. **(A)** 10

First, calculate the value of $g(2)$:

$$g(x) = x + 3$$
$$g(2) = 2 + 3 = 5$$

Then plug 5 into $f(x)$:

$$f(x) = 2x$$
$$f(5) = 2 \times 5 = 10$$

Composite Functions: Calculate the value of the *inside* function first. Then calculate the value of the *outside* function, just as in the example problem.

---

18. **(A)** $x = \frac{-b \pm \sqrt{b^2 - 4ac}}{2a}$

This is a formula you absolutely must memorize.

Quadratic Formula: $x = \frac{-b \pm \sqrt{b^2 - 4ac}}{2a}$

An equation with the variable x and constants a, b, and c written in the form $ax^2 + bx + c = 0$ can be solved with the quadratic formula.

19. **(B)** $y = 2x + 1$
    $3y = 6x + 3$

These two equations have infinitely many solutions because the second equation is 3 times the first equation, making them different expressions of the same equation. Thus, any solution to one equation is a solution to the other as well. Since there are infinitely many solutions to the equations (both equations are linear and a line has infinitely many points), the system itself must have infinitely many solutions.

A system of equations will have **infinite solutions** if the equations are simple multiples of each other. The graphs of the equations are exactly the same.

A system of equations will have **no solutions** if no points are solutions to all equations in the system. Graphically, the graphs of the equations never intersect. In other words, the graphs are parallel.

20. **(A)** $x = 3$

If $x = 3$, the denominator (bottom) of the equation equals zero since $3 - 3 = 0$. If you divide a number by zero, the result is undefined. You cannot divide a number into zero parts.

A function is **undefined** at a point if inputting that value into the function produces an undefined number, such as $\frac{5}{0}$.

21. **(A)** $\frac{11}{12}$

$$\frac{2}{3} + \frac{1}{4} \rightarrow \frac{8}{12} + \frac{3}{12} \rightarrow \frac{11}{12}$$

Add fractions by (1) finding the least common denominator, (2) changing each fraction to have the same denominator, and (3) adding the numerators together.

22. **(B)** $\frac{x}{3} + 1$

$$\frac{x + 3}{3} = \frac{x}{3} + \frac{3}{3} = \frac{x}{3} + 1$$

In general,

$$\frac{xy}{x} = \frac{\not{x}y}{\not{x}} = y \text{ and}$$

$$\frac{x + y}{y} = \frac{x}{y} + \frac{y}{y} = \frac{x}{y} + 1$$

23. **(A)** x^7

$$x^3 x^4 = x^{3 + 4} = x^7$$

24. **(B)** x^{10}

$$(x^2)^5 = x^{2 \times 5} = x^{10}$$

25. **(B)** $\sqrt{x}$

For $x > 0$,

$$\frac{\sqrt[3]{x^2}}{\sqrt[6]{x}} = \frac{x^{\frac{2}{3}}}{x^{\frac{1}{6}}} = x^{\frac{2}{3} - \frac{1}{6}} = x^{\frac{4}{6} - \frac{1}{6}} = x^{\frac{3}{6}} = x^{\frac{1}{2}} = \sqrt{x}$$

Exponent Rules:

$$a^x a^y = a^{x + y}$$

$$\frac{a^x}{a^y} = a^{x - y}$$

$$(a^x)^y = a^{xy}$$

$$a^{-x} = \frac{1}{a^x}$$

$$a^{\frac{x}{y}} = \sqrt[y]{a^x}$$

26. **(A)** 32 $$0.40 \times 80 = 32$$	$$\frac{\text{Part}}{\text{Whole}} \times 100 = \text{Percent}$$ Move the decimal point over two spots to calculate a percentage. $$40\% = 0.40$$
27. **(B)** 50 mph $$\frac{200 \text{ miles}}{4 \text{ hours}} = 50 \text{ mph}$$	$$\text{Distance} = \text{Rate} \times \text{Time}$$
28. **(A)** -2 and 4 For $y = (x + 2)(x - 4)$, y will be zero when x equals -2 and 4.	**Zeros:** The root or zero of a function is the value for which the function has a value of zero. In other words, it is where the function intersects the x-axis.
29. **(A)** $(4, -5)$ In the function $y = 2(x - 4)^2 - 5$, 4 is the h and -5 is the k.	The vertex form of a parabola is $y = a(x - h)^2 + k$ and the vertex (the bottom point of the U-shape) has the coordinates (h, k).
30. **(B)** $-\frac{3}{4}$ For $y = 2x^2 + 3x - 6$, the a is 2 and the b is 3: $$-\frac{b}{2a} = -\frac{3}{2 \cdot 2} = -\frac{3}{4}$$	When a parabola is written in the form $y = ax^2 + bx + c$, the x-coordinate of the parabola's vertex is $x = -\frac{b}{2a}$.

Further Preparation

- Practice with other materials if needed. The PSAT Math sections are very similar to the SAT Math sections. You can use *Barron's SAT* for additional practice. Also, you can find further practice at *Khanacademy.org*, the official College Board practice website.
- Take the most rigorous math courses offered by your school.
- Practice all of the word problems and algebra problems you can find—these are the most prevalent types of problems you will find on the test.

6
Math Strategies, Tactics, and Problem-Solving

How Is the PSAT Math Test Designed?

- Math Test Strcuture:
    - 2 modules, 22 questions each, 35 minutes each
    - First module is of a standard difficulty, second module of an adaptive difficulty (will be easier or more difficult depending on student performance on the first module)
    - 4 of the questions (2 per module) are experimental and will not count towards the score.
    - The questions generally become more difficult as you go.
- Breakdown of math test questions:
    - Algebra (primarily linear equations and systems): approximately 14 questions
    - Problem-Solving and Data Analysis (primarily demonstrating literacy with data and real-world applications): approximately 8 questions
    - Advanced Math (primarily more complicated equations): approximately 13 questions
    - Geometry and Trigonometry: approximately 5 questions

How Can I Prepare for and Be Successful on the PSAT Math Test?

- Brush up on your content knowledge with the "Math Review" chapter.
- Review the timing strategies, question strategies, and math tactics in this chapter.
- Practice PSAT-style math questions in this chapter, targeting the question types that are most challenging to you. They are organized as follows:
    - Algebra
    - Problem-Solving and Data Analysis
    - Advanced Math
    - Geometry and Trigonometry
- Use the "Troubleshooting" guide at the end of this chapter to help you work through strategic issues you have encountered in the past or are finding as you work through problems.

PSAT Math Timing Strategies

1. Take About 1.5 Minutes per Question, Adjusting Based on Where You Are in the Test.

Since the math questions will get gradually more difficult as you progress through each module, spend a little less than 1.5 minutes per question on the earlier questions and a little more than 1.5 minutes per question on the later questions.

If you are having trouble finishing the Math Test, on which questions would it make sense to guess? In general, if you are having difficulty finishing the Math Test, guess on the later questions within a module—these are usually the toughest ones. Every question is worth the same point value, and there is no penalty for guessing; so be sure to try the easy and medium questions.

2. Don't Rush Through the PSAT Math.

Compared to other major standardized tests, like the ACT, the PSAT will be easier to finish in the given time. Practice your pacing on the practice Math Tests in this book, and go into the test ready to be thorough rather than hasty. On school math tests if you finish early, you can typically take the remainder of the class period to do something else. On the PSAT, however, you won't be able to do anything but the test if you finish early—you might as well use all the time available. Rushing to the end may feel good and make you look smart to your fellow test takers, who may glance at you resting on your desk and assume you are a math genius. However, there is no prize for finishing early. There is a prize—thousands of dollars in scholarship money—if you answer the questions correctly. Also, even if you are a fast reader, realize that the dense, technical prose of PSAT Math questions will require more time and focus than other sorts of reading material.

3. Don't Overthink Early Questions, and Don't Underthink Later Questions.

Solutions to earlier questions in the PSAT Math Test will be more straightforward, while solutions to later multiple-choice and student-produced response questions will involve more critical thinking.

4. Do the Questions One Time Well, Instead of Double-checking.

The PSAT Math generally has far more challenging word problems than you may be accustomed to seeing on typical school math tests, making it more difficult to correct careless reading errors. Instead of rushing through the questions and spending time second-guessing and double-checking your work, focus on doing the questions *one time well*. If you misread a PSAT Math question because you are going too quickly and then come back and read it over again quickly to double-check, it is far less likely that you will answer the question correctly than if you had simply taken the time to get it right the first time. If you are very thorough and *still* finish with some time remaining, go ahead and double-check. Go back to problems that are particularly susceptible to careless errors, like ones with negative numbers, fractions, and long word problems. Also, as you go through the test the first time, you can flag any questions you would like to come back to and double-check if time permits.

5. Come Back to Questions You Don't Understand.

Don't underestimate the power of your subconscious mind to work through something while your conscious mind is focused on a different problem. If you have given a problem a decent attempt to no avail, flag the question and come back. While you are working on other problems, your subconscious mind will be unlocking possible approaches to the problem you left behind.

By coming back to the problem later and with fresh eyes, it may seem much easier than it did before. Since the math problems are of gradually increasing difficulty, you will likely want to return to the earlier problems rather than the later ones in the test if you want to attempt them again. Whatever you do, don't allow yourself to become bogged down on a single problem—you can still earn a top score while missing questions.

6. Check Your Pace at Reasonable Intervals.

Every five questions or so on the PSAT Math is typically a good time to see if you are on track with your pacing. If you are going significantly faster than the 1.5 minutes per question, you may want to slow down. If you are going slower than 1.5 minutes per question, speed things up or consider guessing on the harder questions. If you never check your pacing, you may finish way ahead or way behind. If you check the pace too frequently, you will spend too much time looking at your watch instead of solving problems. Use the included timer to monitor your pacing and hide it if you find it distracting.

7. Since the PSAT Is Curved, Do Your Best to Stay Levelheaded.

If the PSAT seems more challenging or less challenging than you anticipated, do your best to keep a level head and not to get too confident or too worried. The curve will reflect the relative difficulty of the test that particular day. As a point of reference, in 2018, a math score of 650 out of 760 would still be in the 95th percentile for a nationally representative sample; a math score of 480 out of 760 was approximately average for all test takers nationwide.[*]

PSAT Math Question Strategies

1. Focus on What the Question Is Asking.

Make notations on your scrap paper to paraphrase the question. Rather than going on autopilot and quickly jumping into solving the question, really pay attention to what the question is asking you to do. Unless you are mindful about focusing on what the questions are asking, you will get tunnel vision and tune out vital information in the questions.

2. Stay in the Moment—Don't Skip Ahead to the Next Step.

When solving a problem, a desire to finish quickly will make you jump ahead to the next step instead of working through the step you are on. Fortunately, the PSAT Math problems generally *do not require many steps to solve them*. Many of the wrong answers, however, will be what many students would calculate if they skipped or rushed through a step. Channel all of your intellectual energy into rigorously solving the problem, one step at a time.

3. Don't Overthink the Questions.

Don't allow yourself to over-complicate the questions at the beginning of the test, as they will be more straightforward and simple to solve than the later questions. The PSAT questions may all be solved in fairly straightforward ways once you get past the surface.

- Drawings and figures are always drawn to scale, unless otherwise noted in the question.
- If a question involves factoring, it will typically use a common factoring pattern, e.g., $(x + 1)(x - 1) = x^2 - 1$.

*https://collegereadiness.collegeboard.org/pdf/psat-nmsqt-understanding-scores.pdf

- If a question involves right triangles, it will often use a special right triangle, e.g., $45°-45°-90°$ or 3-4-5.
- If a question asks you to calculate the value of an expression, like x^3 or $x - 9$, look for ways that the expression can be simplified. For example, if you are asked to solve for x^4 in the equation $x^8 = 49$, simply take the square root of both sides to reach your answer: $x^8 = 49 \rightarrow \sqrt{x^8} = \sqrt{49} \rightarrow x^4 = 7$. This is much easier than solving for just the variable x and having to plug that value back in to x^4.
- Since the PSAT mainly tests algebra, many advanced students who are taking calculus or precalculus may overthink relatively easy questions. You will not need higher-order math to solve the questions on the PSAT—you will just need a firm grounding in the basics. If you have not studied algebra and geometry for a while, be sure to read the "Math Review" chapter in this book thoroughly—it should not take you very long to get back up to speed.

4. Don't Overuse Your Calculator.

PSAT Math problems will not require elaborate calculations, and having a bunch of sophisticated programs on your calculator won't make a difference. In fact, many of the answers to the problems keep radicals and fractions in their non-decimal form, so calculating too far ahead could set you behind. Use the calculator when necessary, but rely on your critical thinking first and your calculator second.

5. Mistakes Can Lead to Success.

If the PSAT problems involved 20–30 steps of calculations, a simple mistake would jeopardize your entire problem-solving process and would waste valuable time. In actuality, the PSAT Math problems do not require great numbers of steps, so a small mistake will not be catastrophic. As long as you find your mistakes quickly and are able to restart your thought process on a problem quickly, you will be fine.

6. Give the Questions the Benefit of the Doubt.

The College Board has spent a couple of years developing the materials you will see on the PSAT, and it has extensively field-tested possible questions on students to ensure the fairness and accuracy of those questions. As a result, when you encounter a tough problem on the PSAT Math, do not immediately assume that it is an unfair or a stupid question. Instead, know that quite a bit of work and care went into crafting the questions, and try to reexamine your understanding of the question.

7. It's Fine If You Cannot Precisely Justify Your Answers.

You simply need to answer the question correctly—you do not need to explain yourself. There are many ways to solve the PSAT Math problems; as long as you have a method that arrives at the correct answer, you are doing things perfectly. Let go of the little voice in your head that tells you that if you can't explain yourself, you must not truly understand it. Trust your intuition.

Math Tactics with Examples

Tactic 1: Translate Word Problems into Algebraic Expressions.

A major difference between the PSAT and school tests is the widespread use of word problems on the PSAT. Many PSAT problems will require you to translate several sentences into an algebraic expression. Table 6.1 lists some of the key phrases that may be used in place of mathematical notations.

Table 6.1 Key Phrases and Mathematical Operators

Wording Examples	Translation
Is, are, was, were, will be, results in, gives, yields, equals	$=$
Sum, increased by, more than, together, combined, total(s), added to, older than, farther than	$+$
Difference, decreased by, less than, fewer than, minus, younger than, shorter than	$-$
Multiplied by, times, of, product of, twice	$\times$
Divided by, per, out of, ratio of, half of, one third of, split	$\div$ or $\frac{x}{y}$

Here is an example of a typical PSAT word problem that is much easier to solve by translating the wording into algebra.

❯ Example

Katie rents an apartment in the spring and will rent it for the rest of the calendar year. To rent it, she must pay a $500 security deposit and a monthly rent of $750. In addition, she must pay monthly utilities of $40 for water and $50 for electricity. What expression gives the total amount of money Katie will spend if she rents the apartment for x months that year?

(A) $840 + 500x$

(B) $500 + 840x$

(C) $500x$

(D) $750x + 500$

✓ Solution

As you read this problem, you can underline key words and write out important information. You should use abbreviations for the sake of time. For instructional purposes, though, everything is written out here using complete words. For example:

$$\$500 = \text{security deposit}$$

$$\$750 = \text{monthly rent}$$

$$\$40 + \$50 = \$90 \text{ for total monthly utilities}$$

To rent the apartment for x months, Katie will need to pay the $500 security deposit one time. Then, she will need to pay $750 in rent each month plus $90 in utilities each month for a total of $840 each month.

So the correct answer is choice (B) because there is a flat fee of $500 plus the $840 per month, varying with how many months she rents. Writing this out, rather than doing it in your head, makes this a much easier problem to solve. If you happen to be taking a digital version of the test, you will have scrap paper provided that you can use.

Tactic 2: Minimize Careless Errors by Writing Out Your Work.

Students often dismiss careless errors as ones that should not concern them in their preparation. However, if you make careless mistakes in your practice, you will likely make them on the real PSAT. Although it may be nice to focus your preparation on learning to solve the most challenging questions elegantly, realize that a couple of careless errors on easier problems may be more detrimental than having conceptual difficulties on a challenging question.

Here is a problem where careless errors can be avoided with careful writing.

❯ Example

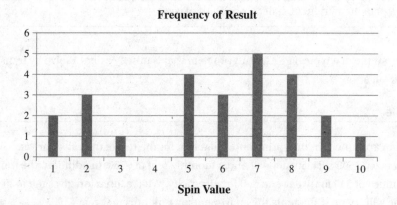

Frequency of Result

Spin Value

A board game has a circular wheel evenly divided into ten segments, each with a numerical value between 1 and 10. For the spins recorded in the above graph, what is the mean value of a spin, rounded to the nearest hundredth?

✓ Solution

If you try to do this in your head, you will likely make a careless mistake. You need to use this formula:

$$\text{Mean} = \frac{\text{Sum of Values}}{\text{Total Number of Values}}$$

The sum of all of the responses is:

$$2(1) + 3(2) + 1(3) + 0(4) + 4(5) + 3(6) + 5(7) + 4(8) + 2(9) + 1(10) = 144$$

The total number of responses is:

$$2 + 3 + 1 + 0 + 4 + 3 + 5 + 4 + 2 + 1 = 25$$

Calculate the mean:

$$144 \div 25 = 5.76$$

Tactic 3: Patiently Visualize What the Parts of an Algebraic Expression Signify.

The PSAT will have questions that require you to interpret algebraic expressions. For many questions, it is helpful to look at the answer choices before solving to see where the question is headed. On questions like these, it is advisable to "look before you leap." The incorrect answers here will likely be very persuasive. So use writing to visualize what the parts of the algebraic expression signify before you evaluate the answer choices. Although this takes more time up front, it will probably save you time in the long run. Here is an example of the kind of problem that applies to this approach.

❯ Example

A book warehouse has an inventory of books, I, that is modeled by the equation $I = 42{,}500 - 600w$, where w represents the number of weeks that have gone by after the beginning of the year. What do the numbers 42,500 and 600 represent in the equation?

(A) The average book inventory throughout the year is 42,500. The number of books at the end of the year is 600.

(B) The book inventory in the warehouse at the end of the year is 42,500. The number of weeks that it takes for the book inventory to be gone is 600.

(C) The initial monetary investment in the book warehouse is 42,500. The weekly revenue from outside book sales is 600.

(D) The warehouse book inventory at the beginning of the year is 42,500. The number of books removed from the warehouse each week is 600.

✓ Solution

Start by rewriting the provided equation:

$$I = 42{,}500 - 600w$$

Next, try plugging in different values for w to see how these impact the inventory, I.

When 0 weeks have gone by, w is 0. So the inventory is 42,500. This means that at the beginning of the year, the inventory is 42,500.

At the beginning of week 1, the initial inventory is still 42,500. At the end of week 1, though, 600 books have been subtracted from the inventory. After 2 weeks go by, the original inventory goes down by 1,200. So a pattern emerges—the 600 in the equation represents the amount by which the book inventory decreases each week. The correct answer is choice (D).

If you just jumped into the answer choices without thinking this question through and making some notes, it would have been quite easy to become trapped by a persuasive answer and over-think the question.

Tactic 4: Plug in the Answer Choices.

One of the most tried-and-true PSAT Math strategies is to plug the answers into an equation, starting with a middle value, like choice (B) or choice (C). Why? That way you will need to try only a maximum of two or three choices instead of potentially all four. The choices are almost certainly going to be in numerical order. So if the first value you choose is too large, you will know which choices to try next. Here is an example of where this technique can save you time.

> **Example**

What is a possible value of x that satisfies the equation below?

$$-(x-3)^2 = -25$$

(A) 6

(B) 8

(C) 10

(D) 12

✓ **Solution**

If you write all of this, it will make for a relatively long, messy calculation. If you work backward from the choices, you will arrive at the answer with ease. Start with choice (C), where $x = 10$, because it is a middle value among your choices:

$$-(10-3)^2 = -25$$
$$-49 \neq -25$$

So choice (C) doesn't work. If you try a larger value, like 12, the difference between the answers will be even larger. So try choice (B) next, where $x = 8$:

$$-(8-3)^2 = -25$$
$$-(5)^2 = -25$$

Since $x = 8$ is true, the correct answer is choice (B). It is unlikely that some of the later, more challenging questions will permit this sort of backsolving. However, this method can save you time on earlier questions, giving you more time to work through the difficult questions.

Tactic 5: Plug in Numbers to Solve Certain Types of Problems More Easily.

A common situation where plugging in numbers can be helpful is when the problem provides a variable within a possible range. In this case, you can pick a number within the given range and plug it in to see the value of the expression. Here is an example.

> **Example**

Assuming that x is not equal to zero, what is the value of the following expression?

$$\frac{1}{4}\left(\frac{(2x)^3}{(3x)^3}\right)$$

Student-Produced Response Question: Write Your Answer _____

✓ **Solution**

Perhaps you see that you can cancel out the x^3 from the top and bottom. If you don't make that intellectual leap, plugging in a value can make things much easier and more concrete. Based on the question, any number that is not equal to zero would work for x. This provides you with infinite options to try for x. Instead of trying a really large number or a fraction, how about plugging in 1 for x? It is not equal to zero, so it is a valid input. It is easy to work with since it will remain 1 when cubed:

$$\frac{1}{4}\left(\frac{(2x)^3}{(3x)^3}\right) =$$

$$\frac{1}{4}\left(\frac{(2\cdot1)^3}{(3\cdot1)^3}\right) =$$

$$\frac{1}{4}\left(\frac{8}{27}\right) =$$

$$\frac{8}{108} = \frac{2}{27}$$

The answer is $\frac{2}{27}$.

Tactic 6: Isolate a Constant in Order to Find Its Value.

If a question asks you to find the value of a constant, simplify the expression so you can isolate the constant and determine its value.

❯ Example

In the equation that follows, a is a constant:

$$(2 - 3x)(x^2 + 4x - 5) = -3x^3 - 10x^2 + ax - 10$$

Given that this equation is true for all values of x, what is the value of the constant a?

(A) -3
(B) 15
(C) 23
(D) 30

✓ Solution

Solve this by first expanding the left-hand side of the equation:

$$(2 - 3x)(x^2 + 4x - 5)$$

Multiply and distribute:

$$2x^2 + 8x - 10 - 3x^3 - 12x^2 + 15x$$

Combine like terms:

$$-3x^3 - 10x^2 + 23x - 10$$

Now that the left-hand side has been simplified, rewrite the original problem to see what matches up to the constant a:

$$-3x^3 - 10x^2 + 23x - 10 = -3x^3 - 10x^2 + ax - 10$$

After looking at this, it becomes clear that 23 corresponds to the constant a. Therefore, choice (C) is the correct answer. Whenever you encounter a problem involving constants, don't worry about solving for multiple variables—just isolate the constant.

Tactic 7: Use the Provided Formulas on Geometry and Trigonometry Problems.

Not many problems use geometry and trigonometry on the PSAT. Because of this, it is easy to forget that the PSAT provides you with several extremely helpful formulas. Although it would be best if you didn't have to look because you have the formulas memorized, here are the provided formulas in case you need them.

Radius of a circle = r
Area of a circle = πr^2
Circumference of a circle = $2\pi r$

Area of a rectangle = length $\times$ width = lw

Area of a triangle = $\frac{1}{2} \times$ base $\times$ height = $\frac{1}{2} bh$

Pythagorean theorem: $a^2 + b^2 = c^2$

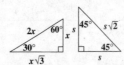

Special right triangles: 30-60-90 and 45-45-90

Volume of a box = length $\times$ width $\times$ height = lwh

Volume of a cylinder = $\pi r^2 h$

Volume of a sphere = $\frac{4}{3}\pi r^3$

Volume of a cone = $\frac{1}{3}\pi r^2 h$

Volume of a pyramid =
$\frac{1}{3} \times$ length $\times$ width $\times$ height = $\frac{1}{3}lwh$

Key Facts:

- A circle has 360 degrees.
- There are 2π radians in a circle.
- There are 180 degrees in a triangle.

The following example is the sort of problem where referring to the formulas can make a big difference.

> **Example**

The area of a sector of a circle represents 20% of the area of the entire circle. What is the central angle that corresponds to this sector in degrees?

(A) 72°
(B) 90°
(C) 120°
(D) 180°

✓ **Solution**

A provided fact is key to solving this:

"A circle has 360 degrees."

If a sector is taking up 20% of the circle, it is also taking up 20% of the degrees in the center of that circle. Since a circle has 360 degrees, the sector is taking up:

$$(0.20)(360°) = 72°$$

The answer is choice (A).

Tactic 8: Use Proportions and Canceling to Solve Unit Conversion Problems.

Converting among different types of units—such as mass measurements, currency conversion rates, and length measurements—is a major component of the PSAT. You can do unit conversions in several ways.

If you are doing a relatively straightforward conversion between just two units, you can set up a proportion or do simple multiplication. Here is an example.

TIP

Many students learn the process for unit conversions in chemistry or other science classes.

> **Example**

A cook needs to measure $3\frac{1}{2}$ cups of flour for a recipe, but he has only a tablespoon available to measure the flour. Given that there are 16 tablespoons in 1 cup, how many tablespoons of flour will the cook need for the recipe?

(A) 32 tablespoons
(B) 56 tablespoons
(C) 64 tablespoons
(D) 73 tablespoons

✓ **Solution**

Option 1: Set up a proportion. There are 16 tablespoons in 1 cup, and the cook needs 3.5 cups. So set up a proportion that has the tablespoons to cup ratio on either side:

$$\frac{16 \text{ tablespoons}}{1 \text{ cup}} = \frac{x \text{ tablespoons}}{3.5 \text{ cups}}$$

Cross multiply to solve for x:

$$3.5 \times 16 \text{ tablespoons} = 56 \text{ tablespoons}$$

The correct answer is choice (B), 56 tablespoons.

Option 2: If you are comfortable enough with conversions, you could simply jump to the last step of the above calculations and multiply 3.5 cups by 16 tablespoons to get the same result.

If you are doing a more intricate conversion that involves three or more units, you can set it up in the same way you probably learned to do unit conversions in your science classes. This method may have been called *dimensional analysis* or the *unit-factor method*. Here is an example.

❭ Example

If John traveled 20 miles in a straight line from his original destination, approximately how many meters is he from his original destination given that there are 1.609 kilometers in a mile and 1,000 meters in a kilometer?

(A) 32.18
(B) 12,430
(C) 24,154
(D) 32,180

✓ Solution

Write this out in an organized way where you can see which units should be canceled:

$$20 \text{ miles} \times \frac{1.609 \text{ kilometers}}{1 \text{ mile}} \times \frac{1,000 \text{ meters}}{1 \text{ kilometer}} =$$

$$20 \text{ miles} \times \frac{1.609 \text{ kilometers}}{1 \text{ mile}} \times \frac{1,000 \text{ meters}}{1 \text{ kilometer}} =$$

$$20 \times 1.609 \times 1,000 \text{ meters} \approx 32,180 \text{ meters}$$

The miles and kilometers cancel, so 20 miles approximately equals 32,180 meters, choice (D).

Tactic 9: Use Estimation When Applicable to Save Time.

Don't be overly reliant on estimation, but use it when it can help avoid a longer calculation. Here is an example.

❭ Example

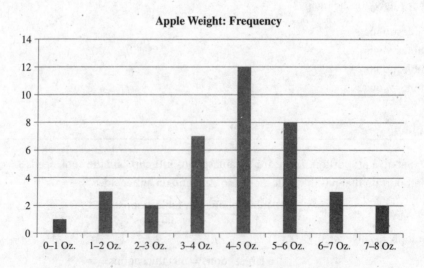

Apple Weight: Frequency

The chart above shows the distribution of individual apple weights that a customer at an apple-picking orchard placed into his bag. Which of the following could be the median weight of the 38 apples in his bag?

(A) 4.6 oz.
(B) 5.1 oz.
(C) 5.4 oz.
(D) 5.7 oz.

✓ Solution

The median of a set of numbers is the middle value when the values are arranged from least to greatest. Although you could come up with sample values and do a laborious calculation, there is no need. The choices have only one possibility that is in the range between 4 and 5 ounces. Since the 4–5 oz. column clearly contains the median value based on a simple eyeball estimation, you can pick choice (A) and move on to the next question.

Another time when estimation is useful is when the numbers in the problem can be rounded to numbers that are easier to manipulate.

❭ Example

Annie initially has $1,997 in her checking account. After shopping for her friend's birthday, the amount of money in her checking account decreases by $603. To the nearest whole number, by what percentage has the amount in her checking account decreased?

(A) 25 percent
(B) 30 percent
(C) 35 percent
(D) 40 percent

✓ Solution

Instead of using the numbers 1,997 and 603, estimate and use numbers that are easier to manipulate: 2,000 for 1,997 and 600 for 603. Use these numbers to estimate the percentage change in the amount of money in her checking account:

$$\frac{\text{Part}}{\text{Whole}} \times 100 = \text{Percentage}$$

$$\frac{600}{2,000} \times 100 =$$

$$\frac{6}{20} \times 100 =$$

$$\frac{3}{10} \times 100 = 30\%$$

This corresponds to choice (B).

Tactic 10: Don't Let Unusual Concepts Intimidate You.

You will be presented with concepts and situations on the PSAT Math that may intimidate you due to their unfamiliarity. Don't respond by quickly giving up because you were never officially taught the concept. Instead, use your intuition and reasoning to think through the problems. Your job is to get the right answer, not to explain your thought process to someone else. If you can devise a clever way to work through the problem, go with it. Remember that the PSAT is designed to assess your general mathematical thinking skills, not your memorization of formulas.

❯ Example

When measuring temperature, the equation to convert degrees Celsius, C, to degrees Fahrenheit, F, is $\frac{9}{5}C + 32 = F$. For the same actual temperature, what is the range of degrees Fahrenheit for which the given number is greater than the given number of degrees Celsius?

(A) $F < -78$

(B) $F > -40$

(C) $F < 26$

(D) $F > 30$

✓ Solution

Although this problem seems as though you may need to incorporate outside knowledge from chemistry, everything you need to figure it out is right in front of you. First paraphrase what the question is asking: "For what temperatures will F be bigger than C?" To determine this, find a value for C and F that is identical. Why? Because if you know the point at which the values are equal to one another, you can then test values greater than or less than that value to determine the direction of the inequality sign.

Let x equal the value for which C and F are the same. Plug it into the equation and solve:

$$\frac{9}{5}C + 32 = F$$

$$\frac{9}{5}x + 32 = x$$

$$32 = -\frac{4}{5}x$$

$$x = -40$$

Since C and F are equivalent at -40 degrees, plug in a simple number for F to see if the expression should be $F > -40$ or $F < -40$. Try 0 for F since it is easy to plug in:

$$\frac{9}{5}C + 32 = F$$

$$\frac{9}{5}C + 32 = 0$$

$$\frac{9}{5}C = -32$$

$$C \approx -17.8$$

From this, you can see that when the F value is 0, it is greater than the value of C, which is a negative number. So the values for which F are greater than the values of C when both numbers represent the actual temperatures are $F > -40$, making the answer choice (B).

Alternatively, you can use an algebraic approach. Since the answers are in terms of F, first solve for C in terms of F:

$$\frac{9}{5}C + 32 = F$$

$$\frac{9}{5}C = F - 32$$

$$C = \frac{5}{9}(F - 32)$$

Then you can make $F > C$ and solve the inequality:

$$F > \frac{5}{9}(F - 32)$$

$$F > \frac{5}{9}F - \left(\frac{5}{9}\right)32$$

$$\frac{4}{9}F > -\left(\frac{5}{9}\right)32$$

$$F > -\left(\frac{9}{4}\right) \times \left(\frac{5}{9}\right) \times 32$$

$$F > -\frac{5}{4} \times 32$$

$$F > -40$$

If you did not realize the algebraic approaches to solving the problem, an alternative would be to take the time to test out the different answers by trying sample values from their ranges to see what would make them true. This approach can work, but it may take you more time than if you can recognize an algebraic solution.

Tactic 11: Approach the Questions Like a Puzzle, Not Like a Typical School Math Problem.

Challenging school math questions often require long calculations and cover tough concepts. The PSAT Math Test questions will not be difficult in these ways. In contrast, the tough questions will involve the patient and creative mindset needed to solve puzzles. Many of the PSAT Math problems can be solved using intuition, trying out sample values, and using the given diagrams. These approaches are not what you would find in a math textbook, yet they often work. Why? Because the PSAT Math Test has generally more *elegant* problems involving pattern recognition than the cut-and-dried problems found on typical school math tests. When you try to do a Sudoku puzzle, a jigsaw puzzle, or a challenging video game, you succeed by setting up the puzzle well instead of going full-speed ahead and doing unnecessary steps. The same applies to answering tough PSAT Math questions.

> **Example**

Consider a set of 25 different numbers. If two numbers are added to the set, one that is larger than the current median of the set and one that is smaller than the current median of the set, which of the following quantities about the set MUST NOT change?

(A) Range
(B) Mean
(C) Mode
(D) Median

☑ **Solution**

On a problem like this, try visualizing what will happen by making up some sample values. Suppose you have a simple set of numbers, something like this:

$$\{1, 1, 2, 3, 4, 5, 6, 7, 8, 9, 10, 11, 12, 13, 14, 15, 16, 17, 18, 19, 20, 21, 22, 23, 24\}$$

The range of the set is 23, which is the difference between the smallest value (1) and the largest value (24).

The mean for this set is all of the above numbers added together and then divided by 25.

The mode is 1 since it appears the most frequently.

The median is 12 since it is the middle value when the numbers are placed in order from smallest to largest.

If you can come up with even one set of values that will make one of these quantities change, that answer is out as a possibility.

If you add −5 and 100 to the set, the range of the set will become much larger—it will be 105. So choice (A) is not correct.

If you add 2 and 1,000 to the set, the mean will change because the average will shift significantly upward. So choice (B) is not correct.

If you add 7 and 17 to the set, it will have 3 different modes instead of just having 1 as the only mode. So choice (C) is not correct.

Choice (D) is correct. As long as you add any number less than 12 and any number greater than 12, the median will remain the same because 12 will still be in the middle of the set of numbers when they are all placed in order from smallest to largest.

You could also solve this more intuitively if you have a solid understanding of the concept of the median of a set. When given a particular median, if you add one number greater than and one number less than the median, the median will not change since it will remain in the very middle of the set.

Tactic 12: Don't Jump to an Answer Too Quickly.

Unlike in traditional math tests where the incorrect answers are often just random numbers, the answers on the PSAT are designed to reflect the errors students can make when solving the problems. Simply because an answer is on your calculator is no guarantee that it is correct. For example, in math class you typically solve for x and the answer is a given solution. On the PSAT, however, the question may be asking for the value of an expression, like $-2x^2 - x$.

If you have absolutely no idea what the correct answer is to a question, then guess. There is no penalty for guessing. The PSAT does not consistently favor one answer choice letter over another. So before you take the test, choose a letter at random. When you have to guess an answer, just use that letter. Choosing a particular letter ahead of time and always using it when you are blindly guessing will help you avoid wasting time during the test deciding which letter to pick.

> **Example**

What is/are the real number value(s) of x in this equation?

$$x = \sqrt{2x + 15}$$

(A) −3 only

(B) 5 only

(C) −3 and 5

(D) Cannot determine based on the given information.

✓ **Solution**

Although this looks fairly easy to solve, more is here than meets the eye. You have to be careful that what seems to be a solution actually is a solution. Start by squaring both sides and determining the potential values for x:

$$x = \sqrt{2x + 15}$$
$$x^2 = 2x + 15$$
$$0 = x^2 - 2x - 15$$
$$0 = (x + 3)(x - 5)$$

So if $(x + 3) = 0$ or if $(x - 5) = 0$, the entire expression equals 0. That means −3 can be a solution since you can set $(x + 3)$ equal to 0 and solve for x:

$$(x + 3) = 0$$

Subtract 3 from both sides:

$$x = -3$$

You can do the same procedure for $(x - 5)$:

$$(x - 5) = 0$$

Add 5 to both sides:

$$x = 5$$

So it appears that both −3 and 5 work as solutions since they both cause $(x + 3)(x - 5)$ to equal 0. When you try these in the original equation, however, only 5 works. Why? Because −3 cannot be the principal square root of 9 since −3 cannot equal the positive square root of a number. So −3 is an "extraneous solution," making choice (B) the answer.

Tactic 13: Know the Student-Produced Response Question Rules.

On the PSAT Math Test, approximately 25% of the questions are student-produced response questions. Here are some key things to know about these types of problems.

- It is possible that a question could have more than one correct answer. Enter just one correct answer.

- Long decimal answers that continue past the five spots allowed for gridding can be rounded up or shortened as long as you use all of the spaces. You can also express a decimal answer as a fraction. For example, you can write $\frac{7}{9}$ as 7/9, .777, or .778.

- You don't need to reduce fractions. For example, since $\frac{2}{3}$, $\frac{4}{6}$, and $\frac{6}{9}$ are equivalent, any of them will work as an answer.

> **Example**

What is the value of x if $(3x + 2) - (5x - 6) = -4$?

✓ **Solution**

On a problem like this, the math is not too difficult. The challenge is to avoid making a careless error because of confusing a negative sign or incorrectly adding numbers. This is especially important on a student-produced response question since you will not have four multiple choices to help you detect a major miscalculation. Avoid making careless mistakes by writing out all of your steps. Start by writing the original equation:

$$(3x + 2) - (5x - 6) = -4$$

Remove the parentheses around $(3x + 2)$ and distribute the -1 through the $(5x - 6)$:

$$3x + 2 - 5x + 6 = -4$$

Check that you distributed the negative sign correctly. Then combine like terms:

$$-2x + 8 = -4$$

Subtract the 8 from both sides:

$$-2x = -12$$

Divide both sides by -2 to solve for x:

$$x = 6$$

You can check your work by plugging in 6 for x into the original equation:

$$(3x + 2) - (5x - 6) = -4$$
$$(3(6) + 2) - (5(6) - 6) = -4$$
$$18 + 2 - 30 + 6 = -4$$
$$-4 = -4$$

It checks out. So the final answer is 6.

Algebra Practice

1. Which ordered pair (x, y) satisfies the pair of equations below?

$$3x + y = -3$$
$$x - 2y = -8$$

   (A) $(2, 4)$
   (B) $(-2, 3)$
   (C) $(-3, 2)$
   (D) $(1, -4)$

2. The United States primarily uses a 12-hour clock with 12-hour periods for the morning (A.M.) and for the afternoon/evening (P.M.). Much of the rest of the world uses a 24-hour clock (e.g., 3:00 P.M. would be expressed as 15 hundred hours). Which of the following inequalities expresses the digits for hours, H, on a 24-hour clock that correspond to the business hours for a restaurant that is open from 7 P.M. until 11 P.M. (Ignore the "hundred" expressed with the hours in the 24 hour clock)?

   (A) $7 \leq H \leq 11$
   (B) $12 \leq H \leq 24$
   (C) $19 \leq H \leq 23$
   (D) $24 \leq H \leq 27$

3. A video arcade charges a set $5 charge to purchase a game card and then charges $0.50 for each video game played. What expression gives the relationship between the number of games played, G, and the total amount of dollars spent using the game card, T?

   (A) $T = 5G - 0.50$
   (B) $T = 4.50G + 5$
   (C) $T = 0.50G - 2.5$
   (D) $T = 0.50G + 5$

4.

Age	Maximum Recommended Heart Rate
50	165
55	160
60	155
65	150

A cardiologist uses the guidelines for maximum recommended heart rate (measured in beats per minute) shown in the table above, which vary based on a patient's age. One of the cardiologist's patients, age 55, wants to start an exercise program. The cardiologist recommends that the patient maintain a heart rate greater than 50% and less than 85% of the maximum recommended heart rate while exercising. Which of the following expressions gives the range in which the patient's heart rate, H, should be during exercise?

   (A) $50 < H < 85$
   (B) $80 < H < 136$
   (C) $85 < H < 160$
   (D) $150 < H < 160$

5. Hannah has only nickels and dimes in her wallet. She has a total of $2.50 and a total of 30 coins. How many nickels does she have?

   (A) 10
   (B) 12
   (C) 15
   (D) 16

6. A two-digit number has a tens place, t, and a units place, u. The digits have the following relationships:

   $$t + u = 8$$
   $$t = 2 + u$$

   What is the value of the two-digit number given by these two digits?

   (A) 41
   (B) 53
   (C) 63
   (D) 79

7. 18-karat gold has 18 parts gold for 24 total parts metal (the difference comes from the 6 parts that are metals other than gold). 24-karat gold is pure gold. In order to make a piece of jewelry that is 2.4 ounces in weight and is 20-karat gold, how many ounces of 18-karat gold, X, and of 24-karat gold, Y, are needed to make this piece of jewelry?

   (A) $X = 0.4, Y = 0.6$
   (B) $X = 0.9, Y = 1.7$
   (C) $X = 1.2, Y = 1.1$
   (D) $X = 1.6, Y = 0.8$

8. For the equation $3 + 4x - 2 = k + 6x - 2x$, what does the constant k need to equal in order for there to be multiple solutions for x?

   (A) 1
   (B) 2
   (C) 3
   (D) 4

9. What is the value of y in the system of equations below?

   $$16x - 4y = 12$$
   $$8x + 2y = 4$$

   (A) 2
   (B) $\frac{3}{2}$
   (C) $-\frac{1}{2}$
   (D) -4

10. What are the solutions for x and y in the equations below?

$$-\frac{3}{4}x + 2\left(y - \frac{1}{2}\right) = 3$$

$$\frac{2}{3}x = 6 - 2y$$

(A) $x = \frac{24}{17}$, $y = \frac{43}{17}$

(B) $x = \frac{2}{13}$, $y = \frac{14}{19}$

(C) $x = -3$, $y = \frac{7}{19}$

(D) $x = -\frac{4}{11}$, $y = \frac{18}{23}$

11. Electrical engineers use Ohm's law, $V = IR$, to give the relationship among voltage (V), current (I), and resistance (R). Which of the following statements is always true about the relationship among voltage, current, and resistance based on Ohm's law?

   I. If the current increases and the resistance remains the same, the voltage increases.

   II. If the voltage increases, the resistance must increase.

   III. If the resistance increases and the voltage remains the same, the current must decrease.

(A) I only

(B) II only

(C) I and III only

(D) II and III only

12. What is the graph of the following function?

$$3 + y = 2 + 3x$$

(A)
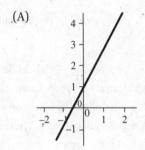

(C)
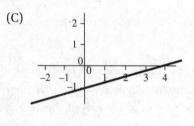

(B)
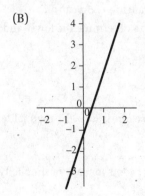

(D)
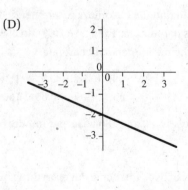

Answer Explanations

1. **(B)** You can use substitution to solve, although elimination could also work.

$$3x + y = -3$$
$$x - 2y = -8$$

Rearrange the second equation to be in terms of y:

$$x - 2y = -8$$
$$x = 2y - 8$$

Substitute into the first equation and solve for y:

$$3x + y = -3$$
$$3(2y - 8) + y = -3$$
$$6y - 24 + y = -3$$
$$7y - 24 = -3$$
$$7y = 21$$
$$y = 3$$

Then plug in 3 for y into the first equation to solve for x:

$$3x + y = -3$$
$$3x + 3 = -3$$
$$3x = -6$$
$$x = -2$$

2. **(C)** Simply add 12 to both 7 and 11 to find the correct range since all of the P.M. times are 12 hours less than the time on a 24-hour clock:

$$12 + 7 = 19 \text{ and } 12 + 11 = 23$$

This makes the range between 19 and 23 hours inclusive, which is expressed as the inequality $19 \leq H \leq 23$.

3. **(D)** There will be a $5 charge no matter how many games are played. So the $5 should be represented as a constant. For each game played, there is an additional $0.50 fee. Since G represents the number of games played, the total cost is $0.50G + 5$ dollars. This can be expressed as $T = 0.50G + 5$. Alternatively, you could make up a number of games played and the total dollars spent. Then find which of the equations gives an identical result.

4. **(B)** Use the table to find the maximum recommended heart rate for a 55-year-old person—160 beats per minute. Then take 50% and 85% of 160 to determine the lower and upper bounds of the recommended heart rate:

$$50\% \text{ of } 160 = 0.50 \times 160 = 80$$
$$85\% \text{ of } 160 = 0.85 \times 160 = 136$$

So the range is between 80 and 136 beats per minute, which is expressed as the inequality $80 < H < 136$.

5. **(A)** Set up a series of two equations. Put everything in terms of cents for sake of simplicity. Use N as the number of nickels and D as the number of dimes:

The total number of coins: $N + D = 30$
The total number of cents: $5N + 10D = 250$

Express D in terms of N based on the first equation:

$$N + D = 30$$
$$D = 30 - N$$

Then, substitute this for D in the second equation:

$$5N + 10D = 250$$
$$5N + 10(30 - N) = 250$$
$$5N + 300 - 10N = 250$$
$$-5N = -50$$
$$N = 10$$

Alternatively, you can solve this by working backward from the answers. Since the total number of cents must be 250, try the different possible values of nickels from the choices to see which one works. You can try choice (B) or choice (C) since they are in the middle. Once you get to choice (A), you will find that if you have 10 nickels, you have 50 cents from nickels. That means there must be 200 cents from dimes, which also means there are 20 dimes. Since 20 dimes and 10 nickels add together to give you 30 coins total, choice (A) is correct.

6. **(B)** Use substitution to solve for t and u:

$$t + u = 8$$
$$t = 2 + u$$

Plug in $2 + u$ for t into the first equation:

$$(2 + u) + u = 8$$
$$2 + 2u = 8$$
$$2u = 6$$
$$u = 3$$

Plug in 3 for u into one of the original equations, and solve for t. This gives 5 in the tens place and 3 in the ones place, making 53 your answer.

Alternatively, you can solve this using elimination.

$$t + u = 8$$
$$t = 2 + u$$

Rearrange the second equation:

$$t = 2 + u$$
$$t - u = 2$$

Then you have this as the set of equations:

$$t + u = 8$$
$$t - u = 2$$

Add the two together to get:

$$2t = 10$$
$$t = 5$$

Then substitute $t = 5$ into the first equation to solve for u:

$$t + u = 8$$
$$5 + u = 8$$
$$u = 3$$

The answer is still 53.

7. **(D)** Set up a system of two equations. One equation models the number of actual gold karats:

$$\frac{18}{24}X + \frac{24}{24}Y = \frac{20}{24} \times 2.4 \rightarrow \frac{3}{4}X + Y = \frac{5}{6} \times 2.4$$

One equation models the weight of the jewelry:

$$X + Y = 2.4$$

You can use either substitution or elimination to solve this system. However, using elimination is better since a Y-term in each equation will be easily canceled. Start by simplifying the first equation:

$$\frac{3}{4}X + Y = \frac{5}{6} \times 2.4$$

$$\frac{3}{4}X + Y = 2$$

Now subtract it from $X + Y = 2.4$:

$$X + Y = 2.4$$
$$-\left(\frac{3}{4}X + Y = 2\right)$$
$$\frac{1}{4}X \quad\quad = 0.4$$

Then solve for X:

$$\frac{1}{4}X = 0.4$$
$$X = 4 \times 0.4$$
$$X = 1.6$$

Now plug in 1.6 for X into one of the equations to solve for Y. Use $X + Y = 2.4$ since it is simpler:

$$X + Y = 2.4$$
$$1.6 + Y = 2.4$$
$$Y = 0.8$$

So the final answer is $X = 1.6$, $Y = 0.8$.

8. **(A)** Before proceeding too far, simplify the equation by grouping like terms:

$$3 + 4x - 2 = k + 6x - 2x$$
$$1 + 4x = k + 4x$$

So if $k = 1$, both sides of the equations are equivalent to one another. The equation reduces to $x = x$, which has an infinite number of solutions.

9. **(C)** Solve this using elimination by taking the first equation and multiplying it by $\frac{1}{2}$:

$$16x - 4y = 12$$
$$\underline{8x + 2y = 4}$$

$$8x - 2y = 6$$
$$\underline{8x + 2y = 4}$$

Subtract the two so we can easily find y:

$$8x - 2y = 6$$
$$\underline{-(8x + 2y = 4)}$$
$$-4y = 2$$

$$y = -\frac{1}{2}$$

10. **(A)** Start by simplifying both equations:

$$-\frac{3}{4}x + 2\left(y - \frac{1}{2}\right) = 3 \qquad \qquad \frac{2}{3}x = 6 - 2y$$
$$-\frac{3}{4}x + 2y - 1 = 3 \quad \text{and} \quad \frac{2}{3}x + 2y = 6$$
$$-\frac{3}{4}x + 2y = 4$$

Then use elimination to solve:

$$-\frac{3}{4}x + 2y = 4$$
$$\underline{-\left(\frac{2}{3}x + 2y = 6\right)}$$
$$-\frac{3}{4}x - \frac{2}{3}x = -2$$

$$-\frac{9}{12}x - \frac{8}{12}x = -2$$

$$\frac{-17}{12}x = -2$$

$$x = \frac{24}{17}$$

Since only choice (A) has x equal to $\frac{24}{17}$, you can save time by just picking it as the correct answer.

11. **(C)** Choice I is correct. Increasing current while keeping resistance constant increases the right side of the equation. This means the left side—the voltage—increases as well. Choice III is correct. If the voltage—the left side of the equation—remains the same while the resistance increases, the current must decrease in order for the value on the right side of the equation to remain the same. Choice II is NOT correct. The current could increase without the resistance increasing if the voltage increases.

12. **(B)** Put the equation into slope-intercept form:

$$3 + y = 2 + 3x$$
$$y = 3x - 1$$

This line has a slope of 3 and a y-intercept of -1, which has the following graph:

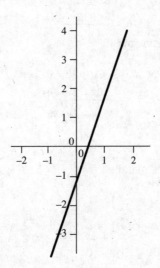

Problem-Solving and Data Analysis Practice

1. A subway map is drawn to scale so that 1 inch on the map corresponds to 2 miles of actual distance on the track. The subway train travels at a constant average rate of 30 miles per hour. How many minutes will a journey on the subway take if the track distance as portrayed on the map is 3 inches?

   (A) 6
   (B) 9
   (C) 12
   (D) 18

2. An electronic reader typically costs $100. However, the price is heavily discounted due to both a coupon and a sale that have the same percent off the regular price. If the price using both the coupon discount and the sale discount is $49, what is the percent off the regular price that the coupon and the sale each provide independently?

   (A) 25%
   (B) 30%
   (C) 35%
   (D) 40%

3. If n percent of 80 is 20, what is n percent of 220?

   (A) 42
   (B) 48
   (C) 55
   (D) 76

4. If 132 men and 168 women are living in a dormitory, what percent of the total dormitory residents are men?

   (A) 28%
   (B) 34%
   (C) 40%
   (D) 44%

5. If 1 Canadian dollar can be exchanged for 0.80 U.S. dollars and vice versa, how many Canadian dollars can a traveler receive in exchange for 120 U.S. dollars?

   (A) 60
   (B) 90
   (C) 150
   (D) 220

6. David is developing a fitness plan and wants to get his weight to a level that will be considered healthy in terms of the body mass index (BMI) calculation. The currently recommended BMI is between 18.6 and 24.9. To calculate BMI using inches and pounds, David takes his weight in pounds and divides it by the square of his height in inches. Then he multiplies the entire result by 703. David is 6 feet, 3 inches tall and currently weighs 260 pounds. To the nearest whole pound, what is the least number of whole pounds he needs to lose in order for his BMI to be within the healthy range?

(A) 61
(B) 68
(C) 75
(D) 83

Questions 7–9 refer to the following information.

A marine biologist has conducted research into the population of blue whales over the past few decades. The estimated global blue whale population is plotted against the given year in the graph below:

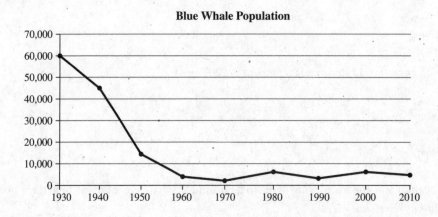

7. From 1940 until 1970, the best-fit equation for the values of the blue whale population has which general characteristic?

(A) Linear decay
(B) Linear growth
(C) Exponential decay
(D) Exponential growth

8. A worldwide treaty prohibiting commercial whaling (i.e., the hunting of whales) was passed at some point between 1930 and 2010. Based on the data, what is the year when this treaty most likely went into effect?

(A) 1930
(B) 1950
(C) 1970
(D) 2000

9. Another scientist is reviewing the results of the marine biologist's observations and assessing the impact of measurement error on such an ambitious project. The scientist is considering two possible sources of measurement error: (1) random error from any factor that would affect the scientist's measurements and (2) systematic error from a problem in the overall setup of the data-gathering project. Which of the following would be the best way that the marine biologist's measurement error could have been minimized?

(A) Collecting whale population data from as many possible points from an even distribution throughout all the world's oceans

(B) Comparing the blue whale data to data of other whales, such as the sperm whale, fin whale, and killer whale

(C) Gathering data from a consistent single point in the Atlantic Ocean, doing so at the same day/time each year

(D) Consistently taking a sample from a 100-square-mile range of the Pacific Ocean and electronically tagging each whale that is observed to ensure no whale is counted twice

Questions 10–11 refer to the following information.

The graph below gives the current GPA of every one of the 389 students at County High School.

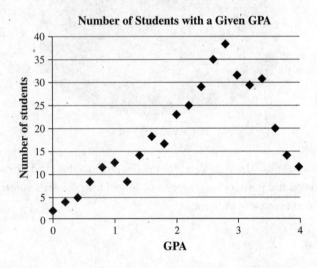

10. Which of these values of the GPA for the students portrayed in the graph is between 2 and 3?

I. Mean

II. Median

III. Mode

(A) I only

(B) II only

(C) I and II only

(D) I, II, and III

11. The school administrators have decided that too much grade inflation occurs at the school. They believe the average GPA is skewed too high by teachers giving too many A's and B's and by not enough students receiving C's, D's, and F's. If the administrators want to ensure that grade inflation is minimized, which of these quantities would be important to bring close to 2.0?

    (A) Median only
    (B) Mean only
    (C) Both mean and median
    (D) Neither mean nor median

Questions 12–13 refer to the following information.

In a recent election in a European country, the political parties divided the vote among the Social Democrats, the Christian Democrats, the Socialists, and the Green Party.

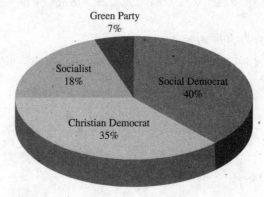

Percentage of Votes

12. If women provided 60% of the total votes for the Green, Socialist, and Christian Democrat parties and if males and females each represent 50% of the country's voters, what percent of the Social Democrat vote was from men?

    (A) 45%
    (B) 49%
    (C) 56%
    (D) 65%

13. The country's constitution states that in order for a party to come to power, it must have a majority of the votes. The constitution also states that the seats in the parliament are allocated proportionally to each party based on the percentage of votes each party received. So if no one political party receives a majority of the vote, a coalition party will have to be formed from 2 or more parties to give a governing majority. Which of the following combinations of political parties from this election would NOT result in a governing coalition?

    (A) Christian Democrat and Social Democrat
    (B) Green Party and Christian Democrat
    (C) Socialist and Social Democrat
    (D) Socialist and Christian Democrat

Questions 14–15 refer to the following information.

300 patients at a hospital were categorized based on whether they had high or low cholesterol and on whether they had high or low blood pressure. The results are tabulated in the table below.

	High Cholesterol	Low Cholesterol	Total
High Blood Pressure	40	30	70
Low Blood Pressure	50	180	230
Total	90	210	300

14. What is the probability that one of the 230 low blood pressure patients has high cholesterol?

(A) $\dfrac{30}{230}$

(B) $\dfrac{50}{230}$

(C) $\dfrac{65}{230}$

(D) $\dfrac{80}{230}$

15. What is the percent chance that one of the 300 patients will have at least one of the conditions—high cholesterol or high blood pressure?

(A) 36%

(B) 40%

(C) 48%

(D) 52%

Questions 16–17 refer to the following information.

A researcher surveyed several residents in a town about the types of vehicles the residents own. The results are shown in the table below.

	Car	Van	Truck/SUV	Total
Gas	104	31	43	178
Hybrid	10	1	m	n
Electric	6	3	0	9
Total	120	35	45	200

16. Jennifer and Bill were members of the group surveyed. They have a car and a van in their garage. What is the probability that both of the vehicles in their garage are hybrids?

(A) $\dfrac{1}{420}$

(B) $\dfrac{1}{380}$

(C) $\dfrac{1}{360}$

(D) $\dfrac{1}{240}$

17. What are the values of m and n in the table above?

(A) $m = 4$ and $n = 8$

(B) $m = 8$ and $n = 26$

(C) $m = 2$ and $n = 13$

(D) Cannot determine based on the given information.

Answer Explanations

1. **(C)** Since 1 inch on the map corresponds to 2 miles of actual distance, double the 3 inches shown on the map to determine that the subway has traveled 6 actual miles. Since the subway is traveling at 30 miles per hour, solve for the number of hours the subway has traveled:

$$\text{Distance} = \text{Rate} \times \text{Time}$$
$$6 = 30 \times \text{Time}$$
$$\text{Time} = \frac{1}{5} \text{ hours}$$

Then multiply $\frac{1}{5}$ by 60 minutes to determine how many minutes the train takes to travel 6 miles:

$$\frac{1}{5} \times 60 = 12 \text{ minutes}$$

2. **(B)** Since both the coupon and the sale provide the same percent discount, you can set up an equation to determine what you must multiply $100 by in order to end up with a price of $49. Alternatively, you can simply multiply $100 by the same variable twice, which will let you determine the correct percentage:

$$(x)(x)(100) = 49$$
$$100x^2 = 49$$
$$x^2 = \frac{49}{100}$$
$$x^2 = 0.49$$
$$x = \sqrt{0.49}$$
$$x = 0.7$$

If x equals 0.7, subtract 0.7 from 1 to find the percent discount:

$$1 - 0.7 = 0.3 = 30\%$$

This means that a 30 percent discount has been applied to the original amount two times.

3. **(C)** Set this up as an equation to determine what n equals. Use the first bit of information in the question:

$$\frac{\text{Part}}{\text{Whole}} \times 100 = \text{Percent}$$
$$\frac{20}{80} \times 100 = n$$
$$\frac{1}{4} \times 100 = n$$
$$n = 25\%$$

Then take 25% of 220:

$$0.25 \times 220 = 55$$

4. **(D)** Since $\frac{\text{Part}}{\text{Whole}} \times 100 = \text{Percent}$, take the number of men and divide it by the total number of residents to determine the percentage of just men:

$$\frac{132}{132 + 168} \times 100 = 44\%$$

5. **(C)** This is easiest to solve using a simple proportion:

$$\frac{1 \text{ Canadian dollar}}{0.80 \text{ U.S. dollars}} = \frac{x}{120}$$

Cross multiply to find the solution:

$$(1 \text{ Canadian dollar})(120) = (0.80 \text{ U.S. dollars})(x)$$

$$x = \frac{120}{0.80} = 150 \text{ Canadian dollars}$$

6. **(A)** First solve for the weight that David must be in order to have a BMI of 24.9 given his height since this would put the BMI within the appropriate range. Use the wording in the question to set up an equation: "To calculate BMI using inches and pounds, David takes his weight in pounds and divides it by the square of his height in inches. Then he multiplies the entire result by 703." This gives the following BMI equation:

$$\frac{\text{Weight}}{\text{Height}^2} \times 703 = \text{BMI}$$

Since David is 6 feet, 3 inches tall, his height is $(12 \times 6) + 3 = 75$ inches. Plug in 24.9 for the BMI and 75 for the height into the equation, and solve for the weight:

$$\frac{\text{Weight}}{75^2} \times 703 = 24.9$$

$$\text{Weight} \times 703 = 24.9 \times 75^2$$

$$\text{Weight} = \frac{24.9 \times 75^2}{703}$$

$$\text{Weight} \approx 199$$

Then subtract the desired weight from David's current weight to determine how many whole pounds he should lose:

$$260 - 199 = 61$$

7. **(C)** Between 1940 and 1970, the blue whale population is decreasing and the function has a substantial curve. So the graph shows exponential decay. Note that if the decay were linear, the graph would have gone down in a straight line.

8. **(C)** After the passage of a treaty banning whaling, it is most reasonable to expect that the population of blue whales would gradually increase. 1970 is the only choice after which there is an increase in the global blue whale population.

9. **(A)** The arrangement described in choice (A) would ensure the most random gathering of data from as large a sample as possible, thereby minimizing both random error and systematic error. The other options focus on irrelevant or extremely narrow samples. Choice (B) has a major systematic error since it does not focus on gathering blue whale data. Instead, this choice focuses on comparing data. Choice (C) minimizes random error for this particular data point due to its consistent measurement. However, this choice has the systematic issue of not gathering a wide enough sample of data. Although choice (D) is superior to choices (B) and (C), it falls short of choice (A). Choice (D) limits the sample to a relatively small part of one ocean instead of considering blue whales all over the world.

10. **(D)** Since there is a large cluster of students with GPAs between 2 and 3, it is possible to estimate that the mean and median will fall in that range. The most frequent value, the mode, will also be in that range since the greatest number of students with a particular GPA is between 2 and 3.

11. **(C)** The median is the middle value of all the GPAs. If the middle value was much above 2.0, it would be a strong indication that there was grade inflation. The mean is the arithmetic average of the GPAs, so if it was much above 2.0, it would also indicate grade inflation. So both the median and mean should be close to 2.0 in order to minimize grade inflation.

12. **(D)** Women provided 60% of the vote for the 60% of the total votes for the Green, Socialist, and Christian Democrat parties. That means that women provided $0.6 \times 0.6 \times$ total votes $= 36\%$ of the total votes, not including the Social Democrat votes. Since women make up 50% of the country's voters, 14% of the country's total voters are women who voted for the Social Democrats since $50 - 36 = 14$. That means that 26% of the total population of the country are males who voted for the Social Democrats. To determine the percentage of Social Democrat votes from males, take 26 and divide it by the total percentage of 40 and then convert that value to a percent:

$$\frac{26}{40} \times 100 = 65\%$$

13. **(B)** The Green Party and Christian Democrat Party together would represent $7\% + 35\% = 42\%$ of the entire vote. Since 42% is less than the 50% majority needed for a governing coalition, these two parties would not be able to form a governing coalition on their own. All of the other options would give combinations that would add up to at least 50% and could therefore form a majority governing coalition.

14. **(B)** There are 50 low blood pressure patients who have high cholesterol. So simply divide 50 by the 230 total patients:

$$\frac{50}{230}$$

15. **(B)** There are 40 patients with both conditions, 50 who have only high cholesterol, and 30 who have only high blood pressure:

$$40 + 50 + 30 = 120$$

Divide 120 by the 300 total to find the percent:

$$\frac{120}{300} \times 100 = 40\%$$

16. **(A)** Multiply the probability that the car is a hybrid, $\frac{10}{120}$, by the probability that the van is a hybrid, $\frac{1}{35}$:

$$\frac{10}{120} \times \frac{1}{35} = \frac{1}{12} \times \frac{1}{35} = \frac{1}{420}$$

17. **(C)** The value of m must be 2. All of the trucks and SUVs must add up to a total of 45, and there are 43 of the other truck/SUV types: $43 + 2 = 45$. The value of n must be 13. The total of all the different types of vehicles must add up to 200. The numbers in the last column show a total of $178 + 9 = 187$ and $187 + 13 = 200$.

Advanced Math Practice

1. Michele wants to design a floor that will have a length and width that add up to 30 feet. She also wants the area of the floor to be 216 square feet. What will the dimensions of the floor need to be?

    (A) 10 feet by 20 feet
    (B) 12 feet by 18 feet
    (C) 14 feet by 16 feet
    (D) 17 feet by 17 feet

2. $\left(\dfrac{n^2 - n^3}{n^4}\right)^{-2}$ is equivalent to which of the following?

    (A) $\dfrac{n^4}{1 - 2n + n^2}$

    (B) $\dfrac{n}{n^8}$

    (C) $\dfrac{1 - 2n + n^2}{n^2}$

    (D) $\dfrac{n^2}{1 + 4n - n^2}$

3. For the real integers x and y, what must $\dfrac{2x + 2y}{4}$ equal?

    (A) The mode of x and y
    (B) $x^2 + y^2$
    (C) The arithmetic mean of x and y
    (D) The median of $2x$ and $2y$

4. Factor: $16a^2 - 9b^2$

    (A) $(2a + b)(a - b)$
    (B) $(3a + 2b)(6a - 3b)$
    (C) $(4a + 3b)(4a - 3b)$
    (D) $(8a + 3b)(2a - 3b)$

5. What are the two solutions for x in the equation $4x^2 + 8x - 4 = 0$?

    (A) $x = 3\sqrt{2}$ and $x = -4$
    (B) $x = 2\sqrt{3}$ and $x = \sqrt{11} + 13$
    (C) $x = -\sqrt{7}$ and $x = -5$
    (D) $x = -1 - \sqrt{2}$ and $x = \sqrt{2} - 1$

6. Simplify: $x^4y^2 + x^3y^5 + xy^6 + 2x^3y^5$

    (A) $xy(x^4 + 3x^2y^3 + y^6)$
    (B) $y^2(x^4 + 4x^3y^4 + y^3)$
    (C) $xy^2(x^3 + 3x^2y^3 + y^4)$
    (D) $x(x^3y^2 + x^2y^5 + y^6 + 2x^4y^4)$

7. $\dfrac{x}{2} = \dfrac{2(n^0)}{2} - \dfrac{1}{2x}$

   What is the value of x?

   (A) 0
   (B) 1
   (C) 2
   (D) 3

8. What is the sum of $3x^3 + 5x - 3$ and $2x^2 - 4x + 6$?

   (A) $x^2 - 9x + 9$
   (B) $2x^3 + 4x^2 - x$
   (C) $3x^3 - x^2 + 2x + 3$
   (D) $3x^3 + 2x^2 + x + 3$

9. $(25\,a^4 + 40\,a^2 b^4 + 16\,b^8) \div (5\,a^2 + 4\,b^4) = ?$

   (A) $5b^4 + 40a^2b^4 + 5a^2$
   (B) $4b^4 + 5a^2$
   (C) $25a^4 + 8a^2b^4 + 4a^2$
   (D) 1

10. The formula used by the National Weather Service to calculate wind chill in degrees Fahrenheit is:

    $$35.74 + 0.6215 \times T - 35.75 \times \left(V^{(0.16)}\right) + 0.4275 \times T \times \left(V^{(0.16)}\right)$$

    T represents the air temperature in degrees Fahrenheit, and V represents the wind velocity in miles per hour.

    Which of these is an accurate statement about the relationship between wind chill and temperature?

    I. The relative impact on wind chill of a particular increase in wind speed is more significant at lower wind speeds than at higher wind speeds.
    II. Wind chill has an impact on the relative temperature feeling only at temperatures greater than or equal to 35.75 degrees Fahrenheit.
    III. Wind chill and temperature are inversely related to one another.

    (A) I only
    (B) II only
    (C) I and II only
    (D) II and III only

11. Consider the function below.

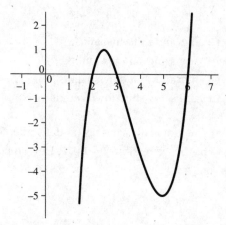

If the function is written as $f(x) = (x - 2) \times A \times (x - 3)$, what is the value of A?

(A) x

(B) $(x + 2)$

(C) $(x - 6)$

(D) $(x - 14)$

12. The function $y = 6x^3 + 19x^2 - 24x + c$ has zeros at the values of $-\frac{1}{2}, \frac{4}{3}$, and -4. What is the value of the constant c in this function?

(A) -16

(B) -9

(C) 2

(D) 14

13. The graph of the function below is given by which equation?

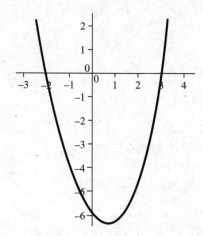

(A) $f(x) = 2x^2 - 2x - 4$

(B) $f(x) = 3x^2 - 6x - 7$

(C) $f(x) = x^2 + x - 3$

(D) $f(x) = x^2 - x - 6$

14. What will happen to the graph of $y = x^2$ in the xy-plane if it is changed to

$$y = (x + 8)^2 + 4?$$

(A) It will shift to the left 8 units and shift up 4 units.

(B) It will shift to the right 8 units and shift up 4 units.

(C) It will shift to the left 8 units and shift down 4 units.

(D) It will shift to the right 8 units and shift down 4 units.

15. Calculating the total cost C, including the sales tax (and no other fees), of a good with an untaxed price of P is given by the expression $C = 1.07P$. How could you calculate the cost of only the sales tax on the good?

(A) P

(B) $0.07P$

(C) $0.13P$

(D) $0.17P$

Answer Explanations

1. **(B)** This is easiest to solve if you work your way backward from the answer choices. The only answer that multiplies to give an area of 216 is choice (B):

$$12 \times 18 = 216$$

If you wanted to solve this algebraically, finding the solution would be much more complicated. This question demonstrates that you should be open to plugging in answers when you anticipate a lengthy calculation. Set up two equations, one equation for the sum of the length and width and one equation for the area:

$$L + W = 30$$
$$L \times W = 216$$

Use substitution to solve:

$$L + W = 30$$
$$L = 30 - W$$

Substitute this in for L in the other equation:

$$L \times W = 216$$
$$(30 - W) \times W = 216$$
$$-W^2 + 30W - 216 = 0$$

This looks rather challenging to solve by factoring, so use the quadratic formula:

$$x = \frac{-b \pm \sqrt{b^2 - 4ac}}{2a}$$
$$x = \frac{-30 \pm \sqrt{30^2 - 4(-1)(-216)}}{2(-1)}$$
$$x = \frac{-30 \pm \sqrt{900 - 864}}{-2}$$
$$x = \frac{-30 \pm \sqrt{36}}{-2}$$
$$x = \frac{-30 \pm 6}{-2}$$
$$x = 15 \pm 3$$
$$x = 12, 18$$

If you plug in 12 as the width, you get 18 as the length. If you plug in 18 as the width, you get 12 as the length:

$$L \times W = 216$$
$$L \times 12 = 216$$
$$L = 18$$

$$L \times W = 216$$
$$L \times 18 = 216$$
$$L = 12$$

So the dimensions are 12 feet by 18 feet, regardless of what you call the length and width.

2. **(A)** Simplify the expression:

$$\left(\frac{n^2 - n^3}{n^4}\right)^{-2} = \left(\frac{n^2}{n^2}\left(\frac{1-n}{n^2}\right)\right)^{-2}$$

Cancel the n^2 terms on the outside:

$$\left(\frac{\cancel{n^2}}{\cancel{n^2}}\left(\frac{1-n}{n^2}\right)\right)^{-2} = \left(\frac{1-n}{n^2}\right)^{-2}$$

Flip the fraction so it has a positive exponent:

$$\left(\frac{1-n}{n^2}\right)^{-2} = \left(\frac{n^2}{1-n}\right)^{2}$$

Square both the numerator and the denominator and simplify:

$$\left(\frac{(n^2)^2}{(1-n)^2}\right) = \left(\frac{n^4}{(1-n)(1-n)}\right) = \frac{n^4}{1-2n+n^2}$$

3. **(C)** $\frac{2x+2y}{4} = \frac{x+y}{2}$, which is the arithmetic mean (simple average) of x and y.

4. **(C)** Both the first term and the second term of the expression are squared terms. So the expression can be restated as the difference of squares, the general form of which is $x^2 - y^2 = (x+y)(x-y)$:

$$16a^2 - 9b^2 =$$
$$(4a)^2 - (3b)^2 = (4a + 3b)(4a - 3b)$$

5. **(D)** Solve by simplifying and completing the square:

$$4x^2 + 8x - 4 = 0$$
$$x^2 + 2x - 1 = 0$$
$$x^2 + 2x = 1$$

Then complete the square by adding 1 to both sides:

$$x^2 + 2x + 1 = 2$$

Then factor the left-hand side:

$$(x+1)^2 = 2$$

Then take the square root of both sides, remembering to include both the positive and the negative values on the right:

$$x + 1 = \sqrt{2} \text{ and } x + 1 = -\sqrt{2}$$

Solve for x to find the solutions:

$$x = \sqrt{2} - 1 \text{ and } x = -\sqrt{2} - 1$$

Alternatively, you could solve this using the quadratic equation. Start by dividing by 4 to simplify:

$$4x^2 + 8x - 4 = 0$$
$$x^2 + 2x - 1 = 0$$

$$x = \frac{-b \pm \sqrt{b^2 - 4ac}}{2a}$$

$$x = \frac{-2 \pm \sqrt{2^2 - 4(1)(-1)}}{2(1)}$$

$$x = \frac{-2 \pm \sqrt{8}}{2}$$

$$x = \frac{-2 \pm 2\sqrt{2}}{2}$$

$$x = \frac{-1 \pm \sqrt{2}}{1}$$

$$x = -1 \pm \sqrt{2}$$

This is equivalent to the answers $x = \sqrt{2} - 1$ and $x = -\sqrt{2} - 1$.

6. **(C)** Combine like terms, and then factor out what is common to all of the terms:

$$x^4y^2 + x^3y^5 + xy^6 + 2x^3y^5 =$$
$$x^4y^2 + 3x^3y^5 + xy^6 =$$
$$xy^2(x^3 + 3x^2y^3 + y^4)$$

7. **(B)** This is probably easiest to solve by plugging in the answers. Start with choice (B) or choice (C) as your first attempt since the answers are in order from smallest to largest. (Note that $n^0 = 1$ since anything to the zero power is 1.) If you plug in 1 for x, it works:

$$\frac{x}{2} = \frac{2(n^0)}{2} - \frac{1}{2x}$$

$$\frac{1}{2} = \frac{2(1)}{2} - \frac{1}{2(1)}$$

$$\frac{1}{2} = 1 - \frac{1}{2}$$

You can also solve the problem algebraically, but doing so may take more time:

$$\frac{x}{2} = \frac{2(n^0)}{2} - \frac{1}{2x}$$
$$x = 2(n^0) - \frac{1}{x}$$
$$x = 2 - \frac{1}{x}$$

Multiply by x:

$$x^2 = 2x - 1$$
$$x^2 - 2x + 1 = 0$$
$$(x - 1)(x - 1) = 0$$
$$(x - 1)^2 = 0$$
$$x = 1$$

8. **(D)** Combine the like terms together to find the sum:

$$\begin{array}{r} 3x^3 + \phantom{2x^2 - {}} 5x - 3 \\ + \phantom{3x^3 + {}} 2x^2 - 4x + 6 \\ \hline 3x^3 + 2x^2 + x + 3 \end{array}$$

9. **(B)**

$$(25a^4 + 40a^2b^4 + 16b^8) \div (5a^2 + 4b^4) =$$

$$\frac{25a^4 + 40a^2b^4 + 16b^8}{5a^2 + 4b^4} =$$

$$\frac{(5a^2 + 4b^4)(5a^2 + 4b^4)}{5a^2 + 4b^4} =$$

$$5a^2 + 4b^4 = 4b^4 + 5a^2$$

10. **(A)** Choice I is correct. Since the velocity is raised to a fractional exponent, the impact of a certain amount of wind speed increase is more significant at lower wind speeds than at higher wind speeds. Choice II is not correct. Wind chill still has an impact when the temperature is less than 35.75 degrees Fahrenheit since this number is a constant, not a minimal temperature. Choice III is not correct. As temperature increases, the perceived temperature due to wind chill also increases.

11. **(C)** The function intersects the x-axis at $x = 6$, making 6 a zero of the function. Therefore, A can be expressed as $(x - 6)$.

12. **(A)** Plug in one of the zeros for x and plug in the number 0 for y since a zero intersects the x-axis. Remember that the y-value must be 0 for an x-intercept since that indicates where the function intersects the x-axis. Use this to solve for the constant c. Use -4 as that x-value so that you do not have to calculate with fractions:

$$y = 6x^3 + 19x^2 - 24x + c$$
$$0 = 6(-4)^3 + 19(-4)^2 - 24(-4) + c$$
$$0 = 6(-64) + 19(16) + 96 + c$$
$$0 = -384 + 304 + 96 + c$$
$$0 = 16 + c$$
$$-16 = c$$

13. **(D)** Since the parabola has zeros at 3 and -2, it can be written in this way:

$$f(x) = (x - 3)(x + 2)$$

Use FOIL:

$$f(x) = x^2 - x - 6$$

Alternatively, you can set $x = 0$. Then see which of the choices results in a y-value of -6 since this is the y-intercept of the parabola based on the graph. Only choice (D) works:

$$f(x) = x^2 - x - 6$$
$$f(0) = 0^2 - 0 - 6 = -6$$
$$f(0) = -6$$

14. **(A)** When you add a number to the x-value itself, the function shifts to the left by that number of places. When you add a number to the function as a whole, the function shifts upward by that number of places. Since 8 is added to the x-value itself and 4 is added to the function as a whole, the function shifts to the left 8 units and shifts up 4 units.

15. **(B)** The cost of the sales tax on the good is found by subtracting the untaxed price from the total cost:

$$1.07P - P = 0.07P$$

You can also visualize this by plugging in a sample value for the price of the good. A helpful sample value to use with percentages is 100 since it gives easily understood results. If, for example, you suppose that the price of the good is $100, the cost with the sales tax included is $1.07 \times \$100 = \$107$. So the sales tax on the good is $\$107 - \$100 = \$7$. This is equivalent to $0.07 \times \$100 = \$7$.

Geometry and Trigonometry Practice

1. If Alaina wishes to paint all six faces of a rectangular box that has dimensions in feet of $8 \times 4 \times 6$, how many square feet of paint does she need?

    (A) 124
    (B) 168
    (C) 208
    (D) 256

2. If a circle has a radius of 3 units, what is the length in units of the arc on the circle that measures $\frac{\pi}{2}$ radians?

    (A) π
    (B) $\frac{3}{2}\pi$
    (C) $\frac{5}{2}\pi$
    (D) 7π

3. If x represents the diameter of a circle, what is the area of a 60-degree sector of the circle?

    (A) πx^2
    (B) $\frac{\pi x^2}{24}$
    (C) $\frac{\pi x^2}{6}$
    (D) $\frac{\pi x^2}{36}$

4.

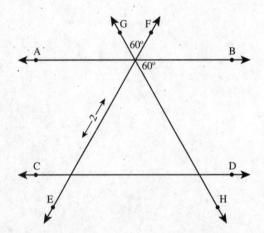

   In the above drawing, lines AB and CD are parallel. Lines EF and GH intersect line AB at the same point and with the angle measures as indicated. What is the perimeter of the triangle formed by lines CD, EF, and GH between lines AB and CD?

    (A) 2
    (B) 4
    (C) 6
    (D) 8

5. A cube with edge length x has all of its edges doubled. Suppose the volume of the original cube is V cubic inches. What is the volume of the new cube in terms of the original cube?

    (A) $2V$

    (B) $4V$

    (C) $8V$

    (D) $16V$

6. The sides of a right triangle are 6, $6\sqrt{3}$, and 12. In a triangle similar to this triangle, what is the measure of the triangle's smallest interior angle?

    (A) $10°$

    (B) $30°$

    (C) $40°$

    (D) $45°$

Answer Explanations

1. **(C)** The box is drawn below:

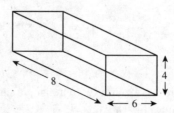

Add up all of the surface areas of the six faces of the box. Since there are 2 of each face dimension, you can set up your equation as follows:

$$2((8 \times 4) + (4 \times 6) + (8 \times 6)) = 208$$

2. **(B)** A measure of $\frac{\pi}{2}$ radians corresponds to $\frac{1}{4}$ of the distance around the circle since 2π radians is the entire distance around the circle. First find the circumference of a circle with radius of 3:

$$2\pi r = 2\pi 3 = 6\pi$$

Then calculate $\frac{1}{4}$ of the circumference:

$$\frac{1}{4} \text{ of } 6\pi \text{ is } \frac{3}{2}\pi$$

3. **(B)** A 60-degree sector of the circle is $\frac{60}{360} = \frac{1}{6}$ of the total circle's area since there are 360 degrees in a circle. The area of a circle is calculated using πr^2. Since the diameter of the circle is x, the radius of the circle is half of x: $\frac{x}{2}$. So the area of this circle equals:

$$\pi r^2 = \pi \left(\frac{x}{2}\right)^2 = \frac{\pi x^2}{4}$$

Multiply the circle area by $\frac{1}{6}$ to find the area of the sector:

$$\frac{1}{6} \times \frac{\pi x^2}{4} = \frac{\pi x^2}{24}$$

4. **(C)** Perimeter is the sum of the side measures of the triangle. The internal angles of the triangle formed are all 60 degrees. Since the angles are all congruent, the sides of the triangle are all congruent as well. Thus, the perimeter of the triangle is $2 + 2 + 2 = 6$ units. You can see this more clearly in the diagram below:

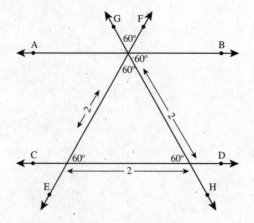

5. **(C)** Each edge of the cube is doubled. So instead of each edge having a length of x, each edge now has a length of $2x$. The volume formula for a cube is $V = x^3$. The original cube has a volume of x^3. The new cube has a volume of $(2x)^3 = 2^3 x^3 = 8x^3$. So the volume of the new cube is 8 times the volume of the original cube, which is $8V$.

6. **(B)** The sides given are a multiple of a special right triangle, the $30°$–$60°$–$90°$ triangle that has sides the length of x, $\sqrt{3}\,x$, and $2x$. In this problem, 6 corresponds to the x, $6\sqrt{3}$ corresponds to the $\sqrt{3}\,x$, and 12 corresponds to the $2x$. In this triangle, $30°$ is the smallest angle.

Troubleshooting

Here are some further pointers for common strategy issues.

"I haven't taken enough math yet."

- Most of the PSAT will be from Algebra 1 and Algebra 2. Don't worry about not having taken precalculus yet—just be comfortable using sine, cosine, and tangent.
- Review the key formulas at the beginning of the chapter. If you memorize these, you will feel much more confident.
- Keep in mind that the test primarily requires critical thinking. If you go into the PSAT Math Test ready to figure out things, you can often overcome a lack of advanced training.

"I take too long."

- Prioritize which problems you do. Don't worry about the last question or two on either PSAT Math module. They will likely be more difficult.
- If a question is taking you more than a couple of minutes to solve, consider flagging it and coming back to it. You are not writing off the problem. You will continue to think about it. If you have time to revisit the problem, it will likely seem quite a bit easier the second time around. Skip very difficult problems here and there. Then go back to them if time is available. Do not initially spend too much time on very difficult problems, because you may not have enough time to finish the test. Because the test is graded on a curve, skipping a problem isn't a big deal. However, not finishing the Math Test because of poor time management could be detrimental to scholarship chances if you leave enough problems incomplete. All problems are worth the same number of points. So it is better to get to the later problems and earn a few more points than just get that one tricky question but not have time for other problems you could be capable of solving. At the very least, be certain that you guess on a very difficult problem because there is no guessing penalty on the test.
- Pace yourself—take about 1.5 minutes per question on average. The earlier questions should take less time than this. The later questions should take more time. Keep yourself moving along.

"I finish too quickly."

- Consider what would be the most effective use of your extra time. For most people, it will be taking more time the first time through the questions. For some, it may be helpful to start with the most challenging questions later in the test so that you will have a couple of chances to try them—both when you start the test and when you finish. Note: Be sure to try this approach first on a practice test before you try it on the actual test. It is not typically an effective strategy; most students end up rushing through easier questions because they become stuck on the more difficult questions.
- Pace yourself—be sure you are taking enough time on each question, on average about 1.5 minutes a question.

"I have math anxiety."

- The confidence that comes with rigorous practice is the best way to overcome your anxiety. If you work through the problem sets throughout this book, you will be ready for the PSAT.
- Realize that some anxiety is welcome—it can help you stay focused and tune out distractions. It can also help push you to work through a challenging problem. Channel your nervous energy into action instead of letting it paralyze your thought process.
- Keep things in perspective. The Math Test represents half of the test; you can still miss several questions and achieve a top score. The PSAT, although vital for National Merit consideration, is primarily preparation for the SAT. You will have plenty of chances to take the SAT and/or ACT, the tests that colleges use for admissions decisions. All the practice you are doing for the PSAT will directly help you prepare for these later tests as well.

TIP

You only have so much energy to devote to thinking on test day. Focus on solving the problems and not on things like overanalyzing the questions, checking your pace too frequently, and excessively reviewing your work.

TIP

Don't forget to try the drills in the next chapter, "Advanced Math Drills," for more challenging practice.

7

Advanced Math Drills

The following 14 drills represent the most challenging types of math questions you will encounter on the PSAT, helping prepare you to earn National Merit recognition. You can practice all of these or focus on your most challenging question types. The drills as a whole are designed to give you comprehensive coverage of the variety of questions you may face on test day. The passages are arranged by topic and type of question:

- Algebra Drill 1
- Algebra Drill 2
- Algebra Drill 3
- Problem-Solving and Data Analysis Drill 1
- Problem-Solving and Data Analysis Drill 2
- Problem-Solving and Data Analysis Drill 3
- Advanced Math Drill 1
- Advanced Math Drill 2
- Advanced Math Drill 3
- Geometry and Trigonometry
- Free-Response Problems Drill 1
- Free-Response Problems Drill 2
- Mixed Drill 1
- Mixed Drill 2

To practice these passages under timed conditions, take about 15 minutes per drill. Answer explanations for each drill appear at the end of the chapter.

Algebra

Algebra Drill 1

1. What is the value of x in the following equation?

$$-\frac{3}{8}x + \frac{5}{16}x - \frac{1}{2}x = \frac{18}{32}$$

   (A) 1
   (B) –1
   (C) 3
   (D) $\frac{117}{8}$

2. What is the value of a in the following equation?

$$\frac{(3a-4)}{5} = \frac{(3a-4)}{8}$$

   (A) $\frac{4}{3}$
   (B) 0
   (C) $\frac{28}{9}$
   (D) $\frac{52}{9}$

3. What is the solution with the least possible y-value that satisfies both of the following inequalities?

$$y \geq 2x + 5$$
$$\text{and}$$
$$4 - y \leq x$$

   (A) $\left(\frac{1}{2}, \frac{5}{2}\right)$

   (B) $\left(\frac{1}{3}, \frac{11}{3}\right)$

   (C) $\left(-\frac{1}{2}, 4\right)$

   (D) $\left(-\frac{1}{3}, \frac{13}{3}\right)$

4. If $|3x - 1| = 4$, what are all of the possible value(s) of x?

   I. -1
   II. $\frac{5}{3}$
   III. 1

   (A) II only
   (B) III only
   (C) I and II only
   (D) All of the above

5. What is the value of x?

$$\frac{3}{2}x - \frac{2}{3} = \frac{x}{6} - \frac{10}{27}$$

   (A) $-\frac{7}{9}$
   (B) $\frac{2}{9}$
   (C) $\frac{17}{54}$
   (D) $\frac{9}{2}$

6. The graph of each equation in the system below is a line in the xy-plane.

$$y = 6x - 2$$
$$-6 = 12x - 2y$$

   What must be true about these two lines?

   (A) The lines are parallel.
   (B) The lines are perpendicular.
   (C) The lines intersect at $\left(\frac{3}{2}, 7\right)$.
   (D) The lines are the same.

7. Towns A and B are 200 miles apart. Caitlin starts driving from Town A to Town B at 3 P.M. at a rate of 30 miles per hour. Hannah starts driving from Town B to Town A at 4 P.M. on the same day at a rate of 40 miles per hour. At what time will they meet (to the nearest minute)?

   (A) 3:42 P.M.
   (B) 5:29 P.M.
   (C) 6:26 P.M.
   (D) 7:32 P.M.

8. A person can ride a roller coaster at an amusement park if he or she is between 36 and 72 inches tall. Which of the following inequalities models all possible values of permitted heights in inches for the ride?

   (A) $|x - 36| < 72$
   (B) $|x - 38| < 34$
   (C) $|x - 30| < 42$
   (D) $|x - 54| < 18$

9. A line in the xy-plane has a slope of $\frac{3}{5}$ and passes through the origin. Which of the following is a point on the line?

   (A) $(15, 10)$
   (B) $(3, 5)$
   (C) $\left(0, \frac{3}{5}\right)$
   (D) $(10, 6)$

10. A salesperson earns a commission (C) on the number of phone plans sold (x) if the value of C is positive. (There is no penalty or cost to the salesperson for a negative value of C; simply no commission is paid.) The amount of commission in dollars is modeled by this equation:

    $$C = 50x + 25(x - 100) - 2,000$$

    What is the least number of phone plans that the salesperson must sell in order to earn a commission?

    (A) 60
    (B) 61
    (C) 75
    (D) 100

Algebra Drill 2

1. If the volume of a pyramid is given by the formula $V = \frac{1}{3}lwh$, where V is the volume, l is the length, w is the width, and h is the height, what is the width of the pyramid in terms of the other variables?

   (A) $\frac{V}{3lh}$
   (B) $\frac{3V}{lw}$
   (C) $\frac{3V}{lh}$
   (D) $\frac{lh}{3V}$

2. What is the negative solution to the following equation, rounded to one decimal place?

   $$18x - \frac{21}{x} = \frac{2x}{3} + 12$$

   (A) 1.5
   (B) −0.8
   (C) −0.6
   (D) −1.5

3. An employee at a company has the following rules for days off from work:

   ▪ Employees are granted 30 flex days paid time off in a year for non-weekend and holiday days.
   ▪ Sick days with a doctor's note count as half a flex day.
   ▪ Personal days count as a full flex day.

   If an employee wants to use at least half of the flex days but less than $\frac{5}{6}$ of them, what inequality would express the total number of sick days, S, and personal days, P, he or she could take in a year?

   (A) $\frac{1}{2} \le \frac{1}{2}S + P < \frac{5}{6}$
   (B) $15 \le \frac{1}{2}S + P < 25$
   (C) $15 \le 2S + P < 25$
   (D) $15 \le S + 2P < 30$

4. If $g(x) = 9x + 2$, what does $g(-4x)$ equal?

   (A) $-36x - 8$
   (B) $-36x + 2$
   (C) $5x + 2$
   (D) $-36x^2 + 2$

5. A carpenter charges a \$40 initial fee for an in-home visit and \$60 for each half hour worked. Which inequality models the total fee, F, for H hours worked where $H > 0$?

   (A) $F(H) = 40 + 30H$
   (B) $F(H) = 40 + 60H$
   (C) $F(H) = 40 + 120H$
   (D) $F(H) = 60 + 40H$

6. What are the values of x and y in the following equations?

   $$0.75x - 0.1y = 1.2$$
   $$2.6x + 3.4y = 15.4$$

   (A) $x = 1, y = -4.5$
   (B) $x = 2, y = 3$
   (C) $x = 3, y = 10.5$
   (D) $x = 4, y = 18$

7. If $\dfrac{m}{n} = -3$, what does $-2\dfrac{n}{m}$ equal?

   (A) -6

   (B) $\dfrac{2}{3}$

   (C) $\dfrac{3}{2}$

   (D) 6

8. If Equation A is defined by $y = \dfrac{2}{3}x - 4$ and if Equation B is defined by $3y = 2x + 3$, what must be done to Equation B so that the system of both Equation A and Equation B will have infinitely many solutions?

   (A) Add 9 to the right side
   (B) Subtract 5 from the right side
   (C) Subtract 7 from the right side
   (D) Subtract 15 from the right side

9. At 1:00 P.M., a blimp and a hot-air balloon are above the cities of Springfield and Washington, respectively. The two cities are 300 miles apart horizontally. The blimp is moving from Springfield to Washington at a horizontal speed of 10 miles per hour; the balloon is moving from Washington to Springfield at a horizontal speed of 200 miles per hour. The blimp starts at an altitude of 5,000 feet and is descending at a rate of 5 feet per minute; the balloon starts at an altitude of 500 feet and is ascending at a rate of 4 feet per minute. At what time will the blimp and balloon be at the same altitude, to the nearest minute?

   (A) 6:20 P.M.
   (B) 7:20 P.M.
   (C) 8:20 P.M.
   (D) 9:20 P.M.

10. Rosa's metabolism is 65 calories per hour when resting and 300 calories per hour when exercising. If Rosa wants to burn more than 2,000 calories per day, what is the range of hours, H, she should spend exercising, calculated to the nearest tenth, assuming that she is either resting or exercising at any time in a given day?

    (A) $24 > H > 1.9$
    (B) $24 > H > 2.4$
    (C) $24 > H > 6.7$
    (D) $24 > H > 22.1$

Algebra Drill 3

1. If $\dfrac{-2x - 4}{5} > 2$, what is the range of x?

   (A) $x > -7$

   (B) $x < -\dfrac{11}{2}$

   (C) $x < -7$
   (D) $x > 7$

2. Susan is given a piggybank for her birthday that can hold a maximum of 500 quarters. The piggybank initially has 120 quarters. Each day after she receives the bank, 4 quarters are added. No coins or other objects are added to the piggybank. Which equation could be used to solve for the number of days (D) after Susan's birthday that it will take to fill the bank?

(A) $500 = 120 + 4D$

(B) $500 = 4D - 120$

(C) $120 = 4D$

(D) $500 = 4 + 120D$

3. In basketball, 1 point is awarded for a free throw, 2 points for a shot within the three-point line, and 3 points for shots outside the three-point line. If the number of points from x two-point shots is at least as great as the number of points from y three-point shots and z free throws, which expression would represent this relationship?

(A) $x \geq y + z$

(B) $x \geq 3y + z$

(C) $2x \geq 3y + z$

(D) $2x \geq y + 3z$

4. What is the value of x in this pair of equations?

$$5 - \frac{2}{3}y = x \text{ and } 4\left(10 - \frac{4}{3}y\right) = 2x + 5$$

(A) -20

(B) $\frac{5}{6}$

(C) $\frac{25}{4}$

(D) $\frac{75}{2}$

5. If $-2|-3| < -3|x + 5|$, what are all possible values of x?

(A) $-7 < x < -3$

(B) $-3 < x$ OR $-7 > x$

(C) $-3 < x$

(D) No solutions

6. Machine 1 can manufacture one box in A hours, and Machine 2 can manufacture an identical box in B hours. When working simultaneously, Machines A and B can produce 1 box in T hours. This relationship is given by the following formula:

$$\frac{1}{A} + \frac{1}{B} = \frac{1}{T}$$

What is the value of B in terms of the other two variables?

(A) $\dfrac{1}{\frac{1}{T} - \frac{1}{A}}$

(B) $\dfrac{1}{\frac{1}{A} - \frac{1}{T}}$

(C) $\frac{1}{T} - \frac{1}{A}$

(D) $\dfrac{AT}{T - A}$

7.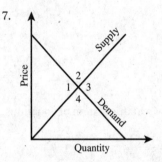

If the manufacturer of the XYZ machine develops new technology that makes creating the machine less expensive, in which zone(s) of the graph would the new supply curve most likely be?

(A) 1 and 2

(B) 2 and 3

(C) 3 and 4

(D) Unchanged

8. Line A has points $(1, -2)$ and $(-1, 0)$. Line B has point $(3, 4)$. What would the y-value of the y-intercept of line B need to be in order for line A and line B to intersect at a 90° angle?

   (A) -7
   (B) -1
   (C) 1
   (D) 4

9. A library fines a patron who fails to return a book on time the replacement cost of the book plus an additional 10 cents each day that the fine is not paid in full. On December 1, Jane borrowed a book with a replacement cost of $30. The book was due to be returned on December 14. Which function models the total amount of dollars (A) that Jane will need to pay x days after December 14?

   (A) $A(x) = 30 + 10x$
   (B) $A(x) = 30 + 0.1x$
   (C) $A(x) = 30 + 1.4x$
   (D) $A(x) = 30 - x$

10. What is the value of a in this system of equations?

   $$a = \frac{2}{3}b + 1 \text{ and } 2 + 3a = -4(2b + 1)$$

   (A) $-\frac{9}{10}$
   (B) $\frac{2}{5}$
   (C) $\frac{11}{15}$
   (D) $\frac{16}{15}$

Problem-Solving and Data Analysis

Problem-Solving and Data Analysis Drill 1

1. In an animal shelter consisting of only dogs and cats, the ratio of dogs to cats is 3 to 1. If there are 360 animals in the shelter, how many dogs must be present?

   (A) 90
   (B) 120
   (C) 270
   (D) 300

2. A reporter finds that on average, a particular politician receives 14 seconds of applause out of every minute of a speech. If the politician were to give a speech for exactly two hours, how many minutes of the speech would be devoted to applause?

   (A) 14
   (B) 28
   (C) 37
   (D) 1,680

3. Whole milk has 3.5% fat content. If you used equal amounts of 1% and 2% milk, how many total gallons of the combined milk would you use to equal the fat content in exactly 1 gallon of whole milk?

   (A) $\frac{1}{200}$
   (B) $\frac{1}{2}$
   (C) $1\frac{1}{6}$
   (D) $2\frac{1}{3}$

4. Katie is interested in running a marathon, which is 26.2 miles long. She just finished a 5-kilometer race, and she wants to see how many 5K races she would have to complete in order to equal a full marathon. Given that there are approximately 0.62 miles in 1 kilometer, how many complete 5K races would Katie have to finish to go at least the distance of a marathon?

(A) 6
(B) 8
(C) 9
(D) 10

5. At the beginning of the year, 1 U.S. dollar can be exchanged for 0.9 euros, and 1 Canadian dollar can be exchanged for 0.7 U.S. dollars. If someone wants to convert 100 Canadian dollars to euros at these exchange rates and assuming that there are no transaction fees, how many euros would the person have after the conversion?

(A) 63
(B) 78
(C) 129
(D) 158

6. **Spread of a Computer Virus**

Day	Number of Computers Infected
1	101
2	110
3	200
4	1,100
5	10,100

The table above gives the number of computers infected with a virus. Which of the following functions models the number of computers infected, $C(d)$, after d days?

(A) $C(d) = 10^{2d} + 10(d - 1) + 1$
(B) $C(d) = 100 + 10^d$
(C) $C(d) = 100 + 10(d - 1) + 1$
(D) $C(d) = 100 + 10^{(d - 1)}$

7. Light travels at approximately 3.00×10^8 meters per second. When the planet Jupiter is at its closest point to Earth, it is 588 million kilometers away. When Earth and Jupiter are this close, approximately how many minutes does light reflected off of Jupiter take to reach Earth?

(A) 3 minutes
(B) 33 minutes
(C) 58 minutes
(D) 18 minutes

8.

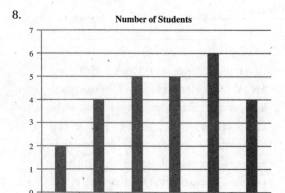

A group of 26 teenagers was asked about their daily smartphone usage. What was the median range of hours that this group used smartphones each day?

(A) Between 1 and 2
(B) Between 2 and 3
(C) Between 3 and 4
(D) Between 4 and 5

Questions 9–10 are about the following table.

	Finished Summer Reading	Did Not Complete Summer Reading	
Mrs. Smith's Class	21	8	29
Mr. Walker's Class	14	17	31
	35	25	

9. Given that the average of Mrs. Smith's and Mr. Walker's classes together represents the average enrollment in each English class at the school and that there are a total of 14 English classes, how many total students are enrolled in English classes at the school, assuming that students are enrolled in exactly one English class?

   (A) 280
   (B) 420
   (C) 560
   (D) 840

10. The high school principal wants to evaluate the effectiveness of the teachers in getting their students to complete the summer reading assignments. The principal assigns 5 points to each student who completes the assignment and gives 0 points to each student who fails to complete the assignment. What is the difference between the mean and the median of the point values given to students in Mr. Walker's class?

   (A) 1.38
   (B) 1.60
   (C) 2.26
   (D) 2.74

Problem-Solving and Data Analysis
Drill 2

1. A student writes a double-spaced typed paper using Times New Roman 12-point font. He finds that each page contains an average of 240 words. If the student changes to Comic Sans 12-point font, each page contains an average of only 170 words. If the student is required to write a 10-page double-spaced report, how many fewer words would he be required to write if the teacher accepts Comic Sans 12-point font instead of Times New Roman 12-point font?

   (A) 70
   (B) 170
   (C) 700
   (D) 1,700

2. On a map of a rectangular fenced-in area, the drawing of the enclosed area has a surface area of 20 square inches. If one side of the fenced-in area drawing is 4 inches long and the key of the map indicates that for every 1 inch drawn on the map there are 6 feet in actual distance, what is the perimeter of the actual fence, assuming there are no gaps or gates?

   (A) 18 ft
   (B) 108 ft
   (C) 120 ft
   (D) 720 ft

3. John's performance on his first test was only 60%. His performance increased by 20% on the next test, and it increased an additional 25% on the third test. What did John earn on the third test, to the nearest whole percent?

   (A) 72%
   (B) 75%
   (C) 90%
   (D) 105%

4. Linda's 15-gallon car tank has only 2 gallons left when she pulls into a gas station. She wants to purchase only the gas she will need to drive 240 miles and still have 1 gallon remaining. Her car gets 28 miles to the gallon. How many gallons should Linda purchase, to the nearest tenth of a gallon?

(A) 6.6 gallons
(B) 7.6 gallons
(C) 8.6 gallons
(D) 9.6 gallons

Questions 5–6 use the following graph.

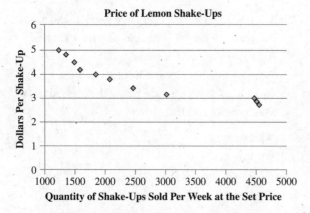

Price of Lemon Shake-Ups

5. If you were to graph dollars per shake-up along the x-axis and quantity of shake-ups sold per week at the set price on the y-axis, which of the following would be a property of the function between the values of 3 and 5 dollars?

(A) It would be a decreasing exponential function.
(B) It would be an increasing exponential function.
(C) It would be a decreasing linear function.
(D) It would be an increasing linear function.

6. At which of the following prices of a lemon shake-up would the total revenue be maximized?

(A) $2.50
(B) $3.00
(C) $3.50
(D) $5.00

Questions 7–8 use the following graph and information.

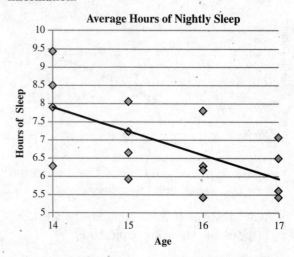

Average Hours of Nightly Sleep

A scientist surveys 16 randomly selected teenage students, recording their ages and their average number of hours of nightly sleep.

7. If x represents the age and y represents the average hours of sleep, which of the following gives the equation of the best-fit line for the survey results?

(A) $y = -0.6x + 7.8$
(B) $y = 0.8x + 7.8$
(C) $y = -0.6x + 16.2$
(D) $y = -1.9x + 16.2$

8. Which of the following would most likely cause the greatest obstacle to the accuracy of the sleep survey results?

(A) If the student survey responses are self-reported
(B) Whether the survey was conducted during the school year or during summer break
(C) If not all of the 16 teenagers respond
(D) If the scientist misreads the number of hours of one responder and records one more hour of sleep on average than what was reported

Questions 9–10 use the following graph.

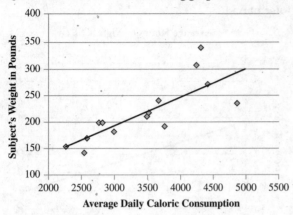

Average Daily Caloric Consumption

9. What choice most closely approximates the slope of the best-fit line of the graph above?

(A) $-\dfrac{1}{10}$

(B) $\dfrac{3}{50}$

(C) $\dfrac{1}{5}$

(D) $\dfrac{50}{3}$

10. What is the most logical explanation as to why the x- and y-axes begin as they do, as opposed to at zero values?

(A) The researcher is not interested in the relationship between weight and caloric intake for a subject less than 100 pounds who eats under 2,000 calories per day.

(B) No person weighs less than 100 pounds.

(C) No person eats under 2,000 calories in a day.

(D) A person cannot weigh zero pounds, and a person cannot consistently eat zero calories each day.

Problem-Solving and Data Analysis Drill 3

1. For every 8 units of x, there are consistently 12 units of y. If the relationship between x and y is given as an equation of the form $y = kx$, where k is a constant, what is the value of k?

(A) $\dfrac{1}{4}$

(B) $\dfrac{2}{3}$

(C) $\dfrac{3}{2}$

(D) 4

2. In a science class, for every two people who are failing, there are three people who have C's and D's. For every one person who has C's and D's, there are two people who have A's and B's. What is the ratio of those who are failing the class to those who have A's and B's?

(A) 1 to 1

(B) 1 to 3

(C) 2 to 3

(D) 1 to 6

3. A restaurant charges a $5 standard delivery fee plus a 15% tip on the amount of the bill before the delivery fee. Which of these expressions would model the total cost to have x dollars worth of food delivered?

(A) $0.15x + 5$

(B) $1.15x + 5$

(C) $5x + 15$

(D) $15x + 5$

Questions 4–5 use the following graph.

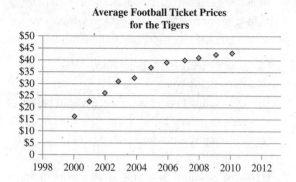

4. Which of the following best describes the general relationship between years and average football ticket price?

   (A) As the years go by, the average football ticket price increases.
   (B) As the years go by, the average football ticket price decreases.
   (C) As the years go by, the average football ticket price stays the same.
   (D) There is no general relationship between years and average football ticket price.

5. Assuming that the trend represented in the graph continues over the next decade (which is not portrayed in the graph), the average price of a football ticket in the year 2014 would most likely be:

   (A) $41
   (B) $47
   (C) $56
   (D) $62

6.

Year	Exchange Rate of Currency X to Currency Y
2000	2.30
2001	15.35
2002	55.42
2003	121.56
2004	237.83

Which of these statements accurately represents the data in the table above?

   (A) As time goes by, Currency X is becoming relatively more valuable than Currency Y.
   (B) As time goes by, Currency Y is becoming relatively more valuable than Currency X.
   (C) As time goes by, Currency X is approaching the same value as Currency Y.
   (D) No relationship can be determined between Currency X and Currency Y.

7.

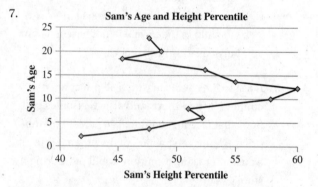

Which of the following is a logical conclusion about the data about Sam's age and height percentile?

   I. Sam's height grew exponentially quickly between ages 12 and 18.
   II. Sam's height relative to that of other men was lower when he was less than 5 years old than when he was between 10 and 15 years old.
   III. Sam continued to experience changes in his height between the ages of 18 and 22.

   (A) I only
   (B) II only
   (C) II and III only
   (D) I, II, and III

8. An amusement park researcher compiles data about the average height of ten-year-old children in a certain town to determine whether this age group will meet the minimum height requirements for a new attraction. The researcher selects 100 ten-year-old children at random from the town and finds that the average height has a 95% confidence interval between 42 and 48 inches. Which of the following conclusions could the researcher most reasonably make?

(A) There is a 5% chance that the average ten-year-old child in the town will have a height between 42 and 48 inches.

(B) It is very likely that the average ten-year-old child in the town will be less than 42 inches tall.

(C) It is very likely that the average ten-year-old child in the town will have a height between 42 and 48 inches.

(D) It is very likely that the average ten-year-old child in the town will not have a height between 42 and 48 inches.

9. If a store has a sale in which all prices are discounted by two-thirds and also distributes coupons that take an additional 20 percent off the price, what is the fraction of the original price that a customer using a coupon would pay during the store's sale?

(A) $\frac{1}{15}$

(B) $\frac{2}{15}$

(C) $\frac{4}{15}$

(D) $\frac{8}{15}$

10. A pollster wishes to project the winner for an upcoming election in her small city. Which of the following approaches to selecting a sample size would give the most accurate polling results?

(A) Interviewing randomly selected shoppers at the grocery store

(B) Contacting residents who live within half a mile of polling locations

(C) Contacting a random selection of registered voters

(D) Inviting voters to submit results to an online survey

Advanced Math

Advanced Math Drill 1

1. A cubic function would be most appropriate when modeling which of the following mathematical relationships?

(A) A sphere's volume and its radius

(B) A circle's circumference and its diameter

(C) A triangle's area and its height

(D) A cube's edge length and its total surface area

2. $\dfrac{a^3 - b^3 + 2a^2b - 2ab^2 + ab^2 - ba^2}{a^2 - b^2}$ equals which of the following, given that $a \neq \pm b$?

(A) $a + b$

(B) $a - b$

(C) $a^2b - ab^2$

(D) $a^2 + b^2$

3. If $-5m^5 + 3m^3 = 2m^7$, what is the sum of all possible values of m^2?

(A) -2.5

(B) 0

(C) 0.5

(D) 2.5

4. Solve for x: $\frac{1}{2}x^2 + \frac{1}{4}x - \frac{1}{8} = 0$

   (A) $\frac{1}{2}(-1 \pm \sqrt{3})$

   (B) $\frac{1}{2}(-1 \pm \sqrt{5})$

   (C) $\frac{1}{4}(-1 \pm \sqrt{3})$

   (D) $\frac{1}{4}(-1 \pm \sqrt{5})$

5. What is/are the solution(s) to the following equation?

$$a + 4 = \sqrt{a^2 - 2}$$

   (A) $-\frac{9}{4}$

   (B) $\frac{9}{4}$

   (C) $\frac{-7}{4}$ and $\frac{9}{4}$

   (D) No solutions

6. How many distinct zeros does the function $f(x) = (x - 3)(x + 7)(x - 3)$ have?

   (A) 0

   (B) 1

   (C) 2

   (D) 3

7. Consider the function $f(x) = x^2 + 2$. What operation could be performed on the right-hand side of the equation to expand the range to include negative values?

   (A) Add 5

   (B) Add -2

   (C) Subtract 3

   (D) Subtract 1

8. What is the vertex of the parabola $(y - 4)^2 = 17(x + 2)$?

   (A) $(-2, 4)$

   (B) $(2, -4)$

   (C) $(-4, 2)$

   (D) $(4, -2)$

9. The root mean squared speed of a molecule, v_{rms}, is calculated using the formula $v_{rms} = \sqrt{\frac{3RT}{M}}$, where R is a gas constant, T is the temperature, and M is the molecular mass. The molecular mass of substance A is most likely to be less than the molecular mass of substance B if the temperature and v_{rms} of substance A compare in which ways to those of substance B?

   (A) Greater v_{rms} and lower temperature

   (B) Lower v_{rms} and greater temperature

   (C) Lower v_{rms} and equal temperature

   (D) Cannot be determined

10. Two different stock portfolios, A and B, have had no new deposits or withdrawals over a ten-year period and had the same initial amount in the account. If stock portfolio A has grown at an annual rate of $x\%$, if stock portfolio B has grown at an annual rate of $y\%$, and if $x > y$, what would represent the ratio of the value of portfolio A over that of portfolio B at the end of the ten-year period?

   (A) $\left(\dfrac{1 + \frac{x}{100}}{1 + \frac{y}{100}}\right)^{10}$

   (B) $\left(\frac{x}{y}\right)^{10}$

   (C) $10\left(\frac{x}{y}\right)$

   (D) $\left(\dfrac{1 - \frac{x}{100}}{1 - \frac{y}{100}}\right)^{10}$

Advanced Math Drill 2

1. A car and a truck are initially 180 miles apart and are driving toward each other on a straight road when an observer measures their respective speeds. The car is driving at a constant speed of x miles per hour, and the truck is going twice this speed. If the car and the truck meet each other after three hours of driving, what is the speed of the truck?

   (A) 20 mph
   (B) 30 mph
   (C) 40 mph
   (D) 60 mph

2. The formula for the area of a trapezoid is $\dfrac{B_1 + B_2}{2} \times H$, where B_1 and B_2 are the bases of the trapezoid and H is its height. If the mean of the bases of the trapezoid is twice the height and if the area of the trapezoid is 72 square inches, what is the trapezoid's height in inches?

   (A) 6
   (B) $6\sqrt{2}$
   (C) 24
   (D) 36

3. $2m^{-2} - 4m^{-3}$ is equivalent to which of the following?

   (A) $\dfrac{2m - 1}{4m^3}$
   (B) $\dfrac{-2}{m^5}$
   (C) $\dfrac{2m - 4}{m^3}$
   (D) $-2m^2 + 4m^3$

4. $(2y^4 + 3x^6) + (5x^6 + 3y^4)$ is equivalent to which of the following?

   (A) $5y^4 + 8x^6$
   (B) $7y^4 + 6x^6$
   (C) $13y^4x^6$
   (D) $5y^8 + 8x^{12}$

5. Which of the following is equivalent to the expression $\dfrac{2x^2 - 12x + 18}{3(x - 3)^3}$?

   (A) $\dfrac{x^2 + 9}{x - 3}$
   (B) $\dfrac{2(x + 3)}{3(x - 3)^2}$
   (C) $\dfrac{2(x - 6)}{(x - 3)}$
   (D) $\dfrac{2}{3(x - 3)}$

6. What are the solutions to $21x^2 = 15x + 18$?

   (A) $\dfrac{5 \pm \sqrt{193}}{14}$
   (B) $\dfrac{15 \pm \sqrt{1527}}{14}$
   (C) $\dfrac{5 \pm \sqrt{67}}{14}$
   (D) No real solutions

7. The supply for a given item at a varying price p (in dollars) is given by the equation $s(p) = 3p + 6p^2$. The demand for the same item at a varying price p is given by the equation $d(p) = 156 - 12p$. At what price are the supply and the demand for the item equivalent?

   (A) $3.50
   (B) $4
   (C) $6.50
   (D) $12

8. If x and y are variables and if c is a nonzero constant, which of the following choices would not necessarily have a y-intercept when graphed?

   I. $x = c$
  II. $y = -c$
 III. $y = cx$

  (A) I only
  (B) I and II only
  (C) II and III only
  (D) None of the above

9.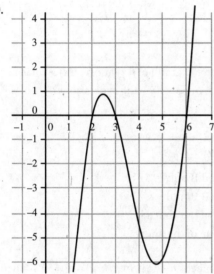

Which of the following equations represents the function graphed above?

  (A) $x^3 + 11x^2 + 36x + 36$
  (B) $x^3 - 11x^2 + 36x - 36$
  (C) $x^3 + x^2 - 24x + 36$
  (D) $x^2 - 5x + 6$

10. The formula for annual compounded interest is $A = P\left(1 + \frac{r}{n}\right)^{nt}$, where P is the initial amount invested, A is the future value of the initial amount, r is the annual interest rate expressed as a decimal, n is the number of times the investment is compounded each year, and t is the number of years the amount is invested. If an initial investment, P, is compounded once every 12 months, which expression is equivalent to the future value of the investment if its interest rate is 5% and if the money is invested for exactly 1 year?

  (A) $0.05P$
  (B) $0.5P$
  (C) $1.05P$
  (D) $1.50P$

Advanced Math Drill 3

1. A square piece of paper is folded in half n times. If L is the length of an edge, what is the area of the piece of paper after it is folded in half n times?

  (A) $\dfrac{L^2}{2^{n-1}}$

  (B) $\dfrac{L^2}{2^n}$

  (C) $\dfrac{L^2}{n}$

  (D) $\dfrac{L^2}{2n}$

2. $\left(81^{-\frac{1}{4}}\right)\left(64^{\frac{1}{3}}\right)$ equals

  (A) -12

  (B) $-\dfrac{4}{3}$

  (C) $\dfrac{1}{12}$

  (D) $\dfrac{4}{3}$

3. Which of the following is equivalent to
$\dfrac{3x^3 + 2x^2 - 5x + 6}{x + 2}$ for x not equal to -2?

   (A) $3x^2 - 4x + 3$
   (B) $3x^2 + 8x + 11$
   (C) $x^2 - 3x + 3$
   (D) $3x^2 + 4x + 12$

4. What relationship must exist between the constants a, b, and c for the equation $ax^2 + bx + c = 0$ to have only real solutions?

   (A) $b^2 \le 4ac$
   (B) $b^2 \ge 4ac$
   (C) $2a > -b$
   (D) Cannot be determined

5. $(3x^3 - 2x^2 + 5x + 7) - (x^4 + x(x + 2)) = ?$

   (A) $2x^3 - x^2 + 7x + 9$
   (B) $-x^4 + 3x^3 - x^2 + 7x + 7$
   (C) $2x^4 - 3x^2 + 5x + 5$
   (D) $-x^4 + 3x^3 - 3x^2 + 3x + 7$

6. How many solutions does the following equation have?

   $$a - \sqrt{a} = 6$$

   (A) 0
   (B) 1
   (C) 2
   (D) 4

7. Out of all possible solutions (x, y) to the pair of equations below, what is the greatest possible product xy that can be obtained?

   $$x(y + 2) - 3x - 4(y + 2) = -12$$
   and
   $$3x - 6 = 3y$$

   (A) 3
   (B) 4
   (C) 6
   (D) 8

8.

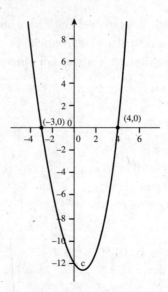

Based on the graph of $f(x)$ above, $f(x)$ is divisible by which of the following expressions?

   I. $x - 4$
   II. $x + 1$
   III. $x + 3$

   (A) I and II only
   (B) I and III only
   (C) All of the above
   (D) None of the above

9. What happens to the vertex (h, k) of $y = x^2 + 3$ if the 3 is replaced by a 6 and if x is changed to $(x - 5)$?

   (A) h decreases by 5, k increases by 6
   (B) h increases by 5, k increases by 3
   (C) h increases by 5, k increases by 6
   (D) h remains the same, k increases by 31

10. If $f(x) = g(x) + 4$ and if $g(x) = x - \dfrac{5}{x}$, what is the value of $f(10)$?

   (A) 9.5
   (B) 10
   (C) 13.5
   (D) 14

Geometry and Trigonometry Drill

1. A right circular cylinder has a volume of $30x$ cubic feet, and a cube has a volume of $21x$ cubic feet. What is the sum of the volumes of a cone with the same height and radius as the cylinder and of a pyramid with the same length, width, and height of the cube?

    (A) $7x$ cubic feet
    (B) $10x$ cubic feet
    (C) $17x$ cubic feet
    (D) $51x$ cubic feet

2. Andrew rides his bike 20 miles directly north and then 15 miles directly to the east. How many miles would he travel if he could fly directly from his starting point to his ending point?

    (A) 25
    (B) 31
    (C) 35
    (D) 625

3. In a right triangle with legs of length a and b, what is the value of the hypotenuse of the triangle?

    (A) $\sqrt{a+b}$
    (B) $\sqrt{a^2 - b^2}$
    (C) $\sqrt{a^2 + b^2}$
    (D) $a^2 + b^2$

4. A rectangle has side lengths of 6 inches and 8 inches. What is the length of the diagonal of the rectangle?

    (A) 9 inches
    (B) 10 inches
    (C) 12 inches
    (D) 13 inches

5. What would be the measure, in radians, of an arc on a circle if the measure of the arc in degrees was 270?

    (A) $\dfrac{2\pi}{3}$
    (B) $\dfrac{3\pi}{2}$
    (C) 270π
    (D) $\dfrac{48,600}{\pi}$

6.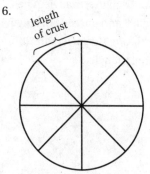

    A circular pizza has a radius of 8 inches. If the pizza is cut into 8 equal sectors as shown in the drawing above, what is the length of the crust on the edge of each piece, rounded to two decimal places?

    (A) 0.13 inches
    (B) 0.79 inches
    (C) 3.74 inches
    (D) 6.28 inches

7.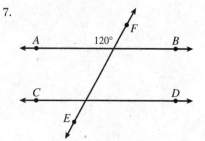

    In the above drawing, lines AB and CD are parallel, and line EF is a transversal. How many angles made from the given lines measure 60 degrees?

    (A) 1
    (B) 2
    (C) 4
    (D) 6

8. A four-sided figure has three interior angles of the same measure and the other interior angle measuring 120 degrees. What is the measure of the smallest interior angle in the figure?

   (A) 40 degrees
   (B) 50 degrees
   (C) 65 degrees
   (D) 80 degrees

9. In two similar isosceles triangles, triangle A has two sides each of length 5 and one side of length 7. Triangle B has exactly one side of length 28. What is the perimeter of triangle B?

   (A) 17
   (B) 20
   (C) 38
   (D) 68

10. Triangle XYZ has a right angle for angle Y and has side lengths of 24 for XY and 26 for XZ. For a triangle that is similar to XYZ, what would be the value of the tangent of its smallest angle?

   (A) $\frac{5}{12}$
   (B) $\frac{5}{13}$
   (C) $\frac{12}{13}$
   (D) $\frac{12}{5}$

Free-Response Problems

Free-Response Problems Drill 1

1. A circle has the equation $x^2 + y^2 = 36$. What is the shortest distance in units from the origin to a point on the circle?

2. Jamie can run $\frac{3}{2}k$ miles in the time that Matt takes to run k miles. If Jamie and Matt run for the same amount of time and their combined mileage is 10 miles, how many miles did Jamie run?

3. What is the product of all solutions to $(x + 2)^2 = (2x - 3)^2$?

4. If $a^4 - 2a^3 + 2a^2 + ma + 2$ has $(a + 1)$ as a factor, what is the value of the constant m?

5. What will be the new slope of the line $y = 2x + 3$ after it is translated 3 units to the right and 2 units down?

Free-Response Problems Drill 2

1. At a particular store, customers can purchase children's outfits for $20 and adults' outfits for $45. If a family purchased 22 outfits for a total of $765, how many children's outfits did the family purchase?

2.

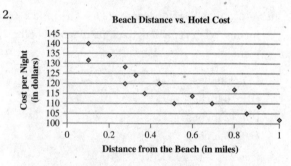

Beach Distance vs. Hotel Cost

The scatter plot above shows the price of a room per night at 15 different hotels versus the distance the hotels are from the beach. If Hotel M is the hotel at the median distance to the beach, how many hotel rooms must be booked for the hotel to make $2,280 in one night?

3. One face of a triangular building is portrayed in a photograph in which 1 inch in the photograph corresponds to 10 feet in the actual building. If the face of the actual building has an area of 960 square feet and a base of 48 feet, what is the building's height (in inches) in the photograph?

Questions 4–5 are about the following table.

| Gender | Major at ABC University | | | Total |
	Humanities	Math/ Science	Engineering	
Male	450	125	140	715
Female	520	100	155	775
Total	970	225	295	1490

4. What is the total percentage of STEM majors (math, science, engineering) out of all the students at ABC University, rounded to the nearest percent? (Ignore the percent symbol when entering your answer. For example, if your answer is 10%, enter 10 as your answer.)

5. What is the probability that a randomly selected student at ABC University will be both a male and a humanities major (calculated to the nearest hundredth)?

Mixed Drills

Mixed Drill 1

1. Solve for x: $\dfrac{12\left(\dfrac{5x - 2x}{2}\right)}{6} = 18$

   (A) 24

   (B) $\dfrac{9}{4}$

   (C) $\dfrac{4}{3}$

   (D) 6

2. A rock is made up by volume of 32% coal, which has a specific gravity (expressed in grams per cubic centimeter) of 1.20. The rock contains 29% granite with a specific gravity of 2.60. The rock also contains 39% of an unknown mineral. If the specific gravity of the entire rock is 1.4, the unknown material has what approximate specific gravity?

   (A) 0.43

   (B) 0.54

   (C) 0.67

   (D) 0.81

3. A train is traveling for 5 hours at a constant rate of x miles per hour and then travels an additional $\frac{x}{10}$ hours at a speed of $\frac{x}{2}$ miles per hour. If the train travels a total of 300 miles during these two segments, which equation could be used to solve for x?

   (A) $x^2 + 100x - 6{,}000 = 0$

   (B) $x^2 + 100x - 300 = 0$

   (C) $x^2 + 5x - 300 = 0$

   (D) $3x^2 + 150x - 6{,}000 = 0$

4. $(6a^3)^3 - (2b)^4 + c^{-2} = ?$

   (A) $6a^9 - 2b^4 + \dfrac{1}{c^2}$

   (B) $18a^9 - 8b^4 + \dfrac{1}{c^2}$

   (C) $21a^6 - 16b^4 + \dfrac{1}{c^2}$

   (D) $216a^9 - 16b^4 + \dfrac{1}{c^2}$

Questions 5–7 use the following graph.

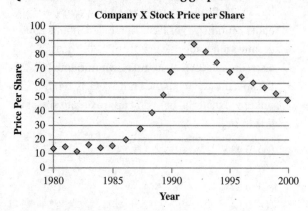

5. The relationship between year and stock price is most exponential during what range of years?

   (A) 1980–1983
   (B) 1984–1991
   (C) 1992–1996
   (D) 1997–2000

6. Between which two-year period does the Company X stock price undergo the greatest percentage increase?

   (A) Between 1983 and 1984
   (B) Between 1986 and 1987
   (C) Between 1988 and 1989
   (D) Between 1989 and 1990

7. A stockbroker sold $1,000 in shares of Company X stock. Approximately how many more shares would she have sold if the stock price is taken at the minimal value in the graph versus at the maximum value in the graph?

   (A) 8
   (B) 20
   (C) 40
   (D) 80

8. If $f(a) = a^2 - 12$, what is $f(b - a)$?

   (A) $a^2 + b^2 - 12$
   (B) $a^3 - b - 12$
   (C) $a^2 - 2ab - b^2 - 12$
   (D) $a^2 - 2ab + b^2 - 12$

9.

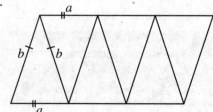

Six identical isosceles triangles are arranged as shown in the figure above. If one side of each triangle has length a and if the other two sides each have length b, what is the outside perimeter of the figure above in terms of a and b?

   (A) $4a + 4b$
   (B) $6a + 2b$
   (C) $6a + 7b$
   (D) $6a + 12b$

10.

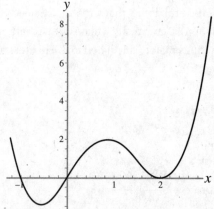

Which of the following could be an equation for the function graphed in the xy-plane above?

   (A) $x(x - 2)(x + 1)$
   (B) $x(x - 2)^2(x + 1)$
   (C) $x(x + 2)^2(x - 1)$
   (D) $x(x + 2)(x - 1)$

Mixed Drill 2

1. What is the value of x in the following equation?

$$15x + \frac{1}{2} = -5\left(x - \frac{5}{2}\right)$$

   (A) $-\frac{3}{20}$

   (B) $-\frac{13}{20}$

   (C) $\frac{3}{5}$

   (D) $\frac{3}{10}$

2. If $i = \sqrt{-1}$, what is the value of $(3 - i)(4 + i)$?

   (A) $11 - i$

   (B) $12 + 7i$

   (C) $13 - i$

   (D) $13 + i$

3. What is the value of the constant c in the equation below?

$$(x - 6)(x - 10) = (x - 8)^2 + c$$

   (A) -4

   (B) 0

   (C) 4

   (D) 16

4.

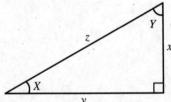

Which trigonometric expression would give the value of angle X?

   (A) $\sin^{-1}\left(\frac{x}{z}\right)$

   (B) $\cos^{-1}\left(\frac{x}{z}\right)$

   (C) $\sin\left(\frac{x}{z}\right)$

   (D) $\sin^{-1}\left(\frac{y}{z}\right)$

5. The ideal gas equation is $PV = nRT$, where P is the pressure, V is the volume, n is the number of moles, R is the gas constant, and T is the temperature. According to the equation, the volume of a gas is inversely related to

   (A) the number of moles.

   (B) gas constant.

   (C) temperature.

   (D) none of the above.

6. In physics, the mirror equation is $\frac{1}{f} = \frac{1}{d_o} + \frac{1}{d_i}$, where f represents the mirror's focal length, d_o is the distance of an object from the mirror, and d_i is the distance of the image from the mirror. Which expression gives d_o in terms of focal length and image distance?

   (A) $\dfrac{1}{\frac{1}{f} + \frac{1}{d_i}}$

   (B) $\frac{1}{f} - \frac{1}{d_i}$

   (C) $\dfrac{1}{\frac{1}{d_i} - \frac{1}{f}}$

   (D) $\dfrac{1}{\frac{1}{f} - \frac{1}{d_i}}$

7. If the following equation is true for every value of x and if a is a constant, what is the value of a?

$$(x + 4)(x^2 + ax + 2) = x^3 + x^2 - 10x + 8$$

   (A) -10

   (B) -3

   (C) -2

   (D) 1

8. $\left(6y^3 + \frac{1}{2}y - \frac{2}{3}\right) - \left(4y^3 - y^2 + \frac{1}{2}y + \frac{1}{6}\right) = ?$

   (A) $2y^3 + y^2 + y + \frac{5}{6}$

   (B) $2y^3 - y^2 + y - \frac{1}{2}$

   (C) $2y^3 - \frac{1}{2}y - \frac{1}{2}$

   (D) $2y^3 + y^2 - \frac{5}{6}$

9. If the slope of line A is $-\frac{x}{y}$, where x and y are positive numbers, what is the slope of a line that is perpendicular to A?

(A) $-\frac{x}{y}$

(B) $-\frac{y}{x}$

(C) $-\frac{x}{y}$

(D) $\frac{y}{x}$

10. The formula for the surface area of a sphere is $A = 4\pi r^2$. If the volume of sphere A is 8 times the volume of sphere B, what is the ratio of the surface area of sphere A to that of sphere B?

(A) 1:2

(B) 2:1

(C) 4:1

(D) 8:1

Answer Explanations

Algebra Drill 1

1. **(B)** To add all of these fractions, you need a common denominator. The least common denominator for the three fractions is 16. However, because the other side has a denominator of 32, let's use 32 for ease. To convert $-\frac{3}{8}x$ to a fraction with a denominator of 32, multiply both the numerator and the denominator by 4. Thus, $-\frac{3}{8}x$ becomes $-\frac{12}{32}x$. Similarly, $\frac{5}{16}x$ becomes $\frac{10}{32}x$ after multiplying both the numerator and denominator by 2. Finally, $-\frac{1}{2}x$ becomes $-\frac{16}{32}x$ after multiplying both the numerator and denominator by 16. Therefore, we're left with:

$$-\frac{12}{32}x + \frac{10}{32}x - \frac{16}{32}x = \frac{18}{32}$$

Combining like terms gives:

$$-\frac{18}{32}x = \frac{18}{32}$$

To isolate x, divide both sides by $-\frac{18}{32}$. Dividing by a fraction is the same as multiplying by its reciprocal, so you're left with:

$$x = \left(\frac{18}{32}\right) \times \left(\frac{-32}{18}\right) = -1$$

So $x = -1$, or choice (B).

2. **(A)** Let's cross multiply here:

$$8(3a - 4) = 5(3a - 4)$$

Next we need to distribute both the 8 and the 5:

$$24a - 32 = 15a - 20$$

Combine both a terms by subtracting $15a$ from both sides:

$$9a - 32 = -20$$

Combine the constants by adding 32 to both sides:

$$9a = 12$$

Finally, solve for a by dividing both sides by 9. So $a = \frac{12}{9} = \frac{4}{3}$, choice (A).

Alternatively, realize that $3a - 4 = 0$ because if we plug in x for $3a - 4$, $\frac{x}{5} = \frac{x}{8}$, meaning $8x = 5x$. Therefore, x must be zero.

3. **(D)** First, get the second inequality in the same form as the first. To do this, subtract 4 from both sides of the second inequality:

$$-y \leq x - 4$$

Then divide by -1, remembering to flip the inequality since you're dividing by a negative:

$$y \geq -x + 4$$

If you graph these two inequalities, you'll see that the point where the lines intersect is the solution that they share that has the lowest y-value.

We can use this knowledge to set both inequalities equal to one another and solve:

$$2x + 5 = -x + 4$$

To solve for x, add an x to both sides to get all of the x-terms on the left. Subtract 5 from both sides to get all constants on the right:

$$3x = -1$$

Dividing by 3 tells us that $x = -\frac{1}{3}$. That's enough to narrow it down to choice (D).

However, if we wanted to know the y-value, we could plug the x-value into the equation for either of the two lines:

$$y = -x + 4 = -\left(-\frac{1}{3}\right) + 4 = \frac{1}{3} + \frac{12}{3} = \frac{13}{3}$$

This also agrees with choice (D).

Alternatively, you can plug in the values of the answers and see which set works for both equations.

4. **(C)** Recall that absolute value can be thought of as the distance of something from the origin. So if the absolute value of something is 4, it is 4 units away from the origin in either direction. This means that it can be either 4 or -4. Therefore, to solve for the values of x, we can set what's inside the absolute value equal to both 4 and -4 and solve. Setting it equal to 4 gives:

$$3x - 1 = 4$$

Adding 1 to both sides results in:

$$3x = 5$$

Dividing both sides by 3 gives us our first solution:

$$x = \frac{5}{3}$$

Next, set the inside of the absolute value sign equal to -4:

$$3x - 1 = -4$$

Adding 1 to both sides gives:

$$3x = -3$$

Dividing by 3 gives us our second solution:

$$x = -1$$

Therefore, there are two solutions, I and II, choice (C).

5. **(B)** To combine the x-terms, you need a common denominator, 6. To combine the constant terms, you also need a common denominator, 27:

$$\frac{9}{6}x - \frac{18}{27} = \frac{1}{6}x - \frac{10}{27}$$

To get all x-terms on the left, subtract $\frac{1}{6}x$ from both sides:

$$\frac{8}{6}x - \frac{18}{27} = -\frac{10}{27}$$

Next, add $\frac{18}{27}$ to both sides to get all constants on the right:

$$\frac{8}{6}x = \frac{8}{27}$$

Finally, divide both sides by $\frac{8}{6}$ (which is the same thing as multiplying both sides by $\frac{6}{8}$) to solve for x:

$$x = \frac{8(6)}{27(8)} = \frac{48}{216} = \frac{2}{9}$$

This matches choice (B).

6. **(A)** Let's get the second equation in $y = mx + b$ form. First, let's get the y-terms on the left by adding $2y$ to both sides:

$$2y - 6 = 12x$$

Next we need to bring the constant to the right side by adding 6 to both sides:

$$2y = 12x + 6$$

Finally, divide both sides by 2:

$$y = 6x + 3$$

Comparing the two lines shows they have the same slope but different y-intercepts. Therefore, they are parallel lines, choice (A).

If their slopes had been negative reciprocals of one another, they would have been perpendicular lines.

If the lines had had different slopes, they would have intersected at exactly one point.

If they had had the same slope and the same y-intercept, then they would have been the same line.

7. **(C)** The women will meet when their positions are equal, so we need to come up with equations to model each of their positions. First, notice that Caitlin leaves a full hour before Hannah. In that first hour, she'll travel 30 miles since she's traveling at 30 mph. Therefore, the women start out 170 miles apart at 4:00 P.M.

Let's say that Caitlin starts at position 0, while Hannah starts at position 170. Caitlin is moving toward 170, so she's moving in the positive direction at 30 mph. Keeping in mind that distance = rate × time, Caitlin's position, s, can then be described as:

$$s = 0 + 30t = 30t$$

On the other hand, Hannah is traveling from position 170 toward position 0, so she's traveling in the negative direction. Therefore, her position can be described as:

$$s = 170 - 40t$$

In order to solve for t, we must set the women's positions equal to one another:

$$30t = 170 - 40t$$

Adding $40t$ to both sides results in:

$$70t = 170$$

Dividing by 70 tells us:

$$t = 2.429$$

Because our rates were in miles per hour, this time is in hours. Therefore, it takes the women two full hours and a fraction of a third hour, so they meet sometime between 6 and 7. This is enough information to narrow down the solution to choice (C).

To find the exact time, we can figure out how many minutes 0.429 hours is by multiplying 0.429 hours by 60 minutes/hour. $0.429(60) = 25.74$ minutes. Therefore, Caitlin and Hannah meet 2 hours and 26 minutes after the time Hannah started traveling, 4:00 P.M. So the women arrive at the same place at 6:26 P.M.

8. **(D)** Recognize that those who are allowed to ride are the ones who aren't too far in either direction from the mean of the permitted heights. If you take the mean height of the constraints, you get:

$$\frac{36 + 72}{2} = 54$$

$72 - 54 = 18$ and $36 - 54 = -18$. Therefore, anyone who is less than 18 units away from 54 is allowed to ride, which is what choice (D) says.

If you didn't recognize this, you could use the process of elimination. You could pick heights that aren't allowed to ride. If you plug in a height that isn't allowed to ride but the inequality is still true, then you'd know that you could eliminate the choice. For instance:

Choice (A): $|35 - 36| = 1$. Since 1 is less than 72, we can rule out this answer choice.

Choice (B): $|35 - 38| = 3$. Since 3 is less than 34, we can rule out this answer choice as well.

Choice (C): $|35 - 30| = 5$. Since 5 is less than 42, we're left with choice (D).

9. **(D)** The answer choices are all positive, so let's come up with some of the positive points on the line. The line has a slope of $\frac{3}{5}$ and passes through the origin (thus has a y-intercept of 0). So the equation for the line is:

$$y = \frac{3}{5}x$$

The line starts at the origin and goes up 3 units and to the right 5 units. So (5, 3) is a point. From there, the line goes up 3 more units and to the right 5 more units, so (10, 6) is also a point, which is choice (D).

Alternatively, you could have used the process of elimination by plugging in the x-coordinates of the answer choices to get the y-coordinate at that value of x.

10. **(B)** In order for the commission to be positive, change the expression to an inequality where the commission will be positive and solve for x:

$$C = 50x + 25(x - 100) - 2,000 \boxed{?}$$
$$0 < 50x + 25(x - 100) - 2,000 \boxed{?}$$
$$0 < 50x + 25x - 2,500 - 2,000 \boxed{?}$$
$$0 < 75x - 4,500 \boxed{?}$$
$$4,500 < 75x \boxed{?}$$
$$60 < x$$

Since the salesperson cannot sell a partial phone plan, the least number of phone plans must be the first integer greater than 60, which is 61.

Algebra Drill 2

1. **(C)** This problem is simply asking you to isolate the w variable. To begin, let's move the constant to the left side of the equation by dividing both sides by $\frac{1}{3}$.

   Dividing by $\frac{1}{3}$ is the same as multiplying by 3. (Remember that dividing by a fraction is the same as multiplying by its reciprocal.) So we're left with:

   $$3V = lwh$$

   Next, let's divide both sides by l:

   $$\frac{3V}{l} = wh$$

   The final step is to divide both sides by h, giving us our final answer:

   $$\frac{3V}{lh} = w$$

   This is choice (C).

2. **(B)** First, we need to get the x out of the denominator by multiplying both sides of the equation by x:

   $$18x^2 - 21 = \frac{2x^2}{3} + 12x$$

   We have two x^2-terms to combine. So we need a common denominator, which is 3:

   $$\frac{54x^2}{3} - 21 = \frac{2x^2}{3} + 12x$$

   This is a quadratic equation since the highest degree of the terms is 2. We bring all terms to the same side so that we can eventually use the quadratic formula:

   $$\frac{52x^2}{3} - 12x - 21 = 0$$

   Recall the quadratic formula for a quadratic equation of the form $ax^2 + bx + c$:

   $$x = \frac{-b \pm \sqrt{b^2 - 4ac}}{2a}$$

   Filling in our values for a, b, and c gives:

   $$x = \frac{12 \pm \sqrt{(-12)^2 - 4\left(\frac{52}{3}\right)(-21)}}{2\left(\frac{52}{3}\right)}$$

   $$x = \frac{12 \pm \sqrt{1600}}{\left(\frac{104}{3}\right)} = \frac{12 \pm 40}{\left(\frac{104}{3}\right)}$$

   So $x = \frac{3}{2}$ or $x = -\frac{21}{26}$.

   We're looking only for the negative value of x, so we only care about the second value. This second value can also be expressed as -0.8077. Rounded to one decimal place, we get choice (B).

3. **(B)** First, figure out what $\frac{1}{2}$ and $\frac{5}{6}$ of 30 are so that you know what range of flex days an employee wants to take:

$$\frac{1}{2}(30) = 15 \text{ and } \frac{5}{6}(30) = 25$$

So the employee wants to take at least 15 days but fewer than 25 days. If we consider F to be the number of flex days taken, this can be expressed as:

$$15 \leq F < 25$$

Now we need an expression for flex days using sick days, S, and personal days, P. A sick day counts as half of a flex day, and a personal day counts as a total flex day. So the number of flex days used will be represented by:

$$\frac{1}{2}S + P = F$$

We can plug in this expression for F in our previous inequality:

$$15 \leq \frac{1}{2}S + P < 25$$

This is choice (B).

4. **(B)** For this question, we simply plug in $-4x$ for every x in the original function:

$$g(-4x) = 9(-4x) + 2 = -36x + 2$$

This answer matches choice (B).

5. **(C)** The carpenter charges a flat fee of \$40, so our equation will have a constant of 40. The carpenter also charges \$60 for each half hour worked. Therefore, the carpenter charges \$120 for each hour, H, worked. Therefore, the carpenter's total fee for working H hours is:

$$F(H) = 40 + 120H$$

This is answer (C).

6. **(B)** Let's use elimination to get rid of the y-terms. Start by multiplying the first equation by 34: $34(0.75x - 0.1y = 1.2)$. This results in:

$$25.5x - 3.4y = 40.8$$

Now we can add this new equation to the second equation to eliminate the y-terms:

$$\begin{array}{r} 25.5x - 3.4y = 40.8 \\ + \quad 2.6x + 3.4y = 15.4 \\ \hline 28.1x = 56.2 \end{array}$$

Dividing by 28.1 tells us that $x = 2$. This is enough to narrow the answer down to choice (B). However, let's solve for y just for practice:

$$2.6(2) + 3.4y = 15.4$$
$$5.2 + 3.4y = 15.4$$

Subtract 5.2 from both sides and then divide by 3.4 to learn that $y = 3$.

7. **(B)** If $\frac{m}{n} = -\frac{3}{1}$, then $\frac{n}{m} = -\frac{1}{3}$. Therefore, $-2\left(\frac{n}{m}\right) = -2\left(-\frac{1}{3}\right) = \frac{2}{3}$, which is choice (B).

8. **(D)** First, you must consider how two lines could have infinitely many solutions. The answer is that they need to have the same slope and the same y-intercept. In other words, they are the same line when graphed.

Let's start by rewriting Equation B in slope-intercept form by dividing both sides by 3:

$$y = \frac{2}{3}x + 1$$

The equations already have the same slope. However, they also need to have the same y-intercept: -4.

Let's subtract 5 from the right side of Equation B so that it matches Equation A:

$$y = \frac{2}{3}x - 4$$

However, we want to know what we need to change about the *original* Equation B. Therefore, we want to get Equation B back in its original form to see what changed. We can do this by multiplying both sides by 3:

$$3\left(y = \frac{2}{3}x - 4\right) \text{ becomes } 3y = 2x - 12.$$

Now we can see that from Equation B to this final equation, we subtracted 15 from the right side to change the y-intercept from $+3$ to -12. This matches choice (D).

9. **(D)** Don't get confused by all of the unnecessary information here! We want to know when the hot-air balloon and the blimp will be at the same altitude. Since altitude deals with only vertical movement, we only care about their vertical movements. The balloon and blimp will be at the same altitude when their vertical positions are equal.

Start with some notation. Let's say that traveling up is in the positive direction. So the balloon is traveling in the positive direction. Let's also say that traveling down is in the negative direction. So the blimp is traveling in the negative direction.

Remember that distance $=$ rate $\times$ time.

The blimp's position can be defined as $s = 5{,}000 - 5t$.

The balloon's position can be described as $s = 500 + 4t$.

The blimp and balloon will be at the same altitude when their positions are equal. So we can set the two expressions equal to one another:

$$5{,}000 - 5t = 500 + 4t$$

Add $5t$ to both sides while subtracting 500 from both sides:

$$4{,}500 = 9t$$

Dividing by 9 tells us that $t = 500$.

Because our rates were in feet/minute, our time is in minutes. Let's divide by 60 to convert this to hours:

$$\frac{500}{60} = 8.333$$

So it takes 8 hours and $\frac{1}{3}$ of the 9th hour. One-third of an hour is 20 minutes since $\frac{1}{3}(60) = 20$. So it takes 8 hours and 20 minutes. Since the balloon and blimp started moving toward one another at 1:00 P.M., they'll meet at 9:20 P.M., which is choice (D).

10. **(A)** Let's first set up an inequality that models this situation. Rosa wants to burn more than 2,000 calories, so we can represent this as $2,000 < \text{calories}$.

Next we need to come up with an expression that represents the number of calories Rosa burns. Rosa is either burning 65 calories per hour by resting or burning 300 calories per hour while exercising. Let's call H the number of hours she spends exercising. Since there are 24 hours in a day and she's not exercising for the rest of the hours outside of H, the hours spent resting will be $24 - H$.

Therefore, the number of calories Rosa burns can be expressed as:

$$2,000 < 300H + 65(24 - H)$$

Now we solve for H. First, distribute the 65:

$$2,000 < 300H + 1560 - 65H$$

Combine like terms:

$$2,000 < 235H + 1560$$

Subtract 1,560 from both sides:

$$440 < 235H$$

Divide both sides by 235:

$$1.87 < H$$

This means that Rosa has to work out for at least 1.9 hours. She can't work out more than 24 hours per day since there are only 24 hours in a day. So the correct answer is (A).

Algebra Drill 3

1. **(C)** Inequalities can be solved just like equations. The only difference is you must remember to flip the inequality sign if you multiply or divide by a negative number.

The first step is to get rid of the denominator by multiplying both sides by 5:

$$-2x - 4 > 10$$

Add 4 to both sides:

$$-2x > 14$$

Divide both sides by -2 to solve for x. Since we are dividing by a negative number, we need to flip the inequality as follows:

$$x < -7$$

The answer is choice **(C)**.

2. **(A)** When the piggybank is full, it will have 500 quarters in it. Let's write an expression for how many quarters the piggybank contains on any given day, D, after Susan's birthday.

Susan starts with 120 quarters on day 0 (her birthday), so 120 is a constant. Every day, 4 quarters are added to the bank. Thus, on day 1, 4 quarters have been added. On day 2, Susan adds an additional 4 quarters to the bank so that $4(2) = 8$ quarters total have been added since her birthday. On day 3, $4(3) = 12$ quarters total have been added, and so on. This part of the expression can be written as $4D$.

Adding in the original 120 quarters she started with gives an expression for the total number of quarters in the bank D days after Susan's birthday:

$$120 + 4D$$

We know the bank is full when it contains 500 quarters. So we can set our expression equal to 500 and solve for D to determine how many days after Susan's birthday the piggybank will be filled. Thus choice (A), $500 = 120 + 4D$, is correct.

3. **(C)** The number of points from x two-point shots will be $2x$. Similarly, making y three-point shots and z free throws corresponds to $3y$ points and z points, respectively. So the number of points earned from y three-point shots combined with z free throws will be $3y + z$. If the number of points from the two-point shots has to be at least as much as (implying at least as much as if not more than) the combined points from three-pointers and free throws, it follows that:

$$2x \geq 3y + z$$

This is choice (C).

Choice (A) doesn't work because it doesn't take into account the different values of each shot.

Choice (B) doesn't account for each two-point shot giving 2 points.

Choice (D) implies that three-point shots score only 1 point and that free throws score 3 points.

4. **(B)** First, let's distribute the 4 in the second equation:

$$40 - \frac{16}{3}y = 2x + 5$$

Next, notice that if you multiplied the first equation by 8, the y-terms (and in fact the entire left-hand side of both equations) would be the same:

$$8\left(5 - \frac{2}{3}y = x\right) = 40 - \frac{16}{3}y = 8x$$

You could subtract the second equation from the first to cancel the y-terms:

$$40 - \frac{16}{3}y = 8x$$
$$-\left(40 - \frac{16}{3}y = 2x + 5\right)$$
$$\overline{0 = 6x - 5}$$

Add 5 to both sides:

$$5 = 6x$$

Now divide by 6 to solve for x:

$$\frac{5}{6} = x$$

This is choice (B).

5. **(A)** Let's start with the left side of the inequality. The absolute value of -3 is 3, so:

$$-2|-3| = -2(3) = -6$$
$$-6 < -3|x + 5|$$

We want to isolate our absolute value. So let's divide by -3, flipping the inequality since we are dividing by a negative number:

$$2 > |x + 5|$$

Because 2 has to be greater than the absolute value, the expression inside of the absolute value symbol can be anything between $(-2, 2)$. In other words, $x - 5$ needs to be greater than -2 but less than 2. To find the x-values such that $x - 5$ is less than 2, simply take away the absolute value signs and solve for x:

$$2 > x + 5$$

Subtracting 5 from both sides gives:

$$-3 > x$$

Next, we want to find the values of x such that $x - 5$ is greater than -2. In other words, we want to solve for x in the inequality $-2 < x + 5$. Subtracting 5 tells us:

$$-7 < x$$

We have found that $-3 > x$ and that $-7 < x$. In other words, $-7 < x < -3$, which is choice (A).

6. **(A)** First, we'll solve for $\frac{1}{B}$. To do this, subtract $\frac{1}{A}$ from both sides:

$$\frac{1}{B} = \frac{1}{T} - \frac{1}{A}$$

Don't be tempted to pick choice (C)! We've solved for $\frac{1}{B}$, not for B as asked in the question. To solve for B, we must take the reciprocal of what we have:

$$B = \frac{1}{\frac{1}{T} - \frac{1}{A}}$$

This matches answer (A).

7. **(C)** If creating the machine is now less expensive, the manufacturer can afford to make more machines for a given price. Therefore, for each price, the quantity will be higher. Thus, the supply curve should shift to the right, shifting it into zones 3 and 4, which is choice (C).

8. **(C)** Let's first find the slope of line A. The formula for slope is Change in y/Change in x:

$$\frac{0 - (-2)}{-1 - 1} = \frac{2}{-2} = -1$$

If the lines are to intersect at a 90° angle, they must be perpendicular. Any line perpendicular to this one would have a slope of 1, since 1 is the negative reciprocal of -1.

We can now use the one given point of line B and the slope in the point-slope formula in order to get the equation of line B.

The point-slope formula is given by the equation $y - y_1 = m(x - x_1)$:

$$y - 4 = 1(x - 3)$$

Distributing the 1 gives:

$$y - 4 = x - 3$$

To get the line into slope-intercept form, add 4 to both sides:

$$y = x + 1$$

Therefore, line B has a y-intercept of 1, which is answer (C).

Alternatively, once it is known that the slope of the new line is 1, the equation must be $y = x + b$. Plug in the point $(3, 4)$ to the line to solve for b:

$$4 = 3 + b \rightarrow b = 1$$

9. **(B)** The book will have a fixed replacement cost of $30, so $+30$ will be a constant term in the function. For each day that the book goes unreturned past December 14, Jane owes another 10 cents. Thus, on day 1 after the return date, she owes a $30 replacement fee and 10 more cents, for a total of $30.10. On the second day, she owes the $30 replacement fee and 2 days' worth of late fees, $(2)(10) = 20$ cents, for a total of $30.20. By continuing in this manner, on day x, Jane will owe the $30 replacement fee and x days' worth of late fees, which is $(x)(10) = 10x$ cents or $0.1x$ dollars. The total cost is shown by $A(x) = 30 + 0.1x$.

This relationship is best described in choice (B).

Choice (A) is tempting, but you must remember that 10 cents is expressed in dollars as $0.10. Choice (A) instead indicates that Jane pays an additional $10 of fees every day plus the $30 replacement fee.

10. **(B)** Since a is already solved for in the first equation, let's plug the right side of that equation into the second equation wherever there is an a:

$$2 + 3\left(\frac{2}{3}b + 1\right) = -4(2b + 1)$$

Next, distribute the 3 and the -4:

$$2 + 2b + 3 = -8b - 4$$

You can combine the constants on the left side of the equation.

$$2b + 5 = -8b - 4$$

Now add $8b$ to both sides and subtract 5 from both sides:

$$10b = -9$$

Dividing by 10 gives you

$$b = -\frac{9}{10}$$

However, the question asks us for the value of a. So let's plug the b-value into the first equation:

$$a = \frac{2}{3}b + 1 = \frac{2}{3}\left(-\frac{9}{10}\right) + 1 = -\frac{18}{30} + 1 = -\frac{3}{5} + \frac{5}{5} = \frac{2}{5}$$

This is choice (B).

This can be solved in other ways, such as by trying elimination instead of substitution.

Problem-Solving and Data Analysis Drill 1

1. **(C)** Let's use the variable d to represent the number of dogs in the shelter and the variable c to represent the number of cats. If the ratio of dogs to cats is 3:1, then there are 3 times as many dogs as cats:

$$d = 3c$$

If there are 360 animals in the shelter:

$$d + c = 360$$

We want to know the number of dogs present. So let's solve the first equation for c in terms of d and plug this into the second equation. Dividing by 3 tells us:

$$\frac{1}{3}d = c$$

Plugging this into the second equation results in:

$$d + \frac{1}{3}d = 360$$

Combining like terms gives:

$$\frac{4}{3}d = 360$$

We can divide both sides by $\frac{4}{3}$ (in other words, multiply both sides by $\frac{3}{4}$) to learn that $d = 270$, which is answer choice (C).

Alternatively, you can solve this as a ratio problem:

$$\frac{d}{c} = \frac{3}{1}$$

As a fraction of the whole, the number of dogs can be expressed as $d = \frac{3}{(3+1)} = \frac{3}{4}$ of the total. Then take $\frac{3}{4}$ of the total number of animals to find the number of dogs:

$$\frac{3}{4} \times 360 = 270$$

2. **(B)** Let's set up a proportion for this problem. The politician receives 14 seconds of applause for every minute of a speech. We want our units to be the same, so let's call that minute 60 seconds. We can model this part of our proportion as $\frac{14}{60}$.

We want to know how many minutes of applause he'll get for 2 hours of speech. Since we want our answer in minutes, let's call 2 hours 120 minutes. We want applause on top again. Therefore, this side of the proportion can be modeled by $\frac{x}{120}$, where x represents the number of minutes of applause the politician will receive in 120 minutes.

You can then set both sides of the proportion equal to one another:

$$\frac{14}{60} = \frac{x}{120}$$

Next, cross multiply:

$$14(120) = 60x$$

$$1{,}680 = 60x$$

Dividing by 60 gives us $x = 28$, choice (B).

3. **(D)** A gallon of whole milk would have 3.5% of a gallon of fat, or 0.035 gallons. If we mix 1% milk and 2% milk in equal parts, we will essentially have 1.5% milk since the fat content will be the average of the two fat contents.

Therefore, the whole milk has $\frac{0.035}{0.015} = 2.333$ times the amount of fat of the 1% and 2% mixture. You would need 2.333 times the amount of milk of the mixture to have the same quantity of fat as in 1 gallon of whole milk. Because 0.333 can be represented as $\frac{1}{3}$, the answer is choice (D).

Alternatively, take the combined average of the lower-fat milks:

$$\frac{1+2}{2} = 1.5$$

Then using x as the number of gallons needed of the combined milks, you can set up this equation:

$$1.5x = 3.5$$

Then solve for x to get $2\frac{1}{3}$.

4. **(C)** Let's first convert the marathon distance to kilometers:

$$26.2 \text{ miles} \times \frac{1 \text{ kilometer}}{0.62 \text{ miles}} = 42.26 \text{ kilometers}$$

If Katie has to run 42.26 km and if she's doing it 5 km at a time, she would need to run:

$$\frac{42.26}{5} = 8.45 \text{ races}$$

Therefore, she would need to run a minimum of 9 whole races to run the distance of a marathon.

Alternatively, you could have done dimensional analysis for the last step, canceling out units that you don't want and leaving only the units that you do want. Katie wants to go 42.26 km, and she's running 5 km/race. Cancel out kilometers, so that we're left with number of races:

$$42.26 \text{ kilometers} \times \frac{1 \text{ race}}{5 \text{ kilometers}} = 8.45 \text{ races}$$

We again need to round up to 9 so that Katie runs the full marathon distance.

5. **(A)** Let's use dimensional analysis, canceling out the units that we don't want and leaving the units that we do want (euros). In the dimensional analysis, let CAD mean Canadian dollars, let USD mean U.S. dollars, and let EUR mean euros:

$$100 \text{ CAD} \times \frac{0.7 \text{ USD}}{1 \text{ CAD}} \times \frac{0.9 \text{ EUR}}{1 \text{ USD}} = 63 \text{ EUR}$$

The correct answer is choice (A).

6. **(D)** The easiest way to approach a problem like this is to test some points with each equation to see which equation works.

Choice (A):

$$C(1) = 10^{2(1)} + 10(1 - 1) + 1 = 100 + 1 = 101$$

So the equation works for day 1. Let's see if it works with day 2:

$$C(2) = 10^{2(2)} + 10(2 - 1) + 1 = 10{,}000 + 10 + 1 = 10{,}011$$

This doesn't match the number for day 2, so we can rule out choice (A).

Choice (B):

$$C(1) = 100 + 10^1 = 100 + 10 = 110$$

This isn't the right number for day 1, so we can rule out choice (B).

Choice (C):

$$C(1) = 100 + 10(1 - 1) + 1 = 100 + 1 = 101$$

This works, so let's try $C(2)$:

$$C(2) = 100 + 10(2 - 1) + 1 = 100 + 10 + 1 = 111$$

This doesn't work, so we can rule out choice (C).

Choice (D):

$$C(1) = 100 + 10^{1-1} = 100 + 1 = 101$$
$$C(2) = 100 + 10^{2-1} = 100 + 10 = 110$$
$$C(3) = 100 + 10^{3-1} = 100 + 100 = 200$$
$$C(4) = 100 + 10^{4-1} = 100 + 1{,}000 = 1{,}100$$
$$C(5) = 100 + 10^{5-1} = 100 + 10{,}000 = 10{,}100$$

Obviously, choice (D) is the correct answer.

7. **(B)** Let's first convert 588 million kilometers to meters:

$$588{,}000{,}000 \text{ kilometers} \times \frac{1{,}000 \text{ meters}}{\text{kilometer}} = 588{,}000{,}000{,}000 \text{ meters}$$

Because distance = rate × time, it follows that $t = \frac{d}{r}$. Therefore, the t in seconds is given by the following expression:

$$t = \frac{588{,}000{,}000{,}000}{3.00 \times 10^8} = 1{,}960 \text{ seconds}$$

Because there are 60 seconds in every minute,

$$1{,}960 \text{ sec} \times \frac{1 \text{ min}}{60 \text{ sec}} = 32.67 \text{ min}$$

This answer rounds to 33 minutes, which is choice (B).

8. **(C)** Since the total number of responses was 26, the median response will be the mean of the 13th and 14th terms.

Terms 1–2 were 0–1 hours.

Terms 3–6 were 1–2 hours.

Terms 7–11 were 2–3 hours.

Terms 12–16 were 3–4 hours.

Therefore, the 13th and 14th terms were both 3–4 hours, which is choice (C).

9. **(B)** Every student in each class either did or did not complete summer reading. So the total number of students enrolled in Mrs. Smith's class is 29, and the total number enrolled in Mr. Walker's class is 31. The average number of students enrolled in the two classes is:

$$\frac{29 + 31}{2} = 30$$

We can assume that each of the 14 English classes has, on average, 30 people. Therefore, the total number enrolled in English classes would be:

$$14(30) = 420$$

The correct answer is choice (B).

10. **(C)** In Mr. Walker's class, 14 students completed summer reading and earned 5 points, accounting for $14(5) = 70$ points. The remaining 17 students received 0 points. So the total points for the class were 70. There are 31 students in the class, so the mean is:

$$70 \div 31 = 2.26$$

To find the median, list the students' point values from smallest to largest. There are 17 students who earned 0 followed by 14 students who each earned 5. The median term in a 31-term series is the 16th term. (There are 15 terms on the left of the 16th term and 15 terms on the right of the 16th term.) The 16th value is 0, so the median is 0. The difference between the mean and the median, therefore, is:

$$2.26 - 0 = 2.26$$

Choice (C) is correct.

Problem-Solving and Data Analysis Drill 2

1. **(C)** First, figure out the number of words that each report would have. We know the number of words per page. So if we multiply this by the number of pages, the pages unit will cancel from the top and bottom. This will leave us with the number of words. If the student uses Times New Roman, he will write:

$$240(10) = 2,400 \text{ words}$$

However, if he uses Comic Sans, he will write only:

$$170(10) = 1,700 \text{ words}$$

We want to know how many fewer words he will write in the second situation.

$$2,400 - 1,700 = 700 \text{ words}$$

So choice (C) is correct.

2. **(B)** The area of a rectangle is given by the formula $A = lw$, where l is length and w is width. If the length of the drawing is 4 inches, we know from dividing both sides of our area equation by the length that:

$$w = \frac{A}{l} = \frac{20}{4} = 5 \text{ inches}$$

The key tells us that each inch on the map represents 6 feet. We can multiply 4 inches by 6 feet/inch to tell us that the length is 24 feet. Similarly, we can multiply the 5-inch width by 6 feet/inch to tell us that the width is 30 feet.

Alternatively, you could have solved for actual distance by setting up a proportion. For the length, the proportion might look something like:

$$\frac{1''}{6'} = \frac{4''}{x'}$$

Cross multiplying gives you:

$$1x = (4)(6)$$

So $x = 24$.

The question wants to know the perimeter of the fence. Perimeter of a rectangle is given by the formula $P = 2l + 2w$. Plugging our dimensions into the formula tells us:

$$P = 2(24) + 2(30) = 48 + 60 = 108$$

The correct answer is choice (B).

3. **(C)** If John's performance increased by 20%, then he performed at 120% of his original performance. 120% can be expressed in decimal form as 1.2, and we can find 120% of his original score of 60 by multiplying the two:

$$1.2(60) = 72$$

So John got a 72% on his second test. His performance then increased another 25%, so his third test performance was 125%, or 1.25, of test 2. Therefore, John's third score was:

$$1.25(72) = 90\%$$

The answer is choice (C).

Alternatively, you could have found John's second score by finding 20% of 60 and adding that to 60:

$$\text{Test } 2 = 60 + (0.2)(60) = 60 + 12 = 72$$

Then you could have found the third score by finding 25% of 72 and adding that to 72:

$$\text{Test } 3 = 72 + (0.25)(72) = 72 + 18 = 90$$

4. **(B)** If you were told that you had to travel 50 miles and that your car got 10 miles/gallon, you may intuitively see that you need 5 gallons of gas. You get that by dividing 50/10. Following this logic, we can get the number of gallons of gas Linda needs to travel 240 miles by dividing 240 by 28:

$$240 \div 28 = 8.57 \text{ gallons}$$

If this doesn't quite make sense, you could also do dimensional analysis to cancel out the units you don't want. You want to cancel out miles and end up with gallons:

$$240 \text{ miles} \times \frac{1 \text{ gallon}}{28 \text{ miles}} = 8.57 \text{ gallons}$$

Linda also wants to have 1 gallon left, so she'll want to have 9.57 gallons in her tank when she starts out. Linda already has 2 gallons in her tank, so she needs to buy $9.57 - 2 = 7.57$ gallons, or 7.6 rounded to the nearest tenth. This matches choice (B).

5. **(A)** We can see from the negative slope that as the quantity of shake-ups increases, price decreases. Therefore, we know that the function will be decreasing, eliminating choices (B) and (D). We can also see that the slope isn't constant. Therefore, it can't be linear, as in choice (C). The graph starts off fairly steep and then it becomes less steep, consistent with exponential decay, as in choice (A).

6. **(B)** Revenue means money made. The amount of money made at any price will be that price times the number of shake-ups sold. Find the approximate revenue at all of the given prices:

$$\text{Choice (A): } \$2.50(4,700) = \$11,750$$

$$\text{Choice (B): } \$3.00(4,600) = \$13,800$$

$$\text{Choice (C): } \$3.50(2,600) = \$9,100$$

$$\text{Choice (D): } \$5.00(1,300) = \$6,500$$

Therefore, the largest revenue occurs with choice (B).

7. **(C)** An equation of a line is given by $y = mx + b$, where m is the slope and b is the y-intercept. The formula for slope is calculated by finding the rise over the run, which is illustrated by this formula:

$$m = \frac{\Delta y}{\Delta x} = \frac{y_2 - y_1}{x_2 - x_1}$$

Plug in values for the endpoints:

$$m = \frac{5.9 - 7.8}{17 - 14} = \frac{-1.9}{3} = -0.633$$

Thus, the slope is approximately -0.6, so we can rule out choices (B) and (D).

Next, we need to determine the y-intercept b. To do this, we can plug a particular point on the line into the equation and solve for b. For instance, $(14, 7.8)$ appears to be a point on the line. Plugging these values into the equation gives:

$$7.8 = -0.6(14) + b$$

So $7.8 = -8.4 + b$.

Adding 8.4 to both sides gives $16.2 = b$. Therefore, choice (C) must be correct.

With this graph, you cannot find the y-intercept, b, just by looking at the where the line crosses the y-axis. On this graph, the y-axis crosses the x-axis at 14, not at 0. However, the y-intercept is, by definition, the value of y when the value of x equals 0.

8. **(A)** Students may be entirely unaware of how many hours they're sleeping. Alternatively, they may modify their answers for a variety of reasons, possibly to give the answers they suspect the researchers want to hear. This makes self-reporting a fairly inaccurate technique, as in choice (A).

   Choice (B) isn't correct because, although students may get a different number of hours of sleep during the school year versus the summer, the study asks for the average number of hours. This should take into account variations due to time of year.

   Choice (C) isn't correct because the researchers could simply ask more teenagers.

   Choice (D) isn't correct because changing one response by a small margin shouldn't have a large result on the accuracy of the entire study.

9. **(B)** We can rule out choice (A) because the slope is clearly positive. Use the slope formula:

$$m = \frac{\Delta y}{\Delta x} = \frac{y_2 - y_1}{x_2 - x_1}$$

   Plug in the values for the approximate endpoints of the line of best fit to get:

$$m = \frac{300 - 150}{5,000 - 2,500} = \frac{150}{2,500} = \frac{3}{50}$$

   The answer is choice (B).

10. **(D)** There's no need to start the y-axis at 0 pounds, because it's impossible to weigh 0 pounds. There's no reason to start the x-axis at 0 calories, because it's not possible to average 0 calories daily. This situation matches choice (D).

Problem-Solving and Data Analysis Drill 3

1. **(C)** When $x = 8$, $y = 12$. We want to know the proportionality constant. We can do this by plugging the values of x and y into the equation and solving for k:

$$12 = 8k$$

Dividing by 8 tells us that $k = \frac{12}{8}$. Reducing this fraction gives choice (C) as the answer, $k = \frac{3}{2}$.

2. **(B)** Let's imagine the simplest version of this and say that there are two people failing. Since for every two failing, three have C's and D's, that means that three in this class do have C's and D's. We also know that for every one person who has a C or a D, two people have A's and B's. Since three have C's and D's, $3(2) = 6$ have A's and B's.

   Therefore, the ratio of those failing to those with A's and B's is 2 to 6, or 1 to 3, which is choice (B).

3. **(B)** Think of this as 3 separate charges. Let's call x the cost of the food. That's the first charge. Then there's a tip charge that is 15% of the cost of food. The 15% tip charge can be expressed as $0.15x$ since x is the cost of food. Finally, there's a \$5 flat fee delivery charge that doesn't depend on the cost of the food. Therefore, the cost can be represented by:

$$C = x + 0.15x + 5$$

Combining like terms gives:

$$C = 1.15x + 5$$

Choice (B) is the correct answer.

4. **(A)** The graph has a positive slope everywhere, so the variables are positively correlated. You can tell that as the year increases from 2000 to 2010, the price increases from about \$16 to about \$43. Choice (A) is the correct answer.

5. **(B)** As you can see from the graph, the trend is a slight decrease in slope each year (while remaining positive). Thus, we would expect ticket prices to rise again but only slightly. You can use the slope from the previous year to get an idea of an approximate increase in the next few years. It looks like from 2009 to 2010, the price increased from \$42 to \$43, so the price increased by \$1. If it continues to increase about \$1 for the next 4 years until 2014, the price will go up a total of \$4, from \$43 to \$47, which is choice (B).

6. **(B)** As time goes by, the exchange rate increases drastically. In 2000, every unit of Currency Y was equal to 2.3 units of Currency X. However, in 2004, 1 unit of Currency Y was equal to 237.83 units of Currency X. That means that Currency Y is becoming more valuable with respect to Currency X because Currency Y is becoming worth more than Currency X. This matches choice (B).

7. **(B)** Go through each possibility.

   Option I: Sam's height percentile actually decreased between ages 12 and 18, so it's extremely unlikely that he experienced exponential growth. By ruling this out, we can eliminate choices (A) and (D).

   Option II: When Sam was less than 5 years old, his height percentile ranged between about the 42nd percentile and the 50th percentile. Between the ages of 10 and 15, he ranged between the 54th and 60th percentile. Therefore, he was taller than more men during these later years, making this statement true.

Option III: We can't say for sure that Sam's height changed between these years, although it's probable. Percentiles measure only your status compared to others. We know only that Sam's height compared to others changed, not that his absolute height changed.

Therefore, the answer is choice (B).

8. **(C)** A 95% confidence interval means that if the study is done at random many times, the average height statistically should fall between these two heights 95% of the time. In other words, choice (C) is correct. It is very likely that an average child will fall between these two heights.

9. **(C)** If prices are discounted by $\frac{2}{3}$, that means you're still paying $\frac{1}{3}$ of the original price. If you also have a coupon that discounts 20%, you're still paying 80% of that price. Since the sale price is $\frac{1}{3}$ of the original price, the price with the coupon is 80% of $\frac{1}{3}$ of the original price. The fraction $\frac{4}{5}$ (or $\frac{8}{10}$ if that makes more sense to you) can represent 80%.

So we can find 80% of $\frac{1}{3}$:

$$\left(\frac{4}{5}\right)\left(\frac{1}{3}\right) = \frac{4}{15}$$

Choice (C) is the answer.

10. **(C)** A random sample is useful if it is truly random and if it is truly representative of the people being studied.

Choice (C) is correct because it polls a randomly selected group and takes into account only registered voters, which is what you would want to sample if you wanted to predict the results of an election.

Choice (A) is incorrect because it polls only people who go to that grocery store and likely excludes voters who shop elsewhere, are too elderly to shop, or don't have money to spend. It also likely samples a significant number of nonregistered voters who won't be counted in the election.

Choice (B) is incorrect because it polls only people in certain geographical locations and therefore likely people of only certain socioeconomic statuses as well.

Choice (D) is incorrect because it polls only those who have access to the Internet and actually take the time to complete the survey.

Advanced Math Drill 1

1. **(A)** A cubic function has a variable raised to the third degree or, in terms of geometry, has 3 dimensions. Therefore, we need a shape that is 3-dimensional. This rules out choices (B) and (C).

Choice (D) may be tempting because a cube is 3-dimensional. However, surface area is actually only 2 dimensions, so this wouldn't be a cubic function.

Choice (A) is correct because volume of a sphere varies proportionally to the cube of its radius. Volume is always in 3 dimensions, hence the reason its units are always in cubic units.

Alternatively, you could have written out all of the relationships depicted in the answer choices.

The volume of a sphere is given by the formula $V = \frac{4}{3}\pi r^3$, which is a cubic function since the radius variable has degree 3. So choice (A) is correct.

The formula for a circle's circumference is $C = 2\pi r = \pi d$, where d represents diameter. This is a linear relationship between d and C, making choice (B) incorrect.

A triangle's area is $A = \frac{1}{2}bh$. This isn't a cubic function, so choice (C) can't be correct.

A cube's surface area is given by the formula $SA = 6x^2$, where x represents the length of each side of the cube. Again, this isn't a cubic function since the degree of x is only 2, so choice (D) is incorrect.

2. **(A)** From all of the answer choices, we can see that the whole denominator cancels out somehow. Let's use polynomial long division to figure out an equivalent expression for our original fraction. Before we use long division, let's first combine like terms in the numerator so that the long division isn't as complicated:

$$a^3 - b^3 + 2a^2b - 2ab^2 + ab^2 - ba^2 = a^3 - b^3 + a^2b - ab^2$$

Now do polynomial long division:

$$
\begin{array}{r}
a + b \\
a^2 - b^2 \overline{)\, a^3 - b^3 + a^2b - ab^2} \\
\underline{-(a^3 \qquad\qquad -ab^2)} \\
-b^3 \;\; +a^2b \\
\underline{-(-b^3 \;\; +a^2b)} \\
0
\end{array}
$$

Thus, our original fraction is equal to $a + b$, which is choice (A).

Alternatively, you could have simplified directly by factoring. Since $a^3 - b^3 = (a - b)(a^2 + ab + b^2)$, we can rewrite the numerator:

$$a^3 - b^3 + 2a^2b - 2ab^2 + ab^2 - ba^2 = a^3 - b^3 + a^2b - ab^2 = (a - b)(a^2 + ab + b^2) + a^2b - ab^2$$

Notice that $a^2b - ab^2 = ab(a - b)$, so our numerator becomes:

$$(a - b)(a^2 + ab + b^2) + a^2b - ab^2 = (a - b)(a^2 + ab + b^2) + ab(a - b) =$$
$$(a - b)(a^2 + ab + b^2 + ab) = (a - b)(a^2 + 2ab + b^2) = (a - b)(a + b)^2$$

Thus, our original fraction can be rewritten as $\dfrac{(a - b)(a + b)^2}{a^2 - b^2}$. Since our denominator is a difference of squares, it can be rewritten as $a^2 - b^2 = (a + b)(a - b)$. Our entire expression becomes:

$$\frac{(a - b)(a + b)^2}{a^2 - b^2} = \frac{(a - b)(a + b)^2}{(a - b)(a + b)} = a + b$$

Choice (A) is correct.

3. **(C)** We can solve for all possible values of m^2 by subtracting $2m^7$ from both sides, factoring the left side, and setting the left side equal to 0:

$$-5m^5 + 3m^3 - 2m^7 = 0$$

First, factor out $-m^3$:

$$-m^3(5m^2 - 3 + 2m^4) = 0$$

Rearrange the polynomial inside the parentheses so that the terms are decreasing in degree for easier factoring:

$$-m^3(2m^4 + 5m^2 - 3) = 0.$$

Next factor the inside:

$$-m^3(2m^4 + 5m^2 - 3) = -m^3(m^2 + 3)(2m^2 - 1) = 0$$

Now set each factor equal to 0 to solve for possible values of m^2:

$$-m^3 = 0$$

Dividing both sides by $-m$ tells you that $m^2 = 0$, so this is one possible value.

$$m^2 + 3 = 0$$

Subtracting 3 from both sides gives $m^2 = -3$. However, you can't square a number and get a negative, so this solution is extraneous.

$$2m^2 - 1 = 0$$

Add 1 to both sides and divide by 2:

$$m^2 = \frac{1}{2}$$

This is another possible value. Therefore, the two possible values of m^2 are 0 and 0.5. Thus, their sum is 0.5, which is choice (C).

4. **(D)** First, multiply by 8 to avoid dealing with fractions:

$$4x^2 + 2x - 1 = 0$$

Next, use the quadratic formula:

$$x = \frac{-b \pm \sqrt{b^2 - 4ac}}{2a} = \frac{-2 \pm \sqrt{2^2 - 4(4)(-1)}}{2(4)} = \frac{-2 \pm \sqrt{4 + 16}}{8}$$

$$= \frac{-2 \pm \sqrt{20}}{8} = -\frac{2}{8} \pm \frac{2\sqrt{5}}{8} = -\frac{1}{4} \pm \frac{\sqrt{5}}{4}$$

This still doesn't match any of the answer choices. All of the answer choices have a fraction factored out of them. We can factor $\frac{1}{4}$ out of our expression to get the answer:

$$\frac{1}{4}(-1 \pm \sqrt{5})$$

Choice (D) is correct.

5. **(A)** Get rid of the square root by squaring both sides. Squaring the right side simply gets rid of the square root, but be careful to FOIL the left side:

$$a^2 + 8a + 16 = a^2 - 2$$

Subtract a^2 from both sides:

$$8a + 16 = -2$$

Next, subtract 16 from both sides:

$$8a = -18$$

Solve for a by dividing by 8:

$$a = -\frac{18}{8} = -\frac{9}{4}$$

This is choice (A).

Note that squaring equations can lead to extraneous answers. In this case, we don't get any extraneous solutions. However, you should get in the habit of checking your solutions by plugging them back into the original equation to ensure that your solution is truly a solution to the original.

6. **(C)** The zeros of a factored polynomial can be found by setting each distinct factor equal to 0 and solving for x. Here there are only 2 distinct factors, $(x - 3)$ and $(x + 7)$. So there will only be 2, choice (C).

$$x - 3 = 0$$
$$x = 3$$
$$x + 7 = 0$$
$$x = -7$$

Note: Although $x - 3$ occurs twice as a factor, this still corresponds to only one zero. We say that 3 is a zero of multiplicity 2 since its corresponding factor occurs twice.

7. **(C)** This function is a parabola. It opens upward because the coefficient in front of x^2 is positive. (In this case, the coefficient of x^2 is 1.) The function has a y-intercept of 2. Therefore, the range is $[2, \infty)$. In order for the range to include negative numbers, the new function either needs to open downward or have a negative y-intercept. In order for it to open downward, you would multiply the right side by a negative number, but this isn't a choice.

The only choice that works is subtracting 3, which would make the y-intercept negative. The y-intercept of the new function would be -1 because $2 - 3 = -1$. The range of the new function would be expanded to $[-1, \infty)$.

8. **(A)** This equation is probably a bit different from the equations of the parabolas that you're used to seeing. To get it into standard form, we need to solve for x instead of the y as we usually do:

$$\frac{1}{17}(y - 4)^2 - 2 = x$$

This is a parabola rotated 90 degrees clockwise. The standard form can be represented by the equation:

$$x = a(y - k)^2 + h$$

Therefore, in this problem, $k = 4$ and $h = -2$. So (h, k) is $(-2, 4)$, as shown in choice (A). Parabola problems like this may not be on the PSAT, but it is included here so that you will be as prepared as possible.

9. **(A)** The relationship is easiest to see if you solve for M first. First, square both sides:

$$(v_{\text{rms}})^2 = \frac{3RT}{M}$$

Multiply both sides by M to get M out of the denominator:

$$M(v_{\text{rms}})^2 = 3RT$$

Now isolate M:

$$M = \frac{3RT}{(v_{\text{rms}})^2}$$

We can now consider how we can lower M. First, M is directly proportional to T. So decreasing T will decrease M. Further, M is inversely proportional to the square of v_{rms}. So increasing v_{rms} will decrease M because you will be dividing by a larger number. Therefore, choice (A) is correct.

10. **(A)** None of the answer choices has a percentage in it, so convert the percentage to a decimal by dividing by 100:

$$x\% = \frac{x}{100} \text{ and } y\% = \frac{y}{100}$$

Suppose P is the initial amount deposited into each portfolio. If portfolio A grows at a rate of $x\%$ yearly, the value after 1 year will be given by the expression:

$$P + \frac{x}{100}P = \left(1 + \frac{x}{100}\right)P.$$

The following year, the amount of money in portfolio A again increases by $x\%$. Therefore, the value after the second year will be given by the following expression:

$$\left(1 + \frac{x}{100}\right)\left[\left(1 + \frac{x}{100}\right)P\right] = \left(1 + \frac{x}{100}\right)\left(1 + \frac{x}{100}\right)P \text{ or } \left(1 + \frac{x}{100}\right)^2 P$$

The third year, the interest will be compounded on the previous value. Therefore, the value will be:

$$\left(1 + \frac{x}{100}\right)^2\left(1 + \frac{x}{100}\right)P \text{ or } \left(1 + \frac{x}{100}\right)^3 P$$

The value after n years is given by:

$$\left(1 + \frac{x}{100}\right)^n P$$

So after 10 years, the value of portfolio A will be $\left(1 + \frac{x}{100}\right)^{10} P$.

Repeat the thought process for portfolio B to arrive at the conclusion that the value of portfolio B after 10 years will be

$$\left(1 + \frac{y}{100}\right)^{10} P$$

since both portfolio A and B start out with the same amount initially, P. Therefore, the ratio of the value of portfolio A to the value of portfolio B is:

$$\frac{\left(1 + \frac{x}{100}\right)^{10} P}{\left(1 + \frac{y}{100}\right)^{10} P} \text{ or } \left(\frac{1 + \frac{x}{100}}{1 + \frac{y}{100}}\right)^{10}$$

This matches choice (A).

Advanced Math Drill 2

1. **(C)** We will use the formula $d = rt$, where d is distance, r is rate, and t is time. Let's define the car's initial position, s, as $s = 0$ and the truck's initial position as $s = 180$.

   The car's position at time t will be its initial position (0) plus the distance it has traveled in that time. We are told that the car's rate r is x, so the distance the car travels in time t is xt. Since the car starts at an initial position of 0, its position at time t will be expressed as $s = xt + 0 = xt$.

   The truck starts at position $s = 180$ and travels toward the 0 position. So the truck's position at time t will be expressed as 180 minus the distance it has traveled in time t. Its speed is twice the speed of the car, or $2x$. So the truck's position at time t will be expressed as $s = 180 - 2xt$.

   They meet where their positions are equal. So set the two equations equal to one another to solve for x:

   $$xt = 180 - 2xt$$

   We know that the vehicles meet after 3 hours, so we can plug in 3 for t:

   $$3x = 180 - 6x$$

   Adding $6x$ to both sides gives:

   $$9x = 180$$

   Dividing both sides by 9 results in $x = 20$.

   However, before selecting choice (A), make sure to finish the problem.

   The question asks you what speed the truck is going. The truck has a speed of $2x$. So its speed is $2(20) = 40$, which is choice (C).

2. **(A)** This problem mentions the "mean of the bases." Notice that $\frac{B_1 + B_2}{2}$, the first part of the area formula, is another way of saying the mean of the bases. Since the mean of the bases is twice the height, we can replace this part of the formula with $2H$:

   $$A = \frac{B_1 + B_2}{2} H = 2H \times H = 2H^2$$

   The area is 72, so plug this in for A and solve for H:

   $$72 = 2H^2$$

   Divide by 2:

   $$36 = H^2$$

   Take the square root of both sides to arrive at the answer $6 = H$, which is choice (A).

3. **(C)** If the negative exponent is in the numerator, it can send whatever is being raised to that exponent to the denominator, but be careful here. In both terms, only the m is being raised to the negative exponents, so the constants stay in the numerator:

   $$2m^{-2} - 4m^{-3} = \frac{2}{m^2} - \frac{4}{m^3}$$

   However, this doesn't match an answer choice. Based on the answer choices, it looks like we may need to add the two fractions together to get just one fraction overall. To add the two fractions, we need a common denominator. If you multiplied the first fraction by $\frac{m}{m}$, both terms would have a denominator of m^3:

$$\frac{2}{m^2} - \frac{4}{m^3} = \frac{2m}{m^3} - \frac{4}{m^3}$$

Now that they have a common denominator, you can add the two fractions together:

$$\frac{2m}{m^3} - \frac{4}{m^3} = \frac{2m - 4}{m^3}$$

Choice (C) is correct.

4. **(A)** Since there's nothing to distribute, you can just drop the parentheses and combine like terms:

$$2y^4 + 3x^6 + 5x^6 + 3y^4 = 5y^4 + 8x^6$$

The correct answer is choice (A).

5. **(D)** Look at the answer choices. All of the choices indicate that at least one $(x - 3)$ factor cancels out, so divide the numerator by $(x - 3)$:

$$
\begin{array}{r}
2x - 6 \\
x - 3 \overline{)\, 2x^2 - 12x + 18} \\
\underline{-(2x^2 - 6x)} \\
-6x + 18 \\
\underline{-(-6x + 18)} \\
0
\end{array}
$$

So the expression can be rewritten as:

$$\frac{(x - 3)(2x - 6)}{3(x - 3)^3}$$

You can cancel an $(x - 3)$ term from the top and bottom:

$$\frac{(2x - 6)}{3(x - 3)^2}$$

The number 2 can be factored out of the numerator:

$$\frac{2(x - 3)}{3(x - 3)^2}$$

Another $(x - 3)$ term cancels:

$$\frac{2}{3(x - 3)}$$

This is choice (D).

Alternatively, you could have factored the numerator directly:

$$2x^2 - 12x + 18 = 2(x^2 - 6x + 9) = 2(x - 3)^2$$

Then you could have canceled out the $(x - 3)^2$ term from the denominator.

6. **(A)** To find the solutions, subtract $15x$ and 18 from both sides to get everything on the left side:

$$21x^2 - 15x - 18 = 0$$

Next, factor out a 3 to make the quadratic equation a bit simpler:

$$3(7x^2 - 5x - 6) = 0$$

Divide both sides by 3:

$$7x^2 - 5x - 6 = 0$$

Notice that the answer choices look similar in structure to the quadratic formula $x = \dfrac{-b \pm \sqrt{b^2 - 4ac}}{2a}$. This suggests that we try to factor our quadratic equation using the quadratic formula. Letting $a = 7$, $b = -5$, and $c = -6$ in the quadratic formula above, we get choice (A).

7. **(B)** Find where the supply and demand are equivalent by setting the two equations equal to one another and solving for p:

$$3p + 6p^2 = 156 - 12p$$

Subtract 156 and add $12p$ to both sides:

$$15p + 6p^2 - 156 = 0$$

Rearrange the equation to get it in $ax^2 + bx + c$ form while simultaneously factoring out a 3:

$$3(2p^2 + 5p - 52) = 0$$

Divide both sides by 3:

$$2p^2 + 5p - 52 = 0$$

Factor to get:

$$(2p + 13)(p - 4) = 0$$

Set each factor equal to 0 and solve for p to get the two possible values of p:

$$2p + 13 = 0 \text{ so } p = -\frac{13}{2}$$

$$p - 4 = 0 \text{ so } p = 4$$

In this situation, p must be positive since it represents the price of the item, which can't be negative. Therefore, p equals only 4, choice (B).

Alternatively, if you didn't recognize that the quadratic equation could be factored, you could have used the quadratic formula:

$$x = \frac{-5 \pm \sqrt{5^2 - 4(2)(-52)}}{2(2)} = \frac{-5 \pm \sqrt{441}}{4} = \frac{-5 \pm 21}{4}$$

$$x = 4 \text{ or } x = -\frac{13}{2}$$

8. **(A)** Look at each option to see whether it is an answer.

Option I: $x = c$ is a vertical line at c. The line will cross the y-axis only if $c = 0$. Since we are told that c is a nonzero constant, this equation does not have a y-intercept.

Option II: $y = -c$ is a horizontal line at the $-c$ value. The line will cross the y-axis at $-c$. This option, therefore, must have a y-intercept.

Option III: $y = cx$ is a line with slope c. Note that when $x = 0$, $y = c(0) = 0$. So the line has a y-intercept at 0.

Thus, only option I is true, which is choice (A).

9. **(B)** The function has zeros at 2, 3, and 6. We can use this to find the factors of the function.

If $x = 2$, $x - 2 = 0$. So $(x - 2)$ is a factor.

If $x = 3$, $x - 3 = 0$. So $(x - 3)$ is a factor.

If $x = 6$, $x - 6 = 0$. So $(x - 6)$ is a factor.

Therefore, the function can be rewritten as $y = (x - 2)(x - 3)(x - 6)$. All of the answer choices are in their unfactored forms, so use FOIL. Start by using FOIL with the first two factors:

$$y = (x^2 - 5x + 6)(x - 6)$$

Then multiply the remaining factors:

$$y = x^3 - 11x^2 + 36x - 36$$

This matches choice (B).

10. **(C)** First, let's identify all of the givens.

Since we're not provided a value for P, we will leave it as is in the formula.

We're also given that the interest is compounded once every 12 months. In other words, it's compounded once every year. Since n is the number of times the investment is compounded yearly, $n = 1$.

We're also told that the investment rate is 5%. Because r is the interest rate expressed as a decimal, $r = \frac{5}{100} = 0.05$.

We want to know A after 1 year, so $t = 1$.

Now plug everything into the equation:

$$A = P\left(1 + \frac{0.05}{1}\right)^{(1)(1)} = P(1.05) = 1.05P$$

Choice (C) is the answer.

Advanced Math Drill 3

1. **(B)**

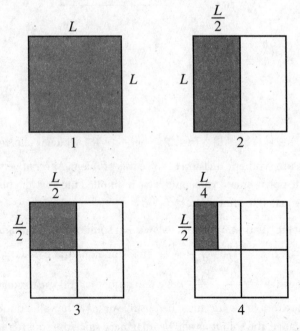

From the drawings, we can see that if the paper is folded in half once, the area is:

$$A = L\left(\frac{L}{2}\right) = \frac{L^2}{2}$$

After the second fold:

$$A = \left(\frac{L}{2}\right)\left(\frac{L}{2}\right) = \frac{L^2}{4}$$

After the third fold:

$$A = \left(\frac{L}{4}\right)\left(\frac{L}{2}\right) = \frac{L^2}{8}$$

We can see that each time, the numerator stays the same while the denominator is multiplied by 2. Therefore, the numerator will always be L^2 while the denominator will be 2^n. Therefore, area can be represented by:

$$A = \frac{L^2}{2^n}$$

Choice (B) is the correct answer.

Alternatively, you could have plugged the values for the areas for each fold into the answer choices to see that only choice (B) works.

2. **(D)** Numbers with negative exponents in the numerator can be rewritten with a positive exponent by moving that number to the denominator (i.e., $a^{-k} = \frac{1}{a^k}$). Fractional exponents are the same as roots. So the entire expression can be rewritten as:

$$\frac{\sqrt[3]{64}}{\sqrt[4]{81}} = \frac{4}{3}$$

The answer is choice (D).

3. **(A)** Let's use polynomial long division to divide the numerator by the denominator:

$$
\require{enclose}
\begin{array}{r}
3x^2 - 4x + 3 \\[-3pt]
x + 2 \enclose{longdiv}{3x^3 + 2x^2 - 5x + 6} \\
\underline{-(3x^3 + 6x^2)} \\
-4x^2 - 5x + 6 \\
\underline{-(-4x^2 - 8x)} \\
3x + 6 \\
\underline{-(3x + 6)} \\
0
\end{array}
$$

Therefore, $(3x^3 + 2x^2 - 5x + 6) \div (x + 2) = 3x^2 - 4x + 3$, which is choice (A).

You could also use synthetic division to solve this problem. Alternatively, if you were unsure of how to divide polynomials, you could have multiplied the answer choices by $x + 2$ to see which choice equaled the numerator.

4. **(B)** Recall that the quadratic formula tells us that solutions to the quadratic equation $ax^2 + bx + c = 0$ are $x = \frac{-b \pm \sqrt{b^2 - 4ac}}{2a}$. Thus, for a quadratic function to only have real solutions, we need $\frac{-b \pm \sqrt{b^2 - 4ac}}{2a}$ to be real numbers. This means that the expression under the square root, $b^2 - 4ac$, must be positive or 0. (If the value underneath the square root sign is negative, the solutions will be imaginary since the square roots of negative numbers are imaginary.)

In other words:

$$b^2 - 4ac \geq 0$$

If we add $4ac$ to both sides:

$$b^2 \geq 4ac$$

The answer is choice (B).

5. **(D)** First, distribute the x in the second part of the expression:

$$x^4 + x(x+2) = x^4 + x^2 + 2x$$

Next, distribute the negative sign:

$$(3x^3 - 2x^2 + 5x + 7) - (x^4 + x^2 + 2x) = 3x^3 - 2x^2 + 5x + 7 - x^4 - x^2 - 2x$$

Next, combine like terms:

$$3x^3 - 2x^2 + 5x + 7 - x^4 - x^2 - 2x = 3x^3 - 3x^2 + 3x + 7 - x^4$$

Rearrange the terms in descending order:

$$-x^4 + 3x^3 - 3x^2 + 3x + 7$$

So choice (D) is correct.

6. **(B)** Add $\sqrt{a}$ to both sides while subtracting 6 from both sides:

$$a - 6 = \sqrt{a}$$

If we square both sides, we can get rid of the square root:

$$a^2 - 12a + 36 = a$$

Subtract a from both sides to set the expression equal to 0:

$$a^2 - 13a + 36 = 0$$

Factoring tells us:

$$(a - 9)(a - 4) = 0$$

So a should equal 9 or 4. However, we have to be careful when square roots are involved. Although squaring both sides was useful when solving for a, this method can produce extraneous solutions. So we have to go back and check our answers to make sure that they are actually solutions to our original equation. Plug both numbers back into the original equation to make sure that they work:

$$9 - \sqrt{9} = 6$$
$$9 - 3 = 6$$

So 9 does work and is a solution to the original equation.

$$4 - \sqrt{4} = 6$$
$$4 - 2 \neq 6$$

So 4 is an extraneous solution. Therefore, there is only one solution, choice (B).

7. **(D)** The second equation is simpler, so solve for y and then plug your expression for y back into the first equation:

$$3x - 6 = 3y$$

Divide by 3 to solve for y:

$$y = \frac{3x - 6}{3} = \frac{3x}{3} - \frac{6}{3} = x - 2$$

Now you can plug $x - 2$ in for y in the first equality:

$$x[(x - 2) + 2] - 3x - 4[(x - 2) + 2] = -12$$

Combine like terms within the parentheses:

$$x(x) - 3x - 4(x) = -12$$

Combine like terms and bring the 12 to the left side:

$$x^2 - 7x + 12 = 0$$

Factor this, or use the quadratic equation if you're not great at factoring:

$$(x - 3)(x - 4) = 0$$

Set each factor equal to 0 to solve for the possible values of x:

$$x - 3 = 0$$
$$x = 3$$
$$x - 4 = 0$$
$$x = 4$$

Next, plug these values into either of the two equations to solve for y. It'll be easiest to plug them into the equation that you already solved for y:

$$y = x - 2 = 3 - 2 = 1$$
$$y = x - 2 = 4 - 2 = 2$$

So x can equal 3 or 4, and y can equal 1 or 2. Therefore, the greatest product xy will be:

$$4 \times 2 = 8$$

Choice (D) is the answer.

8. **(B)** From the graph, the function has zeros at $x = -3$ and at $x = 4$.

Starting with the $x = -3$, add 3 to both sides:

$$x + 3 = 0$$

Therefore, $x + 3$ is a factor. This means that the function must be divisible by $x + 3$.

Similarly, $x = 4$, so:

$$x - 4 = 0$$

Therefore, $x - 4$ is a factor of the function, meaning the function is divisible by $x - 4$. These are the only two zeros. So the function has only two distinct factors, which we have already found. Therefore, Options I and III are correct, which is choice (B).

9. **(B)** The vertex form of a parabola is $y = (x - h)^2 + k$, where (h, k) are the coordinates of the vertex. Our original equation can be written in this form as $y = (x - 0)^2 + 3$. So $h = 0$ and $k = 3$.

The second parabola would be written as $y = (x - 5)^2 + 6$. So $h = 5$ and $k = 6$.

Therefore, h increases by 5 and k increases by 3, which is choice (B).

10. **(C)** First, you must plug the expression for $g(x)$ into $f(x)$ where it's indicated:

$$f(x) = g(x) + 4 = x - \frac{5}{x} + 4$$

Next, plug 10 in for x in $f(x)$:

$$f(10) = 10 - \frac{5}{10} + 4 = 14 - \frac{1}{2} = 13\frac{1}{2} = 13.5$$

Choice (C) is the correct answer.

Geometry and Trigonometry Drill

1. **(C)** Let's do this one in two parts. First, we have a right cylinder with a volume of $30x$. We form a cone with the same height and radius as that cylinder. The formula for the volume of a cylinder is $V = \pi r^2 h$, while the formula for the volume of a cone is $V = \frac{1}{3}\pi r^2 h$.

   Notice that the volume of a cone is just $\frac{1}{3}$ the volume of a cylinder with the same dimensions. Thus, if the volume of the cylinder is $30x$, the volume of a cone with the same dimensions is $\frac{1}{3}(30x)$ or $10x$.

   For the second part of this problem, there's a cube with a volume of $21x$. We have a pyramid with the same length, width, and height as the cube. The formula for the volume of a cube is $V = LWH = L^3$ because the length, width, and height are all the same. The formula for the volume of a pyramid is $V = \frac{1}{3}LWH$.

   In this case, the pyramid has the same length, width, and height as the cube, so the volume for the pyramid can be expressed as $V = \frac{1}{3}L^3$.

   Notice that in this case, the volume of the pyramid is just $\frac{1}{3}$ of the volume of the cube. The volume of the cube is $21x$, so the volume of the pyramid is $\frac{1}{3}(21x) = 7x$.

   The question asked us the sum of the volume of the cone and the pyramid, which can be expressed by:

$$V = V_{\text{cone}} + V_{\text{pyramid}} = 10x + 7x = 17x$$

   Choice (C) is correct.

2. **(A)** The length Andrew would fly would simply be the hypotenuse of a right triangle with side lengths of 20 miles and 15 miles. So we can use the Pythagorean theorem, which states that $a^2 + b^2 = c^2$, where a and b represent the sides and c represents the hypotenuse:

$$(20)^2 + (15)^2 = c^2$$
$$400 + 225 = c^2$$
$$c = \sqrt{625} = 25$$

   Choice (A) is correct.

   Alternatively, you could have saved a bit of time by noticing that this is just a variation of a 3-4-5 triangle:

$$15 = 3(5) \text{ and } 20 = 4(5)$$

   Thus, the hypotenuse will be 5(5) or 25.

3. **(C)** In a right triangle, we can use the Pythagorean theorem to solve for an unknown hypotenuse. $a^2 + b^2 = c^2$ where a and b are the 2 shorter legs and c is the hypotenuse. To solve for c, you take the square root of both sides:

$$c = \sqrt{a^2 + b^2}$$

This matches choice (C).

4. **(B)** You can use the Pythagorean theorem to calculate the length of the diagonal of this rectangle since you know the two side lengths of 6 and 8:

$$6^2 + 8^2 = 10^2$$

Alternatively, you could recognize that 6-8-10 is a multiple of the Pythagorean triple 3-4-5, thus saving you the trouble of calculating using the Pythagorean theorem.

5. **(B)** To convert degrees to radians, simply multiply the number of degrees by $\frac{\pi}{180}$:

$$270\left(\frac{\pi}{180}\right) = \frac{3\pi}{2}$$

Choice (B) is the answer.

Alternatively, you could have realized that 270 degrees is $\frac{3}{4}$ of a circle. A circle is 2π radians, so 270 degrees corresponds to:

$$\frac{3}{4}(2\pi) = \frac{6\pi}{4} = \frac{3\pi}{2} \text{ radians}$$

Note: Radians may or may not be a topic tested on the PSAT. It is definitely something that could be on the SAT. So this problem was included here to prepare you.

6. **(D)** To find the length of the crust, we want to find $\frac{1}{8}$ of the total crust measure. The total crust measure is the circumference of a circle with radius 8. So the crust of one piece is $\frac{1}{8}C$. Because $C = 2\pi r$, the measure we're looking for is:

$$\frac{1}{8}2\pi r = \frac{\pi r}{4} = \frac{8\pi}{4} = 2\pi$$

Note that $2(3.14) = 6.28$, or choice (D).

7. **(C)** The angle next to the 120-degree angle on line AB is 60 degrees because two angles on a given line (supplementary angles) must add up to 180 degrees.

The angle directly opposite that first 60-degree angle must also be 60 degrees, because angles opposite one another (called vertical angles) are equal. Furthermore, that vertical angle is along line EF with the 120-degree angle. So the sum of these supplementary angles must also be 180 degrees, making the vertical angle 60 degrees.

Because lines AB and CD are parallel and line EF is a transversal, opposite interior angles are also congruent. Therefore, the acute angle along line CD is also 60 degrees.

Because that angle is 60 degrees, the acute angle across from it (also along line CD) is also 60 degrees since angles opposite one another (vertical angles) must be congruent.

8. **(D)** The internal angles of a quadrilateral add up to 360 degrees. Since one angle is 120 degrees, the other angles will add up to $360 - 120 = 240$ degrees. Since the other angles are all congruent, divide 240 by 3 to get 80 degrees as the measure of the other angles. 80 degrees therefore is the measure of the smallest interior angle.

9. **(D)** Similar triangles have similar side lengths, meaning that the side lengths vary in fixed proportions. We know that triangle B has exactly one side length of 28. Since exactly one side of triangle A has length 7, this is $28 \div 7 = 4$ times the side length of the unique side in triangle A. Thus, the two shorter sides in triangle B will also be 4 times the side length of the shorter sides in triangle A. Since the two other sides of triangle A have length 5, triangle B has two sides of length $4(5) = 20$ and one side of length of 28.

This could have also been determined using a proportion:

$$\frac{28}{7} = \frac{x}{5}$$

Cross multiplication yields:

$$(28)(5) = 7x$$
$$140 = 7x$$

Dividing both sides by 7 tells us that $20 = x$.

Here we need to be careful. Notice that choice (B) is 20, so you may be tempted to pick choice (B). However, the question is asking us for the perimeter of the triangle rather than for the unknown side length.

The perimeter is $20 + 20 + 28 = 68$, choice (D).

An alternative approach would have been to recognize that the perimeters of similar triangles will vary in the same proportion as the side lengths. We know that triangle B has sides 4 times longer than those of triangle A, so triangle B will also have a perimeter 4 times that of triangle A.

Triangle A has a perimeter of $5 + 5 + 7 = 17$.

Triangle B therefore has a perimeter of $4(17) = 68$.

10. **(A)** We can solve for the unknown side using the Pythagorean theorem:

$$a^2 + b^2 = c^2$$

It follows that

$$b = \sqrt{c^2 - a^2} = \sqrt{26^2 - 24^2} = \sqrt{676 - 576} = \sqrt{100} = 10$$

Similar triangles have the same trigonometric ratios because the similar sides simplify to their lowest multiples.

The smallest angle in this triangle is angle X, as it is across from the shortest side length.

Therefore, a similar triangle will have a tangent of $\frac{\text{opposite}}{\text{adjacent}} = \frac{10}{24}$, which simplifies to $\frac{5}{12}$, choice (A).

Alternatively, you could have saved yourself some time by noticing that this is just a multiple of a 5-12-13 Pythagorean triple. The two known sides are $2(12) = 24$ and $2(13) = 26$. The only side length we were missing was the 5 side, which has a measure of:

$$2(5) = 10.$$

Free-Response Problems Drill 1

1. **(6)** A circle has the formula $(x - h)^2 + (y - k)^2 = r^2$, where (h, k) provides the coordinates for the center of the circle and r is the radius of the circle. This circle, therefore, has a center at $(0, 0)$, otherwise known as the origin. It has a radius of 6. Therefore, a line from the origin to any point on the circle has a distance of 6 units.

2. **(6)** Jamie runs $\frac{3}{2}k$ miles in the time that Matt runs k miles. Their combined distance is 10 miles, so create an equation to show this situation:

$$\frac{3}{2}k + k = 10$$

Get a common denominator so you can add like terms:

$$\frac{3}{2}k + \frac{2}{2}k = 10$$

$$\frac{5}{2}k = 10$$

To solve for k, divide both sides by $\frac{5}{2}$. This is the same as multiplying both sides by the reciprocal, $\frac{2}{5}$:

$$k = 10\left(\frac{2}{5}\right) = \frac{20}{5} = 4$$

However, the question asks how much Jamie runs, so you need to plug this value into $\frac{3}{2}k$:

$$\frac{3}{2}(4) = \frac{12}{2} = 6$$

So Jamie will run 6 miles.

3. $\left(\frac{5}{3}\right)$ Both sides of the equation are squared:

$$(x + 2)(x + 2) = (2x - 3)(2x - 3)$$

If you FOIL both sides:

$$x^2 + 4x + 4 = 4x^2 - 12x + 9$$

To find the solutions, you want to get everything on one side. Moving all terms on the left-hand side to the right side of the equation by subtracting gives:

$$0 = 3x^2 - 16x + 5$$

If you don't see that it can be factored as $(3x - 1)(x - 5)$, then use the quadratic formula:

$$x = \frac{-b \pm \sqrt{b^2 - 4ac}}{2a} = \frac{16 \pm \sqrt{(-16)^2 - 4(3)(5)}}{2(3)} = \frac{16 \pm \sqrt{196}}{6} = \frac{16 \pm 14}{6}$$

Therefore, $x = \frac{1}{3}$ or $x = 5$.

The question asks for the product of all of the solutions, so the answer is

$$5\left(\frac{1}{3}\right) = \frac{5}{3}$$

4. **(7)** If $a + 1$ is a factor, it will divide evenly into the polynomial without a remainder. You can do polynomial long division or synthetic division. We will show the steps for long division:

$$a + 1 \overline{)\begin{array}{l} a^3 - 3a^2 + 5a + (m - 5) \\ a^4 - 2a^3 + 2a^2 + ma + 2 \end{array}}$$

$$\begin{array}{r}
-(a^4 + a^3) \\
\hline
-3a^3 + 2a^2 + ma + 2 \\
-(-3a^3 - 3a^2) \\
\hline
5a^2 + ma + 2 \\
-(5a^2 + 5a) \\
\hline
(m - 5)a + 2 \\
-((m - 5)a + (m - 5)) \\
\hline
2 - (m - 5)
\end{array}$$

In order for there to be no remainder, $2 - (m - 5)$ must be equal to 0. Set it equal to 0 and solve for m:

$$2 - (m - 5) = 0$$

Distribute the negative sign:

$$2 - m + 5 = 0$$

Combine like terms on the right:

$$7 - m = 0$$

Adding m to both sides solves for m:

$$7 = m$$

5. **(2)** Translating the line will merely shift it to the right and down. It will not affect the slope. Therefore, the slope will still be 2. Picture moving a line down and to the right on a graph. Does the slope change? No, so the slope remains the same.

Free-Response Problems Drill 2

1. **(9)** Let's call c the number of children's outfits purchased and a the number of adults' outfits purchased. We can write two equations: one for the number of outfits purchased and one for the amount of money spent.

   We know that the sum of children's outfits and adults' outfits purchased must add up to $22:

   $$c + a = 22$$

   We also know that each children's outfit was $20, so the amount of money spent on children's outfits was $20c$. Similarly, each adult's outfit was $45. So the amount of money spent on adults' outfits was $45a$. We are also told that the family spent a total of $765. Therefore, our second equation is:

   $$20c + 45a = 765$$

   We want to know how many children's outfits were purchased. Let's solve for a in the first equation so that we can substitute a out of the second equation, leaving only c-terms.

   $$a = 22 - c$$

   Plug this into the second equation:

   $$20c + 45(22 - c) = 765$$

   Distributing the 45 gives us:

   $$20c + 990 - 45c = 765$$

   We can now combine both c-terms on the left:

   $$-25c + 990 = 765$$

   Subtracting 990 from both sides leaves:

   $$-25c = -225$$

   Finally, dividing both sides by -25 will tell us the number of children's outfits purchased:

   $$c = 9$$

2. **(19)** The hotel at the median distance in a series of 15 terms will have 7 terms on both sides. Therefore, the hotel that we are looking for is the 8th term. Count 8 points from the left. Then follow that point along to the y-axis to find its cost per night. The cost per night at Hotel M is $120. Let x be the number of rooms the hotel books. Since the hotel wants to make $2,280 and each room costs $120, we have the following equation: $2,280 = 120x$. Divide $2,280 by $120 to tell how many rooms must be booked:

   $$\$2{,}280 \div \$120 = 19$$

   So 19 rooms must be booked. Alternatively, we could have used dimensional analysis in the last step to eliminate units that we didn't want:

   $$2{,}280 \times \frac{1 \text{ room}}{120} = 19 \text{ rooms}$$

3. **(4)** The formula for the area of a triangle is $A = \frac{1}{2}BH$. Plug the given numbers in to solve for the building's actual height:

$$960 = \frac{1}{2}(48)H$$

Divide both sides by $\frac{1}{2}$ (in other words, multiply both sides by the reciprocal, 2):

$$1,920 = 48H$$

Isolate H by dividing both sides by 48:

$$H = 40 \text{ feet}$$

This is the building's actual height, but we want to know its height in the picture. Let's set up a proportion to find the height in the photograph:

$$\frac{1''}{10'} = \frac{x''}{40'}$$

If we cross multiply:

$$(1)(40) = 10x$$

Dividing both sides by 10 gives:

$$x = 4$$

4. **(35)** The number of math/science majors is 225, and the number of engineering majors is 295. So the total number of STEM majors is $225 + 295 = 520$. The total number of students at the university is 1,490. Therefore, the total percentage of STEM majors at the university is:

$$\frac{520}{1,490} \times 100\% = 34.9\%$$

When rounded to the nearest percent, we get 35%.

5. **(0.30)** The probability is given by (number of successes) ÷ number of chances. The number of successes is the number of female humanities majors, which is 450. The total number of chances is the total number of students in the school, which is 1,490. Therefore, the probability is:

$$\frac{450}{1,490} = 0.302$$

When rounded to the nearest hundredth, we get 0.30.

Mixed Drill 1

1. **(D)** We want to isolate what's inside the parentheses with the goal of eventually isolating x. Let's first get that 6 out of the denominator by multiplying both sides by 6:

$$12\left(\frac{5x - 2x}{2}\right) = 108$$

To isolate what's inside the parentheses, we have to divide both sides by 12:

$$\left(\frac{5x - 2x}{2}\right) = 9$$

Now we can get rid of the parentheses:

$$\frac{5x - 2x}{2} = 9$$

To isolate our x-terms, multiply both sides by 2:

$$5x - 2x = 18$$

Combine the like x-terms:

$$5x - 2x = 3x = 18$$

Because $3x = 18$, it follows that $x = 6$.

2. **(C)** Let's imagine the total volume of this rock to be 1 cubic centimeter. Therefore, 0.32 cubic centimeters are coal, 0.29 cubic centimeters are granite, and $1 - 0.32 - 0.29 = 0.39$ cubic centimeters are an unknown mineral. Using the specific gravities, we can calculate the mass of each species.

For coal:

$$0.32 \text{ cm}^3 \times \frac{1.20 \text{ grams}}{\text{cm}^3} = 0.384 \text{ grams}$$

For granite:

$$0.29 \text{ cm}^3 \times \frac{2.60 \text{ grams}}{\text{cm}^3} = 0.754 \text{ grams}$$

For the unknown:

$$0.39 \text{ cm}^3 \times \frac{x \text{ grams}}{\text{cm}^3} = 0.39x \text{ grams}$$

We know that the specific gravity of the whole thing is 1.4 grams/centimeter cubed, so its mass is:

$$1 \text{ cm}^3 \times \frac{1.4 \text{ grams}}{\text{cm}^3} = 1.4 \text{ grams}$$

Because all of the masses together must equal 1.4, it follows that:

$$0.384 + 0.754 + 0.39x = 1.4$$

Subtract the first 2 terms from both sides:

$$0.39x = 0.262$$

Divide both sides by 0.39:

$$x = 0.67$$

3. **(A)** Remember that $d = rt$, where d is distance, r is rate, and t is time. We have two different rates and two different times. We can multiply the coinciding rates and times together and then can add them to obtain the total distance traveled, 300 miles:

$$5x + \left(\frac{x}{10}\right)\left(\frac{x}{2}\right) = 300$$

Multiplying the two fractions together leaves:

$$5x + \frac{x^2}{20} = 300$$

None of the answer choices has a denominator, so let's multiply both sides by 20 to get rid of the denominator:

$$100x + x^2 = 6,000$$

Subtracting 6,000 from both sides and rearranging the terms gives:

$$x^2 + 100x - 6,000 = 0$$

This matches choice (A).

4. **(D)** Take each term one at a time. When you cube $6a^3$, you're cubing both the 6 and the a^3. When you raise an exponent to another exponent, multiply the exponents. Therefore:

$$(6a^3)^3 - (2b)^4 + c^{-2} = 216a^9 - (2b)^4 + c^{-2}$$

Next, raise $2b$ to the fourth power by raising 2 to the fourth power and raising b to the fourth power:

$$216a^9 - (2b)^4 + c^{-2} = 216a^9 - 16b^4 + c^{-2}$$

Lastly, deal with the negative exponent. Something with a negative exponent can be rewritten by moving that something to the denominator and making the corresponding exponent positive:

$$216a^9 - 16b^4 + c^{-2} = 216a^9 - 16b^4 + \frac{1}{c^2}$$

Choice (D) is the correct answer.

An alternative to solving this problem to completion is to realize that once there is the $216a^9$, the answer must have this term in it. Choice (D) is the only option with this term, so you can pick it without having to do the last steps as discussed above.

5. **(B)** Exponential growth has initially slow growth that later becomes fast growth. In other words, it starts with a small slope that quickly turns into a steep slope. Only choice (B) shows this kind of growth.

6. **(B)** Percent change is given by the following equation:

$$\frac{\text{New} - \text{Original}}{\text{Original}} \times 100\%$$

We can rule out choice (A) since stock price decreased between 1983 and 1984. Calculate the approximate percent increase for the remaining answer choices.

Choice (B):

$$\frac{29 - 20}{20} \times 100\% = 45\%$$

Choice (C):

$$\frac{52 - 39}{39} \times 100\% = 33\%$$

Choice (D):

$$\frac{68 - 52}{52} \times 100\% = 31\%$$

Therefore, choice (B) has the greatest percent increase.

7. **(D)** The minimal stock price is about \$11/share. Since the stockbroker sold \$1,000 in shares, she must have sold:

$$1,000 \times \frac{1 \text{ share}}{\$11} = 90.91 \text{ shares}$$

The maximum price is about \$88/share:

$$1,000 \times \frac{1 \text{ share}}{\$88} = 11.36 \text{ shares}$$

She would have sold $90.91 - 11.36 = 79.55$ more shares at the lower price, or about 80 as in choice (D).

8. **(D)** Just plug in $(b - a)$ wherever there is an a in the expression for $f(a)$:

$$f(b - a) = (b - a)^2 - 12$$

Next, use FOIL for $(b - a)^2$:

$$(b - a)^2 = (b - a)(b - a) = b^2 - ab - ab + a^2 = b^2 - 2ab + a^2$$

Plug this back into $f(b - a)$:

$$f(b - a) = b^2 - 2ab + a^2 - 12$$

This can be arranged as $f(b - a) = a^2 - 2ab + b^2 - 12$, choice (D).

9. **(B)** Notice that the top and bottom sides each have a length of $3a$, while the left and right sides will each have a length of b. Therefore, $P = 3a + b + 3a + b$. Combine like terms:

$$P = 6a + 2b$$

The answer is choice (B).

10. **(B)** This function turns 3 times, so it's a quartic function, meaning it must have 4 factors. Right away, we can eliminate choices (A) and (D) because these functions each have only 3 factors; they're cubics. To conceptualize, a quadratic function—a parabola—turns once. A cubic function turns twice.

The function has zeros at -1, 0, and 2. We can use this to solve for the factors.

If $x = -1$, $x + 1 = 0$. So $(x + 1)$ is a factor. From this, you can eliminate choice (C), thus leaving choice (B) as the correct answer. However, if you want to see where the rest of the factors come from, read on.

If $x = 0$, x must be a factor. Why? Because if $x = 0$, the whole function equals zero; so x must be a factor.

If $x = 2$, $x - 2 = 0$. So $(x - 2)$ must be a factor. This factor must actually be squared. In general, if $(x - a)^m$ is a factor of a function, then the function crosses the x-axis at a if m is odd and does not cross the x-axis at a if m is even. In our case, if we look at the graph at $x = 2$, we can see that the graph never crosses the x-axis at 2; it stays above the x-axis right before and after 2. This means that $(x - 2)$ must be raised to an even power. We know that our graph is quartic. Since we already have 2 other distinct factors, the only option is for the exponent to be 2. In other words, $(x - 2)^2$ is a factor. Notice that the graph crosses the x-axis at the other two zeros: -1 and 0. At -1, the graph goes from the positive side to the negative side of the x-axis. The graph goes from the negative side to the positive side of the x-axis at 0. So their corresponding factors must occur an odd number of times (in this case, they each occur once). This matches choice (B).

Mixed Drill 2

1. **(C)** First, distribute the -5:

$$15x + \frac{1}{2} = -5x + \frac{25}{2}$$

Now we want to get all of the x-terms on one side and all of the constant terms on the other side. Let's start by adding $5x$ to both sides:

$$20x + \frac{1}{2} = \frac{25}{2}$$

Now all of the x-terms are on the left, so we want all constant terms on the right. Let's subtract $\frac{1}{2}$ from both sides:

$$20x = \frac{24}{2} = 12$$

Dividing both sides by 20 will isolate the x:

$$x = \frac{12}{20}$$

This simplifies to $x = \frac{3}{5}$, which is choice (C).

2. **(C)** Use FOIL for this like you would anything else. When you FOIL the expression, you get:

$$12 + 3i - 4i - i^2 = 12 - i - i^2$$

Because $i = \sqrt{-1}$, $i^2 = -1$. Thus, we can rewrite our equation as:

$$12 - i - (-1)$$

Therefore, the final answer is $13 - i$, which is choice (C).

3. **(A)** Use FOIL on both sides to get:

$$x^2 - 16x + 60 = x^2 - 16x + 64 + c$$

The coefficients of like terms of both sides of the equation must equal one another. The coefficients of the x^2-terms and of the x-terms are already equal on both sides. However, the constant terms must equal one another as well:

$$60 = 64 + c$$

Subtract 64 from both sides:

$$-4 = c$$

Choice (A) is correct.

4. **(A)** Here we're looking for an angle measure, so we need an inverse trigonometry function. Let's go through the answer choices.

Choice (A) works because sine is the value of the opposite side over the hypotenuse. Side x is opposite of angle X, and side z is the hypotenuse. Thus, $\sin^{-1}\left(\frac{x}{z}\right)$ would provide the measure of angle X.

Choice (B) doesn't work because side x is opposite of angle X rather than adjacent, so we don't want to use $\cos^{-1}$.

Choice (C) won't work because we want an inverse trigonometry function rather than a trigonometry function. The output of an inverse trigonometry function is an angle. In contrast, the output of a trigonometry function is the ratio of two sides of a right triangle.

Choice (D) doesn't work because side y is adjacent to angle X, so $\sin^{-1}$ is not the appropriate inverse trigonometry function to use.

5. **(D)** Solve for V:

$$V = \frac{nRT}{P}$$

Recall that, in general, y is directly proportional to x if $y = cx$ for some constant c, and y is inversely proportional if $y = \frac{c}{x}$. In our case, we are told that R is the gas constant, so we can think of this as our constant. So V is directly proportional to n and T. If you increased either of these variables, V would also increase. V is inversely proportional only to P, which isn't an answer choice. So choice (D) is the correct answer.

6. **(D)** First, isolate $\frac{1}{d_o}$ by subtracting $\frac{1}{d_i}$ from both sides of the equation:

$$\frac{1}{f} - \frac{1}{d_i} = \frac{1}{d_o}$$

We want to find d_o, so we need the reciprocal of $\frac{1}{d_o}$, which is d_o. To find the reciprocal, simply take 1 over both sides:

$$\frac{1}{\frac{1}{f} - \frac{1}{d_i}} = d_o$$

The answer is choice (D).

7. **(B)** First, use FOIL for the left side of the equation:

$$x^3 + ax^2 + 2x + 4x^2 + 4ax + 8$$

Next, combine like terms:

$$x^3 + (a + 4)x^2 + (2 + 4a)x + 8$$

We know that this has to equal the right side of the original equation:

$$x^3 + (a + 4)x^2 + (2 + 4a)x + 8 = x^3 + x^2 - 10x + 8$$

The coefficients of the like terms on both sides of the equation must equal one another. The coefficients on the x^3-terms are already equal and the constants are equal. So we need to worry about only the x^2-terms and the x-terms. Set the coefficients on the x^2-terms equal to one another:

$$a + 4 = 1$$

Subtracting 4 from both sides reveals that $a = -3$, which is choice (B).

We also could have set the coefficients of the x-terms equal to each other to solve for a:

$$2 + 4a = -10$$

Subtracting 2 from both sides and then dividing by 4 gives $a = -3$ as well.

8. **(D)** Distribute the negative sign:

$$\left(6y^3 + \frac{1}{2}y - \frac{2}{3}\right) - \left(4y^3 - y^2 + \frac{1}{2}y + \frac{1}{6}\right) = 6y^3 + \frac{1}{2}y - \frac{2}{3} - 4y^3 + y^2 - \frac{1}{2}y - \frac{1}{6}$$

Next combine like terms:

$$6y^3 + \frac{1}{2}y - \frac{2}{3} - 4y^3 + y^2 - \frac{1}{2}y - \frac{1}{6} = 2y^3 + y^2 - \frac{5}{6}$$

This matches choice (D).

9. **(D)** A line perpendicular to line A has a slope that is the negative reciprocal of $-\frac{x}{y}$.

The negative reciprocal is $-\left(-\frac{y}{x}\right)$, or $\frac{y}{x}$.

10. **(C)** We're given that $V_A = 8V_B$. From the formula for the volume of a sphere ($V = \frac{4}{3}\pi r^3$), it follows that $\frac{4}{3}\pi r_A^3 = 8\left(\frac{4}{3}\pi r_B^3\right)$. The $\frac{4}{3}\pi$ term cancels out on both sides, leaving us with $r_A^3 = 8r_B^3$. Taking the cube root of both sides gives $r_A = 2r_B$. Thus, the radius of sphere A is twice the radius of sphere B. We ultimately want to find the ratio of the surface areas, so consider the surface areas of the two spheres:

$$SA_A = 4\pi r_A^2 = 4\pi(2r_B)^2 = 4\pi(4r_B^2)$$

and

$$SA_B = 4\pi r_B^2$$

To find the ratio of the surface area of sphere A to the surface area of sphere B, we divide the surface area of sphere A by the surface area of sphere B:

$$\frac{SA_A}{SA_B} = \frac{4\pi\left(4r_B^2\right)}{4\pi r_B^2}$$

We can cancel a 4π and an r_B^2 out of both the numerator and the denominator, which leaves us with $\frac{SA_A}{SA_B} = 4$.

Thus, the ratio of the surface area of sphere A to sphere B is $\frac{4}{1}$ or 4:1, which is choice (C).

Practice Tests

Reading and Writing Module 1

1. _____	8. _____	15. _____	22. _____
2. _____	9. _____	16. _____	23. _____
3. _____	10. _____	17. _____	24. _____
4. _____	11. _____	18. _____	25. _____
5. _____	12. _____	19. _____	26. _____
6. _____	13. _____	20. _____	27. _____
7. _____	14. _____	21. _____	

Reading and Writing Module 2

1. _____	8. _____	15. _____	22. _____
2. _____	9. _____	16. _____	23. _____
3. _____	10. _____	17. _____	24. _____
4. _____	11. _____	18. _____	25. _____
5. _____	12. _____	19. _____	26. _____
6. _____	13. _____	20. _____	27. _____
7. _____	14. _____	21. _____	

Math Module 1

1. _____ 7. _____ 13. _____ 19. _____

2. _____ 8. _____ 14. _____ 20. _____

3. _____ 9. _____ 15. _____ 21. _____

4. _____ 10. _____ 16. _____ 22. _____

5. _____ 11. _____ 17. _____

6. _____ 12. _____ 18. _____

Math Module 2

1. _____ 7. _____ 13. _____ 19. _____

2. _____ 8. _____ 14. _____ 20. _____

3. _____ 9. _____ 15. _____ 21. _____

4. _____ 10. _____ 16. _____ 22. _____

5. _____ 11. _____ 17. _____

6. _____ 12. _____ 18. _____

PSAT Test Overview

This PSAT practice test is made up of a Reading and Writing section and a Math section. **Note:** On the previous pages, there is an answer sheet you can use to write down your letter choices and math answers. Feel free to use the sheet to record your answers or simply circle and write down your answers in the test as you go.

Section 1: Reading and Writing (54 Questions)

There are two 27-question modules in the Reading and Writing section.

Section 2: Math (44 Questions)

There are two 22-question modules in the Math section.

Modules

The modules in each section are timed separately. You can review your answers in each module before time expires. When the time reaches zero, you will automatically move on to the next section. You are unable to return to a completed module.

Directions

At the beginning of each section, there are directions for answering the questions.

Practice Test 1

SECTION 1: READING AND WRITING MODULE 1

32 MINUTES, 27 QUESTIONS

> **DIRECTIONS:** You will be tested on a variety of important reading and writing skills. Each question has one or more passages, possibly including a graph or table. Carefully read each passage and question and choose the best answer to the question based on the passage(s).
>
> Every question in this section is multiple-choice with four possible answers. Each question has only one best answer.

1. The housing bubble had finally burst. It wasn't just that a few people defaulted; rather, foreclosures were everywhere you looked. And, even worse, when the banks came by to collect the keys, the houses were now worth only fractions of what the banks lent for them. Consequently, they lost billions.

   In the text, "The housing bubble had finally burst" means what happened?

   (A) Homes were worth less than when they were mortgaged.
   (B) Homes were destroyed across the country.
   (C) No new homes were being built.
   (D) Home prices remained steady for several years.

2. David had just turned fourteen when, walking back from school, he heard the pathetic whimper. The puppy was small—obviously malnourished and feeble—and much too young to be away from its mother. David removed his jacket and coddled the pup against his chest as he walked briskly back to the Hardings, rehearsing what he might say. To his surprise, Mr. Harding's only requests were that David keep the frail animal in his own room.

   As used in the text, the word "coddled" most nearly means

   (A) spoiled.
   (B) humored.
   (C) cosseted.
   (D) indulged.

3. Regrettably, because of the second scribe's large and unwieldy penmanship, the poem's last ten lines or so would not fit on the parchment leaf and are thus lost to history. We are instead left with the compellingly _____ ending (roughly translated): "The white wood rang / Grimly as they hacked each other's shields / Until the linden slats grew lean and splintered / Broken by blades . . ."

Which choice completes the text with the most logical and precise word or phrase?

(A) conclusive

(B) shocking

(C) ecstatic

(D) ambiguous

4. It is easy to notice the endless changes in the recommendations about what foods and beverages people should consume. Coffee is a prime example—it falls out of grace on a regular basis, only to "become healthy" once again a few years later. The same is true of eggs, which are routinely vilified and then exonerated by researchers, regulators, and doctors. However, no food has ever so unjustly gained a bad reputation as dietary fat.

Which choice best states the function of the underlined sentence in the text as a whole?

(A) To provide a specific instance to illustrate a broader point

(B) To anticipate an avenue for further research

(C) To suggest a healthy dietary alternative

(D) To define an unfamiliar term for the reader

5. *The following text is from President Ronald Reagan's 1981 speech to Congress.*

Almost 8 million Americans are out of work. These are people who want to be productive. But as the months go by, despair dominates their lives. The threats of layoff and unemployment hang over other millions, and all who work are frustrated by their inability to keep up with inflation.

One worker in a Midwest city put it to me this way: He said, "I'm bringing home more dollars than I ever believed I could possibly earn, but I seem to be getting worse off." And he is. Not only have hourly earnings of the American worker, after adjusting for inflation, declined 5 percent over the past 5 years, but in these 5 years, federal personal taxes for the average family have increased 67 percent.

The underlined quotation in the text primarily serves to

(A) give concrete statistics.

(B) provide anecdotal evidence.

(C) separate fact from opinion.

(D) acknowledge likely objections.

6. **Text 1**

When it comes to determining what makes a person who they are, a common debate is the effect of nature versus nurture. Are individuals more heavily influenced by their innate attributes or from the environment in which they grew up? The term *nature* refers to someone's genes and how biological family factors lead to their physical and personality traits. On the other hand, *nurture* describes how childhood and upbringing determine who an individual is as an adult.

Text 2

In previous years, the field of psychology was focused on whether individuals are the product of their nature or their nurture. However, the factors are not mutually exclusive. Psychologists today have recognized that both play interacting roles in an individual's development. Donald Hebb, a professional in the field, answered a question of, "Which, nature or nurture, contributes more to personality?" by responding with, "Which contributes more to the area of a rectangle, its length or its width?"

Based on the texts, what would Donald Hebb's attitude towards the presentation of information in Text 1 most likely be?

(A) Appreciation, since it presents both sides of an intractable argument

(B) Disapproval, since it suggests that one must pick sides on this topic

(C) Alarm, since it contradicts the consensus of experts in the field

(D) Curiosity, since it demonstrates a great depth of scholarly research

7. *Text 1 is from Benjamin Franklin's 1771 autobiography. Text 2 is from Booker T. Washington's 1901 autobiography.*

Text 1

I have ever had pleasure in obtaining any little anecdotes of my ancestors. You may remember the inquiries I made among the remains of my relations when you were with me in England, and the journey I undertook for that purpose. Imagining it may be equally agreeable to you to know the circumstances of my life, many of which you are yet unacquainted with, and . . . I sit down to write them for you.

Text 2

Of my ancestry I know almost nothing. In the slave quarters, and even later, I heard whispered conversations . . . of the tortures which the slaves, including, no doubt, my ancestors on my mother's side, suffered in the middle passage of the slave ship while being conveyed from Africa to America. I have been unsuccessful in securing any information that would throw any accurate light upon the history of my family beyond my mother.

It is reasonable to conclude that Booker T. Washington would very much like to have had the opportunity to do which of the following things that Benjamin Franklin spoke about in Text 1?

(A) Obtain anecdotes about his ancestors

(B) Take time to write a memoir

(C) Have a relationship with his children

(D) Relive his life

8. It is hard to imagine what life would be like without the contributions engineers have already made. They have not just helped us to survive, be healthy, explore, and move around better but they have also made life more enjoyable through advances in areas such as communications, computing, and sports. Computer engineers, for example, have helped develop devices and software that we can use to make and share documents and home videos, listen to our favorite music, and talk with co-workers, friends, and family members across the globe. In sports, different engineers have made systems and devices that provide us with better, safer equipment, communications that enable teams to interact better and games to be televised, and environments and infrastructure that improve the playing and watching of games.

What is the point of the text as a whole?

(A) To make the reader feel that engineering is an accessible career

(B) To show how human life would go extinct without engineers

(C) To highlight the contributions of computer and sport engineers

(D) To give examples of how engineers' contributions are used in daily life

9. If one were to set out to form a nation based on democratic principles, there would be essentially two paths to take: presidential or parliamentary. Both hold their own in terms of advantages and disadvantages, and both possess the endorsement of great prosperous nations. Parliamentary is the far more common order, but many attribute its prevalence to the legacy of the British Empire rather than to its superiority.

The author states that a possible reason for the more widespread practice of parliamentary rather than presidential democracy is

(A) majority rule.

(B) historical inheritance.

(C) legislative-executive unity.

(D) centralized authority.

10.

Eye Colors in Ms. Smith's Class

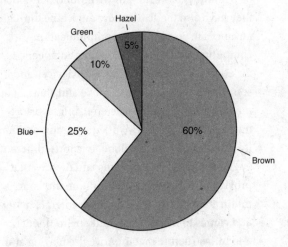

Using the graph, what is true about the relationship between the number of students with green eyes and the number of students with brown eyes?

(A) The number of students with green eyes equals one-sixth of the number of students with brown eyes.

(B) Green eyes are a recessive trait and more uncommon than brown eyes.

(C) Hazel eyes are a variant of green and should be included in the green eyes total.

(D) For every ten students with green eyes there are six students with brown eyes.

11. "Monadnock in Early Spring" is an early 1900s poem by Amy Lowell. In the poem, the speaker alludes to Mount Monadnock's impressive size relative to the other features of the landscape:

_____

Which quotation from "Monadnock in Early Spring" most effectively illustrates the claim?

(A) "Cloud-topped and splendid, dominating all / The little lesser hills which compass thee,"

(B) "Thou standest, bright with April's buoyancy, / Yet holding Winter in some shaded wall / Of stern, steep rock";

(C) "and startled by the call / Of Spring, thy trees flush with expectancy / And cast a cloud of crimson, silently,"

(D) "Above thy snowy crevices where fall / Pale shrivelled oak leaves, / while the snow beneath / Melts at their phantom touch."

12. Lab technicians are able to pinpoint the best antibiotic by measuring the *zone of inhibition* on the microorganism growth plate. The zone with the largest diameter typically signifies that it will be the best at fighting the infection. Prescribing an antibiotic that tests positive for the inhibition of growth or completely stops the growth of the microorganism will hopefully help the patient heal faster and experience fewer side effects.

Antibiotic Tested	*E. coli* Zone of Inhibition	*S. aureus* Zone of Inhibition
Vancomycin	0 mm	20 mm
Ciprofloxacin	17 mm	16 mm
Amoxicillin	10 mm	15 mm

Figure 1 Zone of inhibition measurements to determine the effectiveness of certain antibiotics against the microorganisms *E. coli* and *S. aureus*.

1   1   1

Based on the information in the text and in Figure 1, which of these antibiotics would be most helpful in treating someone with an *E. coli* infection, assuming the patient was not allergic to any antibiotics and had no other illnesses besides the *E. coli* infection?

(A) Vancomycin
(B) Ciprofloxacin
(C) Amoxicillin
(D) Staphylococcus

13. Prior to arranging meetings on behalf of his company, a marketing assistant uses his home kitchen to prepare a packed lunch for his daughter. A graphic designer spends hours a day on her personal PC creating eye-catching brand logos without ever stepping foot outside her apartment. A major shift in a workforce evermore reliant on technology is the increasing number of employees who find themselves _____.

Which choice most logically completes the text?

(A) working in supervisory positions.
(B) increasingly highly compensated for their efforts.
(C) reliant on education to advance their careers.
(D) staying at home during the workday.

14. *The following text is from Upton Sinclair's 1906 novel* The Jungle.

Promptly at seven the next morning Jurgis reported for work. He came to the door that had been pointed out to him, and there he waited for nearly two hours. The boss had meant for him to enter, but had not said this, and so it was only when on his way out to hire another man that he came upon Jurgis. He gave him a good cursing, but as Jurgis did not understand a word of it, he did not object.

It can be reasonably inferred from the text that the supervisors in the meat-packing factories viewed employees as

(A) skillful.
(B) disposable.
(C) valuable.
(D) interesting.

15. The bat species whose diet doesn't consist of insects are frugivores, carnivores, or hematophagous. It is the latter bloodsuckers who attract the most attention. The ecological roles of bats _____ not end with pest control.

Which choice completes the text so that it conforms to the conventions of Standard English?

(A) do
(B) does
(C) don't
(D) do's

16. The ban on foie gras was passed by _____ in an omnibus bill despite the opposition of the city's mayor.

Which choice completes the text so that it conforms to the conventions of Standard English?

(A) Chicago's City Council
(B) Chicagos City Council
(C) Chicagos' Cities Council
(D) Chicagos Cities Council

17. Fitzgerald uses Bernice's transformation to embody modernist ideals of moral relativism and _____ former Victorian standards of custom.

Which choice completes the text so that it conforms to the conventions of Standard English?

(A) the implementation of mockery of
(B) for the mocking of
(C) to mock
(D) mocking

18. Even with Athena—the very core of the Parthenon—missing, the temple _____ still served as a great, inclusive museum of Greek history, tracing the founding of ancient Greece, Athenian democracy, and early western civilization; yet, the Parthenon would endure many other foes.

Which choice completes the text so that it conforms to the conventions of Standard English?

(A) could of
(B) might of
(C) could have
(D) should have been

19. The University of Missouri at Columbia—boasting the number one journalism department in the nation according to *The Huffington Post*—offers more than 30 interest areas, incorporating an intensive liberal arts education along with hands-on experience in media labs and internships for academic credit. Ohio _____ three campus publications plus a broadcasting outlet for students to gain professional experience before graduation, not to mention OU's Institute for International Journalism, which offers opportunities for reporting abroad.

Which choice completes the text so that it conforms to the conventions of Standard English?

(A) University also having, a journalism department ranked in the top ten nationwide offers
(B) University also having a journalism department ranked in the top ten nationwide offers
(C) University, also having a journalism department, ranked in the top ten, nationwide, offers
(D) University, also having a journalism department ranked in the top ten nationwide, offers

20. While our own ancestors were battling drought on the coasts of the African subcontinent, _____ where the Neanderthals developed the tools of flint and bone that have today come to characterize the so-called Mousterian culture of the early Stone Age.

Which choice completes the text so that it conforms to the conventions of Standard English?

(A) the icebound north of modern Eurasia experienced the spread of the evolutionarily distinct species *Homo neanderthalensis*,
(B) the evolutionarily distinct species *Homo neanderthalensis* had spread to the icebound north of modern Eurasia,
(C) the species *Homo neanderthalensis*, being evolutionarily distinct, found itself spread to modern Eurasia in the north icebound,
(D) the north icebound of modern Eurasia experience evolutionarily distinct species spread of the *Homo neanderthalensis*,

21. Strindberg mocked and attacked Ibsen's most successful and enduring play, *A Doll's House*, in a short story of the same title and claimed that his ongoing hostilities with Ibsen had cost him his "wife, children, fortune, and career." Ibsen, meanwhile, somewhat more _____ a portrait of Strindberg in his study where he worked, naming it *Madness Incipient*.

Which choice completes the text so that it conforms to the conventions of Standard English?

(A) soberly—though no less venomously—kept
(B) soberly; though no less venomously kept
(C) soberly though no less—venomously kept
(D) soberly: though no less venomously, kept

1   1   1

22. Quite simply, the days of print-only newsrooms are past. Now, one doesn't wait until the 6 p.m. broadcast to hear what's happening around the world, _____ does one grab the newspaper on Sunday morning for breaking news.

Which choice completes the text with the most logical transition?

(A) nor
(B) because
(C) for
(D) while

23. Alongside the Watson-Crick "Double Helix" and Einstein's "Equation of General Relativity," the Periodic Table of Elements is among the most important and instantly recognizable features of modern science. _____ the table as we know it today emerged just 150 years ago, the story of its conceptual evolution goes all the way back to Ancient Greece, when Aristotle proposed that all mass is composed of a mixture of simple elements.

Which choice completes the text with the most logical transition?

(A) While
(B) Since
(C) Given
(D) If

24. A student has recently started watching movies from Studio Ghibli and wants to learn more about its creator. The student writes down these notes:

- Studio Ghibli was founded by Hayoa Miyazaki, Isoa Takahata, and Toshio Suzuki.
- Hayoa Miyzaki is the animator, director, producer, screenwriter, author, and manga artist.
- The movies appeal to those who are young at heart and enjoy unique storytelling.
- *Spirited Away*, released in 2001 by the studio, has received an Oscar award and is the highest-grossing film in Japanese history.
- Studio Ghibli is sometimes referred to as, "Japan's Disney."

The student wishes to write an essay in which he emphasizes the critical acclaim that the work of Studio Ghibli has received. Which choice most effectively uses relevant information from the notes to accomplish this goal?

(A) The team work of Miyazaki, Takahata, and Suzuki was critical to the success of Studio Ghibli.
(B) The film *Spirited Away* was recognized for its excellence by receiving an Oscar award in 2001.
(C) Young people are the target audience of the works of Studio Ghibli—they particularly enjoy the unique storytelling that their films offer.
(D) Many observers note the similarities between the films of Studio Ghibli and that of the Disney corporation.

25. It is said that Benjamin Franklin suggested the use of foxfire (bioluminescent fungi) as a viable light source on an early variety of submarine, _____ it would consume considerably less oxygen than the combustion reactions of candle or lamplight.

Which choice completes the text with the most logical transition?

(A) but
(B) previously
(C) as
(D) while

26. C. diff is just one example of how the overuse of antibiotics can harm individuals. Within hospitals, it is a serious issue. This does not mean that we should cease use of antibiotics. _____ the lack of antibiotics would kill far more people than C. diff likely ever will.

Which choice completes the text with the most logical transition?

(A) However,
(B) As a result,
(C) In fact,
(D) Due to this,

27. When researching a topic, a student has taken the following notes:

- Bonanza farms were large and incredibly profitable farms on the Great Plains in the 1800s.
- The reapers by Cyrus McCormick and steel plows by John Deere contributed to these farms.
- Another development that supported the development of these farms was displacement of Native Americans onto reservations, thereby opening of huge tracts of land to American settlers.
- The laying of railroad tracks also greatly helped these farmers, as they could now easily bring supplies to their farms and ship their crops East.
- The bonanza farm era continued until the Panic of 1873 and the Great Drought of the 1880s.

The student wants to highlight how changes to national transportation infrastructure positively impacted the development of bonanza farms. Which choice most effectively uses relevant information from the notes to accomplish this goal?

(A) The profits of bonanza farms in the 1800s were without historical precedent.
(B) New railroad tracks enabled bonanza farmers to both obtain supplies from and sell goods to faraway regions.
(C) Ultimately, bonanza farms were doomed to failure because of the economic developments of the late 1800s.
(D) Without the displacement of Native Americans onto reservations, bonanza farmers would not have had the land they wanted to create their large farms.

SECTION 1: READING AND WRITING MODULE 2

32 MINUTES, 27 QUESTIONS

DIRECTIONS: You will be tested on a variety of important reading and writing skills. Each question has one or more passages, possibly including a graph or table. Carefully read each passage and question and choose the best answer to the question based on the passage(s).

Every question in this section is multiple-choice with four possible answers. Each question has only one best answer.

1. After living in a single dorm room as an undergraduate, I had found his apartment listed under the enticing entry "Looking for One Roommate, Cheap Rent for the Quiet and Introverted," and _____ the adventure of graduate school and a roommate who preferred books to parties.

Which choice completes the text with the most appropriate word?

(A) accepted
(B) excepted
(C) inspected
(D) expected

2. *In 1862, Ralph Waldo Emerson delivered the excerpt below as part of a lecture called "American Civilization" at the Smithsonian Institution in Washington, D.C.*

At this moment in America the aspects of political society absorb attention. In every house, from Canada to the Gulf, the children ask the serious father—"What is the news of the war today? and when will there be better times?" The boys have no new clothes, no gifts, no journeys; the girls must go without new bonnets; boys and girls find their education, this year, less liberal and complete. All the little hopes that heretofore made the year pleasant are deferred. The state of the country fills us with anxiety and stern duties.

As used in the text, the word *stern* most nearly means

(A) playful.
(B) terrifying.
(C) serious.
(D) pointless.

3. There are few biochemical compounds as familiar to us as hemoglobin, and as the primary transporter of oxygen in our blood, the celebrity of this curious little compound is not without just cause. Vital to almost every known vertebrate, hemoglobin appears within the very first week of embryogenesis, and while its role may not change throughout development, its molecular structure undergoes a series of significant transformations.

As used in the text, the word *celebrity* most nearly means

(A) notoriety.

(B) disreputability.

(C) personage.

(D) festivity.

4. Each time we cause particles to collide at ever-increasing energies, new constituents are created and investigated. It is as if we continue to peel back the layers of an onion only to find more layers that invite exploration. In the modern era, the field of string theory has been posited, theorizing that the vibrations of tiny string-like mechanisms provide the building blocks of all particles. From string theory, the idea of multiple universes has been proposed and evidence of this mind-blowing idea was reported in late 2015.

Which choice best states the function of the underlined sentence in the text as a whole?

(A) To use an analogy to illustrate a concept

(B) To describe the latest scientific evidence

(C) To make connections between physics and biology

(D) To express dismay at the state of modern science

5. *The following text is from Charles Dickens's 1861 novel* Great Expectations. *In the novel, Pip, a poor orphan who is cared for by his sister and her husband, meets the young girl who will become the lifetime object of his affections while simultaneously becoming aware of his lowly position in the caste system.*

I was very glad to get away [from Miss Havisham's house]. My coarse hands and my common boots had never troubled me before; but they troubled me now, and I determined to ask Joe why he had taught me to call those picture cards Jacks which ought to be called knaves.

The selection from the novel highlights Pip's feeling

(A) a sense of belonging.

(B) a need to show off.

(C) out of place.

(D) ready to argue.

6. For better or for worse, our culture of *germophobia* was hard won by its proponents. From the time it was first proposed in the sixteenth century, the germ theory of disease faced three hundred years' worth of influential naysayers, and it was not until the late 1800s that the theory began to gain the pervasive public vindication it enjoys today. However, an emerging body of research indicates that we have been perhaps overzealous in our crusade to eradicate the germs that live within us.

The text above most directly serves to

(A) articulate that while society has now embraced germ theory, taking the theory too far may be detrimental.

(B) argue that germophobia has continued to be a major obstacle to scientific progress.

(C) point out the shortcomings of germ theory by presenting the valid concerns of germophobics.

(D) present the many ways that germ theory has concrete applications to everyday life.

7. **Text 1**

I saw you from across the room, and I knew immediately. My pulse began to race; I started to sweat; I could barely breathe. From the first moment that I laid eyes on you, I was convinced that you were the one. On our first date, the chemistry was obvious. We laughed and smiled and held hands and talked for hours. I couldn't sleep or eat or even pay attention at work. I just had to be with you.

Text 2

Within one-fifth of a second, your physical appearance and body language caused an excessive release of dopamine in my brain creating feelings of excitement and happiness. We made eye contact for 8.2 seconds; your pheromones were indistinguishable from my mother's. Then, your voice triggered my brain mechanism for generating long-term attachment. Once vasopressin and oxytocin reached my receptors, I knew that I could never be without you.

The different perspectives represented by the first and second texts are generally described as what, respectively?

(A) Ethical, scientific
(B) Trivial, important
(C) Authentic, misguided
(D) Subjective, objective

8. **Text 1**

If you have a driver's license, I expect that you are aware that this is the process by which one registers as an organ donor (at least in most states). Yet, it may surprise you that only 40 percent of American adults have registered; that's only two out of every five. This statistic is particularly jarring when it is contrasted with another: 95 percent of Americans strongly support organ donation (according to a 2005 Gallup poll). That is every nineteen out of twenty people, which is a figure that positively dwarfs the number who have registered.

Text 2

Contrary to tabloid sensationalism, no organ donor has ever been declared dead prematurely; donors are subject to more post-mortem testing than non-donors just to ensure that this scenario never occurs. Thus, you are far more likely to be buried alive as a non-donor than to be declared dead as a donor.

The argument presented in Text 2 could be best used to explain which portion of Text 1?

(A) That the driver's license is the primary way by which one can register to become an organ donor
(B) That premature burial is a major safety concern for most American adults
(C) That most states record one's willingness to become an organ donor through official government documents
(D) That 95 percent of Americans support organ donation, while only 40 percent are registered as organ donors

9. The third step of glycolysis involves the the hormonally-controlled phosphorylation of fructose-6-phosphate into fructose-1, 6-bisphosphate. When glucose is abundant, pancreatic insulin induces the forward glycolytic catalysis of this reaction, allowing the production of fructose-1, 6-bisphosphate, which in turn is cleaved into glyceraldehyde-3-phosphate and dihydroxyacetone phosphate. When glucose is scarce, pancreatic glucagon blocks glycolysis, and induces the gluconeogenic production of fructose-6-phosphate, which is subsequently isomerized into glucose-6-phosphate, and released into the blood.

According to the text, bodily regulation of glucose levels is best described as

(A) artificial.
(B) dynamic.
(C) arbitrary.
(D) static.

10. *The following is an excerpt from Jane Austen's* Mansfield Park *(1814). The novel's protagonist, Fanny Price, returns home after many years of living with her wealthy relatives at Mansfield Park.*

William was gone: and the home he had left her in was—Fanny could not conceal it from herself—in almost every respect the very reverse of what she could have wished. . . . On her father, her confidence had not been sanguine, but he was more negligent of his family, his habits were worse, and his manners coarser, than she had been prepared for.

He did not want abilities; but he had no curiosity, and no information beyond his profession; he read only the newspaper and the navy-list; he talked only of the dockyard, the harbor, Spithead, and the Motherbank; he swore and he drank, he was dirty and gross. She had never been able to recall anything approaching to tenderness in his former treatment of herself. There had remained only a general impression of roughness and loudness; and now he scarcely ever noticed her.

The text characterizes Fanny's father's intellectual interests as

(A) relevant and interesting.
(B) coarse and joking.
(C) overly pragmatic.
(D) arrogantly erudite.

11. A biologist attempts to determine the cause of evolutionary divergence among the populations of a frog found in the Amazonian rain forest. Based on her observations, the biologist supports the *riverine barrier* hypothesis, claiming that dispersion across opposite riverbanks is responsible for the observed differences in the frogs. She notes that the width, depth, and water speed of the rivers form an obstacle that makes it extremely challenging for the frogs to cross.

Which finding, if true, would most undermine the biologist's hypothesis?

(A) Discovery of increased industrial pollutants in one branch of the Amazon River system
(B) Presence of fish and snakes that prey on this species of frog in large portions of the river
(C) Observation of present-day mating of this frog by specimens from opposite riverbanks
(D) The popularity of tourist activities in the river system, including cruises and fishing expeditions

12.

Number of Universities Offering Folklore Degrees / Concentrations

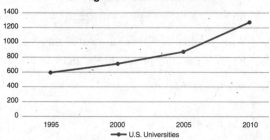

A social scientist would like to make a statement to demonstrate the increasing interest in folklore scholarship. Which statement would be best supported by the information in the graph?

(A) If the number of universities offering folklore degrees and concentrations increases between 2010 and 2015 at the same rate as it did between 2000 and 2005, there will be approximately 2,000 schools in 2015 that offer such programs.

(B) If the number of universities offering folklore degrees and concentrations increases between 2010 and 2015 at the same rate as it did between 1995 and 2005, there will be approximately 1,800 schools in 2015 that offer such programs.

(C) If the number of universities offering folklore degrees and concentrations increases between 2010 and 2015 at the same rate as it did between 2005 and 2010, there will be approximately 1,700 schools in 2015 that offer such programs.

(D) If the number of universities offering folklore degrees and concentrations increases at the same rate between 2010 and 2015 as it did between 1995 and 2010, there will be approximately 1,400 schools in 2015 that offer such programs.

13. In 1812, U.S. president James Madison declared war on the British Empire. There was a variety of reasons for the declaration: British-U.S. relations were strained by England's attempts to thwart international trade between the U.S. and France—with whom the British were already at war—and on several occasions the Royal Navy had endeavored to conscript American sailors by force. However, perhaps no cause for war was more compelling in the U.S. than the desire to expand the nation into the northern territories of modern-day Ontario and modern-day Quebec, which were still British colonies at the time.

It can be reasonably inferred that the author of the text would argue that the most significant motivation for U.S. citizens who wanted to go to war with Canada in the early 1800s was

(A) vengeance towards the British.

(B) territorial ambitions.

(C) the continued capture of American sailors.

(D) defense against Native American incursions.

14. The primary problem with deriving major amounts of dietary sugar directly from fructose rather than from starch lies in the fact that the degradation of fructose—which, upon entry into the cell, is split immediately into dihydroxyacetone phosphate and glyceraldehyde—completely bypasses the first four steps of glycolysis, including the most critical regulatory reaction in the entire process. Thus, how our bodies handle the usage of fructose is utterly dissociated from the hormonal controls of insulin and glucagon, which, over time, invariably predisposes one to obesity, diabetes mellitus, and a host of other dangerous metabolic disorders. The long-term consumption of fructose will lead to _____

Which choice most logically completes the text?

(A) an increasingly well-regulated hormonal balance.

(B) a significant increase in neurotoxins in the blood supply.

(C) a greater likelihood of developing health ailments.

(D) no significant changes to bodily processes.

15. The familiar, somewhat calligraphic anachronism that today we often refer to as "Old English" did not emerge until the twelfth century, around the time of the extinction of the Old English language. The Old English script or, more accurately, blackletter, is in reality not even English, but evolved in medieval universities along the Franco-German border as an efficient alternative to both the highly variable *insular* scripts of England and Ireland, and the consistent though cumbersome Carolingian miniscule of Christian monasteries.

The text suggests that the most significant problem with the insular scripts was what?

(A) They lacked consistency in their letterforms.

(B) They were elaborate and time-consuming.

(C) They were isolated in England and Ireland.

(D) They were only used in Christian monasteries.

16. So, I hope everyone will take heed of this important announcement: "Citizens of the world: *Relax.*" Go on vacation more _____.

Which choice completes the text so that it conforms to the conventions of Standard English?

(A) frequently

(B) frequent

(C) regular

(D) numerous

17. When the skin and the natural flora are compromised and not strong enough to fight off the attack, the body's second line of

_____

Which choice completes the text so that it conforms to the conventions of Standard English?

(A) defense—the innate immune system—kicks in.

(B) defense—the innate immune system, kicks in.

(C) defense the innate immune system—kicks in.

(D) defense the innate immune system; kicks in.

18. Though we can only speculate on its use among preliterate peoples, some historical anthropologists have suggested that the bullroarer's ubiquity across the world's ancient cultures suggests that _____ primary function must have been practical rather than ritual.

Which choice completes the text so that it conforms to the conventions of Standard English?

(A) its

(B) it's

(C) its'

(D) their

2   2   2

19. Once completely oblivious of the damages to the environment caused by pollution, waste, and overpopulation, the world _____ to look seriously upon the depletion of our natural resources. Whether we scrutinize the harmful exhaust gases that pollute our air—carbon dioxide, sulfur dioxide, ammonia, among others—or turn to deforestation and chemical effluents, the situation is clearly out of control.

Which choice completes the text so that it conforms to the conventions of Standard English?

(A) had now began
(B) has now began
(C) has now begun
(D) have now begun

20. Technology and its _____ on all areas of the job market are tedious subjects for the student and young professional.

Which choice completes the text so that it conforms to the conventions of Standard English?

(A) endless affects
(B) endless effects
(C) endlessly affects
(D) endlessly effects

21. Because emission spectra are unique to each element and constant throughout the universe, scientists are able to attach a spectrometer to a telescope, locate a celestial body, and

_____

Which choice completes the text so that it conforms to the conventions of Standard English?

(A) determine, the chemical composition of that body simply, by comparing the resulting spectrum to those of known compounds on Earth.
(B) determine the chemical composition, of that body simply by comparing, the resulting spectrum to those of known compounds on Earth.
(C) determine the chemical composition of that body simply by comparing the resulting spectrum to those of known compounds on Earth.
(D) determine the chemical composition of that body, simply by comparing the resulting spectrum to those of known, compounds on Earth.

22. The oldest known bullroarers were discovered in the Ukraine and are estimated to date from the Paleolithic era, approximately 17,000 B.C.E, but slightly more recent bullroarers have been discovered at archeological sites on every continent _____ Antarctica.

Which choice completes the text so that it conforms to the conventions of Standard English?

(A) apart of
(B) a part of
(C) apart from
(D) a part from

23. Here are three easy ways that we ballet dancers can improve bone mineral density. First, we're athletes. Ensure you are eating enough to fuel a professional athlete. Focus on foods high in calcium and vitamin D. It's not all dairy—seeds, canned fish, beans, lentils, almonds, and leafy greens are also great choices. _____ get your vitamin D level checked. Vitamin D is needed for calcium absorption and almost 42 percent of adults are deficient. Third, go outside. We spend a lot of time in the studio, but sun exposure is a great way to get some more vitamin D. On a break, head outside, roll up your tights and enjoy a little bit of sun.

    Which choice completes the text with the most logical transition?

    (A) Nonetheless,
    (B) Second,
    (C) In contrast,
    (D) Finally,

24. Dark matter—unobserved material inferred to exist by its quantifiable gravitational effect on visible galaxies—is estimated to comprise roughly 23 percent of the universe by density. Visible atoms, _____ , constitute less than 5 percent.

    Which choice completes the text with the most logical transition?

    (A) meanwhile
    (B) as a result
    (C) due to this fact
    (D) precisely

25. Some will contend that the true problem of retro-synthesis lies not in the end-products, but rather in the byproducts and novel synthetic intermediates required to artificially reproduce biochemical compounds. It must be acknowledged that this is indeed a valid concern. The design of stable synthetic intermediates not found in nature has at times led to unforeseen consequences. Methylenedioxymethamphetamine, _____ is a dangerous and highly concerning drug of abuse among youth.

    Which choice completes the text with the most logical transition?

    (A) on the other hand,
    (B) in contrast,
    (C) for example,
    (D) due to this,

26. If you've ever been in the Central or Eastern U.S. around dusk in late summer, you've probably witnessed a peculiar biological phenomenon—all around long, languorous insects begin to appear, with abdomens emitting a flickering, yellow-green glow. These insects, commonly known as "fireflies" or "lightning bugs", produce their glow in a process called bioluminescence. _____ the firefly is perhaps the most familiar species that emits its own light, bioluminescence has been discovered in varieties of fungi, fish, coral, squid, and even a bacterium that lives in elephant mucus.

    Which choice completes the text with the most logical transition?

    (A) When
    (B) For
    (C) Although
    (D) Given

27. While researching a topic, a student has taken the following notes:

- In the United States, people who have been detained by the police have a right to swiftly appear before the court to determine whether the detention is valid.
- This right is known as the writ of "habeas corpus," a Latin phrase that translates as "you should have the body."
- This right prevents people who are being detained from disappearing into a jail or prison without due process of the law.
- Habeas corpus was first set as a right in the Magna Carta, one of the founding documents of the English systems of laws.
- This right today is an important check on the power of police and governments.

The student wants to suggest a possible negative consequence of not having a policy requiring habeas corpus in place. Which choice most effectively uses relevant information from the notes to accomplish this goal?

(A) If the right of habeas corpus were suspended, prisons and jails would be overrun with criminals in an unsafe and unsanitary manner.

(B) While some may want to remove the right to habeas corpus, they should keep in mind what the Magna Carta says about human dignity.

(C) Without the right of habeas corpus, those who are detained could disappear into jail without a proper legal process.

(D) If the United States removed the right to habeas corpus, other countries, like England, may follow its moral lead.

3   3   3

SECTION 2: MATH MODULE 1

35 MINUTES, 22 QUESTIONS

- All expressions and variables use real numbers.
- All figures are drawn to scale.
- Every figure lies in a plane.
- The domain of given functions is the set of all real numbers for which the corresponding value of the function is real.

For **multiple-choice questions**, solve the problem and pick the correct answer from the provided choices. Each multiple-choice question has only one correct answer.

For **student-produced response questions**, solve each problem and enter your answer following these guidelines:

- If you find **more than one correct answer**, enter just one answer.
- You can enter up to five characters for a **positive** answer and up to six characters (this includes the negative sign) for a **negative** answer.
- If your answer is a **fraction** that does not fit in the given spaces, enter the decimal equivalent instead.
- If your answer is a **decimal** that does not fit in the given spaces, enter it by stopping at or rounding up at the fourth digit.
- If your answer is a **mixed number** (like $4\frac{1}{2}$), enter it as an improper fraction (9/2) or its decimal equivalent (4.5).
- Do not enter **symbols** like a comma, dollar sign, or percent sign.

Examples

Answer	Acceptable Entries	Unacceptable Entries That Will Receive Zero Credit
4.5	4.5 4.50 9/2	41/2 4 1/2
$\frac{8}{9}$	8/9 .8888 .8889 0.888 0.889	0.8 .88 0.88 0.89
$-\frac{1}{9}$	−1/9 −.1111 −0.111	−.11 −0.11

3 3 3

1. $3x + 2 = \frac{4}{3}x$

What is the value of x in the above equation?

(A) $-\frac{6}{5}$

(B) $-\frac{2}{3}$

(C) $\frac{1}{4}$

(D) $\frac{5}{6}$

2. A roller coaster requires riders to be at least 48 inches tall. Given that there are approximately 2.54 centimeters in an inch, how tall must a rider be to the nearest whole <u>centimeter</u> to ride the roller coaster?

3. A bus is travelling at a constant rate of 50 miles per hour. At this rate, how far will the bus travel in $3\frac{1}{4}$ hours?

(A) 150 miles

(B) 160 miles

(C) 162.5 miles

(D) 175.5 miles

4. Which of the following is a solution to the equation below?

$$(x - 3)^2 - 81 = 0$$

(A) 12

(B) 11

(C) 9

(D) 8

5. A typist has already typed 3,500 words of a document. How many total words, $W(t)$, of the document will he have typed if he can type 70 words per minute and types for an additional t minutes?

(A) $W(t) = 3,500t$

(B) $W(t) = 70t - 3500$

(C) $W(t) = 3,500t + 70$

(D) $W(t) = 3,500 + 70t$

6. $6a^2 + 8ab - 4ac$ is equivalent to which of the following expressions?

(A) $a(3a + 4b + 2c)$

(B) $2a(3a + 4b - 2c)$

(C) $4a(a + b - 2c)$

(D) $2a(3a - 4b + 2c)$

7. The expression $\left(\frac{2}{3}x + 1\right)\left(\frac{3}{4}x - 1\right) = ?$

(A) $\frac{1}{6}x^2 - \frac{1}{3}x + 1$

(B) $\frac{1}{4}x^2 + \frac{1}{12}x - 4$

(C) $\frac{1}{2}x^2 + \frac{1}{12}x - 1$

(D) $x^2 + \frac{1}{4}x - 1$

8.

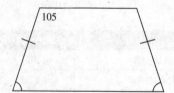

In the isosceles trapezoid above, what is the measure of the smallest interior angle?

$\boxed{3}$ $\boxed{3}$ $\boxed{3}$

9. If $\frac{x}{4} = \frac{1}{2}$, then $\frac{4(x-3)}{(-12)}$ equals which of the following?

(A) $\frac{1}{16}$

(B) $\frac{1}{12}$

(C) $\frac{1}{6}$

(D) $\frac{1}{3}$

10. On a particular college campus, there are two men for every three women. If the total number of men and women on campus is equal to 4,000, how many more women are there on campus than men?

11. When $x > 0$, which of these expressions is equivalent to $\dfrac{1}{\frac{1}{2x}} + \dfrac{3}{\frac{6}{4x}}$?

(A) $4x$

(B) $7x$

(C) $\frac{1}{2}x - 4$

(D) $x^2 - 12$

12. A coffee shop recorded data on the types of beverages ordered by its patrons in a given month. Each patron visited only once during the month and purchased only one beverage, and the four listed beverages are the only ones sold at this coffee shop.

	Cappuccino	Espresso	Latte	Americano	Total
Females under 18	230	125	325	170	850
Males under 18	170	185	240	220	815
Females age 18 and older	425	328	530	290	1,573
Males age 18 and older	350	429	477	313	1,569
Total	1,175	1,067	1,572	993	4,807

What (approximate) percentage of the drinks purchased at the coffee shop in the given month were espresso beverages?

(A) 11%

(B) 17%

(C) 22%

(D) 36%

3   3   3

13. At what point in the *x-y* coordinate plane will the functions $y = 4x - 3$ and $y = -\frac{1}{2}x + 2$ intersect?

(A) $\left(2, -\frac{2}{3}\right)$

(B) $\left(-\frac{3}{4}, \frac{5}{6}\right)$

(C) $\left(\frac{10}{9}, \frac{13}{9}\right)$

(D) $\left(1, \frac{3}{7}\right)$

14. David has two quarters (25 cents each) for every five dimes (10 cents each) in his change dish, with no other coins present. If he has a total of $2 in coins in the dish, how many total coins does he have?

15. The value of money is affected by the inflation rate—the higher the inflation rate, the less valuable money will become over time. The rate of inflation is calculated using the formula below, in which CPI represents the Consumer Price Index, a measure of the average of a typical basket of consumer goods and services (where goods and services are weighted relative to how often they are purchased by a normal consumer):

$$\frac{\text{This Year's CPI} - \text{Last Year's CPI}}{\text{Last Year's CPI}} \times 100$$

The current rate of inflation would *definitely* be zero if the CPI a year ago equaled which of the following?

(A) The CPI a year from now
(B) This year's CPI
(C) Zero
(D) 100

16. A line has the equation $y - 4x = 5$. What is the slope of a line that is perpendicular to this line?

(A) -4

(B) $-\frac{1}{4}$

(C) $\frac{5}{4}$

(D) 4

17.

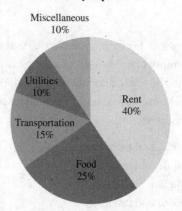

Monthly Expenses

The percentages of Anita's monthly expenses are portrayed in the above chart. If Anita spent $600 on rent, what was the total of her other expenses for the month?

(A) $600
(B) $900
(C) $1200
(D) $1400

3   3   3

18.

Average Number of Hours of Nightly Sleep

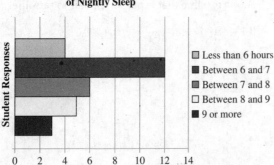

In the above histogram, the distribution of the number of hours of sleep per night as self-reported by thirty students is recorded. Which of the following values would be equal for the above set of values?

(A) Mean and median
(B) Mode and mean
(C) Median and mode
(D) Mean and range

19. An equilateral triangle has a side length of 6 centimeters. What is the area of the equilateral triangle?

(A) 4
(B) $3\sqrt{2}$
(C) $9\sqrt{3}$
(D) $12\sqrt{3}$

20. A wall's width is two-thirds that of its length. If paint to be used to cover the entire wall costs $12 per gallon, and one gallon of paint will cover 60 square feet, what expression gives the cost of the paint (assuming one can purchase partial and full gallons) to cover such a wall that is L feet long?

(A) $\text{Cost} = L^2$
(B) $\text{Cost} = \frac{1}{5}L^2$
(C) $\text{Cost} = \frac{2}{15}L^2$
(D) $\text{Cost} = \frac{3}{64}L^2$

21. An animal shelter can house only cats and dogs. Each dog requires 2 cups of food and three treats a day, while each cat requires 1 cup of food a day and 2 treats a day. If the shelter has a total of 400 cups of food and 500 treats a day, what expressions portray the full scope of the number of c cats and d dogs the shelter could potentially house?

(A) $2d - c \le 400$ and $3d + c < 500$
(B) $2d + c \le 400$ and $3d + 2c \le 500$
(C) $4d + c < 400$ and $d + c < 500$
(D) $2d + 2c \le 400$ and $2d + 3c \le 500$

22.

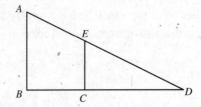

Note: Figure not drawn to scale

In the figure above, both angles ABC and ECD are 90 degrees. If the area of triangle ECD is 20 square inches, the length of EC is 4 inches, and the length of BC is 8 inches, what is the area of triangle ABD?

(A) 32.4 square inches
(B) 64.8 square inches
(C) 320 square inches
(D) 640 square inches

4   4   4

SECTION 2: MATH MODULE 2

35 MINUTES, 22 QUESTIONS

1. What are the solution(s) to the following equation?

   $$5x^2 - 15x + 10 = 0$$

   (A) 0
   (B) 1, 2
   (C) 1, 4
   (D) 2, 5

2. At what x values would the function $y = x(x - 5)(x + 2)$ intersect the x axis?

   (A) −10
   (B) 0, 3, 12
   (C) 2, −5
   (D) 0, 5, −2

3. The function f is given by $f(x) = 2 - |x - 4|$. For what value of x does the function f achieve its maximum value?

   (A) 2
   (B) 4
   (C) 5
   (D) 6

4. If $(x^2)^{\frac{1}{5}} + \sqrt[5]{32x^2} = ax^{\frac{2}{5}}$ for all values of x, what is the value of a?

   (A) 0
   (B) 3
   (C) 5
   (D) 16

5. What is the x coordinate of the minimum of the parabola with the equation $y + 17 = 6x^2 + 12x$?

   (A) −1
   (B) 0
   (C) 2
   (D) 3

6. Given that (x, y) is a solution to the following system of equations, what is the sum of x and y?

   $$2x - y = 3$$
   $$4y = 6x$$

7. Given that $x \neq 0$, find the value of

   $$\left(\frac{2x^4 + 3(2x^2)^2}{x^4} \right)^2$$

8. Which of the following expressions is equivalent to $7 - 2(y - 1)$?

   (A) $9 - 2y$
   (B) $5 - 2y$
   (C) $6 - 2y$
   (D) $4 + 2y$

9. The table below gives the results of a survey of a randomly selected sample of 400 fifteen- and sixteen-year olds. Each respondent selected the method of electronic communication that he or she used the most.

Primary Method of Electronic Communication

	Texting	E-mail	Video Chatting	Other	Total
15-year-olds	110	20	40	30	200
16-year-olds	85	45	30	40	200
Total	195	x	70	70	400

The table omitted the value for x in the bottom row. Based on the structure of the table, what should its value be?

(A) 24
(B) 38
(C) 57
(D) 65

10.

Average Monthly Temperature Degrees Fahrenheit

— Townsville
— Cityberg

The average monthly temperatures for the cities of Townsville and Cityberg were recorded in the last calendar year. Based on the graph, which statement is true?

(A) The temperature on a randomly selected day in Townsville will be greater than the temperature on a randomly selected day in Cityberg.
(B) The temperature on a randomly selected day in Cityberg will be greater than the temperature on a randomly selected day in Townsville.

(C) The average monthly temperature in Townsville was greater than the average monthly temperature in Cityberg for the majority of the year.
(D) The average monthly temperature in Cityberg was greater than the average monthly temperature in Townsville for the majority of the year.

11. If the sale price on a coat is $72, and the original price of the coat was $90, what is the percent discount from this sale?

(A) 14%
(B) 20%
(C) 26%
(D) 80%

12. A chef is making cookies from scratch. He requires a set period of time to gather the ingredients and get everything set up to make the cookies, and then needs a set period of time to make each individual cookie. If c represents the total number of cookies he is making, and t represents the total amount of time it takes to make c cookies, what is the meaning of the 20 in this equation: $t = 20 + 10c$?

(A) How much time it takes to make each individual cookie
(B) The fixed cost of the cookie ingredients
(C) The maximum number of cookies he can make in 10 minutes time
(D) The amount of time it takes him to set things up prior to making a cookie

13. Jasmine has $100,000 in an investment portfolio, divided among only the categories of stocks, bonds, and cash. She has twice as much invested in stocks as she does in bonds, and three times as much invested in bonds as she has in cash. What percent of her portfolio is invested in bonds?

(A) 22%
(B) 27%
(C) 30%
(D) 44%

4   4   4

14. The formula for electric power, P, is $P = I \times V$, where I is the current, and V is the voltage. The formula for voltage is $V = I \times R$, where I is also the current, and R is the resistance. How will the power of a given current be affected if the resistance is doubled and the voltage quadrupled?

(A) It will be doubled.
(B) It will be quadrupled.
(C) It will be 8 times greater.
(D) It will be 16 times greater.

15.

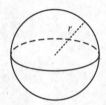

Which of the following expressions would be equivalent to the diameter of the sphere portrayed above, with a radius of r and volume V?

(A) $2\sqrt[3]{\dfrac{3V}{4\pi}}$

(B) πr^3

(C) $4\sqrt{\dfrac{2r^3}{3}}$

(D) $\dfrac{4V^3}{3r^2}$

16. Caitlin opens a checking account to set aside spending money for vacations. Each month she puts the same dollar amount, $50, in the account. Unfortunately, she does not expect to be able to take a vacation at any point in the foreseeable future. What would best describe the relationship between the number of months and the total amount of money in the account?

(A) A linear relationship, with the line of the relationship having a negative slope
(B) A linear relationship, with the line of the relationship having a positive slope
(C) An exponentially increasing relationship
(D) An inverse exponential relationship

17. Which of the following is an equivalent form of $\dfrac{(7x - 7)(7x + 7)}{7}$?

(A) $x^2 - 1$

(B) $49x^2 + 7$

(C) $7(x^2 - 1)$

(D) $\dfrac{(x^2 - 7)}{7}$

18.

Refrigerant ABC: Pressure in Pounds per Square Inch for a Given Temperature

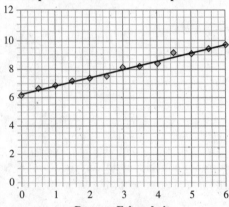

Degrees Fahrenheit

◇ Pressure in Pounds per Square Inch
— Linear (Pressure in Pounds per Square Inch)

A refrigerant manufacturer recorded the pressure associated with certain temperatures in a refrigerator using its new refrigerant, ABC. What would best approximate the equation of the best-fit line portrayed by the data in this graph, using P for pressure and T for temperature (using the same units as portrayed in the graph)?

(A) $P = 0.5T + 6.5$
(B) $P = T + 6.5$
(C) $P = 0.5T - 3$
(D) $P = 7T + 5$

19. A certain cube has edges of length L inches, surface area of A square inches, and volume of B cubic inches. For what value of L would $A = B$?

20. If (a, b) is a solution to the system of equations below, what is the value of a?

$$2a - \frac{1}{2}b = 4$$
$$3a + b = 6$$

21. A currency conversion store at an airport in New York City posts the following conversion rate table:

Currency Type	Currency per 1 U.S. Dollar
U.S. dollar	1.00
Euro	0.90
Indian rupee	68.01
South African rand	16.17
Japanese yen	116.36
Australian dollar	1.41

The conversion store charges 1 percent of the amount converted, plus a $2 flat fee for each total transaction (including multiple-currency exchanges, so long as they take place in a single visit to the store. The fee is assessed *in addition* to the 1 percent conversion fee).

Suppose a customer wanted to see the conversion rate, before doing a transaction with any associated fees, of U.S. dollars to Australian dollars. What is the conversion rate of U.S. dollars to one Australian dollar to the nearest hundredth?

22. Consider the function $f(x) = 2x - 3$. What is the range of the absolute value of this function?

(A) $y < -3$
(B) $y \leq 0$
(C) $y \geq 0$
(D) $y > 5$

ANSWER KEY
Practice Test 1

Reading and Writing Module 1

1. A	8. D	15. A	22. A
2. C	9. B	16. A	23. A
3. D	10. A	17. C	24. B
4. A	11. A	18. C	25. C
5. B	12. B	19. D	26. C
6. B	13. D	20. B	27. B
7. A	14. B	21. A	

Reading and Writing Module 2

1. A	8. D	15. A	22. C
2. C	9. B	16. A	23. B
3. A	10. C	17. A	24. A
4. A	11. C	18. A	25. C
5. C	12. C	19. C	26. C
6. A	13. B	20. B	27. C
7. D	14. C	21. C	

Math Module 1

1. A	7. C	13. C	19. C
2. 122	8. 75	14. 14	20. C
3. C	9. D	15. B	21. B
4. A	10. 800	16. B	22. B
5. D	11. A	17. B	
6. B	12. C	18. C	

Math Module 2

1. B	7. 196	13. C	19. 6
2. D	8. A	14. C	20. 2
3. B	9. D	15. A	21. 0.71
4. B	10. C	16. B	22. C
5. A	11. B	17. C	
6. 15	12. D	18. A	

Digital PSAT Scoring Chart

This will give you an approximation of the score you would earn on the Digital PSAT[1]. Tally the number of correct answers from the Reading & Writing section (out of 54) and the Math section (out of 44). Take the total for each of these and find the corresponding section score in the tables below.

Number of correct reading and writing questions (out of 54)	Reading and writing test score (out of 760)
0	160
1	170
2	180
3	190
4	200
5	210
6	220
7	230
8	240
9	250
10	260
11	270
12	290
13	300
14	310
15	320
16	340
17	350
18	360
19	370
20	390
21	400
22	420
23	430
24	450
25	460
26	470

[1] Keep in mind that some of the questions on an actual SAT test will be research questions that will not count towards your actual score. For the sake of simplicity, we are including possible research questions in your calculation.

Number of correct reading and writing questions (out of 54)	Reading and writing test score (out of 760)
27	480
28	490
29	500
30	510
31	520
32	530
33	540
34	550
35	560
36	570
37	580
38	590
39	600
40	610
41	620
42	630
43	640
44	650
45	660
46	670
47	680
48	690
49	700
50	710
51	720
52	730
53	750
54	760

Number of Correct Math Questions (Out of 44)	Math Section Score (Out of 760)
0	160
1	180
2	190
3	200
4	210
5	240
6	260
7	280
8	300
9	310
10	320
11	340
12	350
13	360
14	370
15	390
16	400
17	410
18	420
19	440
20	450
21	460
22	470
23	480
24	490
25	500
26	510
27	520
28	530
29	540
30	550
31	560
32	570
33	580

Number of Correct Math Questions (Out of 44)	Math Section Score (Out of 760)
34	590
35	610
36	620
37	640
38	650
39	660
40	680
41	710
42	730
43	750
44	760

Add the Reading and Writing score and the Math section score to find your total PSAT test score:

_____ Reading and Writing score +

_____ Math section score =

_____ **Total PSAT test score (between 320 and 1520)**

Approximate your testing percentiles (1st–99th) using this chart:

Total Score	Section Score	Total Percentile	Reading and Writing Percentile	Math Percentile
1520	760	99+	99+	99
1420	710	98	98	96
1320	660	94	94	91
1220	610	86	86	84
1120	560	74	73	75
1020	510	59	57	61
920	460	41	40	42
820	410	25	24	27
720	360	11	11	15
620	310	3	3	5
520	260	1	1	1
420	210	1	1	1
320	160	1	1	1

Scoring data based on information at Collegeboard.org

Answer Explanations

Section 1: Reading and Writing Module 1

1. **(A)** The author explains this line in the following sentences, stating that a majority of borrowers defaulted and the houses' values plummeted, so (A) is the correct choice. The line doesn't refer to actual physical destruction or construction as in (B) and (C). Similarly, we know values greatly fell, making (D) incorrect.

2. **(C)** *Cosseted* makes the most sense here since one of its definitions is "to cuddle or caress lovingly." Choices (A), (B), and (D) can be eliminated because, although they are ways David may treat the dog, they are not reflective of his hugging the animal to his chest.

3. **(D)** The transliterated text presented in the text shows that there is not a clear ending to the story, making *ambiguous* the best option. The other choices would all indicate much more decisive outcomes.

4. **(A)** Before the underlined sentence, it states that there are endless changes to the recommended foods and beverages people should consume. The underlined sentence gives the specific example of coffee, since recommendations have fluctuated over the years as far as its healthiness. This aligns with choice (A) since it is providing a specific instance to illustrate a broader point. It is not (B), because it is not suggesting further research but summarizing the changes in recent opinions. It is not (C), because it is not directly mentioning a healthy dietary recommendation. It is not (D), because coffee is not defined and is likely familiar to readers.

5. **(B)** In the text, Reagan quotes an American worker to illustrate the incongruity of the hourly wage. Since *anecdotal* means an "account based on personal story or experience," (B) is accurate. These lines specifically do not contain *statistics* or address a counterargument. Moreover, choice (C) is wrong because rather than separating them, Reagan uses facts directly after the quote to support the personal testimony.

6. **(B)** Based on Text 2, Donald Hebb argues that nature and nurture are fundamentally interwoven—you can't have one without the other, just like you can't have the length of a rectangle without its width. So, Hebb would most likely disapprove of the description of the topic in Text 1 since it presents it as a two-sided argument. He is unlikely to appreciate this argument, since it does not suggest the possibility of compromise. Choice (C) is too negative, and choice (D) is unsupported since there is no scholarly research presented in Text 1.

7. **(A)** In Text 1, Franklin mentions "obtaining little anecdotes" about his ancestors. The consistent theme in Washington's text is a thirst to know his roots. The ability to obtain such anecdotes would assist him in his quest for knowledge, so choice (A) is the correct answer. Choice (B) is flawed in that Washington is already writing an autobiography, or memoir. Washington makes no reference to children, as in choice (C), or to wishing to relive his life, as in choice (D).

8. **(D)** Text 4 discusses the contributions engineers have made to making life more enjoyable, specifically in the daily areas of "communications, computing, and sports." Hence, (D) is right. The author is not discussing engineering specifically as a career, ruling out (A). (C) is incorrect because the author is considering how engineers from varying fields have impacted communications and sports, rather than focusing on two types of engineers. Choice (B) is

tempting, but the author's purpose is to show how entirely engineers have impacted certain aspects of daily life, not to illustrate how human life would go extinct without them.

9. **(B)** The text states that the prevalence of parliamentary rule is connected to "the legacy of the British Empire," so the answer is (B). Choice (A) is an aspect of presidential rule. (C) and (D), although features of a parliamentary system, are not stated as reasons for its popularity.

10. **(A)** In this graph, "green" takes up 10% while "brown" takes up 60%. Therefore, the ratio is 1:6 or one-sixth.

11. **(A)** The question asks you to find a quote that illustrates that Mount Monadnock has an impressive size relative to the other features of the landscape. Choice (A) states that the mountain is "dominating all the little lesser hills which compass thee," indicating that it is indeed of an impressive size compared to the features surrounding it. The other options do not compare the mountain to the size of the features around it.

12. **(B)** The text states that the "zone with the largest diameter typically signifies that it will be the best at fighting infection." Under the *E. coli* column (2nd column), ciprofloxacin has the largest diameter at 17 mm. It would therefore be the most effective antibiotic in this particular instance, as in choice (B). Vancomycin would be the most effective medication against *S. aureus*, not against *E. coli*. Amoxicillin is the second most effective. Not only is there no data on *Staphylococcus*, but it also is actually a bacterial strain and not an antibiotic.

13. **(D)** The previous examples are of workers who are able to work from home, accomplishing home-based tasks during the workday. Therefore, ending the sentence with *staying at home during the workday* would be most logical. The other options do not relate to at-home work.

14. **(B)** The text states that the boss had intended to hire another man, but, upon finding Jurgis, decided that he would do instead. Really, it seems, *anyone* would do. This is most consistent with choice (B). Workers are *disposable*—they are "easily replaceable, used until they have nothing left and then discarded in favor of someone new." *Skillful*, *valuable*, and *interesting* all convey much more respect for the employees than the supervisor demonstrates.

15. **(A)** *Do* is numerically consistent with the plural subject "roles." Choice (B), *does*, is singular. Choice (C), *don't*, causes a double negative given the "not" that follows. Choice (D), *do's*, is not a word.

16. **(A)** This is the only choice that shows ownership by the singular city of Chicago of the City Council. Choices (B) and (D) do not show possession, and choice (C) shows plural possession.

17. **(C)** *To mock* is parallel with the earlier "to embody" in the sentence and concisely expresses the intended idea. Choices (A) and (B) are too wordy. Choice (D) is not parallel to the earlier phrasing.

18. **(C)** *Could've* sounds like *could of*, but it is short for *could have*. The use of the word *of* in this context is therefore incorrect, making choices (A) and (B) wrong. Choice (C) correctly expresses the verb *have*. Choice (D) makes the sentence *should have been still served*, which is nonsensical.

19. **(D)** This choice correctly places commas around the parenthetical phrase. Choice (A) has a comma at an awkward point, choice (B) lacks the necessary pauses, and choice (C) is too choppy.

20. **(B)** Mention of the Neanderthals at the beginning of the underlined portion is necessary to make a logical comparison with "our own ancestors." Choices (A) and (D) make illogical comparisons since they compare geographic regions to ancestors. Choice (C) has confusing word order at the end, placing *icebound* such that it literally means that the Neanderthals were icebound. Choice (B) puts things in a logical order and makes a logical comparison of people to Neanderthals.

21. **(A)** The dashes properly set aside a parenthetical phrase. Choice (B) does not work, since a complete sentence does not appear after the semicolon. Choice (C) interrupts the thought right in the middle. Choice (D) uses inconsistent punctuation on either side of the parenthetical phrase.

22. **(A)** The sentence is stating two things that do not happen, so stating "doesn't" in conjunction with *nor* makes sense. Choice (B) shows cause and effect. Choice (C) shows a direct connection between two ideas. Choice (D) shows contrast.

23. **(A)** This is the only option to provide the needed contrast between the relatively recent origin of the periodic table and its ancient inspiration.

24. **(B)** "Critical acclaim" involves recognition by other professionals, often through awards. The fact that *Spirited Away* received an Oscar would best illustrate its critical acclaim. The other options relate to other information presented in the notes, but not to critical acclaim.

25. **(C)** "As" conveys a cause-and-effect relationship between Franklin's suggestion and the reason for his suggestion. The other options do not show a cause-and-effect relationship.

26. **(C)** "In fact" leads into the clarification that antibiotics should not be eliminated—the other options would not convey clarification.

27. **(B)** The student wants to highlight the impact that national transportation infrastructure changes had on helping bonanza farms develop—emphasizing how the railroad tracks connected the farmers to faraway regions would accomplish this goal. The other options do not connect to the development of transportation infrastructure.

Section 1: Reading and Writing Module 2

1. **(A)** The sentence requires a word that signifies *to undertake* the adventure/*to embrace* the adventure. *Inspected* the adventure and *expected* the adventure do not communicate that meaning. *Excepted* means "excluded," and doesn't suit our purposes. *Accepted* is the best option.

2. **(C)** According to the text, the state of the country induces "stern duties," so *serious* is the correct choice. A country at war would not connect to anything playful. (B) is too negative. Choice (D) would inaccurately indicate that what's at stake is pointless.

3. **(A)** *Notoriety* refers to fame, so it is the correct choice. *Disreputability* is a close synonym, but it is associated with being well known for a bad deed, which makes it incorrect; although the disorders associated with erroneous hemoglobin may be infamous, hemoglobin itself is not. *Personage* refers specifically to a famous person. *Festivity* refers to a celebration.

4. **(A)** The best indication that this is an analogy is provided by the words "it is as if. . . ." *As* indicates that this is a simile, which is a type of analogy. The author uses the image of peeling an onion to make clearer the concept of physics discoveries of late: peel a layer (discover

something new) only to find that there are more layers (more discoveries yet to be found) beneath the layer just peeled. Choice (D) is incorrect in that the author is celebrating these discoveries, rather than lamenting them. Choice (C) is flawed in that the onion is used metaphorically rather than literally biologically. Choice (B) is flawed in that no new evidence is being *described;* it is merely being compared metaphorically to something else.

5. **(C)** These lines refer to Pip's leaving where he was. Here, he feels ill at ease and disquieted, becoming insecure with himself. The other options don't fit this mood accurately.

6. **(A)** The author suggests that we have been too adamant in our germophobia, making (A) correct. There is no evidence for (B). Choice (C) is contradictive because the valid concerns of germophobics would support rather than refute germ theory. Choice (D) would inaccurately indicate that the purpose of this text was to show the everyday instances of germ theory; in fact, this text gives a historical reminiscence of germ theory before positing the argument that the elimination of all germs is not necessarily the best approach to human health.

7. **(D)** The first text is very personal and emotional in its approach to describing love. The second takes a very scientific and factual approach to love. Since the first is not based on principles of morality, ethical is an inaccurate description. (B) takes an opinion on which basis is more significant, assuming an emotional, heartfelt description of love is trivial or foolish. (C) indicates that the technical approach is misguided. Thus, (D) is the only accurate choice. *Subjective* means "based on personal experience," while *objective* means "based on a representation of facts."

8. **(D)** Text 2 highlights how many people may feel a fear of being declared dead prematurely, which could dissuade them from wanting to be organ donors. This unfounded fear would go a long way in explaining why there would be such a disparity between those who support organ donation—95 percent of Americans—and those who are actually register to be organ donors—just 40 percent. It is not (A) or (C), because there is no focus on the procedure to become an organ donor in Text 2. It is not (B), because Text 1 does not suggest that premature burial is a major safety concern for most adults.

9. **(B)** The text discusses a step of glycolysis and how it works in tandem with the body's current levels of glucose. So, *dynamic*, or in a "state of constant activity and change," is appropriate. *Artificial* means "fake," while *arbitrary* means "random." *Static*, or "unchanging," is the opposite of *dynamic*.

10. **(C)** The text depicts Fanny's father as a man without ambition, curiosity, or knowledge "beyond his profession," making *overly pragmatic* the correct answer. *Pragmatic* means "practical and realistic, uninterested in ideas or theories," so her father's simplemindedness fits this description. She finds him dull rather than interesting as in (A). (B) describes his personality, but not his intellectual interests. And *erudite* means "cultured" or "well-educated," making (D) the opposite of Fanny's description of her father.

11. **(C)** To *undermine* would be to show the flaws with an argument. If present-day frogs mate with one another from across riverbanks, this would hurt the notion that the river poses a barrier to frog mating. It is not (A), because the presence of pollutants in one branch of the Amazon would not determine whether cross-river mating could occur throughout the river system. It is not (B), because that would add support to the biologist's hypothesis, since predators in the river would present another barrier to the frogs' crossing the river. It is not (D),

because tourist activity could also provide a barrier to frog crossing, supporting rather than undermining the hypothesis.

12. **(C)** Between 2005 and 2010, there is a rough increase of about 400 along the y-axis. So, if the number of universities offering folklore increases at the same rate as this between 2010 and 2015, there will be approximately 1,700 schools in 2015 that offer such programs. Choices (A), (B), and (D) do not make conclusions supported by the trends in the presented data.

13. **(B)** The text provides provide the evidence for this choice, stating that "no cause for war was more compelling in the U.S. than the desire to expand the nation into the northern territories." While the other options would motivate U.S. citizens to fight against the British, they do not represent the "most significant" motivation to do so.

14. **(C)** According to the author, consuming your sugars from fructose eventually causes obesity and other health issues. Thus, (C) is correct because it is the only choice that considers the long-term effects of fructose according to the text.

15. **(A)** The text refers to the insular scripts as being highly "variable," meaning that people hand-wrote them in a variety of ways making them more difficult to read. Choice (B) is incorrect, since only the Carolingian miniscule is mentioned as cumbersome. Choice (C) is incorrect, because the text does not support the notion that these scripts were limited to England and Ireland. Choice (D) is incorrect, because the text does not support that these scripts were only used in monasteries.

16. **(A)** An adverb is required as it describes the verb *go*. Choices (B) and (D) are generally used as limiting adjectives, and choice (C) is a multifaceted adjective (but an adjective, nonetheless). *Frequently* is the correct answer. Recall that words that end in -ly are traditionally adverbs.

17. **(A)** *The innate immune system* is a parenthetical phrase: eliminate it, and the sentence still functions acceptably. It can be surrounded with either two commas or two dashes to differentiate it from the main clause. Choices (C) and (D) both neglect the necessary preceding punctuation. Choice (B) starts with a dash, but then uses a comma. It is necessary to be consistent with whichever one (comma or dash) begins the parenthetical phrase.

18. **(A)** *Its* gives the singular possessive adjective needed to refer to "bullroarer" and shows the instrument possessing a "function." Choice (B) is wrong because it's means "it is." Choice (C) is wrong because *its'* is always incorrect. Choice (D) is wrong because *their* is plural.

19. **(C)** The sentence that follows indicates that this essay is written from the present-day perspective. Choice (C) correctly uses the present perfect tense, *has now begun*, and is numerically consistent with the singular subject of "world." Choices (A) and (B) improperly use *began* in the perfect tense (*began* is for the past tense), and choice (D) is plural.

20. **(B)** The adjective *endless* is needed to modify the noun *effects*. Also, *affect* is generally a verb, and *effect* is generally a noun. The incorrect options either use the adverb *endlessly* and/or use the verb *affect*.

21. **(C)** No commas are needed in this long, descriptive phrase. The other options are too choppy.

22. **(C)** *Apart from* works here because it is synonymous with "except for"—the writer is expressing that bullroarers have been found throughout the world except for Antarctica. The

bullroarer would not literally be *a part of* Antarctica, as in choices (A) and (B). Choice (D) gives the incorrect spelling given the needed phrasing.

23. **(B)** This is the only option to be consistent with the numeric listing found elsewhere in the text: "First" and "Third."

24. **(A)** *Meanwhile* provides a logical contrast between the relatively large percentage of dark matter and the relatively small percentage of visible atoms. None of the other options provides a logical contrast.

25. **(C)** The previous sentence makes a broad statement about the unforeseen consequences of synthetic intermediates design, while the final sentence gives a specific elaboration about one of these consequences. Thus, "for example" is the only logical possibility.

26. **(C)** "Although" is the only option that provides a contrast between the familiar firefly and the more obscure species that also utilize bioluminescence.

27. **(C)** Since the student wants to suggest a possible negative consequence of not having habeas corpus in place—the third bullet outlines how this right prevents people receiving jail sentences without the due process of law. This aligns with Choice (C). Choice (A) is a negative consequence but is not supported by the notes, since it is likely that in the absence of habeas corpus, the number of people in prison would increase, not decrease. Choices (B) and (D) do not outline possible negative consequences.

Section 2: Math Module 1

1. **(A)** First, get all x terms on one side by subtracting $3x$ from both sides. To combine the x terms, you need a common denominator, so first convert $3x$ to $\frac{9}{3}x$. After combining the x terms, the equation becomes
$2 = -\frac{5}{3}x$. Next, solve for x by dividing both sides by $-\frac{5}{3}$ (in other words, multiply both sides by $-\frac{3}{5}$):
$-\frac{6}{5} = x$, answer (A).

2. **122** You can use the conversion given in the problem (2.54 centimeters per 1 inch) to cancel out the units you don't want (inches), leaving you with only the units that you do want (centimeters):

$$48 \text{ } inches \times \frac{2.54 \text{ } centimeters}{1 \text{ } inch} = 121.92 \text{ } centimeters \approx 122 \text{ } centimeters.$$

3. **(C)** Recognize that $d = rt$ where d is distance, r is rate, and t is time. In this problem, $r = 50$ and $t = 3\frac{1}{4} = 3.25$. Use this to solve for distance:

$$d = rt = 50 \times 3.25 = 162.5, \text{ answer (C)}.$$

Alternatively, you could have done dimensional analysis to cancel out the units you don't want, leaving you only with the units you do want (miles):

$$\frac{50 \text{ } miles}{1 \text{ } hour} \times 3.25 \text{ } hours = 162.5 \text{ } miles.$$

4. **(A)** First, FOIL the $(x - 3)^2$ term in the equation to obtain:

$x^2 - 6y + 9 - 81 = 0$. Then you can combine like terms:

$x^2 - 6y - 72 = 0$. This factors to

$(x - 12)(x + 6) = 0$. Setting each term equal to 0 tells you that x can either equal 12 or -6. Only 12 is an answer choice, choice (A).

5. **(D)** The typist has already typed 3500 words, so this will be a constant in the expression. The typist types 70 words per minute, so if he types for t minutes, he will type $70t$ more words. Therefore, the total number of words typed, $W(t)$, will be given by the expression

$W(t) = 3500 + 70t$, choice (D).

6. **(B)** First, begin by factoring out all common factors. $2a$ is a factor of all three terms, so it can be factored out, leaving you with $2a(3a + 4b - 2c)$. Alternatively, you could have redistributed the answer choices to eliminate choice (A), (C), and (D), which respectively equal $3a^2 + 4ab + 2ac$, $4a^2 + 4ab - 8ac$, and $6a^2 - 8ab + 4ac$.

7. **(C)** FOIL this like you'd FOIL any other equation:

$\frac{6}{12}x^2 - \frac{2}{3}x + \frac{3}{4}x - 1$. The coefficient in front of the x^2 can be reduced, giving:

$\frac{1}{2}x^2 - \frac{2}{3}x + \frac{3}{4}x - 1$. To combine the x terms, they need to have a common denominator:

$\frac{1}{2}x^2 - \frac{8}{12}x + \frac{9}{12}x - 1$. Combining these terms gives you $\frac{1}{2}x^2 + \frac{1}{12}x - 1$, or (C).

8. **75** Isosceles trapezoids have two sets of congruent angles, and their interior angles add up to $360°$. Therefore, you know that

$360 = 105 + 105 + x + x$. Combine like terms:

$360 = 210 + 2x$. Subtract 210 from both sides:

$150 = 2x$. Dividing by 2 tells you that $x = 75$. Therefore, the smallest interior angle is $75°$.

9. **(D)** First, solve for x by cross-multiplying:

$2x = 4$. Dividing by 2 tells you that $x = 2$. Next, plug 2 in for x in the expression:

$$\frac{4(2 - 3)}{-12} = \frac{4(-1)}{-12} = \frac{-4}{-12} = \frac{1}{3},\text{ answer (D).}$$

10. **800** This is a system of equations. If there are 2 men for every 3 women, the ratio is $\frac{m}{w} = \frac{2}{3}$. If there is a total of 4000 students, $m + w = 4000$. To solve this system of equations, solve the first equation for m and plug this into the second equation using substitution. Solving for m, you get $m = \frac{2}{3}w$, so the second equation becomes $\frac{2}{3}w + w = 4000$. Combine like terms: $\frac{5}{3}w = 4000$. Dividing by $\frac{5}{3}$ (the same as multiplying by $\frac{3}{5}$) tells you that $w = 2400$. To figure out how many more women there are than men, you also need to know how many men there are. Plug 2400 in for w in the equation you already solved in terms of m:

$m = \frac{2}{3}w = \frac{2}{3}(2400) = 1600$.

$w - m = 2400 - 1600 = 800$, so there are 800 more women than men.

11. **(A)** Dividing by a fraction is the same as multiplying by its reciprocal, so $\dfrac{1}{\frac{1}{2x}} = 1 \times \dfrac{2x}{1} = 2x$

and $\dfrac{3}{\frac{6}{4x}} = 3 \times \dfrac{4x}{6} = \dfrac{12x}{6} = 2x$. Therefore,

$$\frac{1}{\frac{1}{2x}} + \frac{3}{\frac{6}{4x}} = 2x + 2x = 4x, \text{ answer (A)}.$$

12. **(C)** 4807 beverages were purchased, and 1067 of them were espresso. Therefore, the percentage of beverages that was espresso is represented by the expression $\dfrac{1067}{4807} \times 100\% = 22.2\%$, answer (C).

13. **(C)** Notice that both functions give equations of lines. To find the point of intersection, you want to find the point (x, y) that is on both lines. Since (x, y) is on both lines, you can find this common x value by setting the right sides of both equations equal to one another:

$4x - 3 = -\frac{1}{2}x + 2$. Combine like terms by adding $\frac{1}{2}x$ to both sides and adding 3 to both sides: $\frac{9}{2}x = 5$. Solve for x by dividing both sides by $\frac{9}{2}$ (in other words, multiply both sides by $\frac{2}{9}$) to learn that $x = \frac{10}{9}$. This is enough to narrow it down to choice (C), but you could solve for y by plugging $\frac{10}{9}$ in for x in either equation:

$$y = 4\left(\frac{10}{9}\right) - 3 = \frac{40}{9} - 3 = \frac{40}{9} - \frac{27}{9} = \frac{13}{9}.$$

14. **(14)** For this problem, you need to create a system of equations. First, having 2 quarters for every 5 dimes means that the ratio of quarters to dimes is $\dfrac{q}{d} = \dfrac{2}{5}$.

Next, you need to come up with an expression that represents the value of the coins. Because quarters are worth 25 cents, the number of cents David has from q quarters will be $25q$. Similarly, the number of cents he has from d dimes will be $10d$. Because these expressions are in cents, you need the amount of money he has to also be in cents. There are 100 cents in 1 dollar, so he has 200 cents. Therefore $25q + 10d = 200$. Since $\dfrac{q}{d} = \dfrac{2}{5}$, you have that $q = \frac{2}{5}d$. Next, plug this in for q in the second equation:

$$25\left(\frac{2}{5}d\right) + 10d = 200. \text{ Combine the } d \text{ terms: } 20d = 200 \rightarrow d = 10$$

Thus, there are 10 dimes. Plug 10 in for d in the equation that expresses q in terms of d:

$$q = \frac{2}{5}d \rightarrow q = \frac{2}{5} \times 10 = 4$$

Thus, there are 4 quarters and 10 dimes, giving David 14 coins total.

15. **(B)** In order for the inflation rate, as given by this formula, to equal 0, the numerator of the fraction must equal 0. This will happen if the current year's CPI is equal to the last year's CPI, because subtracting a number from itself will equal 0. This matches answer (B).

16. **(B)** First, get this line in slope-intercept form so that you can easily tell what the slope of this line is. You can do so by adding $4x$ to both sides to get the equation $y = 4x + 5$. The slope of this line is 4. The slope of a line perpendicular to this one will have a slope that is the negative reciprocal of this, $-\frac{1}{4}$, which matches (B).

17. **(B)** Anita's $600 rent represented 40% of her expenses, while 60% of her expenses were spent on everything else. You want to figure out what this 60% was, so you can set up a proportion:

$\frac{x}{60} = \frac{600}{40}$. Next, cross multiply:

$40x = 36000$. Divide both sides by 40 to determine that $x = 900$. Therefore, she spent $900 on everything else, choice (B).

18. **(C)** In this problem, the mean can't easily be figured out because you can't sum together all of the responses without knowing the actual numerical responses (you only know the range of hours for each student). The mode is between 6 and 7 hours, since this was the most frequent response (12 students chose this range). The median in a series of 30 terms is found by arranging them from smallest to largest, then taking the average of the 15th and 16th terms. In this case, the 15th and 16th terms are both between 6 and 7 hours, so the median will be between 6 and 7 hours. Thus, the median and mode are the same, answer (C).

19. **(C)** Recall that the area formula for an equilateral triangle is:

$$Area = \frac{\sqrt{3}}{4}(Side\ Length)^2$$

So, simply plug in 6 for the side length and solve for the area:

$$\frac{\sqrt{3}}{4}(6)^2 = \frac{\sqrt{3} \times 36}{4} = \sqrt{3} \times 9 = 9\sqrt{3}$$

If you forget this formula, you can use the given 30-60-90 triangle ratio to solve.

20. **(C)** You need to come up with an expression for the area of the wall, then recognize that it will cost $12 for every 60 square feet (paint costs $12 per gallon and one gallon covers 60 square feet).

You know that $W = \frac{2}{3}L$ and $A = LW$ since the wall is a rectangle, so plugging in $\frac{2}{3}L$ for W, you get $A = L\left(\frac{2}{3}L\right) = \frac{2}{3}L^2$.

Multiplying the cost/area by the area will cancel area and leave you with cost:

$$\frac{2}{3}L^2 ft^2\left(\frac{\$12}{60\,ft^2}\right) = \$\frac{24}{180}L^2 = \$\frac{2}{15}L^2,\ \text{answer (C)}.$$

21. **(B)** First, you come up with an expression to represent the amount of food consumed. Each dog consumes 2 cups, so d dogs will consume $2d$ cups of food. Each cat consumes 1 cup of food, so c cats will consume c cups of food. Together, the dogs and cats consume $2d + c$ cups of food. The shelter has 400 cups of food, so $2d + c$ cannot exceed 400. This can be represented by the inequality $2d + c \leq 400$.

Similarly, each dog needs 3 treats daily, so d dogs eat $3d$ treats. Cats eat 2 treats daily, so c cats need $2c$ treats daily. The shelter has 500 treats, so $3d + 2c$ cannot exceed 500:

$3d + 2c \leq 500$. These two equations match answer (B).

22. **(B)** Triangle ECD has an area of 20 and a height of 4. You can plug this into the formula for the area of a triangle ($A = \frac{1}{2}bh$) to obtain the base of the triangle, CD.

$20 = \frac{1}{2}b(4) = 2b$. Divide both sides by 2 to get that the base, $CD = 10$. Therefore, the base of triangle ABD, BD, is $8 + 10 = 18$. Next, you need to find the height of triangle ABD. You can utilize the fact that these are similar triangles to set up a proportion:

$\frac{AB}{4} = \frac{18}{10}$. Cross multiply:

$10AB = 72$. Dividing by 10 tells you that $AB = 7.2$. Plug 7.2 in for the height and 18 in for the base in the area equation:

$$A = \frac{1}{2}(18)(7.2) = 64.8, \text{ answer (B)}.$$

Section 2: Math Module 2

1. **(B)** First, factor a 5 out:

   $5(x^2 - 3x + 2) = 0$. Dividing both sides by 5 leaves you with $x^2 - 3x + 2 = 0$. This can be factored as $(x - 2)(x - 1) = 0$. Set each factor to 0 to solve for possible x values: $x - 2 = 0$, so $x = 2$ or $x - 1 = 0$, so $x = 1$. Therefore, the answer is (B). Alternatively, you could have used the quadratic formula to solve for possible x values.

2. **(D)** A function intersects the x-axis at its roots where $y = 0$: this will occur when any of these three factors equals 0. Set each factor equal to 0 to determine the x values.

   $x = 0$.

   $x - 5 = 0$, so $x = 5$.

   $x + 2 = 0$, so $x = -2$. Therefore, the three x values are 0, 5, and -2, answer (D).

3. **(B)** Notice that the function is 2 minus the absolute value of something. The absolute value of something must always be greater than or equal to 0, so either $f(x) = 2 - 0 = 2$ or $f(x)$ equals 2 minus some positive number. But, this second case will result in a value that is less than 2. (Convince yourself of this. For instance, if the absolute value is 1, then $f(x) = 2 - 1 = 1$.) Therefore, the maximum value of f is 2. So, to find where this maximum will occur, you need to determine which x values give $|x - 4| = 0$. This occurs when $x - 4 = 0$. Thus, $x = 4$, which is choice (B).

   Alternatively, you could have plugged the potential x values in to determine which gave the maximum value for $f(x)$.

4. **(B)** You need to try to simplify the left side of the equation a bit to get it in the same form as the right side.

   When an exponent is raised to another exponent, you multiply those exponents, so $(x^2)^{\frac{1}{5}} = x^{\frac{2}{5}}$.

   Also, $\sqrt[5]{32x^2}$ can be broken up into $\sqrt[5]{32} \cdot \sqrt[5]{x^2}$. Since $\sqrt[5]{32} = 2$, the expression can be further simplified:

   $\sqrt[5]{32} \cdot \sqrt[5]{x^2} = 2x^{\frac{2}{5}}$. Therefore, the left side of the equation simplifies to $x^{\frac{2}{5}} + 2x^{\frac{2}{5}}$. You can then combine like terms:

   $x^{\frac{2}{5}} + 2x^{\frac{2}{5}} = 3x^{\frac{2}{5}}$. If $3x^{\frac{2}{5}} = ax^{\frac{2}{5}}$, then it follows from dividing both sides by $x^{\frac{2}{5}}$ that $a = 3$, answer (B).

5. **(A)** First, get the equation into standard form by subtracting 17 from both sides:

   $y = 6x^2 + 12x - 17$. When a parabola is in standard form, $y = ax^2 + bx + c$, the axis of symmetry is given by the equation $x = -\frac{b}{2a}$. Because the axis of symmetry passes through the vertex and this parabola opens up, the x value that gives the axis of symmetry will also give the x coordinate of the vertex. The y and x values of the vertex give the minimum value and its location on the parabola, respectively, so you want to know the x value of the vertex to solve this problem.

In this case, $a = 6$ and $b = 12$, so $x = -\dfrac{b}{2a} = -\dfrac{12}{2(6)} = -\dfrac{12}{12} = -1$. This corresponds to answer (A).

Alternatively, you could have converted the equation to vertex form by completing the square to get: $y = 6(x + 1)^2 - 17$. Then the vertex is $(-1, -23)$, so $x = -1$.

6. **15** Solve the second equation for y to solve this system of equations using substitution.

$y = \dfrac{6}{4}x = \dfrac{3}{2}x$. Next, plug $\dfrac{3}{2}x$ in for y in the first equation:

$2x - \dfrac{3}{2}x = 3$. In order to combine the x terms, you need a common denominator:

$\dfrac{4}{2}x - \dfrac{3}{2}x = \dfrac{1}{2}x$, so our equation becomes $\dfrac{1}{2}x = 3$. Dividing both sides by $\dfrac{1}{2}$ tells you that $x = 6$. Next, plug in 6 for x in the equation that you already solved for y:

$y = \dfrac{3}{2}x = \dfrac{3}{2}(6) = \dfrac{18}{2} = 9$. Since $x = 6$ and $y = 9$, their sum is $6 + 9$, or 15.

7. **196** First, simplify the second term in the numerator:

$3(2x^2)^2 = 3(4x^4) = 12x^4$, so our entire expression becomes

$\left(\dfrac{2x^4 + 3(2x^2)^2}{x^4}\right)^2 = \left(\dfrac{2x^4 + 12x^4}{x^4}\right)^2$. The x^4 terms of the numerator can be combined:

$\left(\dfrac{2x^4 + 12x^4}{x^4}\right)^2 = \left(\dfrac{14x^4}{x^4}\right)^2$. The x^4 in the numerator cancels with the x^4 in the denominator:

$\left(\dfrac{14x^4}{x^4}\right)^2 = (14)^2 = 196$, so the answer is 196.

8. **(A)** First, distribute the -2:

$7 - 2(y - 1) = 7 - 2y + 2$. Next, combine like terms:

$7 - 2y + 2 = 9 - 2y$, answer (A).

9. **(D)** Look at the bottom row. There are a total of 400 individuals, and each selected one type of communication that they preferred, so the first four numbers in the bottom row must add up to 400:

$195 + x + 70 + 70 = 400$. Combine like terms on the left side of the equation.

$335 + x = 400$. Subtract 335 from both sides to isolate x:

$x = 65$, answer (D).

Alternatively, you could have added up the first two terms in the email column to obtain x: $20 + 45 = 65$.

10. **(C)** From the graph, you can tell that the average monthly temperature in Townsville is greater than that in Cityberg for April, May, June, July, August, September, October, and November, or 8 months. This excessive temperature is sufficient to outweigh the lesser average that Townsville is in the remaining four months to make its average monthly temperature greater than that of Cityberg. Therefore, choice (C) is correct. (A) and (B) are incorrect because the graph doesn't tell you anything about the temperature on any random day. (D) is

incorrect because the average temperature in Cityberg is only greater for January, February, March, and December.

11. **(B)** This question is asking you what percent the discount is of 90. First, you need to know what the discount is, which you can get by subtracting the new price from the original price: $90 - 72 = 18$. Then, you can figure out what percentage 18 is of 90 by setting up a proportion, recognizing that 90 will represent 100% of the quantity:

$\frac{x}{100} = \frac{18}{90}$. Next, cross multiply.

$90x = 1800$. Dividing by 90 yields $x = 20$, so $18 is 20% of $90, answer (B).

12. **(D)** In this equation, the 20 is a constant. Therefore, this is a constant amount of time required that isn't dependent on the number of cookies he makes. Therefore, this is the amount of time he requires to get the ingredients and set things up, which matches choice (D).

13. **(C)** Create a system of equations. First, you know that she has $100,000 invested among the three categories, so if s, b, and c represent the amount of money in stocks, bonds, and cash respectively, then $s + b + c = 100,000$.

She has invested twice as much in stocks as in in bonds, so $s = 2b$.

She has invested three times as much in bonds as in cash, so $b = 3c$.

The question asks how much money is invested in bonds, so you want to get s and c in terms of b, plug these expressions into the first equation, and solve for b. The second equation is already solved for s in terms of b, but you need to solve the third equation for c in terms of b:

$\frac{1}{3}b = c$. Next, plug these expressions in for s and c in the first equation:

$s + b + c = 2b + b + \frac{1}{3}b = 100,000$. You can combine like terms to get

$\frac{10}{3}b = 100,000$. Divide both sides by $\frac{10}{3}$ to get $b = 30,000$. The question asks what percent is invested in bonds, so find what fraction 30,000 is of 100,000, and multiply that number by 100%:

$\frac{30,000}{100,000} \times 100\% = 30\%$, answer (C).

Alternatively, you can figure out the ratio of the investments:

Cash: Bonds: Stocks $= 1 : 3 : 6$

The total of the numbers in this ratio is $1 + 3 + 6 = 10$.

Therefore, as fractions of the whole, the investments are $\frac{1}{10}, \frac{3}{10}$, and $\frac{6}{10}$.

The bonds are $\frac{3}{10}$, which translates to 30%.

14. **(C)** First, you need to get the power equation in terms of just resistance and voltage so that you can tell how changing these two quantities will change the power. Therefore, you need to get rid of current by solving for it in the second equation and plugging this expression into the power formula.

Since $V = IR$, then $I = \frac{V}{R}$. Now plug this in for current in the power equation:

$P = IV = \frac{V}{R}V = \frac{V^2}{R}$. The problem states that resistance is doubled and voltage is quadrupled, so fill these coefficients in:

$P = \dfrac{V^2}{R} = \dfrac{(4V)^2}{2R} = \dfrac{16\,V^2}{2R} = 8\dfrac{V^2}{R}$. Therefore, you can see that power has been multiplied eight-fold, choice (C).

15. **(A)** The volume of a sphere is given by the formula $V = \dfrac{4}{3}\pi r^3$. The diameter is twice the radius, so you can solve for the radius and multiply by 2. To solve for r, first divide both sides by $\dfrac{4}{3}\pi$:

$\dfrac{3V}{4\pi} = r^3$. To solve for r, take the cube root of both sides:

$\sqrt[3]{\dfrac{3V}{4\pi}} = r$. Multiply this by 2 to get an expression for the diameter:

$d = 2\sqrt[3]{\dfrac{3V}{4\pi}}$, answer (A).

16. **(B)** Each month, she adds \$50, so the function will have a constant slope of 50. Because the slope is constant, the function is linear. The slope is positive 50, so the answer is (B). You know that the slope will be positive because the two variables are directly proportional: as time goes on, the amount of money in the account increases.

17. **(C)** First, you can factor a 7 out of both factors of the numerator:

$\dfrac{7(x-1) \cdot 7(x+1)}{7}$. One 7 in the numerator will cancel out with the 7 in the denominator, leaving you with $7(x-1)(x+1)$. Next, FOIL the terms in the parentheses to get $7(x^2 - 1)$, answer (C).

18. **(A)** The y-intercept of the function is somewhere between positive 6 and 8, so you can eliminate choices (C) and (D). Next, find the approximate slope. You can use any two points on the line of best fit, such as the endpoints:

$m = \dfrac{y_2 - y_1}{x_2 - x_1} = \dfrac{9.6 - 6.5}{6 - 0} = \dfrac{3.1}{6} \approx 0.5$, so the answer is (A). The line has a slope of 0.5 and a y-intercept of 6.5.

19. **6** A cube has six sides, so its surface area is given by the formula $SA = 6L^2$. The volume of a cube is given by the formula $V = L^3$. Set these two equations equal to one another:

$6L^2 = L^3$. You can divide both sides by L^2 to obtain that $6 = L$.

20. **2** Multiply the first equation by 2 then add them together to get rid of b:

$$\begin{array}{r} 4a - b = 8 \\ +\underline{(3a + b = 6)} \\ 7a = 14 \end{array}$$

Dividing both sides by 7 tells you that $a = 2$.

21. **0.71** The fees in this case are extra information that you don't even need, because the customer wants to know what the conversion is without taking fees into account.

$1\,USD = 1.41\,AUD$. You want to know how many USD a person would get for $1\,AUD$, so divide both sides by 1.41:

$0.709\,USD = 1\,AUD$. Rounded to the nearest hundredth, the answer is 0.71.

22. **(C)** This question is asking you to determine the range of the function $g(x) = |2x - 3|$. Because the entire function is inside an absolute value symbol, $g(x)$, the range cannot be negative. Therefore, the answer is (C).

ANSWER SHEET
Practice Test 2

Reading and Writing Module 1

1. _____	8. _____	15. _____	22. _____
2. _____	9. _____	16. _____	23. _____
3. _____	10. _____	17. _____	24. _____
4. _____	11. _____	18. _____	25. _____
5. _____	12. _____	19. _____	26. _____
6. _____	13. _____	20. _____	27. _____
7. _____	14. _____	21. _____	

Reading and Writing Module 2

1. _____	8. _____	15. _____	22. _____
2. _____	9. _____	16. _____	23. _____
3. _____	10. _____	17. _____	24. _____
4. _____	11. _____	18. _____	25. _____
5. _____	12. _____	19. _____	26. _____
6. _____	13. _____	20. _____	27. _____
7. _____	14. _____	21. _____	

ANSWER SHEET
Practice Test 2

Math Module 1

1. _____
2. _____
3. _____
4. _____
5. _____
6. _____

7. _____
8. _____
9. _____
10. _____
11. _____
12. _____

13. _____
14. _____
15. _____
16. _____
17. _____
18. _____

19. _____
20. _____
21. _____
22. _____

Math Module 2

1. _____
2. _____
3. _____
4. _____
5. _____
6. _____

7. _____
8. _____
9. _____
10. _____
11. _____
12. _____

13. _____
14. _____
15. _____
16. _____
17. _____
18. _____

19. _____
20. _____
21. _____
22. _____

PSAT Test Overview

This PSAT Practice test is made up of a Reading and Writing section and a Math section. **Note:** On the previous pages, there is an answer sheet you can use to write down your letter choices and math answers. Feel free to use the sheet to record your answers or simply circle and write down your answers in the test as you go.

Section 1: Reading and Writing (54 Questions)

There are two 27-question modules in the Reading and Writing section.

Section 2: Math (44 Questions)

There are two 22-question modules in the Math section.

Modules

The modules in each section are timed separately. You can review your answers in each module before time expires. When the time reaches zero, you will automatically move on to the next section. You are unable to return to a completed module.

Directions

At the beginning of each section, there are directions for answering the questions.

Practice Test 2

SECTION 1: READING AND WRITING MODULE 1

32 MINUTES, 27 QUESTIONS

> **DIRECTIONS:** You will be tested on a variety of important reading and writing skills. Each question has one or more passages, possibly including a graph or table. Carefully read each passage and question and choose the best answer to the question based on the passage(s).
>
> Every question in this section is multiple-choice with four possible answers. Each question has only one best answer.

1. Into the early twentieth century, color cameras themselves remained somewhat _____; this owed largely to the logistical complexities of exposing three separate individually filtered plates on the same subject. One design used a system of prisms and mirrors to split the lens image through three internal filters, which in turn exposed three plates simultaneously.

   Which choice completes the text with the most logical and precise word or phrase?

   (A) unsightly
   (B) unwieldy
   (C) expensive
   (D) precise

2. *From "The New Colossus," by Emma Lazarus in 1883, engraved on the Statue of Liberty—one of the first things that new immigrants to the United States would see if they arrived by boat.*

   Give me your tired, your poor,
   Your huddled masses yearning to breathe free,
   The wretched refuse of your teeming shore.
   Send these, the homeless, tempest-tost to me,
   I lift my lamp beside the golden door!

   As used in the text, what does the word *yearning* most nearly mean?

   (A) Crafting
   (B) Enabling
   (C) Desiring
   (D) Trusting

3. A German patent clerk, Albert Einstein, turned Newtonian mechanics on its head and developed the theory of relativity and the notion of space-time. In the 1920s, scientists studying photographic plates of various star systems took measurements that Edwin Hubble used to demonstrate that the universe is not static at all, but is expanding in all directions, no matter where you might be; this became known as Hubble's law. Hubble's constant—the rate at which the universe is expanding—is currently estimated to be 21 km/s per one million light-years from Earth. This ushered in the notion of the Big Bang as the singular beginning of an expanding space-time and everything in it.

As used in the text, what does the word *singular* most nearly mean?

(A) Odd
(B) Unattached
(C) Definitive
(D) Lonely

4. As the use of antibiotics continues to increase, there is growing concern within the health care community about the development of antibiotic-resistant microorganisms. Microorganisms that cause infections can gain resistance when their DNA spontaneously mutates, or when they receive DNA from another microorganism via conjugation. Once the microorganism has secured the needed DNA sequence, many common antibiotics become ineffective in fighting the infection.

Which choice best states the major concern expressed in the text?

(A) That doctors will lose the capacity to treat bacterial infections
(B) That patients will overdose on their antibiotic prescriptions
(C) That medical professionals will lose their prominence in the community
(D) That Western medicine will not be open to alternative approaches

5. *The following text is from a 1981 speech to Congress by President Ronald Reagan.*

Can we, who man the ship of state, deny it is somewhat out of control? Our national debt is approaching $1 trillion. A few weeks ago I called such a figure, a trillion dollars, incomprehensible, and I've been trying ever since to think of a way to illustrate how big a trillion really is. And the best I could come up with is that if you had a stack of thousand-dollar bills in your hand only four inches high, you'd be a millionaire. A trillion dollars would be a stack of thousand-dollar bills sixty-seven miles high. The interest on the public debt this year we know will be over $90 billion, and unless we change the proposed spending for the fiscal year beginning October 1st, we'll add another almost $80 billion to the debt.

The primary function of the text is to

(A) share relevant first-hand observations.
(B) concretely illustrate the severity of a problem.
(C) verbalize the incomprehensible complexity of a concept.
(D) highlight the widespread interest in a particular solution.

6. *The following text is from Nathaniel Hawthorne's 1852 novel,* The Blithedale Romance.
    Mr. Coverdale, an idealistic young man of the nineteenth century who has recently moved onto a utopian farm, is recovering from a fever.

    All other members of the Community showed me kindness according to the full measure of their capacity. Zenobia brought me my gruel, every day, made by her own hands; and whenever I seemed inclined to converse, would sit by my bed-side, and talk with so much vivacity as to add several gratuitous throbs to my pulse.

    What is the most likely reason that the author has capitalized the word *Community*?

    (A) To be consistent with common cultural practices in the writing of the 1800s
    (B) To label it a formal proper noun, since it likely refers to an idealistic commune
    (C) To demonstrate the narrator's unusual passion for larger urban developments
    (D) To distinguish it from other municipalities discussed earlier in the passage

7. **Text 1**

    Football and basketball players are barred from playing in the NFL and NBA until they are three and one years removed from high school, respectively. They are forced to play college ball before being allowed to earn a real living. Though the athletes are generating billions of dollars in revenue for college athletic departments, they do not receive fair compensation directly from the universities.

Text 2

What happens when a world-class athlete suffers a debilitating injury while biding their time and playing for the NCAA? Consider the case of former South Carolina running back Marcus Lattimore. Marcus was physically ready to be a star NFL player during his junior season, but he was prohibited from doing so. During this time, Marcus suffered a gruesome knee injury; despite rehabilitation, he has never really been the same, and his earning potential is mere decimal points of what it once was.

Which of the following best describes the relationship between the two texts?

(A) Text 1 takes a position in opposition to that expressed in Text 2.
(B) Text 2 provides a specific anecdote in support of the argument in Text 1.
(C) Text 1 considers economics while Text 2 solely focuses on health consequences.
(D) Text 2 addresses the possibility of delayed professional careers while Text 1 does not consider this.

8. **Text 1**

It is through inspiration that a teacher teaches a student to think. Educating is not the business of memorization but the business of inquiry. The student-teacher dichotomy is one of reciprocated wonderment with each party undergoing continuous improvement. And an effective instructor is merely the one responsible for that curiosity in the minds of his or her students. It was Robert Frost who said, "I am not a teacher, but an awakener."

Text 2

I became a teacher because it was the noblest profession I could think of. Get this: I impart knowledge. I am responsible for instilling the foundation in the next generation of professionals and leaders. It all sounds very romantic, but the job comes down to an ability to simplify and explain those concepts that make up the core curriculum. If I cannot communicate clearly with my students, if I cannot come to their level and make the instruction relevant and accessible, then I fail.

Which of the following best describes the relationship between the passages?

(A) Text 1 is more reasonable and Text 2 is more emotional.

(B) Text 1 is more humble and Text 2 is more arrogant.

(C) Text 1 is more dreamy and Text 2 is more contemplative.

(D) Text 1 is more lofty and Text 2 is more practical.

9. *The following text is from John Muir's 1897 work* The American Forests.

So far, our government has done nothing effective with its forests, though the best in the world, but is like a rich and foolish spendthrift who has inherited a magnificent estate in perfect order, and then has left his rich fields and meadows, forests and parks, to be sold and plundered and wasted at will, depending on their inexhaustible abundance. Now it is plain that the forests are not inexhaustible, and that quick measures must be taken if ruin is to be avoided.

Muir's tone in the passage is best described as

(A) urgent and earnest.

(B) arrogant and condescending.

(C) optimistic and cheerful.

(D) hopeless and depressed.

10. In 1950, Enrico Fermi posited the question *Where is everybody?* when considering the apparent contradiction between high estimates of the likelihood of the existence of extraterrestrial life and humankind's lack of contact with, or evidence for, such civilizations. Later referred to as the Fermi Paradox, his provocative query was founded on the assumption that since the sun is quite typical, other Earth-like planets surely exist and have intelligent life, and by now, should have visited or contacted Earth. Extraterrestrial intelligence, or ETI, refers to hypothetical intelligent civilizations that are assumed to exist based on the existence of human intelligence and the vast size of the universe. While popular and scientific opinion on ETI varies greatly—from certainty to skepticism to downright incredulity—the search for alien intelligence is extensive and substantive.

According to the passage, the general scientific attitude toward the existence of extraterrestrial intelligence is best described as

(A) deeply passionate and mostly certain.

(B) quite interested but currently unsettled.

(C) somewhat pessimistic and rather fearful.

(D) fundamentally skeptical but always dogmatic.

1   1   1

11.
**Electromagnetic Waves and
Their Wavelengths**

Wave Type	Wavelength in Meters
Gamma	1×10^{-11}
X-ray	1×10^{-9}
Ultraviolet	2×10^{-8}
Infrared	1×10^{-6}
Radio	1.0

The brain's integration of photons allows humans to perceive colored light with wavelengths between roughly 400 and 700 nanometers (a billionth of a meter), which comprises the entire visible spectrum.

Based on the information in the above text and in the table, light visible to humans would have wavelengths between which two types of waves?

(A) Gamma and X

(B) X and ultraviolet

(C) Ultraviolet and infrared

(D) Infrared and radio

12. A historical passage presents an overview of the history of the War of 1812. Which quotation from the passage best illustrates the claim that the War of 1812 gradually shifted from being fought in the wilderness to being fought in urban areas?

(A) "By concentrating their defenses in Ontario, the Canadians left Quebec vulnerable to invasion along the St. Lawrence River."

(B) "In April of 1814 Napoleon was defeated in Europe, and a greater brunt of the British military fell upon the United States."

(C) "The primary theatres of war, in turn, shifted from the Canadian frontier to coastal American cities such as Baltimore, Washington, D.C., and New Orleans."

(D) "Canada's role in the conflict was by that time essentially at an end, though fighting continued intermittently in the North until the signing of the Treaty of Ghent in December of that year."

13. While we might think of the *cat video* as an invention of the twenty-first century, felines on film have been entertaining humans since the earliest days of cinema over a hundred years ago. Theories abound as to why we love to watch videos of cats, why we find these creatures so entertaining. Perhaps it is because the movements of a cat tend to be far less predictable than those of many other pets, such as dogs. After all, the cat is known for its fickle nature as a species, a fickleness that creates suspense in the viewer who wonders, "what will that cat do next?" Despite being the most common pet in the United States, _____.

Which choice most logically completes the text?

(A) it is easy to know what a cat will want.

(B) cat behavior is anything but familiar to us.

(C) dogs have become increasingly popular among rural dwellers.

(D) other countries do not share the same love of felines.

14. *The following text is from Carrie Chapman Catt's "Address to the Congress on Women's Suffrage" in 1917.*

"There is one thing mightier than kings and armies"—aye, than Congresses and political parties—"the power of an idea when its time has come to move." The time for woman suffrage has come. The woman's hour has struck. If parties prefer to postpone action longer and thus do battle with this idea, they challenge the inevitable. The idea will not perish; the party which opposes it may.

Based on the text, Catt argues that women's suffrage should happen

(A) after a long delay.

(B) when all foreign countries have done so.

(C) after political parties have considered the issue thoroughly.

(D) immediately.

15. But heating proteins isn't the only way to denature them: they can also be denatured by adding certain denaturing substances. Many of these substances, like strong acids and bases, you wouldn't want to add to your food; however, one common denaturing agent is salt. This is why you may want to brine a tougher cut of meat in addition to cooking it. Brining involves soaking something in a solution of salt water. Another benefit of brining is that when the meat absorbs the salt, this draws water into the meat to dilute the salt. Thus, brining also serves to keep meat moist. Some chefs will advise searing the outside of a cut of meat before cooking it through to lock in the moisture. However, chemistry doesn't support this approach: steam is equally capable of escaping through a seared crust as it is through non-seared meat.

According to the text, which of these cooking approaches would have the most negligible effect on the tenderness of meat?

(A) Cooking past protein denaturation

(B) Brining it in salt water

(C) Searing it before further cooking

(D) Using an acid or base to denature

16. In ancient times past, the subtle beauty and architectural refinement of the monument ____ uncontested.

Which choice completes the text so that it conforms to the conventions of Standard English?

(A) is

(B) are

(C) was

(D) were

17. Look through the glass and you'll see that, like a correctional lens, these imperfections distort the images that pass through them. _____ windows were often made using a technique called *glassblowing*.

Which choice completes the text so that it conforms to the conventions of Standard English?

(A) Well into the nineteenth century, glass

(B) Well, into the nineteenth century glass

(C) Well into the nineteenth century glass

(D) Well, into the nineteenth century, glass

18. Without a strong defense system in place, the human body would experience life-threatening consequences from these attacks. Therefore, the body's innate (i.e., natural) immune system and protective mechanisms are crucial to the _____ of humanity.

Which choice completes the text so that it conforms to the conventions of Standard English?

(A) lasting and preservation

(B) survival

(C) essential state of being

(D) continual persistence

19. A commitment to an education in environmental engineering does not go unrewarded. The median annual income is recorded at well over $80,000, and the outlook is promising. Tightening federal regulations _____ expected to only stimulate the need for environmental engineers over the next decade.

Which choice completes the text so that it conforms to the conventions of Standard English?

(A) to meet environmentally safe standards and for the purpose of the cleaning of contaminated sites are

(B) to meet environmentally safe standards and clean up contaminated sites is

(C) in order to meet environmentally safe standards and in order to clean up contaminated sites are

(D) to meeting environmentally safe standards and cleaning up contaminated sites were

20. Colonel Sartoris, or *Sarty*, is trapped in a world stricken by fear, grief, and misery. _____ father, Sarty is continually faced with the paradox of detesting the man who raised him, while also feeling an inherent fidelity to him.

Which choice completes the text so that it conforms to the conventions of Standard English?

(A) While physically similar and often volatile like his

(B) While physically similar, and often, volatile, like his

(C) While physically similar, and often volatile like his

(D) While physically similar and often, volatile like his

21. Dental students, Tim explained, _____ reasons for pursuing the occupation.

Which choice completes the text so that it conforms to the conventions of Standard English?

(A) have many

(B) have much

(C) had much

(D) has many

22. Described by playwright Bernard Shaw as _____ their lingering influences have coexisted and even comingled in drama for more than a century now.

Which choice completes the text so that it conforms to the conventions of Standard English?

(A) "the giants of the theatre of our time,"

(B) the giants of the theatre of our time,

(C) the giants' of the theatre of our time,

(D) 'the giants of the theatre of our time,'

23. The most common application cited by such scholars is that of long-distance communication. _____ no scientific studies on the subject have been published, many witnesses claim that the lower audible frequencies emitted by the bullroarer can travel impressive distances, with listeners clearly discerning its sound from up to two miles away.

Which choice completes the text with the most logical transition?

(A) For the reason that

(B) Because

(C) Since

(D) Though

24. The incubation of blues music began with the first arrival of West African slaves in America. Through the Revolution and the emergence of the United States, to the abolition of slavery and onward, the blues continued to evolve and proliferate, taking on new forms, instrumentations, and significance. _____ today the blues may seem as American as apple pie, we mustn't forget the creative debt that this most American of musical genres owes to its West African ancestors.

Which choice completes the text with the most logical transition?

(A) Whenever

(B) Thus

(C) So

(D) While

25. Medieval alchemists made minor contributions to the creation of the periodic table through their tedious observation of the known elements' physical and chemical properties. _____ inquisitive minds made gradual progress toward understanding matter in its elemental form throughout the millennia, it was not until the 17th century that the discoveries which laid the table's foundation truly accelerated.

Which choice completes the text with the most logical transition?

(A) When
(B) Because
(C) Although
(D) Since

26. In the scholarly debate of gender and class in Renaissance Italy, the writings of historian Samuel K. Cohn, Jr., maintain that Italian women—especially those of the lower classes—experienced a palpable decline in status from the late 14th century until the Counter-Reformation visitations of the 1570s. Cohn's essays are distinct from his contemporaries in that they bespeak a darker and rarely mentioned side of the Renaissance. _____ the broadly encompassing scope of his essays is an attempt to investigate populations as a whole, rather than focusing solely on elites, which, according to Cohn, "has been, with few exceptions, the tendency of women's Renaissance history since the 1970s."

Which choice completes the text with the most logical transition?

(A) However,
(B) Moreover,
(C) Furthermore,
(D) In particular,

27. While researching a topic, a student has taken the following notes:

- Professionals in both law enforcement and forensics need a way to study human body decomposition prior to taking on specific cases.
- To allow people to learn about the decomposition of the human body, a "body farm" can be a great help.
- People can donate their bodies to a body farm upon death, where their bodies may be exposed to different conditions so that learning can take place as to how a human body will decompose under different circumstances.
- FBI agents and other law enforcement professionals may study at a body farm to be better able to work with human remains and gather evidence used to catch criminals.

The student wants to suggest a way that typical readers might contribute to body decomposition research. Which choice most effectively uses relevant information from the notes to accomplish this goal?

(A) Professionals engaged in law enforcement might benefit from studying the latest publications on body decomposition.
(B) Those who are interested in helping body decomposition research can elect to donate their bodies to such research upon their deaths.
(C) Without doing detailed comparisons of bodies from different situations, law enforcement officials will be ill-equipped to apply body decomposition research to actual crimes.
(D) Advances in artificial intelligence will negate the need for further research in bodily forensics.

2   2   2

SECTION 1: READING AND WRITING MODULE 2

32 MINUTES, 27 QUESTIONS

DIRECTIONS: You will be tested on a variety of important reading and writing skills. Each question has one or more passages, possibly including a graph or table. Carefully read each passage and question and choose the best answer to the question based on the passage(s).

Every question in this section is multiple-choice with four possible answers. Each question has only one best answer.

1. Will's parents knew he was a very smart child. He mastered concepts in school much more quickly than other students. However, his grades did not reflect his intelligence. His _____ nature was his downfall as he never completed his homework assignments on time. Perfect test scores were not enough to compensate for missing assignments.

Which choice completes the text with the most logical and precise word or phrase?

(A) lackadaisical
(B) drowsy
(C) moronic
(D) passionate

2. There are a number of more indirect, ecologically-oriented ways in which the microbiome confers protection to its host. Abundant colonization of our bodies by benign microorganisms, for example, inhibits the overgrowth of more dangerous ones through the sheer depletion of microbial nutrients. This notion of ecological balance has been of particular interest to scientists studying the microbiome, as it hinges upon both the variable diversity of species that colonize an individual as well as factors that affect the dynamism of a micro biotic population.

As used in the text, the word *hinges* most closely means

(A) fulcrums.
(B) analyzes.
(C) depends.
(D) joints.

3. *The following text is from Jane Austen's 1814 novel* Mansfield Park. *The novel's protagonist, Fanny Price, returns home after many years of living with her wealthy relatives at Mansfield Park.*

Her disappointment in her mother was greater: there she had hoped much, and found almost nothing. Every flattering scheme of being of consequence to her soon fell to the ground. Mrs. Price was not unkind; but, instead of gaining on her affection and confidence, and becoming more and more dear, her daughter never met with greater kindness from her than on the first day of her arrival. The instinct of nature was soon satisfied, and Mrs. Price's attachment had no other source. Her heart and her time were already quite full; she had neither leisure nor affection to bestow on Fanny. Her daughters never had been much to her. She was fond of her sons, especially of William, but Betsey was the first of her girls whom she had ever much regarded.

As used in the text, the phrase *instinct of nature* most nearly means

(A) maternal feeling.
(B) desire for survival.
(C) thirst for acceptance.
(D) sense of justice.

4. The first great breakthrough in cooking had to be the division of fires into their component functions. <u>That is, a campfire used to produce light or to heat a large area is not typically the ideal fire for cooking.</u> Once a fire ring was designated specifically for the preparation of food, the earliest earthen stoves almost certainly began to evolve shortly afterward and would have significantly increased the degree to which primitive cooks could distribute heat evenly. Discovered in the Ukraine, the oldest known stoves appear to date from about 30,000 years ago and were used primarily to bake mammoth meat.

The underlined sentence serves to clarify what phrase in the text?

(A) "division of fires into their component functions"
(B) "the earliest earthen stoves almost certainly began to evolve"
(C) "Discovered in Ukraine, the oldest known stoves"
(D) "were used primarily to bake mammoth meat"

5. Much like our own cells, a significant portion of bacteria play crucial roles in our metabolic and immunological processes. *Oxalobacter formigenes*, which colonizes the colon, is a primary source of the enzyme oxalyl-CoA decarboxylase, which allows us to safely eliminate dietary oxalate. Without this enzyme, calcium oxalate salts tend to accumulate in the kidney tubules, and eventually precipitate as renal stones. Other colonic bacteria catalyze the reduction of bilirubin into urobilinogen: a reaction critical to our digestion of fats, and absorption of fat-soluble vitamins. Interestingly, many bacteria within our gastrointestinal tracts also directly synthesize several vitamins in excess of their own metabolic needs, and, as a result, represent an important source of both vitamin B12, which is necessary for the production of new red blood cells, and vitamin K, which is a cofactor in the synthesis of several blood clotting factors.

What is the primary purpose of the text as a whole?

(A) To recommend specific bacteriological treatments to common gastrointestinal illnesses
(B) To provide concrete examples of the utility of some bacteria to our metabolic and immunological processes
(C) To address the objections of those who are inherently skeptical towards the existence of bacteria
(D) To explain the metabolic processes whereby bacteria lead to the creation of vitamins B12 and K

6. **Text 1**

If We Were Villains is a novel depicting a group of friends and their journey through an elite arts college. The seven students act in Shakespearean plays throughout the years, each embodying the persona of the character they are given. When it comes to their final play, the students have lost touch of their identity and taken on the character given to them—even that of the villain.

Text 2

Shakespeare is widely regarded as the greatest English writer in history. His works have been published and used as authors' inspiration for decades. Countless books and movies have come out about this poet's life. Surprisingly, most of Shakespeare's inspiration came from historical figures and events, such as *Macbeth* and *Julius Caesar*. Some people question whether the antagonists were also influenced by these people or by those in his personal life.

The example introduced in the beginning of Text 1 is primarily representative of what item mentioned in Text 2?

(A) Figures
(B) Books
(C) Antagonists
(D) Movies

7. **Text 1**

According to Darwin's theory of evolution, all organisms arise and develop through the process of natural selection, or small functional inheritances that boost one's ability to compete and survive in the wild. When small genetic mutations occur and prove beneficial, they are passed on to offspring, allowing a slow evolution to occur while the less competitive organism dies out. Eventually, Darwin argues, these mutations accumulate and form an entirely new organism.

Text 2

Without having a grasp of Gregor Mendel's work on heredity, Darwin couldn't anticipate modern discoveries within genetics such as genetic drift. Darwin himself acknowledged that his theory would encounter challenges if any complex organ were to be found which could not possibly have been formed by successive, slight modifications. With modern advancements in molecular biology and biochemistry, these "irreducibly complex systems" are not only known to exist, but are, in fact, very prevalent on the cellular level.

Which of the following best describes the relationship between the two texts?

(A) Both texts agree on the infallibility of an evolutionary theory.
(B) Text 1 anticipates and addresses an objection presented by Text 2.
(C) Text 2 explains the historical influence of one biologist on another, bolstering Text 1's argument.
(D) Text 2 highlights a shortcoming in the theory presented in Text 1.

8. Ecologically, organic farming is designed to promote and enhance biodiversity, so it must combine scientific knowledge and technologies to stimulate naturally occurring biological processes. For instance, organic farming uses pyrethrin, a natural pesticide found in the chrysanthemum flower, to deter pests, and potassium bicarbonate to control disease and suppress unruly weeds. Furthermore, where conventional farming focuses on mass production of each individual crop, organic farming encourages polyculture, or multiple crops being raised in the same space.

Based on the passage, when compared to a non-organic farm field, an organic farm field will most likely be more

(A) productive.
(B) diverse.
(C) mature.
(D) centralized.

9. *The following text is from Charles Dickens's 1861 novel* Great Expectations. *In it, Pip, a poor orphan who is cared for by his sister and her husband, meets the young girl who will become the lifetime object of his affections while simultaneously becoming aware of his lowly position in the caste system.*

My uncle Pumblechook, who kept a cornchandler's shop in the high-street of the town, took me to the large old, dismal house, which had all its windows barred. For miles round everybody had heard of Miss Havisham as an immensely rich and grim lady who led a life of seclusion; and everybody soon knew that Mr. Pumblechook had been commissioned to bring her a boy.

The text primarily serves to explain

(A) why Pip wanted to be a gentleman.
(B) why Miss Havisham desired companionship.
(C) how Pip came to be at Miss Havisham's.
(D) how Pip came to fall in love with Estella.

10. The infamous *four-letter words* are almost exclusively descended from the Germanic components of English. Even without an expertise in linguistics, one might sense this simply by the way they sound—phonically, most profanity in English is composed of short, terse syllables, and rounds off abruptly with a hard consonant.

A newly formed profane English word with which of the following suffixes would most effectively illustrate the author's claim?

(A) -lah
(B) -ock
(C) -soo
(D) -aly

11. A state is considering increasing the payment it provides to unemployed workers from $300 a week to $500 a week. An economist hypothesizes that this change in policy will discourage unemployed citizens from seeking out work since they will receive increased funds from unemployment.

Which finding, if true, would most undermine the economist's hypothesis?

(A) Observation that in a similar state that when unemployment benefits were doubled, there was no change in those seeking unemployment
(B) Data demonstrating that a 50 percent increase in unemployment benefits in a neighboring state resulted in a 100 percent increase in those seeking unemployment
(C) Analysis of economic statistics showing a strong correlation between an increase in unemployment benefits and a decreased willingness to work
(D) Results from a voluntary survey of 300 people in a particular city showing that respondents would be unwilling to let an increase in unemployment benefits affect their decision about whether to seek out benefits

2   2   2

12.

Population Structure

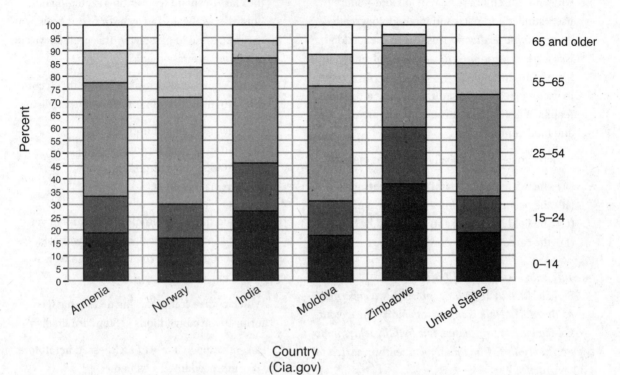

Country
(Cia.gov)

Which of the following is true based on the information in the graph?

(A) Norway has the greatest percentage of people age 65 and older.

(B) Norway has the best health care for older adults.

(C) Most Norwegians choose not to have children.

(D) Norway will soon feel the economic effects of its low birth rate.

13. Folklorists—regardless of their focus within the wide, interdisciplinary field of folklore—often use a similar approach and methodology, called *ethnographic fieldwork*. This means the folklorist's job is not confined to a desk, a university, or a museum; instead, _____ often in exciting, real-world settings in the expressive realms of festival, narrative, faith, art, architecture, and food, among others.

Which choice most logically completes the text?

(A) the work is participatory and engaging,

(B) the occupation is dull and monotonous,

(C) the field is abstract and complex,

(D) the career is highly compensated,

14. *This is an excerpt from Charlotte Bronte's* Jane Eyre, *written in 1847. Jane, previously a governess at Thornfield Hall, is engaged to marry the wealthy homeowner Mr. Rochester. She fretfully relays unexpected events to him that have recently occurred in his absence.*

I dreamt another dream, sir: that Thornfield Hall was a dreary ruin, the retreat of bats and owls. I thought that of all the stately front nothing remained but a shell-like wall, very high and very fragile-looking. I wandered, on a moonlight night, through the grass-grown enclosure within: here I stumbled over a marble hearth, and there over a fallen fragment of cornice. Wrapped up in a shawl, I still carried the unknown little child: I might not lay it down anywhere, however tired were my arms—however much its weight impeded my progress, I must retain it. I heard the gallop of a horse at a distance on the road; I was sure it was you; and you were departing for many years and for a distant country.

In her dream, how did Jane first perceive the presence of Mr. Rochester?

(A) Through sight

(B) Through hearing

(C) Through smell

(D) Through touch

15. In the third grade, my teacher, Mrs. Wabash, asked the class to spend ten minutes sketching our homes, specifically the exterior of our houses as they appeared to passersby. This prelude was part of a larger exercise that I _____

Which choice completes the text so that it conforms to the conventions of Standard English?

(A) have long since forgotten.

(B) had since long forgot.

(C) has long since forgotten.

(D) forgot since long.

16. The good news is technology can work in your favor just as methodically as it can work against you. If you approach the World Wide Web as a tool, it can be _____

Which choice completes the text so that it conforms to the conventions of Standard English?

(A) valuable in a way not witnessed heretofore.

(B) unprecedentedly valuable.

(C) precious beyond your wildest dreams.

(D) more or less a decent outcome.

17. From contracts to design to construction, the architect is there, _____ never done. It is indeed an occupation that encompasses nearly every field of work—engineering, mathematics, marketing, administration, customer service, law, and public safety are all needed in successful architecture.

Which choice completes the text so that it conforms to the conventions of Standard English?

(A) there job

(B) their job

(C) our job

(D) they're job

2   2   2

18. Even a cursory _____ will reveal that the single greatest obstacle to the advent of evidence-based medical science was not—as has often been posited—superstition but Hippocratic humorism itself.

Which choice completes the text so that it conforms to the conventions of Standard English?

(A) analysis of Western medicine's history

(B) analyses of Western medicines' history

(C) analysis of the history of the medicine of the West

(D) analyzing of the history of medical science in Western society

19. While one student may be looking for small class sizes, another may be looking for job placement, while _____ another is in search of a strong study-abroad program.

Which choice completes the text so that it conforms to the conventions of Standard English?

(A) in

(B) from

(C) one

(D) still

20. Rognlie _____ housing wealth as the cause of worsening inequality and shows that Piketty's conclusions are based on the assumption that capital can be substituted for the working class, which is untrue in the housing market.

Which choice completes the text so that it conforms to the conventions of Standard English?

(A) points at

(B) points to

(C) points on

(D) point through

21. More than 300 years ago, the idea was quite _____ gravitational force toward one another with a force proportional to the product of the two masses and inversely proportional to the square of the distance between them.

Which choice completes the text so that it conforms to the conventions of Standard English?

(A) revolutionary: two objects, regardless of their mass, exert

(B) revolutionary, two objects regardless of their mass, exert

(C) revolutionary—two objects regardless of their mass, exert

(D) revolutionary; two objects, regardless of their mass exert

22. *My very educated mother just served us nine pizzas* is a sentence that may not mean much to young students anymore. However, to people of an older generation this sentence is almost universally recognized as a mnemonic device used to aid children in remembering the planets of our solar system. The sentence has changed recently, not because serving nine pizzas is against school lunch health standards, _____ the planets themselves have changed.

Which choice completes the text with the most logical transition?

(A) but because

(B) and since

(C) for a result

(D) and

2   2   2

23. Schrödinger won the Nobel Prize in Physics in 1933 for his work in quantum mechanics, _____ he is most remembered for a theoretical experiment he proposed two years later.

Which choice completes the text with the most logical transition?

(A) but
(B) for
(C) since
(D) and

24. Assessment signifies what we value in the classroom and how we assign that value. _____ to stop testing a subject is to see it all but disappear from the curriculum.

Which choice completes the text with the most logical transition?

(A) In other words,
(B) For these reasons,
(C) Due to this,
(D) Henceforth,

25. After being tasked with writing an essay about Jane Austen, a student has taken the following notes:

- Jane Austen was an English novelist who wrote books from 1811 to 1815.
- She published several novels during her lifetime: *Pride and Prejudice, Sense and Sensibility, Emma,* and *Mansfield Park.*
- Her books centered around women's dependence on marriage for social and economic standing.
- Jane Austen acquired most of her fame after her death when her nephew published *A Memoir of Jane Austen.*
- *Pride and Prejudice* follows a woman who refuses to follow societal norms, turning down suitors even though the financial gain would be of benefit to her family.

The student wants to cite an example of the impact that a posthumous publication had on her reputation. Based on the notes, which of the following of Austen's works should the student cite in order to accomplish this goal?

(A) *Pride and Prejudice*
(B) *Sense and Sensibility*
(C) *Emma*
(D) *A Memoir of Jane Austen*

2   2   2

26. Colleges are invested in helping graduates secure positions, since having large numbers of graduates without jobs makes the colleges look bad and can lead to declining applications and enrollment. _____ it is in the best interest of the college for all students to be employed shortly after graduation.

Which choice completes the text with the most logical transition?

(A) Moreover,
(B) In addition,
(C) However,
(D) Thus,

27. While researching a topic, a student has taken the following notes:

- Creating a stained-glass window masterpiece is a very difficult process that includes many phases.
- In addition to designing the entire piece to be aesthetically pleasing, the artist also must consider the weight of the pieces and the structural integrity of the overall design.
- Pieces that are poorly designed may buckle and fall after being installed in a wall.
- In addition to the design aspect, artists must deal with safety concerns. Artists routinely suffer minor lacerations from their glass work, but also need to worry about chemical poisoning from soldering fumes, lead came, and patina chemicals.

The student wants to outline a possible worst-case scenario as far as the potential health impact on someone who crafts stained glass. Which choice most effectively uses relevant information from the notes to accomplish this goal?

(A) A stained-glass artist faces the possibility of chemical poisoning.
(B) Those who live in buildings with stained glass could see the fragile windows shatter.
(C) The challenges of creating stained glass often intimidate those who consider taking on such a project.
(D) While stained glass is difficult to make, its beauty makes the work well worth the effort.

3   3   3

SECTION 2: MATH MODULE 1

35 MINUTES, 22 QUESTIONS

- All expressions and variables use real numbers.
- All figures are drawn to scale.
- Every figure lies in a plane.
- The domain of given functions is the set of all real numbers for which the corresponding value of the function is real.

For multiple-choice questions, solve the problem and pick the correct answer from the provided choices. Each multiple-choice question has only one correct answer.

For student-produced response questions, solve each problem and enter your answer following these guidelines:

- If you find more than one correct answer, enter just one answer.
- You can enter up to five characters for a positive answer and up to six characters (this includes the negative sign) for a negative answer.
- If your answer is a fraction that does not fit in the given space, enter the decimal equivalent instead.
- If your answer is a decimal that does not fit in the given space, enter it by stopping at or rounding up at the fourth digit.
- If your answer is a mixed number (like $4\frac{1}{2}$), enter it as an improper fraction (9/2) or its decimal equivalent (4.5).
- Do not enter symbols like a comma, dollar sign, or percent sign.

Examples

Answer	Acceptable Entries	Unacceptable Entries That Will Receive Zero Credit
4.5	4.5 4.50 9/2	41/2 4 1/2
$\frac{8}{9}$	8/9 .8888 .8889 0.888 0.889	0.8 .88 0.88 0.89
$-\frac{1}{9}$	−1/9 −.1111 −0.111	−.11 −0.11

1. A bicyclist's distance in miles from her starting point can be modeled by the function $d(x) = 16x$, in which x is given in hours. What does the number 16 represent in this function?

   (A) Her constant speed
   (B) Her varying speed
   (C) Her constant acceleration
   (D) Her varying acceleration

2. $3x\left(\frac{1}{3}x - 5\right)$ is equivalent to which of the following expressions?

   (A) $3x^2 - 30x$
   (B) $6x^2 - 5x$
   (C) $x^2 + 15x$
   (D) $x^2 - 15x$

3. If a line has a slope of 3 and intersects the point $(1, 8)$, what is the y-intercept of the line?

   (A) 5
   (B) 3
   (C) −1
   (D) −3

4. The following chart tabulates the breakfast items ordered at Sam's Breakfast Dine-In & Drive-Thru on a particular Monday.

	Egg Sand-wich	Cinna-mon Roll	Break-fast Burrito	Chicken and Waffles	Totals
Dine-in	73	40	68	110	291
Drive-through	94	26	89	75	284
Totals	167	66	157	185	575

   What is the best estimation of the probability that a randomly selected item sold from the drive-through that Monday is a breakfast burrito?

   (A) 0.28
   (B) 0.31
   (C) 0.36
   (D) 0.43

5. $$\frac{n+3}{2} = 5$$

   What is the value of n in the above equation?

6. A school day at Washington High School is seven and a half hours long. How many <u>minutes</u> long is this school day?

7. What represents the range of values of x in this inequality?

   $$-3(x + 4) > 2x$$

   (A) $x < -\frac{12}{5}$
   (B) $x \leq -\frac{1}{3}$
   (C) $x > \frac{7}{8}$
   (D) $x \geq 3\frac{1}{2}$

8. A retailer sells certain numbers of shirts of the following price ranges during a particular day:

Number of Shirts Sold	Price Range
12	$0 < $ Price $ < \$10$
15	$\$10 \leq $ Price $ < \$15$
10	$\$15 \leq $ Price $ < \$20$
21	$\$20 \leq $ Price $ < \$25$
7	$\$25 \leq $ Price

   Which of the following is justifiable from the given table?

   (A) The range of prices is $25
   (B) The mean price is between $15 and $20
   (C) The median price is between $15 and $20
   (D) None of the above

3   3   3

9. $9a^2 - 81b^2$ is equivalent to which of the following expressions?

(A) $(3a + 3b)(3a - 3b)$
(B) $3(a - b)(a + 3b)$
(C) $9(a + 3b)(a - 3b)$
(D) $9(a - 3b)(a - b)$

10. For how many points in the xy-coordinate plane will the functions $y = 4x$ and $2y = 8x - 5$ intersect?

(A) Infinitely many
(B) 2
(C) 1
(D) None

11. $\frac{1}{3}x + 2\left(\frac{x}{6} + 3\right)$ is equivalent to which of the following expressions?

(A) $\frac{2}{3}x + 6$

(B) $x + 3$

(C) $\frac{4}{6}x + 2$

(D) $3x + 6$

12. A polling company surveys 1,000 randomly selected senior citizens in the state of Connecticut. The senior citizens surveyed are representative of the typical demographics of senior citizens in the state. There are approximately 3.6 million residents in Connecticut, and approximately 14% of these residents are senior citizens. If 23% of the survey respondents indicated they planned on supporting a new tax regulation, what is the best estimate for how many senior citizens in the state as a whole would support the tax regulation?

(A) 83,000
(B) 98,000
(C) 116,000
(D) 828,000

13. A circle has a radius of 4 inches. One sector of the circle has a central angle measure of 60 degrees. What is the area of this sector of the circle in square inches?

(A) $\frac{\pi}{4}$

(B) 2π

(C) $\frac{8\pi}{3}$

(D) $\frac{15\pi}{2}$

14. If $-\frac{2}{3}x = \frac{1}{6}$, then $\dfrac{-\left(\frac{3}{2}\right)}{x}$ is equivalent to which of the following?

(A) $\frac{2}{3}$

(B) 6

(C) -3

(D) $\frac{8}{3}$

15. A customer orders food to be delivered from a restaurant. The cost of the food, including tax, is c. The total price, t, the customer pays upon delivery is given by the equation $t = 1.2c + 2$, which accounts for the cost of the food, a 20% tip on the food, and a \$2 delivery fee. The restaurant doubles its delivery fee, and in response, the customer halves the percent of tip he pays. Which of the following expressions would represent the new total price the customer pays for food of cost c delivered from the restaurant?

(A) $1.2c + 2$
(B) $1.1c + 4$
(C) $0.6c + 4$
(D) $1.4c + 2$

3   3   3

16. At a city park, there are three dogs that weigh an average of 40 pounds each, and three cats. If two of the cats weigh 25 pounds each, what must the weight (in pounds) of the third cat be if the average weight of all six of these animals in the park is 30 pounds?

17. The costs of packages of generic brand soda, G, and name brand soda, N, at a grocery store are directly proportional to each other. If the relationship between the two is modeled by the equation $N = 2G$, where 2 represents the constant of proportionality, which of the following statements would be true?

(A) The name brand soda is twice as expensive as the generic soda.
(B) The name brand soda is half as expensive as the generic soda.
(C) The prices of the generic and name brand sodas are equivalent.
(D) The average number of packages sold of the generic brand soda is twice that of the name brand.

18. If 3 As equal 2 Bs, and 3 Cs equal one B, how many Cs will there be for each A?

(A) 1
(B) 2
(C) 3
(D) 6

19. If a square has a diagonal that measures $3\sqrt{2}$ units, what is the square's perimeter in units?

20. A business starts a social media account at the beginning of the year, beginning with 100 followers. With each month that passes, the number of followers increases by 5%, compounding on the previous month's total number of followers. Which would best represent the relationship between months and the number of followers?

(A) An exponentially increasing relationship
(B) An exponentially decreasing relationship
(C) A linear relationship, with the line of the relationship having a constant slope
(D) A linear relationship, with the line of the relationship having a positive, changing slope

21. The vertex form of parabola f is given by the function $f(x) = x^2 + 3$. The function $g(x)$ is given by the equation $g(x) = -f(x) + 2$. If the vertex of $f(x)$ is point (a, b), what is the vertex of $g(x)$ in terms of a and b?

(A) $(a, b + 2)$
(B) $(-a, -b + 4)$
(C) $(2a, b - 2)$
(D) $(a, b - 4)$

22. Consider a rectangular prism with a height of A, a length of B, and a width of C. How many pyramids of the same length and width of this prism, but half its height, can fit into the prism?

4   4   4

SECTION 2: MATH MODULE 2

35 MINUTES, 22 QUESTIONS

- All expressions and variables use real numbers.
- All figures are drawn to scale.
- Every figure lies in a plane.
- The domain of given functions is the set of all real numbers for which the corresponding value of the function is real.

For multiple-choice questions, solve the problem and pick the correct answer from the provided choices. Each multiple-choice question has only one correct answer.

For student-produced response questions, solve each problem and enter your answer following these guidelines:

- If you find more than one correct answer, enter just one answer.
- You can enter up to five characters for a positive answer and up to six characters (this includes the negative sign) for a negative answer.
- If your answer is a fraction that does not fit in the given space, enter the decimal equivalent instead.
- If your answer is a decimal that does not fit in the given space, enter it by stopping at or rounding up at the fourth digit.
- If your answer is a mixed number (like $4\frac{1}{2}$), enter it as an improper fraction (9/2) or its decimal equivalent (4.5).
- Do not enter symbols like a comma, dollar sign, or percent sign.

Examples

Answer	Acceptable Entries	Unacceptable Entries That Will Receive Zero Credit
4.5	4.5 4.50 9/2	41/2 4 1/2
$\frac{8}{9}$	8/9 .8888 .8889 0.888 0.889	0.8 .88 0.88 0.89
$-\frac{1}{9}$	−1/9 −.1111 −0.111	−.11 −0.11

4   4   4

1. $x^2 - 20 = x$

   What are the solution(s) to the equation above?

   (A) 20
   (B) 12, 5
   (C) −4, 5
   (D) 0, 2

2. What is the smallest possible value for x in this inequality?

   $$-2x + 3 \leq -5$$

   (A) 4
   (B) 1
   (C) 0
   (D) −6

3. Which of the following expressions is equivalent to $12(m + 3) - 4$?

   (A) $2m + 11$
   (B) $m - 7$
   (C) $12m - 15$
   (D) $12m + 32$

4. A speed-reading course teaches students to read 1,000 words per minute. If a graduate from this course were able to read this quickly, how many minutes would it take her to read a book that has 200 pages with an average of 300 words per page?

   (A) 30
   (B) 60
   (C) 90
   (D) 150

5. Which of the following is a solution to the equation below?

   $$(a + 5)^2 + 4 = 68$$

   (A) 2
   (B) 3
   (C) 8
   (D) 13

6. On a test with 40 questions, if someone misses 14 questions on the test and answers the remaining questions correctly, what will be the percent score on the test?

   (A) 35%
   (B) 40%
   (C) 55%
   (D) 65%

7. A teacher gives a five-question pop quiz, and students can score any whole value between 0 and 5, inclusive.

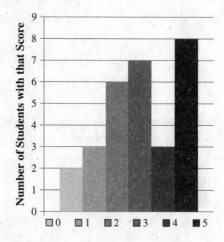

   In the above set of quiz results, which of these quantities would be greatest?

   (A) The median quiz score
   (B) The mean quiz score
   (C) The mode of the quiz scores
   (D) The mean and median will be tied for the greatest value.

8. If $2x\left(\frac{3}{b}\right) = 2(x)^9$ for all values of x, what is the value of b?

   (A) 3
   (B) 1
   (C) $\frac{1}{2}$
   (D) $\frac{1}{3}$

4   4   4

9.

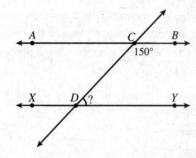

In the figure above, lines *AB* and *XY* are parallel, and line *CD* transverses them. Given that angle *BCD* is equal to 150 degrees, what is the measure of angle *CDY* in degrees?

10. In what quadrants of the *xy*-coordinate plane will solutions to $y > |x| + 1$ be found?

(A) First only
(B) Fourth only
(C) First and second only
(D) Third and fourth only

11. How many zeros does the function
$y = (x - 3)(x - 1)(x + 2)(x - 1)$ have?

(A) 1
(B) 2
(C) 3
(D) 4

12. A copyeditor takes three minutes to edit each page of a book that is *p* pages long. Which of the following expressions gives the total number of <u>hours</u> that the copyeditor would take to edit the book?

(A) $\dfrac{p}{20}$

(B) $3p + 60$

(C) $\dfrac{p}{60}$

(D) $60 - 3p$

13. Consider the following system of equations:
$$y - 4x = 5 \text{ and } y - 13 = 2x$$
What is the *y* value at the point of intersection for these two equations?

14. Given that neither *x* nor *y* is equal to 0, if $\frac{1}{3}x = 2y$, what is the value of $\frac{1}{14}\left(\dfrac{y + x}{y}\right)$?

15. For fiscal year 2017, the State of New York has the following spending allocations for its $96 billion budget:

New York State Government Spending

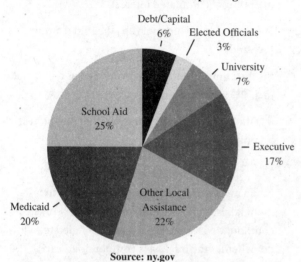

Source: ny.gov

If in the two years after this budget, the budget percentage allocations remain constant and New York state government spending increases at a constant rate of 6% a year, how much money will be spent in the budget two years after this budget on the Executive part (to the nearest tenth of a billion dollars)?

(A) $17.0 billion
(B) $18.0 billion
(C) $18.3 billion
(D) $18.9 billion

16. Acceleration is calculated by taking the change in velocity between two points and dividing it by the change in distance between those same two points. Suppose that a scientist graphs a line of the constant acceleration of a car on the xy-coordinate plane, using distance as the x-coordinates and velocity as the y-coordinates. If this line intersects the y-axis at point b, what property of the line corresponds to the car's acceleration?

(A) Its y-intercept
(B) Its slope
(C) Its y-values (range)
(D) Its x-values (domain)

17. A rectangular fence, which fully encloses a flat area, is 4 times as long as it is wide. If the length of the fence is L feet, what is the perimeter of the fence in terms of L?

(A) $2.5L$
(B) $10L$
(C) $16L$
(D) $16L^2$

18. What are the solution(s) for x in the equation $-|2.4x + 13.5| = 3$?

(A) -4.375 only
(B) -6.875 only
(C) Both -4.375 and -6.875
(D) No possible solutions

19.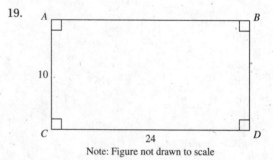
Note: Figure not drawn to scale

In the rectangle drawn above, what is the product of the lengths of the two diagonals, AD and BC?

(A) 50
(B) 52
(C) 625
(D) 676

20. Given that $x > 0$, which of the following is an equivalent form of $\sqrt{(64x^6)^{\frac{2}{3}}x^{-2}}$?

(A) $4x$
(B) $16x^2$
(C) $\dfrac{x^2}{4}$
(D) $\dfrac{2}{3}x^{-\frac{2}{3}}$

4   4   4

21. A conference planner will have equal representation of male and female representatives at a
breakout session in a meeting room. The session
will go ahead as long as people are in the room.
Fire marshal regulations stipulate that no more
than 60 people are permitted in the room at a
given time. Assuming that the breakout session
is proceeding and that no other people are in the
meeting room other than the m male participants
and w female participants, what are the constraints on the values of m and w?

(A) $\begin{cases} m > w > 0 \\ m + w < 60 \\ m = w \end{cases}$

(B) $\begin{cases} m > 0 \\ w > 0 \\ m + w \leq 60 \\ m = w \end{cases}$

(C) $\begin{cases} m < 0 \\ w < 0 \\ m + w \geq 60 \\ m = w \end{cases}$

(D) $\begin{cases} m < 0 \\ w < 0 \\ m - w \leq 60 \\ m - w = 0 \end{cases}$

22. The formula for the compound interest on a mon-
etary investment is $A = P\left(1 + \frac{r}{n}\right)^{nt}$ in which the
variables stand for the following quantities:

A is the total amount of money after n years,
including accumulated interest.

P is the principal amount (i.e., the initial amount
invested).

r is the annual interest rate expressed as a decimal
(e.g., 3% interest is expressed as 0.03).

n is the number of times per year that the interest
is compounded.

t is the number of years the money is invested.

Linda invests $10,000 in a bond fund. Her invest-
ment advisor told her that the fund earns 10%
compounded a year, but the adviser failed to tell
her whether the interest is compounded each
month or just once per year. How much more
interest in the first year of the investment would
she earn if the interest on the fund is compounded
monthly versus compounded annually (enter your
answer to the nearest whole dollar, omitting the
dollar sign)?

ANSWER KEY
Practice Test 2

Reading and Writing Module 1

1. **B**	8. **D**	15. **C**	22. **A**
2. **C**	9. **A**	16. **D**	23. **D**
3. **C**	10. **B**	17. **A**	24. **D**
4. **A**	11. **C**	18. **B**	25. **C**
5. **B**	12. **C**	19. **B**	26. **D**
6. **B**	13. **B**	20. **A**	27. **B**
7. **B**	14. **D**	21. **A**	

Reading and Writing Module 2

1. **A**	8. **B**	15. **A**	22. **A**
2. **C**	9. **C**	16. **B**	23. **A**
3. **A**	10. **B**	17. **B**	24. **A**
4. **A**	11. **A**	18. **A**	25. **D**
5. **B**	12. **A**	19. **D**	26. **D**
6. **B**	13. **A**	20. **B**	27. **A**
7. **D**	14. **B**	21. **A**	

Math Module 1

1. **A**	7. **A**	13. **C**	19. **12**
2. **D**	8. **C**	14. **B**	20. **A**
3. **A**	9. **C**	15. **B**	21. **D**
4. **B**	10. **D**	16. **10**	22. **6**
5. **7**	11. **A**	17. **A**	
6. **450**	12. **C**	18. **B**	

Math Module 2

1. **C**	7. **C**	13. **21**	19. **D**
2. **A**	8. **D**	14. **0.5 or ½**	20. **A**
3. **D**	9. **30**	15. **C**	21. **B**
4. **B**	10. **C**	16. **B**	22. **47**
5. **B**	11. **C**	17. **A**	
6. **D**	12. **A**	18. **D**	

Digital PSAT Scoring Chart

This will give you an approximation of the score you would earn on the Digital PSAT[1]. Tally the number of correct answers from the Reading & Writing section (out of 54) and the Math section (out of 44). Take the total for each of these and find the corresponding section score in the tables below.

Number of correct reading and writing questions (out of 54)	Reading and writing test score (out of 760)
0	160
1	170
2	180
3	190
4	200
5	210
6	220
7	230
8	240
9	250
10	260
11	270
12	290
13	300
14	310
15	320
16	340
17	350
18	360
19	370
20	390
21	400
22	420
23	430
24	450
25	460
26	470

[1] Keep in mind that some of the questions on an actual SAT test will be research questions that will not count towards your actual score. For the sake of simplicity, we are including possible research questions in your calculation.

Number of correct reading and writing questions (out of 54)	Reading and writing test score (out of 760)
27	480
28	490
29	500
30	510
31	520
32	530
33	540
34	550
35	560
36	570
37	580
38	590
39	600
40	610
41	620
42	630
43	640
44	650
45	660
46	670
47	680
48	690
49	700
50	710
51	720
52	730
53	750
54	760

Number of Correct Math Questions (Out of 44)	Math Section Score (Out of 760)
0	160
1	180
2	190
3	200
4	210
5	240
6	260
7	280
8	300
9	310
10	320
11	340
12	350
13	360
14	370
15	390
16	400
17	410
18	420
19	440
20	450
21	460
22	470
23	480
24	490
25	500
26	510
27	520
28	530
29	540
30	550
31	560
32	570
33	580

Number of Correct Math Questions (Out of 44)	Math Section Score (Out of 760)
34	590
35	610
36	620
37	640
38	650
39	660
40	680
41	710
42	730
43	750
44	760

Add the Reading and Writing score and the Math section score to find your total PSAT test score:

_____ Reading and Writing score +

_____ Math section score =

_____ **Total PSAT test score (between 320 and 1520)**

Approximate your testing percentiles (1st–99th) using this chart:

Total Score	Section Score	Total Percentile	Reading and Writing Percentile	Math Percentile
1520	760	99+	99+	99
1420	710	98	98	96
1320	660	94	94	91
1220	610	86	86	84
1120	560	74	73	75
1020	510	59	57	61
920	460	41	40	42
820	410	25	24	27
720	360	11	11	15
620	310	3	3	5
520	260	1	1	1
420	210	1	1	1
320	160	1	1	1

Scoring data based on information at Collegeboard.org

Answer Explanations

Section 1: Reading and Writing Module 1

1. **(B)** The color cameras are described as being cumbersome and challenging to use, which aligns with *unwieldy*. While the cameras were larger than ones used today, the text does not support calling them *unsightly* or ugly. No mention is directly made of their expense. Also, since the cameras were less advanced than ones used today, it is highly unlikely that they would be *precise*.

2. **(C)** The "tired" and "poor" immigrants would be eager to embrace a new life of freedom, making *desiring* the most logical option. The other options do not signify desire.

3. **(C)** In the context of the text, *singular* refers to the type of beginning that the Big Bang was, making *definitive* most appropriate. While the other words can be stand-ins for "singular," they are not consistent with the context of the text.

4. **(A)** The first sentence mentions growing concern in the health care community that there will be microorganisms that will develop antibiotic resistance; therefore, the infections will no longer be able to be treated with antibiotics. There is no concern about potential overdose or a loss of medical prominence. Also, there is no mention about alternative medical approaches.

5. **(B)** The best approach to a question like this is to consider the purpose of the text as a whole. Reagan speaks directly to Congress here, providing visuals and empirical evidence of just how bad the current situation is. So, (B) is the only choice that indicates his intention to illustrate severity.

6. **(B)** The introduction to the text clarifies that Coverdale has moved onto a "utopian communal farm," and it is this commune to which the word *Community* refers. There is no evidence in the text that writers of the 1800s consistently wrote in this manner, as in choice (A). There also is no evidence that the narrator is interested in larger urban developments, as in choice (C), because he has chosen to move to a farming community. And there is no mention of other cities (municipalities) earlier in the text, making choice (D) incorrect.

7. **(B)** Text 1 argues that young athletes miss out on significant earnings opportunities because they are prohibited from starting their careers for certain periods of time. The example of Marcus Lattimore serves to give an example of someone who missed out on significant earnings because of a career-ending injury he suffered in college. Thus, Text 2 provides a specific anecdote in support of the argument in Text 1.

8. **(D)** Text 1 can be generally characterized as high-minded and visionary since it renders a philosophy of education based on inspiration. Text 2 is a realistic approach to a defined, but limited curriculum. Since *lofty* means "exalted" and *practical* means "hands-on" or "sensible," choice (D) is accurate.

9. **(A)** The selection demonstrates Muir's tone of urgency, particularly by saying that it is "now" that action is needed and that "quick measures" must be implemented. He is neither arrogant nor cheerful. And while the current ignorance surrounding environmental conservation may make him depressed, his text is a call to action rather than a hopeless rant.

10. **(B)** The author allows that the search is extensive, but that opinion varies "from certainty to skepticism to downright incredulity," giving evidence for (B). The other options inaccurately indicate that there is a scientific agreement of some sort.

11. **(C)** The text states that humans are visibly able to perceive wavelengths between 400 and 700 nanometers. (A) nanometer is 1×10^{-9} meters, so the visible wavelengths would fall between the ultraviolet and infrared wavelengths.

12. **(C)** This option illustrates a shift from fighting in the wilderness, *the Canadian frontier*, to fighting in urban areas, *cities such as Baltimore, Washington, D.C., and New Orleans*. The other options do not illustrate this sort of shift in setting.

13. **(B)** The text describes cats as being entertaining but "far less predictable" in their behavior than other pets and "fickle." The final sentence creates a contrast between how the cat is a very common pet—to complete that contrast, stating that cat behavior is unfamiliar would be logical. (A) is not supported since the cats are described as unpredictable. There is no evidence in the text to support choice (C). (D) is irrelevant to the focus of the text.

14. **(D)** According to the text, "The time for woman suffrage has come." Hence, *immediately* is the correct answer. None of the other choices refer to instantaneous action.

15. **(C)** *Negligible* means "inconsequential," so this question is asking which approach would not change the end result. (A) removes moisture, so it is consequential even if it is an undesirable effect. (B) locks in moisture. (D) would still denature the protein, impacting tenderness and moistness. According to the author, searing meat doesn't influence tenderness, and so, (C) is the correct answer.

16. **(D)** The sentence refers to "ancient times past," making it most logical to use the past tense. Also, the subject is plural with "beauty and . . . refinement," making the past plural word *were* most fitting.

17. **(A)** *Well* is used similarly to the word *far* in this context, stating that this is for a great duration of time into the nineteenth century. (A) comma is needed after *century* to separate the dependent introductory phrase from the independent clause that follows. Choices (B) and (D) break up the phrase *well into*, and choice (C) has no needed pauses.

18. **(B)** In this instance, simple and concise is superior to long and winded. All four choices demonstrate the same sentiment, but choice (B) is the most succinct and direct.

19. **(B)** This choice is the most concise and uses parallel phrasing. Choices (A) and (C) are too wordy. Choice (D) uses *meeting*, which is incorrect to use in conjunction with *to*—one says *to meet* rather than *to meeting*.

20. **(A)** Keep the entire dependent clause uninterrupted by commas by selecting "No Change." The other options make this phrase too choppy.

21. **(A)** The first decision is whether to use *many* or *much*. The sentence mentions "reasons," which are things that are easily countable. *Many reasons* is the better usage, so eliminate choices (B) and (C). Recall *much* is used to describe things that cannot be counted. The subject is "dental students," which is a plural noun that will require a plural verb like *have*. *Has* is a singular verb. Choice (A), then, is better than choice (D).

22. **(A)** This is the only option that puts quotation marks around a direct quote from Bernard Shaw. Choices (B) and (C) have no quotation marks. Choice (D) would work if this phrase were inside another quotation.

23. **(D)** *Though* is the only option that expresses the contrast needed in the sentence. All of the other options show cause and effect.

24. **(D)** "While" is the only transition provided that shows a contrast between the popular familiarity of the blues and its unfamiliar origin.

25. **(C)** "Although" is the only option that shows a contrast between the long-standing gradual innovation with respect to the periodic table and the relatively recent acceleration of advancement.

26. **(D)** This is the only option to provide a proper transition between the broad statement made in the previous sentence (i.e., that Cohn's essays focus on a darker side of the Renaissance) and the more specific elaboration on what makes his essays distinctive (i.e., that these essays look at people from all social classes instead of only focusing on elites).

27. **(B)** Typical readers are not likely to be law enforcement professionals, so Choice B provides the most viable way that someone without a specific skill set could contribute to this sort of research. It is not A or C because these focus on law enforcement professionals. It is not D because this does not relate to the provided notes.

Section 1: Reading and Writing Module 2

1. **(A)** Will never completes his assignments on time, so you can infer that the intended meaning is *lackadaisical*, as in choice (A). (B) refers more to sleepiness than idleness. (C) would indicate that Will was unintelligent, and would not fit the context. (D) is a near antonym to what is needed, since it refers to eagerness and intensity.

2. **(C)** *Depends* works best here since the line refers to ecological balance being contingent on two things. It would be incorrect to say the balance *fulcrums*, *analyzes*, or *joints* on two things.

3. **(A)** The sentence before indicates that Mrs. Price never showed Fanny more kindness than she did on that first day. The sentence after states that "she had neither leisure nor affection to bestow." So, it can be inferred that the "instinct of nature" that had to be satisfied was her *maternal feeling*. It is not related to *survival*, *acceptance*, or *justice*.

4. **(A)** This sentence clarifies the phrase about the division of fires because it highlights how different fires are needed for different functions, like for heating and for cooking. It does not deal with the history of stoves, like in choices (B) or (C). Also, it does not specifically address the baking of mammoth meat.

5. **(B)** The text furnishes a direct example of the general statement made in the first sentence, pointing out the metabolic and immunological advantages of some natural bacteria. Hence, (B) is correct. (A) and (D) misunderstand details of the text. (C) is appealing because it is true that this example could be used to address an objection toward all germ theory, but this text is more interested in giving that illustrative example rather than responding to objections.

6. **(B)** The example of *If We Were Villains* mentioned in the beginning of Text 1 is described as a *novel*, making it representative of the *books* from Text 2. Whereas *figures* and *antagonists* may

be components of the story, they do not align with what the example primarily represents. *Movies* are not mentioned in Text 1.

7. **(D)** Text 2 argues that because Darwin did not have a grasp of Mendel's work on heredity, he was unable to anticipate the phenomenon of genetic drift. This would be a shortcoming in the theory presented in Text 1 that Text 2 highlights. It is not (A), because neither text claims that the evolutionary theory presented is infallible. It is not (B), because Text 1 does not address any objection from Text 2. It is not (C), because there was a lack of influence of Mendel on Darwin, causing Darwinian theory a problem in the eyes of the author of Text 2.

8. **(B)** According to the author, organic farming "encourages polyculture," so it produces more *diversity*. The text states that conventional farming is more productive and centralized. There is no evidence for (C) either way.

9. **(C)** The selection provides the backstory for how Pip came to the house of Miss Havisham. (A), (B), and (D) all are not presented in this selection.

10. **(B)** *-Ock* is the only option that has a short syllable coupled with a hard consonant ending.

11. **(A)** To *undermine* the hypothesis is to "find a flaw" in it. The economist is arguing that making unemployment benefits more generous will cause fewer people to seek out work. Choice (A) most directly undermines this because it would show that in a similar situation in another state, an increase in unemployment benefits did not result in an increase in unemployment. (B) and (C) would confirm the original hypothesis instead of undermining it. (D) presents a flawed sample of voluntary results that would not be helpful in making a determination on this topic.

12. **(A)** The graph does not provide evidence on health care or birth rates, ruling out choices (B), (C), and (D). Additionally, you can confirm (A) by seeing that about 17 percent of the population is made up of those 65 and older. The only country close to this percentage is the United States with about 15 percent of the population being in this category.

13. **(A)** The sentence states that a folklorist's job is not confined to an academic setting of a university or desk, but is instead highly involved in exciting real-world settings. Therefore, calling the work *participatory and engaging* would emphasize the interesting settings in which the field takes place. It is not (B), because the field is described in a more positive way. It is not (C), because the field is described as being more hands-on instead of abstract. It is not (D), because there is no mention of the pay for folklorists.

14. **(B)** The text states that Jane is first made aware of Mr. Rochester's presence when she hears "the gallop of a horse," which would be perceived through *hearing*.

15. **(A)** This option correctly uses the present perfect tense to indicate that the narrator has forgotten this exercise. Choice (B) incorrectly uses *forgot*, choice (C) incorrectly uses *has*, and choice (D) is nonsensical.

16. **(B)** This choice maintains the original meaning while being concise. Choices (A) and (D) are too wordy, and choice (C) subtly changes the original intent.

17. **(B)** *Their* shows possession in the third person. Choice (A) is wrong, because *there* is used for places. Choice (C) would be used if the subject had been "we" instead of the "architect," and choice (D) is a contraction meaning "they are."

18. **(A)** This choice concisely expresses the needed idea, using the singular possessive apostrophe correctly. Choice (B) uses the plural *analyses*. Choices (C) and (D) are too wordy.

19. **(D)** This is the third item listed in this sentence. To differentiate it from the others, using *still* makes the most sense. The other options do not indicate a third item in this sequence.

20. **(B)** When referring to ideas, the phrase *points to* is fitting. Choice (A) is for pointing at physical objects, and choices (C) and (D) are not idiomatically correct.

21. **(A)** The colon sets off the clarification that follows, and the commas set aside the nonessential yet descriptive phrase, *regardless of their mass*. Choice (B) causes a run-on sentence. Choices (C) and (D) are both missing needed pauses.

22. **(A)** In this sentence, there is a pattern of, essentially, *not for* this *reason,* but *for* that *reason.* That *but* is necessary because it demonstrates the contrasting relationship that is apparent. And *since, and,* and *for a result* fail to capture that pattern of *not for this, but for that.*

23. **(A)** To determine the correct conjunction to use, analyze the relationship between the two clauses. Here, the second clause contrasts with the first. Essentially, although Schrödinger won the Nobel Prize, he is more famous for something else. "Although," like "but," is a contrasting term. Choice (A) is the correct answer. Choices (B) and (C) emphasize a causal relationship. Choice (D) is not contrasting but, rather, conjoining.

24. **(A)** Analyze the relationship between this sentence and the previous statement. Essentially, the second sentence is a restatement of the previous sentence. "In other words" serves to introduce a restatement. Choices (B) and (C) create a cause-and-effect relationship that is not apparent here. "Henceforth" is often used chronologically to signify from this point forward.

25. **(D)** *Posthumous* means "after one's death." Since (*A) Memoir of Jane Austen* is described as being published after Austen's death, this is the only logical option. The other works were not described as being published after Austen's death.

26. **(D)** "Thus" shows a cause-and-effect relationship. It would be appropriate in this context to show that in order for colleges to minimize the possibility of having graduates without jobs, the colleges should make every effort to ensure that its students find employment. Choices (A) and (B) are similar to also, which is not cause-and-effect, and Choice (C) shows a contrast.

27. **(A)** The answer must both outline a worst-case scenario and do so with respect to the user's health impact. Choice (A) is the only option to focus on the worst-case possibility of a stained-glass artist becoming poisoned. Choice (B) does not focus on the health impact of the person making stained glass. Choices (C) and (D) do not connect to worst-case scenarios.

Section 2: Math Module 1

1. **(A)** Distance = (rate) × (time), so $16x$ must represent a rate multiplied by a time.

   You're told that x is the time given in hours, so 16 must represent her rate. *Rate* is another word for speed, so you can narrow it down to choice (A) or choice (B). Because 16 is constant (not changing), the correct answer is choice (A).

2. **(D)** The $3x$ must be distributed to both the $\frac{1}{3}x$ term and the -5 term:

$$3x\left(\frac{1}{3}x - 5\right) = \frac{3}{3}x^2 - 15x$$

Then, the fraction can be reduced, giving $x^2 - 15x$, choice (D).

3. **(A)** Plug the given slope and point coordinates into the point-slope equation: $y - y_1 = m(x - x_1)$, where m is the slope and (x_1, y_1) are the coordinates of a point on the line. Therefore,

$$y - 8 = 3(x - 1)$$

Next, distribute the 3:

$$y - 8 = 3x - 3$$

To get the line in slope-intercept form, add 8 to both sides:

$y = 3x + 5$. Therefore, the y-intercept is 5, choice (A). You could also plug 3 in for the slope and the point $(1, 8)$ into the line when it is in slope-intercept form: $y = mx + b$. Then you could solve for the y-intercept b.

4. **(B)** The drive-through sold a total of 284 items, and 89 of those were breakfast burritos. Therefore, the probability that a randomly selected item will be a breakfast burrito is given by the expression $\frac{89}{284} = 0.31$, choice (B).

5. **7** Start by multiplying both sides by 2:

$$n + 3 = 10$$

Subtracting 3 from both sides tells you that $n = 7$.

6. **450** You can use the conversion 60 minutes per hour to figure out this problem. Use dimensional analysis to cancel out the units that you don't want (hours) and end up with the units that you do want (minutes):

$$7.5 \text{ hours} \times \frac{60 \text{ min}}{1 \text{ hour}} = 450 \text{ min.}$$

7. **(A)** First, isolate what's inside the parentheses by dividing both sides by -3, remembering that dividing by a negative flips the inequality sign.

$x + 4 < -\frac{2}{3}x$. Next, you'll need to subtract x from both sides to get all x terms on the right, but first get a common denominator for the x terms:

$\frac{3}{3}x + 4 < -\frac{2}{3}x$, so $4 < -\frac{5}{3}x$. Finally, divide both sides by $-\frac{5}{3}$, which is the same as multiplying both sides by $-\frac{3}{5}$, again remembering to flip the inequality since you are multiplying by a negative number:

$$-\frac{12}{5} > x, \text{ or } x < -\frac{12}{5}, \text{ choice (A).}$$

8. **(C)** Use process of elimination here. You can eliminate choice (A) because you don't know the range: there is no upper limit provided. You only know that the upper limit is over \$25.

Choice (B) can also be eliminated because you can't figure out an exact mean without knowing what the prices are. For instance, if the prices in the last row were all well above \$25, and thus outliers, the mean would be very skewed.

Choice (C) can be tested. There are $12 + 15 + 10 + 21 + 7 = 65$ terms in this series, so the median term will be the 33rd term (there are 32 terms smaller than this number and 32 terms larger than it). The first row encompasses terms 1–12. The second row encompasses 13–27, and the third has terms 28–37. Therefore, the 33rd term will fall in this third row, and thus will have a price between \$15 and \$20. Therefore, choice (C) is correct.

9. **(C)** First, you can factor out a 9:

$$9(a^2 - 9b^2)$$

Something of the form $(x^2 - y^2)$ is a difference of perfect squares and factors to $(x + y)(x - y)$. In this case, $x = a$, while $y = 3b$ since $(3b)^2 = 9b^2$. Therefore, $a^2 - 9b^2 = (a + 3b)(a - 3b)$. Remembering the 9 you previously factored out gives you $9(a + 3b)(a - 3b)$, choice (C).

Alternatively, you could have FOILed all answer choices to see which choice gave you the expression in the question's statement.

10. **(D)** Get the second equation into slope-intercept form so you can see how the two equations relate. In order to accomplish this, divide both sides by 2:

$$y = 4x - 2.5$$

Therefore, both lines have the same slope, but different y-intercepts. This means that they're parallel lines and never intersect, choice (D).

Alternatively, if you don't recognize this right away, you can set the right side of both equations (in slope-intercept form) equal to each other and attempt to solve for x to see where the two lines intersect:

$$4x = 4x - 2.5$$

Subtracting $4x$ from both sides, you have $0 = -2.5$, which is a false statement, so there are no solutions to this equation, and hence no intersection points.

11. **(A)** First, distribute the 2 in the second term:

$$\frac{1}{3}x + \frac{2}{6}x + 6$$

Reduce the second fraction:

$$\frac{1}{3}x + \frac{1}{3}x + 6.$$

Combine like terms:

$\frac{2}{3}x + 6$. Thus, the answer is choice (A).

12. **(C)** First, you need to know how many senior citizens there are in the state of Connecticut. If 14% of 3.6 million are seniors, then $3,600,000(0.14) = 504,000$ are senior citizens. This also could have been done using a proportion, recognizing that 3.6 million is 100% of the population.

Next, you know that 23% of the survey respondents said that they would support the new tax regulation. Since the question says that those surveyed are representative of the population, it follows that 23% of the senior population would also support the tax regulation. Find 23% of 504,000 by using a proportion (although you could just as easily multiply 504,000 by 0.23 to find the answer).

$$\frac{504,000}{100} = \frac{x}{23}$$

Next, cross-multiply:

$$(504{,}000)(23) = 100x$$

$$1{,}1592{,}00 = 100x$$

Dividing by 100 tells you that $x = 115{,}920$. This most closely matches choice (C).

13. **(C)** First, calculate the area of the circle:

$$\pi r^2 \rightarrow \pi(4)^2 = 16\pi$$

Since the sector has a measure of 60 degrees and a circle has a total of 360 interior degrees, calculate the fraction of the total circle's area that the sector is as follows:

$$16\pi \times \frac{60}{360} \rightarrow 16\pi \times \frac{1}{6} = \frac{16\pi}{6} = \frac{8\pi}{3} \text{ square inches}$$

14. **(B)** Notice that the expression the question is asking about is just the reciprocal of the left side of the first expression. Therefore, it will equal the reciprocal of the right side of the first expression. Because the reciprocal of $\frac{1}{6}$ is 6, the answer is choice (B).

Alternatively, if you do not recognize that it is the reciprocal, you can solve for x in the first equation and then plug this into the second expression:

If $-\frac{2}{3}x = \frac{1}{6}$, then multiplying both sides by $-\frac{3}{2}$ gives $x = \frac{1}{6}\left(\frac{-3}{2}\right) = -\frac{1}{4}$. Plugging this into your

expression gives $\dfrac{-\left(\frac{3}{2}\right)}{x} = \dfrac{-\left(\frac{3}{2}\right)}{-\left(\frac{1}{4}\right)} = \left(\frac{3}{2}\right)\left(\frac{4}{1}\right) = 6$.

15. **(B)** The 2 in the original equation is an added constant, so it is the delivery fee. Doubling the delivery fee would make it a constant \$4. Thus, you can narrow the answer down to choices (B) and (C) since the delivery fee will be the only constant (the cost of food and tip will depend on c). You can eliminate choice (C) as it is unlikely that the restaurant would allow the customer to pay only 0.6 or 60% of the cost of the food.

If you want to see where the correct answer, choice B, comes from, you could separate the original equation into $t = c + 0.2c + 2$, where c is the cost of the food, $0.2c$ is the 20% tip, and 2 is the delivery fee.

Thus, if the tip is halved, it will now be 10% of the cost of food, or $0.1c$. If the delivery fee is doubled, it will now be 4 instead of 2. Therefore, the new equation will be $t = c + 0.1c + 4 = 1.1c + 4$, which matches choice (B).

16. **10** The average of their weight would be the total weight of all six animals divided by 6:

$$\frac{d_1 + d_2 + d_3 + c_1 + c_2 + c_3}{6},$$

where d_i represents the weight of dog i, and c_i represents the weight of cat i. You are told that

the three dogs weigh an average of 40 pounds each, so $\dfrac{d_1 + d_2 + d_3}{3} = 40$ and thus the three

dogs combined weigh $d_1 + d_2 + d_3 = 3(40) = 120$. Also, you know two cats each weigh 25 pounds, so $c_1 = 25 = c_2$.

Thus, the average weight of the six animals is

$$\frac{d_1 + d_2 + d_3 + c_1 + c_2 + c_3}{6} = \frac{120 + 25 + 25 + c_3}{6} = \frac{170 + c_3}{6}$$

You are told that the average weight is 30 pounds, and you want to find the weight of the third cat, so you set your above expression equal to 30 and solve for c_3:

$$\frac{170 + c_3}{6} = 30$$

First, multiply by 6:

$170 + c_3 = 180$. Next, subtract 170 from both sides:

$c_3 = 10$. Therefore, the cat of unknown weight weighs 10 pounds.

17. **(A)** You can determine the answer by assigning particular values to G. For instance, suppose the generic brand soda costs \$1 (i.e., $G = 1$). Since $N = 2G$, it follows that $N = 2(1) = 2$. Thus, the name brand soda is twice as expensive as the generic brand. Similarly, trying other values for G, you always multiply G by 2 to find N, so N is always twice the cost of G, or choice (A).

18. **(B)** Take this step by step. You are told that 3 As equal 2 Bs, or $3A = 2B$, and 3 Cs equal one B, or $3C = 1(B)$. You want to know how many Cs there will be if you have just one (A). You don't know the relationship between (A) and (C) right away, but you do know how (A) is related to (B) and how (C) is related to (B). You can, therefore, use these relationships with (B) to find the relationship between (A) and (C). Since you want to know how many Cs there are for one A, you should first find out how (B) relates to one (A). Since $3A = 2B$, it follows that $A = \frac{2}{3}B$. But, you also know $3C = B$, so plugging this expression in for (B) in your previous equation, you obtain $A = \frac{2}{3}B = \frac{2}{3}(3C) = 2C$. Thus, 2 Cs equal one A, which corresponds to choice (B).

19. **12** A diagonal of a square cuts that square into two 45-45-90 triangles. If the diagonal of the square (the hypotenuse of the triangles) has a length of $3\sqrt{2}$, then that square will have side lengths of 3. This is because a 45-45-90 triangle has legs of length x and a hypotenuse of length $x\sqrt{2}$. (This relationship is given on the formula sheet at provided in the math section).

Therefore, the perimeter of the square will be $4l = 4(3) = 12$.

Alternatively, if you don't recognize this special triangle, you know that this is a square, so the two sides of the triangle will have the same length l. Using the Pythagorean theorem, $l^2 + l^2 = (3\sqrt{2})^2$, so $2l^2 = 18$. Dividing by 2 gives $l^2 = 9$, so $l = 3$.

20. **(A)** Calculate the number of followers in the first few months and see if you can find a pattern.

In the beginning, or month 0, there are 100 followers.

After month 1, the number of followers increases by 5%, so there are now

$$1.05(100) = 105 \text{ followers.}$$

After month 2, the number of followers increases by 5% again, giving $1.05(105)$ followers.

Since $105 = 1.05(100)$ based on your calculation in the previous month, you can substitute this expression in for 105 to get that the number of followers is $1.05(1.05(100))$, or $(1.05)^2(100)$ followers.

Similarly, you get that the number of followers in month 3 is $(1.05)^3(100)$. Continuing in this manner, a pattern emerges, giving you a formula for the number of followers in month n: $(1.05)^n(100)$. This is an exponential relationship between months and number of followers since the months variable is the exponent in your function. Also, the number of followers increases each month, so this is an exponentially increasing relationship. This matches choice (A).

21. **(D)** Note that in general, the vertex form of a parabola is given by $(x - h)^2 + k$, where (h, k) is the vertex of the parabola. You are told that the vertex form of parabola f is $f(x) = x^2 + 3$, which can be rewritten as $f(x) = (x - 0)^2 + 3$. Thus, the vertex of f is $(0, 3) = (a, b)$.
Now, you want to know how the vertex of $g(x)$ compares to (a, b). Note that
$g(x) = -f(x) + 2 = -(x^2 + 3) + 2 = -x^2 - 3 + 2 = x^2 - 1$. Thus, the vertex of g is
$(0, -1) = (a, -1)$. So, you just need to determine how b compares to -1. Since $b = 3$ and
$-1 = 3 - 4 = b - 4$, it follows that the vertex of g is $(a, b - 4)$ when written in terms of a and b, which matches choice (D).

Alternatively, you can think about what is happening in terms of transformations. Suppose (a, b) is the vertex of f. Then $-f(x)$ reflects f across the x-axis, so the vertex (a, b) becomes $(a, -b)$ when reflected. Then $g(x) = -f(x) + 2$ shifts $-f(x)$ up vertically by 2, so the vertex of $g(x)$ is $(a, -b + 2)$. Note that this is not an answer choice. However, the vertex of f is $(0, 3)$ since f shifts the parabola x^2 up 3 units. Thus, $b = 3$. So the vertex of g is $(a, -b + 2) = (a, -3 + 2) = (a, -1)$. Plugging 3 in for b in the answer choices, you see that choice (D) is the only choice that results in vertex $(a, -1)$.

22. **6** You are given the formula for the volume of a rectangular prism, $V_r = lwh$, at the beginning of the math section. In this problem, your rectangular prism has height A, length B, and width C, so the formula becomes $V_r = BCA$. You want to know how many pyramids with the same length and width of the prism, but half of its height, can fit into the prism. You are also given the formula for the volume of a pyramid, $V_p = \frac{1}{3}lwh$, at the beginning of the math section. Since the pyramids have the same length and width as the prism, $l = B$ and $w = C$. The height is half of the prism, so $h = \frac{A}{2}$. Thus, each pyramid has volume
$V_p = \frac{1}{3}BC\left(\frac{A}{2}\right) = \frac{1}{6}BCA$. Note that $\frac{1}{6}BCA = \frac{1}{6}V_r$. Therefore, since $V_p = \frac{1}{6}V_r$, it follows that
$6V_p = V_r$. In other words, you can fit 6 pyramids into the rectangular prism.

Section 2: Math Module 2

1. **(C)** Subtract x from both sides to give the quadratic

$$x^2 - x - 20 = 0.$$

This quadratic easily factors to

$$(x - 5)(x + 4) = 0$$

If either factor equaled 0, the entire expression would equal to 0. Thus, you can find the two solutions to the equation by setting each factor to 0:

$$x - 5 = 0, \text{ so } x = 5.$$

$$x + 4 = 0, \text{ so } x = -4.$$

Therefore, the two solutions are -4 and 5.

Alternatively, if you aren't great at factoring, you could have used the quadratic formula to arrive at the same answer.

If you have no idea how to solve this problem, you could plug each answer choice into the equation to see which numbers actually work. For instance, you can eliminate choice (A) because $20^2 - 20 = 400 - 20 = 380 \neq 20$.

2. **(A)** Solve inequalities just like any other equation, but remember to flip the sign of the inequality any time you multiply or divide by a negative number. The first step is to subtract 3 from both sides so that all of the constants are on the right and all of the variables are on the left:

$$-2x \leq -8$$

Next, you have to divide by -2, remembering to flip your inequality since it is a negative number: $x \geq 4$. Because x must be greater than or equal to 4, it must be at least 4. Therefore, the correct choice is choice (A).

3. **(D)** First, distribute the 12:

$$12m + 36 - 4$$

Next, combine any like terms:

$$12m + 32$$

This answer matches choice (D).

4. **(B)** First, figure out how many words she would have to read. In other words, how many words are in the book?

$$\frac{300 \text{ words}}{1 \text{ page}} \times 200 \text{ pages} = 60{,}000 \text{ words}$$

Next, figure out how long it would take her to read 60,000 words by setting up a dimensional analysis such that you cancel out the units that you don't want (words) and end up with the units that you do want (minutes). Since she can read 1,000 words per minute, you have

$$60000 \text{ words} \times \frac{1 \text{ min}}{1000 \text{ words}} = 60 \text{ min}$$

Therefore, it will take her 60 minutes, choice (B).

5. **(B)** First, you need to FOIL the squared term:

$$(a + 5)(a + 5) = a^2 + 10a + 25$$

Substituting this back into the equation gives you

$$a^2 + 10a + 25 + 4 = 68$$

Bringing everything to the left side of the equation and combining like terms leaves

$$a^2 + 10a - 39 = 0$$

This can be factored to

$$(a + 13)(a - 3) = 0$$

Setting each factor equal to 0 gives

$$a + 13 = 0, \text{ so } a = -13$$

$$a - 3 = 0, \text{ so } a = 3$$

Out of these two choices, only 3 is an option. Therefore, the correct answer is choice (B). Alternatively, you could have used the quadratic formula for the last step.

6. **(D)** In general, to find a percentage, you take $\dfrac{\text{part}}{\text{whole}} \times 100$. In this particular problem, the *whole* test is 40 questions. To find the percent score on the test, you need to determine the *part* of the test, or number of questions, that the person answered correctly. You are told that the person missed 14 questions, which means that they answered $40 - 14 = 26$ questions correctly. Thus, the percent score is

$$\frac{26}{40} \times 100 = 0.65 \times 100 = 65\%$$

7. **(C)** The mode is the quantity that occurs most frequently. Looking at the table, 8 students scored 5 points on the quiz, while fewer than 8 students scored each of the other 5 possible point values. Thus, the mode of the quiz scores is 5 since this is the score that occurred most frequently. Eyeballing the data, it is likely that the median (the middle value) and the mean (the average) are both less than 5, the highest possible score, so you could deduce that the answer is choice (C). But, find the median and mean as well to confirm that the mode is indeed the greatest quantity in this data set. To find the median, you arrange all students' scores from lowest to highest and choose the score in the middle. From the chart, you can see that there are 29 students, so the median will be the score of the 15th student. Going in order from lowest to highest score, there were 2 students who scored 0 points, 3 students who scored 1 point, 6 students who scored 2 points, and 7 students who scored 3 points. In other words, the first 11 students scored 2 points or less, and then the next 7 students all scored 3 points. In particular, the 15th student must have scored 3 points, so the median is 3.

To find the mean, you take the sum of all students' scores and divide by the total number of students. You get

$$\frac{2(0) + 3(1) + 6(2) + 7(3) + 3(4) + 8(5)}{29} = \frac{88}{29} \approx 3.0$$

Thus, the mean and the median are both less than 5, so the mode is the highest quantity.

8. **(D)** In the right side of the equation, only the x is being raised to the 9th power so you can get rid of the parentheses. The 2s cancel giving you

$$x^{\left(\frac{3}{b}\right)} = x^9$$

Because both exponents have the same base, you can set the exponents equal to one another:

$$\frac{3}{b} = 9$$

You need to get b out of the denominator, so multiply both sides by b:

$$3 = 9b$$

Finally, divide both sides by 9 to isolate b:

$$b = \frac{3}{9} = \frac{1}{3}, \text{ choice (D)}.$$

9. **30** Notice that angle *CDY* is an opposite interior angle of angle *ACD*; therefore, these two angles are congruent. Angle *ACD* is on the same line as angle *BCD*, so they must add up to $180°$. Angle *BCD* is $150°$, so angle $ACD = 180° - 150° = 30°$. Therefore, angle *CDY* is also $30°$.

10. **(C)** To solve this problem, first assess the domain and the range of $|x| + 1$. Any value can be plugged into the equation for x, so the domain will be all real numbers.

Next, consider the range. Remember that the absolute value of a number is that number's distance from zero. Since it is a distance, the absolute value of any number must necessarily be nonnegative (i.e., $|x| \geq 0$). Thus, $|x| + 1 \geq 0 + 1 = 1$, so the range is $[1, \infty)$.

This domain and range correspond to a function in the first and second quadrants.

However, notice that the problem is an inequality rather than a function. Therefore, you need to also assess what part will be shaded. The inequality says that y will be greater than the value given by the expression on the right, which means the area above the graph of $|x| + 1$ will be shaded. Therefore, your original answer of the first and second quadrants is valid.

Alternatively, consider this problem graphically: $|x| + 1$ shifts the graph of $|x|$ up by 1, so the graph looks like

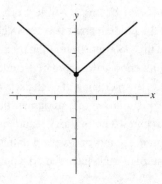

You want y to be greater than $|x| + 1$, so y can only take values in the region above the graph, which is shaded in the picture below:

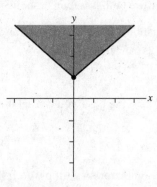

Thus, points (x, y) satisfying the inequality can only be found in the first and second quadrants.

11. **(C)** A function will have a zero for each distinct factor. This polynomial is already factored, so you can assess its factors. It has 4 factors, but only 3 distinct factors: $(x - 3)$, $(x - 1)$, and $(x + 2)$. Thus, there are 3 zeros: 3, 1, and -2. The factor $(x - 1)$ is repeated, meaning this zero will have a multiplicity of two.

12. **(A)** First, figure out what fraction of one hour and three minutes is:

$3 \min \times \dfrac{1 \text{ hour}}{60 \min} = \dfrac{1}{20}$ hours. If he takes $\dfrac{1}{20}$ of an hour per page, multiplying by p, the number of pages, will tell you the total time taken in hours:

$$\frac{1}{20}p = \frac{p}{20}, \text{ choice (A)}.$$

13. **21** These equations can quickly be solved for y. For the first, add $4x$ to both sides to get $y = 4x + 5$. In the second, add 13 to both sides: $y = 2x + 13$. Set the right sides of the equation equal to one another:

$$4x + 5 = 2x + 13$$

Get all of the x terms on the left by subtracting $2x$ from both sides, and get all of the constants on the right by subtracting 5 from both sides:

$$2x = 8$$

Dividing by 2 tells you that $x = 4$. However, the question asks for the y-value at which they intersect. Plug 4 in for x in either equation to solve for y:

$$y = 4(4) + 5 = 16 + 5 = 21$$

So the answer is 21. Alternatively, you could have solved each equation for x and set those equal to one another to directly solve for the y-coordinate of their intersection; you could have also used elimination to solve.

14. **0.5 or ½** Break the part inside the parentheses into its constituent fractions:

$$\frac{1}{14}\left(\frac{y + x}{y}\right) = \frac{1}{14}\left(\frac{y}{y} + \frac{x}{y}\right) = \frac{1}{14}\left(1 + \frac{x}{y}\right)$$

This is a free-response question, so you need to get an actual number as an answer. So, you need to find the value of $\frac{x}{y}$. You can use the relationship $\frac{1}{3}x = 2y$ to solve for $\frac{x}{y}$.

Begin by dividing both sides of the equation by y:

$$\frac{1}{3}\left(\frac{x}{y}\right) = 2$$

Next, divide both sides by $\frac{1}{3}$ (which is the same thing as multiplying both sides by its reciprocal, 3).

$$\frac{x}{y} = 6$$

Plug 6 in for $\frac{x}{y}$ in the expression obtained earlier:

$\frac{1}{14}(1 + 6) = \frac{1}{14}(7) = \frac{7}{14} = \frac{1}{2}$, so the answer is $\frac{1}{2}$, or 0.5.

15. **(C)** You are told that the budget increases by 6% a year. Thus, in one year, the budget will be

$$\$96 \text{ billion} + 0.06(\$96 \text{ billion}) = 1.06(\$96 \text{ billion}) = \$101.76 \text{ billion}$$

Similarly, in the second year, the budget will increase by 6% again to

$$1.06(\$101.76 \text{ billion}) = \$107.87 \text{ billion}$$

Now, you want to know how much of this money will be allocated to the Executive portion. You are told that the budget percentage allocations remain the same, so by the chart, 17% of the budget will still go to the Executive part. Thus, the Executive part is allocated $0.17(\$107.87$ billion$) = \$18.3$ billion, which is choice (C).

16. **(B)** You are told that acceleration is equal to $\dfrac{\text{change in velocity}}{\text{change in distance}}$ between two points. Note that to find the slope of any line, you take $\dfrac{\text{change in } y}{\text{change in } x}$. Now, the scientist graphs the line with distance as the x coordinates and velocity as the y coordinates. So, in your case, change in y corresponds to change in velocity, while change in x corresponds to change in distance. Thus, the slope of your line equals $\dfrac{\text{change in velocity}}{\text{change in distance}}$, which is the formula for acceleration. Thus, the answer is choice (B).

17. **(A)** Let L denote the length and W denote the width of the rectangular fence. You are told that the fence is 4 times as long as it is wide. In other words, $L = 4W$. Now, the formula for the perimeter of a rectangle is $P = 2L + 2W$. The problem asks for the perimeter in terms of L, so you need to replace the W in the perimeter equation with an expression involving L. Since $L = 4W$, you can solve for W by dividing both sides by 4 to obtain $\frac{1}{4}L = W$, or $0.25L = W$. Plugging this expression in for W in your perimeter equation gives $P = 2L + 2W = 2L + 2(0.25L) = 2L + 0.5L = 2.5L$, which is choice (A).

18. **(D)** First divide both sides of the equation by -1 to obtain

$$|2.4x + 13.5| = -3$$

Recall that the absolute value of a number represents that number's distance from zero. Since it is a distance, the absolute value of something must always be nonnegative. In particular, it can never equal -3. Thus, there are no possible solutions to this equation.

19. **(D)** To solve this problem, you need to find the length of each diagonal in the rectangle. Note that since this is a rectangle, the lengths of both diagonals will be the same, so you just need to find the length of one diagonal, say AD. Draw this diagonal (the line connecting points A and D) in your picture, as shown below:

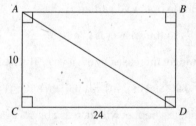

Note that by drawing this line, you create a right triangle whose hypotenuse is the diagonal AD. So, you need to find the length of the hypotenuse. From the picture, two side lengths are 10 and 24. Note that $10 = 2(5)$ and $24 = 2(12)$, so this triangle is just a multiple of the special 5-12-13 triangle; in your case, the side lengths are two times the side lengths of the special triangle. So, the length of your hypotenuse is $2(13) = 26$.

Alternatively, if you don't remember the special 5-12-13 triangle, you can always use the Pythagorean theorem to find the length of the hypotenuse. Since the hypotenuse is your diagonal, it follows that the length of each diagonal is 26. The problem asks for the product of the diagonals, so the answer is $26 \times 26 = 676$, which is choice (D).

20. **(A)** Looking at the four answer choices, you can see that you should simplify your original expression in some way so that there are no longer any square roots. First try to simplify the expression in the parenthesis, $(64x^6)^{\frac{2}{3}}$. This tells you to raise every factor inside the parentheses to the $\frac{2}{3}$ power. In other words, you have $(64x^6)^{\frac{2}{3}} = (64)^{\frac{2}{3}}(x^6)^{\frac{2}{3}}$. Now, $(64)^{\frac{2}{3}} = 16$ since the 3 in the denominator of $\frac{2}{3}$ tells us to take the cube root of 64 (resulting in 4) and the 2 in the numerator tells us to square the result (giving us $4^2 = 16$). Also, $(x^6)^{\frac{2}{3}} = x^{(6)\left(\frac{2}{3}\right)} = x^{\frac{12}{3}} = x^4$. Thus, you can rewrite the expression in parentheses as

$$(64x^6)^{\frac{2}{3}} = (64)^{\frac{2}{3}}(x^6)^{\frac{2}{3}} = 16x^4$$

Now, step back and look at the entire expression inside the square root, $(64x^6)^{\frac{2}{3}}x^{-2}$, which is equivalent to $16x^4x^{-2}$ by your above work. Since $x^4x^{-2} = x^{4-2} = x^2$, your expression becomes $16x^2$.

Thus, the original expression given in the statement of the problem, $\sqrt{(64x^6)^{\frac{2}{3}}x^{-2}}$, can be rewritten as $\sqrt{16x^2}$. Since $x > 0$, $\sqrt{x^2} = x$, so $\sqrt{16x^2} = 4x$, which matches choice (A).

21. **(B)** Let m be the number of male participants and w be the number of female participants. You know that no more than 60 people are permitted in the room. So, the total number of males and females in the room must be 60 or less. In other words, $m + w \leq 60$. You are also told that there will be an equal number of males and females at the session, so necessarily, $m = w$. Finally, you know that the breakout session will occur, so there must be at least one person in the room. But, there are an equal number of males and females present, so there must actually be at least 2 people in the room. In particular, there must be at least one male and one female in the room. So, $m > 0$ and $w > 0$. Hence, your constraints are

$$\begin{cases} m > 0 \\ w > 0 \\ m + w \leq 60, \text{ which matches choice (B).} \\ m = w \end{cases}$$

22. **47** In both cases, $P = 10,000$, $r = 0.10$, and $t = 1$. If interest is compounded yearly, $n = 1$, whereas if it is compounded monthly, $n = 12$. Because she starts with \$10,000 either way, the difference in (A) in the two situations can only be the result of differing amounts of interest. Therefore, you can figure out how much money she would have if it were compounded monthly and subtract the amount of money she would have if it were compounded annually in order to determine how much more interest she would earn in the monthly scenario.

Monthly:
$$A = P\left(1 + \frac{r}{n}\right)^{nt} = 10,000\left(1 + \frac{0.10}{12}\right)^{(12)(1)} = 10,000(1.00833)^{12} = 11,046.69$$

Yearly:
$$A = P\left(1 + \frac{r}{n}\right)^{nt} = 10,000\left(1 + \frac{0.10}{1}\right)^{(1)(1)} = 10,000(1.10)^1 = 11,000$$

Therefore, the difference in the amount of interest earned in the two scenarios is given by the difference $11046.69 - 11000 = 46.69$. Rounded to the nearest dollar, \$47.

Appendix:
After the Digital PSAT

Now that you have prepared for the PSAT, what comes next in terms of the National Merit Scholarship program and your future testing?

When Should I Receive My PSAT Test Results?

PSAT results from the October test date are typically available in mid-December. Be sure to get access to your online score report so that you can review questions you missed and the correct answers. You can find your score report at *www.psat.org/myscore*.

If you forget your online access information, your guidance counselor should be able to help you figure out how to log in.

Some schools also have the hard copies of the test booklets that you used for the PSAT. If so, be sure to ask your school for these so you can use them for future practice.

How Does National Merit Recognition Work?

Each year, about 1.6 million juniors take the PSAT. Out of those 1.6 million students, these are the numbers that receive some sort of recognition:

- **COMMENDED STUDENTS:** About 34,000 top PSAT scorers (approximately the 97th–98th percentile of test takers) receive letters of commendation.
- **NATIONAL MERIT SEMIFINALISTS:** About 16,000 students (approximately the 99th percentile, or the top 1 percent of all test takers)
    - Commended students and semifinalists are notified of their status in the September after taking the PSAT.
- **NATIONAL MERIT FINALISTS:** About 15,000 of the National Merit Semifinalists are named National Merit Finalists by meeting the program requirements (including maintaining high academic standing, confirming their PSAT performance with ACT or SAT scores, and being recommended by their high school principal).
    - National Merit Finalists learn of their status in February of their senior year.
- **NATIONAL MERIT SCHOLARS:** About 7,500 of National Merit Finalists are awarded National Merit Scholarships, ranging from one-time payments of $2,500 to recurring awards depending on the scholarship. (Approximately one-half of 1 percent of PSAT test takers earn a National Merit Scholarship.)
    - National Merit Scholars learn of their status between March and June of their senior year.
    - To earn the National Merit Scholarship, students are evaluated on their test scores, academic record, school recommendation, personal essay, and other factors.[1]

[1]*www.nationalmerit.org*

What If I Was Unable to Take the PSAT Because I Was Sick or Something Unusual Happened at the Test Site That Affected the Test Administration?

You should write to the National Merit Scholarship program and explain your situation as soon as possible. Notify them by November 15 about any testing irregularities. Notify them by April 1 about the need for an alternate entry. Mail requests to the following address:

National Merit Scholarship Corporation
Attn: Scholarship Administration
1560 Sherman Avenue, Suite 200
Evanston, IL 60201-4897

It is advisable to confirm this mailing address at *www.nationalmerit.org*.

How Can I Use My Official PSAT Score Report to Help Me?

You can access your PSAT score online at *www.psat.org/myscore*. Among the key things to check out:

YOUR NMSC SELECTION INDEX: This number determines your eligibility for the National Merit Scholarship competition and is calculated by doubling your scores from the Reading, Writing/Language, and Math section scores. (Each section has a maximum score of 38, so the maximum selection index score is twice the sum of these three section scores—228.)

- To be selected as a National Merit Semifinalist, you will typically need a National Merit selection index of around 218. National Merit Scholarships are allocated on the basis of state representation, and the cutoff scores can be different depending on the state in which you reside. If you live in New Jersey, for example, you may need a selection index of as high as 222. If you live in North Dakota, you may need a selection index of only 207.

QUESTION-LEVEL FEEDBACK: Evaluate which questions you answered correctly and which questions you missed.

- Take advantage of the online resources that allow you to review the actual test questions and answer explanations. This is the best possible diagnostic tool you can use, since you can carefully analyze what gave you difficulty on the PSAT, which is a preview of the SAT.
- As you review the questions you missed, look for patterns in what gave you difficulty:
- Did you have trouble with timing, either finishing too quickly and making careless errors or taking too much time and not attempting later questions?
- Should you focus your future practice on certain types of questions or material, such as grammar concepts, math concepts, or styles of reading passages?
- Did you have trouble with endurance during the test? Did your performance diminish as time went on? Do you need to do a better job getting enough rest in the days leading up to the test?

When Should I Take the SAT?

The SAT is used for college admissions purposes, and your performance on the PSAT will give you a great indication of how you will perform on the SAT. The SAT is offered several times during the year, typically during these months:

- March
- May
- June
- August
- October
- November
- December

You can register for the SAT by going to *www.collegeboard.org*. You should take the SAT at a time that works well with your schedule, and it is fine to take it at least two to three times if need be. Colleges will consider the best score you provide, and some will even "superscore"—i.e., take the best score from each section of the test.

Should I Take the ACT?

Nearly all U.S. colleges will accept either the SAT or the ACT for college admissions purposes, so you will likely want to try the ACT at least once. If you are a faster test taker and you are good at science, the ACT may be a particularly good fit for you—there is a science reasoning section on the ACT, and the ACT has more questions than the SAT to finish in the given amount of time. Fortunately, the ACT and SAT cover many of the same grammar and math concepts, so by preparing for one test, you are essentially preparing for the other.

Index